Rule-Makers or Rule-Takers?

Rule-Makers or Rule-Takers?

Exploring the Transatlantic Trade and Investment Partnership

Edited by

Daniel S. Hamilton & Jacques Pelkmans

Contributors

Freya Baetens

Koen Berden

Steven Blockmans

Jonathan Bonnitcha

Peter Chase

Michelle Egan

Christian Egenhofer

E. Donald Elliott

Joseph Francois

Caroline Freund

Daniel S. Hamilton

Jean Heilman Grier

Barbara Holzer

Tim Josling

Petros Kusmu

Patrick Messerlin

Gergely Molnar

Paolo Natali

Sarah Oliver

Jacques Pelkmans

Lauge Poulsen

Andrea Renda

Stefan Tangermann

Stephen Woolcock

Jason Yackee

Christopher S. Yoo

Center for Transatlantic Relations (CTR), Johns Hopkins University School of Advanced International Studies, Washington, D.C.

Centre for European Policy Studies (CEPS), Brussels

Rowman and Littlefield International, London

Published by Rowman & Littlefield International, Ltd.
Unit A, Whitacre Mews, 26-34 Stannary Street, London SE11 4AB
www.rowmaninternational.com

Rowman & Littlefield International Ltd. is an affiliate of Rowman &
Littlefield
4501 Forbes Boulevard, Suite 200, Lanham, Maryland 20706, USA
With additional offices in Boulder, New York, Toronto (Canada), and
Plymouth (UK)
www.rowman.com

British Library Cataloguing in Publication Data
A catalogue record for this book is available from the British Library

ISBN: 978-1-78348- 711-0

∞™ The paper used in this publication meets the minimum
requirements of American National Standard for Information
Sciences−Permanence of Paper for Printed Library Materials,
ANSI/NISO Z39.48-1992.

Printed in the United States of America

TABLE OF CONTENTS

Part II. Sectoral Issues

LIST OF FIGURES, TABLES & BOXES

LIST OF ABBREVIATIONS

AAPC	American Automotive Policy Council
ACC	American Chemistry Council
ACEA	European Automobile Manufacturers' Association
ACTA	Anti-Counterfeiting Trade Agreement
ADR	Alternative Dispute Resolution
AMP	Advanced Manufacturing Partnership
ANPRM	(US) Advanced Notice of Proposed Rule-Making
ANSI	American National Standards Institute
APA	Administrative Procedures Act
APEC	Asia-Pacific Economic Cooperation
ASME	American Society of Mechanical Engineers
BEUC	European Consumer Organisation
BIAS	broadband Internet access services
BIT	Bilateral Investment Treaty
CBI	confidential business information
CEFIC	European Chemical Industry Council
CEN	European Committee for Standardisation
CENELEC	European Committee for Electrotechnical Standardisation
CETA	(EU-Canada) Comprehensive Economic and Trade Agreement
CFA	Consumer Federation of America
CFR	Code of Federal Regulations
CGE	computable general equilibrium
CJEU	Court of Justice of the European Union
CLP	classification, labelling and packaging
CMP	Canadian Chemicals Management Plan
COPPA	Children's Online Privacy Protection Act
DoC	(US) Department of Commerce
DPD	Data Protection Directive 95/46
DSL	digital subscriber line
ECHA	European Chemicals Agency

ECPA	Electronic Communications Privacy Act
EGA	Environmental Goods Agreement
E-LABEL Act	Enhance Labelling, Accessing, and Branding of Electronic Licenses Act
EPA	(US) Environmental Protection Agency
ETSI	European Telecommunications Standards Institute
ETUC	European Trade Unions Confederation
EU	European Union
EUMS	European Union Member State
FAA	Foreign Intelligence Surveillance Amendment Act
FCC	(US) Federal Communications Commission
FCRA	Fair Credit Reporting Act
FDA	US Food and Drug Administration
FERPA	Family Educational Rights and Privacy Act
FTA	free trade area/agreement
GATS	General Agreement on Trade in Services
GATT	General Agreement on Tariffs and Trade
GHS	(UN) Globally Harmonised System of Classification and Labelling of Chemicals
GLBA	Gramm-Leach-Bliley Act
GLP	(OECD) Good Laboratory Practices
GMOs	genetically modified organisms
GPA	Government Procurement Agreement
GRPs	Good Regulatory Practices
HIPAA	Health Information Portability and Accessibility Act
HLWG	(US-EU) High Level Working Group on Jobs and Growth
HPV	high-production volume
IA	Impact Assessment
ICN	International Competition Network
ICT	information and communication technologies
IEC	International Electrotechnical Commission
IEEE	Institute of Electrical and Electronics Engineers
IMCO	Internal Market and Consumer Protection Committee of the European Parliament
IoT	Internet of Things

ITU	International Telecommunication Union
ISDS	Investor-state dispute settlement
ISO	International Organisation for Standardisation
ISPs	Internet Service Providers
ITA	Information Technology Agreement
KOREU	Korea-EU Free Trade Agreement
KORUS	Korea-US Free Trade Agreement
LTE	long-term evolution
MAD	Mutual Acceptance of Data
ME	mechanical engineering
MEP	Member of the European Parliament
MFN	most-favoured nation
MSR	Market Stability Reserve
NAFTA	North American Free Trade Agreement
NGNs	next-generation networks
NREAPs	National Renewable Energy Action Plans
NRTL	Nationally Recognised Testing Laboratory
NTB	non-tariff barrier
NTM	non-tariff measure
NTTAA	National Technology Transfer and Advancement Act
OIRA	(US) Office of Information and Regulatory Affairs
OMB	(US) Office of Management and Budget
OSHA	(US) Office of Safety and Health Administration
OTT	over-the-top
PDBTS	Policy Dialogue on Borders and Transport Security
PHSMA	Pipeline & Hazardous Materials Safety Admin
PII	personally identifiable information
PMN	pre-manufacture notification
POP	persistent organic pollutant
PP	precautionary principle
PTA	preferential trade agreement
QSAR	quantitative structure activity relationship
RCB	Regulatory Cooperation Body
RCEP	Regional Cooperative Economic Partnership
REACH	Regulation on Registration, Evaluation, Authorisation and Restriction of Chemicals

RIA	regulatory impact assessment
RTA	regional trade agreement
ROO	rules of origin
SAR	structure activity relationship
SDoC	supplier's declaration of conformity
SDOs	standards development organisations
SHEC	safety, health, environment and consumer
SIN	Substitute It Now
SME	small- and medium-sized enterprise
SPS	sanitary and phytosanitary (measures, agreement)
SST	specific selection term
TABD	Transatlantic Business Dialogue
TACD	Transatlantic Consumer Dialogue
TAED	Transatlantic Environment Dialogue
TBT	technical barrier to trade
TEC	Transatlantic Economic Council
TEP	Transatlantic Economic Partnership
TFEU	Treaty on the Functioning of the European Union
TiSA	Trade in Services Agreement
TLD	Transatlantic Legislators' Dialogue
TPA	Trade Promotion Authority
TPP	Trans-Pacific Partnership
TSCA	Toxic Substances Control Act
TISA	Trade in International Services Agreement
TTIP	Transatlantic Trade and Investment Partnership
UL	Underwriters Laboratories
UNECE	United Nations Economic Commission for Europe
USO	Universal Service Obligations Directive
USTR	United States Trade Representative
VoIP	voice over internet protocol
VZBV	Verbraucherzentrale Bundesverband
W3C	World Wide Web Consortium
WCAG	Web Content Accessibility Guidelines
WTO	World Trade Organization

ABOUT THE CONTRIBUTORS

Freya Baetens, Associate Professor of Law, Director of Studies and Head of the Research Centre at Leiden University and Visiting Professor at the World Trade Institute, Berne

Koen Berden, Chief Economist and Senior Partner at Ecorys, Assistant Professor at Erasmus University Rotterdam, and Associate at the World Trade Institute

Steven Blockmans, Head of EU Foreign Policy at CEPS and Professor of EU External Relations Law and Governance at the University of Amsterdam

Jonathan Bonnitcha, Visiting Fellow, Crawford School of Public Policy, ANU College of Asia and the Pacific

Peter Chase, Vice President for Europe, US Chamber of Commerce

Michelle Egan, Associate Professor, School of International Service, American University, Washington, D.C.

Christian Egenhofer, Associate Senior Fellow and Head of the Energy and Climate programme at CEPS and Director of the Energy Climate House

E. Donald Elliott, Professor (adj) of Law, Yale Law School, and Senior Counsel in the Washington, D.C. office of Covington & Burling LLP

Joseph Francois, Professor of International Economics at the University of Bern and Managing Director of the World Trade Institute

Caroline Freund, Senior Fellow at the Peterson Institute for International Economics, Washington, D.C.

Jean Heilman Grier, Principal - Consultant Djaghe, LLC

Daniel S. Hamilton, Austrian Marshall Plan Foundation Professor and Executive Director, Center for Transatlantic Relations at the Paul H. Nitze School of Advanced International Studies, Johns Hopkins University

Tim Josling, Professor Emeritus at the (former) Food Research Institute at Stanford University, Senior Fellow at the Stanford University's Freeman Spogli Institute for International Studies and faculty member at FSI's Europe Center

Patrick Messerlin, Professor of Economics, Sciences Po and Director, Groupe d'Economie Mondiale at Sciences Po (GEM)

Gergely Molnar, Research Assistant in the Energy and Climate Change research programme, CEPS

Paolo Natali, originator at Eni Trading & Shipping and a Visiting Professor at the Paris School of International Affairs (PSIA), Sciences Po

Sarah Oliver, Research Analyst, Peterson Institute for International Economics, Washington, D.C.

Jacques Pelkmans, Senior Research Fellow, CEPS and Visiting Professor at the College of Europe, Bruges

Lauge Poulsen, Lecturer in International Political Economy, University College London

Andrea Renda, Senior Research Fellow, CEPS

Stephan Tangermann, former Director for Trade and Agriculture at the Organisation for Economic Co-operation and Development, Paris

Stephen Woolcock, Associate Professor of International Relations, London School of Economics

Jason Yackee, Associate Professor of Law at the University of Wisconsin Law School

Christopher S. Yoo, Professor of Law, Communication, and Computer and Information Science, University of Pennsylvania Law School

PREFACE

This book is a collaborative effort of the Center for Transatlantic Relations (CTR) at Johns Hopkins University's School of Advanced International Studies, based in Washington, D.C., and the Centre for European Policy Studies (CEPS), based in Brussels. Together we have forged a strong transatlantic network of scholars and experts who have partnered to produce an in-depth, substantive treatment of the important issues involved in the US-EU negotiations on a Transatlantic Trade and Investment Partnership, otherwise known as TTIP. Most chapters are written jointly by European and American authors, whose insights cut through the caricatures, controversies and confusion surrounding TTIP. Authors explain the issues at hand, offer criticisms and recommendations, and provide concrete analytical output as a support for negotiators on both sides.

This project builds on a strong tradition of cooperation between our two centres, which has included the publication of analytical policy research and the organisation of conferences addressing a wide range of contemporary issues, from foreign policy to economic concerns.

We, the project directors, would like to thank our authors for their time, their energy and their insights, and also offer our appreciation to the many other experts and decision-makers who engaged with us over the course of this project.

We would like to express our particular gratitude to Federica Mustilli, Anne Harrington and Els Van den Broeck at CEPS, as well as Miriam Cunningham, Heidi Obermeyer and Benjamin Hilgenstock at CTR, for their tremendous assistance.

This project has been supported by both institutes, as well as by AmChamEU, Repsol and the Konrad Adenauer Foundation, and we are grateful for this funding. CTR acknowledges funding from the European Commission and the Transatlantic Program of the German government, with funds from the European Recovery Program of the German Ministry for Economics and Technology.

All authors have written in their personal capacity, and none of the views expressed here represents those of any government or institution. The organisation, substance and editing of the project results, including this book and its various conclusions, critiques and recommendations, are entirely independent.

Daniel S. Hamilton, Washington, D.C.
Jacques Pelkmans, Brussels

PART I

RULES, NORMS AND STANDARDS

1. RULE-MAKERS OR RULE-TAKERS? AN INTRODUCTION TO TTIP
DANIEL S. HAMILTON
AND JACQUES PELKMANS

1.   The transatlantic economy, now and in the future

Despite the rise of other powers, including many emerging growth markets, the United States and Europe remain the fulcrum of the world economy, each other's most important and profitable market and main source of 'onshored' jobs. The transatlantic economy generates $5.5 trillion in total commercial sales a year and employs up to 15 million workers in mutually 'onshored' jobs on both sides of the Atlantic. It is the largest and wealthiest market in the world, accounting for over 35% of world GDP in terms of purchasing power.[1]

No other commercial artery is as integrated. Every day roughly $1.7 billion in goods and services crosses the Atlantic, representing about one-third of total global trade in goods and more than 40% of world trade in services. Ties are particularly thick in foreign direct investment, portfolio investment, banking claims, trade and affiliate sales in goods and services, mutual R&D investment, patent cooperation, technology flows and sales of knowledge-intensive services. Together the United States and Europe accounted for 70% of the outward stock and 57% of the inward stock of global foreign direct investment (FDI) in 2013. Moreover, each partner has built up the great majority of that stock in the other's economy. Mutual investment in the North Atlantic space is very large, dwarfs trade and has become essential to US and European jobs and prosperity.

But the primacy of the transatlantic economy should not be taken for granted. Due to the rise of emerging markets, the share of global

---

[1] The data cited in this chapter are drawn from Hamilton & Quinlan (2015).

trade accounted for by the EU and the US has fallen and China is set to overtake both soon to become the single most-important trading power in the world. The United States remains by far the largest single bilateral export market for the EU, but its share in overall EU exports has fallen from about 27% to less than 20%, whereas that of China has almost doubled over the last few years. On the import side, the US ranks now only third for the EU. In the longer run, the transatlantic economy is bound to decrease in relative size in the world economy. Extrapolations for 2050 suggest that China will be of an economic size equal to transatlantic GDP, and India, Brazil and other rising economies are becoming increasingly integrated into the global economy.

2.   TTIP's rationale: Three drivers

In short, the world that created the original transatlantic partnership is fading fast. Each side of the Atlantic is facing daunting economic challenges at home and abroad. In this context, the United States and the European Union initiated negotiations on a new Transatlantic Trade and Investment Partnership, known as TTIP, which was born of a realisation on each side of the Atlantic that Americans and Europeans must work with greater urgency to build a partnership that is more effective in generating economic opportunity and confidence at home; engaging rising powers; and strengthening and extending basic norms and principles guiding the international system.

A first and prominent driver behind TTIP is a new and common recognition among US and European leaders that they need to act more urgently to open transatlantic markets in ways that can position each partner, and both together, to succeed in a world of diffuse economic power and intensified global competition. The addition of four billion people to the globalised economy and the rise of other powers, together with recent Western economic turmoil, have convinced US and European decision-makers that the window of opportunity may be closing on their ability to maintain high labour, consumer, health, safety and environmental standards and to advance key norms of the liberal rules-based order unless they act more effectively together.

For more than two centuries, either Europeans or Americans, or both together, have been accustomed to setting global rules. In the post-World War II era, the US and the evolving EU, each in its own way, has been a steward of the international rules-based order. Yet, with the rise of new powers, the resurgence of older powers and the emergence of serious challenges at home, Europeans and Americans now face the prospect of becoming rule-takers rather than rule-makers, unless they act more effectively together to ensure that high standards prevail.[2]

Given these considerations, TTIP's potential economic value extends beyond the transatlantic market itself. Properly constructed, it can also be a useful policy initiative to help open global markets. TTIP reflects a growing recognition on both sides of the Atlantic that the United States and the European Union must invest in new forms of transatlantic collaboration to strengthen multilateral rules and lift international standards. Given the size and scope of the transatlantic economy, standards negotiated by the US and the EU can quickly become a benchmark for global models, reducing the likelihood that others will impose more stringent, protectionist requirements for either products or services, or that lower standards could erode key forms of protection for workers, consumers or the environment. Given deep transatlantic economic integration, the benefits of such an initiative to both parties could be substantial. And given that the transatlantic economy remains the fulcrum of the global economy, there could be significant positive spillovers to third countries in rules, standards and regulatory affairs.

A second driver is the ongoing evolution in the nature and scope of global trade negotiations. Europeans and Americans share an interest in extending prosperity through multilateral trade liberalisation, yet the primary multilateral trade negotiation, the Doha Round, has been at a standstill for some time. Far greater dynamism is apparent with regard to preferential trade agreements (PTAs), which already govern over 50% of world trade and are likely to shape the nature of commercial connections across the Atlantic and around the world in coming decades. Mega-regional trade agreements are likely to be particularly important -- not only TTIP but also the 12-nation TPP (Trans-Pacific Partnership) and the Regional Economic Comprehensive Partnership (RECP) involving more than 20 countries in Asia. Negotiations to establish a preferential Trade Agreement in Services (TISA) currently involve 50 countries accounting for over 68% of global trade in services, including the US and the EU.

These mega-regional arrangements and a number of other 'deep-integration' PTAs seek to go beyond tariff reductions to define new structures and modalities for all sorts of non-tariff barriers to trade, along with new rules for important trade-related issues such as

---

[2] See Hamilton (2014a).

investment and competition, and new concerns e.g. environment, climate, labour, food scarcity, animal welfare, privacy standards and mounting consumer pressures.[3] The EU and Japan, for instance, launched negotiations towards a deep free trade agreement that includes regulatory issues, and the EU-Canada CETA agreement, which also touches on rules, standards and regulatory issues, has been successfully negotiated (although at this writing not yet ratified).

As these initiatives all went forward, it was becoming increasingly odd that leading trading partners such as the United States and the EU had not advanced their own efforts together. On both sides of the Atlantic, more and more voices argued that it was in the enlightened self-interest of both parties to undertake an exemplary initiative in earnest.

Moreover, US-EU agreement via TTIP has the potential to unblock the WTO Doha negotiations and jumpstart multilateral negotiations, just as NAFTA helped jumpstart Doha's predecessor negotiation, the Uruguay Round, and US-EU negotiations on an Information Technology Agreement also eventually became the basic multilateral agreement in this area. Moreover, even a successful Doha Round agreement would not address a host of issues that are not part of its mandate and yet are critical to the United States, the European Union and the global economy. In this regard TTIP can be a pioneering effort to extend the multilateral system to new areas and new members.

Third, global value chains (GVCs), which render a country's exports essentially the product of many intermediate imports assembled in many other countries, are revolutionising trade in both goods and services, with important implications for the conduct and priorities of trade negotiators and for our understanding of the transatlantic economy.

In today's global economy, a good produced in the United States and exported to the EU might include components from Mexico or China, using raw materials from Canada or Australia or services from Turkey or Switzerland. Goods and services are increasingly from 'everywhere', rather than exclusively from 'somewhere', as they are defined today.[4] They are unlikely to be fully "made in Germany", and "made in China" does not necessarily mean "made by China".

---

[3] See Hamilton (2015) and Herfkens & Michalopoulos (2015).

[4] See remarks by OECD Secretary General Angel Gurría (2013) at the launch of the OECD-WTO Database on Trade in Value-Added.

This growing process of international fragmentation is changing our traditional understanding of the patterns and structure of international trade. Traditional measures do not show how supply is driven by the final customer or reveal where the creation of value-added occurs, in terms of wages and profits. They also underplay the role of services in overall trade.[5] The OECD and the WTO have now created tools that are transforming our understanding of trade flows by revealing what was hidden before. This new 'value-added' approach tracks the direct and indirect flows of value-added associated with international trade. It shows where value is actually created. Their findings lead to some surprising conclusions that reinforce our understanding of the dense binding forces of transatlantic integration.

Take German-US trade as an example. Under traditional measures, the United States ranked slightly behind France in 2009 as Germany's major export market and ranked only fourth as an exporter to Germany, behind France, the Netherlands and China. But under the value-added approach, the United States jumps ahead to be both Germany's single most-important export market, accounting for 11% of German exports, and also Germany's most important supplier, accounting for over 12% of German imports.[6] This bilateral trade relationship can also be seen as more lucrative than previously understood, since Germany exports and imports more to and from the United States in value-added terms than in gross terms.

The value-added lens also shows that US bilateral trade with many other EU member states, and with the EU as a whole, is even more important than previously understood. In value-added terms, the EU exports (and imports) relatively more to (from) the United States and relatively less to (and from) China.

The United States also replaces Germany as Italy's top trading partner when exports are viewed on a value-added basis. This is because many of the inputs that Italy provides to other European partner countries, particularly Germany, become part of final goods that ultimately are exported to the United States. The value-added approach gives a similar lift to French-American trade. The United States emerges as France's number one trading partner, in terms of both

---

[5] See www.wto.org/english/res_e/statis_e/miwi_e/tradedataday13_e/paul_schreyer_e.pdf.

[6] All data presented here are drawn from the joint OECD/WTO Database on Trade in Value-Added (see www.oecd.org/sti/industryandglobalisation/TiVA%20Germany.pdf).

exports and imports, whereas conventional measures rank it third behind Germany and Belgium.

The value-added approach does not change America's position as the main destination for UK exports, but it does reveal that it actually received a much higher share of UK exports (21% vs 16%) than when trade is evaluated in gross terms during the baseline year of 2009. This suggests that, like Italy and France, the UK's exports to other EU countries are at least partly intermediate services and inputs, which are then further processed and shipped elsewhere, especially to the United States. Moreover, under the value-added approach, the United States displaces Germany as the UK's main supplier. While the EU as a whole is a more important trading partner for Britain than the United States, more of Britain's lucrative exports head across the Atlantic than previously believed.

The United States is engaged in a variety of dynamic regional value chains with NAFTA partners Canada and Mexico, similar to those that EU member states conduct among themselves. Trade within NAFTA is extensive. But much of it is composed of intermediate goods and services that are processed in Canada or Mexico and re-exported to the United States. The final export destination may lie elsewhere, with Europe garnering a higher share than previously understood. For instance, according to conventional methods, Germany was America's 6th largest export market in 2009. But according to value-added estimates, Germany followed only Canada as the most important export market for the United States, ahead of Mexico and China. In addition, according to value-added calculations, the US trade deficit with China is a quarter lower than estimated under conventional measurements, and is redistributed to Japan, Korea, Germany and other intermediate input suppliers to China.

The value-added approach not only underscores the continuing importance of the transatlantic economy, it is an important consideration as the United States and the EU consider removing tariff barriers across the Atlantic. Since many of these barriers are relatively low, sceptics wonder about the benefits of going to 'transatlantic zero'. But given that many US and EU exports in the end result from many different intermediate imports, and that related-party trade, or trade among affiliates of the same company, is so important in transatlantic commerce, even relatively low tariffs can have multiple knock-on effects all down the value chain. As the OECD (2013) notes: "Success in international markets today depends as much on the capacity to import world class inputs as on the capacity to export. Protection measures against imports of intermediate products increase costs of production and reduce a country's ability to compete in export markets: tariffs and other barriers on imports are a tax on exports." Moreover, given the size of the transatlantic economy, even small changes can have big effect.

Another policy implication of the value-added approach has to do with services. Traditional trade figures suggest that services account for less than one-quarter of global trade. But these new data highlight that services are not just exported through trade in services, they are integral to manufacturing trade as well. Transport equipment, electrical equipment and food products are manufacturing industries with significant services content. For the EU economy as a whole, 55% of the value of all gross exports originates in the services sector. The figure for the United States is 56% – roughly the same. For many EU member states, including the UK, the percentage is even higher; on average, 60% of the value of UK gross exports is comprised of value-added originating from the services sector. And the high value content of Britain's services-sector exports to the United States make them more valuable than they may first appear. Germany is perhaps an even more surprising example. While Germany tends to specialise in manufacturing industries, its exports of manufacturing goods incorporate significant shares of services value-added – over 40% in food, textile products and transport vehicles. In fact, fully half of the value of gross German exports represents services value-added.

In sum, companies and countries keen on improving their manufacturing performance increasingly are pressed to improve their services performance as well. Manufacturing produces for the services sector, and the services sector contributes to manufacturing. The two are increasingly intertwined; the supposed trade-off between manufacturing and services is a false choice. Liberalisation of services trade would not only allow for more-efficient and higher-quality services, it would enhance the competitiveness of manufacturing firms as well.

This is of direct importance to the transatlantic economy. The United States and the EU are the world's most important services economies, and each other's most important and profitable services markets. In the current policy environment, freeing the transatlantic services economy through TTIP could be the single-most important external initiative either side could take to spur growth and create jobs on both sides of the Atlantic.

3.   Why TTIP is different

Given this background and these aims and drivers, TTIP is not just another free trade agreement. According to Pascal Lamy, former Director-General of the World Trade Organization, "TTIP is the first show of the new world of trade".[7] Partly for this reason, TTIP negotiations have been accompanied by a swirl of confusion and controversy manifested in debates in the public domain, particularly but not only in parts of Europe, about their content and ultimate goals. Let us first note why TTIP is different and then set out exactly the structure of the TTIP negotiations.

TTIP is certainly intended to reduce traditional barriers to transatlantic trade. While average transatlantic tariffs are relatively low, at about 3-4% on average, with many tariffs at zero, tariffs remain quite high for some specific products in such categories as agriculture, textiles and apparel, and footwear. So there is room for barriers to come down. In addition, since the volume of US-EU trade is so huge, eliminating even relatively low tariffs could boost trade significantly. A report by the European think tank ECIPE estimated that a transatlantic zero-tariff agreement could boost US and EU goods exports each by 17% – about five times more than expected under the US-Korea free trade deal ratified in 2011.[8] Moreover, since a large percentage of transatlantic trade is intra-firm, or trade in parts and components within the firm or value-chain, even small tariffs add to the cost of production and result in higher prices for consumers on both sides of the ocean. The more intense the intra-industry trade component of trade between two parties, like the one that characterises US-EU commerce, the greater the effects and benefits of lower tariffs. Freer transatlantic trade without tariffs and with lower technical barriers could translate into millions of new jobs in the United States and Europe and improve both earnings and competitiveness for many companies, particularly small- and medium-sized enterprises.

Trade in goods, however, accounts for only about 20% of transatlantic commerce. Even greater gains could be had if TTIP opens the transatlantic services economy, where most jobs could be created; ensures an open rules-based order for investment; tackles technical and other non-tariff barriers and regulatory differences; and repositions the United States and the EU to respond more effectively to greater global competition. These dimensions are central to the TTIP negotiations and

---

[7] See Lamy (2015).
[8] See Erixon & Bauer (2010) and also Berden et al. (2009).

explain why TTIP is more than just another free trade agreement. TTIP's potential and its promise is to go beyond traditional trade arrangements to forge understandings regarding mutual investment, open services markets, non-tariff and regulatory barriers, basic ground rules of the international economic order and new agreements in areas not yet covered by multilateral regimes. All of these elements make TTIP a next-generation negotiation that breaks the mould of traditional trade agreements. At the heart of the ongoing talks is the question whether and in which areas the two major democratic actors in the global economy can address costly frictions generated by their deep commercial integration by aligning regulations and other instruments and setting benchmarks for high-quality global norms and rules.

At its core, TTIP is about far more than trade. It is about creating a more strategic, dynamic and holistic US-EU relationship that is more confident, more effective at engaging third countries and addressing regional and global challenges, and better able to strengthen the ground rules of the international order. TTIP can potentially serve as a symbolic and practical assertion of Western renewal, vigour and commitment, not only to each other but to high rules-based standards and core principles of international order. It is an initiative that can be assertive without being aggressive. It challenges fashionable notions about a 'weakened west'. In this sense, TTIP is poised to be the major political, strategic and economic driver of the transatlantic relationship over the course of this decade.

4.   What is TTIP? Structure and substance

There are many reasons why TTIP debates leave much to be desired. Many discussions zoom in on only one or two aspects, and even then often on the basis of assertions in the (social) media rather than as a result of careful study of the actual documents and/or serious analysis. The present volume should be a considerable help for the reader genuinely interested in the subject.

However, it is useful to simply depict what TTIP is all about and how the negotiations are structured. Figure 1.1 provides an elementary introduction to the substance of TTIP. Apart from a general set of principles and the basic rationale (in the so-called 'chapeau' of a future treaty, see top right), there are three lines of negotiation: market access, regulatory cooperation and 'rules'. The core of TTIP is the middle column (regulatory cooperation) with the addition of public procurement and services (from the left column) as well as GIs (geographical indications) and investor-state dispute settlement (ISDS) from the right hand column. The present volume deals with all these core subjects, including several sectors specified at the bottom of the middle column, but also a few services sectors.

Figure 1.1 What is TTIP all about?

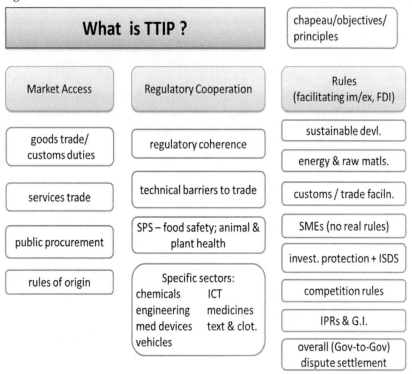

Source: Authors' own configuration.

In addition to opening transatlantic markets, each of TTIP's three pillars has the potential either to strengthen and expand multilateral rules (WTO-plus) or to generate standards and norms in new areas beyond the current system (WTO-extra).

TTIP's market-access pillar, for instance, could potentially result in clearer, more straightforward and transparent rules-of-origin arrangements that could serve as the basis for future preferential rules of origin. Clear, simple and aligned rules of origin would facilitate global trade and thus serve as a common public good.[9]

---

[9] For more on the impact of TTIP on emerging powers and the international system, see Hamilton (2014b).

TTIP's second pillar could pioneer new ways for countries to ensure high standards for consumers, workers, companies and the environment while sustaining the benefits of an open global economy. New consultative mechanisms among regulatory agencies, including as part of TTIP's 'living agreement' provisions, could eliminate redundant regulations, identify more efficient procedures and avoid conflicts that create unnecessary costs for companies and consumers, while ensuring high standards that can prevail not only across the Atlantic but around the world. Mutual recognition of essentially equivalent norms and regulatory coherence across the transatlantic space not only promises economic benefits at home but could form the core of broader international norms and standards.

The standards being negotiated as part of TTIP's third pillar are intended to be more rigorous than comparable rules found in the WTO. Agreement on such issues as intellectual property, services, discriminatory industrial policies or state-owned enterprises could strengthen the normative underpinnings of the multilateral system by creating benchmarks for possible future multilateral liberalisation under the WTO. US-EU agreement on such principles, and agreement to act together to advance such norms globally, could not only take the international trading system further but establish broader political principles regarding the rule of law, human rights, labour, environmental and consumer standards.

The idea of an ambitious transatlantic economic agreement is of course not new; yet over the past two decades such efforts have foundered on a range of US-EU differences. Remaining transatlantic tariff barriers, especially in agriculture, often reflect the most politically difficult cases. Some of the most intense transatlantic disagreements have arisen over differences in regulatory policy. Issues such as food safety or environmental standards have strong public constituencies and are often extremely sensitive in the domestic political arena. To complicate matters further, responsibility for regulation is split in the EU between European and national levels, and in the United States among federal, state and even local governments as well as a range of independent regulatory agencies. Investment barriers, especially in terms of infrastructure and transport-sector ownership, could be very difficult to change. Critics charge that a transatlantic agreement could well subvert the multilateral economic system.

In short, the issues can be tough and complex. TTIP could very well fail to achieve its potential.

The potential payoff for jobs and growth, however, is so high that the United States and the EU have committed themselves to overcome past differences and to forge new types of transatlantic mechanisms to manage future disputes while generating new economic opportunities.

5.   The contribution of this book to the TTIP debate

This volume is intended to cut through the caricatures swirling around TTIP and to illuminate the broad range of complex issues that are being addressed in the TTIP negotiations. We have brought European and American scholars and experts together to explain both the economic and broader geopolitical context of TTIP, and to explore the challenges and consequences of US-EU negotiations across numerous sensitive areas, ranging from food safety and public procurement to economic and regulatory assessments of technical barriers to trade, automotive, chemicals, energy, services, investor-state dispute settlement mechanisms and regulatory cooperation. We believe their insights can also help decision-makers understand how the United States and the European Union can remain rule-makers rather than rule-takers in a globalising world in which their relative influence is waning.

As our work will show, much of the more extreme criticisms of TTIP are either not or at best partially justified. The authors and editors are motivated to show how solid analysis and serious fact-finding can contribute to a better appreciation of TTIP's potential while also offering a more detached assessment of risks and challenges.

The book is divided into two parts.

Part I. Rules, norms and standards

The first substantive section looks at cross-cutting issues of rules, norms and standards. Peter Chase and Jacques Pelkmans explain why TTIP differs from previous US-EU efforts at economic and regulatory cooperation, and the opportunities inherent in 'turbo-charging' regulatory cooperation. They identify the many levels of international regulatory cooperation and provide a detailed annex on what the two parties have accomplished in this area since 1995. They argue that TTIP regulatory cooperation will be significant, but not ambitious, while political and legal limits on cooperation in both the EU and the United States should minimise many concerns. TTIP must accept these political and legal constraints, build trust and confidence among counterpart regulators so each comes to believe that their transatlantic partner can help them do their work better, and provide tools to help regulators on both sides make informed decisions while retaining their regulatory autonomy and accountability to their politicians and citizens. In so doing, TTIP should, over the longer term, provide both the economic and regulatory benefits that the two sides envisage.

Michelle Egan joins Jacques Pelkmans to explain why technical barriers to trade (TBTs) are TTIP's 'hard core' and why they are so difficult to address effectively. Outside of heavily regulated sectors such as chemicals, automobiles or medicines (which have separate chapters in TTIP), TBTs can be caused by divergent (voluntary) standards, technical regulations and conformity assessment. Indeed, in all three areas the United States and the EU have long experienced frictions or indeed, at times, considerable trading costs. However, the authors reject what they believe to be an unproductive 'stand-off' between US and EU negotiators on standardisation and suggest that the two parties clarify the enormous economic 'installed base' of prominent US standards in the world economy and build a solution from there. As for technical regulation, partly due to 'referred' standards (in US law) and partly due to independent agencies' preferences, the prospect of converging regulation (via harmonisation) is often dim, but equivalence (given similar levels of regulatory protection) could be an option.

Koen Berden and Joseph Francois provide an authoritative overview of all important empirical studies on non-tariff barriers and offer a methodology to quantify non-tariff measures (mostly, TBTs) so as to estimate the potential benefits that may be derived from TTIP. They urge policy-makers to dive deeply into sector-specific elements of non-tariff measures (as they differ greatly) and focus on those sectors where the largest potential gains can be made, such as in agriculture, chemicals, automobiles, steel, textiles and insurance services.

Investor-state dispute settlement mechanisms goes to the heart of TTIP's role as a regulatory pace-setter, and yet have been among the most controversial and least understood areas under negotiation. In that spirit, we present two contrasting approaches to the issue. Lauge Poulsen, Jonathan Bonnitcha and Jason Yackee present a cost-benefit analysis of the inclusion of investment protection provisions, including investor-state arbitration, in an investment chapter in TTIP. They argue that there is little evidence to suggest that investor-state arbitration will provide the EU with meaningful benefits, such as increased foreign investment from the United States, and may impose non-trivial costs in the form of litigation expenses and reduced policy space. They conclude that the case for including investor-state arbitration in TTIP is weak. Freya Baetens offers a point-by-point response in her own chapter, and then argues that an investment chapter in TTIP, including, ISDS offers an unprecedented opportunity to incorporate key public policy objectives and protect states' right to regulate.

TTIP's potential impact on levels of consumer protection has also been an issue that has been subjected to great heat yet little light; Stephen Woolcock, Barbara Holzer and Petros Kusmu examine these concerns by studying existing approaches to regulatory cooperation and presenting three short case studies. They find that regulatory powers on both sides of the Atlantic are unlikely to be significantly affected by TTIP, but suggest that European and American legislators will need to ensure that their priorities shape the TTIP regulatory cooperation agenda and not the other way around.

Much analysis and debate has focused on TTIP's potential economic impact. There has been relatively little exploration of its geostrategic implications. TTIP, however, is not just another trade agreement. It is about creating a more strategic, dynamic and holistic US-EU relationship that is more confident, more effective at engaging third countries and addressing regional and global challenges, and better able to strengthen the ground rules of the international order. Steven Blockmans and Daniel S. Hamilton explore TTIP's broader geopolitical ramifications to round out the first section of the book.

Part II. Sectoral issues

In Part II, European and American experts join together to examine TTIP's potential impact on key sectors of the transatlantic economy.

Tim Josling and Stefan Tangermann explore the possibilities and pitfalls of greater openness in transatlantic agricultural commerce and agro-food, which historically has been one of the most contentious issues faced by US and EU negotiators. They argue that progress in this area will largely be determined by the level of ambition in the negotiations as a whole. If ambitions are modest, a low-level agreement could include some limited commitments on agricultural market access and food regulations. Bolder ambitions would imply removing some long-standing irritants in the area of agricultural policy and food regulations: this is where the economic gains are likely to be significant and the spill-overs useful. They argue that it is worthwhile making the effort to secure a constructive and imaginative agreement on agriculture and food regulations in the TTIP, and offer a fairly detailed list of potential sub-deals that could be achieved.

Stephen Woolcock and Jean Heilman Grier look at TTIP's implication for public procurement markets across the North Atlantic in great detail. They propose ways the two sides can use TTIP negotiations to expand their current commitments as well as develop a longer-term approach by making TTIP a 'living agreement'.

Patrick Messerlin examines the transatlantic services economy, with original ideas on how to realise economic gains. He argues that substantial gains are only likely to come from deep discussions of regulatory issues, and that solutions cannot be found in the negotiating techniques normally used for goods. He suggests that a better approach should be based on mutual recognition and equivalence of regulations enforced in the services concerned, preceded by a mutual evaluation to grant such equivalence – all measures to be carried out by the regulatory bodies concerned, not by trade negotiators.

Andrea Renda and Christopher S. Yoo study TTIP's digital dimension in six different aspects. They explore the current divergences between the two legal systems on key digital issues and discuss possible scenarios, from a basic, minimal agreement limited to e-labelling and e-accessibility measures to more ambitious scenarios on network neutrality, competition rules, privacy and interoperability measures.

Donald Elliott and Jacques Pelkmans look at the why and how of greater TTIP ambition in chemicals, and find that the negotiators could approach it differently with better long-run results. They argue that the talks have focused too much on the differences in the two 'systems', rather than on the actual levels of health and environmental protection for substances regulated by both the US and the EU. They critique the two systems, advocate significant improvement of market access where equivalence of health and environmental objectives is agreed and propose to lower the costs for companies selling in both markets by allowing them to opt into the other party's more stringent rules, thereby avoiding duplication while racing-to-the-top.

Paolo Natali, Christian Egenhofer and Gergely Molnar look at TTIP and energy, mainly gas, an area that has been subjected to relatively limited analysis. The US shale revolution, growing interconnectedness of energy markets (recently proven by the disappearance of the 'Asian gas premium') and the EU's quest to diversify its energy supplies set favourable conditions to reinforce energy relations between the EU and the United States. The question is whether there is sufficient political will to tighten relations in a strategic area with implications for national security and sovereignty.

Finally, Caroline Freund and Sarah Oliver look at the automotive industry, a major employer on both sides of the Atlantic, by evaluating the equivalence of US and EU regulations and deriving the potential economic gains that may accrue by aligning such regulations. They estimate that the removal of regulatory differences in autos could increase trade by 20% or more, an effect only slightly smaller than the effect of EU accession on Europe's auto trade. The large economic gains from regulatory harmonisation imply that TTIP has the potential to improve productivity while lowering prices and enhancing variety for consumers.

References

Berden, K.G., J. Francois, S. Tamminen, M. Thelle and P. Wymenga (2009), "Non-Tariff Measures in EU-US Trade and Investment – An Economic Analysis", Ecorys report prepared for the European Commission, Reference OJ 2007/S180-219493.

Erixon, Fredrik and Matthias Bauer (2010), "A Transatlantic Zero Agreement: Estimating the Gains from Transatlantic Free Trade in Goods," ECIPE Occasional Paper No. 4/2010, ECIPE, Brussels.

Gurría, Angel (2013), Introductory remarks by the OECD Secretary-General at the launch of the OECD-WTO Database on Trade in Value-Added, Paris, 16 January (www.oecd.org/about/secretary-general/launchoftheoecd-wtodatabaseontradeinvalue-added.htm).

Hamilton, Daniel S. (2014a), "Transatlantic Challenges: Ukraine, TTIP and the Struggle to be Strategic", in Nathaniel Copsey and Tim Haughton (eds), *Journal of Common Market Studies Annual Review of the European Union in 2013*, September.

_____ (2014b), "TTIP, implicaciones para las potencias emergentes y el orden internacional", *Puentes*, Vol. 15, No. 6.

_____ (2015), "The Future Pan-Atlantic Economy", Atlantic Future Scientific Paper, July.

Hamilton, Daniel S. and Joseph P. Quinlan (2015), "The Transatlantic Economy 2015: Annual Survey of Jobs, Trade and Investment between the United States and Europe", Center for Transatlantic Relations, Washington, D.C.

Herfkens, Eveline and Constantine Michalopoulos (2015), "Multilateral, Plurilateral and Bilateral Trade: Untangling the Knots and Advancing Atlantic Commerce", Working Paper for the 2015 Atlantic Business Forum, Estoril, Portugal.

Lamy, P. (2015), "The New World of Trade", 3rd Jan Tumlir Lecture, ECIPE, 9 March (www.ecipe.org/app/uploads/2015/05/JAN-Tumlir-POLICE-Essays-—-20151.pdf).

OECD (2013), "Trade Policy Implications of Global Value Chains", Paris, May (www.oecd.org/sti/ind/Trade_Policy_Implicatipns_May_2013.pdf).

2. THIS TIME IT'S DIFFERENT: TURBO-CHARGING REGULATORY COOPERATION
PETER CHASE AND JACQUES PELKMANS

1. Introduction

When in June 2013 Presidents Barroso, Obama and Van Rompuy formally called for the launch of negotiations toward a "comprehensive and ambitious" Transatlantic Trade and Investment Partnership (TTIP) between the United States and the European Union, the regulatory part of the agreement was widely heralded as being the most novel and the most important for generating economic growth.

Two years and nine rounds of negotiation later, TTIP's regulatory component is one of the more contentious parts of the agreement. This is attributable both to persistent differences in emphasis between the negotiators and to concerns that regulatory cooperation could lead to a lowering – or, for that matter, an unjustified raising – of consumer, worker, prudential and environmental standards.[1]

In contrast, the authors believe that regulatory cooperation between the United States and the European Union is primarily about enhancing the ability of EU and US regulators to protect their citizens; positive economic gains are a secondary, if important, result. This chapter starts by presenting a framework to understanding regulatory cooperation in general, and briefly discusses developments in US and EU regulatory cooperation since 1995, before presenting, in sections 3 and 4, how TTIP can 'turbo-charge' this by enshrining good regulatory principles and practices, and by introducing new tools to deepen the

---

[1] Note that 'standards' here refer to regulatory *objectives* (e.g. about health, safety, etc.), which the debate has sometimes informally called 'level of protection'.

relationship between transatlantic regulators. Sections 5 and 6 compare this proposal with regulatory provisions in previous US and EU trade agreements, as well as with those the EU Commission has recommended for TTIP.

The central thesis throughout this chapter is that regulatory cooperation between the United States and the European Union should be about helping regulators become more efficient and effective in achieving their goals, and not primarily about removing or reducing 'non-tariff barriers to trade'.[2] While TTIP can help ensure that regulators are better informed about the consequences of their decisions for the transatlantic partner, it must also recognise that changes to regulation must go through our respective domestic decision-making procedures, that the regulators are, and will remain, under political oversight, and that they must retain their autonomy to make decisions appropriate to their jurisdictions, even if those decisions create divergences. This understanding addresses public concerns about transatlantic regulatory cooperation even as, we believe, TTIP will motivate the regulators to do more of it, with all the benefits that this might bring.

2. Regulatory cooperation: What it is and what the EU and US have achieved so far

2.1 Introducing international regulatory cooperation

As a bilateral agreement between two governments that will provide for some regulatory cooperation, TTIP represents merely one form of international regulatory cooperation (IRC), and must be understood in that context.

Governments have engaged in various forms of regulatory cooperation for decades, in everything from informal memoranda of understanding to full international treaties. International regulatory cooperation is pursued bilaterally (e.g. Regulatory Cooperation Councils between the US and Mexico and the US and Canada), multilaterally (the OECD MAD programme on the acceptance of

---

[2] This chapter focuses on the regulatory cooperation as a general matter, rather than on such regulatory issues that are traditionally covered in trade agreements -- sanitary and phyto-sanitary standards, technical barriers to trade such as standards and conformity assessment, etc., although these will of course also be incorporated in TTIP. For SPS and agri-food in TTIP, see Josling & Tangermann (2014); for the TBT chapter in TTIP, see Pelkmans (2015b).

chemical data), in global quasi-hierarchies that provide regulatory 'models' and strong incentives for voluntary implementation (e.g. financial regulation in the G-20 and the Financial Stability Board) and internationally (as treaties such as the Montreal Ozone Protocol, and in such international organizations as APEC, OECD, WTO (especially the SPS and TBT agreements), UNECE (on selected ICT standards, like Bluetooth, and car regulation), and ICAO (on safety in aviation and on minimum environmental requirements). International regulatory cooperation also happens in private international organisations such as ISO (on technical standards) and ILAC (on laboratory accreditation with recognition of conformity assessment results based on strict ILAC/ISO standards). International organisations for regulators have also emerged, such as the International Medical Devices Regulatory Forum, which focuses on global standards as well as a harmonised format of product-registration submissions, and, in medicines, the PIC/S (on common rules for inspections[3]) and the International Conference on Harmonisation (ICH) of technical aspects of marketing approval of medicines, which has issued some 50 guidelines.

This selective list shows that international regulatory cooperation has grown in importance and variety, at different levels and with a range of instruments. The OECD (2013) has done an extensive stock-taking of these various forms of IRC, and has mapped eleven distinct forms.

A convenient summary of the OECD mapping is depicted in Figure 2.1, which distinguishes not 11 but 12 mechanisms and presents international regulatory cooperation as a 'ladder' of increasing ambition, from non-binding and very loose mechanisms at the bottom to stringent, binding, and demanding ones at the top.

The bottom four rungs of the ladder show 'soft' - that is non-binding – IRCs, which can degenerate into a 'talk-shop' if left on their own. With respect to Step 2, principles of 'good regulatory practice' have been developed in the OECD 2012 Recommendations on Regulatory Policy and Governance (and accepted by both the US and the EU). Recognition of international standards (Step 3) is in the WTO TBT Agreement, but this obligation is not 'hard' or easily enforceable given the long-standing discord between the US and the EU about the definition of an international standard. The EU is of the view that 'international standards' are written and promulgated by established international bodies (like ISO and IEC) while the US believes the

---

[3] See www.picscheme.org

Agreement has a much broader application. The economic meaning of Step 3 can be rendered much more powerful if done in conjunction with Step 4, which requires the explicit consideration of international effects when drafting a domestic regulation which might affect trade. Depending on the stringency of the agreed obligations, and without undermining each party's autonomous 'right to regulate,' Step 4 can go quite far.

Figure 2.1 The ladder of international regulatory cooperation

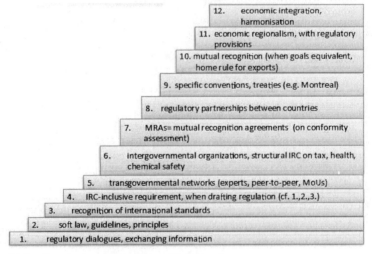

12. economic integration, harmonisation
11. economic regionalism, with regulatory provisions
10. mutual recognition (when goals equivalent, home rule for exports)
9. specific conventions, treaties (e.g. Montreal)
8. regulatory partnerships between countries
7. MRAs= mutual recognition agreements (on conformity assessment)
6. intergovernmental organizations, structural IRC on tax, health, chemical safety
5. transgovernmental networks (experts, peer-to-peer, MoUs)
4. IRC-inclusive requirement, when drafting regulation (cf. 1.,2.,3.)
3. recognition of international standards
2. soft law, guidelines, principles
1. regulatory dialogues, exchanging information

Note: IRC = International Regulatory Cooperation.
Source: Authors' own configuration based on OECD (2013).

Trans-governmental networks of experts and regulators (Step 5) have become important too, both in EU/US relations and embedded in broader country participation. The International Competition Network, for example, goes beyond the EU and US but has been strongly influenced by the two parties. This is also true in the Bank for International Settlement's Basel Committee on banking supervision, which has a wider membership but remains dominated by the EU and the US. Regulators in medicines and medical devices have also developed multilateral or global forums, based in part on initial US-EU bilateral cooperation. This suggests that Step 5 may work bilaterally sometimes, but with global markets and global value chains), the bilateral context could become a stumbling block or be seen as insufficient.

The same may well apply to Step 6 on international organisations. In general, EU-US cooperation is essential to regulatory cooperation in these multilateral forums because work in large international organisations is frequently shallow and soft, hampered by the resistance of some members and/or a divergence in underlying policy objectives. And where IRC in such organisations is successful, it can take years, if not decades, of prudent approximation. A good example of long-winding but eventually successful IRC is the binding OECD MAD agreement on mutual acceptance of chemical safety test data, which took decades.

In Step 7, mutual recognition of conformity assessment, the EU and the US took the lead in the early 1990s, but several other countries caught up on the basis of the EU-US model, the experiences and lessons of which are summarized in Box 2.1 below. Mutual Recognition Agreement (MRAs) on conformity assessment do not affect or put in question any aspect of either party's regulatory regime. Even so, MRAs on conformity assessment are more demanding in that they are also treaties, hence 'hard' law. Equivalence agreements are another option mentioned in the WTO TBT Agreement and the 1998 US-EU Veterinary Equivalence Agreement has been partially successful (see Josling & Tangermann, 2014, for an assessment).

Step 8 (regulatory partnerships) is ill-defined. The partnerships may amount to an ambition greater than MRAs (hence, Step 8 on the IRC ladder) but that is far from certain. Thus, Canada–US regulatory cooperation (with a Council to that effect) is not binding and characterised more by the ambitions and methods of Steps 4 and 5. Such voluntarism may still yield results, though, especially as cooperating regulators build trust in each other and confidence in the partners' rules and enforcement ability. For regulatory partnerships to be as strong and effective as Step 8 would suggest, one would need to specify in much greater detail what regulatory principles, opportunities, disciplines, and cooperative obligations the parties subscribe to in a treaty or other legally-binding agreement. .

The other steps in the IRC ladder go even farther. Step 9 is about narrow treaties that bind countries in a specific area or sector. A leading and successful example is the Montreal Convention on protecting the ozone layer by forbidding or restricting F-gases. Other similar conventions are less successful because they have been drafted in far more circumspect language and with exceptions, carve-outs and other exclusions, or, like UNFCCC, form no more than a general framework for very long-term cooperation (here, on mitigating climate change).

Step 10 on mutual recognition more broadly is even more ambitious. At this level, mutual recognition agreements can stipulate that when the objectives and enforcement of safety, health, environment, investor/saver and consumer protection (SHEIC) risk regulation are 'equivalent', home rules of the exporting countries are regarded as sufficient guarantee for allowing market access into the importing country.[4] Thus, here, the equivalence does not refer to a case-by-case examination of product types by the importing country, in the framework of an 'equivalence agreement' (Step 7), but refers to policy *objectives*. This goes much further and has fairly radical implications.

One huge misunderstanding about mutual recognition is that it might lead to less or less ambitious regulation, once the rules of the exporting country are determined 'sufficient'. This misunderstanding is based on the famous quote from the 1979 Cassis-de-Dijon case,[5] but that quote assumes equivalence of objectives first. In this sense, mutual recognition is about overcoming different technical specifications that reach an equivalent regulatory objective – the latter refers to the market failure that matters and is addressed by that objective; the instruments or technical details are not decisive and should not be (in other words, they may differ).

Steps 11 and 12 are not expected to apply to TTIP as a rule. One should consider Step 11 as far more stringent, perhaps even somewhat centralising, than Step 8 (regulatory partnerships). For instance, the Australia-New Zealand 'Trans-Tasman' Mutual Recognition Agreement builds on mutual recognition but this is occasionally combined with common rules and, in food, with a common enforcement agency. Step 12 proposes harmonisation as a regular element of economic regionalism. TTIP is not meant to assume such ambitions and it is almost certainly not even desirable as a rule. But there are isolated instances of harmonisation between the US and the

---

[4] Extensive analyses of mutual recognition can be found in Pelkmans (2007) and (2012) based on the EU; the practice of MR in Trans-Tasman MRA is analysed in Pelkmans & Correia de Brito (2015a, Annex C).

[5] EU member states must allow 'a product lawfully produced and marketed in another member state into their own market'. Case C-120/78. As formulated, this is the pure origin principle. However, one must read this in conjunction with the logic of the derogations for member states, which are 'justified' if certain regulatory objectives will not be fulfilled. However, the mutual recognition logic consists of establishing whether the objectives of another member state are equivalent (even when not identical) in providing regulatory protection; if so, the origin principle prevails and imports cannot be blocked.

EU which, perhaps surprisingly, have emerged from international organisations (Step 6) and/or specific agreements. One example is far-reaching harmonisation of maritime safety rules in the IMO. As a result, the EU and the US have concluded a separate MRA in 2004 on 49 types of maritime equipment, which works well.

The OECD (2013) study and Figure 2.1 underscore that negotiators and regulators have to think in terms of many different forms for international regulatory cooperation. The spectrum comprises many options, and each option has stringent and less stringent variants. And although one might be correct in suspecting that 'soft' steps near the bottom of the ladder tend to be less effective, this is not always the case. For instance, regulators are loath to bind themselves in treaties and hence might opt for the lower steps in their cooperation. But as shown in medicines and medical devices, the voluntary follow-up in national regulatory regimes of what has been agreed in such sectorial regulatory forums has been active, and many countries adopt such guidelines or allow acceptance of single-form submissions. Regulatory cooperation in TTIP can benefit from these insights as well.

An important conclusion of the sophisticated mapping in the OECD international regulatory cooperation study is that despite "...the growing trend in regulatory cooperation, IRC is not based on a clear understanding of benefits, costs and success factors of the various IRC options" (OECD, 2013, p. 75). This warning must be kept in mind for regulatory cooperation as we look briefly at the history of US-EU regulatory cooperation, and lay out how it could be developed in TTIP. It should be clear in any event that TTIP can be based on, or linked to, many such international initiatives or regimes, or, indeed, it might assume a longer-run process of enhancing the ambitions of such IRC by setting more ambitious TTIP objectives as a leading example.

2.2 Recent US-EU regulatory cooperation: A bird's eye view

While US regulators have been working with their counterparts in major EU member states for many years, cooperation with EU-level counterparts began with the Joint Statement on Regulatory Cooperation at the end of 1997,[6] followed a year later by the

---

[6] "Regulatory Cooperation: Facilitating Trade while Promoting Consumer Protection," Joint Statement released in conjunction with the US-EU Summit in

'Agreement on Mutual Recognition Between the European Community and the United States of America.'[7]

As described in Box 2.1 below, these first agreements were generally limited in scope, applying mainly to recognition of certain laboratories being able to test whether locally-produced products in six sectors (in the 1998 MRA) met the regulatory requirements of the other party.

Box 2.1 The 1998 US-EU MRAs and lessons drawn

As one of their first full forays into bilateral regulatory cooperation, the US and EU concluded a Mutual Recognition Agreement (MRA) on conformity assessment in 1998. The MRA has a general set of principles, rules, and procedures in a 'chapeau' or 'umbrella,' with six distinct annexes in the sectors: telecoms equipment, electromagnetic compatibility (EMC) of equipment and appliances, electrical safety of goods (including machinery), pharmaceutical Good Manufacturing Practices (GMP), medical devices, and recreational craft. Consistent with the practices in Step 7 above, this MRA had the limited objective of allowing designated Conformity Assessment Bodies from each party to certify that products in these sectors met the regulatory requirements of the other party. As such, it reflected a conscious choice not to engage in any regulatory change but to focus solely on reducing transaction costs for market access. The economic gains from such limited MRAs tend to be relatively small, unless the costs of conformity assessment amount to a considerable surcharge on the export price. After carefully reviewing the experience with the MRA, Pelkmans & Correia de Brito (2015b) find:

1. Despite great initial efforts, only three of the six sector MRAs are operational: telecoms equipment, electro-magnetic compatibility, and recreational craft. In terms of trade values, the three MRAs that work cover only one-fifth of the bilateral trade originally foreseen under all six sectoral MRAs. In the other three – pharmaceuticals, medical devices, and electrical equipment – the initial trade policy focus was probably unsuitable for what was seen by US regulators as a loss of control of properly serving their regulatory objectives. Regulators should therefore play a major role in designing regulatory cooperation, even in the case of MRAs, whilst trade policy may generate collateral benefits but cannot be decisive.

Washington, D.C., 5 December 1997 (www.eurunion.org/partner/summit/Summit9712/regulst.htm).

[7] See
http://trade.ec.europa.eu/doclib/docs/2003/october/tradoc_111718.pdf.

2. MRAs are easier in markets which are less heavily regulated, but ironically, in these cases they are also less needed because alternatives to MRAs (in particular, suppliers' declarations of conformity, or SDoCs) can serve as a low-cost and swift solution. When SDoCs are not permitted, alternatives such as subcontracting may nevertheless be used by market players. Thus, in particular, large US and EU exporters with a steady customer base (or as part of a value chain) in the EU and US have a great interest in durable relationships with trusted CABs. The practical working of the MRA will then be significant only for new entrants or occasional exporters or in cases of overload. New entrants may well be SMEs, so for them and possibly the emergence of 'new' competition, the MRA would still fulfil a useful function.

3. MRAs in heavily regulated markets require a considerable degree of convergence in desired levels of protection as well as a gradual build-up of trust and confidence between the regulators. This did not work at first for medicines and medical devices. There are also indications that at the time, in these two sectors, the EU internal market rules and supervision still left something to be desired. Simultaneously, at world level, cautious attempts were initiated to come to greater harmonisation for pharmaceuticals and medical devices [8] in some respects, such as similar data and shorter time-to-market, in which the EU and the US played a leading role. These alternative IRC tracks have meanwhile become quite successful, thereby more or less obviating the 1998 MRA provisions.

4. In electrical goods safety, the third sector that failed (the MRA was suspended by the EU in 2003), the EU attempted in 2008 to convince OSHA (the US regulator for occupational health and safety) to accept SDoCs from EU producers. SDoCs are a form of self-certification customary in the EU 'New Approach' to reducing regulatory barriers. After a two-year investigation, OSHA concluded that the empirical evidence about equivalent or better-risk reduction in the EU was insufficient. This experience underscores that regulators will only enter into agreements with their counterparts where hard evidence exists that both the rules and the enforcement of those rules demonstrate that the counterpart's approach delivers similar regulatory outcomes.

Source: Pelkmans & Correia de Brito (2015b).

---

[8] The Global Harmonisation Task Force for medical devices, active since the mid-1990s, and the International Conference on Harmonisation of Technical Requirements of Pharmaceuticals for Human use (ICH), founded in 1989. For more detail, see Pelkmans & Correia de Brito (2015b).

These efforts were heavily backed by industry, and in particular the Transatlantic Business Dialogue (TABD), which the US and EU had helped create with the 1995 'New Transatlantic Agenda', in part to encourage more direct business engagement and advice in transatlantic trade matters. (Transatlantic Dialogues for consumers, labour, and the environment were established a few years later.) At this time TABD was also strongly encouraging great regulatory cooperation in automotive safety. This failed when the US regulator (the National Highway Transport Safety Agency, NHTSA) undertook extensive studies about certain specific auto safety features (e.g., on standards for side door crash resistance) which demonstrated that EU vehicles were less safe than their American counterparts. This experience again underscores some of the lessons learned in the earlier MRAs – that regulators cannot and will not lower safety standards just to promote trade, and that they depend on hard evidence, rather than political good will.

Despite setbacks, more substantive cooperation began to take off with the first US-EU 'Regulatory Cooperation Roadmap' in 2002, which was successively expanded from six sectors to sixteen over the next three years. An important component to this was a consensus in 2002 on good regulatory practices, which helped strengthen the cooperation and which also helped spur greater dialogue between the US Office of Information and Regulatory Affairs (OIRA) and the Commission's Secretariat General, which also oversees better regulation in the EU. This experience eventually helped in the establishment of the US-EU High Level Regulatory Cooperation Forum (HLRCF) in 2005 to further promote best practices in such cooperation.

By 2007, when the Transatlantic Economic Council (TEC) was founded, transatlantic regulatory cooperation was booming. For example, at that time the US Food and Drug Administration (FDA) informally estimated that its officers were having over 1,000 substantive contacts a year with their European counterparts in DG SANCO, the European Medicines Agency (EMEA), and the European Food Safety Authority (EFSA).

Annex 1 provides a detailed summary list of all the US-EU regulatory cooperation initiatives we have been able to identify since the first agreement on regulatory principles in 1997. This growing cooperation has had a number of significant results, both broadly as with the 2008 report comparing US and EU approaches to import safe products,[9] and in individual sectors, from the November 2007 FDA/EMEA decision to accept a single application for orphan drugs,[10] to the 2008 US Securities and Exchange Commission's (SEC) decision to accept the EU's international accounting standards as equivalent for US capital markets purposes.[11] One of the most ambitious examples was the conclusion in 2009 of the US-EU Bilateral Aviation Safety Agreement,[12] under which the FAA and the European Aviation Safety Agency (EASA) agreed to accept one another's air-worthiness certifications for Boeing and Airbus airplanes, even though an aeroplane is arguably the most regulated product on the market and even amidst an intense WTO trade dispute on the supports both sides give to their respective companies. In 2012, the two governments concluded other agreements, including mutual recognition of their respective approaches to organic produce[13] and to container and air cargo supply chain security systems,[14] as well as joint work in such areas as electric vehicle safety and design requirements.

While the breadth and depth of US-EU regulatory cooperation has been growing, it tends to be technical, and thus known only to those directly engaged in the sectors concerned. Because of this, many outside these areas tend to be sceptical – and at times outright critical – of the cooperation. This may underscore the need for a more basic understanding of what regulatory cooperation is and should be about between the United States and the European Union.

---

[9] See "Toward Enhanced Cooperation between the European Union and United States of America on the Safety of (Imported) Products" (http://ec.europa.eu/enterprise/policies/international/files/tec_safety_en.pdf).

[10] See EMEA press release, "The European Union and FDA Working Together to Create a Single Application for Orphan Designation for Medicines", 26 November 2007 (www.emea.europa.eu/docs/en_GB/document_library/Press_release/2009/11/WC500011002.pdf).

[11] See www.sec.gov/rules/final/2007/33-8879.pdf

[12] See www.faa.gov/aircraft/repair/media/Safety_Agreement_Between_US_and_EC.pdf

[13] See www.ams.usda.gov/AMSv1.0/getfile?dDocName=STELPRDC5097063

[14] See www.cbp.gov/newsroom/national-media-release/2013-02-08-050000/eu-us-fully-implement-mutual-recognition-decision

3. Basic principles and motivation for TTIP regulatory cooperation

The primary role of governments in modern societies is to protect their citizens – from foreign aggression and domestic crime, of course, but also from abusive labour practices, unhealthy environments, and unsafe products and services.

This last function is the most relevant aspect when it comes to trade across borders. But here it needs to be emphasised that the job of regulators is to pre-empt or prevent any market exchange which has unacceptable adverse effects on consumers or workers, or the environment. Regulators want to prevent unsafe products and services from getting into the domestic market whether those products or services are produced at home or abroad.[15]

The level of safety that a regulator demands is primarily a function of the political system and income levels in a society.

➢ **Politically**, in countries with little or no input from citizens, the desired levels of safety will reflect the preferences of government officials; in an autocratic dictatorship, the preference of the ruler. In democratic societies, however, with a transparent and rules-based approach to governance, the level of safety demanded in regulation will in general reflect the risk preferences of the voters as expressed in elections. In this sense, democracy is not just a 'value', but has a very real operational significance with respect to regulation.

➢ **Economically**, increasing levels of protection costs money, and governments need to balance these costs with the benefits in terms of safety that regulation can bring. In a democratic society where the levels of protection will reflect the polity at large, the degree of safety demanded will therefore tend to be a function of income – the higher the level of income, the less important the additional costs of risk mitigation and the higher the level of protection demanded. This is a wholly domestic affair – democratic governments will regulate to the risk preference

---

[15] Governments may of course also regulate international trade to minimise the economic risks of competition from foreign firms, otherwise known as protectionism. That aspect of risk mitigation is not considered here, as both the US and the EU nominally eschew it.

demanded by their voters even in the absence of imports from another jurisdiction.

This somewhat theoretical discussion is directly relevant to the issue of regulatory cooperation in TTIP. As democratic societies with comparable levels of income and wealth and transparent and politically accountable[16] regulatory systems, the United States and the European Union have in general identified the same sorts of goods and services as posing risks to their citizens (and voters), and strive for the same level of safety in those areas—that is, their regulatory objectives and outcomes are generally similar.

This general observation is based on both impressions and empirical studies. Impressionistically, over 25 million people travel each way between the United States and Europe each year, staying in hotels, eating local foods, renting cars, buying products, and otherwise engaging in daily activities; they do not seem to perceive any difference in the level of safety provided. More academically, a 2010 study published by Resources for the Future (RFF), based on 20 case studies and 3,000 observations of risk-reducing regulatory decisions in the US and EU, found that overall risk stringency is about the same, with the differences largely due to non-safety related issues.[17]

It is precisely this political and economic foundation that permits, and indeed encourages, a truly ambitious level of regulatory cooperation in TTIP. US and EU legislators and regulators have traditionally determined the level of safety they desire based on domestic costs and benefits. The US and EU economies are so tightly integrated, however, that these inward-looking approaches are insufficient, missing both the costs and the benefits of the transatlantic implications of these domestic choices. The EU and the US have the largest trading relationship in the world, with over $1 trillion in two-way trade in goods and services each year. Further, US firms have invested over $2.3 trillion in the EU, while EU firms have invested some $1.7 trillion in the US. These investments together generate nearly $5

---

[16] In the United States, Congress actively oversees the activities of US regulatory agencies. In the European Union, the Council, representing the elected governments of the 28 member states, 'co-decides' the level of safety in regulation with the directly elected European Parliament, while member state governments and parliaments will be the 'first responders' to failures in market surveillance and enforcement. For an authoritative and detailed exposition of the US and EU regulatory system, see Parker & Alemanno (2014).

[17] See Wiener et al. (2010).

trillion in sales each year. Nearly half of all trade is intra-industry and intra-firm. When legislators and regulators on either side make decisions without considering this integration, even if they are separately trying to achieve the same level of safety, they may do so in ways that require products and services to be designed and produced differently to be sold in each market.

This raises costs to producers, at times to the point where they cannot profitably supply a product or service to the other side of the Atlantic. This is particularly so for smaller firms, many of which only know that the regulatory requirements and standards are different, and don't have the ability to research or re-tool to meet them. But it also affects large firms – the cost of crashing over a hundred custom-made models to meet different safety, testing, and certification requirements in automobiles, for instance, run to hundreds of millions of euros. This makes it almost impossible for smaller French and Italian car manufacturers to sell into the US market. The same can happen for medicines, especially for rare illnesses. And this, of course, raises costs to consumers, who may be wholly denied products and services that they wanted or needed.

One of the most politically interesting examples was the pressure put on the FDA in the 1980s and 1990s to fast-track approval of HIV medicines that had been working effectively in Europe for years. And both societies as a whole lose the gains in productivity that would come from more companies competing in their markets, and the advantages of synergy and global competitiveness that firms working on both sides of the Atlantic could have if they did not face these 'unnecessary' regulatory divergences: 'unnecessary' in the sense that the intended levels of safety are similar (see also Box 2.2).

The disadvantages of insufficient consideration of the transatlantic costs and benefits of greater regulatory compatibility between the United States and the European Union are, however, only one part of problem. Potentially more important is the adverse impact on the regulators themselves, and their ability to achieve their goal of keeping their citizens safe. Regulators devote their resources to ensure that rules are being observed for the products and services being sold in their market. The enormous volumes of transatlantic trade require a correspondingly large amount of resources to police. At the same time, globalisation has also greatly increased trade with many other partners. With ever-increasing volumes of imports from other - potentially more risky - jurisdictions, sophisticated and ever-lengthening supply chains, and ever-decreasing budgets, the regulators are in danger of being stretched too thinly to do their job. If, however, they have evidence demonstrating that their transatlantic counterparts are able to enforce levels of protection similar to their own, they can develop a partnership with that counterpart regulator, allowing them to focus their enforcement resources on higher-risk problems. Indeed, it was precisely this broader gain from international regulatory cooperation that motivated President Obama to issue Executive Order 13609,[18] encouraging US regulators to be more active in this area, especially with places like the EU, which share US regulatory values.

Box 2.2 Potential economic gains from regulatory cooperation in TTIP

In the sense of our discussion above, many of the gains from regulatory cooperation cannot be easily measured. However, a number of empirical economic simulation studies on TTIP have been published in 2013 and 2014; two – Francois et al. (2013) for the Commission Impact Assessment, and Fontagne et al. (2013) - explicitly study TTIP regulatory cooperation in detail. These two studies, both of which are based on a broader ECORYS study from 2009, attempt to estimate the costs of regulatory differences as a percentage of export invoice costs (the so-called 'tariff equivalent' of technical barriers to trade, or TBTs). The studies estimate these TBT tariff equivalents between the US and the EU to range from 15-72%, depending on the sector. Such percentages are a large multiple of US and EU nominal tariffs on industrial goods and many agricultural products. Francois et al. estimate that no less than 56% of TTIP's economic gains arise from an assumed 50% cost reduction of TBTs (their ambitious scenario). Even with the difficulty of properly estimating the benefits of TBT reduction (see Pelkmans et al., 2014) as well as the limitations of even the best econometric models, the reduction of TBT costs through regulatory cooperation is obviously important to the overall economic gains of TTIP.

The ability for enhanced transatlantic regulatory cooperation to increase the efficiency and therefore the effectiveness of US and EU regulators is one of the most misunderstood benefits of TTIP, even by some of the regulators themselves. Given their political accountability at home, whether to Congress, the European Parliament or the EU member states, their ability to cooperate with a foreign counterpart is directly proportional to the level of trust and confidence that they have

---

[18] See www.whitehouse.gov/sites/default/files/omb/inforeg/eo_13609/eo13609_05012012.pdf

in that counterpart. And that comes only with time and experience. In this sense, the US and the EU are now better positioned for an ambitious approach to regulatory cooperation in TTIP, as the US and EU regulatory systems have improved, and as regulatory cooperation has grown over the past 15 years.

4. Turbo-charging regulatory cooperation in TTIP[19]

The most important question now is how TTIP can build upon the experiences US and EU regulators have had over the past 15 years in collaborating with one another, given the broader political, economic, consumer, and regulatory benefits of greater transatlantic regulatory cooperation.

4.1 General considerations

As discussed above, the single most important consideration is understanding that regulatory cooperation can only work if the regulators on both sides have the full trust and confidence of one another, that the levels of protection are similar, and that the enforcement of those regulatory requirements is effective. While TTIP aims to enhance regulatory collaboration and compatibility, regulators in the end must make decisions that reflect the political will of their electorate.

A second critical consideration is a clear delimitation of the scope of regulatory cooperation under TTIP. Regulatory cooperation in TTIP should focus on laws and regulations that directly apply to goods and services traded between the two parties. Laws and regulations that go to wholly domestic matters, such as those on working hours, wage levels, air pollution standards, etc., should be outside the scope of any general disciplines on regulatory cooperation, even though those measures may have an indirect effect on trade

A third consideration which also affects the scope is that the obligations on regulatory cooperation in TTIP should apply to the EU Commission and the US Executive branch and independent agencies, not the respective legislatures (Congress in the United States, the

---

[19] The comments in this section are jointly drafted but reflect the first author's experiences in transatlantic regulatory cooperation as well as his work in the US Chamber; see, for instance, www.uschamber.com/sites/default/files/ regulatory_coherence_regulatory_cooperation_-chamber_ttip_paper_- _final_3-02.pdf, February 2015.

Council and European Parliament in the EU). This third consideration is elaborated upon below.

With these three considerations in mind, the regulatory part of TTIP (here, not counting SPS and TBTs, see before) should have three essential components:

- agreement on principles and best practices in domestic regulation (sometimes referred to as 'regulatory coherence'),
- general (or 'horizontal') provisions governing regulatory cooperation and
- sectoral annexes reflecting agreements that have been, and will be, agreed between counterpart US and EU regulators, both during and after the TTIP treaty negotiations.

This structure, and in particular the use of sectoral annexes, is essential to the acceptance and functioning of transatlantic regulatory cooperation in the context of the TTIP negotiations. It is essential, firstly because it recognises pragmatically that trust and confidence between counterpart sectoral regulators is the core of regulatory cooperation; secondly because it guarantees, for citizens and politicians alike, that the regulators themselves (rather than trade negotiators) are in charge of the details of the cooperation for which they are politically accountable; and thirdly because it allows the regulatory part of TTIP to be a 'living' agreement, with the inclusion of additional regulator-to-regulator agreements even after the TTIP is concluded, as additional experience, trust, and confidence are gained between the counterpart agencies.

The remainder of this section will focus on the regulatory coherence and cooperation aspects of TTIP, as well as the sectoral annexes, since these are the most novel aspects of the regulatory part of the agreement.

4.2   Regulatory coherence

The opening section of a TTIP regulatory chapter must lay out the principles and practices that are the foundation on which the trust and confidence of regulators are to be built – a common understanding of what constitutes a strong, democratically accountable regulatory system. This should not be difficult to draft: the US and EU have twice issued joint statements on this (2002[20] and 2011[21]), focusing in particular on the need for transparency, stakeholder participation, and accountability in rule-making, as well as the need for quality impact assessments, evidence-based decision-making and the like, as described in Box 2.3 below.

Box 2.3 US-EU consensus on regulatory principles and practices

The US and the EU have been developing a consensus on regulatory principles and practices since the late 1990s. In fact, its origin may be traced back to the 1995 recommendation of the OECD Council on Improving the Quality of Government Regulation. In addition to the 1997 US-EU guidelines on regulatory cooperation, the three main expressions of this consensus include the joint statements of 2002 and 2011 noted earlier and, more recently, the 2012 recommendation of the OECD Council on Regulatory Policy and Governance.[22] The 2011 'Common Understanding' demonstrates that the two partners have already developed regulatory principles that are very similar, if not the same. The Understanding reaffirms their shared commitment to good regulation, and is based on EU and US documents that already guide domestic regulatory policy. When regulation is to be developed, it should be evidence-based (with impact assessment or equivalents), include an analysis of relevant alternatives, evaluate the effectiveness of existing regulation, and apply approaches that minimise the burden while aiming for simplicity. The regulatory process should be transparent and should solicit, evaluate, and respond to input from all stakeholders.

Further, the 2011 Common Understanding says explicitly that "regulatory measures should aim to avoid unnecessarily divergent or duplicative requirements between the US and the EU, when appropriate". Moreover, the US and the EU "should also explore a process to exchange regulatory information of the Unified Agenda and Work Programme, respectively, ... and have a fixed agenda item at the High Level Regulatory Cooperation Forum" with a view to seeing whether the two parties can work together on areas both are considering. The Understanding also encourages new regulatory

---

[20] See www.whitehouse.gov/sites/default/files/omb/oira/irc/2002-guidelines-on-reg-coop-and-transparency.pdf, April 2002

[21] See www.whitehouse.gov/sites/default/files/omb/oira/irc/common-understanding-on-regulatory-principles-and-best-practices.pdf, 8 June 2011.

[22] See www.oecd.org/gov/regulatory-policy/49990817.pdf. Note that between the US and the EU, the starting point is still the 2011 Common Understanding.

cooperation measures, and obliges both to flag upcoming regulatory proposals likely to have international trade and investment effects, and/or publishing an Annual Notice to solicit public comments.

The 2002 guidelines are more detailed but otherwise very similar. They begin with seven steps which "will help minimise and resolve trade frictions and facilitate trade." None of these seven steps are surprising or controversial, and are presumably often, if not always, in the domestic public interest, too. Among other things, they include the commitment to "pursue... harmoni[s]ed, equivalent or compatible solutions.... and to minimize... or eliminate unnecessary divergence in regulations" through dialogue at all phases of the regulation development process. Transparency is strongly emphasised, as is the need for adequate time to provide meaningful comments, and their reasonable consideration, on draft proposals. These should be performance-oriented and cost effective, and hence have fewer adverse effects. These and other suggestions are by now well accepted throughout the OECD.

The issue being addressed in the TTIP negotiations now is how precisely the two sides think these principles and practices should be implemented, and indeed how to go beyond the 2011 Common Understanding. The United States, which has emphasised the importance of the concepts of transparency, participation, and accountability, argues in particular that the Commission should publish draft legislation and regulation ('implementing measures' and 'delegated acts' under the EU's 'comitology' procedures) on the internet for comment from all stakeholders, and that it should then summarise and respond to the substantive comments and evidence provided through that process when it finalises the proposal.

These ideas are less straightforward than they seem in the EU context. When it comes to legislative proposals, publication of a draft for comment prior to adoption of a proposal by the College of Commissioners is a sensitive issue for the Commission, as it is seen as undermining one of the central powers of the Commission under the EU treaties – the right to initiate legislation. The Commission is concerned that the member states in the Council and Members of the European Parliament would be among the most active participants in the public consultations about the drafts, which would essentially eliminate its right to initiate legislation. It therefore balks at making such a radical constitutional change in the context of a trade negotiation.

But it should be stressed that the idea of providing an opportunity to comment on draft legislation is not just a request of the US government, but one made by many European stakeholders as well, both in the business sector, in civil society, and by a 2009 broad Task Force of an EU think-tank.[23] As such, changes that might come about here can and should happen independently of TTIP, and be consistent with the Commission's own efforts to improve its domestic regulatory processes. And indeed, First Vice-President Timmermans and the Secretariat General of the Commission are now considering responses to the June 2014 request for comments on guidelines on the use of stakeholder input in the legislative and regulatory process.[24]

There are a number of ways input on legislative proposals could be handled without endangering the right of initiative. Publishing a draft after the initial inter-services consultation might be one approach; at this point, the serious politics (and thus the sensitivities) in the Commission have not yet begun. An alternative might be to stay with the current system and publish legislative proposals after adoption by the College - after all, these are proposals that must go through the legislative process in the Council and European Parliament. The Commission could accept comments on the proposals for, say, 60 days; these comments would be published on the Commission website, and the Commission's analysis and response to them could then be made available to the Council and Parliament upon formal presentation of

---

[23] See, e.g., the many responses to the request of the Commission's Secretariat General on 1 July 2014 for comments on draft guidelines concerning impact assessments and stakeholder consultation, which can be found respectively at http://ec.europa.eu/smart-regulation/impact/consultation_2014/contributions/index_en.htm and http://ec.europa.eu/smart-regulation/impact/planned_ia/consultation_2014/contributions/index_en.htm. For the Task Force report, see a CEPS book on reforms of EU regulation and policy-making (Renda, 2009, p. xii and pp. 36-37, as 'idea no. 13').

[24] As this chapter was being prepared for publication, the Commission adopted "Better Regulation for Better Results – An EU Agenda" (COM(2015) 215 of 19 May 2015, which includes an open eight-week comment period on Commission legislative proposals after the College adopts them; comments will be provided to the European Parliament and Council. The Commission will also introduce a four-week comment period on delegated acts and implementing measures.

the proposals to those institutions (see footnote 24 acknowledging this idea).

In the case of such regulatory measures as delegated acts and implementing measures, where the Commission has considerably more authority over the proposal, the idea of publishing drafts for notice and comment should be far less controversial, as acknowledged in the new Better Regulation package of the Commission. However, these two types of technical implementation refer to a massive quantity of acts/measures, many of which are actually of little importance, so there may well be a practical issue of overload.[25]

The EU too has demands of the United States when it comes to regulatory coherence. The legislative process in the United States appears more chaotic to Europeans than that in the EU, with literally thousands of bills being offered each Congress. Many of these are never acted on, yet can form the basis for amendments of a significant nature that (in the Senate at least) can often come to the floor for a vote with little or no notice, never mind an opportunity to comment. (That said, US legislation tends to be much more general in nature than it does in the EU, so that the effects on traded products and services are more likely to come later in the process, when legislation is implemented during the regulatory phase.)

Under the US Constitution, the executive branch has no control over the legislative process, just as the EU Commission has no control over the Council or the European Parliament. Nor will any of those political bodies surrender in a trade agreement their autonomy to legislate. This is why the third key consideration noted in section 3 above is necessary, and one of the first things both sides need to do in TTIP is to recognise that they can only demand some semblance of coherence between the Executive and the Commission, acknowledging that the political and legislative process outside those two bodies is necessarily a bit messy on both sides.[26]

---

[25] In COM (2015) 215 (ibid., p. 50), the Commission writes that delegated acts can be commented on by stakeholders, but does not refer to, say, a selection of them. This is not the case for the other category where only 'important implementing acts' which are 'subject to Committee opinion' will be made public for comments.

[26] But legislation could still be TTIP-relevant, if the administrations on both sides can take on commitments and attempt to convince Congress and EP/Council to incorporate them. Also, the legal dichotomy between legislation

Even so, the Europeans could ask the US executive branch to take steps to make the US legislative process less confusing for its largest trading partner. Proposed bills are only serious if they are brought to the relevant Congressional committee for a hearing and mark-up. At this stage, the Executive branch is almost always requested to testify. If it is, and if the proposal would affect a product or service traded between the US and EU, TTIP could oblige the Administration to alert the EU of the hearing, and provide a copy of the Administration's testimony as a courtesy. In addition, if and when legislation is to be voted on, the Executive branch often issues a statement of the administration's position. This too could be provided to the EU if the bill affects a product or service that the EU exports to the US. In both instances, the Office of Management and Budget (OMB) is responsible for coordinating the Administration's agreed position on the legislation, and should be the point of contact for these efforts to enhance transparency.[27]

In contrast, by law under the Administrative Procedures Act, the US regulatory process is already generally open for participation by any stakeholder, including those in Europe. Proposed rules are published well in advance; all comments must be received and published, and must be responded to by the regulatory agency in adopting its final rule. Violations of these procedures can – and frequently are – brought before administrative court, which can – and frequently does – require the agency to undertake additional evaluation before a rule is implemented. The system is not perfect[28] (no system is), but it is generally open, transparent, and accountable.

In addition, for the US side to truly provide coherence, it must recognize that TTIP must also cover the activities of US 'independent' regulatory agencies. These agencies, generally known as Commissions (Federal Communications Commission, etc.), are outside the Executive branch and answer to both Congress and the President. Although such Commissions do not and legally cannot come under OMB, and so will

---

and administration is not always followed in practice. Thus, recent Acts like the Jobs Act, the Affordable Care Act, and a recent one on cybersecurity were drafted by the administration and (mostly) taken over by Congress.

[27] In fact, this procedural courtesy is already often practiced with respect to the European Commission, and the OMB already de facto coordinates.

[28] See, e.g. statement of Michelle Sager, Director, Strategic Issues, Government Accountability Office, to the US Senate Committee on Homeland Security and Governmental Affairs, 11 March 2014 (www.gao.gov/assets/670/661540.pdf).

need to be treated differently in some respects, the legislation that implements TTIP can provide Congressional assent to bring them into the scope of transatlantic regulatory cooperation. This is particularly important in the context of financial services regulation.

The EU too must assure institutional coherence by fully including its autonomous agencies (the European Chemicals Agency, the European Food Safety Authority, the European Banking Authority and the like) in TTIP, for while these are, strictly, not rule-making bodies (but often risk assessors), they are instrumental and increasingly influential in the rule-making process and/or as supervisors. Legally, the EU might not follow our advice to include these agencies fully, as they are not independent regulators, but we advocate the strongest possible involvement, without affecting ultimate regulatory responsibility.

4.3   Regulatory cooperation

While the regulatory coherence part of TTIP should help improve both sides' understanding of and trust and confidence in the domestic rule-making procedures of the other side, the regulatory cooperation part should establish obligations that apply generally to all regulatory agencies on both sides to ensure that their decisions are informed about the impact of proposals on the transatlantic partner. And, as noted above, it should also include annexes that reflect regulator-to-regulator agreements in specific product and service areas.

Again, it's important to re-emphasise here the three considerations spelled out in section 3 above: the need to explicitly affirm regulator autonomy, primarily through the use of the annexes; the focus on regulations that directly affect products and services that are or could be traded between the United States and the EU; and the application of these regulatory cooperation commitments to the Executive branch and independent agencies in the United States, and the Commission and relevant autonomous agencies or advisory bodies in the EU.

Within this scope, the horizontal regulatory cooperation provisions of TTIP should:

- establish the explicit goal of making US and EU regulatory regimes increasingly compatible,
- provide the necessary tools to regulators to achieve this goal and
- create an institutional framework to oversee and guide this process.

The goal should be simple, and unbounded by time. It provides a direction to the ongoing regulatory cooperation process, but should not mandate that that goal must be achieved in all instances (it won't). Further, it cannot be subject to a timetable, in the recognition that building trust and confidence between counterpart regulators takes time, and indeed can be quickly lost. TTIP will set the trajectory for greater and deeper collaboration, but it will not reach an end-point, for among other things, laws and regulations in our society are and should be dynamic (in contrast, for instance, with the static tariff levels that are a normal subject of trade talks).

The 'tools' that should apply to all sectors falling within the specified scope should both inform the individual sectorial agreements and the regulatory processes of each side. Among other things, they should explicitly provide regulators on either side the legal authority to enter into agreements with their transatlantic counterpart, consistent with their existing legislative authority and on the understanding that such agreements will be subject to political oversight on either side. It should also affirm that all regulator-to-regulator agreements under TTIP can be suspended immediately, should something happen that leads a regulator on one side to lose confidence in the other, and that the agreements can be unilaterally terminated within a specified period of time, should the trust and confidence not be restored following consultation.

But more specifically, the general disciplines should ensure that regulators on both sides of the Atlantic are better informed about the costs and benefits of their domestic regulation as it affects the other party, and the trade in goods and services between them. This applies to both proposed new regulation, and to existing regulatory provisions affecting products and services. In both cases the objective is to inform decisions, not to determine them. While better informed of the transatlantic consequences, the regulator will in the end make the choice appropriate for its jurisdiction.

For new regulations that will a) have a significant cost of compliance to the economy and b) affect a product or service in which there is a significant amount[29] of transatlantic trade, TTIP should

---

[29] What is meant by a 'significant' amount of trade could be defined in the agreement, for example, if a regulation would affect a product or service where there is $100 million or more of trade. This level could even be sliding (from, say $500 million to $50 million) over a period of time to allow regulators to

mandate that regulators include a regulatory compatibility assessment (RCA) in the impact assessment process they would normally undertake in any event. While the details and methodology of this would need to be spelled out in more detail, the RCA would, in any case: a) require the regulator to contact its transatlantic counterpart, b) ascertain whether the product or service is regulated on the other side of the ocean, c) determine whether the counterpart had a similar or different definition of the problem the regulation is meant to address, d) assess whether the proposed approach is compatible with that of the counterpart and e) evaluate the costs and benefits of adopting a non-compatible approach. As this impact assessment is to be made available for public comment, all stakeholders would be able to see and provide new evidence related to the RCA. Again, a non-compatible approach that would affect trade between the two parties could be adopted, but the decision would be informed by an evaluation of the consequences for transatlantic trade.

For existing regulations, TTIP could establish a regulatory equivalence assessment (REA) process. Under this process, interested parties could send a petition to the relevant regulator stating that the levels of safety, or the required tests or manufacturing processes, for a specified product or service (or groups of products or services) achieve the same regulatory outcomes on both sides of the Atlantic. The petition should be accompanied by evidence supporting the contention of equivalence. The regulator receiving the petition would share it with his or her counterpart, and both would publish the petition and the evidence provided for public notice and comment. The two would then review the responses, and hold hearings on them. They would then write a joint or separate report in response to the petition, including what, if any, follow-on steps they would propose. Again, there would be no requirement that any specific result comes from this.

The RCA and REA procedures would be applicable to all regulated sectors, including, for instance, financial services. But, as noted above, they would not jeopardise a regulator's autonomy, only ensure better informed regulatory decisions. If agreements for enhanced regulatory cooperation emerge from the process, those agreements (after going through the appropriate domestic approval process) could then be reflected in the relevant TTIP sectoral annex.

---

grow accustomed to the process. Indeed, it might be worthwhile to have different values of 'significance' for different sectors.

Arguably, regulators on both sides are already meant to consider the trade implications of their proposed regulations, and additional transparency, participation and accountability would help provide information about these impacts. Further, regulators on both sides probably already could receive and consider petitions asserting equivalence. But enshrining these procedures as obligations under TTIP would ensure that they are followed, and that there is increased consultation between the regulatory agencies. It would also give grounds for one party to complain if it had reason to believe that a regulatory agency on the other side did not undertake the required consultation steps.

The regulatory cooperation section should also establish an institutional mechanism to oversee the regulatory cooperation process. This could be the existing US-EU High Level Regulatory Cooperation Forum (HLRCF)[30] established in 2005, although it would make sense in the context of the increased requirements in TTIP to enhance it. In the Executive Order on international regulatory cooperation, mentioned above, President Obama recommended the establishment of regulatory cooperation councils (RCCs) with certain partners. The US currently has RCCs with Canada[31] and Mexico.[32] These RCCs meet once or twice a year, bringing together select regulatory agencies to develop work plans for regulatory cooperation, report on progress to date, discuss best practices and other such steps. They have no law-making capability as regulatory agencies on both sides must go through their domestic decision-making procedures to change any rules. This would be true as well for whatever oversight body TTIP creates. In addition to helping set the regulatory cooperation agenda and ensuring public reports, the oversight body would review experience, identify best practices among regulators, help resolve misunderstandings, expand and update the RCA and REA methodologies, and the like.

In contrast to the HLRCF, which is fairly ad hoc in its participation, TTIP should identify the bodies which should participate. Ideally it would be co-chaired by the two bodies which oversee the regulatory activities of the two governments, the Office of Information and Regulatory Affairs (OIRA) of the US Office of Management and Budget (OMB), and the European Commission

---

[30] See www.whitehouse.gov/omb/oira_irc_europe.

[31] See www.whitehouse.gov/omb/oira_irc_north_america#canada. See also OECD (2013b) for a report on how it works in actual practice.

[32] See www.whitehouse.gov/omb/oira_irc_north_america#mexico.

Secretariat General. All relevant agencies, including those dealing with risk assessment or regulation directly, should participate.

The RCC name, while legally significant in the US context, has slightly different political connotations in the EU, where 'Councils' are ministerial-level bodies that make law. This may be one reason why some in Europe distrust the idea. Another name should be chosen for the oversight body in TTIP to avoid this misperception. Indeed, the EU first draft on Regulatory Cooperation in TTIP speaks of a 'body'.

4.4   The sectoral annexes

Structurally, one of the most important components of the regulatory cooperation part of TTIP is a set of sectorial annexes, for it is this structure which most clearly demonstrates that regulators are in the lead on regulatory cooperation, not trade negotiators. It is the former who are responsible for implementing the laws governing the level of safety of the products and services they regulate, and which are thus politically accountable to the relevant political oversight committees of Congress, the European Parliament and Council, and the national governments and parliaments. And it is this structure which clearly demonstrates to the legislative bodies, and to the public, that the desired levels of safety cannot be arbitrarily reduced (or increased) because of TTIP.

Indeed, in both the US and EU, changes in the level of regulatory protection would undoubtedly require legislative or at least regulatory measures. In the US, any such change would be subject to the requirements of the Administrative Procedures Act, and thus subject to legal challenge, should the public notice and comment process not be followed. Similar requirements exist on the EU side.

In this sense, TTIP can only occasionally be expected to bring about changes in underlying law; rather, it is a way to build bridges between two regulatory regimes. And bridges can only be built if the two sides are relatively close to one another. If the regulatory outcomes demanded by the two sides are far apart, then, at the very least, spans will need to be constructed to bring them closer together before anything further can be accomplished.

The annexes should be kept simple, but should encourage results in TTIP: each should have a heading reflecting the class of regulated products or services being referred to (autos, pharmaceuticals, medical devices, cosmetics, toys, apparel, banking, insurance, etc.); each should list the relevant regulatory agencies on both sides and perhaps points of contact in them; and each should reflect agreements that have been reached between the relevant regulators. One annex, for instance, could be on large civil aircraft: the Federal Aviation Administration and the European Aviation Safety Agency would be listed as the regulators, and the 2009 Bilateral Aviation Safety Agreement, mentioned above, should be linked on it.

As this example highlights, the annexes should include existing agreements between counterpart US and EU regulators (such as on organic produce and supply chain security systems), any additional ones agreed during the TTIP negotiations, and any that may be agreed subsequent to agreement on TTIP. In other words, concrete results in regulator-to-regulator exchanges should find their way into the annexes, so that they are anchored in TTIP, now or later.

It is this last part, i.e. the ability to add new regulator-to-regulator agreements in the annexes, that makes TTIP a 'living' agreement. As described previously, over the past decade and a half, many of our regulatory agencies have reached agreements with one another; they didn't need TTIP to do this. But TTIP, with its horizontal obligations for such things as the RCA and the REA, will provide direction to that cooperation and 'turbo-charge' it, without undermining our respective regulatory processes.

And this 'living' agreement both recognises that such regulator-to-regulator agreements can only come where regulators have trust and confidence in one another, and that such trust and confidence takes time to build. TTIP as a trade agreement should not and need not be delayed as that process unfolds.

Annex 1 to this report provides an illustrative list of existing US-EU regulatory agreements in over 20 different sectors, on which these annexes should be built.

5. Comparing regulatory cooperation chapters in three FTAs

In order to get an idea of the ambition, nature, and level of intensity of bilateral regulatory cooperation between the US and of the EU so far, it might seem instructive to compare the regulatory chapters of recent bilateral trade agreements concluded by the parties. However, this is only partly true. Because no published information of any substantive detail is available about TPP (the Asia-Pacific FTA of 12 parties including the US),[33] the only recent FTA concluded by the US is KORUS, the Korea-US FTA. The EU has concluded three recent FTAs, with Korea (KOREU in 2010), Singapore, and CETA. The latter two are still being legally scrubbed prior to signature and subsequent ratification. In the present section, some comparative remarks will be made about KOREU and SINGEU, on the one hand, and KORUS on the other. The relevant chapters in these three FTAs are all about transparency, only one aspect of regulatory coherence. What there is about regulatory cooperation is linked to sectors or may arise from general clauses for future initiatives of the ministerial-level body governing the FTA. No specific regulatory cooperation framework or chapter is included. This is different in CETA (see section 6).

KOREU[34] does not include a chapter entitled 'Regulatory Cooperation'. Instead, chapter 12 is entitled 'Transparency'. There is a possibility that this is caused by the simultaneity of the negotiations on KORUS and KOREU. It has often been suggested that KORUS served as a lead example for KOREU, and indeed the structure and substance of the two agreements are quite similar, and KORUS also has a chapter (21) called 'Transparency'. The substance of chapter 12 of KOREU goes some modest distance towards what one would expect from a chapter on horizontal regulatory cooperation, knowing that sectorial and other specific regulatory cooperation is also scattered throughout the treaty and annexes. Article 12.2 on objective and scope clarifies that: "Recognising the impact which their respective regulatory environment may have on trade between them, the Parties shall pursue an efficient and predictable regulatory environment for operators, especially small ones doing business in their territories." The chapter lays down clarifications and improved arrangements for transparency, consultations, and better administration of measures of general application. Subsequent articles re-iterate some of the OECD guidelines and recommendations referred to in Box 2.3 – most EU member states as well as Korea are members of the OECD – such as on timely publications, with the opportunity to comment and endeavours to take

---

[33] From Schott, Kotschwar and Muir (2013, p. 13), it appears that regulatory coherence texts focus on promoting transparency and streamlining standards, certification, and regulatory processes. In any event, the Honolulu APEC Ministerial was also the occasion for TPP to release a broad mandate, with regulatory coherence as one of the priorities. But no details are available beyond these generalities.

[34] OJEU L 127 of 14 May 2011, pp. 6-1450.

such comments into account before legislating for the measures. These are followed by provisions on mechanisms for enquiries and contact points, administrative proceedings, review and appeal, and cooperation in promoting regulatory quality. Chapter 14 of the provisional text of SINGEU[35] on transparency is almost a copy of KOREU's chapter 12. The objective, scope and structure is essentially the same, and often textually identical.

KORUS's chapter 21 is concerned with transparency. For TTIP purposes, it looks rather elementary. Compared to chapter 12 of KOREU, it lacks a broader objective on an 'efficient and predictable regulatory environment for operators,' although one surmises that drafters must have had this in mind. Article 21.1 goes into great detail about several aspects of publication of laws, regulations, procedures and administrative rulings, such as timely publication in advance of proposals, providing a reasonable opportunity for stakeholders to comment, and a host of details ensuring easy access to information (e.g. a single official journal, a comment period of 40 days, setting out the rationale, and addressing significant comments). Article 21.2 reiterates this for 'requests'. Article 21.3 insists on administering 'in a consistent, impartial and reasonable manner', complemented with, again, reasonable notice and opportunity. Somewhat similar provisions apply (Art. 21.4) to review and appeal. Presumably because of occasional informal past campaigns in Korea against certain imported goods, Art. 21.5 seeks confirmation that that is not standing policy. A detailed anti-corruption and anti-bribery provision is found in Art. 21.6. In the light of recent APEC initiatives on regulatory reform and principles, largely overlapping with those of the OECD, one suspects that Chapter 21 of KORUS is more a reflection of the past (KORUS was negotiated up to 2007) than of today.

Whereas it is often suggested that KORUS is the template of how modern FTAs are negotiated by the US, this is clearly not true for the transparency chapter, and even less so for the US and the EU together, which have moved beyond the KORUS-type provisions in their regulatory cooperation during the last few decades. Nevertheless, for purposes of transparency for business in TTIP, one might go much further still. One example: wouldn't it be a good idea to facilitate two-way business for SMEs, by creating a one-stop-shop on both sides, with easy access to regulatory requirements, both at the federal (or EU) and the sub-central (or member state) levels? Demanding surely for both

---

[35] See http://trade.ec.europa.eu/doclib/press/index.cfm?id=961

partners, but undoubtedly extremely helpful for SMEs, lowering the costs - and perceived costs - of entry.

6.   TTIP's regulatory cooperation: What CETA and the EU TTIP proposal tell us

Regulatory cooperation is dealt with very differently in CETA. One important explanation for this difference in ambition is the existence of regulatory cooperation under the Canada-EU Framework on Regulatory Cooperation and Transparency, which dates back nearly a decade. Chapter 26 of the provisional consolidated text of CETA[36] - which is about regulatory cooperation - states (in Art. 26.2 sub 5) that the chapter replaces the earlier framework, which implies an upgrade. Given the parallel histories of regulatory cooperation between the US and the EU and Canada and the EU, and the fact that Canada and the US have enjoyed a considerable degree of market integration in NAFTA for more than two decades, it is reasonable to regard CETA as a possible benchmark for a regulatory chapter in TTIP. However, it is not sure whether the TTIP negotiators see it that way; in any event, the US position on this chapter is as yet unknown. In Table 2.1 we compare the CETA chapter with the EU draft proposal on regulatory cooperation in TTIP.[37]

Table 2.1 shows that CETA and – probably – TTIP are going to be very different from recent FTAs in terms of regulatory coherence and cooperation. Although there are differences between the two texts, and some confusing disparities in structure, the overlap in the substantial provisions about regulatory cooperation and coherence is quite large. Both also envisage a joint body with a fairly wide and flexible remit which enables future cooperation in many ways. It would also facilitate the idea and operation of a 'living agreement'. In the regulatory coherence part, the reference to the OECD 2012 recommendations (in the EU proposal) re-affirms a common set of principles and practices in an explicit and well-codified form which effectively overlaps with what CETA Articles 2 and 3 contain. In the EU TTIP text the 'regulatory exchanges' are to be led by the regulators (Art. 9.4); this is not explicit in CETA. On the other hand, one would surmise, at this stage, that the TTIP approach as proposed by the EU is more ambitious in terms of commitments and procedures than CETA, as the hard core of the CETA

---

[36] See http://trade.ec.europa.eu/doclib/2014/september/tradoc_1528

[37] See http://trade.ec.europa.eu/doclib/docs/2015/february/trade_153120

chapter are (19) voluntary cooperative 'activities' whereas TTIP regulatory cooperation is far more about commitments in law. Still, much will depend on the actual functioning of the chapter under each treaty. In any event, TTIP already has (tentatively) agreed on as many as nine sectorial chapters or annexes, and the EU proposal suggests that more might eventually emerge from the 'living agreement', whereas in CETA it does not look nearly as ambitious when taking the text literally.

Table 2.1 Comparing regulatory cooperation in CETA and the EU TTIP proposal

CETA on	Specifications in CETA	Specifications in EU TTIP proposal
Scope (Art. 1)	Development, review, and methodological aspects of regulatory measures of the Parties; reference to WTO SPS and TBT, plus GATT and GATS ; and to six chapters in the draft treaty, including environment and labour	Art. 3: applies to regulatory acts at central level on goods and services; with 'significant impact'; and regulatory acts concerning specific or sectorial provisions (to be determined later). The type of regulatory acts at central level are precisely defined in Art. 2, a and b for resp. the EU and the US] [note, that the first EU draft will be completed with provisions on regulatory acts at sub-central level][reference to WTO elsewhere in CETA]
Principles (Art. 2)	Quite detailed. Their cooperation is to be open to other trading parties; should 'enhance the climate for competitiveness and innovation, including through pursuing regulatory compatibility, recognition of equivalence and convergence'; promote regulatory processes that ....better ... fulfil the mandates of regulatory bodies... [and] 'enhanced use of best practices'	Art. 1.3 : 'the Parties reaffirm their shared commitment to good regulatory principles and practices, as laid down in the OECD Recommendation of 22 March 2012 on Regulatory Policy and Governance'

Objectives (Art. 3)	Four very detailed objectives, i.e. contributing to SHIEC objectives (by leveraging international resources and helping risk assessment), building trust and deepening mutual understanding of regulatory governance (in seven ways, typical 'good regulatory practices' items, including transparency and predictability), facilitating bilateral trade and investment (e.g. by reducing unnecessary regulatory differences), and contributing to competitiveness and efficiency of industry (by e.g. minimizing administrative costs and reducing duplicative regulatory requirements, plus pursuing compatible regulatory approaches e.g. recognition of equivalence or the promotion of convergence)	Art.1.1 comprises four objectives: a. 'to reinforce regulatory cooperation thereby facilitating trade and investment…. to stimulate growth and jobs while pursuing a high level of protection..' in SHEIC but also working conditions, personal data, cybersecurity, cultural diversity or preserving financial stability; b. 'reduce unnecessarily burdensome, duplicative or divergent regulatory requirements…. by promoting … compatibility of… EU and US… acts' c. 'promote an effective, pro-competitive environment… transparent and predictable ' d. 'to further… international instruments … to strive towards consistent regulatory outcomes'
Regulatory cooperation activities (Art. 4)	A very wide and ambitious set of provisions on 19 (!) regulatory cooperation activities, many of those on sharing / exchange of information on a host of areas, examining opportunities to minimise unnecessary divergences, cooperation on developing international standards and guides, data collection, cooperative research agendas, conducting post-implementation reviews, reducing adverse trade effects by e.g. greater	In the draft EU proposal, many (not all) regulatory cooperation activities, as they are called in CETA, are found in different articles: Art. 5 (on early and public information on planned acts) and Art. 6 (on stakeholder consultations) are under a subsection 'transparency', whereas the first (early information) is in Art. 26.4 of CETA, that is not the case for stakeholder participation (except for a very open clause in Art. 26.8, CETA).

	convergence, mutual recognition, minimising the use of trade-distorting instruments, and the use of international standards, etc.	Provisions on impact assessment (in CETA Art. 26.4, item 6b) are in Art. 7 in the EU proposal. Some of what CETA calls 'activities' are the subject of 'regulatory exchanges' in the EU proposal (art. 9 and 10), the essential difference being a greater precision in procedures and timing. (For the CETA provision on post-implementation reviews, there is a weak counterpart in the EU draft, in Art. 7.3c) On the other hand, CETA has no explicit provision on promoting international regulatory cooperation, as in Art. 13 of the EU draft.)
Compatibility of regulations (Art. 5)	'With a view to enhancing convergence and compatibility between regulatory measures of the Parties, each Party shall, when appropriate, consider the regulatory measures or initiatives of the other Party on the same or related topics...'	Compatibility is in Art. 8.1 as well as in Art. 11, following from (in some cases) so-called 'regulatory exchanges', specifying mutual recognition of equivalence (of regulatory acts or outcomes), harmonization or simplification; goes further than CETA via a proposal for joint examination.
Role and Composition of the Regulatory Cooperation Forum (Art. 6)	'...to facilitate and promote regulatory cooperation between the Parties'; functions: i) a setting for discussion of regulatory policy issues of mutual interest, ii) assist individual regulators (identifying partners; model confidentiality agreements); iii) reviews of whether regulatory initiatives	The TTIP Regulatory Cooperation Body will have seven functions (Art. 14): i) Annual Regulatory Cooperation Programme; ii) monitoring of the implementation and reporting; iii) technical preparation of new or added sectoral provisions; iv) considering new proposals for regulatory cooperation,

	'provide potential for cooperation'; iv) encourage bilateral regulatory cooperation activities (as the 19 types in Art. 4) and review sectorial initiatives. The RCF reports to the CETA trade Council	including on compatibility; v) preparation of joint proposals of international regulatory instruments; vi) ensuring transparency; vii) open clause on relevant 'other issue'
Further cooperation of the Parties (Art. 7)	Is about monitoring forthcoming regulatory projects, as well as exchange of information on a host of issues, e.g. standardisation, market surveillance, risk assessment methods and product recalls and early warnings. Endorsement of other initiatives are encouraged too.	Not explicit but probably subsumed in Art. 14; presumably, market surveillance, risk assessment and product recalls may require more specific provisions
Consultations (Art. 8)	'In order to gain non-governmental perspectives, the Parties may jointly or separately consult' all kinds of private entities	Much more detailed and forthcoming or encouraging on consultation in Art. 15 of EU proposal
Contact points (Art. 9)	Specified for both Parties	Not (yet) specified

Of course, the EU text is still incomplete with respect to sub-central governments. Neither the CETA nor the EU text is very detailed with respect to some 'coherence' aspects discussed in our section 4 above. For example, there is not much detail on early information of planned drafts for the other party or the public at large. With respect to the horizontal aspects of cooperation, nothing even nearly as ambitious as Regulatory Compatibility Assessments for new regulations and/or Regulatory Equivalence Assessment for existing regulations is referred to in either text.

In the absence of a publicised US text proposal or a revision after nine rounds of negotiation, it would be wrong to draw any further conclusion at this stage.

7. Conclusion: Building bridges and enhancing social objectives

The purpose of the Transatlantic Trade and Investment Partnership is to build on the unique trade and investment-based US-EU economic relationship to promote growth and, most importantly, jobs on both sides of the Atlantic.

It will do this in many ways, but one of the key steps will be in tackling unnecessary differences in regulation, which create unintended obstacles to trade without any corresponding regulatory or social benefit. The US and EU can do this, as they are both democratic, high-income economies that in general seek similar levels of consumer, worker, environmental and prudential safety.

But TTIP can succeed only if it frames this process correctly. TTIP will not be, and perhaps cannot be, the most ambitious form of regulatory cooperation, as seen in some treaties focused on discrete issues. But it can, and probably will, be more than either side has done in any previous trade agreement. Done properly, regulatory coherence and cooperation under TTIP will enhance regulatory efficiency and effectiveness, increasing consumer safety even as it improves the competitiveness of US and EU firms. TTIP should help ensure that regulators on both sides of the Atlantic agree on the principles and practices that make for a robust, evidence-based and transparent regulatory system, as confidence in each other's domestic systems is a prerequisite for cooperation.

It should set the clear goal for our regulators of improving regulatory compatibility, while reaffirming their autonomy and their accountability to their political oversight bodies and their citizens. It should give them tools such as the Regulatory Compatibility Assessments and the Regulatory Equivalence Assessments, to ensure informed decision-making without trying to predetermine the outcomes. And it should recognise that regulatory cooperation can succeed only where there is trust and confidence between the regulators, and that TTIP must be patient enough and flexible enough with a living agreement, to allow for this trust and confidence to be built on sufficiently strong foundations.

For only with these foundations will TTIP be able to build a bridge between the US and the EU, one that is safe, that meets the needs and concerns of our politicians and our citizens, while at the same time fostering economic growth and job creation.

References

Francois, J., M. Manchin, H. Norberg, O. Pindyuk and P. Tomberger (2013), "Reducing Transatlantic barriers to trade and investment: An economic assessment", study for the European Commission supporting the Impact Assessment of TTIP (http://trade.ec.europa.eu/doclib/docs/2013/march/tradoc_1507 37.pdf).

Fontagne, L., J. Gourdon and S. Jean (2013), "Transatlantic trade: whither partnership, which economic consequences?", CEPII Policy Brief No. 12, CEPII, Paris, September (www.cepii.fr).

Josling, T. and S. Tangermann (2014), "Agriculture, Food and the TTIP: Possibilities and pitfalls", CEPS Special Report No. 99, CEPS, Brussels, December and chapter 9 in this volume.

Kommerscollegium [Swedish Board of Trade] (2014), "Regulatory cooperation and TBTs within TTIP", Stockholm, April (www.kommers.se).

Morrall, John III (2011), "Determining Compatible Regulatory Regimes between the US and the EU", US Chamber of Commerce, Washington, D.C. (www.uschamber.com/sites/default/files/documents/files/Determining%2520Compatible%2520Regulatory %2520Regimes.pdf).

OECD (2012), Recommendations of the Council on Regulatory Policy and Governance, Paris (www.oecd.org/gov/regulatory-policy/499908.pdf).

_____ (2013), *International Regulatory Cooperation*, Paris.

Parker, R. and A. Alemanno (2014), "Towards Effective Regulatory Cooperation under TTIP: A comparative overview of the EU and US legislative and regulatory systems", CEPS Special Report No. 88, Brussels, May (www.ceps.eu).

Pelkmans, J. (2007), "Mutual Recognition in goods, on promises and disillusions", *Journal of European Public Policy*, Vol. 14, No. 5, pp. 699-716.

_____ (2012), "Mutual recognition: economic and regulatory logic in goods and services", in T. Eger and H-B. Schaefer (eds), *Research Handbook on the Economics of EU Law*, Cheltenham: E. Elgar, pp. 113-145.

_____ (2015), EP Briefing Paper for the IMCO and INTA Committees on TBTs in TTIP; working title: "The TTIP: Challenges and opportunities for the internal market and consumer protection in the area of standards", April, forthcoming on EP website.

Pelkmans, J. and A. Correia de Brito (2015a), "Study on Mutual Recognition Agreements", OECD, Paris, forthcoming.

_____ (2015b), "Transatlantic MRAs: Lessons for TTIP?", CEPS Special Report No. 101, Brussels, February (www.ceps.eu).

Pelkmans, J., A. Lejour, L. Schrefler, F. Mustilli, J. Timini et al. (2014), "The impact of TTIP: The underlying economic model and comparisons", CEPS Special Report No. 93, Brussels, October (www.ceps.eu; also published as report to the EP (www.europart.europa.eu/RegData/etudes/etudes/join/2014/528798/IPOL_JOIN_ET%282014%29528 798_EN.pdf).

Renda, A. (2009), *Policy-making in the EU: Achievement, challenges and proposals for reform*, CEPS, Brussels (www.ceps.eu).

Schott, J., B. Kotschwar and J. Muir (2013), *Understanding the Trans-Pacific Partnership*, Peterson Institute of International Economics, Washington, D.C.

Wiener, J., M. Rogers, J. Hammitt, and P. Sand (2010), *The reality of precaution, comparing risk regulation in the US and Europe*, Resources for the Future Press, Washington, D.C. and London.

US-EU High Level Group (2013), Final Report of the High Level Working Group on Jobs and Growth, February (http://trade.ec.europa.eu/doclib/docs/2013/february/tradoc_15 0519.pdf).

US Chamber of Commerce (2015), "Regulatory Coherence and Cooperation in the TTIP", February, Washington, D.C. (www.uschamber.com/sites/default/files/regulatory_coherence_regulatory_cooperation_-chamber_ttip_paper_-_final_3-02.pdf).

Annex 1. 20 Years of US-EU Regulatory Cooperation

Regulators in the United States and the European Union (as opposed to individual EU member states) have been collaborating since the 1995 US-EU "New Transatlantic Agenda" declaration. While there are a number of agency-to-agency agreements, much of the early work was captured in the general reports on progress under the Regulatory Cooperation Roadmaps (starting in 2002), to the High Level Regulatory Cooperation Forum (established 2005) and ultimately the Transatlantic Economic Council (TEC), created in 2007. A review of these general reports, listed in the first section below, gives a good overview of progress in the many sectors covered.

Issue/Agencies	Description
General (All)	US-EU Joint Statement on Regulatory Cooperation (Dec. 1997)
	US-EU MRA Agreement (December, 1998)
	Guidelines for use of the MRAs, 2001
	Transatlantic Economic Partnership Report (Bonn Summit, June 1999)
	Transatlantic Economic Partnership; Commission Overview and Assessment, October 2000
	Guidelines on Regulatory Cooperation and Transparency Implementation Roadmap (April 2002)
	Regulatory Roadmap – 2004
	Regulatory Roadmap – June 2005
	Joint Report on the Roadmap, June 2006
	Joint Report on the Roadmap, April 2007
	HLRCF Report, April 2008
	Joint Report on Impact Assessments and Trade, May 2008
	HLRCF Report, October 2008
	HLRCF Report, July 2009
	HLRCF Report, June 2010
	HLRCF Report, December 2010
	Common Understanding re Regulatory Principles and Best Practices, June 2011
Standards US: National Institute of Standards and Technology (NIST)	EU and US Extend Scientific Cooperation on Measurements and Standards July 2013 (JRC news release)
	Building Bridges between the US and EU Standards Systems Nov 2011
	Memorandum of Understanding Dec 2010

EU: DG Enterprise (GROW); Joint Research Centres	US–EU HLRCF Joint Statement on Standards in Regulation Dec 2010 Collaborative Arrangement regarding cooperation in the fields of metrology and measurement standards Feb 2008 Memorandum of Understanding regarding cooperation on scientific research and measurement standards Dec 2007
Import Product Safety US: OIRA EU: DG Enterprise	Implementation of Recommendations Report, December 2008 Safety of Imported Products, April 2008: looks at motor vehicle, food, pharmaceutical, cosmetic, toy, consumer–use electrical equipment sectors
Agriculture US: FDA, USDA, FSIS, APHIS EU: DG SANCO/SANTE, DG AGRI	National Organic Program June 2012: the US and EU created an equivalence arrangement in regards to organic standards USDA press release Competent authorities responses of the US to recommendations from DG SANCO 2011 FCA and EFSA information sharing agreement July 2007: the two agencies signed the first EU–US agreement in the area of assessing food safety risk. EFSA Statement FDA Statement EU-US Safe Food 2005-2007: A program that ran for two years in order to contribute to and communicate knowledge about food-born zoonoses Report, 2007: complete Implementation Plan under their confidentiality arrangement; experts hold joint meeting on nanotechnology in food to share perspectives on the issue
Chemicals US: EPA EU: DG ENVI, ENT; ECHA	ECHA and EPA statement of Intent Dec 2010: The document asserts the agencies intent to enhance technical cooperation and share information regarding chemical management. EPA press release US-EU Conference Draft Nanotechnology in the Workplace July 2012: Establishing standardization OSH principles for developing best practices applied to nanotechnology work settings
Pharmaceuticals	EC wavier for export of US pharmaceutical manufactures June 2013

US: FDA EU: DG ENT, EMEA	Update on the implementation of recommendations made by Transatlantic Taskforce on Antimicrobial Resistance (TATFAR) Feb 2013
	Programme to rationalize international GMP inspections Feb 2012
	Enhancing GMP Inspection Cooperation between EMA and FDA Dec 2011
	Report on the Pilot EMA-FDA GCP Initiative July 2011
	Implementation Report on Transatlantic Administration Simplification action plan July 2011
	Interactions between EMA and FDA June 2011
	Report on the International API inspection Pilot May 2011
	EMA-FDA pilot program for parallel assessment of Quality by design applications March 2011
	Transatlantic Taskforce on Antimicrobial Resistance Report 2011
	EMEA and FDA statements re non-disclosure of confidential information from partner agency (September 2010)
	FDA EMEA Administrative Simplification Implementation Report Oct 2009
	EMEA-FDA Good Clinical Practice (GCP) Initiative Terms of engagement and procedures for participating authorities: Sep 2009
	EMEA-FDA GCP Initiative July 2009
	EMEA-DFA Parallel Scientific Advice July 2009
	Confidentiality Commitment between the FDA and EDQM May 2009
	Update on pilot project to collaborate on international GMP inspection activities Jan 2009
	FDA/EMEA Joint Press Release re Cooperation on Medicines, Oct 2008
	Medicines Regulation: Transatlantic Administrative Simplification Action Plan June 2008

Veterinary Medicines US: FDA, USDA EU: EC, EMEA	(See also above re medicines and reports on TATFAR) CVM / EMA Exchange of Experts 2012 FDA EDQM Confidentiality Commitment, May 2009: EMEA/Veterinary Medicines and Inspections Unit – Parallel Scientific Advice Meetings, May 2008 Implementation Procedures for Veterinary Medicinal Products Cluster, May 2008
Medical Devices US: FDA EU: DG ENTR – EMEA	October 2012 EU proposed changes to Medical Device laws and allowed US comments Statement From the International Medical Device Regulators' Forum October 2011 Exchange of Letters to facilitate information sharing re the safety, quality and efficiency of medical devices, July 2007
Cosmetics US: FDA EU: DG Enterprise and Industry (cosmetics unit), ECVAM	ICCR (International Cooperation on Cosmetic Regulation): made up of the US, EU, Japan, and Canada Meeting reports: 2012, 2011, 2010, 2009, 2008, 2007 FDA – DG Enterprise – Related to Cosmetics July 2007: Press Release
Automotive Safety US: NHTSA EU: DG ENT	Europe, USA, Japan will harmonise electric Vehicle Regulations Nov 2011 Proposal for two working groups re e-Vehicles November 2011 Global Technical Regulations 2004-2011 Memorandum of Cooperation Automobiles June 2008
Aircraft Safety US: FAA, TSA EU: DG ENT, EASA	Cooperation Agreement on Civil Aviation Safety, March 2011 Regulation of Civil Aviation Aircraft
Marine Equipment US: USCG EU: DG Energy and Transport; European Marine Safety Agency	Memorandum of Understanding regarding marine optical radiometry, March 2011 US-EC Marine Equipment MRA Joint Committee, February 2009 US-EU Mutual Recognition Agreement for Conformity Assessment for Marine Equipment, June 2001

Energy Efficiency, Eco-Design US: DOE, FERC, EPA EU: DG EVN, DG ENER, DG ENT	EU – US Energy Council Press statements following meetings of the Council o December 2012 o November 2011 o November 2010 o Website on the council is here EU US Energy Council Working Group on Technology, Research, Development and Demonstration 2009 Establishment of EU-US Energy Council, 2009 EU U.S advance Energy dialogue, March 2008 Energy Star Agreement renewed, Jan 2013 Implementing Arrangement for Environmental Research and Ecoinformatics, Feb 2007: Energy star agreement, December 2001 Working link First Energy Star Agreement – November 2001
Consumer Products, Toy Safety US: CPSC EU: DG SANCO	China–US – EU trilateral meetings o Sep 2008 Joint Press Statement o October 2010 Joint Press Statement o June 2012 Joint Press Statement Roadmap Feb 2010: Council grants mandate for the EC Nov 2009: EU US HLRCF Report on the Safety of Imported Products, Dec 2008 EU US HLRCF Report on Safety of Imported Products May 2008 Report, 2007 Guidelines for Information Exchange and on Administrative Cooperation on consumer product safety Report, 2006 Toy Safety, January 2010
Financial Regulation/Supervision US: Treasury, Federal Reserve, SEC, CFTC, NAIC, FASB, PA EU: DG Market, EBA, ESMA, EIOPA	Derivatives Agreement, July 2013 (Press release and text from CFTC) SEC and CESR Announcement Nov 2010: The SEC abolished reconciliation to GAAP for foreign companies using IFRS Nov 2007 CESR and SEC Protocol to implement work plan Sept 2007 SEC and CESR Work Plan Aug 2006

	Insurance US-EU Dialogue Project Update, April 2013 EU-US Dialogue Project Report, Dec 2012 EU-US Dialogue Project: The Way Forward, Dec 2012
Transportation Security US : DHS/CBP and TSA, FAA, FMC EU: DG JHA	CBP, EU Sign C-TPAT Mutual Recognition Decision, May 2012 (Implement this report Feb 2013) Air Cargo Agreement June 2012. TSA press release, EU press release US-EU Joint Declaration on Aviation Security, January 2010 Joint Statement, September 2008 Agreement Between the United States of America and the European Union on the Use and Transfer of Passenger Name Records to the United States Department of Homeland Security, December 2011 Agreement re: Passenger name Records, July 2007 Trusted Trader Program, May 2012

Source: Compiled by Peter Chase.

3. TTIP's Hard Core: Technical Barriers to Trade and Standards

Michelle Egan
and Jacques Pelkmans

1. Introduction and structure

The Transatlantic Trade and Investment Partnership (TTIP) is viewed as the single most-important trade deal undertaken by the US and the EU. The two partners have undertaken it in response to the changing geopolitical environment, resulting from, among other things, the stalled Doha Round of multilateral trade negotiations, the rise of Asia and Asian regionalism, and the economic slowdown and sovereign debt crisis. Although the deal is expected to promote jobs and growth and strengthen existing economic ties, the prospect for an ambitious preferential trade agreement is also derived from building on earlier initiatives and experience to promote trade, regulatory and financial cooperation between two economies that are highly interdependent (Hamilton, 2014; Pollack & Shaffer, 2001; Egan, 2005).

The progressive elimination of tariff barriers has shifted attention. The import-weighted tariffs have been reduced over time to less than 4% (with many tariff lines being zero), so the issue in many traditional regional free trade agreements (FTAs) is no longer tariffs, but rather technical barriers to trade (TBTs). These barriers consist of standards, technical regulations and conformity assessment procedures that have emerged in different administrative bodies and standardisation organisations at domestic, regional and international levels, often independently from one another, thereby creating duplicative costs of compliance (see Box 3.1). Standards are usually developed by private standards development organisations (SDOs), to avoid redundant variety (e.g. of components), for compatibility, but also to ensure the health, safety and quality of products, as well as processes, production methods and other related technical matters. They can define a specific design or performance characteristics, determine performance criteria, or provide guidelines and definitions (NRC, 1995).

Standards are formally voluntary when adopted, but can acquire legal effect when 'referenced' in legislation, or may become dominant in the marketplace through widespread acceptance. Conformity assessment methods and procedures are used to assess whether a particular material, product, or process conforms to a specified standard. Conformity assessment bodies, which can be public or private entities, include testing, certification and inspection organisations. When technical standards are integrated into regulatory requirements, they can create or enhance technical barriers to trade, due to differences in performance, design, testing, and certification measures. Since these requirements are indispensable for entering their respective markets, it can lead to extra costs as the imported product has to be tested and certified acceptable or safe, or, in other words, meet specific safety, health, environment and consumer (SHEC) protection objectives.

TBTs do not concern the level and scope of regulation, i.e. SHEC objectives, but rather reduce the costs of given regulatory differences of instruments that impact market access. Such differences have become a central issue in the ongoing US-EU trade negotiations, so that standards and conformity assessment practices on both sides of the Atlantic remain one of the greatest challenges in TTIP. Removing or reducing the cost of such transatlantic TBTs is likely to result in possibly significant economic gains – which may vary by sector – but this does not mean that regulatory objectives in terms of levels of SHEC protection will diminish, as asserted – without any justification – in social and conventional media as well as stakeholder meetings. At issue are differences in instruments, methods or testing to meet given, specified objectives.

The chapter proceeds in section 2 to establish the significance of TBTs that stem from standards, testing and conformity assessment practices for the costs of international trade and the particular challenges of resolving them. The prior transatlantic efforts to address them are considered in section 3 and the scope of the TTIP TBT approach is addressed in section 4. Section 5 outlines the standards regimes and their respective legal and policy differences in order to illustrate the areas of contention for the ongoing TTIP negotiations. Section 6 shows how these regime distinctions impact bilateral trade and section 7 focuses on the current state of negotiations in TTIP. The chapter concludes by elucidating the prospects and implications for achieving some form of agreement on TBT issues.

Box 3.1 TBT definitions for understanding TTIP negotiations

A *technical regulation* lays down product characteristics or their related processes and production methods, including the applicable administrative provisions, with which compliance is mandatory. It may also include or deal exclusively with terminology, symbols, packaging, marking or labelling requirements as they apply to a product, process or production method (Annex 1, TBT Agreement).

A *standard* is a document approved by a recognised body that provides for common and repeated use, rules, guidelines, or characteristics for products or related processes and production methods, with which compliance is not mandatory. It may also include or deal exclusively with terminology, symbols, packaging, marking or labelling requirements as they apply to a product, process or production method (Annex 1, TBT Agreement). A technical standard is written by standard bodies and is always voluntary, whether in the US, the EU or elsewhere. This suggests that standards should not normally be regarded as a TBT. Although this is often correct, there are instances where different (voluntary) standards amount to barriers (e.g. no compatibility, requirements for insurance, etc.), that is, they raise the costs of effective market access. Most standards written by standard bodies are purely market-driven, for reasons which market players, including consumers, are expected to appreciate. The principal reasons why standards are advantageous (see Pelkmans & Costello, 1991; Swann, 2010; Blind, 2013) include:

i)   well-defined information on measures, weights, or a host of other technical 'codes' which reduce the costs of information for engineers, designers, etc., whilst avoiding confusing differences for technicians;

ii) well-defined codification of certain quality features of goods (including intermediate goods, parts, components) – quality *can* of course include aspects of goods serving safety, health of consumers or workers, environment and/or consumer protection (and often will because markets appreciate it);

iii) agreed specifications needed for interoperability or compatibility of intermediate or final products; and

iv) agreed ways to reduce clear redundancy of variety in order to facilitate economies of scale.

> Industry spends resources to write standards, because they want markets to function better and codify new technologies or production solutions, while also allowing variety to ensure competition, innovation and coordination across firms, sectors and supply chains.
>
> An *international standard* (or guide or recommendation, as the World Trade Organization specifies) is widely understood as a standard issued by world bodies such as the International Organization for Standardization (ISO), the International Electrotechnical Commission (IEC) and the International Telecommunication Union (ITU), except in ICT where other consortia often play a role. The WTO TBT Committee has defined a set of six *principles* for determining whether a standard is 'international': openness, transparency, impartiality and consensus, relevance and effectiveness, coherence and the development dimension (see, e.g. USTR (2014), 2014 Report on TBTs, pp. 25-26).
>
> *Conformity assessment procedures* are any procedure(s) used, directly or indirectly, to determine that relevant requirements in technical regulations or standards are fulfilled (Annex 1, TBT Agreement).

2. The meaning of TBTs for trade

Unlike conventional trade restraints, such as voluntary export restraints, quotas or tariffs, technical barriers to trade (TBT) that include conformity assessment procedures are not explicitly designed as trade protection measures to restrict market access and shield domestic markets from competition (Budetta & Piermartini, 2009). Although they are not explicitly discriminatory, as exporters may meet local, national or regional technical standards, regulations and conformity assessment procedures to achieve market access so that the same rules apply to both domestic and foreign products, this tends to impose disproportionate costs on foreign producers that have to conform to different sets of rules and requirements for different markets. Duplicative testing and certification can also constitute a barrier to trade, as this increases costs in meeting the administrative requirements, as well as testing and certification procedures in the importing country, and if different, it places foreign firms at a competitive disadvantage in comparison to domestic firms. Governments and industries may define specific requirements that provide strategic advantages to certain industries or firms.

Germany has recently imposed additional administrative requirements on the sale of pyrotechnic products, as the Federal

Institute for Material Research and Testing (BAM) has required an additional notification fee, and user amendments, beyond that of the EU Pyrotechnics Directive. Since the Directive applies in the automotive sector for safety restraints such as airbags and seatbelts, the issue has become a technical barrier to trade for other car manufacturers, resulting in EU infringement proceedings against Germany. In the US, the slow pace of approval for sunscreen ingredients by the Food and Drug Administration (FDA) has led to applications pending for 12 years, due to the cumbersome regulatory process that has thwarted new European products from accessing the market despite their widespread approval and use in Europe and Asia.[1]

Companies often have to make design or manufacturing changes to sell in both European and American markets, or, especially for SMEs, forego market access due to the costs of adaptation, or perform redundant and duplicative testing to demonstrate compliance with both sets of rules. Differences between toy safety standards, for example, cost $3 billion annually despite the relative convergence of many of the design and testing specifications, which has led both sides together to promote a presumption of equivalence, so that toys compliant with either the US or European standard would be considered 'safe'. This would still allow each jurisdiction to determine the means to establish conformity to lower the costs of two-way market access.[2]

TBTs may take many forms in actual practice and many variations of such forms, often specific to sectors. If differences are slight and procedures light, the costs of TBTs may be small and little might be heard about them. However, the typical TBTs long discussed in transatlantic regulatory fora and exchanges are costly and influence more than marginally the costs of market access. It is exceedingly hard to estimate authoritatively the costs of TBTs (see Berden & Francois, 2015, chapter 4 in this volume), but the TBTs relevant for trade negotiations in bilateral FTAs carry costs equivalent to anywhere from 10% to 80% of the invoice price. This means that, in such sectors, the

---

[1] The Sunscreen Approval Act was signed into law in 2014, amending Chapter V of the Federal Food, Drug, and Cosmetic Act (21 U.S.C. 351 et seq.). The Public Access and Sunscreen Coalition (PASS) lobbied hard for the regulatory changes during the FDA review process.

[2] Comments Concerning Proposed Transatlantic Trade and Investment Agreement (Docket number USTR-2013-0019) from Toy Industry Association and Toy Industries of Europe.

full removal of tariffs does little to open up markets because TBTs might entail multiple tariffs and thus render market access quite – or even very – costly, or, for SMEs, simply impossible.

The TTIP negotiations are, however, embedded within a larger context of recent and concurrent trade negotiations involving the US or EU as negotiating partners. Not surprisingly, both sides have exhibited a willingness to advance their trade interests through bilateral FTAs with the larger goal of promoting trade, market access, investment and development. Both sides have separately pushed for stronger market-opening commitments from third countries as bilateral and regional trade agreements have become their preferred trade strategy. To that end, the EU has indicated that it will play a leading role in sharing best practice and developing global rules and standards as well as promoting convergence towards EU or international standards in select policy areas (see European Commission, 1996).

The US has also engaged in a similar strategy to implement WTO TBT commitments, supplemented with technical assistance, and sector specific provisions (see below) (Lesser, 2007). But what adjustment costs are they willing to make when the trade giants are negotiating with each other? Whose standards or, more specifically, regulatory requirements will prevail? Or indeed, should one necessarily prevail, or would 'equivalence' be an option to pursue? Should the US and the EU renew their efforts to improve and extend their 1998 Mutual Recognition Agreement (MRA), which works only for some of the six industrial sectors selected? Their differing regulatory policies in some specific areas have been the constant target of trade disputes, resulting in the US and EU being the most prolific initiators of complaints in the WTO (Young).

3. Prior transatlantic efforts at addressing TBTs

Over the past 20 years, the US and EU have engaged in a variety of efforts to foster transatlantic regulatory cooperation with many pre-existing dialogues, initiatives and commitments (Barker, 2013; Lester & Barbee, 2013). While there are differences between the US and EU that matter for TTIP, collaboration has evolved as the product of prior efforts at promoting trade and investment cooperation. One has to acknowledge that the optimism of the mid-1990s, when it was thought that a relatively simple and 'light' approach such as an MRA in several industrial sectors would be a quick route to lowering the costs of EU/US TBTs, was largely mistaken. An MRA aims to accomplish the acceptance of all relevant aspects of conformity assessment of the trading partner for the purpose of testing and certifying export goods on the requirements of the importing economy. It works for telecom equipment and EMC (electromagnetic compatibility of equipment) but not for medical devices, GMP in medicines or electrical goods and machinery (a huge sector).

On both sides lessons have been learned about how difficult the creation of a New Transatlantic Marketplace (NTM), deemed in 1995 to be feasible, would be, given the many problems in implementing MRAs in providing effective market access. Moreover, it was also better realised that MRAs are a rather heavy construction for a relatively minor cost advantage: even with a well-functioning MRA, the main reason for TBT costs (regulatory differences and requirements) remains intact. Consequently, regulatory cooperation since 2002, and more so since 2007 in the framework of the Transatlantic Economic Council (TEC), has deepened mutual understanding and also helped to develop practical forms of regulatory cooperation, without formal obligations, linked in cases like medical devices and medicines to global fora of regulators.[3] Moreover, the TEC has emphasised the pre-emption of TBTs in new or emerging product markets or in new technologies (such as electric vehicles). The TTIP TBT chapter is meant to decisively move beyond this status quo and genuinely address the cost of TBTs.[4]

Both sides have struggled to coordinate their administrative approaches, with early warning systems,[5] mutual recognition agreements, exchanges of information, as well as the adoption of broad regulatory principles and guidelines.[6] The two administrative cultures have fundamentally different market and regulatory regimes, which has led to many proposals that, unfortunately, have failed to promote the expected regulatory coherence (Nicolaïdis & Egan, 2001). Nevertheless, in some special instances, there are success stories in transatlantic regulatory cooperation, such as the 2009 EU/US certification of aircraft agreement, the EU/US Veterinary Agreement

---

[3] For a detailed analysis of MRA implications for TTIP, see Pelkmans & Correia de Brito (2015).

[4] On regulatory cooperation, see Chase & Pelkmans (2015).

[5] http://useu.usmission.gov/062199_report_bonn.html.

[6] http://trade.ec.europa.eu/doclib/docs/2011/july/tradoc_148030.pdf.

(see Josling & Tangermann, chapter 9, in this volume) and the 2012 agreement on organic farming recognition.[7]

The US-EU High Level Working Group on Jobs and Growth (HLWG) laid out its goals regarding transatlantic trade barriers, emphasising the importance of preventing future barriers to trade as well as addressing the current divergences that impede cross-border trade (US-EU High Level Working Group on Jobs and Growth, 2013). The report focused on broad goals in addressing technical barriers with the inclusion of a 'TBT plus' chapter, building on horizontal disciplines in the WTO Agreement on Technical Barriers to Trade, including establishing an ongoing mechanism for improved dialogue and cooperation for addressing bilateral TBT issues, which is not unique to the transatlantic free trade negotiations. The HLWG also promotes greater openness, transparency, and convergence in regulatory approaches and requirements and related standards-development processes; reduces redundant and burdensome testing and certification requirements; promotes confidence in the respective conformity assessment bodies; and enhances cooperation on conformity assessment and standardisation issues globally. The goal is to strengthen horizontal cooperation among regulators through early consultations, impact assessment, upstream cooperation and good manufacturing practices to prevent unnecessary costs and delays, and to enhance cooperation on standards-related issues.

In February 2013, both sides announced they would embark on an FTA together after a decade of competitive liberalisation in which they sought to disseminate new rules in international trade and employ free trade negotiations to establish closer economic links with security partners or use them to isolate economic competitors by excluding them from economic cooperation agreements negotiated with other nations. While many observers felt that TTIP would have an easier time in soliciting agreement than other recent trade agreements, the reality has been more complex. In an FTA, trade negotiations typically seek least trade-restrictive rules and procedures, and not the codification of existing practices. The legal basis of GATT/WTO rules for regional trade agreements (RTAs) (Art. XXIV.5) allows for RTAs as a special exception provided a) duties and other trade regulations of commerce are reduced on or removed from all trade and b) the RTA does not raise the overall protection vis-à-vis other WTO members.

---

[7] See Chase & Pelkmans (2015) for an annex with all US-EU regulatory cooperation initiatives since the mid-1990s.

While the US and EU have been the main proponents of WTO-plus commitments in RTAs, with both conditional and promotional elements that include incentives, sanction and monitoring, they differ on what should be included as part of a gold standard agreement for TTIP.[8] Though the TBT, SPS (sanitary and phytosanitary) and GATT Agreements provide a source of discipline regarding technical barriers to trade, the multilateral agreement on Technical Barriers to Trade (TBT) seeks to ensure that technical regulations, standards and procedures for assessing conformity do not create unnecessary obstacles to trade. It requires that applicable regulations are transparent, justifiable, non-discriminatory and based on international standards whenever possible. However, in terms of their respective FTA templates, they have varied in terms of their approach. The US follows a standard template focused on fairly light WTO-plus commitments whereas the EU is more varied, although both have included additional issues focusing on governance rather than trade (Baldwin, 2015).

Despite various calls to phase in different elements of the agreement, the US has steadfastly focused on a comprehensive agreement. However, there have been disagreements within the US about the coverage and inclusion of issues in any negotiated agreement, providing a stark reminder of the need to address different domestic constituencies. Congressional demands have focused on opposition to broadening of 'geographical indications', on the maintenance of 'buy American' and 'buy local' provisions, and on the improvement in biotechnology approval, thereby providing a stark reminder of the need to address different domestic constituencies. There is also resistance from some regulatory agencies about their inclusion in the talks. While the US pushed for the exclusion of financial services at the behest of the Treasury and SEC, the FDA has sought to undertake regulatory cooperation with the EU outside of the TTIP negotiations (Inside U.S. Trade, 18 July 2014 – www.insidetrade.com). In the EU, there has been concern over the impact of TTIP on food and safety issues and medicinal products. Therefore, the EU is keen to negotiate

---

[8] For example, the US did not want the inclusion of competition policy and so instead promoted the idea of the International Competition Network (ICN), which was accepted but differed from the initial EU preference to include competition and binding principles, e.g. most favoured nation (MFN), cartels and other non-binding principles such as vertical restraints.

both a healthcare and SPS chapter as well as addressing regulatory cooperation on medical devices.

4.   TBTs in TTIP: What sectors and why?

TBTs addressed in TTIP are not confined solely to the TBT chapter; they are dealt with in four different contexts:

i)   the TBT chapter as is traditionally the case in most FTAs;

ii)   issues of food safety and animal and plant health (which are dealt with separately in a SPS chapter, based on the WTO SPS Agreement);

iii)   the sectoral sub-chapters or annexes (as proposed in TTIP on chemicals, cosmetics, engineering, medical devices, ICT, pharmaceuticals, textiles, and automotive);

iv)   a chapter on horizontal regulatory cooperation in TTIP, with a view to future questions in a 'living agreement', which is a continuous process of addressing regulatory barriers to enhance cooperation.

The economic gains from any agreement have received significant attention. The headline figures are of annual GDP gains of €119 billion for the EU and €95 billion for the US derived from two key economic studies on EU/US trade liberalisation commissioned by the European Commission.[9] The economic study by Francois et al. (2013)[10] for the Commission Impact Assessment of TTIP deals with all these segments of TBTs, though measuring the costs of TBTs with some degree of reliability is exceedingly difficult. Francois et al. (2013) is based on ECORYS estimates of 'tariff equivalents' of TBTs, i.e. regarding the TBT costs as equivalent to an import tariff. These costs (in percent of the invoice price, like a tariff) are no less than 21% (EU

---

[9] See Berden & Francois (2015) for an overview; the U.S. International Trade Commission (ITC) conducted a confidential investigation on the potential economic effects of providing duty-free treatment for US imports from the EU, pursuant to Section 131 of the Trade Act of 1974 (19 U.S.C. 2151) and Section 2104(b)(2) of the Trade Act of 2002 (19 U.S.C. 3804(b)(2)) which it submitted to the USTR in September 2013.

[10]   See   http://trade.ec.europa.eu/doclib/docs/2013/march/tradoc_150737.pdf; see also Pelkmans et al. (2014), for a non-technical explanatory study for the INTA Committee on the Francois (or CEPR) report, underlying model and alternatives estimates.

TBTs for US exports) and 25% (US TBTs for EU exports) on average, with peaks for agro-food (respectively, 57% and 73%), and fairly high TBTs for automotive (25% and 27%), chemicals (14% and 19%), electrical machinery (13% and 15%), other transport equipment (19% and 19%) and metals and metal products (12% and 17%). All these TBT costs are much higher than transatlantic tariffs. By contrast, Fontagné et al. (2013), using a different technique in which the average TBT costs for manufacturing are much higher, with costs amounting to 43% (EU TBTs) and 32% (US TBTs), suggest that the reports result in robust findings on the economic benefits of addressing TBTs.[11]

In addition, strictly regulated sectors such as medicines, automotive, chemicals and cosmetics do not fall under the TBT chapter. In the EU, none of these sectors fall under the New Approach (New Legislative Framework), thus voluntary standards are not used for the simple reason that regulation is highly specific and intrusive while conformity assessment typically relies on pre-market type approval and inspections. However, in engineering (including machinery), there is a preponderant reliance on the 'new legislative framework' that allows compliance with European standards to provide a presumption of conformity in the European internal market.

In the US, Congress appears keen to promote third-party verification, having mandated or authorised its use in recent legislation including the 2011 Food Safety Modernization Act, which strengthened authority to regulate imported food by recognising accreditation bodies to accredit third-party auditors to certify foreign food facilities and imports. In some areas, Congress has directed federal agencies to develop a third-party programme; in others, regulatory agencies have developed programmes under existing statutory authority. In medical devices, there is mandatory pre-market notification (unlike in the EU) and inspection of facilities, whereas cosmetic products do not require preapproval, with some exceptions in terms of colour additives by the FDA. Besides these four sectors with specific annexes, there are of course other sectors and specific goods that may encounter TBTs when trying to access the US or EU market. Thus the TBT chapter attempts to organise a framework to address existing TBTs as well as pre-empt new ones. TTIP also contains a horizontal regulatory cooperation chapter

---

[11] Berden & Francois (2015) suggest several reasons why Fontagné et al. (2013) might show an upward bias.

aimed at providing greater regulatory coherence and joint governance on issues pertaining to TBTs.[12]

The goal is to promote common principles and good regulatory practices, providing for mutual exchange of information through notice and comment procedures, which can involve stakeholders, and discipline both governments to take account of the trade and investment effects of future regulations. A Regulatory Cooperation Body would be established to identify common priorities, negotiate follow-up draft agreements for discussion and adoption in the respective EU and US legislative and regulatory processes, and implement regulatory provisions of agreement in both goods and services.[13]

5. Understanding US and EU standards and related regulatory regimes

The US and EU have each developed a set of procedures and policies to regulate goods and processes that have resulted in different technical standards and conformity assessment procedures that can be viewed as potentially significant barriers to trade (Pelkmans, 2015). As long as regulation is not linked to standards, the goals are fundamentally similar in that standards reflect market needs and are not simply about techniques or engineering but about improving the functioning of markets (see Box 3.1). However, owing to differences in their origins and development, both sides use private standards in their existing legislation as a means to demonstrate conformity with mandated laws and statutory requirements. In Europe, national governments have established close ties with private standards bodies, often providing public funding for specified 'public' assignments, resulting in a system that recognises a *singular* standards body (per country), which may be autonomous under private law, as a private or non-profit, independent

---

12 http://trade.ec.europa.eu/doclib/docs/2015/february/tradoc_153120.pdf; see also Chase & Pelkmans (2015).

13 Though not the focus of this chapter, there have been widespread efforts at regulatory coordination, not just across sectors, such as marine safety equipment or consumer products in terms of safety recalls, but also efforts between OMB-OIRA and the Secretariat General of the European Commission to address methodological issues, i.e. related to good regulatory practice, such as impact assessment, stakeholder consultation, etc., in order to improve the understanding of each other's regulatory systems and practices.

or public agency regulated by government statutes (Egan, 2005; Bremer, 2015).[14]

These national standards bodies are then part of a Europe-wide network that creates European standards through CEN, CENELEC and ETSI. In the US, the government took a more informal approach towards collaboration with standards bodies, and the result has been multiple standards development organisations (SDOs), creating a highly decentralised and fragmented system. Though some 200-plus are accredited by the American National Standards Institute (ANSI), an umbrella organisation that brings together standards bodies, conformity assessment bodies, companies and government agencies, there are other SDOs, consortia and fora outside of ANSI, which can also develop their own standards. Although ANSI is a member of ISO/IEC and provides a platform for promulgating standards, there are no officially recognised standards bodies. Standards are developed primarily in the private sector, predominantly by a handful of independent standards bodies that are autonomous and do not receive government funding.

Though ANSI is often viewed as the coordinating umbrella for US professional and trade associations engaged in standard-setting, ANSI does not develop its own standards. ANSI does not determine which standards should be developed but provides a coordination and accreditation function among the various bodies. Thus many prominent standards are developed by a fairly limited number of independent bodies in the US, including ASME, the National Fire Protection Association (NFPA), ASTM and IEEE – perhaps a dozen or at most two dozen in all, which also have a recognised status in many markets in the world. In addition, there are many small or highly specialised sectoral bodies, sometimes even competing on standards. It is estimated that there are 600 standards bodies in the US with more than 100,000 private standards currently in use (Bremer, 2015: 28). The US ITA has defended this system as providing "technological innovation", with proponents arguing that it is "open and accessible" (International Trade Administration, 2009: 2).

Both the US and EU use private technical standards in their regulations to support government mandates. Both have established

---

[14] Note that the EU countries with public agencies for standardisation are typically former communist countries – the West/North European standardisation tradition is strictly private (industry).

procedures for the public use of private standardisation: the US policy is set out in a statute[15] and executive order,[16] and the EU's is outlined in an annual programme on European standardisation and delineated in a European regulation (No. 1025/2012). What occurs in both the European and American contexts is that standards are incorporated into regulations by reference, so that 'law-making' is not limited to public institutions. Incorporation by reference is the practice of codifying material published elsewhere by referring to it in the text of a regulation (Bremer, 2014). In the US, there is no obligation to have a single standard and any standard may be referenced, if the correct procedure for incorporation by reference is followed. Although this has resulted in more than 360 organisations providing voluntary standards for 26 federal agencies, 10 SDOs provide the majority of standards incorporated into public law (Bremer, 2015; NIST, 2013). In fact, federal, state and local agencies have to justify the development of "government unique standards" when a private consensus-based standard is available (Mendelson, 2013).[17] In terms of the possible misapplication of legal standards, in the US, the antitrust agencies act as enforcement bodies in ways similar to other business review bodies but not as adjudicators of the legality of standards development activity itself.[18] Thus, even if, as has happened, standard-setting provides commercial advantages for participants over competitors, congressional limitations and court decisions have prevailed, allowing private standards to be incorporated into public law (Sagers, 2004; Strauss, 2013).

In Europe, there is an obligation to eliminate all conflicting standards (CEN & CENELEC, 2013). The standards developed by the three European standards bodies are valid in all the EEA countries plus Turkey and Switzerland, and once adopted, member states must withdraw any existing national standard that overlaps or might compete with it. The European Standards Organizations, CEN,

---

[15] See National Technology Transfer and Advancement Act of 1995 (NTTAA), Pub. L. No. 104-113, § 12(d), 110 Stat. 775 (1996)

[16] Office of Management and Budget Executive Office of the President, OMB Circular No A- 119.

[17] NIST notes that since the passage of the NCAA Act only 53 government unique standards have been proposed with voluntary consensus standards providing solutions for government legislative mandates.

[18] HR House Report 108-125, Part 1, 108th Congress, Standards Development Organization Advancement Act, 2003.

CENELEC and ETSI provide the standards to meet "essential requirements" (mainly, the technical expressions of SHEC objectives from specific EU directives or regulations) based on a contractual agreement with the European Commission through General Guidelines for Cooperation that provides specific designation to ESOs as monopoly providers. However, the so-called 'mandates' or 'requests' of the European Commission to CEN/CENELEC are full of obligations about verifying all relevant standards in the world, connecting with bodies outside the EU where this would be promising, involving non-EU expertise where relevant, etc. Although the European standards remain voluntary (unless they are US 'referred standards', which become compulsory), once 'harmonised European standards' have been accepted as fulfilling the 'essential requirements' and published by the European Commission, they give a 'presumption of conformity' with the relevant essential SHEC requirements, and thus free movement inside the single market.

In fact, free movement is granted to all goods having a CE mark – a symbol indicating conformity with EU technical laws – whether based on a harmonised standard or not. But the harmonised standard greatly facilitates conformity owing to the full access it allows to 28 countries in the EU single market, which is much appreciated by manufacturers. Note that EU member states do not have regulatory autonomy in areas where EU regulation has been enacted; again, in the US, the states often have regulatory discretion despite federal risk regulation, based on referred standards. It should be understood that such a European harmonised standard remains voluntary and a manufacturer is free to use another standard or present its own (innovative) solution to abide with the 'essential requirements' (basically, SHEC objectives), but in the latter case, the manufacturer has to go through third-party certification by a Notified Body (a recognised conformity assessment body).

This is critical in terms of good regulatory practices because what matters is that the SHEC *objectives* (essential requirements) are met properly, but the instruments or innovative other solutions of doing so are at best secondary, and hence should not be prescribed or restricted unnecessarily.[19] The European Commission has set out broad operating principles that encompass "transparency, openness, consensus,

---

[19] This system is based on Reg. 2008/765, Decision 768/2008 and Reg. 1025/2012 (the latter on European standardisation). See also the 'Blue book' issued by DG Grow of the European Commission.

independence of vested interests, and efficiency" through national representation. It has pushed the European standards bodies to be as inclusive as possible to ensure wide-ranging participation in technical committees with multiple stakeholders (in particular, SMEs, consumers and labour unions).

Many US government agencies use technical standards created by different American SDOs, and do not give preference to any specific standards bodies, in contrast to their European counterparts that require the adoption of European or internationally agreed standards. Federal law and executive policy have long required agencies to use available voluntary consensus standards instead of creating so-called 'government unique' standards solely to serve regulatory purposes. Currently, there are over 10,000 citations of standards in the Code of Federal Regulations. Over 80% of these references are private sector standards and more than 3,900 are government unique standards that have been replaced by private-sector standards.[20] These standards are rarely the result of government mandates, although this may change as a result of the changes proposed to the OMB Circular A-119, to allow agencies to solicit standards from qualified SDOs. [21]

While the US is deeply committed to private standards development, and although private standards outnumber public standards, the number incorporated into public law is relatively small. However, it was the dissatisfaction with the closed nature of standard-setting in the 1960s and 1970s that led to the expansion of federal consumer and safety protection through the creation of OHSA and CPSC, which pushed the private standards development bodies into reforms towards a voluntary consensus-based process built on the principles of transparency, due process, openness and the promise that standards would be agreed by consensus.[22] These changes allowed the federal government to use such voluntary standards in their federal regulations. Yet this masks the scope of private standards that are not incorporated by reference, and the degree to which statutory requirements allow government agencies ranging from transportation,

---

[20] It should be noted that the government unique standards issue hardly plays a role in Europe, except in network industries (which used to be state-owned and not subject to competition, e.g. rail or telecoms infrastructure).

[21] *Source*: Author's interview with former USTR official.

[22] Allied Tube & Conduit Corporation v. Indian Head, Inc., and American Society of Mechanical Engineers v. Hydrolevel Corp.

energy, consumer protection, federal emergency management and homeland security, to participate in private standards development.[23]

Europeans have expressed concern when a designated private standard subsequently becomes part of US law; European suppliers find that few alternative methods or innovative solutions can be used or demonstrated to serve equally well the designated public policy objectives, unless alternative standards are specified in the regulation. Because multiple standards (may) exist, US regulators or federal government agencies choose the most suitable existing standard. This implies that, for an EU company, this system of 'incorporation by reference' risks creating many TBTs for EU exporters, the more so as few US standards are ISO/IEC standards anyway, and more than one referred standard may be encountered at different (US) levels of government. There are also concerns that once a standard has been incorporated by reference in agency rule-making, these can force the private sector to lag behind, as the vast majority of incorporated standards were adopted prior to the new rules outlined in the NTTAA.[24] Recognising that private standards can evolve, and thus that referred standards need updating, the US is trying to avoid continual notice, rule and comment efforts, by updating standards through statutory improvements. Agencies differ in approaches to updating standards referenced in their regulations. While OSHA issues *de minimis* violations to manage updated standards by regulated entities, the Coast Guard allows "equivalence" for an updated standard, and the Environmental Protection Agency updates final rule-making to incorporate changes proposed by SDOs (Bremer, 2013).

The intersection of public law and private standards has generated debates in the US about transparency and copyright issues resulting in tension between the public right to access the law and private intellectual property rights. The Pipeline and Hazardous Materials Safety Administration (PHSMA), asserting their copyright restrictions, refused to allow access to Congress, which then compelled PHSMA by statute to ensure that all its IBR standards were freely available online beginning in 2013. They were then revised, due to

---

[23] See National Technology Transfer and Advancement Act of 1995 (NTTAA); federal agencies participated in 552 SDOs according to NIST's latest report (2013).

[24] Several authors in criticising the incorporation by reference to standards indicate that many predate 1996 when the NTTAA was signed. This has been difficult to verify.

intense lobbying efforts about the revenue implications for SDOs. Due to the pressure for transparency, changes in administrative procedures have meant that US agencies must ensure the reasonable availability of incorporated materials and also summaries of those materials when standards are incorporated by reference (Strauss, 2013; Bremer, 2013).

6. How the US and EU standards systems impact trade

Europe's standards bodies have worked closely with the international standards bodies, the ISO and the IEC, based on the Vienna and Dresden Agreements which offer a framework for writing new ISO/IEC standards together with European ones, with the same (European) experts, in addition to experts from the rest of the world (including, often, US experts). Over time, this has gradually cumulated in no less than 72% of CENELEC standards being identical to IEC ones, and some 31% of CEN standards being identical to ISO ones. As long as standards – by definition voluntary – are not linked to regulations, European exporters and investors can live with the US landscape in which many standards – at least, from the dozen or so leading prestigious bodies – are well-known and often have a worldwide reputation through use in the marketplace. However, the US rarely adopts either fully or partially ISO or IEC standards, which can create disadvantages in electronic and electrical goods, including machinery, where safety and compatibility issues have been addressed internationally for decades.

However, a longstanding complaint, mainly from US companies but nowadays also from the combined EU and US ICT business sector (see DigitalEurope & (US) ITI, 2015), is that EU member state governments do not (always) recognise global ICT standards in their public procurement. Indeed, until changes were introduced to EU Regulation 1025/2012, governments were obliged to refer only to European standards and – since many global ICT standards are not formally ISO/IEC (or European) standards but developed (rapidly) in consortia or special ICT fora – numerous well-accepted ICT standards could not be listed in public procurement. Furthermore, because the sector is fast-moving, with continual innovation, industry preferred using alternative institutional frameworks rather than the designated European standards bodies.

In the US, the argument has traditionally been that as a technological leader, its standards were often those used in industrial production. However, the result has been that in the Code of Federal Regulations (CFR), the US government has only referenced a limited number of ISO, IEC and ITU standards. Currently, of the 397 total international standards, the US references 172 from ISO, 156 from IEC, 25 combined ISO/IEC, 37 from ITU and seven from other bodies.[25] Some US standards promulgated by well-known US engineering societies, such as ASTM (which alone has written some 12,000 standards!), are de facto world standards, e.g. for aircraft, computers, power grids, cars, etc., and, in these cases, multinational businesses (including many EU companies) are used to living with two standards.

Usually, two reasons are given for US reluctance to adopt international, i.e. ISO and IEC, standards. The first is that historically, the Europeans have had many votes (when voting together) and the US has only one single vote, creating a permanent fear of being outvoted, especially in the first decades of the ISO. This argument has weakened a great deal because ISO/IEC membership is now worldwide and the EU cannot dominate such an international organisation.[26] In fact, ANSI has whether ISO/IEC standardisation is still subject to block voting by CEN/CENELEC members and found that it is no longer the case. Second, it is asserted that ISO/IEC standards are often too much of a compromise, and US bodies feel they ought to deviate for quality reasons, or promulgate their own. Much more important, it is also difficult and very costly to alter engineering traditions built on familiar standards. The issue of adjustment costs and enormous structural change in designs, production lines, materials, etc., for literally thousands of companies (and not just US multinationals but local ones in numerous countries) would seem to be the root of EU/US friction in the debate over the use of 'international standards'.

The key US standard bodies with an international reputation see their standards used by many companies all over the world. For some of these bodies, their standards are used in local production or in segments of global value chains in more than 100 countries, by thousands of multinationals and SMEs. Even in Europe, there are a large number of 'American' standards in use in markets simply because they are of high quality and usually highly specialised, although they

---

[25] Two under American National Standards Institute, two under European Standards, two under International Civil Aviation Organization and one under International Maritime Organization.

[26] IEC has 60 members and 23 associate members; ISO has 163 members.

need not always be related to regulation. In the economics of technical standards, this property is called the 'installed base', having (a) enormous 'sunk costs' and (b) formidable 'switching costs', that is, immense adjustment costs when changing to alternative standards (say, IEC/ISO standards).[27] It is first of all crucial that this property and its economic consequences are spelled out far more clearly in the TBT debate in TTIP. Expecting US standards bodies to adjust and radically rewrite their (many) standards, if markets have long embraced them, will be pointless if there is no sense of whether ISO or IEC standards are in fact superior. The degree to which many of these American standards are de facto global standards or, alternatively, compete with similar IEC/ISO standards is not known or analysed authoritatively. To the extent they are truly global, there would be very large adjustment costs for (US and other) companies or value-chains when switching would become the norm. These are exceptionally difficult issues to address.

It is counterproductive for the TTIP negotiators to keep on talking in abstract generalisations about what exactly an 'international standard' is and is not, without publicly recognising fully the economic and market issues underlying the positioning and without seeking a constructive long-term way out of this gigantic 'installed base' issue. Nevertheless, it is and remains true that the very idea of standardisation is to do away with multiple specifications, as long as this can be justified, because a *single* high quality technical standard will, more often than not, be of formidable long-term economic benefit. Following the 'one standard, one test, valid everywhere' which was advocated by the Transatlantic Business Dialogue (TABD) more than 20 years ago, at long last some longer-term and credible forms of accommodation must be found and, if possible, begin to be recognised in TTIP regarding TBTs.

Sometimes standards bodies also act as conformity assessors, mixing up the two functions and risking conflicts of interest. Conformity assessment may present the largest and least understood obstacle to trade. The many NTB notifications in the WTO seems to suggest it, in spite of the TBT Code Agreement encouraging the acceptance of conformity assessment procedures, provided that they conform with equivalent technical regulations or standards equivalent

---

[27] In the economics of network standards, the examples are typically different, say, a rail infrastructure network or high-voltage transmission system, having very high sunk costs. The economic idea is the same.

to their own procedures. However, there are differences between the US and the EU with respect to conformity assessment, in particular when components or final products have to demonstrate conformance with a prescriptive regulation (often based on 'referred standards').

While the EU uses supplier declaration of conformity (SDoC), the US is more likely to use third-party testing, inspection and market surveillance as a prerequisite for market access, so that mutual recognition is difficult given the different forms of conformity assessment. Of concern in Europe is that conformity with EU essential SHEC requirements are not tested or certified in the US; rather, once a standard is referred to (presumably because it serves one or more SHEC objectives), it is to be followed and no alternative method or solution is accepted (unless already in the regulation). However, accrediting certification bodies is challenging, even more so if the agency is a foreign body, as agencies cannot perform the same kind of oversight that would take place in a domestic context. In the EU, under many directives, alternative solutions can be certified by a Notified Body as long as the relevant SHEC objectives are served.

In the US, much of the US risk regulation is in fact managed by independent federal regulators such as OSHA (protection of workers in the workplace), the Federal Communications Commission (safety and health aspects of telecoms equipment, etc.), the Consumer Protection Safety Agency, the Environmental Protection Agency (many aspects including chemicals), the FDA (medicines and medical devices, as well as food law), the Federal Aviation Administration (aircraft certification), the US Coast Guard (boat and maritime safety), among others.[28] Many firms in the US are reluctant to use third-party inspection. Although inspection might satisfy regulatory requirements in multiple jurisdictions, there has been a low rate of participation in some areas regulated by the FDA, whereas the FCC has found that third-party certification has become the norm.[29]

The practical aspects of conformity assessment depend then on federal agencies, and the degree to which private accreditation bodies

---

[28] The FDA established the AP Program, allowing manufacturers of Class II and III (medium- and high-risk) devices to contract with an AP to conduct a third-party inspection, in lieu of an FDA inspection, using the Quality System regulation and other device requirements in the FD&C Act.

[29] www.acus.gov/sites/default/files/documents/Third-Party-Programs-Report_Final.pdf, p. 58. Examples of third-party testing FDA inspection for medical device production facilities, medical devices, and FCC TBC program.

can be recognised directly by federal agencies, either through a designated domestic programme or by an international organisation, such as the IAF (for accreditation of certification bodies) or ILAC (for accreditation of laboratories), can determine the degree to which conformity assessment creates TBTs. There have been longstanding frictions in conformity assessment, with options including mutual recognition agreements, unilateral recognition of another country's conformity results, and acceptance of supplier declaration of conformity. For the EU, problems with OSHA, due to its policy of assigning Nationally Recognised Testing Laboratories (NRTLs) for mandatory third-party certification of electrical goods including machinery, a stronghold of EU exporters, have generated trade frictions.[30]

At first, for all practical purposes, UL was the only NRTL and EU exporters long felt that UL abused its de facto monopoly by higher prices and unjustified complications.[31] Nowadays, a dozen NRTLs have been recognised, but UL does not accept certification of components and parts of other NRTLs (hence, testing is duplicative). Moreover, some 30 US states have enacted provisions singling out UL as the mandatory conformity assessment body, which strengthens UL's dominant position and creates delays and unjustified rigidity. Fortunately, there are reforms emerging in the US with a view to improving such conformity rules and practices. While both Circular A-119 and OSHA's policy with respect to NRTLs are under review, NIST and OMB are revising their guidelines on conformity assessment (Federal Register 19357, 30 March 2012). TTIP is a good opportunity to remove these frictions and costly TBTs, especially for the electrical and machinery sector.

Both the US and EU have accredited conformity assessment bodies on the basis of ISO standards for laboratory accreditation relying on private third-party programmes for conformity assessment (ILAF

---

[30] Note that, in the EU, the regime is 'light': conformity assessment is based on SDoC (self-declaration), in turn based on a technical file demonstrating compliance, which must be shown on request of the authorities.

[31] Explained in detail in Orgalime (2011 and 2012). The latter provides a number of details about excessive pricing (compared to other NRTLs, and also due to unnecessarily cumbersome procedural requirements). EU stakeholders hold that the US Department of Justice should have long ago acted against UL on the basis of antitrust law.

and IAF), which results in recognition of results.[32] Moreover, the 1998 MRA between the US and the EU in six sectors (telecoms equipment, EMC, electrical goods, medicines GMP, medical devices and recreational crafts[33]) was expected to focus purely on conformity assessment issues, without ever touching on domestic regulation or standards at all. The results of this MRA were mixed, if not disappointing, but much has been learned from this seemingly modest exercise. While MRAs were widely touted in the late 1990s, they merely accept certification of designated third-party assessment, and hence are much more limited than the TTIP TBT debate. While duplicative testing is expected to be done away with, this will *not* address the underlying differences in rules/standards, which are normally the main costs of TBTs.

7. State of play within TTIP negotiations

While differences in product standards can constitute barriers to trade, they also reflect differences in perceptions of health and safety, environmental requirements and preferences that have mobilised opposition on both sides of the Atlantic, as public opinion and civil society have questioned proposals across many sectors and issues.[34] Though the EU has published a proposal on technical barriers to trade that it made public in January 2015, the US has been less transparent and public in promoting its objectives in the negotiations. The EU proposal on technical barriers focuses on addressing the burdens created by divergent technical regulations, standards and conformity assessment.[35] The EU proposal would also include the WTO Agreement on Technical Barriers to Trade in the agreement. In addition, the proposed TBT chapter focuses on greater regulatory cooperation between both public and private organisations in areas of accreditation, standards and conformity assessment, and promotes global harmonisation within existing international bodies not defined

---

[32] See, e.g. International Laboratory Accreditation Cooperation, www.ilac.org/; see Pelkmans & Correia de Brito, (2015).

[33] GMP = good manufacturing practices, an OECD standard for factories; EMC = electro-magnetic compatibility, preventing interference between different pieces of electric/electronic equipment.

[34] As an example of this view, see Chemnitz (2014). The U.S. Chamber initially wanted the trade negotiations to focus on tariffs, which in their view would realise significant immediate gains.

[35] http://trade.ec.europa.eu/doclib/docs/2015/january/tradoc_153025.pdf.

in the text and a single certificate of approval, authorisation or acceptance of conformity to foster mutual equivalence. The TBT chapter as proposed by EU negotiators is much more ambitious than the US template for such FTA-type negotiations, namely, the KORUS.

The US has stated that its trade priorities are to go beyond the existing WTO TBT commitment, increase the transparency and openness of the decision-making process regarding European standards and technical regulations, ensure that US bodies are permitted to test and certify products sold in Europe without the need for duplicative conformity assessment, and promote the recognition in Europe of internationally accepted standards that are used by US exporters and producers. The US also wants to establish an ongoing mechanism to discuss TBT concerns. In May 2015, the US tabled a new proposal on technical barriers to trade, and both sides have worked on an agreement on a 'consolidated text' on horizontal regulatory cooperation. The EU has pushed for a mechanism to promote strategic engagement with each other to prevent future regulatory differences that could create barriers to transatlantic trade. This seems to have much in common with an EU notification system for national draft laws in non-harmonised areas of goods regulation, in which regulations and standards are notified, and may be subject to a 'standstill measure' if the EU wishes to pursue regulatory action.[36] The process is aimed at ex-ante prevention in terms of trade barriers, having achieved significant success by covering both public and private sector activities (Correia de Brito & Pelkmans, 2012).

The US, by contrast, has focused on "good regulatory practices", which in reality is the promotion of their own notice rule and comment procedures that it believes will promote more transparency and reduce regulatory divergences if there are opportunities to comment on early draft proposals. Though pushing the notion in the Administrative Procedures Act (APA) for a public comment period has been a consistent proposal from the US side, the process provides for public feedback after significant inter- and intra-agency reviews of the proposed regulation. However, the US also uses negotiated rule-

---

[36] In fact, it is tougher: any notification automatically leads to a three-month standstill, which, by committee decision, can be extended to four (routine), six or 12 months (depending on the feared TBTs). All of these merely to iron out the problems with the member state in question. If, however, the possible TBT is so serious and/or might be imitated by EU countries, the standstill becomes 18 months for an EU proposal to be made and adopted by the Council and the European Parliament.

making under the Negotiated Rulemaking Act of 1990, where interested parties are asked to develop a proposal that the agency can then use as a basis for a more widely accepted regulatory proposal, although this approach is not often used. The US process requires a rule-making record so that if legally challenged there is a record of agency deliberations, and hence the US has pushed for a similar means to provide more visible public comments on European rule-making before it becomes adopted into law. Europeans have pushed for transparency in terms of the negotiating texts, having released a significant number on various topics, but without the US positions, the state of the talks is difficult to assess.

American trade officials might argue that their attention has been on securing the so-called 'fast track', i.e. the Trade Promotion Authority (TPA), intended to send a credible signal that any subsequent trade deal will receive a singular vote in Congress without amendments. The passage of the H.R. 1295 Trade Preferences Extension Act, in which the US Administration fought hard to overcome the strident opposition within their own party, will provide significant momentum for trade talks, although the US is also pushing forward with negotiations on the Trans-Pacific Partnership (TPP), the Trade in International Services Agreement (TISA), the Information Technology Agreement (ITA), and the Environmental Goods Agreement (EGA), all in addition to TTIP. As a result, the US focus on concluding TPP has meant that the past six months of transatlantic negotiations have focused on technical issues, in terms of regulatory cooperation across specific sectors, leaving some of the more controversial issues off the table (Inside U.S. Trade, 30 January 2015 – www.insidetrade.com).

Given the paucity of official documents on US proposals, an evaluation of current suggestions from different interest groups may provide some insights into the efforts of addressing TBTs. The Business Coalition for Transatlantic Trade is focusing on regulatory cooperation aimed at providing input on TBTs and developing new regulatory coherence and coherence efforts. This business group also supports the adoption of specific sectoral annexes in any agreement. Equally important, it has emphasised the importance of a common definition of 'international standards' by referencing WTO TBT Committee decisions, as well as referencing equivalence standards that could be applied within the EU 'new approach' directives. It has also requested more open and direct participation in standard-setting – all goals that reflect US trade objectives.[37]

Yet in other sectors, there is the emergence of transatlantic alliances between industry associations that have voiced common positions in addressing trade barriers. In the case of the automobile, chemical and pharmaceutical sectors, trade associations submitted joint proposals to address regulatory barriers to trade.[38] Part of this is due to integrated supply chains, intra-firm investment and trade patterns that push these associations to seek to reduce trade barriers.[39] While these associations have focused on addressing barriers to trade, they have eschewed harmonisation by pushing for the promotion of mutual equivalence in terms of inspections and the exchange of information for regulatory approvals to avoid making costly adjustments and choosing one standard over another (Egan & Nicola, 2015). There are some associations that have pushed for transatlantic harmonisation, with the pesticides associations wanting agreement on the US standard, and the automotive partners also wanting harmonisation through the UN Economic Commission for Europe Working Group on Global Technical Regulations (GTRs).[40]

However, the opposition to the agreement on both sides has come from different civil society groups, focusing on agriculture and investor disputer settlement, rather than domestic oriented firms, and labour groups such as the AFL-CIO and ETUC (European Trade Unions Confederation). The latter have also coordinated their views in stakeholder meetings in which they have indicated that trade

---

[37] http://www.transatlantictrade.org/issues/regulatory-cooperation/.

[38] Active Pharmaceutical Ingredients Committee (APIC) / European Fine Chemicals Group (EFCG) / Society of Chemical Manufacturers and Affiliates (SOCMA); European Automobile Manufacturers' Association (ACEA), the American Automotive Policy Council (AAPC) and the Alliance of Automobile Manufacturers (Auto Alliance); European Chemicals Industry Council (CEFIC) / American Chemistry Council (ACC) and Motor and Equipment Manufacturers Association/ European Association of Automotive Suppliers Pharmaceutical Research and Manufacturers Association (Pharma) / European Federation of Pharmaceutical Industries and Associations (EFPIA). See Young (2015).

[39] Young (2015).

[40] European Automobile Manufacturers' Association (ACEA), the American Automotive Policy Council (AAPC) and the Alliance of Automobile Manufacturers (Auto Alliance).

agreement could be beneficial, provided that it maintains high levels of worker protection that are not constituted as barriers to trade.[41]

The USTR continues to solicit feedback, drawing on expertise in industry and trade associations, standards bodies, professional and academic communities. Some of the debates are not new, as the US pushes its view that transparency does not require a flat obligation to use international standards. The TBT Code provides for notification if international standards are not used. For American trade negotiators, the issue is one of access to European standard-setting. Regional standards are neither international standards nor 'open to all' participants. As such, standard-setting in Europe does not (have to) follow trade principles of non-discrimination and national treatment. The goal is to ensure that there is no preferential treatment given to European standards bodies but fair and equal treatment to American standards bodies, with the option of being recognised in some way.

For Americans, any entity can be recognised as providing standards, whether it is a trade association, consortium, industry-based or local government, and they want to apply the same principle to European standardisation. They view European standards as a tool of industry policy, and want more flexibility, noting that consortia in the ICT sector have evolved and reformed to increase flexibility, which is something that the Europeans have had to belatedly recognise, given their competitive disadvantage in the ICT sector. For Americans, competition within established bodies might create innovation. While recognising that the initial idea of European standardisation has been beneficial in addressing internal barriers to trade, the goal of a unified transatlantic market cannot emerge if the relationship between European standards and New Approach Directives remains exclusive. However, there is no such thing as a TTIP goal of a 'unified transatlantic market' in any of the TTIP official documents.

In terms of concrete efforts, the European standards bodies (SDOs) and the American National Standards Institute (ANSI) have indicated that they plan on building upon their informal contacts to generate a memorandum of understanding (MoU), which is not widely supported by other trade associations and standards bodies in the US that do not want codification of existing practices. However, making progress toward bridging the differences between the US and Europe on what constitutes an international standard based on a set of rules

---

[41] www.aflcio.org/content/download/132421/3553131/AFL-CIO+TTIP+ Report_6+%282%29.pdf.

approved in the WTO by the Committee on Technical Barriers to Trade will be challenging. The US has repeatedly indicated that the global relevance of the standard is not which organisation developed the standard, or where it was developed, but its usage in the global marketplace (Froman, 2013). The number of 'international standards' in the formal sense incorporated by reference in the US is 397, primarily from the ISO, IEC and ITU.[42] The US believes that international standards can be developed by any SDO that adheres to WTO TBT principles. For the US, this multiple path approach means that standards can be agreed upon by international organisations such as the ISO and IEC or through direct participation in SDOs such as the IEE and ASTM or through consortia such as the IGRS. This difference in what constitutes an international standard is nothing new according to US participants but does constitute a lingering difficulty in promoting a memorandum of understanding or intent between the two sides that have been in discussions since 2013.

Although increasing cooperation on standards-setting and international accreditation arrangements is the overall goal, the issue is not specific to the transatlantic relationship, as similar discussions have emerged in recently approved negotiations for a non-binding memorandum of intent concerning standards and conformity assessment between the US and Brazil on this same issue, in which Brazil is much closer to the EU position on international standards and also relies on government agencies to conduct conformity assessment. European standards bodies have come under criticism as US officials have argued that the EU promotes its standards as part of trade agreements, aggressively pushing its 'market power', so that its standards are frequently adopted in other markets.

The US has consistently stated in trade talks that there should be openness and transparency in terms of standard-setting. This is an implicit criticism of the structure of European standard-setting in which European SDOs receive formal 'mandates' to adopt European wide standards in turn strengthened by a framework for regulatory cooperation with the ISO and IEC that often leads to the uploading or acceptance of European standards at the international level. With more than 65% of US exports subject to one or more New Approach Directives, US companies are anxious to address the inconsistencies in regulatory approval. The annual trade barrier report noted, "U.S.

---

[42] Data from Regulatory Standards Incorporated by Reference (R-SIBR) Database.

persons are not able to participate directly and effectively in the development of regulations, standards and conformity assessment procedures in the EU. In particular, some institutional arrangements in the EU appear to either accord exclusive rights to, or effectively favour, EU entities in the development and implementation of such measures. Further, there appears to be no effective mechanisms to ensure accountability to non-EU interests in the adoption and implementation of measures" (USTR, 2014). It is useful to put such remarks in perspective: many experts from US companies do in fact participate in writing European standards at the national level in the EU as well as with the ISO and IEC (sometimes with a US expert even serving as chair!).

Despite a surge in US SME exports to the EU from $67 billion in 2010 to $76 billion in 2011, the US International Trade Commission was asked to survey SMEs across the US as part of its evaluation of the TTIP negotiations.[43] It found significant problems in relation to standards, regulations and conformity assessment, and expressed concern that the lack of national treatment of certification bodies, costly compliance with European standards, and regulatory differences between the US and EU made it disproportionately difficult for SMEs to access the European market.[44] Most of the suggestions focused on harmonisation or mutual recognition, arguing that in a range of sectors from automotive to toy safety, the standards are functionally equivalent, with the same regulatory objectives but different methods to achieve them, e.g. vehicle emissions EPA certification and Euro VI vehicle certification. Many trade associations suggested that the mutual equivalence of conformity assessment to allow domestic testing in the US be accepted in Europe.

This preference begs the question why MRAs in various sectors are not pursued by the US or, alternatively, why the 1998 MRA is not modernised via today's global accreditation quality networks. Some SMEs even suggested that firms should incorporate components that already have the CE symbol to ease compliance problems, or seek government support or financial assistance from public certification or testing facilities.[45] In the TTIP negotiation, a recurrent critique put forward by the US administration is that while European SDOs are centralised, the procedural requirements concerning certification are

---

[43] www.usitc.gov/publications/332/pub4455.pdf.

[44] Ibid.

[45] www.usitc.gov/publications/332/pub4455.pdf.

highly decentralised, with substantial variation in consistency between and little control over the quality of the accreditation bodies in EU member states, which makes US approval difficult. However, one should distinguish the EU situation after 2008: Reg. 765/2008 and its follow-up, with the new European system of accreditation, much improved the level and consistency of accreditation and the quality of conformity assessment bodies.

A similar study by DG Trade on the impact of TTIP on SMEs found that 28% of the exports to the US were from SMEs, totalling €77 billion.[46] The study found that compliance with food and safety regulations and technical regulations for goods acted as barriers to market access and exports, making TBT and SPS issues the most cited factor in terms of trade barriers.[47] Across sectors, SMEs cited barriers to pharmaceuticals, chemical, and plastic and rubber products, and firms in both the pharmaceutical and medical devices sectors advocated for good manufacturing practice so that they could reduce conformity assessment costs. Their concerns may be warranted regarding pharmaceuticals, as companies are concerned that the FDA review process is almost twice as long as that of its European counterpart, the European Medicines Agency (Holtzman, 2012).[48] For chemical firms, conformity assessment along with the labelling requirements that do not follow UN standards impose higher costs on European exporters.

8.　Conclusion

On both sides of the Atlantic, there is a widespread recognition that TBTs arising from different standards, testing and conformity assessment practices can impede trade and raise market entry barriers. Though technical standards are developed by private SDOs through a voluntary consensus process, once they become part of statutory requirements, the result can create trade impediments, as the public law obligations differ. The different procedural requirements have created difficulties in negotiating regulatory cooperation, as 'reference to standards' and 'incorporation by reference' have different market and regulatory effects. In the past, governments on both sides have chosen a variety of tools to reduce or eliminate TBTs, with varying

---

[46] http://trade.ec.europa.eu/doclib/docs/2015/april/tradoc_153348.pdf.

[47] Ibid., p. 15.

[48] Starting in 2014, with the passing of the Affordable Care Act, a 2.3% medical excise tax was imposed on all sales of devices, regardless of country of origin, which may shift medical device manufacturers to new markets.

success. The goal is to ensure that standards-setting processes are transparent and inclusive, and that the resulting standards do not have anti-competitive effects that impede the prospect of alternative means to meet regulatory requirements for market access.

Conformity assessment (whether in-house labs or third-party testing) must demonstrate its competence to meet specific legal and standards-based requirements. But this will require accreditation of conformity assessment bodies so that their mutual acceptance (or national treatment and non-discrimination) will avoid duplicative testing, certification and other measures. After the long and complex process of a trade negotiation, most governments realise that the task is not complete when a trade agreement has been signed and ratified.

Rather, new challenges must be addressed in order to successfully implement an FTA, which has led to greater emphasis on the institutional framework to address perceived problems as well as future issues in a so-called 'living agreement'. There are previous FTA examples with provisions for regulatory cooperation, technical committees and regulatory councils. However, the according of national treatment to conformity assessment bodies, based on modern global accreditation principles and networks,[49] would build on the strong example set out in the CETA agreement. The TBT Agreement indicates that conformity assessment procedures should not be more trade restrictive than necessary, and should determine merely whether regulatory objectives are similar. It follows that the relevant products should not be subject to additional product approval – this principle should be central to the TTIP, as they often only differ in their origin. In the case of standards, the mandatory versus voluntary status in public law when incorporated into legislation is difficult to change. However, greater transparency, access and non-discrimination in standards (or mutual recognition based on specified SHEC objectives) would facilitate market access.

Finally, TTIP negotiators have to transcend the pointless stand-off over the definition of an 'international standard'; explain in market and economic terms the underlying issues (e.g. widespread use of US standards in numerous markets around the world and in global value chains)); stimulate exploration of the extent of this market-driven 'installed base' problem for thousands of firms all over the world (and

---

[49] In chapter 27 of the CETA Agreement, an MRA Protocol is elaborated in many sectors, based on accreditation.

not only for the relevant dozen of leading US SDOs); and constructively seek longer-term answers in a 'living agreement'.

References

Baldwin, R. (2015), "WTO 2.0: Governance of Twenty-First century Trade Agreements", *Review of International Organizations*, Vol. 9, No. 2, pp. 261-283.

Barker, T. (2013), "For Transatlantic Trade, This Time is Different", *Foreign Affairs*, 26 February (www.foreignaffairs.com/articles/139027/tyson-barker/for-transatlantic-trade-this-time-is-different).

Berden, K. and J. Francois (2015), "Quantifying non-tariff measures for TTIP", CEPS Special Report No. 116, CEPS, Brussels and chapter 4 in this volume.

Blind, K. (2013), "The impact of standardisation and standards on innovation", NESTA Working Paper No. 13/15, NESTA, London.

Bremer, E.S. (2014), "Incorporation by Reference in an Open-Government Age", *Harvard Journal of Law and Public Policy*, Vol. 36.

_____ (2015), "American and European Perspectives on Private Standards in Public Law", Unpublished manuscript.

Budetta, M. and R. Piermartini (2009), "A Mapping of Regional Rules on Technical Barriers to Trade", in A. Estevadeordal, K. Suominen and R. Teh (eds), *Regional Rules in the Global Trading System*, Cambridge: Cambridge University Press.

CEN and CENELEC (2013), Position Paper on EU-US Transatlantic Trade and Investment Partnership (TTIP) – Technical Barriers to Trade – Initial EU Position Paper, Brussels (www.cencenelec.eu/news/policy_opinions/PolicyOpinions/PositionPaperTTIP.pdf).

CEPR (2013), "Reducing Transatlantic Barriers to Trade and Investment, An Economic Assessment", paper prepared for the European Commission (J. Francois et al.), London/Brussels.

Chase, P. and J. Pelkmans (2015), "This time it's different: Turbo-charging regulatory cooperation in TTIP", CEPS Special Report No. 110, CEPS, Brussels, June and chapter 2 in this volume.

Chemnitz, C. (2014), "TTIP: Selling out Standards", Heinrich Böll Foundation, 28 August (http://us.boell.org/2014/08/28/ttip-selling-out-standards).

Comments concerning Proposed Transatlantic Trade and Investment Agreement (Docket number USTR-2013-0019) from Toy Industry Association and Toy Industries of Europe.

Correia de Brito, A. and J. Pelkmans (2012), "Pre-empting TBTs in the single market", CEPS Policy Brief, CEPS, Brussels, July.

DG Grow (nd), 'Blue book' issued by of the European Commission, Brussels.

DigitalEurope and (US) ITI (2015), "ICT industry recommendations for regulatory cooperation in the TTIP", Brussels and Washington, D.C., 2 February.

Egan, M. (2001), *Constructing a European Market: Standards, Regulation and Governance*, Oxford: Oxford University Press.

_____ (ed.) (2005), *Creating a Transatlantic Marketplace: Government Policies and Business Strategies*, Manchester: Manchester University Press.

Egan, M. and F. Nicola (2015), "Reframing Regulatory Cooperation under TTIP: The Role of Private Law Making and Industry Standards", paper presented at EUSA, Boston, MA, March.

European Commission (1996), "The Global Challenge of International Trade: A Market Access Strategy for the European Union", COM(96) 53, 14 February.

Froman, M. (2013), "The United States, the European Union, and the Transatlantic Trade and Investment Partnership", remarks by the US Trade Representative, German Marshall Fund, 30 September, Brussels (www.gmfus.org/events/ustr-froman-gives-first-major-address-brussels-transatlantic-trade-agreement-gmf).

Hamilton, D.S. (2014), "America's Mega-Regional Trade Diplomacy: Comparing TPP and TTIP", *International Spectator*, Vol. 49, No. 1, March, pp. 81-89.

Holtzman, Y. (2012), "The U.S. Medical Device Industry in 2012: Challenges at Home and Abroad", MDDI, 17 July (www.mddionline.com/article/medtech-2012-SWOT).

International Trade Administration (2009), "The Voluntary Standards System: A Dynamic Tool for U.S. Economic Growth and Innovation", Seminar Program, U.S. Department of Commerce, Washington, D.C., 24 July.

Lesser, C. (2007), "Do Bilateral and Regional Approaches for Reducing Technical Barriers to Trade Converge towards the Multilateral Trading System?", OECD Trade Committee Working Paper 58, TAD/TWP(2007)12/FINAL, Organization for Economic Co-operation and Development, Paris.

Lester, S. and I. Barbee (2013), "The Challenge of Cooperation: Regulatory Trade Barriers in the Transatlantic Trade and Investment Partnership", *Journal of International Economic Law*, Vol. 16, No. 4, December.

Mendelson, N. (2013), "Private Control Over Access to Public Law: The Puzzling Federal Regulatory Use of Private Standards", *Michigan Law Review*.

National Research Council (NRC) (1995), "Standards, Conformity Assessment and Trade in the Twenty-First Century", National Academic Press, Washington, D.C.

Nicolaïdis, K. and M. Egan (2001), "Transnational Market Governance and Regional Policy Externality: Why Recognize Foreign Standards?", *Journal of European Public Policy* 8.3.

NIST (2013), Federal Agency Use of Voluntary Consensus Standards (http://nvlpubs.nist.gov/nistpubs/ir/2013/NIST.IR.7930.pdf).

Orgalime (2011), "EU manufacturers suffer from malfunctioning of the US certification market: potential abuse of dominant position", Position Paper of 24 October.

_____ (2012), "Orgalime priorities for the upcoming EU-US trade and investment negotiations", Position Paper of 5 October.

Pelkmans, J. (2015), "TTIP: Opportunities and Challenges in the area of Technical Barriers to Trade", study prepared for the Internal Market and Consumer Protection Committee, European Parliament, June, Brussels (www.europarl.europa.eu/RegData/etudes/STUD/2015/542225/IPOL_STU%282015%29542225_EN.pdf).

Pelkmans, J. and D. Costello (1991), "International Product Standards", Working Paper, United Nations Industrial Development Organisation (UNIDO), Vienna.

Pelkmans, J. and A. Correia de Brito (2015), "Transatlantic MRAs: Lessons for TTIP?", CEPS Special Report No. 101, CEPS, Brussels, March.

Pelkmans, J., A. Lejour, L. Schefler, F. Mustilli and J. Timini (2014), "EU-US Transatlantic Trade and Investment Partnership: Detailed Appraisal of the European Commission's Impact Assessment", European Parliament Ex-ante Impact Assessment Unit, April (www.europarl.europa.eu/RegData/etudes/etudes/join/2014/528798/IPOL-JOIN_ET%282014%29528798_EN.pdf).

Pollack, M.A. and G.C. Shaffer (eds) (2001), *Transatlantic Relations in the Global Economy*, Lanham, MD: Rowman and Littlefield.

Sagers, C. (2004), "Antitrust Immunity and Standard Setting Organizations: A Case Study in the Public-Private Distinction", 25 *Cardozo Law Review* 1393, Vol. 25.

Strauss, P.L. (2013), "Private Standards Organizations and Public Law", *William & Mary Bill of Rights Journal*, Vol. 22, p. 497.

Swann, P. (2010), "The economics of standards, an update", report for Department of Business, Innovation and Skills, UK Government, London.

United States Trade Representative (USTR) (2014), "Report on Technical Barriers to Trade", Washington, D.C.

US-EU High Level Working Group on Jobs and Growth (2013), Final Report, 11 February (www.ustr.gov/about-us/press-office/reports-and-publications/2013/final-report-us-eu-hlwg).

Young, A. (2015), "TTIP as 21st Century Trade Politics", paper presented at the 14th Biennial Conference of European Union Studies Association (EUSA), Boston, MA, March.

_____. (nd), "The European Union's use of the WTO**Error! Bookmark not defined.** Dispute Resolution Process" (www.gla.ac.uk/media/media_36176_en.pdf).

4. QUANTIFYING NON-TARIFF MEASURES FOR TTIP
KOEN BERDEN AND JOSEPH FRANCOIS

1. Introduction

The Transatlantic Trade and Investment Partnership (TTIP) is not like any other free trade agreement negotiated or signed into existence (Fontagné et al., 2013; Berden et al., 2009). The communicated objectives of TTIP make it clear that its goals include but go beyond traditional market-access elements such as goods and services trade and customs duties, and rules. It is envisaged that TTIP will concentrate in particular on the areas of 'regulatory cooperation' and 'rules'.

Traditional economic (ex-ante) impact analyses used to focus on tariffs, quotas and subsidies (and increasingly also on barriers to services trade) as the main trade policy instruments. With an enlarged scope of trade agreements, like TTIP, which include regulatory cooperation, these analyses were no longer sufficient to estimate the potential impact of TTIP – or any TTIP-like agreement. The main challenge that needed to be addressed in order to be able to quantify the potential economic effects was *how to quantify economically the area of regulatory differences* – in this case between the European Union and the United States.[1]

Several studies have looked at the potential economic effects of TTIP, ranging from Berden et al. (2009) to Fontagné et al. (2013), Francois et al. (2013) and Felbermayr et al. (2013). These studies have been compared by Pelkmans et al. (2014) in their comparative work for the European Parliament. All of these studies focus on the likely macroeconomic and sectoral impacts of TTIP. For that they take as

---

[1] The comprehensive approach to include regulatory cooperation and rules in trade agreements has first been used in the EU-Canada CETA negotiations and is currently also used by the EU – in parallel with the TTIP negotiations – in the EU-Japan FTA negotiations and the negotiations over the renewal of the EU-Mexico FTA.

input for their methodological approaches different ways to quantify economically regulatory differences, or non-tariff measures (NTMs) as they are also called. NTMs – as opposed to non-tariff barriers (NTBs) – are compatible with the WTO charter. The term NTM is therefore often used as the collective name for regulatory differences or barriers that include technical barriers to trade (TBT) and sanitary and phyto-sanitary (SPS) measures.

In this chapter, we will first identify the methods that have been employed to quantify NTMs (section 2). We then compare some of the most important methods and analyse their differences and look at what they mean for the TTIP negotiations (section 3). We start with a short literature review of past approaches to measuring the costs of non-tariff measures (NTMs). We then look in more detail at four seminal studies to quantify NTMs over the past several years: Dean et al. (2009), Berden et al. (2009), Fontagné et al. (2013) and Egger et al. (2015). These four studies contain cornerstone elements on how to approach NTMs – and these studies thus serve as the basis for most of the quantitative research into the realm of 'regulatory cooperation'.

We find several similarities in the approaches taken. For example, all studies find that trade costs caused by NTMs matter significantly and significantly more than remaining tariff barriers. Also the studies find significant variation of NTMs across sectors and a few sectors where NTMs are particularly high (e.g. processed foods). Differences between the approaches (and thus in results) come from a difference in basic approach (i.e. price- or quantity-based), differences in the data sources used for NTMs (e.g. business survey, UNCTAD TRAINS, past FTA data), econometric specifications (e.g. general equilibrium versus partial equilibrium), and levels of country and sector disaggregation and coverage.

Because all studies conclude that NTMs matter, policy-makers are right to focus on 'regulatory cooperation' in TTIP. Given the significant differences in NTMs across sectors, policy-makers should dive deep into sector-specific elements of NTMs and focus on those sectors where the largest potential gains can be made (i.e. where NTMs are highest, such as in agriculture, automobiles, steel, textiles and insurance services).

An area identified for further research is the fact that unlike trade taxes (i.e. tariffs), regulatory barriers to trade are not generally targeted at trade as the primary policy objective, but rather stem from other strategic policy concerns like consumer safety and/or social and environmental protection. This element should be further investigated.

2.   Review of NTM quantification methods

In the past 20 years, we have witnessed two important trends regarding both multilateral and bilateral trade agreements. The first is a relative shift in focus of trade negotiations from tariff reductions to the removal of NTMs. For surveys of earlier work, see Deardorff & Stern (1998) and Ferrantino (2006). The second is an increase in the depth of trade agreements being negotiated (see for example Dür et al., 2014, and Egger et al., 2015). Because of these shifts, the importance of quantifying the impact of NTMs has increased significantly over the past 10 years, and more research into this specific field has been carried out.

There are two basic avenues one can follow in order to estimate in a systematic way the economic and trade effects of NTMs: quantity- and price-based approaches. Quantity-based approaches (or actually value-based approaches as indicated by Ferrantino, 2009) use gravity equations to estimate by how much the presence of an NTM reduces trade flows compared to potential trade. This allows for the estimation of an ad valorem equivalent (AVE) or trade cost equivalent (TCE), essentially a 'fictitious' import tariff, that – if real – would reduce imports by exactly the height of the NTM. Earlier work was done by Baldwin (1975), and Bhagwati & Srinivasan (1975), but also others have since looked at this: Leamer (1988), Trefler (1993), Kee et al. (2008, 2009), Berden et al. (2009), Fontagné et al. (2013), Francois et al. (2013) and Egger et al. (2015). The approaches based on price compare the prices in the importing country with prices of comparable products in free markets, i.e. without distortions. Using detailed price data, a distinction can be made between the impact of NTMs and the impact of local distribution costs in raising the price. Through an instrumental variables approach to incorporate the endogeneity of NTMs, the height of NTMs can be estimated. The 'price gap' or tariff equivalent is then the difference between the price of imports (higher because of the NTM) and the lower world price (in the absence of the NTM). Among those using a price-based approach are Bradford (2003, 2005), Ferrantino (2006), and Dean et al. (2009).

The debate between those proposing price-based approaches (Ferrantino, 2006; Dean et al., 2009) and those favouring quantity-based approaches (Fontagné et al., 2013) is ongoing. According to Ferrantino (2006, p. 20 and Annex 2): "There are several reasons for preferring price gaps to quantity gaps in most cases. First, price gaps measure the difference between two observed values, a distorted (NTM-ridden) price and a non-distorted price. Quantity or value gaps measure the difference between an observed (distorted) value and an estimated ('normal') value of trade, and are thus influenced by the quality of the estimated value, which is subject to the various uncertainties surrounding econometric specifications." Fontagné et al. (2013), on the other hand, argue that although price-based approaches allow for a direct estimation of NTMs – in contrast to the more indirect quantity-based approaches – "largely due to data issues, quantity-based approaches prove more convenient for large-scale analyses such as the one [eds: economic impact assessment of TTIP] conducted here" (Fontagné et al., 2013, p. 8).

Apart from a methodological discussion between price- and quantity-based approaches, we need to be careful here for another reason: unlike trade taxes, regulatory barriers to trade are not generally targeted at trade as the primary policy objective. Rather, we are talking about regulatory approaches to issues such as consumer safety, the stability of financial markets, and environmental protection from – for example – dangerous chemicals. In this case, higher costs (identified by regressions, for example) most certainly reflect the balance between costs of regulation (including trade costs) and benefits linked to the primary policy objective. This point, while acknowledged in passing, is not given full due in quantitative analyses of NTM reductions. Where consumers (aka voters) in the US and EU place different values on such objectives, we need to be careful not to assume that identified barriers are not offset by benefits.

Tariff equivalents/Trade cost equivalents (TCEs)

Despite the methodological debate on the differences between price- and quantity-based approaches, authors from either strand agree that the ultimate goal of the quantification exercise is to yield tariff equivalents (or synonymously, ad valorem equivalents or trade cost equivalents). A TCE is in essence the aggregate height of the differences in regulatory systems expressed in one number: a 'tariff equivalent'. Expressing the total of differences in regulatory systems (estimated through either price- or quantity-based approaches) as one number has several major advantages. First of all, a tariff equivalent makes it conceptually much easier for readers to get a ballpark idea of the degree of regulatory divergence between the EU and US in a specific sector, i.e. for US exports to the EU, the difference in regulations adds up to a 26% TCE in the automotive industry. Second, tariff equivalents make it easy to compare tariff rates and regulatory differences (expressed in tariff equivalents). Third, a tariff equivalent can be compared across sectors, as the measuring unit is the same, i.e. for EU exports to the US, a 73% difference in the food sector is much higher than a 21% difference in the chemicals sector. Fourth, the removal of regulatory differences, i.e. liberalisation scenarios that are used to estimate the consequence of TTIP through regulatory cooperation, can be modelled by lowering tariff equivalents in a sector (or multiple sectors) in a partial or general equilibrium setting. This 'lowering of TCEs' represents any form of regulatory cooperation to address regulatory differences.[2] Please note that this implies that a lowering of a TCE implies a lowering of NTMs, which is lowering of the *differences* between regulatory systems, not lowering the levels of protection or lowering of standards (which goes back to our earlier point on consumer and environmental protection). Fifth, a TCE – being a numerical value – can be inserted into an international trade or macro-economic model to look at the effects of regulatory cooperation on GDP, firm production, consumer prices, wages, jobs, etc., as has been done by Berden et al. (2009), Fontagné et al. (2013), Francois et al. (2013) and Felbermayr et al. (2013).

In order to do justice to both strands of work to quantify NTMs in the remainder of this section, we will cover four different studies: the price-based NTM estimation work of Dean et al. (2009) and the quantity-based NTM estimation work of Berden et al. (2009), Fontagné et al. (2013) and Egger et al. (2014). It needs to be noted that Dean et al. (2009) do not focus on measuring the potential economic impact of TTIP in particular, while the other three studies aim to do that – and as such some model specifications are different (e.g. sector selection).

While we have stressed regulatory cooperation and reduction of differences in the discussion so far, it is not so clear that empirical evidence to date actually reflects this. In particular, trade costs may follow from differences in approach to the same objective, or from differences in the objectives themselves. We discuss this point further when we turn to the concept of actionability. At this point, however, we wish to stress the risk that we, as economists, may focus too much here on cost and not enough on the benefit side of regulations that happen to have trade and investment effects.

---

[2] In this chapter we look at the econometric techniques of quantifying the economic costs and benefits of NTMs, not at the different ways in which regulatory alignment can be achieved. Whether it is better to aim for harmonisation of standards, harmonisation of regulations, mutual recognition of standards, mutual recognition of regulations or mutual equivalence is outside the scope of this chapter, and is covered in chapter 3 of this book.

2.1 The Dean et al. (2009) NTM quantification methodology (price-based)

Dean et al. (2009) employ a price-based approach. This means they use city-level retail price data to estimate the impact of core NTMs on prices and assess their significance. In doing so they base themselves on Bradford (2003, 2005) for price data for many products in many countries, and on Kee et al. (2008, 2009) for NTM incidence data. They go through four distinct steps in their price-based approach.

The four-step approach:

I.   NTM incidence and retail price data
II.   Price gap
III.   Variable coefficients
IV.   From variable coefficients to sector-specific TCEs

I.   NTM incidence and retail price data

Dean et al. (2009) needed to collect two types of data for their analysis. First, in order to get a better understanding of the extent and types of NTMs across countries and products, they draw upon two complementary datasets: the UNCTAD TRAINS database and the USITC database (Donelly & Manifold, 2005). These data bases document EU (from the EU Market Access Database) and US (USTR National Trade Estimate Report on Foreign Trade Barriers – which includes information from the WTO Trade Policy Reviews) private-sector complaints about NTMs. The UNCTAD TRAINS database (including WITS) collects data from publicly available sources and reports in detail at the tariff line level. The authors used the potentially complementary information from the two databases, while at the same time there was overlap in the reported NTMs. This is why Dean et al. compare the two datasets and conclude that NTMs appear to be widespread, and the two databases partially overlap but also provide specific independent information. This is why they used the two databases combined.

In addition to the NTM incidence, Dean et al. (2009) required extensive amounts of price data in order to carry out a 'price gap' analysis. They used city-level retail price data for 47 products from around 115 cities from the EIU CityData for 2001. This allowed the authors to examine inter- and intra-country price differences, some of which can be attributed to NTMs. They found that price differences are both product- and country-specific – again an indication for the widespread nature of NTMs.

II.   Price gap

Dean et al. (2009) also employed the data from Step I in a differentiated product model. This model takes into account different varieties, in particular a distinction between imported and domestic varieties. This approach matters because a big challenge for the price-based approach is product differentiation: "The model captures the fact that the retail price in a particular location will likely be an average of the retail prices of all the imported and domestic varieties sold locally, and that these products are likely to be differentiated by source" (Dean et al., 2009, p. 4).

Then, using the EIU CityData for 2001, they observe price differences – in deviation from purchasing power parity (PPP). This they define as the Price Gap or 'PG' – the dependent variable.

III.   Variable coefficients

In order to capture the NTM effect (NTM rent of country i, Q_i), the retail price gap between the home country and foreign country (PG_{ii^*}) is regressed on local distribution margins (μ), transport costs (D), and specific tariffs (T). The authors also correct for endogeneity of NTMs by adding two interaction terms – one with country income and one with tariffs. This is depicted in equation (1) as:

$$PG_{ii^*} = \beta(\mu_i - \mu_{i^*}) - \gamma(D_i - D_{i^*}) - \delta(T_i - T_{i^*}) + \sigma_0(Q_i - Q_{i^*}) + \sigma_1(Q_i\tilde{Y}_i - Q_{i^*}\tilde{Y}_{i^*}) + \sigma_2(Q_i\tilde{T}_i - Q_{i^*}\tilde{T}_{i^*}) + \varepsilon_{ii^*} \qquad (1)$$

where σ_0 is the average price premium due to NTMs. This is the coefficient that is the core of the chapter: a regression analysis coefficient to single out the additional price effect of NTMs by country and sector. If this coefficient is statistically significant and positive, we can conclude that the NTM effect is one that increases the price gap. The coefficient information is presented in column (A) of Table 4.1 below. Dean et al. (2009) do this for 65 countries. In Table 4.1, we only report findings for the EU and US – as this chapter focuses on the quantification of NTMs in the area of TTIP, hence on the EU and US.

IV.   From variable coefficients to country-specific, sector-specific TCEs

Step III above (Variable Coefficients) yields country-specific, sector-specific regression coefficients for the NTM effect. The variable coefficient of the NTM effect can be changed into trade cost estimates (tariff equivalents) as follows:

$$TCE = 100 \, x \, (e^{\varepsilon} - 1) \qquad (2)$$

where ε is the NTM effect regression coefficient. The TCE (in percent) is the estimated increase in prices in a country, per sector, as a consequence of NTMs. This information is presented in column (B) of Table 4.1 below.

Table 4.1 Country estimates NTM coefficients and NTM TCEs

Country and Sector	NTM effect regression coefficients (A)	NTM TCEs (%) (B)
EU (average 18 EU member states)		
- Fruits/vegetables		48.2
- Bovine meat		68.2
- Processed food		35.6
- Apparel		46.3
United States		
- Fruits/vegetables	0.47	60.6
- Bovine meat	0.59	80.0
- Processed food	0.30	34.6
- Apparel	0.20	22.6

Data source: Dean et al. (2009).

Final results

The Dean et al. (2009) study leads to some interesting findings. First, they find for 65 countries and four sectors TCEs through direct NTM price-based estimation (above we report only for the EU and US because these NTMs are relevant for the TTIP negotiations). Second, they find that NTMs complement tariffs – in some sectors the presence of a tariff reduces the price effect of the NTM. Third, in some sectors there is a correlation between the restrictiveness of NTMs with country income (some positive, some negative).[3] Fourth, the level of NTMs displays some significant sector- and country-variation. Finally, they find that NTMs matter significantly in explaining trade restrictiveness in the sectors examined.

2.2 The Berden et al. (2009) NTM quantification methodology (quantity-based)

In order to quantify NTMs, the Berden et al. (2009) study develops five distinct steps in line with the quantity-based approaches to quantifying NTMs. This basic quantification work has been used to quantify the potential effects of TTIP (combined with CGE analysis) by Berden et al. (2009), Francois et al. (2013), and Capaldo (2014). The five steps take the reader from grass-roots views on regulatory divergences by firms that do business across the Atlantic to an estimate of trade cost equivalents (TCE) involved for EU-US and US-EU trade at sectoral level.

The five-step approach

The five steps to go from survey results on transatlantic regulatory barriers to TCE are the following:

I.   Business survey to get bilateral NTM survey numbers
II.   From NTM survey numbers to NTM index
III. From NTM index to gravity regression variable coefficient
IV.   From variable coefficient to transatlantic, EU and NAFTA[4] TCEs
V.   From transatlantic, EU and NAFTA TCEs to sector specific TCEs

I.   Business survey to get bilateral NTM survey numbers

Is it more difficult to trade between France and the US for a French exporter than to trade between France and Spain? Or between Poland and Italy, Poland and India and Poland and the US? Or for a US exporter to export to Mexico or to Germany? In light of the definition of an NTM, the costs for a French producer to produce and sell inside

---

[3] It seems logical to us that, where regulatory barriers reflect income sensitive demand for higher consumer protection (as in food products and consumer goods), we would see such a positive correlation.

[4] NAFTA = North American Free Trade Agreement.

France are not zero, because regulatory differences, e.g. to protect food safety or the safety of a car we drive in, lead to various costs.

The business survey then collected two types of data. First, firms were asked to indicate on a scale from 0 to 100 how restrictive each of their export markets was (compared to their home market as a benchmark).[5] The 5,500 data points from both large firms and SMEs that were the result of this survey allowed Berden et al. to generate exporter-importer specific survey numbers of NTMs with a country-pair specific NTM variable between 0 and 100. These survey numbers were – for statistical reasons – then aggregated into specific exporter destination NTM values, averaging the indicated NTM for each country. This information is presented in column (A) of Table 4.2. Second, firms were asked to list the main (sector-specific) barriers that they ran into when exporting. The lists of barriers were prioritised based on the firm survey responses, discussions with (sector) experts and literature information. The lists of barriers were also used to look at whether barriers involved economic rents and/or costs and the degree to which each of the barriers would be 'actionable' or not. The concept of actionability contains the sub-concepts of 'technical actionability' and 'political actionability'. For example, the electricity systems in the EU and US differ (220 volts a.c. vs. 110 volts) – which would require such an investment that this difference is deemed 'technically non-actionable'. In some sectors, e.g. aerospace, national security concerns imply that some regulatory differences are 'politically non-actionable'.

The additional survey information on costs-rents and on actionability are significant, because this information allows us to be more accurate in our estimations: they reduce the scope for TTIP impact to only those regulatory differences that can logically be addressed, i.e. are 'actionable'. And they give a better insight into the redistribution effects of TTIP from producers to consumers or vice versa (redistribution of economic rents) and the cost effects of TTIP (costs). Both the degrees of actionability and costs-rents differ per sector and for EU exports to the US and US exports to the EU (bi-directional).

---

5 Whereby a value of '0' presents a completely open and 'free trade' environment and a value of '100' a completely closed environment. A scale from 0 to 100 was chosen to allow for enough variation in the survey responses.

II. From NTM survey numbers to NTM index

The NTM survey numbers (Step I) are transformed into an NTM index in log scale conforming to OECD best practice:

$$Trade/investment\ level\ of\ restrictiveness = \ln (1 + 0.01 * NTM\ survey\ value) \tag{3}$$

This is done so that the coefficients on the index can be interpreted as elasticities with respect to changes in the level of restriction across the index. Shifting the origin is done to handle zero values in the original data. This information is presented in column (B) of Table 4.2.

III. From NTM index to gravity regression dummy-variable coefficients

The way to measure the impact of trade agreements, in this case TTIP, on trade and investment is through employing the gravity equation (Tinbergen, 1962; Linneman, 1966; Aitken, 1973). The gravity equation derives its name from Newton's law of gravitation. In international trade this has come to mean that the trade flow of goods (services) from one country to the other is related to the economic sizes of the two countries and the physical distance between them. In addition various control variables are added, e.g. dummies for sharing a common border or speaking a common language, as are policy-based trade costs, e.g. tariffs, or NTMs.

The gravity equation has a remarkable explanatory power and as such has become the work horse in looking at the impact of trade agreements (Sapir, 1981; Bergstrand & Egger, 2007; Berden et al., 2009). In Berden et al., three different dummies have been defined to capture the potential effect of the TTIP agreement. These three dummies – when interacted with the NTM index constructed in Step II – capture effects that, when added up, yield the total effect of NTM reductions because of TTIP. First an EU dummy is defined that has a value '1' if both countries in the bilateral trade pair are members of the EU and '0' if otherwise. This dummy captures the intra-EU preferential treatment given to other EU members compared to external partners.

This means that a reduction in non-EU NTMs, e.g. EU-US through TTIP, will make the US more and other EU members relatively less attractive and thus divert trade and investment away from European partners to – for example, in the case of TTIP – the US. Second, a NAFTA dummy is constructed that has a value '1' if both countries in the bilateral trade pair are members of NAFTA and '0' if otherwise. As with the EU, this dummy captures the intra-NAFTA preferential treatment given to other NAFTA members compared to external partners. This means that a reduction in non-NAFTA NTMs, e.g. EU-US through TTIP, will make the EU more and other NAFTA members relatively less attractive and thus divert trade and investment away from NAFTA partners to – for example, in the case of TTIP – the EU. Finally, the authors define a transatlantic dummy, i.e. a dummy that has a value '1' if there is a transatlantic pair and '0' if this is not the case. The transatlantic dummy measures the increase in transatlantic trade and investment in case of a once percent decrease in the NTM index. For service sectors, the business survey did not yield sufficient numbers of responses and therefore the OECD FDI restrictiveness indicators have been used instead.

IV.   From variable coefficient to transatlantic, EU and NAFTA trade cost equivalents (TCE)

Step III yields – overall and sector level – regression coefficients for the EU dummies, NAFTA dummies and transatlantic dummies for trading block membership. These are variables with a bi-directional dimension (exporter and importer). The coefficients on the EU, NAFTA and transatlantic dummy variables can be changed into trade cost estimates as follows:

$$TCE = 100 \, x \, (e^{\varepsilon} - 1) \tag{4}$$

where ε is the gravity regression coefficient. The TCE (in %) is the estimated increase in trade costs as a consequence of NTMs (regulatory differences) in the EU, NAFTA and transatlantic market place. This information is presented in columns (C), (D) and (E) of Table 4.2.

V.   From transatlantic, EU and NAFTA TCEs to sector specific TCEs

Having calculated in Step IV the TCE values (%) for the intra-EU preference margins (EU dummy), intra-NAFTA preference margins (NAFTA dummy) and transatlantic offset margins (transatlantic dummy), it is possible to derive the total NTM effects for the EU and US of TTIP. For the EU the total NTM effect is the intra-EU preference margin minus the transatlantic offset margin. For the US, the total NTM effect of TTIP is the intra-NAFTA preference margin minus the same transatlantic offset margin. That is, it is assumed that the preferential intra-EU and intra-NAFTA treatment is extended across the Atlantic. This information is presented in columns (F) and (G) of Table 4.2.

Table 4.2 From NTM values to trade cost equivalents for trade flows (Steps I to V)

Sector	NTM values (Step I) (A)		NTM index (Step II) (B)		Intra-EU preference margin (Steps III-IV) (C)	Intra-NAFTA preference margin (Steps III-IV) (D)	Transatlantic offset margin (Steps III-IV) (E)	Net NTM effect EU to US (Step V) (F)	Net NTM effect US to EU (Step V) (G)
	EU to US	US to EU	EU to US	US to EU				EU to US	US to EU
Aerospace & space	56.0	55.1	0.44	0.44	18.8	19.1	0.0	19.1	18.8
Automotive	34.8	31.6	0.30	0.27	16.3	17.6	-9.2	26.8	25.5
Chemicals	45.8	53.2	0.38	0.43	23.9	21.0	0.0	21.0	23.9
Communication services	44.6	27.0	0.37	0.24				1.7	11.7
Electronics	30.8	20.0	0.27	0.18			-6.5	6.5	6.5
Cosmetics	48.3	52.2	0.39	0.42	34.6	32.4	0.0	32.4	34.6
Financial services	29.7	21.3	0.26	0.19				31.7	11.3
Insurance services	29.5	39.3	0.26	0.33				19.1	10.8
Food & beverages	45.5	33.6	0.38	0.29	56.8	73.3	0.0	73.3	56.8
OICE	37.9	32.3	0.32	0.28	8.9	12.7	-10.2	22.9	19.1
Pharmaceuticals	23.8	44.7	0.21	0.37	24.0	18.2	8.7	9.5	15.3
Transport services	39.9	17.6	0.34	0.16					
Biotechnology	46.1	50.2	0.38	0.41					

Sector	NTM values (Step I) (A)		NTM index (Step II) (B)		Intra-EU preference margin (Steps III-IV) (C)	Intra-NAFTA preference margin (Steps III-IV) (D)	Transatlantic offset margin (Steps III-IV) (E)	Net NTM effect EU to US (Step V) (F)	Net NTM effect US to EU (Step V) (G)
ICT	20.0	19.3	0.18	0.18				3.9	14.9
Construction services	45.0	37.3	0.32	0.37				2.5	4.6
Machinery	50.9	36.5	0.31	0.41					
Medical equipment	49.3	44.5	0.37	0.40					
Other business services	42.2	20.0	0.18	0.35				3.9	14.9
Personal, recreational services	35.8	35.4	0.30	0.31				2.5	4.4
Steel	35.5	24.0	0.22	0.30	11.9	17.0	0.0	17.0	11.9
Textiles	35.6	48.9	0.40	0.30	11.0	8.5	-8.2	16.7	19.2
Wood & paper products	30.0	47.1	0.39	0.26	11.3	7.7	0.0	7.7	11.3
Travel services	35.6	17.6	0.16	0.30					
Total average	38.1	35.2	0.30	0.33	21.8	22.8	-2.3	17.7	17.5

Data source: Berden et al. (2009).

Final results

The Berden et al. (2009) study reaches some interesting conclusions and yields specific insights. First of all, the study has been able to generate bi-directional, i.e. EU-US and US-EU, TCEs at sector level for 18 different sectors. Since agriculture was not in the scope of the study, no results have been reported for agriculture. Second, the study shows that there is significant NTM-level variation across sectors and depending on the direction of the trade flow. Third, combining the NTM approach with OECD FDI restrictiveness indexes, the study also finds NTM levels for service sectors. Fourth, because an NTM index is used, the study was able to employ a friction-variable approach[1] to determine the effect of NTMs *per se*, staying away from the problem that residual approaches suffer from: measurement errors or omitted variables lead directly to errors in the estimated NTM levels. They find that NTMs matter more than tariffs in creating barriers to trade and that the level of restrictiveness varies significantly.

2.3 The Fontagné et al. (2013) NTM quantification methodology

Fontagné et al. (2013) come up with estimates of NTMs for goods and services. For goods, they base themselves on Kee et al. (2009), while for services they draw from Fontagné et al. (2011). This section summarises the approaches by Kee et al. (2009) and Fontagné et al. (2011).

I. Quantifying NTMs for goods – Kee et al. (2009)

Kee et al. (2009) go through three steps: they define three types of restrictiveness indicators, they describe the approach to estimate ad valorem equivalents (AVEs) of NTMs at tariff line level, which is equivalent to the trade restrictiveness indexes (TCEs).

---

[1] A friction-variable approach is one where the specific variable – in this case the 'NTM index' – is used as an independent variable on the right-hand side – and as such has a coefficient to be measured. The friction variable approach is set against the 'residual' approach, whereby it is assumed that the regression (with all its control variables) captures everything, except for the NTM effect which is the residual. This means that any effect not captured by the regression equation ends up in the residual – and as such in the level of NTMs. The residual approach is clearly considered inferior to the friction-variable approach because of the risk of mis-estimation (especially over-estimation), which is why the latter approach has been chosen in Berden et al. (2009).

Tariff and NTM data

The main sources that Kee et al. (2009) use for tariff data come from the WTO's Integrated Database and UNCTADs TRAINS. In addition, the MAcMap database is used for specific tariffs as well as for data on unilateral, bilateral and regional preferences. The main source for core NTM data (see below) is the UNCTAD's TRAINS database. NTMs are price control measures, quantity restrictions, monopolistic measures and technical regulations. In addition, the authors use the WTO's Trade Policy Reviews and the EU's Standard's Database (Shepherd, 2004). The agricultural domestic support is obtained from the WTO members' notifications (see Hoekman et al., 2004, for a discussion on this variable).

TRI, OTRI and MA-OTRI restrictiveness indicators

Kee et al. (2009) start by arguing that in order to measure TCEs properly, in line with Anderson & Neary (1992), two aggregation problems need to be addressed: the aggregation of different forms and types of trade policies and the aggregation across different goods that have different degrees of economic importance. Anderson & Neary (1994, 1996) find that *"one single indicator cannot provide a measure of trade distortions a country imposes on itself while simultaneously capturing trade distortions imposed on its trading partners"* (Kee et al., 2009, p. 173). In line with Anderson & Neary, Kee et al. define the Trade Restrictiveness Index (TRI) – domestic welfare effect of domestic trade policies; the Overall Trade Restrictiveness Index (OTRI) – effect of domestic trade policies on domestic imports; and the Market Access-Overall Trade Restrictiveness Index (MA-OTRI) – effect of domestic trade policies on domestic exports.

AVE equivalents of NTMs at tariff line level and trade restrictiveness

Kee et al.'s theoretical foundation comes from Leamer (1990) with an 'n-good n-factor' general equilibrium model. The import value of a good is regressed on exogenous world prices, tariff line dummies, country characteristics, economic size, a dummy for islands and a measure for distance to world markets as well as three variables that are the focus of the analysis: a dummy indicating the presence of a core NTM, a variable measuring the degree of agricultural domestic support, and ad valorem tariffs for that good. Various corrections are applied to this basic regression to correct for – for example – tariff endogeneity and lack of time variation. In its essence, Kee et al. (2009)

estimate the impact of core NTMs and agricultural domestic support on imports at tariff line level.

In order to make the estimated core NTM variable comparable to ad valorem tariffs, the quantity impact needs to be transformed into price-equivalents:

$$AVE = \frac{\partial \ln p^d}{\partial NTM} \qquad (5)$$

The AVEs are calculated in each country at the tariff line level. The AVE is positive when the NTM is binding and 'zero' when the NTM is not binding. In Table 4.3 below, the main empirical results of Kee et al. (2009) for NTM TCEs are reported for the EU and US.

II. Quantifying NTMs for services – Fontagné et al. (2011)

In addition to the estimates for NTMs in goods by Kee et al. (2009), Fontagné et al. (2013) base themselves on Fontagné et al. (2011) regarding services NTM estimates. They use a quantity-based approach using gravity, while addressing specific services-related problems along the way. For example, in services – as opposed to goods – non-discriminatory market access is not influenced by the presence of tariffs but rather by NTMs, e.g. regulatory divergences. Also, measuring cross-border trade in services implies an analysis of only one of the four modes, mode 1.

Services trade data

Fontagné et al. (2011) use the GTAP database as the main source for services trade data, providing them with bilateral trade in services for 14 services sectors (in 2004): construction, communication, trade, finance, other services (education, health, defence, public services), business, transport (air, water, other), insurance, recreational services, dwelling, water, and energy – reducing this to seven sectors through some aggregations. The authors use IMF data on GDP and Producer Price Indexes and population data from the World Development Indicators of the World Bank. For trade in services the authors use the OECD data because of better country coverage and annual frequency. This implies that they miss some countries but still 89% of all global services trade is covered.

Tariff equivalents of NTMs for services

It is regulatory differences, i.e. NTMs, that constitute barriers to trade in services. Because we cannot observe directly the individual regulations (in a quantity-based approach to quantifying NTMs), through gravity, Fontagné et al. (2011) compare actual trade with the theoretical situation of free trade in services without any trade costs associated. This yields a ratio that represents the deviation of actual imports of services of a country compared to its potential free trade imports. Because the free trade imports can also not be directly seen, Fontagné et al. (2011) define a benchmark country as the 'free trader' and calculate everything else compared to this benchmark. This allows Fontagné et al. (2011) to estimate the tariff equivalent – under the assumption of a constant elasticity of substitution (something that is most likely not the case as is suggested by Francois et al., 2009). The TCEs that Fontagné et al. (2013) find are reported below in Table 4.3.

Table 4.3 Country estimates NTM coefficients and NTM TCEs

Country and Sector	NTM TCEs EU (%) (A)	NTM TCEs US (%) (B)
Agriculture	48.2	51.3
Manufacturing	42.8	32.3
Services*	32.0	47.3
- Communication	38.6	36.9
- Construction	53.2	95.4
- Financial services	51.2	51.3
- Insurance services	44.9	43.7
- Business services	32.6	42.3
- Other services	39.1	8.8
- Trade	48.0	61.5
- Transport	29.1	17.5
- Water	65.3	98.4

* For services, we report the unweighted average of EU member states from Fontagné et al. (2011) as the EU results.

Data sources: Kee et al. (2009) and Fontagné et al. (2011).

Final results

The Fontagné et al. (2013) study reaches some interesting conclusions. First of all, they combine the import elasticity and TCE for goods estimates of Kee et al. (2009) with the services NTM estimates of Fontagné et al. (2011) to get NTM estimates across agriculture, industry and services. Second, the results from Kee et al. (2009) results are based on an elaborate dataset and they use different trade restrictiveness indicators. They find NTMs at tariff line level using an approach that comes close – but is not exactly equal – to a price-based approach.

2.4 The Egger et al. (2015) NTM quantification methodology

Egger et al. (2015 forthcoming) focus on the quantification of NTMs while taking into account the depth of free trade agreements (Dür et al., 2014). They then use the estimated TCEs of NTMs in a CGE model to look at the potential effects of TTIP. The focus of this section is on the first part of their work: estimating the TCEs of NTMs. Like the other authors, Egger et al. (2015) recognise that the challenge in quantifying the effects of deep agreements is that most of the elements under negotiation cannot be directly measured quantitatively, something that is possible with tariffs.[2] Egger et al. (2015) go through two steps to get to TCEs: first, they estimate levels of NTMs through a gravity model using historical evidence from (depth of) FTAs and then they take those estimates to turn them into ad valorem TCEs.

Three-step approach

I.   FTA data
II.   Estimations of NTMs
III.   Calculating TCEs

I.   FTA data

In order to get estimates of NTMs, Egger et al. (2015) look at evidence from past FTAs. The EU has engaged for decades in reducing NTMs in its internal market project; many (bilateral) FTAs have been signed over the past decade and the depth of these FTAs has increased over time. Through the DESTA – *Design of Trade Agreements* – database, a solid

---

[2] Tariffs allow us to more easily measure the difference between domestic prices and the world price, deriving the price wedge that then can be analysed straightforwardly with existing models and methods.

measure for the depth of trade agreements has become available. The DESTA data is used as a variable in the gravity analysis of Step II.

II.   Estimations of NTMs

Egger et al. (2015) specify a gravity equation, modelling bilateral trade flows as a function of country-specific fixed effects, bilateral control variables, e.g. geography, culture, history, a measure of political distance (polity),[3] tariff margins by country-pair (within or outside FTAs). Egger & Larch (2011) have shown that the NTM effect of FTAs corresponds to the combined effect of FTAs conditional on tariffs and the depth of FTAs. This is important, because it means that the NTM effect of FTAs can be estimated as 'beyond tariff reductions'. The gravity regressions are run for each sector separately for two reasons: first, to allow for trade elasticities to vary across sectors as evidenced by Broda & Weinstein (2006) and Egger et al. (2012); second, to allow NTMs to vary across sectors as was shown by Cadot & Malouche (2012) and Berden et al. (2009).

In order to estimate the importance of NTMs, the authors include two variables: a dummy indicator for intra-EU relationships and an integer-value DESTA variable (ranging from 0 to 7) that indicates the depth of non-EU FTAs based on Dür et al. (2014). Egger et al. (2015) estimate a separate parameter for EU membership because it allows them to single out the EU internal market effects compared to other FTAs – since EU membership and the EU internal market clearly go beyond liberalisation policies in other FTAs. The results of this gravity estimation are presented below in Table 4.4 for goods (Columns (A) and (B)) and in Table 4.5 for services.

For NTMs in services – as already alluded to in the previous section by Fontagné et al. (2013) – various other issues matter (see also Francois & Hoekman, 2010, for a general discussion). Egger et al. (2015) do not estimate these NTMs themselves but rather work with estimates of trade restrictions in services from the World Bank (Borchert et al., 2014), AVEs for trade barriers in services based on the World Bank data (Jafari & Tarr, 2015), and assessments of GATS bindings and how these

---

[3] Egger et al. (2015) also include a measure of political distance based on measures from the political science literature. They use the Quality of Governance expert survey dataset (Teorell et al., 2011), in particular the pairwise similarity of polity, reflecting evidence that homophily is important in explaining direct (economic and) political linkages (De Benedictis & Tajoli, 2011).

compare to PTA services commitments from the WTO (Roy, 2011 database, updated 2013).

III. Calculating TCEs

The estimates obtained under Step II for the coefficients for FTA depth (DESTA) and the EU membership dummy are taken by Egger et al. (2014) to derive potential changes in ad valorem trade costs along the same lines as Berden et al. (2009):

$$TCE = 100 \times (e^\varepsilon - 1) \qquad (6)$$

The results of the TCE equivalents for goods are presented below in Table 4.4 and for services in Table 4.5. Both in Columns (C) and (D) NTM TCE values are reported. Column (C) shows the results when the gravity regression is run with the EU dummy as a benchmark, i.e. the NTM effect compared to the EU because it is the deepest FTA we know of today. Column (D) shows the NTM TCE estimates when the gravity regression is run with the DESTA variable (for depth of FTAs), comparing the existing NTMs to an average depth of an FTA as the benchmark.

Table 4.4 Gravity results and TCE equivalents (%) for goods (EU membership and FTA depth)

Sector	Gravity coefficients EU IM (A)	Gravity coefficients FTA depth (B)	NTM TCE (%) EU dummy (C)	NTM TCE (%) FTA depth (D)
Goods	0.575	0.087	12.9	13.7
Primary food	1.610	0.150	25.2	15.8
Energy	-0.001	0.169	-0.01	16.1
Processed food	1.499	0.158	48.4	33.8
Beverages & tobacco	1.498	0.215	41.8	42.0
Petrochemicals	0.270	0.173	7.9	24.2
Chemicals & pharma	0.889	0.110	20.6	29.1
Metals	1.268	0.086	38.5	16.7
Motor vehicles	1.299	0.184	19.5	19.3
Electrical machinery	0.631	0.009	19.4	1.8
Other machinery	0.133	0.071	1.6	6.2
Other goods	0.468	0.043	5.7	3.6

Data source: Egger et al. (2015).

Table 4.5 Gravity results and TCE equivalents (%) for services (EU membership and FTA depth)

Services	AVEs of current policies (%)	
	EU	US
Services	12.8	12.9
Construction*		
Air transport	25.0	11.0
Maritime transport	1.7	13.0
Other transport	29.7	0.0
Distribution	1.4	0.0
Communications	1.1	3.5
Banking	1.5	17.0
Insurance	6.6	17.0
Professional and business	35.4	42.0
Personal, recreational		
Public services		

* Construction is taken from Berden et al. (2009).

Data source: Egger et al. (2015).

Final results

Egger et al. (2015) employ a new approach to estimating the height of NTMs through a quantity-based approach framework. For goods, they do not employ detailed NTM data – either from existing databases or a business survey – but they look at (the depths of) past FTAs, with the EU Internal Market project singled out in particular and use the evidence from the past to look at NTM potential. For services, they build on the work done by Borchert et al. (2014) on trade restrictions in services and Jafari & Tarr (2015) on ad valorem tariff equivalents for trade barriers in services. They find that NTMs pose significant trade restrictions, but more in goods than in services. This could be explained in part by the fact that for services, only modes 1 and 2 and to an indirect extent mode 3 are captured, and that services have a much larger non-tradable share. They also find that compared to the EU benchmark this effect is (on average) larger than compared to the FTA depth. This is the case because the EU dummy captures the deepest FTA there is, while the FTA depth is an average of the depth of the FTAs (which is less deep than the EU post-WWII project).

3. Analysing and summarising the results

"Give me a one-handed economist", US President Harry Truman told the press, frustrated by his economic advisors who kept on saying "on the one hand … on the other hand …". Reading this chapter thus far, you may have similar feelings. Indeed, there are many differences between the studies carried out, but let's start out this section with some important similarities across the studies, followed by the differences.

3.1 A systematic comparison of empirical studies

Similarities in approaches

The first important similarity is the fact that all the studies – although to slightly differing degrees – find that TCEs of NTMs are significant and of a higher order of magnitude than tariff barriers today. The second important similarity is that those studies that could look at a more disaggregate level find that the variation of TCEs across sectors is significant: trade barriers and regulatory divergences differ significantly across sectors. The third important similarity is that they all agree that summarising NTMs in terms of TCEs or tariff equivalents is the best way to incorporate the multi-dimensional and complex issue of regulatory cooperation into a manageable variable to work with further, at least at the moment. In other words, the approach is certainly not ideal, but is the best we have given the state of the art in terms of data availability and applicable methodologies. This caveat is an important one. We can expect improvements as better data and methods become available.

Differences in approaches

As highlighted in the chapter so far, there are many different ways to approach the issue of quantifying regulatory cooperation/NTMs. In order to structure these differences, we categorise them into the following components, which we then use to compare the studies in Table 4.6 below: basic approach to quantifying NTMs: quantity- or price-based; data sources to start measuring NTMs; econometric specifications; level of disaggregation and coverage of service sector NTMs.

Basic approach to quantifying NTMs: quantity- or price-based approaches – row (A) in Table 4.6

In line with the two main strands in the literature one of the differences between the recent studies is that one uses the price-based approach (Dean et al., 2009), which means they use detailed price data to estimate the impact of core NTMs on prices and assess their significance. From there they can estimate TCEs of the NTMs. The other authors use the quantity-based approaches (Berden et al., 2009; Fontagné et al., 2013; Egger et al., 2015). They use gravity equations to estimate by how much the presence of an NTM reduces trade flows compared to potential trade. This then allows for the estimation of a tariff equivalent or TCE.

Data sources to start measuring NTMs – row (B) in Table 4.6

The most pronounced difference between the covered approaches is the set of input data used (in combination with the econometrics). Dean et al. (2009) focus on detailed price data to create the dependent variable – the price gap. They have price data for 47 products which they can aggregate into four agricultural sub-sectors. The authors also employ the UNCTAD TRAINS and USITC databases for NTM incidence – to measure the share of NTMs in explaining this gap. They use both datasets combined because – though they overlap in part – they also contain distinct information and are partially complementary. Berden et al. (2009) conducted a large business survey with 5,500 responses to create a bilateral import-export NTM index that – together with data from GTAP (2007) – was inserted into a gravity equation to estimate the statistical and economic significance of NTMs for the dependent variable, trade and investments in goods. For services – as the business survey responses were too few, they used the OECD FDI restrictiveness indicators. The survey also yielded information on specific barriers, how important they were according to firms and an assessment of whether the individual barriers would affect costs or economic rent (or a combination of both). Fontagné et al. (2013) base themselves on Fontagné et al. (2011) for services NTM estimates – using the GTAP database (2004) – and on Kee et al. (2009) for goods NTM estimates – who use the UNCTAD TRAINS database for NTM information supplemented by MAcMaps and WTO Trade Policy Reviews as well as WTO notifications. Finally, Egger et al. (2015) use a combination of GTAP (2011) data and data from past FTAs – by means of an EU dummy and the DESTA variable to measure the depth of FTAs. DESTA have a value between 0 and 7 whereby 7 is the deepest form of a trade agreement. Recently, trade agreements have increased in depth.

Econometric specifications – row (C) in Table 4.6

The detailed econometric specifications differ between the studies. Most distinct is the approach by Dean et al. (2009) since they carry out a regression analysis with retail price gaps as the dependent variable and tariffs and NTMs – adjusted for differences in local distribution mark-ups, transport costs and specific tariffs. The other three studies all use the gravity equation and the same dependent variable – but the gravity equations are not specified in the same way. In Berden et al. (2009) the gravity equation contains the NTM index on the right-hand side, allowing the authors to measure the contribution of NTMs to the trade gap (and thus indirectly the price gap). Egger et al. (2015) employ the gravity equation with an EU dummy and the DESTA variable for depth of FTAs on the right-hand side as two independent variables. They also add a variable called 'polity' to correct for political distance. Finally, Fontagné et al. (2013) – using Kee et al. (2009) for goods NTM estimation – use the gravity equation but run it per sector, employing a partial equilibrium and not a general equilibrium approach. For services, they rely on Fontagné et al. (2011), whereby a gravity equation is used.

Level of sector disaggregation – row (D) in Table 4.6

The level of disaggregation differs across the studies. Dean et al. (2009) focus on four agricultural sub-sectors – at a high degree of disaggregation, but for only a small part of the economy. It is clear that the large amount of data needed for the price-based approach limits the scope in terms of the number of sectors that can be studied. Fontagné et al. (2013) explore a limited number of goods sectors, but a comparable number of service sectors to Berden et al. (2009) and Egger et al. (2015). In terms of goods sector disaggregation Berden et al. (2009) and Egger et al. (2015) use the GTAP database (2007 and 2011) to reach the highest level of disaggregation covering the entire economy.

Coverage of service sectors – row (E) in Table 4.6

Dean et al. (2009), using detailed price data, focus on four agricultural sectors but do not look at service sectors. Berden et al. (2009), using the business survey, cover nine service sectors that are also in GTAP (2007). Fontagné et al. (2013) cover the same nine service sectors but use the GTAP (2004) database. Finally, Egger et al. (2015) use the broadest service sector coverage available in GTAP (2011), looking at NTMs in 11 sectors.

Table 4.6 Structured comparison of different approaches to quantifying NTMs

Components	Dean et al. (2009)	Berden et al. (2009)	Fontagné et al. (2013)	Egger et al. (2015)
Basis approach to quantifying NTMs (A)	Price-based approach	Quantity-based approach	Quantity-based approach	Quantity-based approach
Data sources to start measuring NTMs (B)	UNCTAD TRAINS and USITC for NTM incidence + retail price data for 47 products EIU City data 2001	Business survey (5,500 responses), OECD FDI restrictiveness indicators, GTAP 2007 pre-release	UNCTAD TRAINS, MAcMaps, WTO TPR, WTO member notifications, GTAP 2004	EU dummy and FTA depth dummy (past FTA results); GTAP 2011
Econometric specifications (C)	Regression analysis with retail price gap as dependent variable and tariffs and NTMs (and other control variables) as independent variables	Friction variable gravity analysis with goods & services trade (and investment) as dependent variable and NTMs (and control variables) as independent variables	For goods NTMs estimation use the gravity equation but run it per sector – employing a partial equilibrium and not a general equilibrium approach. For services NTMs a gravity equation is used	Gravity analysis with goods & services trade as dependent variable and EU/FTA depth variables (and control variables) as independent variables
Level of disaggregation (D)	Fruits & vegetables, bovine meat, processed food, apparel	Aerospace & space, automotive, chemicals, communication, electronics, cosmetics, financial, insurance,	Agriculture, manufacturing, services – communication, construction, financial,	Overall goods, primary food, energy, processed food, beverages & tobacco, petrochemicals, chemicals & pharma,

Components	Dean et al. (2009)	Berden et al. (2009)	Fontagné et al. (2013)	Egger et al. (2015)
		food & beverages, OICE, pharmaceuticals, transport, biotechnology, ICT, construction, machinery, medical equipment, other business services, personal & recreational, steel, textiles, wood & paper, travel	insurance, business, other services, trade, transport, water	metals, motor vehicles, electrical machinery, other machinery, other goods, overall services, air transport, maritime transport, other transport, distribution, communications, banking, insurance, professional and business services, personal, recreational, public services
Coverage of services sectors (E)	No	Yes, 9 sectors	Yes, 9 sectors	Yes, 11 sectors
Country coverage (F)	60 countries	EU, US and other countries combined into ROW	Goods: 78 countries Services: 65 countries	12 regions

Country coverage – row (F) in Table 4.6

The three GTAP-based studies (Fontagné et al., 2013; Berden et al., 2009; and Egger et al., 2015) cover the entire world economically, but aggregate countries into relevant groups. Berden et al. (2009), focusing on TTIP, aggregate all GTAP countries into the EU, US and Rest of World (ROW). Egger et al. (2015) – also focusing on TTIP – define the EU, US, EFTA, Turkey, Other Europe, Mediterranean, Japan, China, TPP countries, Other Asia, Other middle-income, and low-income countries. Fontagné et al. (2013) specify 78 countries for goods trade and 65 for services trade. Finally, Dean et al. (2009) cover 60 countries.

Strengths and weaknesses of the different approaches

Each of the covered approaches has its merits and challenges. And in light of the complex discussion of how to quantify NTMs it is important to at least summarise some of the main strengths and weaknesses of each of the approaches in order to aid policy-makers in deciding what model they deem best-suited to the policy questions at hand. In Table 4.7 below, we present a short summary of the main strengths and weaknesses per approach.

Table 4.7 Summary of main strengths and weaknesses of NTM quantification approaches

Study	Strengths	Weaknesses
Dean et al. (2009)	• The direct estimation of the contribution of NTMs on the price gap • The direct link at product level (if price data available) to NTMs that could explain the price gap • The treatment of NTMs as endogenous and in combination with tariffs and income (through interaction terms) • The careful assessment of both the UNCTAD TRAINS database and USITC database and	• The large amounts of price data needed for all products affected by large-scale FTA effects is not available – so not suitable to large-scale FTA policy questions • NTM incidence is needed to distinguish NTMs from other factors that influence the price gap – how to measure the presence of NTMs? • Some of the TCEs attributed to NTMs could represent price premia because of

Study	Strengths	Weaknesses
	combining the (partially complementary) information available in each of these datasets	product differentiation, not because of the existence of NTMs
Berden et al. (2009)	• The use of a business survey that leads to the construction of an NTM index (values 0-100) that allows for a friction variable gravity regression approach • The combination of business survey and OECD FDI restrictiveness indexes to yield bi-directional and sector-specific NTM estimates • The characterisation of NTMs into cost and/or economic rent inducing – very important for estimating welfare impacts of NTMs • Information on actual barriers faced while exporting to the EU/US by small and large firms	• Indirect estimation of the price gap: first the quantity gap, then with price elasticities the price gap – adding risk of the quality of the estimation • The explained trade gap cannot be directly linked to NTMs at product level • The risk of a biased business survey (checked econometrically and no bias found) • The concept of 'actionability' in order to divide NTMs into those that can potentially be addressed and those that cannot/are not likely to be addressed limits the potential of regulatory cooperation, but is empirical only
Fontagné et al. (2013)	• The estimation work of Kee et al. is grounded in theory (Anderson & Neary) • The method of Kee et al. allows for estimation of bootstrap standard errors for the TCEs that take into account sampling and	• Indirect estimation of the price gap: first the quantity gap, then with price elasticities the price gap – adding risk of the quality of the estimation • In addition to the above, any mis-estimation of transport

Study	Strengths	Weaknesses
	estimation errors (indicating whether the quality of the estimation is a risk) • Kee et al. use very detailed NTM incidence data at tariff line level using detailed import elasticities – coming closer to product-level barriers	costs also affects the NTM impact (Dean et al.); • The explained trade gap cannot be directly linked to NTMs at product level (even though Kee et al. are close) • The partial equilibrium approach chosen by Kee et al. may lead to a bias (overestimation) of NTMs – direct impact, no income effects and no substitution effects possible • Kee et al. depend on ability of Heckscher-Ohlin model specification to explain trade flows
Egger et al. (2015)	• The approach to estimate potential NTMs based on a very large amount of information from past FTAs • The use of DESTA as a variable in the gravity equation to insert a measure of the depth of FTAs • The careful treatment of political variables ('polity') and sensitivity analysis to take the Berden et al. concept of actionability to a new (tested) level	• Indirect estimation of the price gap: first the quantity gap, then with price elasticities the price gap – adding risk of the quality of the estimation • The explained trade gap cannot be directly linked to NTMs at product level

Source: Compiled by the authors.

3.2   Juxtaposing the four approaches

Comparison of study results, policy recommendations and relevance for TTIP negotiations

The four studies covered in detail in this chapter have been used to various degrees to look at the potential effects of TTIP. It is important to note that in order to measure the potential effects of TTIP, quantifying the level of NTMs is only one – and the first – methodological step. In order to come up with economic estimates of a potential TTIP agreement, four methodological steps need to be taken:

1)   Quantification of NTMs as explained in this chapter
2)   Combining the quantified NTM estimates with tariff line information
3)   Developing liberalisation scenarios that could be the result of the TTIP negotiations
4)   Employing a macro/trade model (partial or general equilibrium) to look at the macro-economic effects

Figure 4.1 NTM quantification work used in different TTIP impact studies

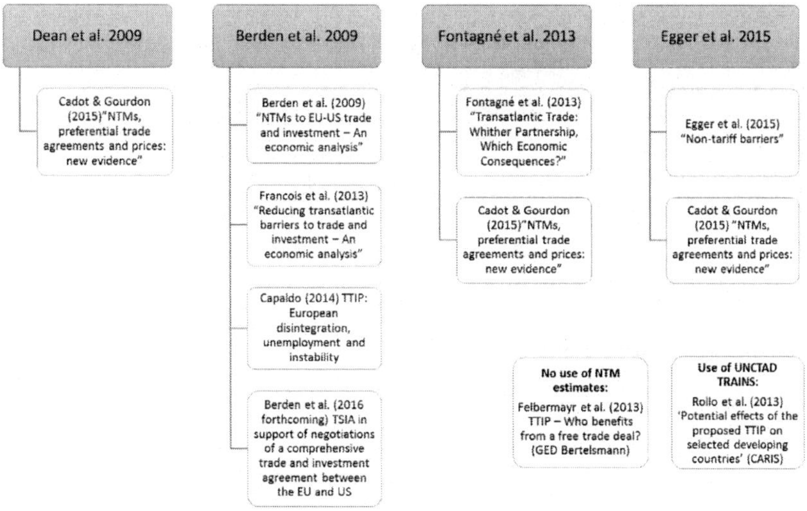

Source: Authors' own configuration.

Link between NTM quantification and TTIP impact studies

Many studies have in recent years worked through these four steps in order to quantify the potential effects of TTIP. And these studies have shown different results of a potential TTIP agreement because of different choices made in any of these four steps: different estimations of NTMs (the topic of this chapter), different tariff line data depending on what year the study was carried out, different liberalisation scenarios, i.e. anticipated levels of ambition, and different macro/international trade models to look at the final welfare effects. In Figure 4.1, we show what NTM estimation work has been used in some of the main studies carried out to estimate the potential impact of TTIP.

Comparison of NTM estimation results and link to policy-making

In Table 4.8 we present the summary of estimated NTM results per study and per sector (or aggregate thereof). This is in essence a meta-results table for the most important NTM estimates carried out so far, focusing on the EU and US from the TTIP perspective. From this table some interesting conclusions can be drawn.

First of all, it becomes clear from all studies that NTMs matter significantly in terms of their effect on international trade. The studies confirm that NTMs matter more than tariffs (2.2% for the US and 3.3% for the EU on average, according to Fontagné et al., 2013). This result matters for policy-makers because it suggests they should focus their attention relatively more on regulatory cooperation than on tariffs when negotiating new free trade agreements, as that is the area where potential barriers are highest. In fact, Egger et al. (2015) show that this is indeed what policy-makers are doing in recent trade agreements – stemming from the fact that the depth of FTAs negotiated and under negotiation has increased significantly in recent years.

Second, when we look across sectors, there appears to be a significant degree of variation between NTMs at sector level and depending on the direction of EU-US trade. For example, in processed foods, the NTMs found are much higher than in electrical machinery (electronics), and in general manufacturing goods NTMs are found to be higher than services NTMs (with the exception of Fontagné et al., 2013). This result implies that policy-makers should drill down into NTMs at sector level. They could focus first on those sectors where the differences are significant (and thus the scope for reduction is larger) based on as broad a range of studies as possible.

Third, in some sectors the studies show strikingly similar results. For example, when comparing the results of both the price-based and quantity-based approaches for processed foods, we find that the results are quite comparable across all studies. Furthermore, in some sectors like agriculture, automotive, steel, textiles, and insurance services – though level estimates vary – all studies find significant levels of NTMs.

Finally, when comparing estimated service sector NTM levels – though the height of NTMs differs – all studies that looked at services NTMs find that financial services, insurance services and maritime transport services are much more restrictive in the US than in the EU. Policy-makers can take note of the reported sectors and trends found across the studies as cross-validated, and treat them as 'more likely to be accurate' (as compared to those sectors or results where divergences in findings are high – see next point).

Fourth, the studies show some important differences in results. Dean et al. (2009) and Fontagné et al. (2013) find on average much higher levels of barriers from NTMs than Berden et al. (2009) and Egger et al. (2015). It is not easy to compare the studies because they use different levels of sector aggregations, e.g. Fontagné et al. (2013), only use report aggregate manufacturing results, not sector-specific ones. However, when we attempt to analyse where the differences in results come from, we find that the answer lies in part in what sectors are estimated and in what data and methodological approaches are used.

- First, when turning to what sectors have been estimated, we note that Berden et al. (2009) do not include estimations on the agricultural sector. Dean et al. (2009) and Fontagné et al. (2013) find high agricultural barriers – which explains in part why on average for all sectors the Berden et al. (2009) study finds lower NTMs, i.e. agricultural barriers are not included. So if policy-makers want to focus on the NTM levels in agriculture, they should turn to one of the other three studies.

- Second, we find that Dean et al. (2009) and Fontagné et al. (2013) – based on Kee et al. (2013) for manufacturing sectors – both use the UNCTAD TRAINS database, which collects NTMs and gives them a value '1' if present and '0' if absent. Berden et al. (2009) rely on the business survey results while Egger et al. (2015) use past FTAs as the benchmark (EU and FTA depth) – which do not have a binary nature. We believe that an important driver of the results is the binary nature of the NTMs in the UNCTAD TRAINS database versus the scaled variables of the Berden et al. business survey and FTA depth variable in Egger et al. Because the presence of any NTM is given a value '1' it is possible to overestimate NTMs using UNCTAD TRAINS. There are large data limitations to measure the incidence, impact, nature and importance of NTMs. All approaches are approximations that could help policy-makers focus on 'the biggest bang for the buck' – especially if the studies cross-validate each other's results.

- Third, it is important to note that Kee et al. (2009) themselves indicated that – as already outlined by Anderson (1998) – employing a partial equilibrium assumption on the estimation approach *"may lead to overestimating the degree of trade restrictiveness as the potential for substitution across markets is frozen in our setup..."* (Kee et al., 2009, p. 196). Since Fontagné et al. (2013) take the results for NTM estimations in goods from Kee, this estimation bias may also be present in their work. For policy-makers it is therefore important to realise that the Fontagné et al. (2013) results could be biased upwards.

- Fourth, Dean et al. (2009) use the price-based approach where they directly estimate the price gap and estimate the share of the price gap that can be attributed to NTMs, corrected for various factors. They however acknowledge that any measurement error in any of the control variables, e.g. transport costs, could lead to mismeasurement of the NTM variable (Q) as the residual variable that is measured. This implies that if any control variable is under-valued or if there is any effect that is not captured by the control variables, the potential NTM effect increases, thus possibly overestimating the impact of NTMs. For policy-makers it is therefore important to realise that the Fontagné et al. (2013) results could be biased upwards.

- Fifth, especially in services, the differences in NTM estimates between Berden et al. and Egger et al. on the one hand and Fontagné et al. on the other are large. This cannot be attributed to the GTAP database, because both Berden and Fontagné use the same GTAP 2007 version. Instead, we believe the different results stem from the fact that Kee et al. (2009) use a partial equilibrium approach to estimating NTMs, taken subsequently by Fontagné, combined with the use of the UNCTAD TRAINS dummy variable. For policy-makers, this means that NTMs are high, but maybe not as high as presented by Fontagné.

Finally, the price-based approaches require very large amounts of data at product level to work. If policy-makers are looking to estimate NTMs for specific products, and if price data are available in sufficient quantities, then the price-based approach is a very useful one to use. However, for estimating the impact of – for example – TTIP requires measuring the impact on tens of thousands of products in many sectors. For such an exercise price data are not available. Hence, using price-based approaches for all encompassing trade agreement impacts is not recommended.

Table 4.8 Summary of NTM quantification results per study

Sector	NTM TCE estimates by Dean et al. (2009)		NTM TCE estimates by Berden et al. (2009)		NTM TCE estimates by Fontagné et al. (2013)		NTM TCE estimates by Egger et al. (2015) – EU dummy (goods)/current policy (services)		NTM TCE estimates by Egger et al. (2015) – FTA depth (goods)/current policy (services)	
	(A)	(B)	(C)	(D)	(E)	(F)	(G)	(H)	(I)	(I)
	EU	US	EU to US	US to EU	EU	US	EU	US	EU	US
All goods							12.9	12.9	13.7	13.7
Agriculture					48.2	51.3	25.2	25.2	15.8	15.8
- Bovine meat	68.2	80.0								
- Fruits & vegetables	48.2	60.6								
Manufacturing					42.8	32.3				
- Aerospace & space			19.1	18.8						
- Automotive			26.8	25.5			19.5	19.5	19.3	19.3
- Beverages & tobacco							41.8	41.8	42.0	42.0
- Biotechnology										
- Chemicals			21.0	23.9			20.6	20.6	29.1	29.1
- Cosmetics			32.4	34.6						
- Electronics (electrical machinery)			6.5	6.5			19.4	19.4	1.8	1.8

Sector	NTM TCE estimates by Dean et al. (2009)		NTM TCE estimates by Berden et al. (2009)		NTM TCE estimates by Fontagné et al. (2013)		NTM TCE estimates by Egger et al. (2015) – EU dummy (goods)/current policy (services)		NTM TCE estimates by Egger et al. (2015) – FTA depth (goods)/current policy (services)	
	(A)	(B)	(C)	(D)	(E)	(F)	(G)	(H)	(I)	(J)
	EU	US	EU to US	US to EU	EU	US	EU	US	EU	US
- Energy							-0.01	-0.01	16.1	16.1
- Machinery							1.6	1.6	6.2	6.2
- Medical equipment										
- Office, Info & comm equip.			22.9	19.1						
- Other goods							5.7	5.7	3.6	3.6
- Petrochemicals							7.9	7.9	24.2	24.2
- Pharmaceuticals			9.5	15.3			20.6	20.6	29.1	29.1
- Processed food	35.6	34.6	73.3	56.8			48.4	48.4	33.8	33.8
- Steel (metals)			17.0	11.9			38.5	38.5	16.7	16.7
- Textiles	46.3	22.6	16.7	19.2						
- Wood & paper products			7.7	11.3						
Services			8.5	8.9	32.0	47.3	12.8	12.9	12.8	12.9
- Air transport services							25.0	11.0	25.0	11.0
- Communication services			1.7	11.7	38.6	36.9	1.1	3.5	1.1	3.5

Sector	NTM TCE estimates by Dean et al. (2009)		NTM TCE estimates by Berden et al. (2009)		NTM TCE estimates by Fontagné et al. (2013)		NTM TCE estimates by Egger et al. (2015) - EU dummy (goods)/current policy (services)		NTM TCE estimates by Egger et al. (2015) - FTA depth (goods)/current policy (services)	
	(A)	(B)	(C)	(D)	(E)	(F)	(G)	(H)	(I)	(J)
	EU	US	EU to US	US to EU	EU	US	EU	US	EU	US
- Construction services			2.5	4.6	53.2	95.4	4.6	2.5	4.6	2.5
- Distribution							1.4	0.0	1.4	0.0
- Financial services (banking)			31.7	11.3	51.2	51.3	1.5	17.0	1.5	17.0
- ICT			3.9	14.9						
- Insurance services			19.1	10.8	44.9	43.7	6.6	17.0	6.6	17.0
- Maritime transport services					65.3	98.4	1.7	13.0	1.7	13.0
- Other business services			3.9	14.9	32.6	42.3	35.4	42.0	35.4	42.0
- Other transport services							29.7	0.0	29.7	0.0
- Pers., recreational services			2.5	4.4						
- Trade					48.0	61.5				
- Transport services					29.1	17.5				
- Travel services										
Total average	49.6	49.5	17.7	17.5	41.0	42.2	17.0	18.7	16.4	18.1

Data sources: Dean et al. (2009), Berden et al. (2009), Kee et al. (2009), Fontagné et al. (2011) and Egger et al. (2015).

References

Aitken, N.D. (1973), "The e ect of the EEC and EFTA on European trade: A temporal cross-section analysis", *American Economic Review* 63(5), pp. 881-892.

Anderson, J. (1998), "Trade restrictiveness Benchmarks", *Economic Journal*, Vol. 108(449), July, pp. 1111-1125.

Anderson, J. and P. Neary (1992), "Trade reforms with quotas, partial rent retention and tariffs", *Econometrica*, Vol. 60(1), pp. 57-76.

_____ (1994), "Measuring the restrictiveness of trade policy", *World Bank Economic Review*, Vol. 8(2), May, pp. 151-169.

_____ (1996), "A new approach to evaluating trade policy", *Review of Economic Studies*, Vol. 63(1), January, pp. 107-125.

_____ (2003), "The Mercantilist index of trade policy", *International Economic Review*, Vol. 44(2), May, pp. 627-649.

_____ (2007), "Welfare versus market access: the implications of tariff structure for tariff reform", *Journal of International Economics*, Vol. 71(2), March, pp. 627-649.

Baldwin, R. (1975), Foreign Trade Regimes and Economic Development: The Philippines, National Bureau of Economic Research, New York, NY: Columbia University Press.

Berden, K.G., J. Francois, S. Tamminen, M. Thelle and P. Wymenga (2009), "Non-Tariff Measures in EU-US Trade and Investment – An Economic Analysis", Ecorys report prepared for the European Commission, Reference OJ 2007/S180-219493.

Berden, K.G., J. Bergstrand and E. van Etten (2014), "Governance and Globalisation", *The World Economy*, Vol. 37, No. 3, March, pp. 353-386.

Berden, K.G. and J. Vermeulen (2016 forthcoming), "Trade Sustainability Impact Assessment (Trade SIA) in support of negotiations of a comprehensive trade and investment agreement between the European Union and the United States of America", Ecorys report prepared for the European Commission under the Framework Contract TRADE/2013/E1/E03.

Bhagwati, J. and T.N. Srinivasan (1975), Foreign Trade Regimes and Economic Development: India, National Bureau of Economic Research, New York, NY: Columbia University Press.

Borchert, I., B. Gootiiz and A. Mattoo (2011), "Services in Doha: What's on the table", in W. Martin and A. Mattoo (eds), *Unfinished Business? The WTO's Doha Agenda*, Washington, D.C.: World Bank/CEPR, pp. 115-143.

_____ (2014), "Policy barriers to international trade in services: Evidence from a new database", The World Bank Economic Review, 28, 1 pp. 62-188.

Bradford, S. (2003), "Paying the price: final goods protection in OECD countries," Review of Economic and Statistics, 85(1), pp. 24-37.

_____ (2005), "The Extent and Impact of Final Goods Non-Tariff Barriers in Rich Countries," in P. Dee and M. Ferrantino (eds), Quantitative Methods for Assessing the Effects of Non-Tariff Measures and Trade Facilitation, Singapore: World Scientific Publishing.

Broda, C. and D. Weinstein (2006), "Globalization and the gains from variety", Quarterly Journal of Economics, 121, pp. 541-585.

Cadot, O. and J. Gourdon (2015), "NTMs, Preferential Trade Agreements, and Prices: New evidence", CEPII Working Paper, No. 2015-01, CEPII, Paris, February.

Cadot, O. and M. Malouche (eds) (2012), Non-Tariff Measures – A Fresh Look at Trade Policy's New Frontier, London and Washington, D.C.: CEPR and World Bank.

Capaldo, J. (2014), "The Trans-Atlantic Trade and Investment Partnership: European Disintegration, Unemployment and Instability", Global Development and Environment Institute, Working Paper No. 14-03, October.

De Benedictis, L. and L. Tajoli (2011), "The world trade network", The World Economy, 34, pp. 1417-1454.

Dean, J.M., J. Signoret, R. Feinberg, R. Ludema and M. Ferrantino (2009), "Estimating the Price Effects of Non-Tariff Barriers", B.E. Journal of Economic Analysis & Policy, Vol. 9, No. 1 (Contributions), Article 12.

Deardorff, A.V. and R.M. Stern (1998), Measurement of Nontariff Barriers, Ann Arbor, MI: University of Michigan Press.

Donnelly, W. and D. Manifold (2005), "A Compilation of Reported Non-Tariff Measures: Description of the Information", USITC Working Paper EC2005-05-A, International Trade Commission, Washington, D.C.

Dür, A., L. Baccini and M. Elsig (2014), "The design of international trade agreements: Introducing a new database", Review of International Organizations, 9, pp. 353-375.

Egger, P., J. Francois, M. Manchin and D. Nelson (2015), "Non-tariff barriers", Economic Policy, Vol. 2.

Egger, P., M. Larchand and K.E. Staub (2012), "Trade preferences and bilateral trade in goods and services: A structural approach", CEPR Discussion Paper No. DP9051, Centre for Economic Policy Research, London.

Felbermayr, G., B. Heid, and S. Lehwald (2013), "Transatlantic Trade and Investment Partnership (TTIP) – Who benefits from a free trade deal?", GED Bertelsmann Foundation.

Felbermayr, G., B. Jung and M. Larch (2013), "Icebergs versus tariffs: a quantitative perspective on the gains from trade", CESifo Working Paper 4175, Center for Economic Studies, Munich.

Ferrantino, M.J. (2006), "Quantifying the Trade and Economic Effects of Non-Tariff Measures", OECD Trade Policy Papers, No. 28, OECD Publishing, Paris.

_____ (2009), "Methodological approaches to the quantification of non-tariff measures", chapter IX in Mia Mikic with Martin Wermelinger (eds), Rising Non-Tariff Protectionism and Crisis Recovery, study by the Asia-Pacific Research and Training Network on Trade (ARTNeT) of the UN Economic and Social Commission for Asia and the Pacific (www.unescap.org/sites/default/files/tipub2587.pdf).

Fontagné, L., J. Gourdon and S. Jean (2013), "Transatlantic Trade: Whither Partnership, Which Economic Consequences?", CEPII Policy Brief No. 1, CEPII, Paris.

Fontagné L., A. Guillin and C. Mitaritonna (2011), "Estimations of Tariff Equivalents for the Services Sectors", CEPII Working Paper 2011-24, CEPII, Paris.

Francois, J.F. and B. Hoekman (2010), "Services trade and policy", *Journal of Economic Literature*, 48, pp. 642-692.

Francois, J., M. Manchin, H. Norberg, O. Pindyuk and P. Tomberger (2013), "Reducing Transatlantic Barriers to Trade and Investment – An Economic Analysis", Report prepared for the European Commission under implementing Framework Contract TRADE10/A2/A16, March.

Francois, J., O. Pindyuk and J. Woerz (2009), "Trends in International Trade and FDI in Services: a global dataset of services trade", Technical Report Discussion Paper 2009-08-02, Institute for International and Development Economics, Rotterdam.

Hoekman, B., F. Ng and M. Olarreaga (2004), "Agricultural tariffs versus subsidies: what's more important for developing countries", *World Bank Economic Review*, Vol. 18(2), May, pp. 175-204.

Jafari, Y. and D. Tarr (2015), "Estimates of Ad Valorem Equivalents of Barriers Against Foreign Suppliers of Services in Eleven Services Sectors and 103 Countries", *World Economy*, forthcoming.

Kee, H., A. Nicita and M. Olarreaga (2008), "Import Demand Elasticities and Trade Distortions", *Review of Economics and Statistics*, 90(4), pp. 666-682.

_____ (2009), "Estimating Trade Restrictiveness", *Economic Journal*, 119(534), pp. 172-199.

Leamer, E. (1988), "Measures of Openness", in R.E. Baldwin (ed.), *Trade Policy Issues and Empirical Analysis*, Chicago, IL: University of Chicago Press and NBER.

_____ (1990), "Latin America as a target of trade barriers erected by the major developed countries in 1983", *Journal of Development Economics*, Vol. 32(2), April, pp. 337-368.

Linnemann, H. (1966), *An econometric study of international trade flows*, Amsterdam: North Holland Publishing.

Park, S.-C. (2002), "Measuring Tariff Equivalents in Cross-Border Trade in Services", Trade Working Papers 353, East Asian Bureau of Economic Research.

Rollo, J., P. Holmes, S. Henson, M. Mendez Parra, S. Ollerenshaw, J. Lopez Gonzalez, X. Cirera and M. Sandi (2013), "Potential Effects of the Proposed Transatlantic Trade and Investment Partnership on Selected Developing Countries", Report by CARIS, University of Sussex for the Department for International Development.

Roy, M. (2011), "Services Commitments in Preferential Trade Agreements: An Expanded Dataset", Staff Working Paper ERSD-2011-18, World Trade Organization, Geneva, 9 November.

Shepherd, B. (2004), "EU standards database", mimeo, Science Po, Paris.

Teorell, J., C. Dahlström and S. Dahlberg (2011), "The Quality of Governance Expert Survey Dataset", Quality of Government Institute, University of Gothenburg, Sweden.

Tinbergen, J. (1962), *Shaping the World Economy: Suggestions for an International Economic Policy*, New York, NY: The Twentieth Century Fund.

Trefler, D. (1993), "Trade Liberalization and the Theory of Endogenous Protection: An Econometric Study of U.S. Import Policy", *Journal of Political Economy*, 101(1), pp. 138-160.

5. TRANSATLANTIC INVESTMENT TREATY PROTECTION

LAUGE POULSEN, JONATHAN BONNITCHA AND JASON YACKEE*

1.   Introduction

This chapter presents an informal cost-benefit analysis of including investment protection provisions, including investor-state dispute settlement (ISDS), in the TTIP. Our analysis is conducted from the perspective of the EU, although it covers many of the same issues that would also be relevant in a cost-benefit analysis conducted from the perspective of the US.

Provisions on investment protection, if included in TTIP, will be important. Almost one-third of all outward FDI stock from 28 member states of the EU will be covered by the agreement and almost 40% of all FDI coming from outside of EU28 (Table 5.1). These figures dwarf those of the Canada-EU Comprehensive Economic and Trade Agreement (CETA), the first EU-negotiated agreement with significant investment protection provisions and ISDS. For the US, the shares are even greater: 50% of US outward stock will be covered by TTIP and almost 62% of total US inward stock (Hamilton & Quinlan, 2014, Table 7). Assessing the implications of an investment protection chapter is therefore crucial.

---

* The discussion in this chapter closely follows a series of reports that we were commissioned to produce for the UK Department of Business, Innovation and Skills (BIS) (see www.gov.uk/government/uploads/system/ uploads/attachment_data/file/260380/bis-13-1284-costs-and-benefits-of-an-eu-usa-investment-protection-treaty.pdf). Our conclusions in those reports, and here, should not be taken as necessarily representing the views of BIS or the UK government. We are grateful to the BIS for permission to reproduce parts of the report.

Table 5.1 FDI stock coverage of free trade agreements, 2012
(€ bn, unless otherwise specified)

	Transatlantic Trade and Investment Partnership	Comprehensive Economic and Trade Agreement
EU outward FDI stock to...	2,182	340
% of EU total	32%	5%
EU outward FDI stock from...	2,026	188
% of EU total	39%	4%

Source: Authors' own computations.

Scarce availability of data makes a rigorous cost-benefit analysis unfeasible, so we rely on our reading of the best and most relevant evidence. Note also, that although an investment chapter could liberalise foreign direct investment (FDI) entry regimes in both the EU and US by requiring pre-establishment national treatment in most sectors, this is not covered in our analysis. The extent to which TTIP would provide liberalisation over and above what the parties would offer is uncertain at this point, and our ability to calculate the net predicted costs and benefits to the EU of marginal changes in openness to FDI across numerous sectors is limited. (On the other hand, it should be noted that the US and the majority of EU member states already provide pre-establishment national treatment in most economic sectors and for most activities as a matter of domestic law). Our analysis thus examines only the inclusion of post-establishment investment *protection* provisions in the TTIP and takes no account of possible investment *liberalisation*.

The analysis proceeds on the assumption that these post-establishment investment protections would be enforceable through ISDS. A cost-benefit assessment of a treaty that did not contain ISDS would look very different. Most of the potential benefits – for example, its theoretical ability to promote investment by offering reliable legal protection against certain political risks to investors – stem from investors' ability to enforce their rights under the treaty through ISDS. Similarly, most of the potential economic and political costs associated with the risk of claims stem from investors' ability to enforce their rights under the treaty through ISDS.

ISDS is controversial. In the public hearing organised by the European Commission, more than 145,000 European citizens agreed with non-governmental organisations that investment arbitration should not be included in TTIP (European Commission, 2015a). This meant that 97% of responses were overtly negative and there were only 60 companies that thought the issue was important enough to warrant separate replies apart from submissions from their industrial organisations. Among these 60 firms, two were tobacco companies – including Phillip Morris – and then there were a number of small firms as well, many of which did not express strong support for ISDS. The results made European Trade Commissioner Cecilia Malmström conclude: "The consultation clearly shows that there is a huge scepticism against the ISDS instrument."[1]

Among academics, as well, the merits of ISDS are disputed. It is easy to find respectable academics arguing that it is something close to an unmitigated good, and others, just as respectable, arguing the opposite. For this particular agreement, our conclusions can be simply summarised: ISDS, considered by itself, is unlikely to provide the EU or its member states with significant benefits; moreover, the benefits that ISDS may provide are unlikely to outweigh the associated costs. The inclusion of ISDS in TTIP is, in our view, largely unjustified by the available evidence. Whether the inclusion of ISDS would be a prudent concession on the part of the EU in order to assume some greater benefit in another part of the overall agreement would depend on the scale of the concession offered in return for the inclusion of ISDS, and an assessment of whether there were any less costly ways to secure those additional concessions.

The chapter proceeds as follows. After considering the likely investment-protection-related provisions in a TTIP investment chapter, we provide an overview of expected benefits and costs. We focus on both economic and political dimensions of the investment protection chapter and conclude by briefly offering a set of policy recommendations.

---

[1] "Public backlash threatens EU trade deal with the US", *Financial Times*, 13 January 2015.

2.   Treaty provisions: The likely content of the "I" in the TTIP

Since the beginning of its bilateral investment treaty (BIT) programme in the early 1980s, the US has negotiated these treaties on the basis of a detailed model text. Investment chapters in US FTAs generally follow the same model. Historically, the US has not been willing to deviate considerably from its model treaty (Vandevelde, 2009, p. 108). This means that successful investment treaty negotiations with the US typically resulted in agreements almost exactly mirroring the US template. One notable exception is the investment chapter of the US-Australia FTA, which generally follows the US model BIT except that it does not provide consent to investor-state dispute settlement.

The US has relatively few BITs in place with EU member states and no BITs in place with the EU's most powerful and developed members. The US-EU member state BITs include the following: Bulgaria (1992), Czech Republic (1991), Estonia (1994), Latvia (1995), Lithuania (1998), Poland (1990), Romania (1992), Slovakia (1991) and Croatia (1996). All of these BITs contain comprehensive dispute settlement and pre- and post-establishment national treatment, as well as other provisions common to the US model.

The US released its most recent model BIT in 2012, which is the intended basis for all current and future US BIT negotiations (Vandevelde, 2009, p. 108).[2] Given the US negotiating position in the past, it is very likely that Washington will insist that its 2012 model text provides the starting point for negotiations in the TTIP. In Europe, however, it is not entirely clear which direction the EU is going to take at this point given what Maupin accurately refers to as "the confusing range of objectives set forth by the Council, the Parliament, and the Commission." (Maupin, 2013, p. 196; see also Reinisch, 2013). For the purpose of this chapter, we assume that the EU could accept the 2012 US model, or something close to it, as a starting point for negotiations. This assessment is based on our understanding that the proposed investment chapter in the CETA reflects a US-style (or NAFTA) approach to investment protection. We therefore assume for the

---

[2] The 2012 US model BIT can be found at www.state.gov/documents/organization/188371.pdf.

purposes of this chapter that the text of TTIP investment provisions would follow the CETA/2012 US model BIT approach.[3]

The US model BIT is considerably more detailed and more comprehensive than the existing BITs typical of EU member states. Unlike EU member state BITs, US BITs mandate national treatment (NT) and most-favoured nation (MFN) treatment at both the pre-establishment and post-establishment phases. With the exception of Canadian and Japanese BITs, the BITs of most other countries do not address pre-establishment rights. The US model can thus be seen as requiring the liberalisation of inward FDI policy in addition to investment protection. The US model BIT also includes typical post-establishment provisions, such as guarantees of the international "minimum standard of treatment" (Art. 5), full compensation for expropriation (Art. 6), and the right to free transfer of capital (Art. 7). Finally, the US model contains comprehensive investor-state dispute settlement (ISDS) (Sec. B), which unlike the simple ISDS provisions in many European BITs, specifies required ISDS procedures in significant detail, including mandatory "transparency" of arbitral proceedings (Art. 29).

The comprehensive nature of the US model is evident in other provisions that go beyond the traditional core of favourable standards of treatment backed up by access to ISDS. For example, the US model bans many types of 'performance requirements', beyond what is already prohibited under the WTO TRIMs agreement (Art. 8). It also encourages the implementation a US-style 'notice and comment' system for the development and promulgation of investment-related administrative regulations (Art. 11). And it contains provisions concerning the host state's right to implement treaty-consistent measures to protect the environment (Art. 12) and the desirability of not weakening domestic labour laws in order to attract investment (Art.

---

[3] It is likely that the TTIP investment chapter will include a most-favoured nation MFN clause. Unlike the MFN clauses of other investment treaties, the MFN clause of the US 2012 model BIT does not apply to dispute settlement. Also, US BIT practice contains some examples of treaty-based limitations on the applicability of MFN clauses. For example, some US BITs include sectoral or subject matter exceptions to MFN treatment in an annex. The US has also sometimes excluded from its MFN clause treaty provisions in *earlier* BITs ensuring that the MFN clause only applies to more favourable treatment provided in *later* BITs. Our analysis is based on the assumption that the MFN provision of the TTIP would be drafted to exclude the application of MFN to early treaties.

13). These latter two articles are largely hortatory, however. The US model is also notable for its inclusion of various explanatory footnotes and annexes that attempt to clarify the meaning of otherwise vague or ambiguous treaty text. For example, the "minimum standard of treatment" is defined as equivalent to the "customary international law minimum standard of treatment of aliens" (Annex A).

Finally, the US model contains a number of exceptions designed to enhance the host state's policy space. For example, Article 18 provides a self-judging 'essential security' exception that allows the host state to apply otherwise treaty-inconsistent measures "that it considers necessary for the fulfilment of its obligations with respect to the maintenance or restoration of international peace and security, or the protection of its own essential security interests." The self-judging nature of the essential security exception ("that it considers necessary") means that the host state's invocation and application of the exception will be difficult or perhaps impossible for an investor to challenge in arbitration.[4] Article 20 of the US model provides another exception, for prudential measures designed to ensure the "integrity and stability of the financial system". Crucially, the investor's right to challenge state decisions taken under this exception is subject to numerous important limitations drafted into the article's text. Moreover, the US model limits the ability of investors to challenge 'taxation measures' as treaty-inconsistent (Art. 21).

A key question for the cost-benefit assessment, of course, is whether the chapter will be backed up by comprehensive ISDS. While the US did agree to remove ISDS from the investment chapter of its 2004 PTIA with Australia – at Australia's request – several stakeholders in the EU and the US desire comprehensive ISDS.[5] For our purposes, we assume that if negotiations are concluded, the investment protection chapter will indeed include comprehensive ISDS. Our assessment is conducted on this basis.

---

[4] For an overview of these so-called 'non-precluded measures', see Burke-White & von Staden, 2008.

[5] The US-Australia FTA, in addition to *not* including ISDS, also *does* include the various exceptions discussed above: essential security (Art. 22.2), taxation (Art. 22.3) and prudential regulation of financial services (Art. 13.10).

3. Potential benefits of ISDS

3.1 Promotion of US investment in the EU

The main potential economic benefit of an EU-US investment chapter lies in its theoretical ability to promote additional inbound investment to the EU by providing US investors with valuable international legal protections that they currently do not enjoy. In other words, is an EU-US investment chapter likely to increase the volume of US FDI in the EU? In our view, there is little convincing empirical evidence that investment treaties containing ISDS actually promote FDI in any significant way.

First of the all, the types of risks an investment protection chapter would cover are not generally considered present in most EU member states. This is clear from the US government's official "Investment Climate Statements", summarised below in Table 5.2. Even in what would typically be considered the most 'risky' investment destinations in Eastern Europe, the US government considers foreign investments there generally safe from expropriation and post-establishment discrimination, and advertises it as such to potential American investors.

Table 5.2 Summary of US Investment Climate Statements 2014 for 28 EU member states

	Post-establishment discrimination	Expropriation	Courts
Austria	No concerns	No concerns	No concerns
Belgium	No concerns	No concerns	No concerns
Bulgaria	Concerns about frequent changes in regulatory framework, but no significant concerns about discrimination	No concerns, except for intellectual property rights	Some concerns about corruption and nepotism and serious concerns about efficiency But while slow and bureaucratic, courts do resolve investment disputes and Bulgaria is seen as having effective means of enforcing property and contractual rights

Croatia	Some concerns about transparency and efficiency, but no specific concerns about discrimination	None except for a potential concern that Ministry of Justice oversees expropriation complaints over real property	Some concerns about efficiency and speed of court proceedings, but no concerns about independence of courts or the enforcement of property and contractual rights
Cyprus	No concerns	No concerns	Some concerns about speed of court proceedings, but no concerns about independence of courts or the enforcement of property and contractual rights
Czech Republic	A few concerns about corruption in procurement practices	No concerns	Some concerns about efficiency and speed of court proceedings, but no concerns about independence of courts or the enforcement of property and contractual rights
Denmark	No concerns	No concerns	No concerns
Estonia	No concerns	No concerns	Some concerns about efficiency and speed of court proceedings, but no concerns about independence of courts or the enforcement of property and contractual rights
Finland	No concerns	No concerns	No concerns
France	A few concerns about publicly held firms	No concerns	No concerns
Germany	No concerns	No concerns	No concerns
Greece	No concerns	No concerns, except for intellectual property rights	Some concerns about efficiency and speed of court proceedings and some foreign firms complain about bias

			Overall, however, no concerns about independence of courts or the enforcement of property and contractual rights
Hungary	Some concerns about transparency and efficiency, but no specific concerns about discrimination	Concerns over IPRs and compensation expressed by a few non-US firms, but later settled in court	Some concerns about independence of courts, but no concerns about the enforcement of property and contractual rights
Ireland	No concerns apart from transparency of government tenders	No concerns	No concerns
Italy	A few concerns about advantages to parastatal firms in procurement decisions	No concerns, except for IPRs	Some concerns about efficiency and speed of court proceedings, but no concerns about independence of courts or the enforcement of property and contractual rights
Latvia	No concerns	No concerns	Some concerns about speed of lower court proceedings, but no concerns about independence of courts or the enforcement of property and contractual rights
Lithuania	No concerns	No concerns	No concerns
Luxembourg	Not available	Not available	Not available
Malta	No concerns	No concerns	Some concerns about speed of court proceedings, but no concerns about independence of courts or the enforcement of property and contractual rights

Netherlands	No concerns	No concerns	No concerns
Poland	No concerns	No concerns	Some concerns about efficiency and speed of court proceedings, but no concerns about independence of courts or the enforcement of property and contractual rights
Portugal	No concerns	No concerns	Some concerns about efficiency and speed of court proceedings, but no concerns about independence of courts or the enforcement of property and contractual rights
Romania	Significant concerns about transparency and predictability in regulatory framework, but no significant concerns about discrimination	No concerns, except for IPRs and some outstanding disputes from Communist era	Serious concerns about efficiency and speed of court proceedings, but no concerns about independence of courts
Slovakia	No concerns	Some expropriation cases but no significant concerns about state's commitment to provide full compensation	Some concerns about efficiency and speed of court proceedings, but no concerns about independence of courts
Slovenia	No concerns	No concerns	Some concerns about efficiency and speed of proceedings about private property expropriated by Socialist Yugoslav government, but no concerns about independence of courts

Spain	Some concerns about advantages to SOEs	No concerns	Some concerns about speed of court proceedings, but no concerns about independence of courts or the enforcement of property and contractual rights
Sweden	No concerns	No concerns	No concerns
UK	No concerns	No concerns	No concerns

Source: Compiled by authors based on US investment climate statements (www.state.gov/e/eb/rls/othr/ics/2014/index.htm).

A recent survey of Chinese investors in the EU by the EU Chamber of Commerce in China supports the conclusions that we draw from the US Investment Climate Statements. That survey reports that Chinese investors view the EU as a "safe and stable place to invest, with a transparent and predictable legal environment…. Chinese companies are confident about the long-term prospects of their investments there, which were contrasted with regions such as Africa and Southeast Asia."[6] While the report includes some complaints by Chinese investors about certain difficulties encountered in operating in the EU, those complaints seemed to concern issues that are not typically dealt with in investment treaties, such as inflexibility of labour laws, difficulties in obtaining visas and work permits, and high costs and taxes.[7]

Our sense that many EU member states are already viewed as attractive places for US investors, despite, in many cases, the lack of a US BIT, is further confirmed by quantitative indicators of the investment climate. For example, the Investment Profile index published by the PRS Group in its International Country Risk Guide (ICRG) rates countries on a 12-point scale as to the favourability of their investment climates. Indexes such as this suffer from a number of methodological problems (Yackee, 2014), but it is nonetheless interesting to note that EU member states tend to rate very well. The average ICRG Investment Profile index score for EU member states in 2011 (the last year for which we have data) was 10.14 (where a higher rating means a more favourable investment climate), only Portugal and Greece fall below a rating of 8.0 (see Figure 5.1, below). In contrast, the world average ICRG Investment Profile rating for 2011 was 7.56.

---

[6] European Union Chamber of Commerce in China (2013).

[7] Ibid., p. 33.

There are a few exceptions to the generally high quality of EU domestic legal systems, such as Bulgaria and Romania, where US Investment Climate Statements indicate that serious concerns persist about procurement practices, intellectual property rights protection and inefficient courts. In the case of Bulgaria, the courts are also seen as subject to political influence – a relevant factor to consider for investment disputes against the government. However, the US already has BITs with Romania and Bulgaria. Thus, including investment protection provisions in TTIP would not result in a significant change to the status quo for US investors considering investing in Bulgaria and Romania.

Figure 5.1 2011 ICRG Investment Profile Index, EU member states

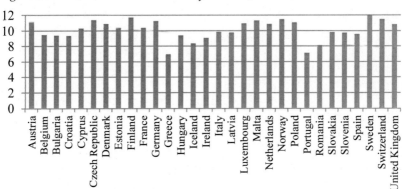

Source: Authors' own configuration.

Moreover, even in Bulgaria and Romania, existing US BITs do not appear to have helped promote investment. A 2012 study found that past US treaties with investment protection clauses rarely had a tangible impact on US outward investment – even in far more risky jurisdictions than European economies (Table 5.3).[8] For those treaties

---

[8] Econometric analyses of the impact of investment treaties often suffer from an absence of high-quality investment data and the problem of reverse causality: Do investment treaties cause investment flows, or is it the other way around? Investigating American agreements only allows the authors to use more complete investment data than panel-type studies, as American FDI flows are more readily available. Also, to account for the endogeneity of the relationship between FDI and investment treaties, the authors analyse the impact of each investment treaty in isolation with one or more lagged dependent variables. This further prevents questionable assumptions of homogeneity of effects across different countries, as is otherwise standard in panel data studies.

that have had a measurable impact, it has been only marginal. Crucially, not a single investment treaty with a developed country – including Canada, Australia, Israel and Singapore – has had an impact on US investment outflows. Nor is there evidence that BITs with Eastern European members of the EU were effective in promoting American investment.

Table 5.3 Estimation of investment effects of US BITs and PTIAs*

	Sustained positive effect on US FDI (increase in net US inflows/yr)	No sustained effect on US FDI	Insufficient data
BITs	Bangladesh ($28 million) Honduras ($83 million) Trinidad & Tobago ($254 million) Turkey ($155 million)	Albania, Argentina, Azerbaijan, Bahrain, Bolivia, **Bulgaria**, Cameroon, Rep. of Congo, DR Congo, **Croatia**, Ecuador, Egypt, **Estonia**, Georgia, Grenada, Jamaica, **Latvia**, Mongolia, Morocco, Mozambique, Panama, **Poland**, **Romania**, Senegal, Sri Lanka, Tunisia and Uruguay	Armenia, **Czech Republic**, Jordan, Kazakhstan, Kyrgyz Republic, **Lithuania**, Moldova, Serbia, **Slovakia** and Ukraine
PTIAs	Morocco ($72 million)	Australia, Bahrain, Canada, Chile, El Salvador, Guatemala, Honduras, Israel, Mexico, Morocco, Nicaragua and Singapore	Jordan

* Preferential trade and investment agreements.

Notes: Analyses regressed each country's net FDI inflows from the US on a one-year lag of net FDI inflows, a one-period pulse for the first full year after the agreement entered into effect and a dummy variable taking the value of one in each year the agreement has been in effect. Further details explained in the source. EU member states in bold.

Source: Adapted from Peinhardt & Allee (2012).

Figure 5.2 Response from general counsel within American multinational corporations about awareness and importance of BITs

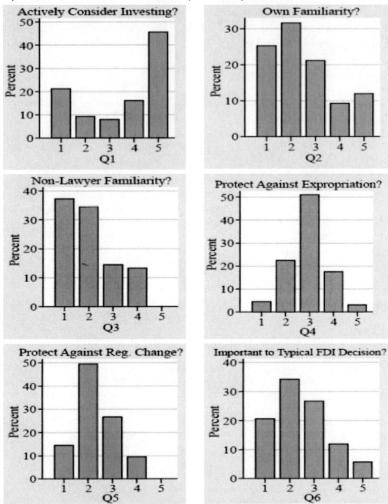

Notes: Histogram reports responses from in-house legal counsel in major American multinationals to: i) To your knowledge, how regularly does your company actively consider investing in foreign (non-US) operations, businesses, joint ventures, or other projects? ii) How familiar are lawyers in your office with the basic provisions of BITs? iii) How familiar are non-lawyer senior executives in your corporation with the basic provisions of BITs? iv) In your view, how effective are international treaties like BITs at protecting foreign investments from expropriation by a foreign government? v) In your view, how effective are international treaties like BITs at protecting foreign investments from adverse regulatory change in the foreign country? vi) How

important is the presence or absence of a BIT to your company's typical decision to invest in a foreign country? For the first question, 1 indicates 'Never or rarely' and 5 indicates 'Frequently'. For the next two questions, 1 indicates 'Not at all familiar' and 5 indicates 'Very familiar.' For questions four and five, 1 indicates 'Not at all effective' and 5 indicates 'Very effective'. For the last question, 1 indicates 'Not at all important' and 5 indicates 'Very important'.
Source: Yackee (2010).

These 'negative' findings are supported by feedback from American investors themselves. In 2010, a survey of in-house legal counsel in the 100 largest American multinationals showed that not only did many find BITs less effective to protect against expropriation and adverse regulatory change than commonly assumed, hardly any saw the treaties to be critical to their companies' investment decisions (Figure 5.2). This survey concerned the US BIT programme, which consists almost exclusively of treaties with developing and transition economies. In our view, this is a strong indication that US investors are highly unlikely to factor the availability of ISDS with EU countries into their investment decisions.

This is important, as investment protection treaties have arguably been more likely to be considered by US firms compared to European firms (Poulsen, 2010). Apart from their legally binding liberalisation provisions, the inclusive and open debates in Washington on investment protection treaties following the very public investment claims under NAFTA (see below) has led to a greater awareness of the treaties among US multinationals. This contrasts with Europe, where BITs have hardly ever been politicised until recently. Yet, irrespective of the greater awareness of investment treaties in the US, they do not appear to have played a considerable role in promoting American investment abroad.

Finally, it is worth highlighting that most public political risk insurance agencies in Europe do not find investment treaties important for pricing of availability of insurance even in otherwise risky jurisdictions (Poulsen, 2010). The same is the case for the Overseas Private Investment Corporation (OPIC). So even if ISDS in the TTIP could hypothetically have an impact on the transaction costs of foreign investment via the provision and pricing of insurance, this does not seem likely either.

In sum, we find it unlikely that investment protection provisions in the TTIP would have a tangible impact on the amount of US investment flowing to the EU.

3.2 Protecting EU investment in the US

A couple of very large European companies like Repsol and Total have told the European Commission that they are in favour of strong ISDS protections in TTIP and so have a number of European industrial organisations.[9] This, of course, is not surprising. A comprehensive investment protection chapter would add yet another layer of protection to European investors operating or seeking to operate in the US – without the investors having to pay for such protections themselves (as they would when taking up political risk insurance for instance). But the proper question is not whether some firms or industrial groups would like TTIP to include strong investment protections but rather whether the treaty would mitigate significant concerns actually experienced by European investors in the US. We find this unlikely as well.

To our knowledge, there are very few aspects of the US investment climate that concern EU investors. EU investors in the US have no restrictions on repatriation of profits, dividends, interest or royalties. And with respect to discrimination, it is true that 'buy American' provisions in the 2009 American Recovery and Reinvestment Act raised concerns about discrimination against foreign investors. However, despite these provisions foreign firms commonly receive national treatment in the US with respect to local, state and federal government fiscal or financial incentives.[10] More generally, there are hardly any discriminatory measures against foreign investors after establishment. Exceptions from national treatment are clearly set out in the OECD's National Treatment Instrument and both local, state, and federal level deviations from treatment proscribed by investment treaties are set out in the non-conforming measures annexes of recent US BITs and FTAs.[11]

---

[9] European Commission, "Online public consultation on investment protection and investor-to-state dispute settlement (ISDS) in the Transatlantic Trade and Investment Partnership Agreement", Brussels, 13.1.2015, SWD(2015) 3. After reading an initial draft of this chapter, a representative from Repsol (a Spanish firm) responded that strong investment protections in TTIP were necessary to protect against political risks in southern Europe, yet it is our understanding that there are no plans to have the chapter protect intra-European investment flows.

[10] See e.g. the United States report on its investment regime to APEC (APEC, 2011).

[11] Available at: www.ustr.gov.

With respect to discrimination when it comes to M&As or takeovers, the administration, via the Committee on Foreign Investment in the United States (CFIUS), has become increasingly politicised in recent years when reviewing security implications of such transactions. CFIUS decisions are unlikely to be challengeable in investment arbitration, however, given the likely national security exception in an EU-US investment chapter. This means that even if EU investors are concerned about the politicisation of CFIUS – which we do not have evidence to sustain – an EU-US investment treaty is unlikely to provide them with any other recourse than is currently available. It is also important to note that while acquisitions by EU investors account for the largest share of notices to CFIUS (60% in 2011), few of these result in legally binding mitigation measures. Rather, actual restrictions have primarily been targeted at sovereign-owned or -controlled investments, particularly from China (see e.g. Fagan, 2010).

With respect to expropriation, property rights are protected under the US Constitution, constitutions of individual states, as well as federal, state, and local laws. As in BITs, US 'takings' jurisprudence addresses both direct and indirect forms of expropriation and provides for compensation at fair market value at the time of the 'taking'. Enforcement of contracts is not a problem either. Due to the efficiency of the US judicial system in enforcing contracts, the US ranked 6th in the World Bank's *Doing Business 2013* report on this indicator.

Finally, US courts are characterised by both high quality and a high level of independence. In its arguments in favour of including ISDS in TTIP, the European Commission, in a statement dated 27 January 2014, suggested that there is nonetheless evidence that US courts are biased against foreign investors. The Commission presented a small number of examples, which we quote at length:

> In the US there have been occasions where investors found reasons to complain. The Commission can cite two well-known examples of denial of justice, which were eventually defeated in investment arbitration for jurisdictional grounds, Loewen v United States (an investor involved in a contractual dispute worth $5m was ordered to pay damages of $500m before he could appeal) and Mondev v United States (an investor could not sue the Boston Redevelopment Authority because of an immunity clause). An example of expropriation without compensation is the Havana Club case: Pernod Ricard, a French investor, has been prevented from using one of its trademarks for over 10 years. The EU has also successfully challenged this in a WTO dispute settlement

case; however, the US has yet to bring itself into compliance with the WTO. One of the first WTO cases brought by the EU against the US (the Helms-Burton) case, concerned restrictions placed by the US on investors from the EU, on account of investments they had made in Cuba.[12]

In our view, these examples of questionable conduct by the US government are not persuasive evidence of the need for ISDS to protect EU investors in the US. Both the Havana Club and the Helms-Burton cases involve the unique circumstances of US restrictions on business with Cuba. Moreover, the Havana Club case can be read as illustrating the strong US commitment to protecting property rights, and not the opposite, as the Commission statement suggests. Pernod Ricard acquired the trademarks from the Cuban government, which had taken (expropriated) the marks from the previous Cuban owners, the Arachabala family. From Washington's viewpoint, US law served to discourage expropriation by preventing the expropriating government (Cuba) from seizing and then selling intellectual property. Understood in this way, the case is hardly a useful indicator of US disregard for property rights.

Nor are the *Loewen* or *Mondev* cases particularly relevant. It is true that *Loewen* is widely regarded by international investment law experts as being very poorly reasoned, and perhaps objectively 'incorrect'. The case involved a state-court trial of a contract dispute between a large Canadian funeral home operator and a much smaller Mississippi funeral home operator. A Mississippi jury awarded the Mississippi plaintiff $500 million, most of which entailed punitive damages for allegedly unsavoury business practices. Many observers of the case may view the facts as illustrating something approaching a 'denial of justice'. On the other hand, the Commission mischaracterises the case in describing it as involving a "court order to pay damages of $500 million before [the defendant] could appeal". In fact, the court order was to post a performance bond of 125% of the jury award (which, as indicated, included punitive damages for allegedly egregious behaviour on Loewen's part) in order to pursue an appeal, as was the law in Mississippi. Loewen refused to post the bond, declined to appeal to the United States Supreme Court, and settled the case for a fraction of the jury award. The NAFTA Tribunal declined to

---

[12] Answer by Karel de Gucht on behalf of the Commission to Parliamentary Question NO/E-013215/13, 27 January 2014.

reach the merits of the case, and the United States was never found to have committed a denial of justice.

There are aspects of the underlying trial in *Loewen* that are admittedly disturbing, especially to European eyes unused to the sight of trial by jury, or of outsized punitive damage awards. On the other hand, it is remarkable that there are thousands of foreign investment projects in the United States and there have been hundreds of cases in US courts involving foreign investors, and yet *Loewen* – a case which the foreign investor *lost* in ISDS – is only one of two concrete examples of 'bias' in the US court system that the Commission can identify. Think what one may of *Loewen*, but it is a stretch to view the case as illustrating widespread anti-investor bias in the US justice system. Indeed, given the tremendous amount of FDI in the US, the lack of other examples would seem to illustrate the very high quality of the US justice system, and not the opposite.

Mondev is an equally problematic example. There, a Canadian real estate company sought to overturn a Massachusetts State Supreme Court decision in its contract dispute with a local government entity over a failed commercial redevelopment project. The Tribunal found that the state court's decisions were perfectly acceptable as a matter of international investment law. The Canadian plaintiff also challenged a state law that limited immunity in tort – not contract – to the local government actors. The Tribunal firmly rejected this challenge as well, upholding the grant of immunity as consistent with international investment law. Neither Massachusetts law nor Massachusetts courts violated plaintiff's international law rights.

In short, both *Loewen* and *Mondev* are exceptional cases; furthermore, they are cases in which the investor *lost* in ISDS, Loewen due to a lack of jurisdiction and Mondev on the merits. They are not evidence of systematic, serious flaws in the US judicial system's treatment of foreign investment.

While the high quality of the US judicial system (and US laws) concerning foreign investors is beyond debate, we have heard concerns from some European parties that without ISDS, EU investors will not be able to enforce their TTIP rights in US courts. This argument is not particularly convincing. It makes sense only insofar as there is an underlying justification for including enforceable investment protection provisions in TTIP. Our analysis in this chapter suggests that such a justification is lacking.

Even assuming, for the purposes of argument, that there were a coherent policy rationale for ensuring that TTIP provides EU investors in the US with a set of enforceable investment protections that go beyond what they would otherwise be entitled to under US law, the inclusion of ISDS in TTIP would be unnecessary. It is true that, under the US Supreme Court's *Medellin* case law (which raises a number of subtleties regarding so-called 'non-self-executing treaties' that we do not delve into here), some US treaties may indeed be difficult or impossible for private parties to enforce in US court. However, access to US courts can be assured either by clearly indicating in TTIP that the US considers the treaty to be 'self-executing', or by having the US pass appropriate implementing legislation. In other words, if one believed that was a problem of domestic-court enforceability of TTIP rights in the US, the appropriate response by the EU would be to insist in its negotiations that the US pass implementing legislation securing a right to access US courts for certain TTIP violations, not to include ISDS in TTIP.

3.3 The possibility of investment diversion and treaty-shopping

Related to our discussion of the potential of a TTIP investment chapter to promote FDI into the EU is the possibility that the investment chapter may in many cases simply divert US investment from one EU member state to another. For example, an investment chapter might, in theory, make western European states that currently lack a BIT with the US more attractive as destinations for US foreign investment by increasing the level of investor protection above the status quo. So, for example, we might imagine that an EU-US investment chapter would make the UK (or France or Germany) marginally more attractive to US investors because the chapter would give US investors considering investing in those countries international legal rights that they currently do not enjoy. On the other hand, an investment chapter would probably not change the status quo vis-à-vis those EU member states that already have a BIT with the US. For those states, an investment chapter would be largely redundant with the protection that US investors in those states already enjoy. Conceivably, the differential impact of an investment chapter on, say, Bulgaria (as an EU member state that has a BIT with the US) and the UK (which does not have a US BIT) may even divert some investment away from the former to the latter, as the EU-US investment chapter would eliminate any international investment law 'advantage' that Bulgaria currently enjoys over the UK.

However, in assessing the likelihood of diversion effects, it is important to note our analysis above, which suggests that the presence or absence of an investment treaty is unlikely to play a significant role in the location decisions of US investors, especially as to those EU member states that enjoy strong rule-of-law traditions and institutions. This observation implies that, even if an EU-US investment treaty alters the relative strength of investment protections available to US investors in various states within the EU, this legal change is unlikely to induce significant diversion effects.

Our conclusion here is also influenced by the possibility that US investors may currently be able to structure their EU investments in ways that provide BIT protections even where the ultimate EU destination for the investment does not have a BIT with the EU – a phenomenon called 'treaty shopping'. For example, if US investors in, say, Germany (which does not have a BIT with the US) route their investment via an intermediary incorporated in a third state that *does* have a BIT with Germany, the investment may be entitled to the protection of the Germany-third state investment treaty. Germany, like the UK, France, and many other EU member states, has an extensive network of BITs, most of which contain ISDS. If US investors in EU member states like Germany currently structure their investments in such a way as to gain BIT coverage, then an EU-US investment chapter is likely to have little impact on the amount or location on inbound investments to the EU. This is because, again, an EU-US investment chapter will likely be redundant with international legal protections that the US investor already enjoys, or that the US investor can enjoy through appropriate corporate structuring.

We are not aware of any evidence that US investors in the major EU member states actually do (frequently or otherwise) structure their investments via third states for the purpose of accessing the protection of existing investment treaties. This is not surprising because, as we explained above, evidence suggests that neither US investors in the EU nor EU investors in the US have expressed significant concerns about the sort of risks against which an investment treaty might protect, nor do they seem to particularly value the protections that ISDS may offer. Nevertheless, in cases where investors have specific concerns about future government measures, it is conceivable that they could structure the investment with investment treaty implications in mind. For example, in the dispute between *Philip Morris Asia v Australia*, the Australian government has argued that the Philip Morris group structured its investment in Australia so as to bring its trademarks within the coverage of the Hong Kong-Australia BIT.[13] Insofar as there is a possibility to structure investment between the US and EU member states so as to bring it under the protection of existing investment treaties, this would have implications for our estimation of both the costs and the benefits of a US-EU investment protection chapter, as ISDS in TTIP would be redundant with what US investors can already obtain via restructuring.

Just as US investors might use corporate structuring to take advantage of existing third-state BITs when investing in the EU, so too might EU investors seeking to invest in the US also attempt to gain BIT coverage by routing their investments through any of the 40-some states which currently have a BIT with the US. However, EU investors would face two challenges. The first is that the US has included 'denial of benefits' provisions in a number of its investment treaties and FTA investment chapters. According to a commentary on the 2012 US model BIT, the main purpose of denial of benefits provisions is to provide "safeguards against the problem of treaty shopping through the creation of 'sham' enterprises." (Caplan & Sharpe, 2013, p. 812). For example, NAFTA Article 1113(2) allows the United States (and the other Parties to NAFTA) to:

> deny the benefits [of NAFTA's investment chapter] to an investor of another Party that is an enterprise of such Party and to investments of such investors if investors of a non-Party own or control the enterprise and the enterprise has no substantial business activities in the territory of the Party under whose law it is constituted or organized.

The term "substantial business activities" is not further defined. Equivalent denial of benefits provisions are included in the 2012 and 2004 US model BITs (Art. 17 in both cases), and in other non-NAFTA free trade agreements, including the United States-Central America-Dominican Republic FTA (CAFTA, Art. 10.12).[14]

A second difficulty is that the US lacks investment treaties with states such as the Netherlands, Cayman Island and the Virgin Islands,

---

[13] *Philip Morris Asia v Australia*, Australia's Response to the Notice of Arbitration, 21 December 2011 [4]-[6].

[14] CAFTA's denial of benefits provision was, in fact, recently successfully invoked by El Salvador to defeat jurisdiction in a claim filed by a US-based holding company that, in the Tribunal's view, was only a "passive actor" in the US. *Pac Rim Cayman LLC v Republic of El Salvador* (ICSID Case No. ARB/09/12) (Decision on Jurisdiction).

which are likely to be attractive for tax reasons. This is an important consideration as tax planning plays a far greater role in corporate structuring than concerns related to investment treaties.

In sum, US investors in the EU may currently be able to obtain investment treaty coverage of their investments even in the absence of an investment treaty between the US and the EU host state. If this is the case, ISDS in TTIP will prove largely redundant with the coverage US investors can already enjoy, if they wish. On the other hand, US investment treaty practice makes it more difficult for EU investors in the US to engage in such 'treaty shopping' under existing arrangements. If, contrary to our analysis in this section, the availability of investment treaty protection were a decisive factor for EU investors considering investing in the US, then the difficulties associated with 'treaty shopping' under existing US treaties would mean that ISDS in TTIP would prove a greater benefit to such EU investors.

3.4   De-politicisation of transatlantic investment disputes

One potential benefit of investment arbitration is if it 'de-politicises' investment disputes. One version of this claim is that investment arbitration reduces the role of the home state in the resolution of specific conflicts between foreign investors and their host states (Shihata, 1986). This has also been used as a core argument against relying on inter-state dispute resolution in the investment protection chapter. Yet, in our view, concerns about politicisation of transatlantic investment disputes are often exaggerated.

First of all, it is rarely clear what exactly is meant by de-politicization of investment disputes (Paparinskis, 2012). While the involvement of home states in a dispute is one *type* of politicization, it is not the only one. Few would argue that the Phillip Morris claim against Australia is not politicised, for instance, and the same could be said of Vattenfall's claims against Germany. More broadly, the controversial nature of investment arbitration to resolve public law disputes has brought about considerable political controversy in Europe – potentially at the expense of broader foreign policy agendas, such as a swift negotiation of TTIP.

Secondly, while the de-politicisation thesis is widely shared amongst lawyers, it has never been subject to any rigorous empirical testing. Moreover, we are aware of no evidence to suggest that investment disputes across the Atlantic have spilled over into broader diplomatic conflicts. In the case of the Netherlands, interviews with diplomatic officials indicate that this has never happened – despite the large bilateral investment flows between the two countries (Tietje & Baetens, 2014, pp. 69-72).

Third, an investment chapter in TTIP is unlikely to provide meaningful access to ISDS for the kinds of investment disputes that are most likely to raise political sensitivities. As mentioned above, an EU-US investment chapter is almost certain to include a self-judging national security exception similar to Article 17 of the 2012 model US BIT. In that case, decisions by the US government to block acquisitions by European investors on national security grounds may be essentially unreviewable in arbitration, leaving diplomatic protection as the investor's only option to challenge the denial of permission to invest.

Finally, and with respect to US pressure on European states, the US Department of State formally maintains a restrictive policy toward diplomatic espousal of investment claims, requiring, for instance, full exhaustion of local remedies.[15] And while the US executive has historically been drawn into investment disputes in numerous developing countries,[16] the high quality of the US-EU political relationship combined with Europe's favourable investment climate makes us expect that incidences of strong US pressure on European states on behalf of US investors are rare. Diplomatic representations are bound to take place, but the type of politicisation of investment disputes seen in the mid-20th century between Western and developing states is highly unlikely. Transatlantic investment flows have flourished for decades without significant politicisation of the dispute settlement process.

3.5   Impact on future negotiations with third parties

A final potential benefit of including ISDS in the TTIP is if it increases the bargaining power of both the US and the EU in future negotiations with countries such as China. Although difficult to assess *ex ante*, we urge caution about the plausibility of this scenario.

First of all, with respect to China, Beijing has adopted investment treaties for decades and the Chinese leadership has developed a somewhat distinct investment treaty practice tailored to its perception of China's national interest (Gallagher & Shan, 2009). China has indicated considerable interest in an investment treaty with the EU –

---

[15] www.state.gov/s/l/c7344.htm.

[16] Maurer (2013).

also before knowing the outcome of the TTIP negotiations – and has not expressed concerns about extending ISDS to post-establishment provisions. China also recently signed an investment treaty with Australia that included ISDS. This was despite the fact that Australia had previously refrained from enshrining ISDS provisions into its preferential trade and investment agreement (PTIA) with the United States. As noted by Berger & Poulsen (2015, p. 2), "Beijing was thereby not deterred from including investment arbitration in an agreement with a developed country, which had previously refused to include similar provisions in a treaty with the US. This seems to be the final nail in the coffin for the already implausible argument that China's support of ISDS depends on the nature of investment protection agreements among developed countries."

Secondly, both European countries and the United States have refrained from signing BITs with developed countries for decades, but that has not prevented them from expanding their already widespread BIT networks with developing countries. Similarly, although OECD countries failed to agree to the Multilateral Agreement on Investment in the 1990s among themselves, this didn't prevent OECD countries from continuing to sign BITs with developing countries. The reason is simple: the main purpose of ISDS is to act as a substitute for poor judicial systems, so it is not clear why it should be seen as illegitimate to exclude ISDS in agreements where there are for the most part developed legal systems on both sides.

This was the argument used by Australia and the US for not including ISDS in their 2005 agreement and the logic behind the European Parliament's 2013 vote to clarify that future EU investment agreements should include ISDS "[i]n the cases where it is justifiable".[17] Similarly, Commissioner De Gucht implied that the EU would not necessarily push for ISDS if parties had well-developed legal systems, like the United States: "[o]bviously you need [ISDS] when it is an agreement with a third country that does not have a properly-functioning judicial system, where one can have doubts about the rule of law."[18] The United States is not such a country and nor are any of the

---

[17] See Committee Report tabled for Plenary, 1st Reading/Single Reading, 26 March 2013 (www.europarl.europa.eu/oeil/popups/summary.do?id= 1255871&t=d&l=en).

[18] See Remarks of Commissioner De Gucht, EUR. PARL. DEB. (339), 22 May 2013) (www.europarl.europa.eu/sides/getDoc.do?type=CRE&reference= 20130522&secondRef=ITEM-019&language=EN&ring=A7-2013-0124).

EU member states that do not currently have BITs with the United States, so we find it unlikely that investment protection provisions in the TTIP would have a tangible impact on the extent to which third parties will agree to ISDS with the US and/or the EU.

4.   Potential costs

4.1   Risk of claims and adverse awards

The primary cost to the EU of ISDS-backed investment protection is the increased risk of successful investment treaty claims against the EU or its member states. In estimating the scale of this cost, the first step is to assess the size of US investment stocks in the EU, as the likelihood of claims against the EU can be expected to increase roughly in proportion with the size of the investment stock in the EU covered by the treaty. As mentioned initially, the EU possesses a very large stock of US-origin investment.

This is important. An often-heard argument in European debates about TTIP is that since (western) EU member states have been subject to only a few claims after having signed hundreds of BITs for decades, there is no reason to expect that the number of claims should rise significantly after TTIP. But this argument is based on a comparison between BITs signed with (mostly) insignificant sources of FDI and a potential future treaty signed with a very significant source of inward investment. Take the case of Germany, for instance, which has signed more than 150 BITs – the vast majority with developing countries. In 2011, 3% of FDI stock in Germany came from developing countries, 9% came from the United States.[19] Similar patterns emerge when looking at other western EU member states. In France, 4% of its 2011 FDI stock came from developing countries and 10% from the United States. In Sweden, 2% came from developing countries, 7% from the United States. And in the United Kingdom, 28% of inward FDI stock came from the United States, 8% from developing countries.

Two further issues relate to the type of US investments in the EU: their size and sectoral composition. These issues are relevant because investment treaty claims involving investors in certain sectors and of certain sizes have been more common. Given the tremendous quantity

---

[19] The following calculations are based on UNCTAD's FDI statistics (http://unctad.org/en/Pages/DIAE/FDI%20Statistics/FDI-Statistics-Bilateral.aspx). Note that bilateral FDI statistics are subject to considerable measurement error.

of US investment in the EU, there are undoubtedly a great number of investment projects that are of sufficient size to make the economics of an investment treaty claim (i.e. ratio of legal costs to potential award) viable in theory. With respect to the distribution of sector-specific investment, US companies have made significant investments across virtually all sectors of the EU economy.[20]

A different consideration concerns the culture and practice of dispute resolution among US investors in the EU. For example, American investors appear to be especially litigious. Accordingly, the British government warns UK investors operating in the US:

> Americans are, in general, inclined to start litigation or to threaten it – probably more so than the British. It is not just American lawyers that exhibit this tendency, but also American business people. Americans often sue or threaten suit as a strategic device to obtain some sort of amicable settlement (e.g., a money payment, a new contract, an agreement by the other side to abandon its claim). The great majority of commercial litigation started is never decided by the court or an arbitration panel. It is settled by the parties after the legal proceeding has begun; sometimes, the threat of legal action is sufficient to bring about a settlement. (UKTI, 2013, p. 32).

This also seems relevant in the context of investment treaty arbitration. A 2007 empirical analysis of the 83 investment treaty disputes that were known at the time to have resulted in awards found that 32 of those cases – over 38% – involved an investor from the United States (Franck, 2007, p. 28). The second-most-frequent nationalities were Canada and Italy, with just six cases each. In the absence of a theoretical model for predicting baseline expectations for investor participation in investment treaty arbitration, it is difficult to draw any definitive conclusions from these figures. For example, the US is a major source of outward FDI, and for that reason it may not be entirely unexpected that many investment treaty claims would involve US investors. On the other hand, the high proportion of claims by US investors may be seen as striking, given the relatively low number of US investment treaties in force (approximately 40, plus investment chapters in US FTAs, such as NAFTA). Unfortunately, Franck's data do not control for such things as the amount of FDI from the home country, so it is impossible to say whether the level of US investor claims is

---

[20] See US Bureau of Economic Analysis data (www.bea.gov/scb/pdf/2013/07%20July/0713_direct_investment_positions.pdf).

objectively "high". Franck's data also show that investors won damages in 38.5% of claims that were finally resolved in an award (Franck, 2007, p. 49 & p. 58). Franck's data do not break out these statistics by the home state of the investor, so we are not able to say whether US investors win more often, or win more, than other investors.

Canada's experience under NAFTA Chapter 11 is relevant here, as Canada is a developed country with a strong rule-of-law tradition – just like most EU member states. As of February 2015, Canada had been the target of 35 NAFTA investment-chapter claims, all but one brought by US investors.[21] If anything we would expect that EU member states would be more prone to US claims than Canada, as Canada hosts less than 8% of US outward FDI stock, whereas the EU hosts more than 50% (UNCTAD, 2014, Table II.7). Table 5.4 shows all known Chapter 11 notices of intent filed by US investors against Canada. The table lists the claimant's name, the minimum amount of damages sought (as indicated in the notice of intent), the year the notice of intent was filed, a short description of the dispute and the dispute's outcome.

Table 5.4 illustrates the breadth of Canadian government actions that US investors have challenged: electricity regulation, changes in tax laws, the revocation or denial of various licenses, export bans on hazardous materials, health care regulations, patent decisions and more. The table also shows that a significant proportion of notices of intent are eventually withdrawn or become inactive (14/35). Unfortunately, the Canadian government does not indicate the reason for withdrawal or inactivity. We think it likely that many withdrawn or inactive notices of intent are withdrawn or become inactive because the investor realises that the claim has little chance of success, or that proceeding with arbitration will be too costly.

However, we have no hard evidence to support this hypothesis. Eleven notices of intent have proceeded to arbitration and led to an award or a formal settlement. Of those eleven, only five have resulted in payments to the investor. In total, it appears that Canada has paid investors approximately CDN 156 million, with the bulk of that total consisting of a CDN 130 million settlement in *AbitibiBowater*. (Damages are still pending in the recent award in *Mobil Investments*). Eight disputes are on-going. US investors appear to have become more active in filing Chapter 11 notices of intent in recent years, with nine notices

---

[21] See www.naftaclaims.com/disputes_canada.htm. By "claims" we mean that a notice of intent to file a Chapter 11 claim was filed by the investor.

filed since 2010. Those nine notices together claim a minimum of over $3 billion in damages, including a claim for $1.5 billion in the *Detroit International Bridge Co.* case. However, it is probably safe to say that those damage claims are exaggerated and intended by the investors to increase pressure on Canada to settle in the investors' favour.

Table 5.4 Claims against Canada by US investors pursuant to NAFTA chapter 11

	Claimant(s)	Minimum damages sought	Year notice intent	Dispute description	Outcome
1	Signa S.A. de C.V.	CDN 50 million	1996	Drug patent decision	Withdrawn
2	Ethyl Corp.	USD 201 million	1997	Import ban on gasoline additive	Settled; investor paid approx. CDN 20 million
3	Pope & Talbot Inc.	USD 30 million	1998	Softwood lumber	Partial award for investor, USD 408 thousand
4	S.D. Meyers Inc.	USD 10 million	1998	Export ban for PCB waste	Award for investor, CDN 6 million
5	Sun Belt Water, Inc.	NA	1998	Denial of license for water export	Inactive
6	Ketcham Investments, Inc. and Tysa Investments	CDN 30 million	2000	Softwood lumber	Withdrawn
7	United Postal Service of America, Inc.	USD 100 million	2000	Anti-competitive practices of Canadian postal service	Investor claims rejected on merits
8	Chemtura Corp.	USD 100 million	2001	Regulation of crop pesticide	Investor claim rejected on merits
9	Trammel Crow Co.	USD 32 million	2001	Abuse of postal service procurement process	Withdrawn
10	Albert Connolly	NA	2004	Forfeiture of mining claim site	Inactive

11	Contractual Obligation Prod. LLC et al.	USD 20 million	2005	Denial of television programming subsidy	Inactive
12	Peter Nikola Pesic	NA	2005	NA	Withdrawn
13	GL Farms LLC and Carl Adams	USD 78 million	2006	Milk export programme	Inactive
14	Merrill & Ring Forestry LP	USD 25 million	2006	Export controls on logs	Investor claims rejected on merits
15	V.G. Gallo	USD 355 million	2006	Expropriation of landfill	Investor claims dismissed for lack of jurisdiction
16	Gottlieb Investors Group	USD 6.5 million	2007	Change in tax laws	Inactive
17	Mobil Investments Inc. & Murphy Oil Corp.	USD 50 million	2007	Imposition of performance requirements	Award in investor's favour; compensation TBD
18	Centurion Health Corp.	USD 155 million	2008	Restrictions on private health care	Investor claim terminated by tribunal
19	Clayton Bilcon	USD 188 million	2008	Environmental assessment of quarry project	Pending
20	David Bishop	USD 1 million	2008	Revocation of license for wilderness outfitter	Inactive
21	Dow AgroSciences LLC	USD 2 million	2008	Ban on lawn pesticides	Settled with no compensation paid
22	Georgia Basin L.P.	USD 5 million	2008	Export controls on logs	Inactive
23	Janet Marie Broussard Shiell et al.	USD 21 million	2008	Fraudulent bankruptcy proceedings	Inactive
24	William Jay Greiner and Malbaie River Outfitters Inc.	USD 5 million	2008	Revocation of license for wilderness outfitter	Withdrawn

25	AbitibiBowater Inc.	CDN 300 million	2009	Termination of water and timber rights	Settled; investor paid CDN 130 million
26	Christopher and Nancy Lacich	USD 1.2 thousand	2009	Change in tax laws	Withdrawn
27	Detroit International Bridge Co.	USD 1.5 billion	2010	Regulation of toll bridge	Pending
28	John R. Andre	CDN 4 million	2010	Emergency caribou hunting restrictions	Inactive
29	Mesa Power Group LLC	CDN 775 million	2011	Renewable energy regulation	Pending
30	St. Mary's VCNA, LLC	USD 275 million	2011	Denial of license for quarry	Settled with no compensation paid
31	Eli Lilly & Co.	CDN 100 million	2012	Invalidation of pharmaceutical patent	Pending
32	Lone Pine Resources Inc.	CDN 250 million	2012	Revocation of mine permit	Pending
33	Mercer International Inc.	CDN 250 million	2012	Electricity generation	Pending
34	Windstream Energy LLC	CDN 475 million	2012	Renewable energy regulation	Pending
35	J.M. Longyear	$12 million	2014	Forestry taxes	Pending

Notes: "Minimum damages sought" are taken from Notices of Intent and do not include pro forma requests for costs, interest and the like; actual amounts claimed in arbitration may be higher. Where "US" or "CDN" is not listed, the Notice of Intent is ambiguous as to whether the investor is requesting monetary relief expressed in US or Canadian dollars. Last updated 4 February 2015.

Sources: Compiled by authors from information on the website of the Department of Foreign Affairs and International Trade (www.international.gc.ca/trade-agreements-accords-commerciaux/topics-domaines/disp-diff/NAFTA.aspx) and NAFTAClaims.com.

We think that it is fair to say that Canada has a relatively successful record in defending itself against investor-state claims, at least in the sense of avoiding frequent and/or large adverse awards.[22] This contrasts with the experiences of some developing countries, such as Argentina and Ecuador, which have seen very large adverse awards as a result of investor-state arbitration initiated by US investors (Gallagher & Shrestha, 2011, Table 1).

If an EU-US investment chapter provided US investors with more generous rights than they would otherwise have under the laws of European states, the risk of investor lawsuits and adverse arbitral awards would rise, perhaps considerably. It is beyond the scope of this chapter to offer a general survey of the legal regimes of all EU member states. Instead, we provide an illustrative case study, using the UK as an example. It is probably fair to say that the UK has a legal regime that, both in terms of substantive content and implementation by local courts, is among the best in the EU at protecting the property rights of both domestic and foreign investors. We nonetheless find some meaningful risk of adverse awards for the UK; *that risk will necessarily be higher for member states that do not have as high-quality legal regimes as does the UK*. In other words, we expect that an analysis of all EU member states would indicate that, on average, the risk of adverse awards is *higher* than we estimate that risk to be for the UK considered alone.

4.2   The UK as an example of the risk of adverse awards

In general, our view is that an EU-US investment chapter is unlikely to grant US investors in the UK *significantly* greater rights than they would otherwise have under UK law. As we explain below, however, an EU-US investment treaty may provide opportunities or incentives for investors to bring claims that they would not bring under UK domestic law. The content of international investment law remains contested and uncertain, and it is possible that an ISDS tribunal formed under an EU-US investment chapter would grant a US investor significant damages for conduct that would not normally be actionable under UK domestic law.

We say that an EU-US investment chapter would not grant US investors in the UK *significantly* greater rights than they currently enjoy because most successful investment treaty claims concern circumstances that would clearly be inconsistent with UK law, such as the unilateral abrogation of contracts by government authorities, or serious procedural failures in administrative or judicial processes.

---

[22] While Canada, as indicated, has lost a small number of investor-state arbitrations, the US has never lost an investment treaty arbitration.

While in some cases investment tribunals have interpreted investment treaty text in ways that go beyond the protections contained in UK law – for example, on the question of 'legitimate expectations' or the granting of regulatory permits and licenses (Poulsen, Bonnitcha & Yackee, 2013) – we believe that an EU-US investment chapter is likely to contain relatively restrictive formulations of the minimum standard of treatment, regulatory expropriation and other standards that have, when drafted without qualification, been interpreted more expansively. Since the well-known *Methanex* NAFTA Chapter 11 arbitration, in which a Canadian investor unsuccessfully challenged a California environmental regulation, the US has appeared to be particularly concerned with protecting its right to change the legal or regulatory regime in non-discriminatory ways (Caplan & Sharpe, 2013, p. 756). We see that sensitivity in the various explanatory footnotes and annexed text in the 2012 US model BIT that, for example, limit the fair and equitable treatment standard to the customary international law standard for the treatment of aliens,[23] or that reaffirm that "except in rare circumstances, non-discriminatory regulations that are designed and applied to protect legitimate public welfare objectives…do not constitute indirect expropriation",[24] or that clarify that whether a regulatory grant of permission to engage in an activity is not a covered "investment" if the grant of authority does not also "create any rights protected under domestic law".[25]

On the other hand, and despite such attempts to narrow and clarify the protections provided by the US model BIT, there remains significant debate and uncertainty as to the content of such terms as "fair and equitable treatment".[26] That lingering uncertainty leaves open the possibility that an arbitral tribunal might interpret the language of an EU-US investment chapter expansively, despite the addition to the treaty text of cautionary footnotes and annexed clarifications. In turn, continued uncertainty as to the content of international investment law means that investors may have an incentive to bring 'long-shot' claims against the UK, in particular where the investor has suffered large damages. In some cases, a long-shot claim may result in an arbitral

---

[23] 2012 US model BIT, Annex A.

[24] 2012 US model BIT, Annex B.

[25] 2012 US model BIT, Art. 1 footnote 2.

[26] Kläger (2011, pp. 87-88) (discussing the failure of the US model BIT's clarifications on the meaning of "fair and equitable treatment" to actually clarify the meaning of the phrase).

interpretation and application of treaty text that goes beyond UK domestic law.

For example, the tribunal in the recent case of *Occidental v. Ecuador II* read into the fair and equitable treatment provision of the US-Ecuador BIT an obligation on the state to treat the investor "proportionately" when the state exercises a contract-based right to terminate its commercial relationship with the investor upon the investor's breach of the contract.[27] While the principle of proportionality has some operation as a ground of review in the administrative law of the UK, English *contract* law does not require an innocent party to exercise a right to terminate a contract proportionately. If one party breaches a contract and if that breach creates a right to terminate, the innocent party is entitled to exercise that right to terminate at its discretion.[28] While there are other complexities in *Occidental II* that may bear on how the case would be resolved if it had been litigated under the English law of contract, we think a dispute akin to *Occidental II* may well be decided differently if it were litigated under English law. As such, the case provides a helpful illustration of the point that apparently restrictive concepts such as the minimum standard of treatment required by customary international law are sometimes interpreted by arbitral tribunals in ways that can grant foreign investors more generous rights than would be recognised under UK law.

The EU appears to have recognised that vague investment treaty terms like "fair and equitable treatment" give ISDS tribunals a great deal of leeway to rule against host states if they wish.[29] The Commission has proposed that EU investment agreements "will set out precisely what elements are covered and thus prohibited" under the fair and equitable standard. The Commission proposes that the fair and equitable treatment would be defined as covering issues such as "manifest arbitrariness, abusive treatment (coercion, duress or harassment), or failure to respect the fundamental principles of due process".[30] While we agree that the standard formulation of fair and

---

[27] *Occidental v Ecuador II*, ICSID Case No. ARB/06/11, Award, 5 October 2012 [383].

[28] *Union Eagle Ltd v Golden Achievement Ltd* [1997] AC 514 per Lord Hoffmann.

[29] See the EU Commission Fact Sheet, "Investment Protection and Investor-to-State Dispute Settlement in EU agreements", November 2013 (http://trade.ec.europa.eu/doclib/docs/2013/november/tradoc_151916.pdf)

[30] Ibid.

equitable treatment could certainly be improved to make its content more certain (and to make tribunal holdings more predictable *ex ante*), the Commission's proposed clarifications would still leave tribunals significant discretion to interpret such terms as "arbitrariness" or "duress" expansively. This is especially so as the current draft suggests that the application of such principles should take into account "legitimate expectations" of the investor that are based on "specific representations" made by officials of the host state.

Despite the potential of expansive interpretations of uncertain treaty text, an EU-US investment chapter would still probably *by design* confer greater rights on US investors that they would be entitled to under UK law, at least in certain areas. The general rule in the UK is that legislation passed by Parliament cannot be challenged in the courts. This is relevant also when considering political costs, as noted below, as investment tribunals authorised to override acts of Parliament is politically sensitive. Moreover, while the actions of the executive can be challenged in UK courts, pecuniary remedies are only rarely awarded in such cases (Craig, 2012). In both respects, the position under an EU-US investment treaty would differ from the position under UK law.

Overall, our view is that the UK faces meaningful risk that US investors will seek to invoke an EU-US investment chapter's ISDS provisions to bring claims against the UK government, and that EU member states with weaker legal systems will face even greater risk. This assessment is primarily due to i) the large amount of US investment in the UK, and in the EU more generally; ii) the fact that US investors appear to have been relatively aggressive in bringing actions against other states, including Canada, under investment protection instruments that are likely to be very similar to an EU-US investment chapter; and iii) the continued uncertainty over the proper meaning of key concepts in international investment law, such as 'fair and equitable treatment'. In particular, investors can be expected to bring some number of 'long-shot' claims against the UK, some of which the UK may lose.

Moreover, so long as the investor has some chance of success, the mere act of filing an arbitral claim may give the US investor leverage against the UK government in terms of encouraging the UK government to settle the case, even if only to avoid litigation costs and any possible damage to the UK's reputation as a welcoming environment for foreign investment. This is an important point. For example, in the well-known Ethyl NAFTA litigation, Canada settled the case by agreeing to pay the US investor $13 million. Thus, while we do not expect the UK to incur many high-value awards in favour of US investors, this does not mean the UK will not incur considerable litigation-related costs under an EU-US investment chapter. These include the costs of more favourable settlements than would otherwise be agreed, as well as fees to lawyers and tribunals. The latter are expected to average at approximately $4 million per claim per party, as discussed below. We view it as virtually certain that such costs under an EU-US investment chapter will be higher than under the status quo, as we assume that currently the vast bulk of existing US investment in the UK is not covered by an investment treaty. In contrast, under an EU-US investment chapter, all US investment in the UK would be covered.

Our analysis, as applied to other EU member states, would obviously depend on whether investments in those other member states are already covered by a US investment treaty and on the quality of the domestic legal system. But the UK illustration is important, as we expect that some EU member states will have legal systems that are of generally lower quality than that of the UK and, as such, at greater risk of adverse awards.

4.3 Legal costs

We expect that the EU and its member states would be able to develop a defence capacity of a quality roughly comparable to that of the US and Canada, especially given that EU government institutions are unlikely to engage in the kinds of mistreatment of US investors that are likely to be viewed as clear or egregious violations of international law. However, it must be recalled that the EU and its member states are likely to incur additional costs (lawyers' fees; tribunal fees) in defending itself against investor lawsuits. Whether the EU itself or a particular member state will bear the costs of ISDS litigation will depend on EU regulations governing cost allocation (European Commission, 2012). We do not discuss intra-EU cost allocation here as our focus is on the costs and benefits of ISDS as to the EU and its member states considered collectively. More precisely, our analysis focuses on the magnitude of legal costs, and the way they are distributed between investors (in their capacity as claimants in ISDS proceedings) and the EU and the member states (in their capacity as respondents).

A recent OECD scoping paper on ISDS reported the results of a survey showing that total "legal and arbitration costs for the parties in recent ISDS cases have averaged over $8 million [or $4 million per party] with costs exceeding $30 million in some cases." (OECD, 2012, p. 18). These figures are consistent with a briefing by the law firm Allen & Overy, which puts average costs at slightly over $4 million per party, with minor variations of tribunal costs as between cases under differing sets of procedural rules (Hodgson, 2012). Additional costs (such as the costs to the government of maintaining an office dedicated to investment-treaty defence) would add some amount of 'overhead' to the per-dispute averages reported in the OECD report. It should also be noted that ISDS costs can be significantly higher than the average figure mentioned above. For example, in the recent *Abaclat* decision on jurisdiction, the claimants had spent some $27 million on their case to date, and Argentina had spent about $12 million (OECD, 2012). These costs were solely for a decision addressing jurisdiction but not the merits. In our own experience, costs for the respondent states and claimants are roughly equivalent on average, albeit with significant variation between cases. This impression is broadly consistent with available evidence.[31]

Moreover, international investment law is currently *not* characterised by reliable a 'loser pays' rule as to costs, and "it is widely recognised that outcomes on cost shifting in ISDS cases are highly uncertain". (OECD, 2012, p. 21). Even when investors are required to pay the costs of the tribunal, considerable legal fees can still be borne by the 'winning' party. In *Plama v Bulgaria*, for instance, Bulgaria had to spend more than $6 million in legal fees in a case the Bulgarian government 'won'.[32]

On the other hand, EU treaty negotiators appear to be considering the inclusion of language on cost shifting in TTIP that would establish a 'loser pays' rule.[33] Depending on the specific text (for example, is cost shifting allowed only for 'frivolous' losing claims or for all losing claims?), the provision – if the US agrees to it – may significantly reduce litigation costs for the EU and its member states,

---

[31] Between $100,000 and $350,000 higher on average, depending on whether outlying cases are excluded from average figures.

[32] *Plama Consortium Limited v. Bulgaria*, ICSID Case No. ARB/03/24, Award, 27 August 2008.

[33] See the European Commission Fact Sheet, "Investment Protection and Investor-to-State Dispute Settlement in EU agreements", November 2013 (http://trade.ec.europa.eu/doclib/docs/2013/november/tradoc_151916.pdf).

either by shifting government expenses to the losing investor, or by discouraging investors from bringing claims in the first place. But it should be realised that a 'loser pays' rule will also leave the EU and its member states potentially liable for the *investors'* legal costs in the event that the US investor wins. Whether a 'loser pays' rule will result in a net benefit or cost to the EU over the status quo of each side pays its own costs will depend on assumptions about the distribution of losers and winners and the likely magnitude of the costs on each sides.

In their commissioned study by the Dutch Government, Tietje & Baetens (2014, p. 75) suggest that the cost to a host state of defending an investor-state arbitration may well be less than the costs of defending the same claim if it had been brought in the courts of the host state. They rightly point out that the costs of the court proceedings themselves (as opposed to the parties' legal costs) are always borne by the state, whereas in arbitration the costs of the tribunal are either divided between the parties or borne by the losing party. Nevertheless, we have doubts that investor-state arbitration is a more cost-effective procedure for resolving disputes, either from the perspective of a host state or from the perspective of society as a whole. In our view, it is impossible to say whether investor-state arbitration is more cost-effective than resolving disputes through national court proceedings in the absence of significantly more comprehensive evidence than is currently available.

First, EU countries will need to maintain court systems regardless of whether they agree to ISDS in TTIP or, indeed, any other investment treaty. This has important implications for how the avoidable cost of resolving disputes through arbitration rather than national courts should be calculated. Regardless of whether ISDS is included in investment treaties, all the fixed costs of maintaining a court system - for example, those associated with the construction of court buildings and the appointment of judges - are already incurred. The only institutional costs avoided through arbitration are the variable costs incurred in relation to the particular dispute in question - for example, the value of the time that judges and other court officials would have spent on the case had it been resolved in court.

Second, the parties' legal and witness costs (party costs) constitute the vast majority of the costs associated with investment treaty arbitration (Hodgson, 2014). Average tribunal costs were $746,000 - less than 10% of the total costs of the proceedings. While we are not aware of any equivalent data in relation to the costs of national court proceedings (which may, in any case, vary significantly by country), the data we have for arbitration suggest that any assessment of the relative costs of arbitration and national court proceedings must take into account any differences between party costs in the different types of proceedings.

Third, there are reasons to think that party costs associated with domestic litigation will generally be lower than those associated with litigating the same dispute through investor-state arbitration. This is because most European countries have well-developed systems of administrative, corporate and contract law. In contrast, arbitration under investment treaties involves the application of vague and imprecise standards, such as the obligation to provide 'fair and equitable treatment'. Lack of clarity in the applicable law is likely to increase the range of factual and legal questions at issue in a dispute, which would tend to increase party costs.

To give an example, a challenge to Australia's tobacco plain-packaging laws, brought by Japan Tobacco International, proceeded to final judgment in Australia's highest court in less than a year from the initiation of the claim. In contrast, by the time of this publication it has taken more than three years for the challenge to Australia's tobacco plain-packaging laws brought to investor-state arbitration by Philip Morris to reach a hearing on *preliminary objections*. While this example is not necessarily representative, it illustrates the need for further evidence about the average party costs of comparable investor-state disputes that are litigated in national courts.

Fourth, Tietje & Baetens (2014, p. 75) suggest that arbitral proceedings are more likely to conclude with a complete and final resolution of a dispute, reducing the costs of subsequent proceedings. We think better evidence is needed before such a claim can be made. Whilst it is normally possible to appeal the decisions of a national court of first instance, it is also possible to challenge the decisions of arbitral tribunals. As Tietje & Baetens note, the decisions of ICSID (International Centre for Settlement of Investment Disputes) tribunals are subject to annulment proceedings under the ICSID Convention. The decisions of non-ICSID tribunals are also subject to challenge in the form of set-aside and recognition proceedings in national courts. In the past, many investor-state arbitral decisions have been the subject of expensive and protracted proceedings in national courts. For example, the award in *BG v Argentina* was the subject of further proceedings in both the US Court of Appeals and the US Supreme Court. Any overall comparison of the costs of proceedings would need to consider the full range of possibilities for further litigation following the decisions of both arbitral tribunals and courts of first instance, the costs of such further proceedings, and the frequency with which these procedural options are pursued.

All in all, we are less than convinced about the claim of Tietje & Baetens that comparable domestic court/law proceedings involve lower costs for the host state than investment arbitration. The claim is impossible to test without comparable data. But given our comments above, there are reasons to expect that it is in fact the other way around.

4.4 Risk of reduced policy space

The inclusion of ISDS-backed investment protections in the TTIP would impose costs on the EU to the extent that it prevents the EU and its member states from regulating in the public interest. This potential cost encompasses both the effect of TTIP on legislative decision-making (e.g. if the existence of ISDS-backed investment protections dissuaded a state from enacting new tobacco control laws) and the effect of TTIP on executive decision-making (e.g. if the existence of ISDS-backed investment protections dissuaded a regulatory agency from shutting down a foreign-owned hazardous waste facility on account of the investor's failure to comply with environmental conditions attached to its operating permit). We use the term 'policy space' to refer to this potential cost.

Assessing the extent of this cost raises two initial conceptual difficulties. The first of these stems from the fact that the EU itself and the EU member states are already bound by their own systems of law. Insofar as the TTIP 'constrains' the EU and its member states from adopting or applying policy measures that are, in any event, prohibited by other laws, no 'policy space' is lost. A useful first approximation is the principle that investment treaties only restrict a state's policy space insofar as they prohibit the EU and the member states state from acting in a way that would otherwise be permissible. Therefore, any assessment of political costs associated with TTIP must begin with a close legal analysis of the provisions of the TTIP in light of comparable provisions of EU law,[34] and the law of the member states. However, this is only a starting point for the analysis. Constitutional principles aside, national laws are subject to regular change, whereas the terms of TTIP would be exceedingly difficult to amend.

---

[34] For an example of such an exercise focusing specifically on EU law, see Kleinheisterkamp (2012).

A second conceptual issue concerns valuation of the 'cost' that the additional restrictions imposed by an investment treaty would place on the member state's policy space. One of the most contentious issues in existing legal and academic debates about investment treaties is whether the constraints they impose on the exercise of government powers should be understood as 'costs' or, rather, as standards of 'good governance' that it would be in the interest of every state to meet, even in the absence of investment treaties (Bonnitcha, 2014, sec. 2.4.3). This debate raises complex and contested questions about the manner and extent in which governments should intervene in their economies. In this chapter we do not propose an overarching theory of desirable and undesirable forms of government regulation. All the member states of the EU are democracies. We suggest that, in a democracy, the appropriate benchmark for valuing the cost associated with any restriction on policy space is the government of the day's own assessment of the public interest. Accordingly, the impact of TTIP's investment protection provisions on EU policy space can be understood as the extent to which the treaty prevents the EU and the EU member states from adopting or applying policies that the relevant government would have preferred to apply in the absence of the treaty.

Assessing the likely size of this cost raises many of the same issues that were considered in our assessment of the likely economic cost of adverse arbitral awards under TTIP. Given the sheer size of the stock of US investment in the EU, the likelihood of disputes between US investors and the EU and its member states is high. The composition of US investment in the EU is also potentially relevant because investments in particular sectors have proven more likely to result in investment treaty disputes in the past. We note that there are substantial stocks of US investment spread across almost every sector of the EU economy, including sectors that have proven particularly prone to investment treaty claims in the past.

In reconciling our assessment of the political costs associated with lost policy space under an EU-US investment treaty and our assessment of the economic costs associated with adverse arbitral awards, it is important to acknowledge the risk of double-counting the same costs. If the EU and the EU member states fully comply with their obligations under TTIP, they would not incur any economic costs as a result of adverse arbitral awards. However, they may refrain from regulating in ways that they would otherwise regard as desirable. In contrast, if the EU and the EU member states ignore the risk of claims under TTIP, they will not suffer from any reduction in policy space *in practice.* They would, instead, expose themselves to the risk of economic costs associated with adverse arbitral awards. In practice, we think the risk of ISDS is likely to affect the behaviour of EU member states in a way that falls somewhere between these two extreme scenarios.

There are other ways in which the treaty could affect EU policy space. We have noted the size of US outward FDI stocks in the EU and the fact that US investors seem particularly likely to rely on their legal rights as a bargaining tool. If TTIP did include ISDS, we expect that the EU and its member states would be regularly faced with US investors opposing new policies on the grounds of the treaty. This opposition could be expressed either through lobbying, through submissions to government inquiries or by initiating arbitration proceedings under the treaty. To the extent that these activities encouraged EU decision-makers to modify or abandon preferred measures, it would count as a political cost of the treaty. In assessing the ability of US investors to persuade the EU or its member states to modify or abandon preferred policies, two considerations are relevant: the quality of legal advice available to the EU and its members states' decision-makers; and the extent to which the EU-US investment treaty grants US investors greater rights than they would otherwise have under relevant EU and national law.

We do not have access to any direct measure of the quality of legal advice available to EU member states. It may be that there is a degree of variation in the internal legal capacity of member states. We would expect member states with stronger internal legal capacity to be better placed to manage tactical use of threats of litigation by US investors, insofar as those threats lack legal foundation.

On the other hand, the availability of high-quality legal advice may make governments of the member states *more* likely to amend or withdraw policies when those policies raise serious risks of non-compliance with the investment protection provisions of TTIP. A clear example of this phenomenon is the recent announcement by New Zealand relating to its policy on tobacco plain-packaging. While the New Zealand government has made it clear that its preferred policy would be to introduce tobacco plain-packaging, in light of legal objections raised by tobacco companies it has decided to delay the enactment of legislation until after the investment treaty claim concerning Australian tobacco plain-packaging, *Philip Morris v Australia*, has been resolved (Turia, 2013; Wilson, 2014). Similarly, in *SD Myers v Canada* the Canadian government revoked a ban on hazardous waste exports to the US after a US investor initiated arbitration.[35] The Canadian government judged – correctly as it turned out – that it was likely that the measure would be found to be inconsistent with NAFTA. A third example of this potential political cost associated with investment treaties is the case of *Ethyl v Canada*, a claim brought by a US investor under NAFTA. It seems that this claim played at least some role in encouraging the Canadian government to abandon the environmental measure that was the subject of the dispute (Tienhaara, 2009). The settlement agreement required the payment of damages (as noted above) and the withdrawal of the measure, thereby entailing both economic and political costs to Canada.[36] In short, in circumstances where a foreign investor opposes a preferred government policy on the basis of an investment treaty, and where that policy is at serious risk of non-compliance with the investment treaty, developed states comparable to the EU member states have amended, delayed or withdrawn preferred policies.

In this light, the second question – the extent to which TTIP would grant US investors in the EU more generous legal rights than they would otherwise have under relevant EU and national laws – assumes particular importance. In earlier sections of this chapter we observed that an EU-US investment treaty would likely follow the US model BIT in including text that limits and clarifies the substantive protections provided by the treaty. These clarifications redress some of the most obvious ways in which an EU-US investment chapter could confer greater rights on US investors that are otherwise available under the law of some EU member states – notably, some of the broader interpretations of the doctrine of 'legitimate expectations' adopted by earlier arbitral tribunals. Nevertheless, in our section on Economic Costs, we identified particular ways in which an EU-US investment treaty would still grant US investors legal rights that they would not otherwise have in particular member states, referring to the example of the UK. For example, this could strengthen the bargaining position of US investors in negotiations to settle contractual disputes with the EU member states.

---

[35] *SD Myers v Canada* Partial Award, 13 November 2000.

[36] There are some complications in assessing the extent of political cost implied by the events surrounding the Ethyl case, as the abandoned measure, in its original form, was also ruled inconsistent with Canadian law.

4.5   Risk of controversial claims

Another potential political cost concerns the possibility that high profile claims against EU member states may provoke controversy within domestic political systems. Disputes resolved through investor-state arbitration may be the subject of public controversy especially if the investor's claims or the arbitral tribunal's decision are seen as threatening the government's policy space in sensitive areas.

The evaluation of this potential cost should of course be handled with great caution. In a democratic society, the fact that a policy, judicial decision or – in the present circumstances – a claim before an arbitral tribunal becomes the subject of popular debate and controversy should not be understood as constituting a cost in itself. Disagreement about public affairs is a normal and healthy incident in democratic government. Nevertheless, if the controversy around a *specific* claim against a party triggers widespread opposition to treaties and international cooperation *in general*, then in extreme cases this backlash could limit the ability of the government of the day to pursue preferred policies on the international plane.

US investors have brought controversial claims against other developed countries arising from: banking regulation (*Genin v Estonia*); domestic ownership and domestic content requirements on media organisations (*CME v Czech Republic*); regulation of the trans-boundary movement of hazardous waste (*SD Myers v Canada*); regulation of national monopolies (*UPS v Canada*); the ability of private health providers to operate alongside a host state's public health system (*Howard and Centurion Health v Canada*); the phasing out of carcinogenic pesticides (*Chemtura v Canada*); invalidation of patent rights (*Eli Lilli v Canada*); and plain-packaging regulation (*Philip Morris v Australia,* via Hong Kong BIT). While the majority of these claims were resolved in favour of respondent governments, the fact that US investors are known to frequently bring controversial claims is important, as a particularly sensitive case can provoke a broader political backlash. EU investors, as well, have brought numerous highly controversial claims arising from, for instance, affirmative action policies (*Foresti et al. v South Africa*); reactions to financial crises (*Marfin v Cyprus & Postova banka and Istrokapital v Greece*); and the phase-out of nuclear energy (*Vattenfall v Germany*).

The US government itself has realised that sensitive claims can result in a political backlash. When a Canadian company, Loewen, filed a NAFTA claim concerning its treatment by a Mississippi state court, one of the arbitrators was told informally by the US Department of Justice that "if we lose this case, we could lose NAFTA".[37] Similarly, if a US investor seeks to override an act of one or more European parliaments, or files a claim concerning sensitive areas of public regulation, such as environmental or public health regulation, this could potentially provoke a political response with systemic consequences for the ability of the EU to support investor-state arbitration in agreements where it is more necessary than in the TTIP. Perhaps an even-greater risk is the possibility that controversy about investor-state claims could reduce the level of political support within the EU for international economic cooperation on matters where the potential benefits are much greater – for example, trade liberalisation.

5.   Conclusion

Based on our analysis, we conclude that including an investment protection chapter in TTIP that is accompanied by ISDS is unlikely to generate significant economic or political benefits for the EU. Our analysis also suggests that the inclusion of such provisions would lead to significant economic and political costs for the EU. While it is important not to exaggerate the scale of potential costs, our overall assessment is that the costs are highly likely to exceed any potential benefit to the EU. Accordingly, we would suggest that unless ISDS is accompanied by considerable concessions by the United States so as to offset ISDS-related costs, it would be prudent for the EU to consider alternatives.

One of the authors has previously recommended a number of pragmatic proposals – such as relying on inter-state dispute settlement or, at a minimum, restricting recourse to investment arbitration through a significant local litigation requirement and a comprehensive state 'filter' of claims (Kleinheisterkamp & Poulsen, 2014). If such proposals fail to attain support, another option would be to simply exclude investment protections from the agreement. The economic benefits of a transatlantic free trade agreement could be considerable for the EU, as outlined elsewhere in this volume, but hardly any of those benefits are likely to accrue from the investment protection chapter. Excluding such a chapter may thereby be politically prudent if it prevents further opposition to the TTIP based on a set of rules which are not necessary to protect American investment in Europe or European investment in the United States.

---

[37] See the discussion in Schneiderman (2010).

References

APEC (2011), "2010 Guide to Investment Regimes of APEC Member Countries", 2nd revised edition, APEC Secretariat, Asia-Pacific Economic Cooperation, Singapore.

Berger, Axel and Lauge Poulsen (2015), "The Transatlantic Trade and Investment Partnership, investor-state dispute settlement and China", *Columbia FDI Perspectives*, No. 140.

Bonnitcha, Jonathan (2014), *Substantive Protection under Investment Treaties: A Legal and Economic Analysis*, Cambridge: Cambridge University Press.

Burke-White, William and Andreas Von Staden (2008), "Investment Protection in Extraordinary Times: The Interpretation and Application of Non-Precluded Measures Provisions in Bilateral Investment Treaties", *Virginia Journal of International Law*, 48.

Caplan, Lee M. and Jeremy K. Sharpe (2013), "United States", in Chester Brown (ed.), *Commentaries on Selected Investment Treaties*, Oxford: Oxford University Press.

CFIUS (Committee on Foreign Investment in the United States) (2012), Annual Report to Congress, Washington, D.C.

Craig, Paul (2012), *Administrative Law*, Oxford: Oxford University Press.

European Commission (2021), Draft Financial Responsibility Regulation, COM(2012) 335 final, 2012/0163 (COD), 21 June.

_____ (2015a), "Online public consultation on investment protection and investor-to-state dispute settlement (ISDS) in the Transatlantic Trade and Investment Partnership Agreement", Brussels, 13.1.2015, SWD(2015) 3.

_____ (2015b), "The 2015 EU Justice Scoreboard", Brussels, COM(2015) 116.

European Union Chamber of Commerce in China (2013), *Business Confidence Survey*, available at: www.europeanchamber. com.cn

Fagan, David (2010), "'The U.S. Regulatory and Institutional Framework for FDI", in Karl Sauvant (ed.), *Investing in the United States: Is the U.S. Ready for FDI from China?*, Cheltenham: Edward Elgar.

Franck, Susan (2007), "Empirically Evaluating Claims about Investment Treaty Arbitration", *North Carolina Law Review*, 86.

_____ (2011), "Rationalizing Costs in Investment Treaty Arbitration", *Washington University Law Review*, 88.

Gallagher, Kevin and Elen Shrestha (2011), "Investment Treaty Arbitration and Developing Countries: A Re-Appraisal", Working Paper No. 11-01, Global Development and Environment Institute, Tufts University, Somerville, MA.

Gallagher, Norah and Wenhua Shan (2009), *Chinese Investment Treaties*, Oxford: Oxford University Press.

Hamilton, Daniel and Joseph Quinlan (2014), *The Transatlantic Economy 2014*, Center for Transatlantic Relations, Johns Hopkins University. Washington, D.C.

Hodgson, Matthew (2012), *Counting the Costs of Investment Treaty Arbitration*, Allen & Overy.

Kläger, Roland (2011), *Fair and Equitable Treatment in International Investment Law*, Cambridge: Cambridge University Press.

Kleinheisterkamp, Jan (2012), "European Policy Space in International Investment Law", *ICSID* Review, 27:2.

Kleinheisterkamp, Jan and Lauge Poulsen (2014), "'Investment Protection in TTIP: Three Feasible Proposals", Policy Brief, Global Economic Governance Program, University of Oxford.

Maurer, Noel (2013), *Empire Trap*, Princeton, NJ: Princeton University Press.

Maupin, Julie (2013), "Where Should Europe's Investment Path Lead? Reflections on August Reinisch, Quo Vadis Europe?", *Santa Clara Journal of International* Law, 12:183.

OECD (2012), "Scoping Paper for Investor-State Dispute Settlement Public Consultation" (oecd.org/investment/internationalinvestmentagreements/50291642.pdf).

Paparinskis, Martins (2012), "Limits of Depoliticization in Contemporary Investor-State Arbitration," *Select Proceedings E Soc Int'l L* 3:271.

Peinhardt, Clint and Todd Allee (2012), "Failure to Deliver: The Investment Effects of US Preferential Economic Agreements", *World Economy*, 35:6.

Poulsen, Lauge (2010), "The Importance of BITs for Foreign Direct Investment and Political Risk Insurance: Revisiting the Evidence", *Yearbook on International Investment Law & Policy 2009-2010*, Oxford: Oxford University Press.

Poulsen, Lauge, Jonathan Bonnitcha and Jason Yackee (2013), "Costs and Benefits of an EU-China Investment Treaty", study prepared for the UK Department for Business Innovation and Skills, November (www.gov.uk/government/publications/costs-and-benefits-to-the-uk-of-an-eu-china-investment-protection-treaty).

Reinisch, August (2013), "The EU on the Investment Path – Quo Vadis Europe?", *Santa Clara Journal of International* Law, 12:111.

Schneiderman, David (2010), "Judicial Politics and International Investment Arbitration: Seeking an Explanation for Conflicting Outcomes", *Northwestern Journal of International and Business Law*, 30.

Shihata, Ibrahim F.I. (1986), "Towards a greater depoliticization of investment disputes", *ICSID Review*, Vol. 1, No. 1.

Tienhaara, Kyla (2009), *The Expropriation of Environmental Governance*, Cambridge: Cambridge University Press.

Tietje, Christian and Freya Baetens (2014), "The Impact of Investor-State-Dispute Settlement (ISDS) in the Transatlantic Trade and Investment Partnership", study commissioned by the Ministry for Foreign Trade and Development Cooperation, Ministry of Foreign Affairs, The Netherlands.

Turia, Tariana (2013), "Government moves forward with plain packaging of tobacco products", *Beehive.govt.nz: The Official Website of the New Zealand Government*, 19 February.

UKTI (UK Trade and Investment) (2013), "Establishing a business presence in the USA", London.

UNCTAD (2014), *World Investment Report 2014*, Geneva: United Nations.

Vandevelde, Kenneth J. (2009), *U.S. International Investment Agreements*, Oxford: Oxford University Press.

_____ (2010), *Bilateral Investment Treaties: History, Policy and Interpretation*, Oxford: Oxford University Press.

Wilson, Peter (2014), "Plain packaging bill passes first reading," available at: www.3news.co.nz.

Yackee, Jason W. (2010), "Do Bilateral Investment Treaties Promote Foreign Direct Investment? Some Hints from Alternative Sources of Evidence", *Virginia Journal of International Law*, 51:2.

_____ (2014), "Political Risk and International Investment Law", *Duke Journal of Comparative and International Law*, 24:3.

6. TRANSATLANTIC INVESTMENT TREATY PROTECTION – A RESPONSE TO POULSEN, BONNITCHA & YACKEE

*FREYA BAETENS**

1. Introduction

A number of preliminary comments apply to the *Poulsen, Bonnitcha & Yackee* chapter as a whole: firstly, while its focus on investor-state dispute settlement (ISDS) is valid, it is important to keep in mind that there is more to the investment chapter in TTIP than solely its dispute settlement clause. As such, it would be productive for future work to address how the bulk of the investment chapter, namely its substantive standards, could be improved upon. Secondly, the authors chose not to cover pre-establishment national treatment – a regrettable exclusion, as this might well be included in the final text of the agreement, following the US approach in its other investment treaties. Furthermore, the authors' assumption that post-establishment investment protection will be enforceable by way of ISDS is not necessarily correct, in light of the ongoing debate of the issue, and as such it would have been interesting to conduct a cost-benefit analysis of investment protection in TTIP *without* an ISDS clause, if only to assess whether this is a viable option.

* This chapter is intended as a response to the thought-provoking ideas presented in chapter 5 by Lauge Paulson, Jonathan Bonnitcha and Jason Webb Yackee, focusing on some of their findings that are open to discussion and structuring the arguments made below along the lines of their chapter. As such, the present chapter does not intend to raise any new topics in this debate but serves only as a response to the original chapter.

The author would like to express her gratitude to Sophie Starrenburg for her assistance in preparing this chapter.

2. Treaty provisions: The likely content of the 'I' in 'TTIP'

Poulsen, Bonnitcha & Yackee offer an overview of US practice in negotiating investment treaties, for example drawing attention to the prudential measures taken to ensure its ability to regulate the finance sector, but also including references to safeguard domestic labour laws and the environment in order to preserve the host-state's policy space. Another pertinent example is the manner in which the 'minimum standard of treatment' is defined in Annex A of the US model BIT as "the customary international law minimum standard of treatment of aliens". However, one aspect of this practice – relevant when it comes to assessing the legitimacy and desirability of such treaties – is *not* mentioned, namely the fact that the US has been among the first states to include provisions concerning an ISDS appeals mechanism in several investment agreements (Annex 10-H of the US-Chile FTA, Annex 10-F of CAFTA, and the 2012 US model BIT). Admittedly, none of these proposals has yet materialised, but the foundation stones have been laid, making clear that the US is open to creating such a mechanism.

One further aspect of US practice – the transparency of ISDS proceedings as for example adopted in NAFTA Chapter 11 disputes – is only cursorily mentioned. However, this increased level of transparency might prove vital in the future, as "justice should not only be done: it must also be seen to be done", and this will contribute to the legitimacy of the entire ISDS process.

3. Potential benefits of ISDS

Poulsen, Bonnitcha & Yackee note that the benefits of TTIP could materialise in two possible ways: firstly, by promoting US investment in the EU; and secondly, by protecting EU investment in the US.

3.1 Protection of US investment in the EU

On the question of whether TTIP – or any other investment agreement – will promote US investment in the EU, the authors argue that past practice has shown that investment treaties with investment protection chapters have negligibly (or not at all) affected investment flows. As such, TTIP would not provide much benefit to the EU in terms of higher investment rates by the US, as the region is already considered 'safe' from the perspective of US investors. However, this argument is made on the basis of limited empirical evidence, and such evidence often cuts both ways: for every study that claims that there is a significant economic benefit that can be gained by the inclusion of an investment chapter,[1] another can be found that says that this is not the case.[2]

In any event, just because there may be no impressive increase in FDI as a result of the conclusion of a BIT, this does not mean that BITs are valueless. They may not be a direct gateway to massively increased investment rates, but rather a tool that is considered by a given company as part of its investment strategy. Ultimately, a company's decision to invest in a country will be based upon a range of factors about the country or region in which they are seeking to invest, of which the availability of ISDS is one, serving as a "confidence and credibility-inspiring signal".[3]

There are several other aspects of this discussion that merit further mention. Firstly, *Poulsen, Bonnitcha & Yackee* argue that the types of risks an investment protection chapter would cover are generally not considered present in most EU member states. However, one type of risk that is certainly present in several EU member states relates to the possibility of not being granted a fair trial before a domestic court. According to a recent country ranking of 'judicial independence' performed by the World Economic Forum,[4] some EU countries are among the best in the world (Finland and Denmark are in the top five), but others perform rather poorly (Slovakia ranks at 130 out of 140, Bulgaria at 126) – at place 30, the US is still below countries with which ISDS is planned to be concluded, such as Canada (place 9) or Singapore (at 20), or with which it can be expected to be concluded, such as Uruguay (at 21) or Saudi Arabia (at 26). The extensive jurisprudence of the European Court of Human Rights shows that some EU member states such as Italy, France and Germany have repeatedly violated Article 6 of the European Convention on Human Rights through their

---

[1] See e.g. Sauvant & Sachs *(2009)*; UNCTAD (1998), Banga (2003), Tobin & Rose-Ackerman (2006), Salacuse & Sullivan (2005), Neumayer & Spess (2005), Aisbett (2007) and Busse et al. (2008).

[2] See e.g. Hallward-Driemaier (2003), Tobin & Rose-Ackerman (2003) and Gallagher & Birch (2006).

[3] Interview with Eric Neumayer, Kevin P. Gallagher and Horchani Ferhat at www.iisd.org/itn/2009/04/30/do-bilateral-investment-treaties-lead-to-more-foreign-investment/;

[4] See http://reports.weforum.org/global-competitiveness-report-2014-2015/rankings/

inability to provide a hearing and/or a decision within a 'reasonable time'.[5] This also shows why investors may prefer international arbitration: in the large majority of cases, a final decision will be rendered much sooner than if such disputes were to be decided through the domestic court system.

Secondly, the authors mostly focus on whether US or Chinese investors consider the EU a safe place to invest, but do not address whether the converse is true.

Thirdly, *Poulsen, Bonnitcha & Yackee* rely upon a 2010 survey of legal counsel within the 100 largest American multinationals in order to underscore their argument that investment treaties have little impact on investment flows, given that the majority of counsel stated that these treaties did not play a (critical) role in their decisions to invest abroad. However, the ISDS system is not employed to a great extent by the large multinationals, but rather by middle-sized or smaller ones. An OECD survey concluded that 22% of all ISDS claims are brought by individuals or "very small corporations".[6] Medium and large multinational companies account for 50% of the claims, and the rest of the cases (28%) were brought by investors about which there is little public information. The fact that larger companies do not rely as frequently upon ISDS as one might expect due to their relative size, is arguably because the largest companies have other means of leverage,

---

[5] See, e.g. landmark cases: *H. v. France*, 24 October 1989, Series A no. 162-A; *X. v. France*, 31 March 1992, Series A no. 234-C; *Caloc v. France*, no. 33951/96, ECHR 2000-IX; *Kress v. France* [GC] no 39594/98, ECHR 2001-VI; *Frydlender v. France*, [GC] no 30979/96, ECHR 2000-VII; *Katte Klitsche de la Grange v. Italy*, 24 October 1994, Series A, no 293-B; *Scordino v. Italy (no. 1)* [GC] no 36813/97, ECHR 2006-V; *Capuano v. Italy*, 25 June 1987, Series A no. 119; *Bottazzi v. Italy*, [GC] no 34884/97, ECHR 1999-V; *Di Pede v. Italy*, 26 September 1996, ECHR 1996-IV; *Vocaturo v. Italy*, 24 May 1991, Series A no. 206-C; *Cappello v. Italy*, 27 February 1992, Series A no. 230-F; *Fisanotti v. Italy*, 23 April 1998, ECHR 1998-II; *Bock v. Germany*, 29 March 1989, Series A no. 150; *Pammel v. Germany*, 1 July 1997, ECHR 1997-IV; *Probstmeier v. Germany*, 1 July 1997, ECHR 1997-IV; *Sürmeli v. Germany*, [GC] no 75529/01, ECHR 2006-VII; *Blake v. UK*, no 68890/01, 26 September 2006; *Robins v. UK*, no. 22410/93, 23 September 1997; *H. v. UK*, 8 July 1997, ECHR 1997-VIII. For a more complete overview see European Court of Human Rights, *Guide to Article 6 – Right to a Fair Trial* (2013) p. 51 et seq.

[6] OECD (2012), "Investor-State Dispute Settlement", Public Consultation Doc, p. 16 (www.oecd.org/investment/internationalinvestmentagreements/50291642.pdf).

and thus do not need to resort to the courts in order to achieve their goals.

This author agrees with *Poulsen, Bonnitcha & Yackee* that, in Europe, BITs have not been widely publicised or 'politicised' – at least not until quite recently. It is important that the public is informed of the role that BITs play in the international realm, as the current level of knowledge about these instruments – even amongst media and NGOs claiming to specialise in this area – is shockingly low. This is dangerous because they play such an important role in informing civil society – as was evident by their impact on the recent consultation of the European Commission. There, many of the replies to the survey circulated by the Commission indicated fears that ISDS inclusion in TTIP would place too great a limit on states' policy space. However, the majority of these replies "were based on copy-and-paste templates circulated by non-governmental organisations campaigning against TTIP",[7] much like pressing a 'dislike' button on Facebook or signing an online petition, without the need for any actual knowledge or substantiated contribution to the debate. Such tactics are not new; they were applied by Philip Morris in order to allege that public opinion was against the EU Tobacco Products Directive[8] – an example which suggests that mass automatic replies ought to be interpreted cautiously.

3.2 Protection of EU investment in the US

Turning to the second strand of *Poulsen, Bonnitcha & Yackee*'s argument – whether TTIP will protect EU investment in the US – several comments can be made. The authors argue that TTIP is unlikely to improve the situation for EU investors in the US, because, in general, the protection level of foreign investors in the US is already high, and TTIP will not offer much additional protection. In general, it is indeed true that there is no evidence of systematic, serious flaws in the US system. But do *Poulsen, Bonnitcha & Yackee* mean to state that domestic courts should deal with all private claims in countries where the rule of law is strong, to the exclusion of international judicial review?

Following this line of reasoning to its logical conclusion, they should in that case also be advocating the abolishment of the various regional courts for human rights as the legal systems of the European

---

[7] C. Olivier, "Public Backlash Threatens EU Trade Deal with the US", *Financial Times*, 13 January 2015.

[8] See e.g. article at: www.theguardian.com/society/2013/jun/07/tobacco-firm-stealth-marketing-plain-packaging

member states and the US already contain strong human rights protection. The only difference would be that the European Convention on Human Rights for example, does require applicants to exhaust local remedies – as a result, there can easily be 10-15 years or more between the injury and the remedy. However, an argument could be made for allowing a state to first attempt to address a violation in relation to a protected investment via its own court system and only if this does not result in an appropriate solution within an acceptable time frame (for example, two years after bringing a claim), the investor could revert to an international tribunal. This option is further discussed below, in the Conclusions.

To state that domestic courts should 'suffice' for the handling of investment claims overlooks the fact that many domestic courts are not allowed – meaning that it is not within their legal scope of jurisdictional competence – to apply public international law, such as BITs, directly. Moreover, US courts that are in theory allowed to do so have a track record of nevertheless not accepting any claims of individuals based on any form of international law.[9] (Indeed, the same is true in Europe.[10] For example, on 13 January 2015, the Grand Chamber of the European Court of Justice held, inter alia, that the NGO *Stichting Natuur en Milieu* was not entitled to invoke the Aarhus Convention of 1998 on access to information, public participation, and access to justice in environmental matters, in spite of an explicit reference in the EU regulation implementing this Convention.[11] Importantly, this was decided upon at the request of the European Commission, Council and Parliament – some members of which are now arguing that investment protection standards in international treaties should be enforced by domestic and EU courts. Why would private investors be allowed to rely upon international treaties before such courts, while NGOs are not?)

Hence stating that "the appropriate response by the EU would be to insist in its negotiations that the US pass implementing legislation securing a right to access US courts for certain TTIP violations", as

---

[9] See e.g. Haljan (2014), Wojcik (2013) and Hix (2013).

[10] See Bronckers (2015).

[11] Joined cases C-404/12 P and C-405/12 P, *Council of the European Union and European Commission v Stichting Natuur en Milieu and Pesticide Action Network Europe*, Judgment of the Court (Grand Chamber) of 13 January 2015, not yet published (Court Reports - general).

Poulsen, Bonnitcha & Yackee do, shows a lack of knowledge about US negotiation policy and the actual practice of domestic courts. Looking at US practice concerning domestic enforcement of individual rights under international treaties,[12] it is highly unlikely that the US would ever agree to pass legislation that would make substantive treaty standards domestically enforceable. For example, the US only ratified the International Covenant on Civil and Political Rights on the condition that its standards would not be enforceable before US courts.[13] In practice, if substantive protection for investors is included in TTIP, the only option of redress for violations of such standards would be through some form of international dispute settlement mechanism.

Another common misconception is that investment arbitration is consistently more expensive than national court proceedings; this is not necessarily the case. *Poulsen, Bonnitcha & Yackee* argue that "it is impossible to say whether investor-state arbitration is more cost-effective than resolving disputes through national court proceedings in the absence of significantly more comprehensive evidence than is currently available". But they proceed to examine precisely that question, making four points. First, EU countries will need to maintain court systems regardless of whether they agree to ISDS. That may be so, but referring more cases (and in particular, more complex cases concerning matters in which domestic judges are not specialised) to domestic courts, already overburdened and prone to delays, is not an obvious remedy.

Secondly, it is true that the parties' legal and witness costs constitute the vast majority of costs associated with investment treaty arbitration (although tribunal costs are not negligible either). For this reason, the 'loser pays' principle, whereby the claimant who brings a manifestly unfounded claim has to reimburse the state's legal and witness costs, would form a valuable safeguard – one that cannot be offered under most domestic court systems (including the US). In *Chemtura*, to take a salutary example, the unsuccessful claimant was ordered to pay Canada's costs, including an allowance for the time

---

[12] See Powell (2001, p. 245); Roth (2001, p. 891); Spiro (1997, p. 567); Kaye (2013, p. 95).

[13] International Covenant on Civil and Political Rights, adopted 16 December 1966, S. Exec. Doc. E, 95-2 (1978) 999 UNTS 171, ratified by the US 8 June 1992.

invested by government officials in preparing Canada's defence.[14]
Other cases in point are *ADC v Hungary, Plama v Bulgaria, Europe Cement v Turkey,* and *Gemplus v Mexico.*[15]

Thirdly, arbitrators who are specialised in the interpretation of 'vague and imprecise' standards should have less trouble deciding the factual and legal questions in an investment dispute than local judges would have who would be called upon to decide such cases (particularly if investment standards would be 'copied and pasted' into national legislation, as the authors seem to envisage). This is not to say that some investment standards such as 'fair and equitable treatment' or 'indirect expropriation' as such would not benefit from the incorporation of more clearly defined standards. Additionally, if treaty standards would have to be implemented in national legislation, this risks exacerbating interpretation problems due to the well-known problem of translation differences across the EU.[16] The same standard in Portuguese, for example, may be interpreted by local courts as meaning something different in Latvian – thereby nullifying the stability and predictability that a uniform treaty could bring.

Finally, in the majority of cases, arbitral proceedings offer a complete and final resolution of a dispute. Under any ISDS system, except the one set up by International Centre for Settlement of Investment Disputes (ICSID), annulment and appeal are not possible. The ICSID system cannot be included in TTIP because the EU, as a regional organisation is not, and cannot, be a member of the Convention; but even if it were, its annulment procedure is intended to be rare and limited to five strictly defined grounds,[17] unlike an appeal before a national court which reviews the entire case. In most countries, even an appeal is not the end of the dispute: there is a possibility to ask for a third consideration of the case before a supreme court or court of cassation. Furthermore, arbitral awards and national court decisions

---

[14] *Chemtura Corporation v. Government of Canada,* UNCITRAL (formerly *Crompton Corporation v. Government of Canada*) 2 August 2010.

[15] *ADC Affiliate Limited and ADC & ADMC Management Limited v. The Republic of Hungary,* ICSID Case No. ARB/03/16, 2 October 2006; *Plama Consortium Limited v. Republic of Bulgaria,* ICSID Case No. ARB/03/24, 27 August 2008; *Europe Cement Investment & Trade S.A. v. Republic of Turkey,* ICSID Case No. ARB(AF)/07/2, 13 August 2009; *Gemplus S.A., SLP S.A., Gemplus Industrial S.A. de C.V. v. The United Mexican States,* ICSID Case No. ARB(AF)/04/3 16 June 2010.

[16] See for example, Künnecke (2013, pp. 243-260) and Pozzo (2006).

[17] Article 52 of the ICSID Convention.

alike can subsequently be subjected to review as soon as the claimant attempts to enforce them in a different country – so there is no difference in this regard. Admittedly, annulment procedures have become more frequent in recent years and as the European Commission proposal for TTIP is putting forward the inclusion of an appeal mechanism, the gap in time and cost is, in this respect, narrowing.

4.   Potential costs

In their fourth section, *Poulsen, Bonnitcha & Yackee* posit that the costs of the agreement significantly outweigh any possible benefits to the EU in general. However, this argument is not systematically supported by evidence and appears to be based on a number of challengeable extrapolations. Firstly, they argue that the likelihood of claims against the EU can be expected to increase roughly in proportion with the size of the investment stock in the EU covered by the treaty, but do not properly underscore why this would be this case. The authors make a number of further claims in their chapter, without specifying how they arrived at or calculated them, such as the fact that a great number of investment projects are of sufficient size to make the economics of an investment claim viable in theory; or that, with respect to sectors, US companies have made significant investments across virtually all sectors of the EU economy.

They also state that an investment treaty with the US would be disadvantageous given that 'American' investors tend to be the most litigious. This statement is, however, outdated; in 2013, it was investors from the Netherlands, Germany, Luxembourg and the United States that brought the largest number of claims. This also corresponds with overall trends throughout the history of ISDS.[18] By the end of 2013, US investors had brought 125 claims against states, followed by the Netherlands (61), the United Kingdom (42) and Germany (39). Comparing US investor claims to all EU investor claims helps put this hypothesis into perspective – six of the top ten home states for investors are member states of the European Union, which have brought a total of 225 claims.

Poulsen, Bonnitcha & Yackee note that there remain several important factors that would increase the risk of adverse awards, one of which is the fact that certain important terms within investment law remain undefined (such as 'fair and equitable treatment') and are thus capable of being interpreted expansively by an arbitral tribunal in a

---

[18] Tietje & Baetens (2014, p. 26).

manner unfavourable to the EU. Whilst this is true, one must pause to consider the other alternative: would this situation not be as bad if such treaty provisions were to be interpreted by various domestic courts?

The mere fact that arbitral tribunals have significant discretion to interpret the terms of investment law should not be an argument against the conclusion of an investment treaty, as this role is also performed by domestic judges – interpretation is what adjudicatory bodies do for a living. Another option would be through state-to-state dispute settlement, i.e. espousal of investors' claims by their home state. However, it was precisely to prevent the problems arising from the essentially political and arbitrary character of espousal that ISDS procedures as well as human rights adjudicatory bodies were created, establishing private standing for injured individuals.

Poulsen, Bonnitcha & Yackee furthermore argue that the legal costs of investment disputes are disproportionately high, even if the respondent state 'wins' the case. As stated above, several tribunals have recently adopted some form of the 'loser pays' approach, ordering the losing party not only to bear all arbitration costs of an adverse award, but also to make a substantial contribution to the winning party's legal fees – in particular when a case concerns a frivolous claim. This approach has also been taken in the discussions surrounding the Comprehensive Economic and Trade Agreement (CETA) between the EU and Canada, where frivolous claims can be terminated at an early stage in proceedings, and generally the unsuccessful party is required to cover all the costs made in the process of a case.[19] Ultimately, even if the costs of ISDS are considered too high, there are ways of lowering them. One could think of negotiating the fees with the registry office and arbitrators, or capping lawyers' fees and negotiating an hourly rate – given that the market for arbitrators and lawyers is sufficiently saturated in order to survive a payment cap.

Two risks are raised as possible political costs of TTIP: i) the risk of reduced policy space, and ii) the risk of controversial claims or adverse awards. Particularly the first emerged as one of the main grounds of concern in the results from the recent consultations on TTIP conducted by the European Commission. The results from these consultations indicated that one of the most prevalent fears amongst

---

[19] Kuijper (2014, p. 111).

respondents was the perceived negative effects that the inclusion of ISDS in TTIP would have on national sovereignty.[20]

Essentially, all obligations that a state undertakes, 'limit' its policy space: promising to do A, may affect how one can do B. Also, governments will not infrequently wait with the enactment of new legislation until the result of a domestic or EU court case emerges, the same as if a state would postpone a certain measure pending the outcome of an arbitral award. Investment claims are mostly brought against executive decisions made with respect to one particular investor or in the context of a particular concession, permission or promise granted to an investor, *not* against legislative acts (with a limited number of notorious exceptions). When looking at all ISDS disputes, the respondent states have *won* in approximately 60% of the cases.[21] In the few cases where claims have been brought against acts of legislation, the investor quasi-invariably ended up on the losing side, as tribunals recognised and protected the policy space and the right to regulate of the respondent state.[22] As such, the inclusion of ISDS would not threaten or reduce policy space, because most arbitral awards would not encroach upon it.

An example of this was the *Vattenfall/Germany* arbitration, where the government first granted licenses to a coal plant (which resulted in the awarding of voluntary damages to the investor) and for a nuclear plant (of which the case is still pending), and subsequently retracted these licences.[23] These cases have not had a measurable impact on Germany's environmental regulations – only on the procedures followed with regards to transparency in the decision-making process (benefitting not only investors but also other stakeholders), as well as the fact that 'disclaimers' are now incorporated into any licenses granted by the state; such developments could hardly be seen as negative. Even if there is an adverse award, one must recall that the state will *not* be forced to make any changes in policy: a tribunal can only require a state to pay appropriate damages to the individual investor, and investors usually receive much less compensation than what they asked of the tribunal (as the authors show). Ultimately, the

---

[20] C. Olivier, "Public Backlash Threatens EU Trade Deal with the US", *Financial Times*, 13 January 2015.

[21] Tietje & Baetens (2014).

[22] Tietje & Baetens (2014, p. 47).

[23] Tietje & Baetens (2014, p. 103).

fear of regulatory chill expected from the inclusion of ISDS, due to which states allegedly would refrain from adopting certain legislative, executive or administrative acts, has not been empirically (beyond the mere anecdotal or purely hypothetical) established.[24] In other words, there is no scientific ground to assume there would be more regulatory chill because of the risk of ISDS cases, than there is based on the looming possibility of domestic court cases.

Furthermore, the apparent widespread fear of ISDS inclusion in TTIP might appear more endemic than it actually is, when one takes into account that many of the negative responses to the consultations that vocalised this fear "were based on copy-and-paste templates circulated by non-governmental organisations campaigning against TTIP", as stated above.[25] Similarly, with regard to the risk of controversial claims, public controversy also surrounds domestic court decisions. One would be greatly pressed to prove that the societal impact would not be demonstrably greater than a 'notorious' case at the national level. If fears still remains that ISDS inclusion will limit policy space to too great an extent, the stakeholders could opt to include *"an express general clarification in TTIP and other investment treaties that foreign investors should get the same high levels of protection as domestic investors receive in domestic law, but not higher levels of protection"*.[26] They could also make explicit statements that the treaty is not to impinge upon the good-faith exercise of public policy objectives by the state; such statements would need to be taken into account by arbitral tribunals in their interpretation of the relevant investment agreement.[27] Another option, would be to restrict ISDS access for the more controversial issues which are related to the exercise of public policy objectives of the State, such as *bona fide* environmental measures.[28]

Poulsen, Bonnitcha & Yackee posit that it is unlikely that TTIP will change much of the already close relations between the EU and the US, nor would it, they argue, make it more likely that China and India

---

[24] Tietje & Baetens (2014, p. 48).

[25] C. Olivier, "Public Backlash Threatens EU Trade Deal with the US", *Financial Times*, 13 January 2015; see also www.vieuws.eu/eutradeinsights/exec-to-struggle-for-way-out-of-controversy-after-release-of-isds-consultation-results/

[26] Kleinheisterkamp & Poulsen (2014).

[27] Kuijper et al. (2014, p. 42).

[28] Kuijper et al. (2014, p. 87).

would enter into an investment treaty with the EU. The US and the EU member states have to date concluded many more BITs with developing than with developed countries. It is important to keep in mind the signal that might be sent out if the EU somehow refuses to incorporate ISDS into TTIP, given that "the EU has 1,400 bilateral ISDS agreements … Rejecting ISDS completely would open up European countries to a charge of double standards in that they are seeking to deny US companies the same safeguards that their businesses enjoy".[29] Apart from being a potentially detrimental starting position in further treaty negotiations, this is ultimately sending out a signal of distrust and inferiority towards developing states, forming a strong and, in this author's opinion, highly unfortunate reminiscent of certain colonial attitudes.

5.   Conclusion

Four possible alternatives to the inclusion of ISDS in TTIP are frequently mentioned. The first would be to opt for state-to-state arbitration. However, such an option would hardly be preferable, as it will invariably politicise a dispute and blow it far out of proportion, potentially influencing the international relations between states as a whole. As these cases are not actually located at the inter-state level, they should not be framed as disputes between states. In order for such cases to proceed to the inter-state level, investors would need to rely upon diplomatic protection, which is sporadic, arbitrary in its incidence and prone to politicisation, as there is no control over the process or any form of remedy for the individual whose claim is espoused. Furthermore, the decision whether to espouse a claim is often not taken on legal grounds but is rather dependent upon other factors such as the relative size of a state and potential need for foreign aid. As such, espousal of claims has rightly been superseded by investment protection and human rights law.

A second option would be for the home state to be able to block any claims brought by investors. Some of the problems of this second approach could be mitigated by allowing the home state to be a third-party intervener – which is perhaps a route that could still be explored.

The third option would be to require the exhaustion of local remedies before allowing a claim to be brought under ISDS. However, the problem with this is that the amount of time and costs required are

---

[29] C. Olivier, "Public Backlash Threatens EU Trade Deal with the US", *Financial Times*, 13 January 2015.

significantly higher for all parties involved. A possible solution to such issues would be to rely upon 'fork-in-the-road' clauses (where the investor has to initiate national court proceedings or international arbitration, but not both). Also, one could establish mediation as a mandatory precursor or alternative to ISDS proceedings.

Another possible solution would be to adopt a fixed or elastic time period for pursuing local remedies. The latter could be based on a "third-party index measuring the potential of domestic courts to produce effective solutions to claims of remedies rule". The more such an index would indicate that a domestic court system is 'reliable', the greater emphasis would be placed upon domestic courts being the first port of call, as opposed to other, more internationalised paths to dispute resolution.[30] Other potential procedural safeguards could include protection against frivolous claims, by virtue of offering tribunals a way to reject manifestly unfounded claims at a preliminary stage or by forcing a frivolous claimant to pay not only its own legal costs but all costs of the proceedings and potentially the legal costs of the respondent also.

The fourth, and ultimately most honest option, would be to exclude substantive investment provisions from the agreement entirely. If TTIP is to include a right, there should also be a remedy for violations of that right; if one is to take away the remedy of ISDS, then it is better not to grant the right.

One final issue that was raised during the discussion of the original paper at the Brussels Conference in 2014 was the question of whether a standing court for investment claims would be preferable over an *ad hoc* method of procedure, as is currently the case. Poulsen (presenting the paper) argued in favour of the former and this author recognises the merits of such argument – in part because of the aversion the term 'arbitration' seems to provoke among the general public. However, some important problems remain. Crucially, there is no single legal instrument giving jurisdiction to a single court, but instead there is a network of BITs. As such, to argue in favour of a standing court raises the issue of how one could confer competence upon such a court – or would the idea be to create a standing court for each and every treaty the EU concludes? In the latter case, possibly the TTIP Court could serve as a model court for subsequent treaty partners. Further potential problems would arise in the appointment of the judges to the Court – who is to be appointed, and what would happen

---

[30] Kuijper et al. (2014), p. 44.

if the integrity of a judge is called into question? Such problems could be solved by careful treaty drafting.

However, at present it seems unrealistic to hope for the creation of an overarching international investment organisation with a separate dispute settlement body, such as the WTO. Both options – a standing court or a permanent international organisation – have been tried and failed, notably in the case of the Multilateral Investment Agreement and the International Trade Organisation, which was to be established by the Havana Charter. Ultimately, the issue with ISDS, as often becomes clear in heated public discussions, is that certain segments of civil society simply do not want 'foreigners' to examine the legality of state actions – whether this examination is done by a standing or *ad hoc* body could be seen as being of little import, in the broader scheme of things.

Poulsen, Bonnitcha & Yackee distinguish broadly two camps in the discussion surrounding ISDS in TTIP: those who see its inclusion as an unmitigated good, and those who see it as the exact opposite. But there remains a large number of scholars who choose the middle path, arguing that the system currently catering to the settlement of investment disputes needs to be reformed but that the risks of ISDS inclusion are overestimated. The present author would see herself in the last category, based on her view that domestic law *does* sufficiently protect investors most of the time and that domestic courts *do* a good job at applying the law in most disputes. As is the case for the European and American Conventions on Human Rights and their respective courts, investment law and its international enforcement (whether by means of arbitration or a new court) should serve only as a safety net, to provide a remedy in those cases (no doubt rare but by no means unknown) where the domestic system has not been able to provide a fair remedy.

It is necessary that, in the future, investment disputes are depoliticised, and that a general international standard of treatment is established. Much work remains; one can think of further defining and limiting of the scope of application of investment law, so that not all and sundry qualifies as an investor; or further definition of the scope of the more vague standards of protection, such as fair and equitable treatment and indirect expropriation. There is a need to incorporate more justifications for state action with regard to environmental, health and labour issues; the inclusion of an appeals system within the ISDS framework; greater transparency, or a review of the methods to calculate damages. Unfortunately, few of these issues are discussed in *Poulsen, Bonnitcha & Yackee's* chapter.

There are many ways in which safeguards could be built into the arbitral process, in order to refine the current procedures and make them more amenable to those stakeholders currently opposed to ISDS inclusion. Firstly, with regards to transparency, one can think for example of the publication of information about the dispute at hand; whilst final awards are in the large majority of cases already in the public domain, further actions can be taken, such as allowing open hearings, or making written submissions and evidence publicly accessible online (where the information concerned is not classified information or confidential business knowledge, as determined by the tribunal). Secondly, there should also be an active role given in proceedings to other states that are parties to the treaty, as well as third-party stakeholders, such as NGOs, industry groups, or international and regional organisations. Furthermore, it would be desirable to establish a code of conduct with clear disclosure rules and methods of avoiding conflicts of interests, as well as to create a roster of arbitrators ahead of any conflict between states and investors.

Fourthly, one could perhaps envisage the creation of an appellate mechanism, as suggested by the European Commission. It is frequently argued that such a mechanism would add to the stability, predictability and legitimacy of investment law; whilst the opportunity for appeal would add to the duration and cost of proceedings, it is likely that – over time – the number of appeals would decrease (as has been the case for the WTO Appellate Body), thus offsetting a potential increase in cost by the probable increase in stability within investment procedures. If such an appeals mechanisms were to prove politically unfeasible, one could envision the creation of a treaty committee or an *ad hoc* procedure through which the parties to TTIP could give "authoritative interpretations of the provisions of the investment instrument",[31] thus ultimately providing for some measure of consistency and perceived fairness between cases. Such an option – the establishment of a treaty committee that interprets controversial treaty provisions in order to provide clarity and consistency – appears to also be currently taken by the EU and Canada in the context of the CETA negotiations, with the establishment of a Committee on Services and Investment.[32]

---

[31] Kuijper et al., pp 40-41 and p. 68.

[32] Kuijper et al., p. 70.

In sum, an investment chapter in TTIP offers an unprecedented opportunity to reform and improve the system of investment law, in a way that gradual renegotiation of individual BITs never would be able to achieve. This author hopes that the EU and the US will grasp this opportunity to rewrite international investment law by setting an important precedent in treaty-drafting, allowing for the incorporation of public policy objectives, thereby protecting states' right to regulate. Ultimately, the type of concerted strategy that could result from TTIP is likely to be far stronger than the individual country strategy necessitated by the present system of over 3,000 international investment agreements (IIAs). Perhaps the most important conclusion that should emerge from the current discussions – irrespective of whether TTIP will actually include an investment chapter – is that that there is a need for correct, timely and complete information for law and policy-makers as well as the broader public, in relation to international investment law and ISDS procedures.

References

Aisbett, E. (2007), "Bilateral Investment Treaties and Foreign Direct Investment: Correlation versus Causation", CUDARE Working Paper 1032, University of California at Berkeley, Department of Agricultural and Resource Economics and Policy, Berkeley, CA (http://repositories.cdlib.org/are.ucb/1032).

Banga, Rashmi (2003), "Impact of Government Policies and Investment Agreements on FDI Inflows", Working Paper No. 116, Indian Council for Research on International Economic Relations, New Delhi, November.

Bronckers, M. (2015), "Schizophrenia in the EU about International Law", 21 January (http://ssrn.com/abstract=2555622).

Busse, M., J. Koeniger and P. Nunnenkamp (2008), "FDI Promotion through Bilateral Investment Treaties: More Than a Bit?", Kiel Working Paper No. 1403, Kiel Institute for the World Economy, February.

Gallagher, K.P. and M.B.I. Birch (2006), "Do Investment Agreements Attract Investment? Evidence from Latin America", *Journal of World Investment and Trade*, Vol. 7, No. 6, pp. 961-974.

Haeck, Y. and E. Brems (eds.) (2014), *Human rights and civil liberties in the 21st century*, Dordrecht: Springer.

Haljan, D. (2013), *Separating powers: International law before national courts*, The Hague: T.M.C. Asser Press.

Hallward-Driemaier, M. (2003), "Do Bilateral Investment Treaties Attract FDI?. Only a bit and they could bite", World Bank Policy Research Paper, WPS 3121, World Bank, Washington, D.C.

Hix, J.P. (2013), *Indirect effect of international agreements: Consistent interpretation and other forms of judicial accommodation of WTO law by the EU courts and the US courts*, Volumes 3-13 of Jean Monnet Working Papers, NYU School of Law, New York, NY.

International Covenant on Civil and Political Rights, adopted 16 December 1966, S. Exec. Doc. E, 95-2 (1978) 999 UNTS 171, ratified by the US 8 June 1992.

Kaye, D. (2013), "State Execution of the International Covenant on Civil and Political Rights", *University of California at Irvine Law Review*, Vol. 3. No. 1.

Kleinheisterkamp, Jan and Lauge Poulsen (2014), "Investment Protection in TTIP: Three Feasible Proposals", Global Economic Governance Programme and Blavatnik School of Government (http://www.globaleconomicgovernance.org/sites/geg/files/Kleinhe isterkamp%20and%20Poulsen%20December%202014.pdf).

Kuijper, P.J., I. Pernice, S. Hindelang, M. Schwarz and M. Reuling (2014), "Investor-State Dispute Settlement (ISDS) Provisions in the EU's International Investment Agreements", Vol. 2, study requested by the European Parliament's Committee on International Trade, Brussels, September.

Künnecke, M. (2013), "Translation in the EU: Language and Law in the EU's Judicial Labyrinth", *Maastricht Journal of European and Comparative Law*, Vol. 20, No. 2, pp. 243-260.

Neumayer, E. and L. Spess (2005), "Do bilateral investment treaties increase foreign direct investment to developing countries?, World Development, Vol. 33, No. 10, pp. 1567-1585.

Neumayer, E., Kevin P. Gallagher and Horchani Ferhat (2009), "Do Bilateral Investment Treaties Lead to More Foreign Investment?", interview in *Investment Treaty News*, April (www.iisd.org/itn/2009/ 04/30/do-bilateral-investment-treaties-lead-to-more-foreign-investment/).

OECD (2012), Investor-State Dispute Settlement, Public Consultation Document, Paris.

Olivier, C. (2015), "Public Backlash Threatens EU Trade Deal with the US", *Financial Times*, 13 January.

Poulsen, Lauge, Jonathan Bonnitcha and Jason Yackee (2015), "Transatlantic Investment Treaty Protection", CEPS Special Report No. 102, CEPS, Brussels, March and chapter 5 in this volume.

Powell, C. (2001), "Dialogic Federalism: Constitutional Possibilities for Incorporation of Human Rights Law in the United States", *University of Pennsylvania Law Review*.

Pozzo, B. (2006), *Multilingualism and the harmonisation of European law*, Amsterdam: Kluwer Law International.

Quinn, Ben and Mark Sweney (2013), "Tobacco firm begins 'stealth-marketing' campaign against plain packaging", *The Guardian* (www.theguardian.com/society/2013/jun/07/tobacco-firm-stealth-marketing-plain-packaging).

Roth, B.R. (2001), "Understanding the 'Understanding': Federalism Constraints on Human Rights Implementation", *Wayne Law Review*, Vol. 47, p. 891.

Salacuse, J.W. and N.P. Sullivan (2005), "Do BITs really work? An Evaluation of Bilateral Investment Treaties and Their Grand Bargain", *Harvard International Law Journal*, Vol. 46, pp. 67-130.

Sauvant, Karl P. and Lisa E. Sachs (2009), *The Effect of Treaties on Foreign Direct Investment: Bilateral Investment Treaties, Double Taxation Treaties, and Investment Flows*, Oxford: Oxford University Press.

Spiro, P.J. (1997), "The States and International Human Rights', *Fordham Law Review*, Vol. 66, p. 567.

Tietje, C. and F. Baetens (2014), *The Impact of Investor-State Dispute Settlement (ISDS) in the Transatlantic Trade and Investment Partnership*, study prepared for the Ministry of Foreign Affairs of The Netherlands (www.rijksoverheid.nl/documenten-en-publicaties/rapporten/2014/06/24/the-impact-of-investor-state-dispute-settlement-isds-in-the-ttip.html).

Tobin, J. and S. Rose-Ackerman (2003), "Foreign Direct Investment and the Business Environment in Developing Countries: The Impact of Bilateral Investment Treaties", William Davidson Institute Working Paper No. 587, Ann Arbor, MI: University of Michigan Business School.

_____ (2006), "Bilateral Investment Treaties: Do They Stimulate Foreign Direct Investment?", Yale University, mimeo, June.

UNCTAD (1998), *Bilateral Investment Treaties in the Mid-1990s*, United Nations Conference on Trade and Development, United Nations, New York and Geneva.

Wojcik, M.E. (2013), "Legislative Attempts to Prohibit the Use of International Law and Islamic Law in US Courts", in Kyriaki Topidi and Lauren Fielder (eds), *Transnational Legal Processes and Human Rights*, Farnham, Surrey: Ashgate.

World Economic Forum, Global Competitiveness Index (GCI), Competitiveness Rankings (http://reports.weforum.org/global-competitiveness-report-2014-2015/rankings/

7. TTIP AND CONSUMER PROTECTION

STEPHEN WOOLCOCK, BARBARA HOLZER AND PETROS KUSMU

1. Introduction

This chapter examines options for regulatory cooperation within the Transatlantic Trade and Investment Partnership (TTIP) and assesses its implications for consumer protection. Its goal is to discuss the TTIP's potential opportunities and challenges and to discuss how it might affect the regulatory sovereignty of the respective legislatures. While the analysis focuses on the impact on EU regulatory sovereignty, the findings will also be relevant for the US. Will it contribute to a lowering of 'standards' and consumer protection rules? What will be the impact of the use of methods such as equivalence on regulatory requirements? Will the TTIP influence the regulatory or legislative agendas and if so, how should the European Parliament ensure that its priorities are properly represented? From the European perspective, which will be the 'competent body' representing the EU in any regulatory cooperation body and how can it be ensured that this body reflects balanced EU preferences?

The second section sets the scene by providing a short overview of the EU's past agreements and existing practices in international negotiations, and it also looks specifically at past initiatives in transatlantic regulatory cooperation. Against that background, section 3 then discusses the opportunities and challenges inherent in the TTIP negotiations in terms of the general approach to regulatory cooperation. This includes a discussion of the approach proposed in the European Commission's Textual Proposal of February 2015. Section 4 then provides some illustrations of the opportunities and challenges in specific sectors, before the final section offers some conclusions.

2.   Past agreements and existing practice

Regulatory cooperation in the TTIP builds on several existing international agreements, such as the Technical Barriers to Trade (TBT) Agreement in the WTO, numerous past transatlantic attempts to promote regulatory cooperation and, more recently, initiatives in preferential agreements negotiated by the EU and, to a lesser extent, the US. This section sets the scene for the current debate by summarising the experience with other relevant agreements.

2.1   Shaping multilateral rules

The EU has led the way in raising awareness of the impact of divergent regulations as a barrier to trade. The EU's so-called 'new approach' to such barriers in the 1980s had a significant impact on international agreements in the WTO and the work of the international standards-making bodies, e.g. ISO, CEN and CENELEC. These EU-shaped international agreements are incorporated in virtually all PTAs (preferential trading arrangements) and it is expected to be reaffirmed in the TTIP.

    The existing international rules take the form of the 1994 TBT Agreement, which contains a binding commitment to national treatment (non-discrimination) in the application of regulation and conformity assessment, 'best endeavours' wording on mutual recognition and a Code of Good Practice for standard-making bodies. As experience within the EU has shown, however, national treatment does not remove regulatory barriers/trade costs resulting from divergent regulations or standards. The GATT Agreement on the Application of Sanitary and Phytosanitary Measures, also known as the SPS Agreement – covering human, animal and plant life and health – seeks to prevent the use of SPS measures that unnecessarily distort trade. The SPS Agreement is largely 'science-based' but also provides for the use of precaution (Art. 5(2) SPS). But the SPS Agreement has not prevented transatlantic disputes on GMOs (genetically modified organisms) or hormones in beef, etc. Finally, the General Agreement on Trade in Services (GATS) provides a framework for commitments on national treatment and mutual recognition, but the option of mutual recognition has seldom been used.

2.2   Past transatlantic regulatory cooperation initiatives

In addition to being the main actors shaping existing multilateral rules, the EU and the US have engaged in numerous bilateral attempts to promote regulatory cooperation. These have taken place within the framework of bilateral cooperation established by the Transatlantic Declaration of 1990, a largely politically motivated effort to redouble transatlantic cooperation at the end of the cold war. In 1995, a renewed effort to deepen transatlantic economic relations resulted in a Joint Action Plan and the New Transatlantic Agenda Task Force, which had, among other things, the aim of promoting regulatory cooperation. This resulted in mutual recognition agreements on telecommunications equipment, electrical safety, pharmaceutical and medical devices and recreational crafts being implemented with varying degrees of difficulty (Pelkmans & Correia de Brito, 2015). It is also worth recalling that stakeholder dialogues, e.g. the Transatlantic Business Dialogue (TABD), the Transatlantic Consumer Dialogue (TACD) and the Transatlantic Environment Dialogue (TAED) were established at this time with a view to promoting a common understanding of regulation and regulatory policy aims. The Transatlantic Legislators Dialogue was also set up to strengthen European Parliament–US Congress contacts.

The limited success of the New Transatlantic Agenda led to a redoubling of efforts in the form of the 1998 Transatlantic Economic Partnership (TEP), which also had an Action Plan, including regulatory cooperation. This led to the adoption of a Veterinary Equivalence Agreement and the introduction of an 'early warning system' to help identify and head-off potential conflicts over regulation. These efforts were disappointing, especially the lack of progress on mutual recognition, and were not able to head-off trade disputes (European Commission, 2000). In an attempt to reframe the transatlantic trade agenda in a positive light following a number of high-profile disputes – stemming in no small measure from differences in regulation – the Positive Economic Agenda was launched in 2002. At this time a number of new regulatory dialogues were established, such as the Financial Market Regulatory Dialogue between DG Market and the US Treasury and Securities and Exchange Commission in 2002 and the Policy Dialogue on Borders and Transport Security (PDBTS) to address security concerns following 9/11.

Without dwelling on the past (see Chase & Pelkmans, 2015, for an exhaustive list of US-EU regulatory cooperation since 1995), it is therefore worth recalling previous efforts at regulatory cooperation and learning from them. The broad conclusion is one of rather disappointing results due to the difficulty in reconciling the different regulatory philosophies, a lack of consistent political support for detailed regulatory work and reluctance on the part of legislators to cede any regulatory autonomy. Regulatory requirements in the US and the EU result from the respective market structures and well-established consumer preferences that make regulatory cooperation inherently difficult. Where regulatory differences result from diverging policy choices, it is fair to assume that the reasons that have prevented a closer alignment of regulation in the past will not suddenly disappear with the TTIP (Gerstetter, 2014, p. 5). Surmounting the 'transatlantic deadlock' (Alemanno, 2009, p. 27) will be the main challenge for negotiators and regulators on both sides.

2.3   The EU-Korea FTA

The EU-Korea agreement reaffirms the parties' obligations under the TBT Agreement and sets out a general aim of joint cooperation in order to avoid unnecessary divergence in regulatory approaches (Art 4.3, EU-Korea FTA). It encourages cooperation between public and private standards and conformity assessment bodies.

The approach to technical regulations is based on intensified cooperation. The parties agreed to ensure the notification of the other party when a regulatory change is envisaged, allowing the other party time to respond and to participate in any formal public consultation. This is little more than a requirement to ensure that the TBT commitments are effectively implemented, which is not always the case. On voluntary standards, the EU-Korea agreement is also not TBT-plus. On conformity assessment, it simply offers a series of alternatives in the form of a) the mutual acceptance of the test results of the other party, b) the recognition of the conformity assessment of the other party or c) acceptance of suppliers' declaration of conformity. In two respects the EU-Korea agreement is new. It introduces a series of sectoral working groups covering, for example, automobiles and parts, machinery, chemicals, etc. These working groups report to the Trade Committee (on which the EU is represented by the European Commission). Secondly, it introduces TBT Coordinators in each party, who have the job of finding speedy remedies in cases of unnecessary barriers to trade, something that is seen as helping small- and medium-sized firms in particular.

With regard to the SPS chapter in the EU-Korea agreement, it reaffirms the existing obligations of the parties under the WTO SPS Agreement. In line with the practice established first in the EU-Chile FTA, it includes detailed procedures on how principles set out in the SPS Agreement can be implemented, for example, equivalence or the designation of disease- or pest-free regions. Thus, as for TBTs, the agreement really seeks only to implement more fully the existing SPS commitments.

With regard to services, the EU-Korea agreement builds on the GATS by encouraging the professional bodies responsible for determining qualifications to make recommendations to the Trade Committee on mutual recognition. The Trade Committee is then to decide on whether to negotiate a mutual recognition agreement that would be negotiated by 'the competent authorities'. A Working Group on Mutual Recognition is also established to monitor this aspect of the agreement.

2.4 The EU-Canada Comprehensive Economic and Trade Agreement (CETA)

The approach employed in CETA is broadly in line with that in the EU-Korea agreement, but with a number of innovations.

On technical regulations (Chapter 6), CETA also reaffirms commitments under the TBT agreement, but appears to go further by adding a provision according to which a party may request recognition of equivalence with the existing regulation of the other party (Art. 4 (4) CETA). In other words, the EU can request Canada to accept EU regulations as equivalent to Canadian requirements or vice versa. This request would be considered by the Committee on Trade in Goods, which will make recommendations to the (overarching) Trade Committee. In CETA, the parties also agree to apply the (voluntary) Code of Good Practice for Standards Making Bodies.

CETA includes separate protocol (as chapter 27 of the draft treaty) on conformity assessment, with an Annex. This strengthens the case for mutual recognition of the results of conformity assessment by stating that Canada will recognise conformity assessment bodies established in the EU if accredited by Canadian authorities or designated by an EU member state. The EU in turn agrees to recognise third-party conformity assessment in Canada (i.e. in cases where self-certification by producers is not allowed). The protocol also identifies priority sectors. Included is the safeguard that 'nothing shall be interpreted as requiring recognition' of conformity assessment.

On SPS, the CETA follows the same approach as the EU-Korea FTA by reaffirming obligations under the existing SPS agreement and then adding detail provisions on how the SPS agreement should be applied.

Likewise in services, CETA adopts the approach of encouraging professional bodies to initiate the process of negotiating mutual recognition agreements by making recommendations to the Committee on Trade in Services, which will then make a recommendation to the Trade Committee.

Finally, CETA includes the establishment of a Regulatory Cooperation Forum that will have the role of promoting cooperation across all sectors. This is perhaps the model for the Regulatory Cooperation Body (RCB) proposed by the European Commission for TTIP (see discussion below).

2.5 The general approach to recent PTAs in the US

This section draws primarily on the KORUS agreement between the US and Korea, which is an indication of US preferences in this policy area.

The US also reaffirms commitments under the TBT agreement in Chapter 9 of KORUS. There is an article on joint cooperation (9.4), which encourages general mutual understanding and provides for sectoral initiatives. On conformity assessments, KORUS is less ambitious than the EU–Korea FTA in that the former merely lists a range of six mechanisms, including mutual and autonomous recognition of conformity assessment, accreditation and supplier declarations. If recognition is requested but not granted, the reasons for not granting recognition must be given (see Pelkmans & Correia de Brito (2015) for a detailed comparison of the TBT chapter in KORUS with that of the EU-Korea FTA). There is a reference to the APEC Mutual Recognition Arrangement for Conformity Assessment in Telecommunications, of which Korea is a member. KORUS broadly follows the TBT approach on transparency and urges the use of electronic forms of communication. But here, as in the general provisions on technical regulations, there is only 'best endeavour" wording for the 'level directly below that of central government'. In other words, state level government in the US is not bound. Analogous to the EU-Korea agreement, there is a sectoral committee on regulatory requirements for_automobiles, which is to work towards joint implementation of the regulatory requirements set out by UNECE (United Nations Economic Commission for Europe). Additionally, the TBT provisions are to be monitored by a Committee on Technical Barriers to Trade on which USTR represents the US.

The KORUS provisions on SPS are even briefer than those on TBTs. Chapter 8 reaffirms the SPS Agreement and establishes an SPS

Committee that should ensure that SPS measures rely on 'science and risk-based assessments.' (Chapter 8(3)).

In services, KORUS provides some further 'best endeavours' wording on transparency and the provision of information. Article 12(9) provides for the recognition of qualifications either mutually or autonomously, but stresses that there is no requirement to recognise.

3.   Opportunities and challenges

3.1   Opportunities

3.1.1   *Reduced costs and more competitive markets*

For the Parties, industrial transatlantic regulatory cooperation offers the opportunity of reducing the waste of complying with competing – but equivalent – regulatory requirements. Better regulatory cooperation can also enhance market access for EU exporters, especially small- and medium-sized companies. This is particularly of interest for the leading EU exporters to the US in sectors such as automotive, machinery and chemicals in terms of regulatory requirements_and to US exporters in food and health products and machinery. Strong sectors in the EU such as financial services, public transport equipment and construction also stand to benefit from increased cooperation in services regulation and procurement. All sectors, as well as traders and wholesalers, stand to benefit from a reduction in trade costs due to border controls and improved trade facilitation. The TTIP therefore offers an opportunity to strengthen international competitiveness and to create more wealth and jobs in the EU and the US. The scale of the welfare and trade gains has been the subject of much debate (Pelkmans et al., 2014) but gains from reduced costs due to different but equivalent regulation represent the most important economic gains from the TTIP.

3.1.2   *Shaping international trade rules and consumer protection levels*

In addition to improving economic growth, the TTIP has been justified on the grounds that it will enable the EU and the US to share leadership of the international trading system and shape the trade rules 'democratically'. Transatlantic trade does account for a significant share of world trade. The EU and US are also the most active and advanced actors when it comes to addressing regulatory issues in trade and investment. On this view, agreeing to common approaches through regulatory cooperation offers the opportunity of setting international norms and high levels of consumer protection_in this respect.

It should, however, be remembered that the EU and the US have been doing this for some time, whether in the form of shaping the approach to rules on trade in services in the OECD, WTO and now in the TiSA (Trade in Services Agreement) or in the negotiations on government procurement in the (GPA) Government Procurement Agreement of the WTO. In these fora, the agendas and outcomes have been largely shaped by the transatlantic dialogue. In the area of technical standards and regulation, this has been much less the case. The EU has simultaneously promoted international standards through the markets and bodies such as the ISO and IEC. But the success of some leading American standards-making bodies selling their technical standards internationally has meant that it has eschewed binding commitments on standards. Progress on regulatory cooperation in this area could therefore have a real impact on shaping international norms.

Another area is that of rules of origin. Here the EU and the US are the main actors in shaping preferential rules of origin, with the PanEuro and NAFTA models being the two dominant but different models. Regulatory cooperation that could bring about a convergence and ideally a simplification of these two models would have significant benefits for the rest of the trading system.

Lastly, the existing system of investor-state dispute settlement (ISDS) is subject to reform within the TTIP, hence implying the shaping of international trade rules 'democratically'. In response to the EP's recent resolution, EU Trade Commissioner Cecilia Malmström emphasised that the old system of ISDS should not and cannot be reproduced in TTIP, and that the Parliament's call for a "new system" must be heard, and it will be (European Commission, 2015c).

3.1.3 Increase consumer welfare and levels of safety

Increased competition, due to progress in regulatory cooperation, offers the prospect of lower prices and an increased variety of goods and services for consumers (Diels & Thoran, 2014). Regulatory cooperation could also bring about improved consumer protection and safety. The assumption that the level of consumer protection is basically higher or more sophisticated in the EU is not sustainable. In place of the EU's precautionary principle, the US has a stringent civil liability system that acts as a means of ensuring high levels of health and safety, via liability insurance requirements or induced regulations. For instance, the strong and high level of consumer protection regulations on toys and infant and toddler products in the US could greatly increase consumer protection and welfare for Europeans in this sector (CFA, 2014). Rather than fearing that the EU might trade away their precautionary principle approach to regulation, it could be seen as an opportunity to learn from each other's experience, to strengthen regulatory collaboration and to provide more transparency on the use of the PP.

An intensified exchange of information offers an opportunity to advance consumer policy interests. Intensified exchange of information is in line with the existing practice in dealing with regulatory divergence and barriers to trade and forms a central element in the proposals on regulatory cooperation. Where the TTIP leads to shared approaches, those are more likely to be followed around the world, meaning a regulatory race to the top rather than a race to the bottom.

The TTIP negotiations carry the potential to promote the interests of consumers. For example, negotiators could expand opportunities for consumers and micro-businesses by removing duties for personal imports, eliminating excessive pricing of telecommunications (i.e. roaming fees) and broaden access by consumers to the digital market, for instance, by preventing online geographical price discrimination (European Consumer Organisation/BEUCBilate, 2015; Renda & Yoo, 2015). However, this potential will only be fully tapped if the narrow focus of negotiations is extended to a modern and broad comprehension of consumer welfare (Diels & Thorun, 2014, p. 48).

Making regulations more compatible does not mean going for the lowest common denominator, but rather seeing where divergence is unnecessary and where coordination is beneficial for both economic interests and consumer welfare. Therefore, impact assessments for the purpose of transatlantic regulatory cooperation must not be limited to the impact on trade, but also consider consumers' interests, such as safety, information and sustainable consumption as is the case with the holistic approach to impact assessment. The use of impact assessment on both sides of the Atlantic also provides scope for the engagement of a variety of stakeholders, for example in the common definition of concrete tools to measure the impact on consumer safety.

3.1.4   Momentum for continued EU reform

In order to keep pace with international competition, the EU should maintain the momentum needed for further domestic reforms as a means of boosting its own competitiveness. External pressure in the shape of international competition or negotiations with key trading partners has always played a role in the development of EU commercial policy and the creation of the Single Market. Negotiating TTIP or any agreement with a major developed market economy poses more of a challenge for the EU than PTAs with smaller, less-developed economies or arguably negotiations in the WTO (with the possible exception of agriculture). But such negotiations also offer an opportunity to provide the additional external driver that may be needed to break domestic deadlocks on policy reforms due to entrenched vested interests, resulting in breakthroughs that will be beneficial for EU consumers and firms as a whole.

3.2   Challenges

3.2.1   Making regulatory cooperation a success

The essential challenge is to make transatlantic regulatory cooperation a success and thus tackle the additional (trade) costs resulting from different but equivalent regulation, standards or conformity assessment in the US and the EU, whilst ensuring there is no diminution of consumer safety and protection or environmental policy objectives. Inevitably, some sectors will prove to be difficult or near impossible for substantial regulatory cooperation to take place due to grave and irreconcilable concerns that the public may have. Consequently, the EU has been explicit in stating the issues that will be exempt from negotiations, such as GMOs and beef-with hormones (see Josling & Tangermann, 2014 for more information on agriculture and the TTIP) food and data-privacy laws. However, relevant consumer protection associations, such as BEUC (European Consumer Organisation, 2015) and the TACD (2015), have expressed major concerns that this is not enshrined in the European Commission's Textual Proposal document. Furthermore, in order to ensure that regulatory cooperation is a success, citizens and consumer advocacy groups need increased transparency and involvement, which means that the US should follow the EU's lead in publicising their negotiation proposals and increase the public's involvement (CFA, 2014a; TACD, 2015; and European Consumer Organisation/BEUC, 2015).

It is also worth recalling that there have been various previous attempts to promote transatlantic regulatory cooperation that have at best been only partially successful. With the main economic gains from TTIP projected to come from addressing regulatory barriers, the main challenge is to tackle them effectively.

3.2.2 Dealing with differences in regulatory philosophies and practice

Beyond the technical difficulties that are involved with regulatory cooperation, one of the greatest challenges facing TTIP will be reconciling the different regulatory philosophies, such as the difference between the EU's use of the precautionary principle (PP) and the US reliance on science-based risk assessment, cost-benefit analysis and cost-effectiveness analysis ('science-based approach') (Bergkamp & Kogan, 2013, pp. 495-497). The following section will provide a brief overview of both philosophies.

The precautionary principle enables the EU to invoke more stringent levels of regulation or standards in cases when a potential adverse impact on human health or the environment can take place and/or there is scientific uncertainty, such as scientific controversy, disagreements or a lack of scientific knowledge (von Schomberg, 2006). Prior to drafting legislation, the EU normally drafts Impact Assessments as a means of understanding a piece of legislation's far-reaching impact (Alemanno, 2014). Even with the European Commission's Delegated and Implementing Acts, Impact Assessments are normally conducted when significant economic, environmental or social impacts are expected as a result of the act (Alemanno, 2014). It is worth noting that part of the EU's precautionary principle is anchored in Art. 191(2) TFEU, which states that environmental policy should be based on the precautionary principle. So it cannot be 'negotiated away'. That said, this does not prevent the European Commission from entering into an agreement that could potentially nullify some of its effects (Bergkamp & Kogan, 2013).

The US scientific approach to regulation is supported by the central role of the White House Office of Information and Regulatory Affairs (OIRA) and the Regulatory Impact Assessments (RIAs) that agencies are required to produce. Both are simply based on a science-based cost-benefit analysis (Alemanno & Parker, 2014), which stands in contrast to the EU's more precautionary and holistic examination of the potential societal and environmental impacts that a piece of legislation may have. In place of the precautionary principle, the US has a stringent civil liability system that acts as a means of ensuring that health and safety regulations and product standards are not lax (Bergkamp & Kogan, 2013). In multiple cases, the US Supreme Court has ruled that the US Office of Safety and Health Administration must have demonstrated "significant risk" prior to regulation (Wiener & Rogers, 2002, p. 318).

There may be some signs that the US is inching towards a greater use of precaution in their regulatory approaches. For instance, President Obama made reference to precaution in his statement on a deep seabed mining policy and the US House of Representatives decided to highlight "scientific inadequacy" in its regulatory decision on endangered species (Bergkamp & Kogan, 2013, p. 500). However, it would be relatively naïve to believe that the US will significantly alter its regulatory philosophy any time soon.

Differences in regulatory principles in the EU and US have led many to be concerned that any attempt at regulatory convergence in the TTIP may imply deregulation of European consumer protection. The greatest concern is that the science-based approach to risk assessment in the US differs from the use of the precautionary principle in EU risk assessment. Science-based risk assessment has not always been sufficient, as shown in the case of the mad-cow disease epidemic. This was an example of science-based risk assessment getting it wrong. This and other episodes have influenced thinking in the EU towards more scope for the use of precaution, such as in the field of chemicals with the introduction of REACH in the EU (Karlsson, 2015). (For a detailed discussion of consumer concerns, see Diels & Thorun, 2014 and Alemanno, 2014.) However, several studies have demonstrated that, with some possible exceptions, the high standards required by both the EU and the US will ensure a high level of consumer, health and environmental protection (Bergkamp & Kogan, 2013, p. 507). A further study by Fabry & Garbasso (2014, p. 4) suggests that differences between precaution and science-based risk assessment have been overplayed and that differences are more due to a selective application of precaution to different risks in different places and times.

3.2.3 Selecting the best options for regulatory cooperation

The recent literature on approaches to regulatory cooperation from a consumer protection standpoint has identified harmonisation, mutual recognition or equivalence and intensified exchange of information as options in addressing regulatory divergence.

Harmonisation

Harmonisation has been used for voluntary standards but has proven difficult or, at best, very time consuming. For consumer protection, the issue is whether the common levels of consumer protection represent a levelling up or down. The work on this suggests that contrary to fears of a 'race to the bottom', there is some evidence of a levelling upwards, as has been the case within the US where higher levels of consumer protection in some states have led to a levelling up in the quality of consumer protection in a variety of states: the so-called 'California effect' (Vogel, 1997).

Mutual recognition or equivalence

Mutual recognition in its various forms or equivalence can be appropriate when the policy goals are the same but the approach used to meet these goals differs. This approach offers the prospect of being more effective in reducing the costs of incompatible provisions. It poses no threat to consumer protection, provided the goals are indeed equivalent. From a consumer perspective, the interest here is to ensure that regulatory cooperation is geared towards satisfying consumer interests and not unduly focusing on the removal of regulatory barriers to trade or increased trade costs. This is, of course, the basis for the 'new approach' to technical harmonisation and standards within the EU that led to the success of the Single Market programme in the 1980s and 1990s. But in the EU case, it was based on a harmonisation of minimum essential requirements as well as a broad approximation of regulatory aims.

Intensified exchange of information

Considerable opportunities lie in an intensified exchange of information and research between European and US regulators. Informational coordination on issues of common interest promises not only greater but also increased consumer protection through mutual learning. However, this free flow of information that benefits consumers should never be confused with the flow of commercially valuable personal information regulated under data protection and privacy frameworks on both sides of the Atlantic. Moreover, a free flow of information is also not necessarily the same as an increased level of transparency.

In practice, the way in which regulations and standards have been dealt with in trade agreements is a little more complicated. Here it is helpful to differentiate between several elements.

Transparency constitutes a fundamental basis of trade agreements. In this context, it involves the publication of all regulations and testing procedures as the first essential step to the removal of barriers to market access. This can be facilitated by the requirement to use modern electronic communications and by ensuring there is a central focal point to answer any enquiries concerning regulations.

Technical regulations are defined in the WTO as measures that are obligatory and laid down in national or EU legislation. The TBT agreement requires national treatment, but this does not, of course, deal with the trade costs resulting from differing regulations. The alternative approach is mutual recognition of regulations, but there are only 'best endeavours' wording on mutual recognition in the WTO TBT Agreement and most other trade agreements. Standards are defined as voluntary measures that may or may not provide a means of showing compliance with regulatory requirements. International standards-making bodies cover goods, e.g. the International Standards Organisation (ISO), CENELEC (for electrical equipment) and for minimum requirements underlying SPS measures, the Codex Alimentarius.

Both the TBT and SPS agreements make reference to international standards. In the former, there are 'best endeavours' wording only on the use of international standards and a voluntary Code of Good Practice on Standards Making. The SPS agreement urges the use of Codex regulatory requirements, but only where these are appropriate (e.g. too low), thus allowing significant scope to waive the requirements. Conformity assessment relates to the process or procedure by which compliance with agreed standards or regulations are tested. Most trade agreements, including the TBT agreement, require national treatment for conformity assessment, so that imported products must be tested in the same way as nationally produced products. As for technical regulations, this does not address the additional costs of complying with unnecessarily complex or different conformity assessment measures. So again there is the option of mutual recognition or equivalence of conformity assessment.

Institutional provisions are included in agreements. These usually take the form of committees to monitor and promote the application of regulatory cooperation. There may also be specific committees, such as in the case of the recent EU–Korea FTA or KORUS discussed above.

The options discussed above have different implications for regulatory sovereignty and thus the scrutiny function of the EP and its committees. Taking each of these in turn, harmonisation of voluntary standards is carried out by standards making bodies, the representation in these is through the national standards making bodies and on detailed technical work there is strong involvement of private sector experts. Agreed international standards are adopted by voting in the international bodies in which the European standards-making bodies have a very strong presence, which is often still seen in the US as skewing the balance against the 'more industry-led' approach to standards used in the US.

Mutual recognition can take a number of forms. In the past mutual recognition agreements have been based on legislation. If this is the case, legislatures on both sides of the Atlantic will retain regulatory sovereignty. But, as noted above, the reluctance of the regulators and legislators to make changes has been a significant impediment in the past. The European Commission and the USTR have stated that regulatory cooperation provisions in the TTIP will not imply rule-making powers. At this level therefore there would seem to be no threat to the regulatory autonomy. The respective legislatures would however, have to exercise effective scrutiny.

The third alternative of intensified exchange of information raises few issues for regulatory scrutiny. This option seeks to influence the preparatory phase of regulation. Through exchanges of research and thinking on the form and stringency of regulation, incompatibilities should be reduced from the outset. The proposed legislation would then be compatible or more compatible, but the EP and US Congress would still retain legislative sovereignty.

3.2.4   Identifying suitable priorities

In order to make progress, it has been recognised by negotiators on both sides that what is needed is to identify those areas where levels of consumer protection are equivalent but the means of achieving them differ. In these areas it should be possible to reconcile the procedural differences through mutual recognition or acceptance of equivalence, subject of course to effective scrutiny to ensure that this does not lead to a reduction in consumer protection_that would be detrimental to consumer/environmental interests. This chapter suggests that this should be possible in sectors such as engineering and automobiles and perhaps in aspects of trade facilitation such as supply chain security.

It will equally be necessary to recognise, as the negotiators appear to have done, that there will be some areas in which levels of consumer protection diverge so that the more ambitious forms of regulatory cooperation such as mutual recognition in its various forms are inappropriate. Such sectors appear to be in REACH in the chemical sector (see Elliot & Pelkmans, 2015) and probably significant areas of food safety. In these areas it will be necessary to recognise that regulatory cooperation will have to take the form of less ambitious instruments, such as intensified exchange of information or joint research on future standards as a means of limiting future divergent standards.

3.2.5 Getting the process right

The nature of these challenges suggests that regulatory cooperation will have to be a continuous process. As has long been recognised in the debate on TBTs, the conclusion of an agreement is only the beginning. Real progress in removing regulatory barriers requires more or less continuous efforts Again, this is a lesson that has been learned in the EU's attempts to reduce such barriers to the cross-border intra-EU movement of goods, services and factors of production. A key challenge in the TTIP is therefore getting the process right. This means ensuring that the framework established to carry the work forward is appropriate. In the context of the TTIP this means ensuring that the mechanisms, such as the proposed Regulatory Cooperation Body (RCB), are effective and transparent. Calls from the TACD (2015) have proposed that as a way to boost the effectiveness and transparency of the RCB, consumer groups and citizens should be integral to its design and that the good practices of meaningful, public and transparent consultations should be enshrined in the TTIP.

Another key challenge in getting the process right is ensuring that future attempts to implement new regulations do not become overly burdensome – more specifically, costly and time-consuming. It is important to note that this may have greater implications for the US compared to the EU due to a difference in regulatory systems and legislative functions (TACD, 2015; VZBV, 2015).

In the European Commission's textual proposal document, it states that impact assessments and meaningful consultations are required to take place on planned regulatory acts at the central level.

Furthermore, each Party is required to inform the other Party about proposed regulatory acts (at the central level) that will likely have a "significant impact" on "international trade or investment...between the parties" (European Commission, 2015a).

The European Commission's proposed IA (impact assessment) and consultation process may slow down future attempts of implementing new regulations and make it more costly for legislators complying with regulatory requirements for three reasons. First, the European Commission's proposal for an increased usage of IAs will most likely result in a greater administrative workload when regulations are being proposed. This is especially true for the US where IAs are not as frequently employed as it is in the EU (TACD, 2015). This proposal may prove difficult for the administrative departments or agencies that are responsible for drafting IA if they are overstretched or under-resourced.

Second, since IAs are not clearly defined in the European Commission's textual proposal, these IAs may be more extensive than the IAs that the US normally conducts. More specifically, beyond a cost-effectiveness analysis (which the US IAs primarily focus on), European IAs are more 'holistic' in that they will also analyse, for instance, social and environmental impacts (Alemanno & Parker, 2014). However, US consumer advocacy organisations, such as the CFA, are in favour of IAs with a more holistic analysis (CFA, 2014b).

Third, the European Commission's interest in binding the US's sub-federal units to the TTIP (i.e. US states) may also magnify the potentially burdensome impacts of IAs and consultation (TACD, 2015).

While some groups, such as the TACD (2015), BEUC (2015) and the VZBV (2015), believe that this may cause a "significant slowdown and chill on regulatory processes", these concerns may be over-exaggerated in that the European Commission's latest textual proposal document outlines that each Party will be charged to determine whether a regulatory act will have a "significant impact" (European Commission, 2015a). Furthermore, US federal agencies proposing "significant" new regulation, already conduct stringent regulatory IAs and normally opt for a more consultative process as a means of averting potential judicial reviews (Alemanno & Parker, 2014). As for the EU, the European Commission conducts at least broad consultations with parties impacted by new proposals for delegated acts and publicises the consultation process of an implementing act's proposal (Alemanno & Parker, 2014). The European Commission's May 2015 proposal for "Better Regulation(s)" will result in a more frequent use of Impact

Assessments in the Commission's delegating measures (European Commission, 2015d).

In addition to ensuring that regulatory cooperation is a continuous process once the TTIP is concluded, negotiators need to ensure that future attempts of implementing new regulations are not overly burdensome.

3.2.6   Safeguarding regulatory sovereignty: The case of the EU

A question of interest to MEPs is whether the proposed process poses a challenge for the EU's regulatory sovereignty. The present analysis argues that the European Parliament's regulatory sovereignty, in terms of legislative rule-making authority, is unlikely to be affected by the TTIP. In the discussion so far it has become clear that the RCB will have no rule-making powers.

The EU's proposed approach to the TTIP has been set out in the initial European Commission's Textual Proposal made public on the 9th February 2015. It should be understood that this is only an indication of what might be in the TTIP. The outcome of the negotiations is of course unknown at this stage. No US textual proposal has been made available for discussion even though regulatory cooperation was the subject of discussion in the 9th round of negotiations in New York in the week of the 20th April. The EU text sets out the general aim of 'reinforcing regulatory cooperation' (Art 1) without restricting the right to regulate in pursuit of legitimate public policy objectives, such as 'a high level of protection of inter alia: the environment; consumers; working conditions; human, animal and plant life, health and safety; personal data; cyber security; cultural diversity; or preserving financial stability.' Both the EU and US negotiators have repeatedly emphasised that there is no intention to restrict the right to regulate levels of consumer protection or any other regulations, neither to lower such standards (Fabry & Garbossa, 2014). As the US supports this position there is no reason to believe that the final outcome will diverge from this position.

One area of contention is coverage. The EU's proposed text refers to cooperation at the level of central government (Art. 3), although there is a note that the scope will be reviewed at a later stage of the negotiation. At issue here is whether the US will accept an extension to the sub-federal, i.e. state level regulation. In a number of regulatory policy areas, the states play an important role. In other trade agreements, the US has offered no more than best endeavours for the coverage of sub-federal regulation, so including state level regulation in the process will be a challenge for the EU.

According to the EU proposal, transparency provisions would require the parties to provide a list of planned regulations 'at least once a year'. The EU's proposed approach under regulatory policy instruments is that the parties 'affirm their intention' to carry out impact assessments of planned regulatory acts at the central level (this would mean the EU level and the US federal level). In carrying out such impact assessments, the parties shall i) consider how the regulation relates to relevant international instruments and ii) take account of the regulatory approaches of the other party and the impact on international trade or investment (including investors) (Art 7).

In the course of such impact assessment, the parties would be required to exchange information and promote the exchange of experience. Stakeholders would also have to be given a 'reasonable opportunity' to provide input through public consultations (Art 6). The US and the EU currently use impact assessments, but it will be important to assess how this meshes with the EU's regulatory and legislative processes. Impact assessments are widely used in the pre-legislative phase in the EU and normally take place for delegated or implementing measures (Alemanno & Parker, 2014; Alemanno, 2014). Regulatory cooperation in the TTIP could therefore result in a greater use of impact assessments.

An Annual Regulatory Cooperation Programme would be established to set priorities for regulatory cooperation. This is similar to previous transatlantic approaches to regulatory cooperation, but an annual programme suggests greater intensity. Since such an approach would effectively shape the priorities for the RCB, it would be important for the European Parliament to have an input into and provide scrutiny of the programme.

Articles 9 and 10 of the EU textual proposal deal with information and regulatory exchanges. These are in line with the well-established approach used in long-standing trade agreements, such as the provisions on TBT or SPS in WTO or preferential agreement already concluded by the EU. The EU proposal does, however, include specific reference to an obligation to inform the other party of proposed regulatory acts that 'do not originate from the executive branch'. This appears to be designed to ensure that rule-making emanating from US regulatory agencies is also included, and is necessary given the nature of the US system. The regulatory exchanges will take place between regulators and competent authorities.

In Article 11, the proposal includes the central element of promoting regulatory compatibility. This shall apply to areas where 'mutual benefits can be realised without compromising the achievement of legitimate public policy objectives' as set out in Art 1. The text includes a number of options, namely:

- 'mutual recognition of equivalence of regulatory acts, in full or in part' ... based on equivalent outcomes as regards the fulfilment of the public policy goals pursued by both parties;

- harmonisation of regulatory acts, or their essential elements through the application of existing 'international instruments' (e.g. international standards);

- the approximation of rules and procedures on a bilateral basis; or

- simplification of regulatory acts in line with shared principles and guidelines.

This approach seems balanced and would not undermine the EP's regulatory sovereignty provided the RCB has no rule-making powers.

The RCB would be composed of 'regulators and competent authorities'. The expectation must be that the competent body on the part of the EU would be the European Commission's Directorate General responsible for the regulatory policy concerned. If this is the case, then there can be some assurance that regulatory policy objectives, such as consumer interests, would not be less likely to be compromised in the interests of 'trade' or market access. But this is something the European Parliament should monitor.

The RCB would have the power to create sectoral working groups. This seems to be in line with the typical powers granted to similar committees in other preferential trade agreements (PTAs). This is necessary due to the technical nature of regulation and regulatory barriers to competition in markets. The RCB would hold a meeting open to the participation of stakeholder 'at least once a year', prepared with the involvement of the co-chairs of the Civil Society Contact Groups. Therefore, formal consultations with civil society are envisaged.

In summary, the EU's proposals are based on intensified exchange of information with a view to reinforcing regulatory cooperation. The options offered are fairly simple and include equivalence/mutual recognition, harmonisation or 'simplification'. The text includes a safeguard in the sense that it expressly reserves the right to regulate in pursuit of high levels of protection for consumers and other legitimate public policy objectives. MEPs will wish to ensure that this is the case in the final text and that they have an input in the priorities in regulatory cooperation, such as through scrutiny of the Annual Regulatory Cooperation Programme.

The research for this chapter has focused on the case of the EU. When it comes to the US, regulators and the US Congress have a solid record of defending their regulatory sovereignty. As noted above, there is as yet no (published) US textual proposal on the approach to regulatory cooperation. If the (unofficial) text for regulatory cohesion in the TPP is a model, however, the US approach would appear to pose no threat at all to regulatory sovereignty as the emphasis would be on promoting coherence within the US (and the EU if this approach were used in the TTIP). The role of any joint body to set agendas for regulatory cooperation across the Atlantic would therefore be less, so there could be no danger that such a body might somehow undermine regulatory sovereignty.

4. Case studies

4.1 Chemicals

The area of chemicals entails considerable divergence between US and EU legislation and thus marked interest in greater regulatory consistency (for more on chemicals, see Elliot & Pelkmans, "Great TTIP ambition in chemicals: Why and how".) The EU's central piece of legislation is the Regulation on Registration, Evaluation, Authorisation and Restriction of Chemicals (REACH), which entered into force in June 2007, and streamlines the legislative framework on chemicals of the EU. Classification and labelling of substances is governed by the so-called CLP (classification, labelling, and packaging) Regulation. Basically, under REACH, producers or importers must register chemicals to be put on the market in quantities exceeding a certain threshold with the European Chemicals Agency (ECHA). As part of the registration, they must provide specific information on the properties of the chemicals to ECHA. Registrants must also conduct a chemical safety assessment. Certain chemicals, included in Annex XIV of the Regulation, are subject to pre-marketing authorisation; criteria for including substances into the list are defined (Gerstetter, 2014, p. 30).

In May 2014, the European Commission published a position paper for the TTIP negotiations on chemicals, stating that "neither full harmonisation nor mutual recognition seems feasible on the basis of the existing framework legislation in the US (Toxic Substances Control Act, TSCA) and EU (REACH)" and that proposals for greater consistency have to be within the existing legislative framework of the EU. Although current EU and US regulations on chemicals differ, there are areas where the two systems allow for joint work. The position paper outlines four areas for which the European Commission proposes to assess possibilities for enhanced cooperation with the US via the TTIP:

1. Prioritisation of chemicals for assessment and assessment methodologies;

2. Promoting alignment in classification and labelling of chemicals;

3. New and emerging issues (e.g. endocrine disruptors, nanomaterials); and

4. Enhanced information sharing among regulators while protecting Confidential Business Information (CBI) (e.g. on test data to reduce animal testing).

This suggests an intensified exchange of information approach, which means in practice that US and EU regulators might agree to work together during their assessment through evaluating the same substances at the same time and exchanging respective information. This bears cost-saving potential for both the companies and the regulators, but it would not change the level of protection offered by EU law. The EU decision-making process might be concerned by decisions emanating from an US-EU regulatory cooperation, for instance on the inclusion of substances in any of the Annexes. In such a case, the European Commission would formulate a proposal and the relevant Committee, composed of member state representatives, would be involved. In other decisions under REACH, ECHA itself or the competent authorities of member states are involved. Thus, TTIP will not change the fundamental decision-making structure of the EU.

The example of chemicals regulation shows that the scope for autonomous decision-making by the European Commission is limited, as in major implementing acts a number of actors are involved. The goal is to seek opportunities for cooperation between the relevant regulators in order to better coordinate certain practices and therefore increase efficiencies and reduce costs for authorities and economic units, but without lowering any existing consumer protection levels.

4.2 Automotive sector

The automotive sector is another industry that could benefit greatly from regulatory convergence. (For more on the automotive sector, see chapter 15 in this volume by Freund & Oliver). The EU's automotive industry is, after China, the second-largest manufacturer of motor vehicles worldwide and it generates millions of jobs – directly and indirectly – EU-wide. The US represents by far the largest market for EU automobile exporters (followed by China, Russia and Turkey).

A significant stimulus for transatlantic trade of motor vehicles and parts can be created by addressing trade related costs which arise from NTBs, such as different product standards or regulations, testing methods, classifications and product labelling. The EU and the US have different regulations in relation to lights, door-locks, seat belts, steering and electric windows. As these regulations assure a similar level of safety across the Atlantic, there is a wide range of regulations where mutual recognition seems possible (Kolev & Matthes, 2014, p. 8). Nevertheless, the processes by which the US and EU establish product regulations in the automotive industry have very different paths. Contrary to the US system of self-certification, the safety of motor vehicles is attested via pre-market government approval in the EU. The European vehicle regulations include both EU directives, which must be implemented by the member states, and regulations promulgated through UNECE with optional implementation by the national governments of the member states. Signatories to the UNECE Agreement commit to mutual recognition of approvals for vehicle components. However, the US did not join the agreement, as it was not ready to recognise regulations generated outside the US. What this means for manufacturers is that they have to run tests twice in order to get cars approved in both markets. Besides safety, there exist main differences of regulatory requirements between the US and EU concerning fuel economy and emissions requirements (Canis & Lattanzio, 2014, p. 5).

The European Commission's May 2014 proposal for regulatory cooperation on motor vehicles outlines a possible approach to promote regulatory compatibility while achieving the levels of health, safety and environmental protection that each side deems appropriate. The ultimate goal pursued in the TTIP negotiations concerning the automobile manufacturers is according to the EU's position twofold:

- "Firstly, the recognition of motor vehicles (and their parts and components, including tyres) manufactured in compliance with the technical requirements of one party as complying with the technical requirements of the other. [...]

- Secondly, a significant strengthening of EU-US cooperation also in the framework of UNECE 1998 Agreement, especially on new technologies."

The first step in the process of mutual recognition of technical requirements is the development of a methodological approach enabling regulators to assess whether the regulations of one side are equivalent (in terms of, for example, safety levels and environmental protection). In areas where equivalence of regulatory outcome can be confirmed, "the relevant regulations of the other TTIP partner would have the same legal effect as compliance with domestic regulations". Regarding the second point, the hope is that the EU-US cooperation in the framework of the UNECE 1998 Agreement should lead to the adoption of Global Technical Regulations in the near future. Strengthening EU-US cooperation is considered essential regarding the role of the EU and US as potential regulatory requirement-setters in the global automotive industry. The reinforcement of EU-US cooperation is already a central element in the field of new technologies such as hydrogen and electric vehicles, test-cycle on emissions and advanced safety technologies (Kolev & Matthes, 2014, p. 26).

In the context of future regulatory cooperation, it is important to clearly define which measures concern TBTs and redundant administrative burdens and which measures are linked to desired levels of consumer protection and regulations and should not be altered. The EP's democratic scrutiny over EU regulatory processes will be crucial when creating the framework for future cooperation. At the same time, it has to be vigilant about a balanced involvement of stakeholders such as the European Automobile Manufacturers' Association (ACEA) and the American Automotive Policy Council (AAPC) within the stakeholder consultations included in the development of a regulatory proposal.

In summary, it is of particular interest for the EU to achieve an ambitious TTIP incorporating the commitment of the parties to promote regulatory convergence without sacrificing vehicle safety or environmental performance.

4.3 ICT

The Information and Communications Technology (ICT) industry – which is a "combination of manufacturing and services industries that capture, transmit and display data and information electronically" (OECD, 2012) – is one that can greatly benefit through increased regulatory convergence between the US and the EU. However, a sensitive area to consumer protection – data privacy measures – may make it particularly challenging for negotiators to bridge the regulatory transatlantic divide (for more on the ICT sector, see Renda & Yoo, 2015).

With the regards to the European Commission's offensive interests in the ICT sector (European Commission, 2015b), regulatory cooperation does not seem to be a significant challenge on ICT goods (Renda & Yoo, 2015) For instance, efforts in establishing e-labelling requirements are expected to have little difficulty in regulatory cooperation since the US's E-LABEL Act was enacted in November 2014. This measure will especially help SMEs in reducing manufacturing costs of digital devices since it gives them the ability to not place labels, stickers and etches of regulatory compliance on their (electronic) devices by providing the regulatory compliance information digitally in the device's screen and/or software. Additionally, issues of e-accessibility – making ICT easier to use by people with disabilities – and interoperability – allowing users to exchange data between different products easier – do not seem to be highly contentious. The same could also be said about the European Commission's objectives in establishing better enforcement regulations and common principles for certifying ICT products, especially in the realm of cryptography.

In spite of the EU's offensive ICT interests, where consumers and firms alike will reap large benefits from increased regulatory cooperation, a more uncertain aspect of TTIP's regulatory cooperation lies in one of the European Commission's primary defensive interests – ICT services issues relating to the free flow of data – which has large implications for consumer protection.

Recent concerns with data privacy has prompted the EU to adopt increasingly stricter data protection measures, resulting in some countries adopting data localization efforts – legal requirements that an organization containing critical data of EU citizens must be physically stored in data servers in their respective country (Lakatos, 2014). Stringent data requirements, such as the EU's 1998 Directive on Data Protection, make it challenging for businesses abroad to do provide digital goods and services to the EU. In order to streamline digital trade between the EU and US and to ensure that the data of EU citizens were highly protected, the US-EU Safe Harbour Agreement was created in 2000. Consequently, organisations in the US that register to the US-EU Safe Harbour programme must provide certain protections, rights and assurances to EU citizens that their data is well-protected.

However, increased concerns surrounding data privacy in 2013 prompted the European Commission to review the US-EU Safe Harbour Agreement as they proposed a series of reforms to improve the security of personal data. While substantial progress has been made in negotiating a reformed Safe Harbour agreement, the EU and US have also been negotiating a Data Protection Umbrella Agreement to protect the personal data transferred between the two countries for law enforcement purposes since 2011 (European Commission, 2014).

Despite the European Commission making it clear that it does not want to negotiate on the topic of data privacy in TTIP (European Commission, 2013), the US has been keen on including some commentary on this in TTIP's e-commerce chapter as they have tabled a proposal to prohibit data localization measures (Lakatos, 2014; Järvinen, 2014). The US Trade Representative (USTR) increasingly faces pressure from lawmakers that have made multiple attempts in Congress to pass legislation that would give the USTR a stronger mandate against data localisation efforts in trade agreements (Bendrath, 2014). For instance, the "Law Enforcement Access to Data Stored Abroad Act", introduced in February 2015, states, "the (USTR) should pursue open data flow policies with foreign nations." However, there is a challenge within the EU as different countries are now exceeding the EU's requirements on data protection by having data localization efforts, which may make regulatory convergence all the more difficult on this issue.

In conclusion, it would be of interest to the EU if they could negotiate provisions similar to those in CETA, where Parties are required to respect the international requirements of relevant international organisations they are a part of, in TTIP. This would be of great interest to consumer advocacy groups, such as the TACD, that demand issues surrounding data flows to not be negotiated with (TACD, 2013). In addition to this, it would ideal if such provisions could reference the US-EU Safe Harbour agreement and the currently negotiated Data Protection Umbrella Agreement. If such provisions could be negotiated to protect the personal data of consumers, the EU stands to benefit from regulatory cooperation in the ICT sector in the TTIP.

5.   Conclusion

Focusing on the area of consumer protection, this chapter argues that regulatory sovereignty of American and European legislators – in terms of the legislative, rule-making ability – is unlikely to be affected by the

TTIP. The discussion of the European Commission's recently published paper on regulatory cooperation has shown that the provisions are procedural and intended to promote, guide, monitor and help facilitate regulatory cooperation. There is, of course, as yet no final agreement. The EU's approach to TTIP as set out in the Textual Proposal and the existing EU and US approaches to regulatory cooperation in other PTAs does not suggest much of a challenge to the present regulatory sovereignty. The three options for addressing regulatory divergence – harmonisation, mutual recognition and intensified exchange of information – have different implications for the scrutiny function of the legislators and its committees. Transatlantic regulatory cooperation, such as through the proposed Regulatory Cooperation Body, will have to identify which areas of regulation are suitable for harmonisation, which for mutual recognition/equivalence and which for intensified exchange of information. Decisions on this will be taken in the RCB, but any action requiring legislative change will be dealt with under existing policy-making procedures. The American and European legislators should, along with other institutions, ensure that the work of the RCB is transparent. The priorities in regulatory cooperation that will be set by the Annual Regulatory Cooperation Programme should be scrutinised to ensure that they reflect the broader consumer priorities.

A final assessment of the impact of transatlantic regulatory cooperation on consumer protection can only be made once the process can be observed. Further work will therefore be needed to monitor the procedures established and assess whether they are successful in making progress on the reducing the costs of different approaches, while ensuring that consumer interests are safeguarded.

References

Alemanno, A. (2009), "How to get out of the Transatlantic Regulatory deadlock over GMOs? This is Time for Regulatory Cooperation", IGS Center on Institutions and Governance, UC Berkeley, June.

_____ (2014), "The Transatlantic Trade and Investment Partnership and the Parliamentary Dimension of Regulatory Cooperation", European Parliament, Directorate-General for External Policies of the Union – Policy Department, Brussels.

Alemanno, A. and R. Parker (2014), "Toward Effective Regulatory Cooperation under TTIP: A Comparative Overview of the EU and

US Legislative and Regulatory Systems", CEPS Special Report No. 88, CEPS, Brussels.

Bendrath, R. (2014), "Analysis – TTIP and TiSA: big pressure to trade away privacy" (www.statewatch.org).

Bergkamp, L. and L. Kogan (2013), "Trade, the Precautionary Principle, and Post-Modern Regulatory Process: Regulatory Convergence in the Transatlantic Trade and Investment Partnership", *European Journal of Risk Regulation*, Vol. 4 No. 4, pp. 493-507.

Canis, B. and R.K. Lattanzio (2014), "U.S. and EU Motor Vehicle Standards: Issues for Transatlantic Trade Negotiations, Congressional Research Service Report", Washington, D.C.

CEPR (2013), "Reducing Transatlantic Barriers to Trade and Investment, An Economic Assessment", paper prepared for the European Commission (J. Francois et al.), London/Brussels.

Chase, P. and J. Pelkmans (2015), "This time it's different: Turbo-charging regulatory cooperation in TTIP", CEPS Special Report No. 110, CEPS, Brussels, June and chapter 2 in this volume.

Consumer Federation of America (CFA) (2014a), Comments of Consumer Federation of America Concerning Proposed Public Interest Trade Advisory Committee, DOC NO: USTR-2014-0005, March.

_____ (2014b), "How the EU/US Trade Agreement Impacts Product Safety and Regulatory Process", May.

Diels, J. and C. Thorun (2014), "Chancen und Risiken der Transatlantischen Handels- und Investitionspartnerschaft (TTIP) für die Verbraucherwohlfahrt", WISO Diskurs, November.

Ecorys (2009), "Non-Tariff Measures in EU-US Trade and Investment – An Economic Analysis", study commissioned by DG Trade, European Commission, 11 December, (http://trade.ec.europa.eu/doclib/html/145613.htm).

Elliott, E.D. and J. Pelkmans (2015), "Greater TTIP ambition in chemicals: Why and how", CEPS Special Report No. 113, CEPS, Brussels, July and chapter 13 in this volume.

European Commission (2000), "The Transatlantic Economic Partnership: An Overall Assessment".

_____ (2013), "European Commission calls on the U.S. to restore trust in EU-U.S. data flows", Press Release.

_____ (2014), "Factsheet EU-US: Negotiations on Data Protection".

_____ (2015a), "Textual Proposal on Regulatory Cooperation", February (http://trade.ec.europa.eu/doclib/docs/ 2015/february/tradoc_153120.pdf).

_____ (2015b), "Information and communication technologies (ICT) in TTIP".

_____ (2015c), Statement by EU Trade Commissioner Cecilia Malmström on the European Parliament's vote on the TTIP resolution.

_____ (2015d), Communication from the Commission to the European Parliament, the Council, The European Economic and Social Committee and the Committee of the Regions: Better regulation for better results – An EU agenda.

European Consumer Organisation (BEUC) (2015), "Consumers at the heart of Trade Policy: BEUC position on the Future Trade and Investment Strategy", Ref.: BEUC-X-2015-060, June.

European Parliament (2015), Resolution of 8 July 2015 containing the European Parliament's recommendations to the European Commission on the negotiations for the Transatlantic Trade and Investment Partnership (TTIP) (2014/2228(INI)).

Fabry, E. and G. Garbasso (2014), *The Reality of Precaution: Comparing* Risk *Regulation in the US and Europe,* J. Wiener, M. Rogers, J. Hammitt and P. Sand (eds), Jacques Delors Institute, Paris, July.

Freund, C. and S. Oliver (2015), "Gains from Harmonizing US and EU Auto Regulations under the Transatlantic Trade and Investment Partnership", Policy Brief No. PB15-10, Peterson Institute for International Economics, Washington, D.C., June, and chapter 15 in this book.

Gerstetter, C. (2014), "Regulatory cooperation under TTIP – a risk for democracy and national regulation?", Heinrich Böll Stiftung: TTIP Series, September.

Heydon, K. (2015), "The Transatlantic Trade and Investment Partnership (TTIP): Challenges and Opportunities for the Internal Market and Consumer Protection in the Area of Services", In-depth analysis for the European Parliament, IMCO Committee.

Järvinen, H. (2014), "US wants to undermine privacy in TTIP negotiations", European Digital Rights (https://edri.org/us-wants-to-undermine-privacy-in-ttip-negotiations/).

Josling, T. and S. Tangermann (2014), "Agriculture, Food and the TTIP: Possibilities and Pitfalls", CEPS Special Report No. 99, CEPS, Brussels, December, and chapter 9 in this book.

Karlsson, M. (2015), "TTIP and the environment: The case of chemicals policy", *Global Affairs*, Vol. 1, No. 1.

Kolev, G. and J. Matthes (2015), "The Transatlantic Trade and investment Partnership (TTIP): Challenges and Opportunities for the Internal Market and Consumer Protection in the Area of Motor Vehicles", Briefing, IMCO Committee, July (forthcoming as EP publication).

Lakatos, A. (2014), "Striking a transatlantic data deal: The smart decision", *Data Protection: Law & Policy*, Vol. 11, No. 9.

OECD (2002), "Annex 1. The OECD Definition of the ICT Sector", *Measuring the Information Economy*, Paris.

Pelkmans, J., F. Mustilli and J. Timini (2014), "The Impact of TTIP: The underlying economic model and comparisons", CEPS Special Report No. 93, CEPS, Brussels, October.

Pelkmans, J. and A. Correia de Brito (2015), "Transatlantic MRAs: Lessons for TTIP?", CEPS Special Report No. 101, CEPS, Brussels, March.

Renda, A. and C. Yoo (2015), "Telecommunications and Internet Services: The digital side of the TTIP", CEPS Special Report No. 112, CEPS, Brussels, July and chapter 12 in this book.

Transatlantic Consumer Dialogue (TACD) (2013), Resolution on Data Flows in the Transatlantic Trade and Investment Partnership, DOC NO: 50/13, October.

_____ (2015), Resolution on Regulatory Cooperation in the Transatlantic Trade and Investment Partnership, DOC NO: 17/15, April.

Vogel, D. (1997), *Trading Up: Consumer and Environmental Regulation in the Global Economy*, Cambridge, MA and London: Harvard University Press.

Schomberg, R. von (2006), "The precautionary principle and its normative challenges", in E. Fisher, J. Jones and R. von Schomberg (eds), *Implementing the Precautionary Principle: Perspectives and Prospects*, Cheltenham, UK and Northhampton, MA: Edward Elgar Publishers, pp. 19-42.

Wiener, J.B. and M.D. Rogers (2002), "Comparing precaution in the United States and Europe", *Journal of Risk Research*, Vol. 5, No. 4, pp. 317-349.

Woolcock, S. et al. (2015), "The Transatlantic Trade and Investment Partnership (TTIP): Challenges and Opportunities for the Internal Market and Consumer Protection in the Area of Public Procurement", Briefing for the European Parliament, IMCO Committee, forthcoming as EP publication.

VZBV (2015), "Frage- und Problemstellungen sowie Empfehlungen aus Verbrauchersicht", Verbraucherzentrale Bundesverband, Berlin, March.

8. TTIP's Broader Geostrategic Implications
Daniel S. Hamilton
and Steven Blockmans

1. Introduction

Much analysis has been conducted into the potential economic impact of TTIP, but little consideration has been given to its political and geostrategic implications. This chapter builds on earlier research by the lead author and attempts to fill that gap.[1] Our research has been guided by a number of questions:

- Will TTIP strengthen or subvert the multilateral rules-based order?

- How might such a partnership affect the broader debate about the so-called 'decline of the West'?

- Would a transatlantic economic partnership restore a sense of common purpose to the US-EU relationship, and in what way?

- How might TTIP influence the way in which the US and the EU engage with other important actors, such as China, and the degree to which emerging powers choose to challenge the prevailing order, or accommodate themselves to it?

- What geopolitical dynamics might be unleashed by the interaction among TTIP, the Trans-Pacific Partnership (TPP) and various EU bilateral trade negotiations with Asian countries?

- How might a transatlantic economic partnership affect the EU's Eastern Partnership countries, NAFTA partners Canada and Mexico, or NATO-ally Turkey? How might such a partnership affect each partner's respective relations with Russia?

---

[1] See e.g. the contributions to Hamilton (2014), in particular the summary chapter by the editor, pp. vii-xxxii.

- What might be the consequences of failure to reach a TTIP deal or the rejection of that deal by legislators or the general public on either side of the Atlantic?

We set the scene by analysing the strategic considerations that define the (perceived) need for transatlantic renewal (section 2), and then discuss the geo-economic impact of TTIP on emerging powers (section 3) and poorer countries (section 4). We argue that TTIP has the potential to be a catalyst for trade liberalisation at the global level (section 5). In this context, we address the question of the openness of TTIP (section 6) and conclude with remarks on the challenges and opportunities that lie ahead (section 7).

2.   The setting

2.1   The perceived need for transatlantic renewal

TTIP is not a new idea. Talks of an ambitious transatlantic deal stretch back over 20 years. Serious negotiations have never been launched, however, primarily because of concern for their potential impact on the multilateral trading system. Moreover, some critics have argued that such a deal would be "too small," since transatlantic tariffs and other trade barriers have not been that consequential. Others have argued that such a deal would be "too big," encompassing so many issues and with such reach into American and European societies that it would invite opposition by too many interest groups.[2]

Both of these arguments have since waned. First, the Doha Round of multilateral trade negotiations has been in stalemate for years. The recent and unexpected agreement on the so-called 'Bali Package' at the WTO's Ninth Ministerial Conference in December 2013 is an exception that proves the rule about the demise of global trade liberalisation: the package deal was reached with great difficulty but in July 2014 India decided against signing onto the trade facilitation protocol that was agreed upon as a key deliverable in Bali. It was only after the US and India came to a permanent agreement regarding India's food subsidies in November 2014 that the Bali Package received the final seal of approval. This saga shows that both the development spectrum and the appetite for liberalisation inside the WTO are rather variable. This is especially so in some of the more modern trade policy areas that are important to Washington and Brussels, such as

---

[2] See Ries (2014).

competition frameworks, intellectual property protection and market access for financial services. As noted by former European Commissioner for Trade Peter Mandelson:

> If GATT had been a club of self-described liberalisers, the WTO had become a club of guardians of the global trade rule book. For members who see global trade liberalisation as a work in progress the WTO can be a frustrating place to be, moving as it seems to do at the speed of the slowest of its members.[3]

Second, transatlantic tariffs may be low, but the size of the transatlantic economy is so huge that even small reductions could be more important than bigger tariff cuts in smaller markets, and tackling tariffs makes it easier to tackle regulatory differences, where even more substantial gains could be made.

Third, TTIP is indeed a big negotiation. But deep integration between the US and EU economies means that greater alignment and coherence on issues ranging from services and investment to regulatory differences could do far more to generate jobs and economic growth than a narrow focus on trade alone. This is especially so in areas like automotive and pharmaceuticals, where regulation is essentially science-based and the desired outcomes are basically the same on both sides of the Atlantic. Also, the value of agreeing better regulatory process frameworks (i.e. identical standards for regulatory consultation, impact assessments and other forms of transparency) should not be underestimated.[4]

The backdrop to the negotiation is a widely held perception that support for the multilateral institutions and the post-WWII principles on which they rest is eroding. This is due in part to ambivalence among rising powers about the nature of the international order, including a sense among some political elites in those countries that their moment in history has come (back) and that models other than those promoted by the US and the EU may be more relevant to future growth and prosperity. The creation of a BRICS Development Bank and the Chinese-led Asia Infrastructure Investment Bank are cases in point.

The need felt on both shores of the pond to strengthen the transatlantic partnership is fuelled by the fear that perceptions of a weakened 'West'– Europe afflicted by the worst economic and financial crisis since the Great Depression and the US unwilling to police crucial

---

[3] See Mandelson (2014).

[4] See chapter 2 in this volume, Chase & Pelkmans (2015).

hotspots of the world – will take hold and lead to more robust challenges to the international financial institutions and security arrangements that have traditionally been controlled by the US and Europe. China's pinpricks in the East and South China Seas could indeed be seen as attempts to undermine American maritime dominance in Asia-Pacific, just as Russia's aggression in Ukraine is a direct challenge to the EU and NATO.

In short, TTIP reflects a new transatlantic consensus that the international order inspired and supported by the transatlantic alliance is fading fast, and that Americans and Europeans must work together more urgently to build a partnership that is more effective in generating economic opportunity at home, dealing with new competitors, especially in emerging growth markets, and shoring up basic norms and principles guiding the international system.

2.2 The economic dimension

The transatlantic economy generates $5.5 trillion in total commercial sales a year and employs up to 15 million workers. It is the largest and wealthiest marketplace in the world, accounting for three-quarters of global financial markets, over half of world trade, and 35% of global GDP in terms of purchasing power. No other commercial artery is as integrated. Nonetheless, much more can be done to lower tariff and non-tariff barriers, kick-start services and investment and tackle unnecessary and costly regulatory differences.[5]

TTIP is first and foremost an economic negotiation seeking agreement in three areas. The first addresses such market access issues as tariffs and rules of origin. The second seeks to reduce, where feasible, non-tariff barriers and to find coherence, convergence or recognition of essential equivalence on regulatory issues. The third area seeks common agreement on a range of norms and standards regarding such issues as investment, intellectual property rights, discriminatory industrial policies and state-owned enterprises. Some of these standards are likely to extend prevailing WTO standards (WTO+); others could go beyond existing multilateral norms (WTO-extra).

In addition, the TTIP will not necessarily be concluded with a final document. TTIP is essentially a process whereby negotiators seek a 'living agreement' consisting of new consultative mechanisms

---

[5] For more on jobs, trade and investment between both sides of the North Atlantic, see Hamilton & Quinlan (2015).

regarding regulatory and non-tariff issues as they evolve in response to developments in trade, technology or other changes. Taken together, these elements underscore that TTIP is not just another trade agreement, it is a new-generation negotiation aimed at repositioning the US and European economies for a more diffuse world of intensified global competition.

TTIP's economic impact depends upon the final nature of any arrangement.[6] Its importance will be a function of the depth and content of the binding commitments and rules achieved, particularly whether or not it is seriously a WTO+ agreement. If TTIP eliminates or reduces most transatlantic tariffs; lowers barriers to the services economy; aligns or reduces inefficiencies in regulatory discrepancies; and ensures continued high standards in such areas as labour, consumer, safety and health and environment, then it is likely to boost jobs and growth significantly on both sides of the Atlantic.

2.3   Strategic considerations

TTIP is about more than just trade. It is about creating a more strategic, dynamic and holistic US-EU relationship that is better positioned with regard to third countries to open markets and to strengthen the ground rules of the international order.

TTIP is politically important to the US-EU relationship itself. The bilateral relationship encompasses a diffuse array of issues, but many are mired in process without overarching purpose. Revelations of National Security Agency (NSA) spying have also polluted the political environment in which the transatlantic partners confront global challenges and opportunities. The transatlantic engine is sputtering and needs some fuel. TTIP offers a framework for a concrete set of ambitious objectives to forge a more global partnership. It is the first real transatlantic initiative for the 'post-post' Cold War world and would be the first congressionally ratified agreement between the United States and the European Union. It could give the US-EU relationship new life, new focus, and new direction.

In this sense TTIP could be both a symbolic and practical assertion of transatlantic renewal, vigour and commitment, not only for the US and the EU towards each other but also to high rules-based standards and core principles of international order. It is an initiative

---

[6] For simulations, Erixon & Bauer (2010) and Francois et al. (2013). See also Fontagne et al. (2013).

that could be assertive without being aggressive: it challenges fashionable notions about a 'weakened West,' that are prevalent in the context of the 'rise of the rest'.

TTIP is rooted in a core truth: despite the rise of other powers the US and Europe remain the fulcrum of the world economy, each other's most important and profitable market and source of onshore jobs, each other's most important strategic partner, and still a potent force in the multilateral system – when they work in concert. The US-EU relationship remains a foundational element of the global economy and the essential underpinning of a strong rules-based international order. Americans and Europeans literally cannot afford to neglect it. TTIP is evidence that the two partners are committed to open transatlantic markets, to strengthen global rules and leverage global growth.

In this respect, TTIP could also be an operational reflection of basic values shared by democratic societies across the Atlantic, even if differences on specific values exist (e.g. GMOs). Surely, the values dimension should be extolled, not suppressed, for it is certain to have broader resonance. Revolutionary advances in communications technologies mean that governments are no longer able to control what information citizens receive.

There is also a reassurance element to the TTIP. When plans about TTIP were unfolded, NATO was wobbly and many Europeans were worried that the US 'pivot' to Asia would translate into less US attention and commitment to Europe. While Russia's shock to the European – even global – security order has given NATO a new lease on life in defence of its original mission, the bigger picture still reflects a strategic rebalancing of America's military might towards Asia Pacific. In this context, TTIP is strategically important. The creation of what would essentially be an EU-US marketplace, together with a commitment to work together to advance shared ('Western') norms and standards, would offer reassurance that the EU is in fact America's 'partner of choice' and that the pivot to Asia is not a pivot away from Europe. To be sure, TTIP will not be an 'economic NATO'[7] – a term that can easily be misinterpreted – but it could be what former Secretary of State Hillary Clinton called a "second anchor" for the transatlantic relationship, rooted in the deep and growing integration of our economies and societies.

---

[7] See remarks by then NATO Secretary General Anders Fogh Rasmussen at a conference organised by the Confederation of Danish Industry (Rasmussen, 2013).

TTIP is also important to each partner's own goals for itself. A successful agreement could help lessen America's political polarisation and generate significant economic opportunities. If TTIP and TPP are successful, the US and its partners will have opened trade and investment across both the Atlantic and the Pacific with countries accounting for two-thirds of global output. As the only party to both initiatives, the negotiations give the US a distinct advantage in leveraging issues in one forum to advance its interests in the other, while potentially reinvigorating US global leadership. TTIP is also important to generate growth and jobs in EU member states, to win greater popular support for the European Union, particularly in members like the United Kingdom, and to spur implementation of some of the EU's own goals, such as completion of the Single Market. TTIP is important for the EU – its member states and institutions alike – to off-set its relative decline on the global stage.[8]

The rise of the US as a global energy power has given the TTIP negotiations added importance. Energy-dependent European allies, particularly in Eastern Europe, as well as energy-dependent Pacific partners such as Japan are looking to the US as a new energy source. US law, however, currently limits natural gas exports to countries with which the United States has a free trade agreement. This gives some partners considerable motivation to move quickly to such an agreement with the US. A surge in transatlantic energy trade would generate even greater benefits for both sides of the Atlantic than most calculations have shown.

For all these reasons – much as war is too important to be left to generals – TTIP is too important to be left to economists. The foreign policy community has a fiduciary responsibility for the success of TTIP, which could offer new glue for the transatlantic relationship.

3.   Geo-economics: Impact on rising powers

America's wars in Iraq and Afghanistan revealed the limits of military might. In spite of Russia's sabre-rattling in the neighbourhood it shares with the EU, and the turmoil in the Middle East, today's great political games revolve mostly around another dimension of power: geo-economics. The rise of China is central to this story.

There are four sets of big international negotiations under way: TTIP, TPP, EU efforts to forge bilateral deals with India and Japan, and

---

[8] See Gros & Alcidi (2013).

US-EU led talks between more than 20 advanced and rising economies to liberalise trade in services (the Trade in Services Agreement, TiSA). Pull the strands together and – despite rhetoric to the contrary – the message is that the US and the EU have given up on the grand multilateralism that defined the post-World War II era and are repositioning themselves for the world of tomorrow. The outcomes of all four sets of negotiations promise to draw the geo-economic contours of the globalised world, fix the point of balance between advanced and rising states, and circumscribe China's place in the world. They will decide what can be salvaged from the present multilateral system. The choice lies between open global arrangements and an economic order built around competing blocs.

TTIP is important in terms of how the transatlantic partners together might best relate to rising powers, especially the emerging growth markets. Whether those powers choose to challenge the current international order and its rules or promote themselves within it depends largely on how the US and the EU engage, not only with them but also with each other.[9] The stronger the bonds among core democratic market economies, the better their chances of being able to include rising partners as responsible stakeholders in the international system. The more united, integrated, interconnected and dynamic the international liberal order is – shaped in large part by the US and the EU – the greater the likelihood that emerging powers will rise within this order and adhere to its rules. The looser or weaker those bonds are, the greater the likelihood that rising powers will challenge this order. Thus, the US and the EU have an interest in protecting and reinforcing the institutional foundations of the liberal order, beginning with their own partnership and extending it to the WTO. This means not only refraining from imposing such national protectionist measures as trade tariffs, export subsidies or 'buy national' policies, but coordinating efforts to ensure high standards globally that can lift the lives of their own people and create economic opportunity for billions of others around the globe.

There are already signs that TTIP is affecting third countries. TTIP was 'the elephant in the room' at the 2013 EU-Brazil summit; it is causing Brazilian leaders to reframe how they think of their evolving role and position.[10] Japan's decision to join the TPP was due as much to the start of TTIP negotiations as to intra-Asian dynamics. With the EU

---

[9] See Eizenstat (2013).

[10] See e.g. Thorstensen & Ferraz (2014).

now also negotiating a bilateral trade agreement with Japan, both the US and the EU are in direct talks with Tokyo about opening the Japanese market – a goal that for decades has seemed unattainable. There is also reason to believe that the trade facilitation deal struck by WTO members in Bali in December 2013 was due in part to concern from various holdout countries that with the TTIP and TPP the global trading system was moving ahead without them. There is no denying that TTIP and related initiatives are injecting new impetus into efforts to open markets and strengthen global rules.[11]

China has woken up to fact that it is being left behind in today's most important sets of trade negotiations. China has long sought to translate its economic clout into military influence (e.g. in the South China Sea) or into diplomatic and political influence (e.g. by holding down the value of its currency to boost its companies), but Beijing has changed its position and signalled a willingness to join plurilateral talks on services (TiSA) and has suggested that negotiations with the EU on investment rules could be followed by the negotiation of a trade pact. The responses from Washington and Brussels have been distinctly lukewarm. The US and the EU want evidence that Beijing is ready to open up its economy. China has been the big winner from the open global economy but is seen as a free-rider on the multilateral system. The US is asking why it should further expand arrangements that empower its rival. The US response to China's rise has long been to engage and hedge – to draw Beijing into a rules-based system while refurbishing old alliances as an insurance policy. The emphasis now is on hedging.

TTIP is a values-based, rules-based initiative that is likely to strengthen international solidarity and cohesion, facilitate US energy exports to Europe, and enhance the attractiveness of the transatlantic model of liberal democratic economies. All this is anathema to the current leadership in the Kremlin.[12] Russia is engaged in a bidding war with the EU over the shared neighbourhood. Realising that the promise of accession to the future Eurasian Economic Union (EEU) does not exert enough power of attraction,[13] the Kremlin has been using military and economic coercion in an effort to drive a wedge between the EU

---

[11] As noted above, India eventually made good on its change of heart (i.e. not signing the TFA in July 2014) by agreeing in November 2014 with the US on its food security and public stockholding concerns.

[12] See Lucas (2014).

[13] See Blockmans et al. (2012).

and countries like Armenia (which caved in and joined the EEU on 2 January 2015), Ukraine, Moldova and Georgia. Although the European Commission has initiated proceedings before the dispute settlement body DSB against Russia for its alleged infringement of WTO rules under four separate counts, the EU's overall pushback on Russia's actions has been weak, which reinforces views in Eastern Europe that TTIP could offer advantages that a multilateral framework might not.[14] Meanwhile, the Kremlin is reported to be conducting active measures in Eastern Partnership countries and in the EU itself to foment opposition to the TTIP.[15]

The risks of fragmentation of international trading rules are obvious enough. A positive sum can quite quickly become a zero sum game, carrying the unfortunate flavour of a contest between "the West and the rest". Sidelining China would carry threats to the existing fabric of the global system; and history throws up some ugly examples of how disputes about trade are the precursor to more serious conflict.

4.   Addressing concerns of poorer countries

A related consideration has to do with how the United States and the EU approach poorer countries. Much depends on the way the US and the EU handle the multiple trade agreements that each has with third countries and regions. The two parties would do well to send a clear signal that the TTIP is about common efforts to open markets by harmonising their current hodgepodge of trade preference mechanisms for low-income African countries.

Sub-Saharan Africa, the poorest region in the world, accounts for a minuscule 2% of world trade. This marginalisation of the region is holding back its development at a time when its economic governance is rapidly improving. Sub-Saharan Africa needs generous access to developed consumer markets to spur investment in labour-intensive export sectors that can spark growth and contribute to its successful economic transformation.[16]

Both the United States and the European Union give trade preferences for (some) products from (some) countries in Sub-Saharan Africa. The EU provides duty-free and quota-free access to its markets for all products – but only to the 27 least-developed countries in the

---

[14] See Hamilton (2014b). See also Novák (2014).

[15] See Lucas (2014).

[16] See e.g. Herfkens (2014).

region. It also offers less generous access to former colonies through preferential deals. The US scheme benefits 40 of the 48 countries in the region, but excludes key agricultural products (such as cotton) that African countries can produce competitively. These schemes may look good on paper, but they are actually underutilised because of their administrative complexity and outdated rules. Local content requirements are too high, and the rules of origin required for product eligibility were created decades before the development of today's value chains, which involve many countries specialising in fragmented tasks. Moreover, the US and the EU use different methods to define origin, forcing exporters to cope with a myriad of rules.[17]

It will be difficult to justify or implement a North Atlantic deal in which the participants have differing rules for developing countries. What foreign policy interest is served, for example, if the EU and the US provide different access to Kenya's products? In addition, once TTIP is in place it will make no sense to have differing access arrangements for companies from third countries. The United States and the European Union could gain considerable political advantage while following through on the logical consequence of their own negotiations if they were to harmonise their trade preference schemes for sub-Saharan Africa, either as part of or as a complement to their partnership pact.

The scheme should cover all products, since excluding just a few could encompass most products that these countries can produce competitively. Rules of origin need to be relevant, simple and flexible for beneficiaries to be able to use the schemes and benefit from the growth of value chains. Such value chains have virtually bypassed the Sub-Saharan region so far, but they hold considerable potential for less-developed African countries. It is much easier for these countries to develop capabilities in a narrow range of tasks (e.g. at the low end of global value chains) such as simple assembly, as long as infrastructure is sufficient to attract FDI) than in integrated production of entire products or processes.

Updating these rules to the realities of 21st century production networks is long overdue. WTO negotiations on clarifying rules of origin are likely to take decades; the US and the EU could do something together now. As an interim solution the European Union and the United States could recognise each other's product origin regime. If an import is eligible for preferential treatment in the US, it should also be

---

eligible in the EU, and vice versa. By doing so, the US and the EU would also demonstrate that TTIP is about opening markets rather than diverting trade. This is admittedly very tough politically, given protectionist measures in both the US and the EU. But the logic of an ever-closer transatlantic market will raise this question sooner or later. If the US and the EU address the issue sooner, they gain some additional political advantages. If they address it later, those advantages disappear and domestic political infighting over the removal of cotton subsidies in the US, for instance, is likely to grow.

5.   TTIP and multilateralism

Europeans and Americans share an interest in extending prosperity through multilateral trade liberalisation. The December 2013 Bali agreement on trade facilitation is a sign that piecemeal progress can be made. But the overall Doha Round has been underway for over 13 years with no agreement in sight, and the WTO system is under challenge, especially from emerging growth markets that have benefited substantially from the system. A number of rapidly emerging countries do not necessarily share the core principles or basic structures that underpin open rules-based commerce and show little interest in new market-opening initiatives. As a result, the global economy is drifting dangerously towards the use of national discriminatory trade, regulatory and investment practices.

In this regard, TTIP could indeed represent a new form of transatlantic collaboration to strengthen multilateral rules and lift international norms. Given the size and scope of the transatlantic economy, standards negotiated by the US and EU could become a benchmark for future global rules, reducing the likelihood that others will impose more stringent, protectionist requirements for either products or services. Mutual recognition of essentially equivalent norms and regulatory coherence across the transatlantic space, in areas ranging from consumer safety and intellectual property to investment policy and labour mobility, not only promise economic benefits at home but could also form the core of broader international norms and standards.[18] TTIP's first market access pillar could result in clearer, more straightforward and transparent rules of origin arrangements that could serve as the basis for future preferential rules of origin – a common public good. In many cases, the standards being negotiated are intended to be more rigorous than comparable rules found in the

---

[18] See Chase & Pelkmans, chapter 2 in this volume.

WTO. Agreement on such issues as intellectual property, discriminatory industrial policies or state-owned enterprises could strengthen the normative underpinnings of the multilateral system by creating benchmarks for possible multilateral liberalisation under the WTO.

There is a precedent for this. When the Uruguay Round stalled in the early 1990s, the US, Canada and Mexico negotiated the North American Free Trade Agreement in just 14 months in 1992; it came into force in 1994. This plurilateral effort had a catalytic effect on the multilateral system;[19] the Uruguay Round restarted and concluded successfully. The Information Technology Agreement negotiated by the US and EU also eventually became the basic multilateral agreement in this area. With the Doha Round stalled, we may again be at a point where plurilateral initiatives could ultimately re-energise the multilateral system. TTIP may spur others to come back to the Doha table.

TTIP may be useful not only to shore up the multilateral system but to extend it to new areas and new members. Even a successful Doha Round agreement would not address a host of issues that were not part of its mandate and yet are critical to the transatlantic partners and the global economy. Transatlantic initiatives in investment or clean technologies, for example, could be extended to WTO members who are willing to take up the same responsibilities and obligations covered by such agreements.

Hence, the 'multilateral vs. transatlantic' dichotomy is a false choice. The US and EU should advance on both fronts simultaneously; push multilateral liberalisation while pioneering transatlantic market-opening initiatives in areas not yet covered by multilateral agreements. The alternative to this WTO+ agenda is not drift; it is growing protectionism, US-EU rivalry in third markets, and the triumph of lowest-common-denominator standards for the health and safety of our people. The absence of agreed rules and procedures weakens the leverage of our two regions to ensure that high standards prevail.

In this regard, those who worry that TTIP could threaten the multilateral economic system should consider that the opposite may in

---

[19] Other developments were also significant to moving the Uruguay Round forward, such as the deepening and widening of economic cooperation between European Community member states (1992) and the effect this had on the states belonging to the European Free Trade Association. In 1994, the EC and EFTA states joined the newly created European Economic Area.

fact be true. Although the notion of an ambitious transatlantic compact has been discussed for two decades, the US and EU refrained from going ahead, and yet the Doha Round still didn't work. TTIP could be a laboratory for the WTO and a vanguard for the rest of the world.

TTIP is not just about regulatory coherence across the Atlantic, it is about setting global benchmarks. In this regard it is more ambitious than the TPP. In fact, a successful TTIP would actually be a TPP+ agreement with regard to regulatory coherence. TTIP is likely to have more impact on Asian economies than TPP is likely to have on European economies.

There are still some concerns, however. Political energy is finite, and mega-regional deals could take the oxygen out of multilateral efforts.[20] Also, the values argument loses some of its punch if TTIP is perceived to be about trade diversion rather than trade creation. TTIP could spur multilateral liberalisation, but only if and when other states go along with the transatlantic agreement and if no great trading powers work against it. In fact, much may depend on the outcome of the two other sets of negotiations promising to test allegiance to multilateralism. One will decide whether it is possible to secure a global accord on climate change (COP 21 in Paris in December 2015); the other whether rich nations are ready to extend help to poorer nations enshrined in the soon-to-expire 2015 Millennium Development Goals. The debates in both cases centre on rights and responsibilities. How to share out the burden of cutting carbon emissions; how much should rich countries pay for development? Should their largesse be matched by greater responsibility on the part of the recipients? Do governments from north and south, or west and east have the political will and energy to recognise their mutual interest in new multilateral agreements? While modest progress has been made (e.g. with the December 2014 Lima Call for Climate Action), success on both multilateral tracks remains elusive. Governments elsewhere pay lip service to the facts of interdependence while jealously guarding outdated notions of national sovereignty. Enlightened self-interest is an approach lost on most of today's world leaders. Then again, globalisation without global rules may work for a while, but it may not last.

In short, while multilateral agreement is preferable, it is not currently available. TTIP represents a very significant second-best

---

[20] See Straubhaar (2014).

option. However, a weak element to the TTIP thus far relates to openness.

6.   The issue of openness

Governments have not stated whether and how TTIP, once concluded, might be open to others willing and able to commit to similar goals and ground rules. United States Trade Representative (USTR) Mike Froman has characterised TTIP as an "open platform" but the two parties have made no official statement to this effect.[21] This stands in contrast to the TPP, where the United States and its negotiating partners have stated explicitly that the TPP is open to other APEC members (including China and Russia) and in principle much of the Asia-Pacific region.[22]

Framing the TTIP as an element of 'open architecture' accessible to others could give the US and the EU tremendous leverage in terms of ensuring ever broader commitment to the high standards and basic principles governing modern open economies, much as NATO and EU enlargement gave them significant leverage over transitional democracies in Central and Eastern Europe. One reason why many Turks are interested in TTIP, for instance, is that it represents a "transatlantic form of governance" as opposed to other models, and is thus important as a means to influence Turkey's own modernisation.[23] Yet the US and EU have not been clear about whether Turkey could in fact accede at some point. Turkey has a Customs Union with the EU, but nothing similar with the US, which means that under a TTIP US goods could flow via the EU onto the Turkish market without Turkish engagement on the terms. NAFTA countries Canada and Mexico face similar issues, as do EFTA states such as Switzerland, Iceland, Norway and Liechtenstein. The issue of 'open architecture' is also likely to have great resonance for Eastern Partnership countries like Georgia, Moldova and Ukraine, with which the EU has recently concluded deep and comprehensive free trade arrangements, integral to their Association Agreements. As noted above, it is also likely to influence countries such as Brazil and other emerging economies.

The US and the EU could issue a leaders' statement that TTIP is part of an open architecture of trade. The leaders' statement could also

---

[21] See remarks by Ambassador Froman (2014).

[22] TPP Leaders' Statement, Honolulu, 12 November 2011 (www.apec.org/ Meeting-Papers/Leaders-Declarations/2011/2011_aelm.aspx).

[23] See e.g. Kirişci (2014).

announce that the two parties are initiating consultative/information mechanisms for third parties potentially affected by a final agreement, recognising that some of this is already under way. Once such a statement is made, further internal work should be done to make it operational. The underlying premise is that the TTIP package would be opened only once it has been negotiated. On this basis, various options may be worth exploring. One would be straightforward accession: countries that are willing and able to meet the same high standards as negotiated could accede to the agreement. There may be an option to open individual elements to others, for instance market access or signing on to basic investment principles. This option would recognise that there are likely to be limits as to how open TTIP can be. For instance, it will be difficult simply to open some regulatory arrangements that might emerge from TTIP, or to open the 'living agreement' aspect of a TTIP process, because such elements are likely to be based on the trust and confidence generated among US and EU regulators, legislators and certifiers.

But countries may be able to join or attach themselves to certain provisions. For instance, when the US and the EU finalised their Open Skies agreement on transatlantic air transport in 2007, legal texts were created enabling a range of additional countries, not only in Europe but in other parts of the world, to also implement provisions of the agreement through separate accords.[24] Another option would be for the US and the EU to negotiate new or additional WTO-compatible agreements. There is some precedent for this option. For instance, since Chile could not accede to NAFTA, the US negotiated a separate bilateral arrangement. The latter option may convince true multilateralists that TTIP should not be seen as an alternative to WTO frameworks but rather as a catalyst in reforming them by 'uploading' key aspects of TTIP onto the multilateral plane. Such an approach would do justice to the twin-track approach advocated above.

Whatever modalities are chosen, once the agreement is concluded the two parties should be proactive about making the 'open architecture' of TTIP a reality.

---

[24] For instance, a Euro-Mediterranean Aviation Agreement between the European Union and Israel was signed on 10 June 2013, published in the *Official Journal* of the EU, 2013 L 208/3.

7.   Concluding remarks

There should be no illusions about the difficulties involved in achieving a TTIP. Remaining transatlantic tariff barriers, especially in agriculture, often reflect the most politically difficult cases. Some of the most intense transatlantic disagreements have arisen over differences in regulatory policy. Issues such as food safety or environmental standards have strong public constituencies and are often extremely sensitive in the domestic political arena. There is considerable debate about how and whether to include financial services and energy. For the EU, TTIP will really only be worth its salt if export barriers to energy products are lifted. Yet it is questionable whether either side is prepared to gore its sacred cows on the TTIP altar – audio-visual for the EU, the Jones Act[25] for the United States. Defence trade is off-limits. To complicate matters further, responsibility for regulation in the EU is split between Brussels and member states, and in the US between federal and state governments.

Investor state dispute settlement mechanisms envisaged under TTIP could present the biggest risk of all. Some view the issue as a self-inflicted wound, offering little gain at great pain. Investment flows freely across the Atlantic; few potential investors are deterred due to fear of arbitrary, discriminatory court action or regulatory takings. Yet the issue has awoken an unholy alliance of sovereigntists and populists on both sides of the Atlantic. Others argue that the investor state issue goes to the heart of TTIP's role as a regulatory pace-setter and that it is essential to a ground-breaking agreement.[26]

This list of difficult issues has raised concern that TTIP could divide rather than unite Europeans and Americans. The regulatory elements in particular have elicited a generalised concern in the EU that TTIP could enable the American 'system' to steamroll the European way of life. GMO issues feed these fears, even though GMOs are not part of the negotiations; NSA revelations offer further nourishment.

---

[25]The Jones Act is a common reference for the U.S. Merchant Marine Act of 1920. In essence a protective tariff, it dictates that all waterborne cargo shipped between domestic ports-known as cabotage - be handled exclusively by US built, owned, and crewed vessels. For more, see Justin Lewis, "Veiled Waters: Examining the Jones Act's Consumer Welfare Effect", Issues in Political Economy, Vol. 22, 2013, pp. 77-107.

[26] See the debate between Freya Baetens and L. Poulsen, J. Bonnitcha and J. Yackee in chapters 5 and 6 of this volume.

Both US and EU officials have been clear that TTIP will not undermine existing levels of protection. It will reinforce each side's right to regulate, but now informed by common consultations and a process that should create greater trust and confidence in each other's regulatory processes and decisions. Yet this message has not really come through. Part of the problem is that TTIP costs can be translated into negative, personalised anecdotes, whereas TTIP benefits are more abstract and broad. Arguably, US and European officials could do more to raise awareness with average citizens about the benefits of TTIP.[27]

These concerns and uncertainties underscore the importance of managing expectations while building a more energetic and effective outreach effort to both public and elite audiences. Such strategies should convey not only what TTIP is, but what it is not. It is not the first step towards, or justified by, 'globalisation.' It isn't a supranational regime and it poses no threat to the American or European way of life. It is a means to generate jobs, open markets, and ensure high standards for the food we eat, the products we buy and the services we receive.

Thus far both parties have signalled strong political commitment to a successful TTIP agreement. But as the going gets tough and other issues intrude, the open question remains whether both sides will consider that they need each other enough to make TTIP a priority and invest the necessary political capital to see the deal through to a successful ratification.

Unanticipated third issues might also emerge that could damage or even scuttle the negotiations, for instance a British referendum rejecting EU membership; renewed economic crisis; an environmental disaster or a terrorist attack, among others. The most prominent issue is still the disclosure of extensive spying operations by the US National Security Agency against European allies and other governments, which has eroded mutual trust and confidence to such an extent (especially in Germany) that some in Europe have called for the EU to suspend various agreements with the United States and to halt TTIP negotiations.[28] Thus far European leaders have resisted such demands, as they know that TTIP is far more than just another trade agreement and that the EU has a great stake in a successful outcome to the

---

[27] The European Commissioner for Trade Cecilia Malmström has been particularly active in this area since she assumed her new position in November 2014.

[28] See German Marshall Fund, "Transatlantic Trends 2014" (http://trends.gmfus.org/files/2012/09/Trends_2014_complete.pdf).

negotiations. But the issue remains unresolved and may become a bone of contention with a more critical European Parliament. It is also unclear whether an ultimate TTIP deal will be considered a final agreement to be ratified only by the European Parliament, or a so-called 'mixed agreement' to be ratified by all 28 EU member states as well, an issue that may run into trouble with Members of the US Congress who may find it difficult to explain to their constituents that the entry into force of the agreement might be upheld by a single disgruntled EU member state.

TTIP is ambitious. It will be tough to conclude. But the potential payoff is high, and the geostrategic impact of such an agreement could be as profound as the direct economic benefits.

References

Blockmans, S., H. Kostanyan and I. Vorobiov (2012), "Towards a Eurasian Economic Union: The Challenge of Integration and Unity", CEPS Special Report No. 75, CEPS, Brussels, December.

Chase, P. and J. Pelkmans (2015), "This time it's different: Turbo-charging regulatory cooperation", chapter 2 in this volume.

Eizenstat, S. (2013), "Transatlantic Trade and Investment Partnership (TTIP) Remarks", Woodrow Wilson International Center for Scholars, Washington, D.C., 21 March (www.acus.org/files/transcripts/seizenstat130321wilsonremarks.pdf).

Erixon, F. and M. Bauer (2010), "A Transatlantic Zero Agreement: Estimating the Gains from Transatlantic Free Trade in Goods", ECIPE Occasional Paper No. 4/2010, Brussels, ECIPE.

Fontagne, L., J. Gourdon and S. Jean (2013), "Transatlantic trade: whither partnership, which economic consequences?", CEPII Policy Brief No. 12, Paris, September.

Francois, J. et al. (2013), "Reducing Transatlantic Barriers to Trade and Investment: An Economic Assessment", Centre for Economic Policy Research, London.

Froman, M. (2014), "The Strategic Logic of Trade", New York, remarks by the US Trade Representative at the Council on Foreign Relations, New York, NY, 16 June (www.cfr.org/trade/us-trade-negotiations-aim-raise-labor-environmental-standards/p33141).

German Marshall Fund (2014), "Transatlantic Trends 2014" (http://trends.gmfus.org/files/2012/09/Trends_2014_complete.pdf).

Gros, D. and C. Alcidi (eds) (2013), "The Global Economy in 2030: Trends and Strategies for Europe", CEPS, Brussels.

Hamilton, D. (ed.) (2014a), *The Geopolitics of TTIP: Repositioning the Transatlantic Relationship for a Changing World,* Center for Transatlantic Relations, Washington, D.C.

Hamilton, D. (2014b), "Transatlantic Challenges: Ukraine, TTIP and the Struggle to be Strategic", *Journal of Common Market Studies,* pp. 1–15.

Hamilton, D. and J. Quinlan (2015), "The Transatlantic Economy 2015: Annual Survey of Jobs, Trade and Investment between the United States and Europe", CTR, Washington, D.C.

Herfkens, E. (2014),"TTIP and Sub-Saharan Africa: A Proposal to Harmonize EU and U.S. Preferences", in D. Hamilton (ed.), *The Geopolitics of TTIP: Repositioning the Transatlantic Relationship for a Changing World,* CTR, Washington, D.C., pp. 151-166.

Kirişci, K, (2014), "TTIP and Turkey: The Geopolitical Dimension", in D. Hamilton (ed.), *The Geopolitics of TTIP: Repositioning the Transatlantic Relationship for a Changing World,* Center for Transatlantic Relations, Washington, D.C., pp. 71-95.

Lucas, E. (2014), "TTIP, Central and Eastern Europe, and Russia", in D. Hamilton (ed.), *The Geopolitics of TTIP: Repositioning the Transatlantic Relationship for a Changing World,* Center for Transatlantic Relations, Washington, D.C., pp. 49-56.

Mandelson, P. (2014), "TTIP - what to play for?", keynote address, Caplin Conference on the World Economy, University of Edinburgh, 2 May.

Novák, T. (2014), "TTIP's Implications for the Global Economic Integration of Central and Eastern Europe", in D. Hamilton (ed.), *The Geopolitics of TTIP: Repositioning the Transatlantic Relationship for a Changing World,* CTR, Washington, D.C., pp. 57-70.

Rasmussen, A.F. (2013), "A New Era for EU-US Trade", speech by NATO Secretary General at the Conference of the Danish Industry Confederation, Copenhagen, 7 October.

Ries, C. (2014), "The Strategic Significance of TTIP", in D. Hamilton (ed.), *The Geopolitics of TTIP: Repositioning the Transatlantic Relationship for a Changing World,* CTR, Washington, D.C.

Straubhaar, T. (2014),"TTIP: Don't Lose Momentum!", in D. Hamilton (ed.), *The Geopolitics of TTIP: Repositioning the Transatlantic Relationship for a Changing World,* Center for Transatlantic Relations, Washington, D.C., pp. 33-48.

Thorstensen, V. and L. Ferraz (2014), "The Impact of TTIP on Brazil", in D. Hamilton (ed.), *The Geopolitics of TTIP: Repositioning the Transatlantic Relationship for a Changing World,* Center for Transatlantic Relations, Washington, D.C., pp. 137-149.

PART II

SECTORAL ISSUES

9. AGRICULTURE, FOOD AND TTIP: POSSIBILITIES AND PITFALLS

*TIM JOSLING AND STEFAN TANGERMANN**

1. Introduction

Agriculture is always a difficult area in trade negotiations. The US and the EU have butted heads on the issue of market access and export subsidies for 50 years, as each tries to protect its own farm interests and farm programmes. However, a combination of domestic reforms, WTO constraints and firmer world market prices has reduced the gap between US and EU farm product prices and led to a possible opening up of trade across the Atlantic. Food trade issues are also tricky: countries are hesitant to change engrained regulatory habits. In the last 20 years there have been significant disagreements between the US and the EU over food regulations, and in particular food safety standards. In some instances there has been convergence of standards; in other areas the differences in regulations and standards appear unbridgeable. Moreover, the differences in food safety regulations have played into the public debate about TTIP, narrowing the room for flexibility, particularly on the side of the EU. But with the extensive development of supply chains in the food industry, the need for more cohesion in food safety and food quality rules is becoming increasingly urgent.

The progress in agriculture and food issues in the TTIP talks will largely be determined by the level of ambition in the negotiations as a whole. If ambitions are modest, a low-level agreement could probably be reached that included some limited commitments on agricultural market access and food regulations. These could include promises of mutual support in the area of opening up agricultural markets through

* Helpful comments on an earlier draft received from Daniel Hamilton, Jacques Pelkmans and Jo Swinnen are gratefully acknowledged.

the WTO and of further transatlantic cooperation in trying to resolve conflicts over food regulations. Bolder ambitions would allow more scope for tackling the difficult problems, although at the cost of time. It would be unfortunate if the opportunity were not taken to make some significant progress in removing some long-standing irritants in the area of agricultural policy and food regulations: this is where the economic gains are likely to be significant and the spill-overs useful. This chapter will make the case that it is worthwhile making the effort to secure a constructive and imaginative agreement on agriculture and food regulations in the TTIP.[1]

2. Agriculture and food in transatlantic trade

To put the agricultural issue in perspective, it is useful to review the extent and nature of transatlantic trade flows in agriculture and food products and the tariff and non-tariff barriers that exist. These non-tariff barriers mainly reflect differences in food regulations and standards, and have attracted public attention beyond their economic significance. The TTIP agenda in agriculture will reflect the balance between the economic interests of the US and the EU in these areas and the extent to which each of the negotiating partners have room to make accommodating changes to policies.

2.1 Trade flows in agricultural and food products

The value of transatlantic trade in food and agricultural products (chapters HS 1-24 of the tariff code) has been increasing modestly over the past 20 years mainly as a result of increased exports of food and beverage products. Trade values slumped a little with the economic downturn in 2007-08 but the expansion of trade has been rather rapid since 2009, reaching $23 billion in 2012. The EU has generally exported more agricultural and food products to the US than it imports from that source, and now shows a surplus of $9 billion on transatlantic agricultural and food trade (see Figure 9.1). Much of this surplus is accounted for by buoyant exports of beverages and spirits and of processed foods. EU producers have been reasonably successful in gaining access to the US market, up 48% since 2000. Although the importance of the US as a trading partner in agriculture and food for

---

[1] For a detailed discussion of the 50-years history of agricultural trade relations between the US and the EU and implications for the TTIP negotiations, see Josling & Tangermann (forthcoming).

the EU is somewhat less than it is for total merchandise trade, the US remains the largest single export market for the EU's agriculture and food industry.

Figure 9.1 Food and agricultural trade between the EU-27 and the US, 2000-12

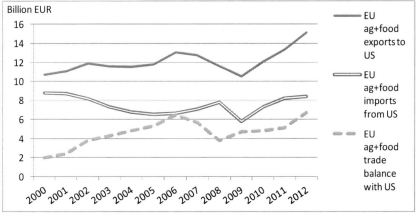

Source: Josling & Tangermann (forthcoming).

With respect to food and agricultural imports into the EU, the US is a relatively minor supplier (only 8%) of EU food and agricultural imports. The US trails well behind Brazil as a source of the EU's food and agricultural imports: Brazil sells 70% more agricultural and food products to the EU than does the US. Correspondingly, the EU is a relatively unimportant market for US agricultural and food exports. Moreover, the importance of the EU as an agricultural trading partner for the US has declined steadily over time with the growth of markets in Asia: the 'pivot to Asia' has certainly taken place in US agricultural trade. US exporters to the EU of food and agricultural products have found themselves with a stagnant market for the past decade, down 6% since 2000. This difference between the US and the EU in the significance of transatlantic agricultural trade could prove an important aspect of the political backdrop to the TTIP negotiations.[2]

---

[2] This raises the question as to whether it is successful exporters who take the lead in trade negotiations or those who are frustrated by slow growth in certain markets. One assumes that exporter concerns focus on import barriers into potentially lucrative markets.

Certain types of food and agricultural products dominate these trade flows. By far the largest item in the EU's exports of agricultural and food products to the US is accounted for by beverages and spirits (HS 22), where EU exports of spirits, wine and beer figure most prominently (and in that order).[3] That sector makes up one-half of all EU food and agriculture exports to the US. No other sub-sector in the field of food and agriculture (at the 2-digit HS level) accounts for more than 6% of the EU's transatlantic food and agricultural exports.[4] The largest category of imports into the EU in food and agriculture trade from the US is edible fruit and nuts (HS 08), such as almonds and walnuts, followed by oilseeds and oleaginous fruit (HS 12) including soybeans. These two subsectors represent 18% and 16% respectively of the total of all EU imports from the US in the food and agriculture sector, and are more important than beverages and spirits (14%), and cereals (6%). The difficulties in selling genetically modified (GM) products in Europe has been in part a cause of the slow growth, but as significant has been the success of Latin America in providing bulk commodities to Europe.

One might expect in such a two-way trade pattern that there would be significant trade flows in both directions within each individual product sector, at least for processed foods that are less homogeneous than raw agricultural commodities. This 'intra-industry trade' could be as politically significant as trade among sub-sectors. One widely-used measure of the extent of intra-industry trade is the Grubel-Lloyd index (Grubel & Lloyd, 1975). That index lies between 1, indicating that all trade in the sub-sector concerned is of an intra-industry nature, and zero, signalling that there is no two-way trade flow within the sub-sector concerned. The Grubel-Lloyd index for EU-US trade in food and agricultural products (at the level of 2-digit HS product groups) is presented in Table 9.1, where product sectors are arranged in decreasing order of their share in total EU-US trade.[5] The

---

[3] Trade shares reported here relate to the average of 2010-12.

[4] For convenience we use 'transatlantic' to refer to US-EU trade and not trade between the EU and Canada.

[5] That share is defined as the percentage of EU exports to the US plus EU imports from the US of the product sector concerned in the aggregate of all EU exports plus imports in food and agriculture in trade with the US, for the average of 2010-12. Table 9.1 contains all product sectors where that percentage is 3% or more. The broad definition of the sectors might lead one to expect that relatively high degrees of intra-industry trade would be found.

Grubel-Lloyd index shows that for the nearly all of the most important product sectors in agricultural and food trade between the EU and the US (including the major trade flows in the beverages sector) there is relatively little intra-industry trade. Major exceptions are three rather heterogeneous product sectors (animal or vegetable fats and oils; miscellaneous edible preparations; preparations of vegetables, fruit, nuts) where such inter-industry trade is to be expected.

Table 9.1 Intra-industry trade in major EU-US trade flows in the food and agriculture sector

HS	Product sector	Grubel-Lloyd index	Share in total EU-US agricultural and food trade
22	Beverages, spirits and vinegar	0.273	35.6%
08	Edible fruit and nuts etc.	0.157	7.0%
12	Oilseeds and oleaginous fruits etc.	0.226	6.5%
15	Animal or vegetable fats and oils etc.	0.624	4.5%
21	Miscellaneous edible preparations	0.983	3.8%
20	Preparations of vegetables, fruit, nuts etc.	0.587	3.7%
23	Residues and waste from the food industries etc.	0.308	3.3%
04	Dairy produce, birds' eggs etc.	0.165	3.3%
18	Cocoa and Cocoa preparations	0.101	3.1%
19	Preparations of cereals etc.	0.229	3.0%

Source: Authors' own calculations.

On this basis it might appear that in the agriculture and food sector the US and the EU are primarily engaged in trade where the respective exporter has a clear comparative advantage, i.e. where there is not much of an issue of competition between these trading partners but rather the less-contentious trading relationship of complementarity. However, the existing structure of trade is the result of the current regime of trade and regulatory policies – i.e. of precisely the policies that are set to be liberalised and harmonised as a result of the TTIP. So the low degree of intra-industry trade could be interpreted as an indication of a potential for an increase in such trade if barriers could be reduced.

2.2 Tariff barriers

As a result of many rounds of multilateral trade negotiations, tariff barriers on transatlantic trade are already relatively low. Average trade-weighted tariffs on imports into the US stand at 4.7%: the corresponding average tariff for the EU is 6.4%. Even in the case of agriculture and food products, the average MFN tariff applied on all agricultural and food products by the US is only 3.9%.[6] In the EU, the average tariff is more than double that figure, at 8.6%, but even that appears reasonably low compared to agricultural tariffs in other countries. However, these averages hide significant tariff peaks in sensitive products (agriculture, textiles, beverages, etc.). Figure 9.2 shows tariff profiles across individual product groups within agriculture. The EU maintains a tariff level above 50% to protect dairy products, above 30% in the sugar and confectionary sector, and around 20% for animal products as well as for beverages and tobacco. In the US, tariffs are highest in dairy products, beverages and tobacco and sugar. In all product sectors, with the exception of cotton (where EU output is close to zero), EU tariffs are considerably higher than those of the US.

Figure 9.2 EU and US tariff profiles in agriculture: MFN applied duties

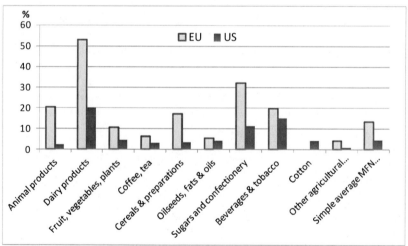

Data sources: WTO, ITC & UNCTAD (2013).

---

[6] Source of tariff information discussed here is WTO, ITC and UNCTAD (2013), as well as European Parliament (2014).

Moreover, trade-weighted tariff averages tend to under-represent these tariff peaks as import volumes of such products tend to be small. And the average includes those tariffs in agriculture (at the 6-digit HS level, MFN applied) that are already duty free, accounting for 30.7% of tariffs in the US and 31.2% of tariffs in the EU 31.2%. High tariffs themselves are somewhat unevenly distributed: tariffs above 15% are found in only 5.3% of all agricultural product categories in the US, while in the EU 26.2% of all product categories in agriculture have tariffs above that level.

This disparity is even more apparent if one examines more disaggregated information on tariff levels: this is more likely to identify the so-called 'sensitive' products that can pose particularly potent political problems. Some of the levels that these mega-tariffs can attain are shown in Figure 9.3.[7] The dairy sector in the EU is protected, for example, by a mega-tariff of up to 600% and in other agricultural sectors there are four cases of tariffs above 100%.[8] In the US, the highest tariff, at 350%, is found in the beverages and tobacco sector, and there are two other sectors with a tariff above 100%.[9] Thus, the common view that tariffs, including those for agricultural products, will not be a major obstacle in the TTIP negotiations may be somewhat premature. Free bilateral trade will cause some disruption. There will be a request for long transition periods and safeguards for sensitive products (Trachtenberg, 2012). The political economy of trade negotiations will be fully on display as interest groups, from sugar, beef and dairy to fruits, nuts and vegetables, will play their cards. The dilemma for trade negotiators will be whether to exclude sensitive sectors that are protected by high tariffs, so as to avoid the talks getting bogged down, or to hope that lofty ambitions will carry enough weight to overcome sector resistance.

---

[7] It should be noted that the vertical axis of Figure 9.3 extends to much higher tariff levels than that of Figure 9.2.

[8] Mega-tariffs are often specific tariffs, and their estimated *ad valorem* equivalent depends on the import price assumed. This is one reason why alternative sources report different levels of maximum (*ad valorem* equivalent) tariffs.

[9] It is also worth noting that mega-tariffs of such orders of magnitude are an exclusive agricultural phenomenon. Outside the agricultural sector, the highest tariff rate reported for the EU is 26% (in the product group fish & fish products), and that for the US is 55% (in the group leather, footwear, etc.).

Figure 9.3 EU and US tariff profiles in agriculture: maximum applied MFN duty within the respective product group

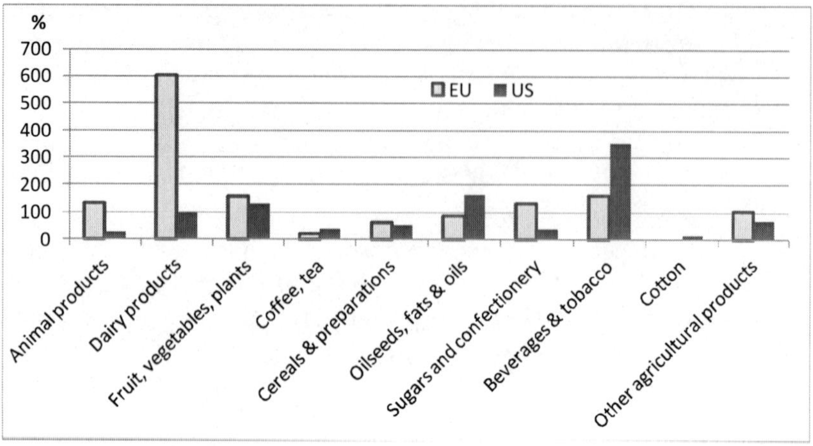

Data source: WTO, ITC & UNCTAD (2013).

2.3   Non-tariff trade impediments

Even though it may be difficult to approach complete tariff elimination in agricultural trade between the US and the EU, the biggest hurdle in the trade part of the TTIP negotiations is reduction of the trade barriers resulting from non-tariff measures (NTMs).[10] However, this is also the element that can generate the largest benefits. Thus it will be crucially important to find an effective way forward in dealing with the many NTMs, both at and behind the border, that result from diverging regulatory approaches used in the two entities. In many cases these NTMs stand in the way of harmonious trade relations across the Atlantic, and in a number of instances they have caused, and continue to cause, serious acrimony and legal disputes in the WTO. Though NTM issues cause difficulties in US-EU trade relations across the board in all sectors, they are particularly pronounced and troublesome in the agriculture and food sector, where particular problems result from health and safety (sanitary and phytosanitary – SPS) measures.

---

[10] The value of removing non-tariff barriers to trade is notoriously hard to quantify. As shown below, studies find considerable economic benefits from the harmonisation of regulatory measures in the transatlantic marketplace, benefits that by far exceed those resulting from tariff elimination.

The main impetus behind dealing with NTMs will come from the US. Agricultural businesses in the US want a number of long-standing regulatory issues with the EU resolved. They perceive these as the major impediments to market access. These include the use of growth additives in livestock, methods of pathogen reduction in slaughterhouses and approval of genetically modified varieties of corn and soybeans (Grueff, 2013).[11] But not all the offensive interests are on one side of the Atlantic. Agricultural and food producers in the EU would like better access to the US market, specifically for dairy products and meats. As EU milk quotas are abolished, the need to find overseas markets for cheeses and other high-value dairy products will increase. Moreover, the EU would like more protection for geographical indications (GIs) in the US, for cheese and for specialty meats (as well as wines), an issue that has led to stalemate in the context of the TRIPS negotiations.

3.   Estimates of benefits from TTIP

A number of recent studies have aimed at estimating the potential quantitative impacts of a TTIP on variables such as GDP, trade and output in the US, the EU and third countries.[12] These models include agriculture, although often at a highly aggregated level. Most of the studies have employed some type of a computable general equilibrium (CGE) model for the analysis, representing the whole economy, disaggregated into several sectors, and including all important feedback mechanisms, in particular linking income generation with expenditures for both consumers and governments. In the models a number of individual countries are identified, in particular the US and the EU, while the rest of the world, closing the global model, is often treated as one country.

As one might expect, results differ from study to study, depending on factors such as the structure of the model and its parameters, underlying data, the baseline assumed (in the absence of TTIP) and the scenarios considered. A study by Fontagné et al. (2013)

---

[11] GM crops are approved for sale on the EU market only after an extensive scientific investigation as to their safety to health and the environment. The slowness of this process was at the root of a WTO challenge by the US on the EU's biotech approval process.

[12] See, for example, Ecorys (2009 and 2012), Felbermayr et al. (2013), Fontagné et al. (2013), Francois et al. (2013), Kinnman & Hagberg (2012) and European Parliament (2014).

conveys the types of impacts of agricultural trade liberalisation suggested by such models, and their orders of magnitude. The modelling framework used in that study is dynamic, generating future time paths for all variables. The results shown below are those for the year 2025, expressed as percentage deviations from the baseline (in which no TTIP is assumed), in constant prices.

3.1 Impact on trade flows

Estimated impacts on bilateral trade flows are summarised in Table 9.2, for the 'reference' scenario, assuming a complete phasing out of all tariffs, and a 25% cut in the trade restrictiveness of all NTMs, for all sectors of the US and EU economies. The impacts of liberalising trade between the US and the EU are found to be significant: bilateral trade between the US and the EU would increase by around half overall, indicating the extent to which current barriers prevent the transatlantic trade potential from being fully tapped.

Table 9.2 Estimated impacts of TTIP on bilateral trade flows ('reference' scenario percentage deviation from baseline in 2025)

Exporter	Importer	Total	Agriculture	Industry	Services
Transatlantic trade					
US	EU27	52.5	168.5	66.4	14.0
EU27	USA	49.0	149.5	61.8	24.0
Other trade flows					
US	RoW	-1.4	-1.9	-1.3	-1.6
EU27	RoW	-1.4	-0.4	-1.4	-1.4
RoW	USA	-2.5	-0.8	-2.8	-0.7
RoW	EU27	0.2	-1.5	0.1	0.6
EU27	EU27	-1.2	-2.6	-2.3	2.8
RoW	RoW	0.1	-0.0	0.2	0.2

Note: RoW refers to the rest of the world.
Source: Fontagné et al. (2013).

As the highest trade barriers in both the US and the EU are currently found in agriculture, agricultural trade flows are estimated to expand significantly in both directions, by 150% and more. The estimated strong expansion of bilateral trade within a US-EU free trade area (FTA), indicating a potential for large trade creation, might be expected to result in considerable trade diversion at the expense of third countries, as their exports to the US and the EU would no longer be so competitive. Yet, perhaps surprisingly, the authors find that trade diversion would be rather small under a TTIP, with US and EU trade flows from and to third countries declining by less than 3%. The study also estimated the impact of the components of the tariff and NTM package separately.

These results are summarised in Table 9.3, for the 'reference' case and four alternative policy scenarios. In the 'tariffs only' scenario, only tariffs are phased out. Under 'targeted NTM cuts', NTMs that are more restrictive than the median of the respective sector (agriculture, industry or services) are reduced by 30%, while the remaining ones are cut by 15%. The scenario 'harmonisation spillovers' looks into the benefits that third countries may reap as they find it easier to deal with harmonised standards in the US and the EU, and in this scenario the authors assume that the trade restrictiveness of NTMs maintained by the US and the EU vis-à-vis third countries is reduced by 5%. [13]

Table 9.3 Estimated impacts of TTIP on US and EU real income and exports for alternative scenarios (percentage deviation from baseline in 2025)

	Alternative scenarios				
	Reference	Tariffs only	Targeted NTM cuts	Harmonisation spillovers	Ecorys NTMs
	Real income				
US	0.3	0.0	0.3	0.5	0.2
EU27	0.3	0.0	0.2	0.5	0.1
Rest of world	-0.1	0.0	-0.1	0.1	0.0
	Exports				
US	10.1	2.1	10.4	14.5	5.4
EU27	2.3	0.4	1.9	3.4	1.3
Rest of world	-0.3	- 0.1	-0.3	0.9	- 0.2

Source: Fontagné et al. (2013).

3.2 Trade impacts of NTMs

It is difficult to provide a quantitative overview of the significance of NTMs. Anecdotal evidence of particularly notable cases helps to foster

---

[13] For a more recent and more detailed discussion and analysis of such spill-over effects, see Lejour et al. (2014).

an impression of the nature of the problem, but the amount of trade displaced is more difficult to calculate. The most important conflicts in agricultural trade between the US and the EU revolve around regulatory differences, and the attention given to them indicates the weight of the issues the TTIP negotiations on NTM matters will have to deal with. Yet, there are many more barriers of this type that would require action if trade across the Atlantic were to be truly liberalised.[14] To what extent do these NTMs impact on trade flows, compared to the incidence of tariffs?

One way of trying to make information on NTMs comparable to tariff information is by estimating their price impact. Where a given NTM acts as an effective barrier to imports, the domestic market price of the product concerned in the importing country is kept above the international market price (where necessary corrected for a relevant tariff). The resulting price gap, expressed as a percentage of the international price, provides a yardstick of the NTM's price impact that is directly comparable to an *ad valorem* tariff.[15] Aggregate results for the whole food and agriculture sector, as well as for manufacturing and services, reported in two different studies are presented in Table 9.4, along with average tariff levels in the agriculture and food sector. Even though the two studies (Ecorys, 2009; and Fontagné et al., 2013) arrive at somewhat different estimates for NTMs, they both agree on three interesting findings.[16] First, in agricultural and food trade between the EU and the US, NTMs result in higher trade barriers than tariffs prevailing in that sector. Second, trade barriers resulting from NTMs are higher in the food and agriculture sector than in manufacturing and services.[17] Third, while tariffs in agriculture and food are higher in the

---

[14] For a list of relevant NTMs in trade between the EU and the US, based on various sources, including an extensive business survey, see Ecorys (2012).

[15] There are, however, alternative and more complex approaches to estimating *ad valorem* equivalents of NTMs. For studies applying such alternative approaches, see for example Ecorys (2009).

[16] The 'Ecorys NTMs' scenario, finally, is identical to the 'reference' scenario, except that the Ecorys estimates of NTM restrictiveness in the US and the EU are used instead of those estimated by Fontagné and his colleagues (see Table 9.4).

[17] Alternative studies yield different results in this regard. For example, Francois et al. (2013) find that NTMs are highest in the sectors of cars and chemicals, followed by processed foods.

EU than in the US, NTMs in that sector are more pronounced in the US than in the EU.[18]

Table 9.4 Estimates of ad valorem equivalents of NTMs and tariffs in the sector of agriculture and food in the EU and the US

	EU	US
NTMs: Fontagné et al.	48.2%	51.3%
NTMs: Ecorys	56.8%	73.3%
Tariffs in agriculture: simple average MFN applied	13.2%	4.7%

Data sources: Ecorys (2009); Fontagné et al. (2013) and WTO, ITC and UNCTAD (2013).

4. Possible modalities for the negotiations

The way in which the US and the EU have negotiated agricultural and food issues in other bilateral agreements suggests the likely modalities for the TTIP. The US and EU trade negotiators have accumulated ample experience with negotiating agricultural provisions in FTAs, and there are many other such agreements that provide examples.[19] A general overview and a few concrete examples from existing FTAs will suffice to illustrate some of the major elements that trade diplomats find on the FTA negotiating table, and the room for manoeuvre they can potentially use.

4.1 Negotiations on market access

A significant part of FTA negotiations traditionally deals with tariff cuts. The simplest techniques of cutting tariffs in an FTA is to establish a timeline over which tariffs on bilateral trade would go to zero. Products are often grouped into categories, depending on whether the tariffs are to disappear immediately on the FTA coming into force or

---

[18] Using data at a more disaggregate level, another study finds the tariff equivalent of NTMs to vary considerably across individual products within the food and agriculture sector (Felbermayr et al., 2013). It also finds, contrary to the studies cited above, that tariff equivalents of NTMs in the EU are higher than those in the US, where estimates are available for both entities.

[19] For a more comprehensive overview of the treatment of agriculture in existing FTAs, see Fulponi, Shearer and Almeida (2011) and the literature referenced there.

over a specified time-period. Many agricultural and food items could be liberalised on such a schedule. But in the case of particularly sensitive sectors, several options are available for introducing modalities specific to agriculture. One of these is exclude some agricultural lines from the duty-free treatment.[20] As was shown above, there are several sectors, including dairy products and sugar, where high tariffs are found in both the US and the EU. The existence of these 'sensitive' products in the agricultural sector, often protected by mega-tariffs, is the major reason why most regional trade agreements (RTAs) do not achieve complete tariff elimination on all agricultural products. For example, the EU's RTA with South Africa, in force since 2000, foresees zero duties on the EU side for no more than 73% of all agricultural tariff lines; the RTA between the EU and Korea, on the other hand, in force since July 2011, provides for zero duties for imports into the EU on 97.9% of all tariff lines in agriculture (WTO, ITC & UNCTAD, 2013). Under the RTAs the US has with Chile and Morocco, the US is committed to apply zero duties to 100% of the agricultural tariff lines, while in the case of its RTA with Peru that share is 97.1% (WTO, ITC & UNCTAD, 2013). One notable exception is that in the FTA with Australia sugar was excluded altogether from the tariff elimination commitment.

A second option that can be used in FTA negotiations over agriculture is the length of the transition period over which tariff cuts are phased in.[21] Obviously, where tariff elimination is considered politically difficult, a longer transition period can be used to attenuate some of the pain. Fulponi et al. (2011) have analysed 55 selected RTAs and found that on aggregate they provided for duty-free treatment of slightly more than 90% of all tariff lines in agriculture, although that level is on average reached only after a transition period of somewhat more than 15 years. Within the product groups of dairy and sugar, however, only 72% of tariff lines were agreed to see complete tariff elimination in this set of RTAs. The US regularly uses the device of categorising products into categories, where one category is liberalised

---

[20] GATT Article XXIV:8(b) requires that duties are eliminated "on substantially all trade" between the partner countries in an FTA. Although often discussed, a legal definition of which share of trade constitutes "substantially all the trade" has never been agreed.

[21] In this context, GATT Article XXIV(5c) speaks of a "reasonable length of time", which the Understanding on the interpretation of Article XXIV of the GATT says "should exceed 10 years only in exceptional cases".

on signing and other categories reach zero tariffs over different lengths of time. Eventually these transition periods end, and the degree of certainty given by such reduction schedules is itself a useful signal for investors and farmers.

A third relevant option regarding 'sensitive' products is to agree on tariff cuts for only limited quantities of imports, implemented through **tariff rate quotas** (TRQs). For example, under its FTA with Egypt, the EU applies TRQs to the importation of 34 agricultural products, while the US-Australia FTA specifies TRQs for imports of 17 agricultural products into the US (Fulponi et al., 2011). An important consideration in negotiating TRQs is whether the import quantities concerned can grow over time, and at which rate. After all, if the TRQ provides for sufficiently fast expansion of the preferential quantity, then it can eventually become equivalent to an unconstrained tariff cut.

Fears that trade liberalisation might result in import surges and consequent pressure on domestic farmers have led negotiators of some FTAs to include "special agricultural safeguards" in the agreements, based on price and/or quantity triggers. Fulponi et al. (2011) found several examples in their sample of 55 FTAs, including all six FTAs involving the US. Fundamentally the nature of these safeguards often resembles that of the Special Safeguards Provisions in the WTO Agreement on Agriculture, although the specific details and parameters vary considerably. The applicable product lists also vary from case to case, although livestock, dairy, poultry, and fruits and vegetables are frequently covered. The remedies allowed also vary, including the option to halt tariff reductions or even to revert to the MFN tariff. Typically, however, the special safeguard provisions expire when the FTA has reached the end of its transition period. Even though special safeguards may create some uncertainty for trade flows, if they allow agreement on deeper and faster tariff cuts in an FTA they could help in completing the negotiations. Many agreements also contain provisions for general trade remedies, i.e. anti-dumping and countervailing duty measures. They tend to make reference to the general rules under the GATT, but also sometimes modify them for trade within the FTA.

4.1.1   Rules of origin

Since partners of an FTA typically want to avoid trade deflection, i.e. re-routing of imports from third countries through the FTA partner with the lowest tariff, rules of origin (ROOs) are also an important element of FTAs. Partners of an FTA maintain, contrary to those of a customs union, their national MFN tariff schedules applicable to imports from third countries. There is, hence, an incentive to re-route imports into an FTA partner with a high MFN tariff through the territory of an FTA partner with a lower tariff. Such trade deflection would effectively undermine the tariff protection maintained by the high-tariff partner. In order to prevent this from happening, FTAs require that goods imported into any of the partner countries must, in order to qualify for duty-free treatment, originate wholly or primarily inside the FTA. It is reasonably straightforward to define what "wholly" should mean in this context. However, many goods contain intermediate products (including agricultural commodities) imported from third countries. With a growing tendency for value chains to be extended across several countries, there are more and more products that include components imported from anywhere in the world, including of course from countries outside the FTA. Under these conditions it is a matter for negotiation to define which criteria must be fulfilled for a product to be considered to originate "primarily" from inside the FTA. Resolution on the question of ROOs can require considerable negotiation. The outcome will however be important to the relevance of the TTIP to agricultural and food trade (see Box 9.1).

Box 9.1 ROOs and EU FTAs

When negotiating the ROOs for TTIP, two fundamental issues are relevant. First, the overall 'philosophy' needs to be chosen, in the sense that decisions are required as to how restrictive or liberal the US and the EU want the ROO to be. That philosophy will determine the criteria to be set for all the individual products, but it would also be reflected in a number of more general rules. In particular, most ROOs include a tolerance/*de minimis* clause specifying that inputs from third countries are allowed as long as their share in the value of the final product is below a given threshold, even where these third-country inputs would otherwise exclude the product concerned from preferential treatment. In most FTAs, that threshold is in the range of 7% to 10% (Donner Abreu, 2013). In the EU-South Africa FTA, however, it is generally set at 15%, but reduced to 10% for some agricultural products. Lower-than-the-generally-applicable thresholds are also set for certain agricultural products in many other FTAs. In the TTIP negotiations, the US and the EU could consider setting an example by agreeing on a comparatively high *de minimis* threshold, including for all agricultural products.

Such a 'liberal' philosophy for ROOs could also include exemption from otherwise applicable rules where MFN tariffs meet given conditions. In particular, it could be agreed that ROO requirements do not apply to products where the difference between MFN tariffs of the US and the EU does not exceed a given margin, say five percentage points. The reasoning behind such an approach is that ROO requirements are not needed where the cost of trans-shipment through the partner country is higher than the difference in MFN tariffs. Given the geographical distance between the US and the EU, trans-shipment through the partner territory is rather costly, and hence the acceptable margin between their MFN tariffs could also be set at a reasonably generous level.

Another expression of a liberal 'philosophy' behind ROOs is the degree of flexibility provided to producers. A free choice, e.g., could be allowed between two alternative criteria, say between a change in tariff classification and a minimum share of value added.

A second fundamental choice for ROOs is the scope for so-called 'cumulation'. It is typical for ROOs in FTAs to allow cumulation of inputs and value added across all FTA members when determining whether the product concerned has originated inside the FTA. Moreover, several FTAs also allow for 'diagonal' cumulation, i.e. inputs originating in third countries that benefit from some form of preferential treatment by the FTA partners. The EU has spearheaded the inclusion of such diagonal cumulation principles in its FTAs, in particular in its 'PanEuroMed' system of trade preferences with countries in the Mediterranean basin, but also in many of its other preferential schemes (Donner Abreu, 2013). The US also makes use of diagonal cumulation in several of its FTAs.

It would appear only natural for a TTIP agreement to allow for diagonal cumulation to include all countries with which both the US and the EU have FTAs, and also those developing countries to which both the US and the EU have extended unilateral preferences under the GSP regime. In a way, this would be a generalisation of the suggestion to exempt products from ROO requirements where the difference between MFN tariffs of the US and the EU does not exceed a given margin: that criterion could be applied not only to MFN tariffs but also to preferential tariffs that the US and the EU charge on imports of a given product from the country concerned.

When deciding on the design of ROOs in the food and agriculture sector, it is worth remembering two implications for the functioning of markets which result from the fact that many agricultural products are so homogeneous in nature that their origin is essentially irrelevant. This means that, first, imported produce can replace the domestically produced output in consumption, with the result that an FTA country can (theoretically) export all its domestic output to the partner country, fully meeting even the most stringent ROO requirements. Where that is the case, no ROO can effectively exclude trade deflection (Josling, 1993 and 1997). Second, where the partner countries of an FTA are on aggregate a net exporter of a given product, the price of that product will in any event be at the world market level and not reflect tariffs that any partner maintains vis-à-vis third countries. In that case, trade deflection is not an issue, and no ROO for the product concerned will be effective in protecting its producers inside the FTA.

4.2 Negotiations on subsidies

Agricultural subsidies have been a large part of the contentious trade relations between the US and the EU over the years (Josling & Tangermann, forthcoming). In the context of the TTIP it is useful to separate out subsidies given on exports from that given to domestic producers through various farm programmes. The former is a more likely candidate for inclusion in a TTIP agreement.

4.2.1   Export subsidies

As export subsidies for agricultural products are still legal, within given constraints, under the Agreement on Agriculture (AoA), they could potentially also be used to distort trade flows between partners of an FTA. That is why many FTAs require the elimination of subsidies on within-FTA exports, although sometimes only after a phasing-out period. Some FTAs also contain provisions aimed at avoiding distortions caused by subsidised exports from a third country to one of the FTA partners. NAFTA, for example, allows the US and Canada to subsidise exports of certain products to Mexico if Mexico imports products from third countries that subsidise their exports.

4.2.2   Domestic subsidies

Domestic subsidies pose an interesting problem for FTA negotiations. In principle, like in the case of export subsidies, partners of an FTA may well have an interest in seeing domestic subsidies on intra-trade disciplined so as to avoid distortions. However, it is technically difficult, if not impossible, to cut domestic subsidies to only that part of output that will be exported to an FTA partner country: once output has left the farm gate, it can go anywhere. Hence, if FTA partners wanted to discipline domestic subsidies, the only feasible way to do so is to constrain them for all of domestic output. As this is precisely what is being dealt with in the WTO negotiations on agriculture, the conventional wisdom is that discipline on domestic subsidies can be agreed only at the multilateral level. This is probably also the reason why nearly all FTAs are essentially silent on domestic subsidies (except for remedies, see below). As a matter of fact, the need to discipline domestic subsidies effectively is sometimes used as one of the central arguments for continuing multilateral negotiations rather than leaving trade liberalisation to regional arrangements.

However, one can also argue that there may well be good political reasons for considering the possibility of agreeing on domestic subsidy discipline in TTIP. Among these reasons is the fact that the US and the EU still have 'rights' to trade-distorting domestic support of about $90 billion under the AoA (Orden et al., 2011). Thus, in a way, negotiations on domestic support between the two cover a large part of the ground that is being debated in the WTO. By agreeing on reduction commitments between them, the US and the EU could set an example that the rest of the WTO membership would find difficult not to follow. This consideration resembles strategic ideas that some countries, including the EU, have in mind in the context of global climate talks, where they feel that pushing ahead with unilaterally set reduction commitments might persuade others to go along. The US and the EU could even try to inspire amendment of the WTO rules on domestic support by adopting a modified regime, for example by giving up on inclusion of market price support in calculating domestic support levels, on the grounds that price support is anyhow effectively constrained by tariff bindings and export subsidy constraints. The counter-argument, however, is that bilateral agreement on domestic subsidy disciplines in TTIP would give away negotiating chips that the US and the EU may need in the multilateral negotiations in the Doha Round, in particular vis-à-vis developing countries, which are trying to change the rules of that game in their favour in the current negotiations. It would, therefore, appear unlikely that the TTIP negotiations deviate from the tradition of not including disciplines on domestic subsidies in agriculture in FTAs.

4.3 Negotiations on regulatory convergence

The most important, and at the same time the most difficult issue for liberalising trade between the US and the EU, will be to manage regulatory divergences and the resulting trade barriers in the form of NTMs. It is not unusual for regulatory issues to be problematic in trade negotiations. Several reasons can be offered for these difficulties. Traditional trade issues such as tariffs and subsidies are more transparent and quantitative: the effects of reductions in these trade impediments are easier to estimate. The reduction of tariffs also has an apparent objective (such as free trade) that can guide a process of transition and measure progress: no such clear objective is apparent with regulatory convergence or increasing compatibility. Neither is there an easy way to define when regulatory differences are themselves desirable, even if they have emerged from administrative happenstance or protectionist pressures. And, above all, the issues facing negotiators discussing regulatory convergence attract the interest of a wider constituency than does tariff reduction. Much of the (surprising) public interest in the TTIP negotiations, in particular in Europe, revolves around minor differences in such regulations as those dealing with the washing of chicken carcasses.

Past FTA negotiations have adopted several different approaches to dealing with the question of regulatory divergence. While that issue is relevant across the board in all sectors, the trade problems caused appear to be particularly pronounced, acute and intractable in agricultural and food trade, above all those resulting from SPS matters. Although most, but not all, existing FTA agreements have some provisions relating to SPS matters and other NTMs, there is no obligation to include them at all in regional trade arrangements. WTO rules (GATT Article XXIV:8(b)) require FTAs and CUs to eliminate "duties and other restrictive regulations of commerce" on "substantially all the trade" among the partners, but explicitly exclude from that requirement those NTMs that are permitted under certain GATT Articles, including Article XX (which covers, among others, measures "necessary to protect human, animal or plant life or health"). However, a TTIP that, in its trade part, does not go beyond eliminating duties on US-EU trade is simply not conceivable. When the political leaders from both sides launched the negotiations in February 2013, they explicitly made the point that TTIP would address regulatory and other non-tariff barriers.

This promise would also not be fulfilled if TTIP were to limit itself to an option that comes only marginally higher in the hierarchy, namely just reaffirming the intention of the participating countries to fully respect their rights and obligations under the relevant WTO provisions, in particular the Sanitary and Phytosanitary (SPS)

Agreement. That option is used in several existing FTAs. There is nothing to be said against including a formula like that in an FTA, but there is also not much that speaks for it: governments of WTO member countries should anyhow live up to their obligations under the WTO. For TTIP this option is certainly not sufficient. After all, the existing WTO rules have not prevented barriers from inhibiting the free flow of trade across the Atlantic, and indeed have not guaranteed the absence of serious trade conflicts. There is, therefore, the expectation that TTIP goes beyond stating the obvious need to respect WTO obligations. Whether this means that TTIP would have to include some type of explicit and specific arrangement for all relevant trade barriers in agriculture is, however, a different question. But even if some negotiators might privately dream of sweeping some of the most intractable NTM issues under the rug so as to prevent them from getting in the way of concluding the overall deal, they will feel pressed to move at least one further step up in the hierarchy of options, which is to include at least some procedural provisions in the agreement, envisaging future efforts to come to grips with the issue concerned.

Rather than only making general reference to given WTO rights and obligations, an FTA can also contain provisions going beyond multilaterally agreed rules, specifying how the FTA partners intend to implement WTO provisions in practice. In this regard, too, there are different ways of shaping this option, with varying degrees of concreteness and exigency. For example, the EU-Korea FTA has a chapter on sanitary and phytosanitary measures where a text of less than two pages contains fairly general provisions on how the two sides intend to deal with SPS matters. A much different example is the EU-Chile FTA, for which negotiators have worked out a whole agreement on SPS measures, annexed to the FTA. The agreement is rather specific and runs over nearly 40 pages. It also aims at developing a common understanding concerning animal welfare standards between the EU and Chile, although finally this focused exclusively on the stunning and slaughter of animals. This EU-Chile Agreement also includes provisions for matters which, as far as trade in animal products between the US and the EU is concerned, are laid down in the US-EU Veterinary Equivalency Agreement signed, after six years of negotiation, in 1999 (see below).[22] It would, therefore, appear

---

[22] The EU also has sanitary and phytosanitary agreements with several other countries, either as separate agreements or as parts of FTAs. For a list of the agreements, see http://ec.europa.eu/food/international/trade/agreements_en.htm

conceivable, if not likely, that this 1999 agreement, with amendments later agreed and possibly with further modifications, could also be annexed to a TTIP agreement.

The Task Force that anticipated the agenda of the TTIP[23] addressed the issue of regulatory change by defining the objective as to find "new and innovative ways" to reduce non-tariff barriers to trade and investment. This phrase may conceal a lack of agreement on which approach to take. One approach would be to tackle differences in regulatory philosophy, particularly in such areas as the role of science in regulations where public opinion is not fully convinced by research conclusions. The use of the 'precautionary principle' in EU legislation has generally been regarded in the US as a sign of weakness, allowing public opinion to intrude on matters that can be addressed by scientific enquiry. But any direct assault on these differences in the context of TTIP is likely to be counterproductive, hardening opinions on both sides of the Atlantic and reducing the chances of success.

So the Task Force modestly called for the reduction of "unnecessary costs and administrative delays" arising from regulations. No one could be against that, nor could one argue against the consequent aim of improving the competitiveness of US and EU companies in third markets. And the key questions of harmonisation of standards and the mutual recognition of each other's standards are addressed with caution: greater compatibility in standards is to be "promoted" "where appropriate".

To throw some more light on this part of the heavy package that US and EU officials find on the TTIP negotiating table, it is useful to consider the range of options as to how to deal with regulatory divergences in FTA negotiations, from the least to the most demanding in terms of negotiating effort. Clearly, none of these options would be applied universally to all NTMs: some cases may qualify for more progressive treatment than others. Also, the range can be multidimensional, and individual elements of each approach can be combined in dealing with a given issue.

---

[23] A High Level Working Group on Jobs and Growth (HLWG), established in November 2011 and led by US Trade Representative Ron Kirk and EU Trade Commissioner Karel De Gucht, was tasked with identifying "policies and measures to increase EU-US trade and investment to support mutually beneficial job creation, economic growth, and competitiveness". Within less than 15 months, on 11 February 2013, the HLWG issued its final report (see HLWG, 2013).

4.3.1 Harmonisation

At the top of the hierarchy of options for dealing with NTMs appears the approach of harmonisation, where both partners decide to use the same measure. The SPS Agreement urges WTO members to harmonise their SPS measures, as far as possible, by basing them on international standards, guidelines or recommendations, where they exist. One may expect that in a TTIP agreement, the US and the EU will reaffirm their intention to do so, in general terms. However, they could also go further than that, by agreeing to harmonise their measures for given product sectors, either with international standards where they exist, or on a bilateral level. Such a step would be constructive in helping to minimise the cost of having different standards co-existing in the transatlantic marketplace. At some stage it may even be feasible to establish a common agency to administer such standards. Yet, this solution is unlikely to be adopted for any but the least controversial areas of trade. NAFTA envisaged a degree of harmonisation in regulations but the efforts to reconcile Canadian and US standards on such matters as border inspection have not met with great success. The model for any such cooperation could be the Australia-New Zealand Closer Economic Relations Agreement that has a joint food standards agency for those two countries. But the economic relations across the Atlantic may never be as close as those across the Tasman Sea.

Harmonisation of standards raises political red flags. Some NGOs claim that convergence of standards implies the destruction of the gains made on health, nutrition, environmental protection and human rights. Such a widespread accusation hardly constitutes constructive criticism, but it does raise the possibility that agreements, whether in TTIP or just in MOUs between regulatory agencies could become a lightning rod for opposition. Moreover, as the definition of a standard and the related procedures for its implementation is a highly technical matter requiring substantial detail, it appears unlikely that concrete decisions on any harmonised measures could become part of a TTIP agreement. What is conceivable, however, is that agreement is sought on the establishment of bilateral bodies that would be tasked to work towards harmonised measures.

4.3.2 Mutual recognition

At a somewhat lower level in the hierarchy of options for dealing with NTMs is mutual recognition in the sense that each partner accepts the products legally sold domestically in the other partner's markets. In establishing its Single Market, the EU very much relied on (and still upholds) a strong version of mutual recognition.[24] Mutual recognition can apply to the regulations themselves or the conformity tests. At first glance it may appear as if there is not much difference between this and equivalence (see below). Equivalence also means that partner countries mutually recognise each other's standards and procedures. Yet, MR in its strong form goes very much further than equivalence. The main difference is that mutual recognition implies acceptance of a product that conforms with the domestic regulations of the exporting country, whereas equivalence refers to the product conforming to the standards of the importing country. Moreover, equivalence is implemented on a case-by-case, and only where positive comity is found in the market opened up to imports from the partner country. In other words, equivalence agreements are based on a positive list approach. Where mutual recognition governs, however, there is an *a priori* presumption that all standards and procedures in the partner country are acceptable and hence products from there can be freely imported. If the importing country has specific concerns, it must prove that imports of the partner country's product would violate one or more of a list of agreed criteria (say, public health). Mutual recognition, hence, uses a negative list approach, and the criteria are typically defined so stringently that it is very difficult to move a product onto the negative list.

The mutual recognition approach has the great advantage that only one decision is needed: partner countries agree to accept the validity of each other's standards and procedures, and from then on trade can flow freely. In a purely practical sense, negotiators don't need to spend much time and specific expertise on this approach. They simply agree on mutual recognition and move on to other items on the negotiating agenda. However, there are reasons why different countries have diverging regulatory regimes, some more and some less convincing. And there are reasons why such divergences are difficult to remove and hence can result, and have resulted, in trade tensions. It would be unrealistic to assume that once it comes to FTA negotiations such divergences can be resolved by the stroke of a pen. Hence, mutual recognition is an option that will most likely have a minor role in the outcome of the agricultural and food part of the TTIP negotiations.

---

[24] This strong definition of mutual recognition is sometimes referred to as the "Cassis de Dijon" version in reference to a decision by the European Court of Justice relating to the free circulation of that French drink in the German (and by implication the whole EU) market.

For its Single Market, the EU has adopted the mutual recognition approach across the board. One could, however, also imagine the application of that option to selected product sectors. That approach would establish some sort of a half-way house between equivalence and overall mutual recognition. It would still go further than equivalence as it would open up markets for the products concerned on a permanent basis, without the need to verify the partner's procedures time and again. It would, thus, create more certainty for producers and traders. But it also requires a significant additional amount of mutual trust between the FTA partners. It might be worth considering whether (some of) the products for which the US and the EU have already determined full equivalence in both directions might qualify for a product-specific mutual recognition. Later the two parties could aim at widening product coverage under that approach.[25]

4.3.3   Equivalence

At a rather lower level of ambition is the option to establish equivalence between US and EU regulations on particular topics. This approach is closely interlinked with the concepts of mutual recognition and conformity assessment, and all of them represent important approaches to reducing non-tariff barriers to trade. The equivalence approach has been employed in several areas of standards and was one of the strategies supported in the WTO SPS Agreement. Three requirements for establishing full equivalence can be identified: first, the aims of the standard have to be the same; secondly, the effectiveness of the standards has to be comparable; and thirdly the importing country has to trust the exporting country to carry out its inspection and verification with at least equal diligence (conformity assessment).

Where agreement on the equivalence of each other's standards (in reaching the set objectives) and testing methods is feasible, this represents a more significant step forward in terms of reducing trade barriers. The US-EU Veterinary Equivalency Agreement, for example, defines those animal products for which the US and/or the EU recognise each other's measures as achieving the importing party's

---

[25] Under the US-EU Veterinary Equivalency Agreement, the degree of 'equivalence' is ranked, and only where a product is assigned the highest rank, the importing party agrees that the exporting party's measures achieve the importing party's appropriate level of sanitary protection, and only for a subset of products have both the US and the EU assigned that highest rank (McNulty, 2005).

appropriate level of sanitary protection, and sets out the procedures that allow such equivalence to be determined for products not yet covered. Where full equivalence is agreed, the importing party commits to allowing the products concerned in its market without further sanitary restrictions. Agreements of this nature constitute an approach that would appear to merit serious consideration in the TTIP negotiations. However, practical experience with the US-EU veterinary agreement cautions against too high expectations. The six-year period that was required to negotiate that agreement indicates how difficult the issues involved were at the time in the eyes of the negotiating officials. Also, although very far from all products were granted full equivalence status in the original agreement, only very few products were added to the equivalence list after the agreement went into force. Nevertheless, it is worth serious negotiating efforts to make TTIP an effective door opener for more equivalence agreements, or even to add some equivalence agreements to the TTIP agreement.

Agreement on equivalence of conformity assessment procedures, including those in the food and agriculture sector (though the term conformity assessment is not typically used there), is certainly useful and hence another step up the hierarchy. Nevertheless, although they help to reduce the costs of exporting somewhat, they don't really open up EU and US markets much more widely for each other.

4.4 Alternative approaches

Although the trio of approaches discussed above – harmonisation, mutual recognition and equivalence – are the usual ways of achieving a resolution of differences in standards, they imply that the standards themselves are a necessary part of market regulation. But other options exist in many areas of food and agricultural marketing that could help to resolve trade differences. Two of these alternatives are discussed here: the reliance on labelling as a way of providing consumer information hence avoiding the use of mandatory public (non-safety) standards, and the decision to allow different standards to exist in parallel in the marketplace. This would generally imply a greater role for the private sector to handle (and potentially benefit from) the range of transatlantic consumer attitudes to foods in conjunction with the national standards.

4.4.1 Labelling as a positive strategy

This approach could be called "resolution of differences through consumer information", making use of the ability of consumers to make decisions on purchases, subject to general or specific laws on misrepresentation. The boundary between safety and quality standards may be shifting over time, but it still provides a framework for deciding on the role of public and private actors in the food system. A key to informing the public about the quality of food products is the use of labelling. Wherever risks to health, safety or the environment are not so serious that banning a particular product characteristic or a process is necessary, or requiring a warning label, citizens are generally trusted to make their own choices, based on appropriate information provided through product labelling.

Governments, however, often come under pressure from civil society groups and special interests to assume responsibility for dealing with all types of risks. This tendency is prominent in the food sector and has led administrative levels of government to regulate extensively. The EU has arguably suffered more from this 'regulatory creep' than the US in food standards, although in farming it could be that the reverse is true. Such over-regulation in itself complicates the process of integrating the transatlantic marketplace. An alternative approach is to recognise that in most cases their citizens are perfectly capable of making their own judgments on what is good and not so good for them, provided they have sufficient evidence-based information. Thus, rather than banning particular products, including imported goods, from the market, they could also require appropriate labelling and leave people to choose whether they want to buy them. Many trade conflicts could be avoided if labels were allowed to replace standards. Thus, one conceivable outcome of TTIP negotiations might be that in certain areas the two partners agree to deregulation by switching to labelling requirements rather than marketing restrictions.

4.4.2 Hands-off approach: Diversity is good

At the other end of the continuum of approaches to regulatory differences is the apparently trivial but by no means unimportant option of leaving NTMs untouched in the agreement. This may be called a *vive la différence* solution. Not all issues will prove amenable to regulatory negotiation. There will always be issues on which convergence is not possible or even desirable. Ultimately there may have to be an agreement to differ – and "live and let live". In such cases the aim of negotiations such as TTIP should then be to make sure that information on the respective standards is readily available and the discussions can continue in appropriate venues. This does not preclude activities to build trust among agencies that might eventually lead to closer and less provocative trade relations.

The private sector would play a natural role in such a 'hands-off' approach to regulatory compatibility. Two standards, one applying in the US and the other in the EU, may seem to be a negative situation for business, as transactions costs are increased. But it also represents an opportunity for product differentiation. If consumer sensitivities are different across the Atlantic and different regulatory standards have been adopted to meet those concerns, then a firm marketing in both the US and the EU must adapt production and marketing strategies accordingly. So instead of viewing standards harmonisation as the only approach to reducing costs, the firms themselves could tailor their products more specifically to particular markets. Of course, this happens all the time as a matter of marketing strategy, but it is striking that many of the regulatory issues in transatlantic food trade do not seem to be seen in this light.

5.   Possible landing zones

What are the possible outcomes of the negotiations in the area of agricultural and food issues? Which areas lend themselves to broad agreement and which situations offer little chance of agreement without considerable delay or significant domestic opposition? And how will that relate to the resolution of trade problems between the EU and the US? Table 9.5 provides an overview of some of the possible outcomes that could be negotiated over the next two years.

On issues of market access, the US is unlikely to settle for an agreement that does not include significantly better access to the EU agricultural market. This could include the removal of EU tariffs on all food and agricultural products at no slower a pace than that granted to Canada in the CETA (i.e. 94% immediate and 95% within 7 years). Indeed, one could imagine an agreement to accelerate this pace in the third year to catch up with Canada. There would also no doubt be provision for EU TRQs for a limited number of sensitive commodities (dairy, beef and pork), but the US would expect these to expand regularly. Within-quota imports could be duty-free. In effect, access for US exports would be as good as in FTAs with Mexico and Korea and the countries that have negotiated Economic Partnership Agreements

(EPAs), although not as good as for LDCs under EBA where TRQs do not apply.

The EU will in turn expect the removal of all US tariffs on food and agricultural goods at a comparable pace to the schedules of the Trans-Pacific Partnership (TPP – involving 12 countries throughout the Asia-Pacific region), if that set of negotiations is also successful. This could mean 95% zero tariffs on signing, with further reductions over five years. If the TPP were to include the removal of all tariffs, including sensitive commodities, then there would be pressure for similar market access to be given to the EU. This would imply that TRQs for sugar and dairy would be increased over time until removed in (say) year five.

Other market access outcomes could further open up the transatlantic marketplace. There could be an agreement not to use agriculture-specific safeguards, including the SSG allowed under the WTO. Agreement on broad principles for ROOs, based on WTO rules, could also include a commitment to avoid the use of ROOs to protect markets. This could include an agreement on diagonal cumulation of ROOs over NAFTA and EEA countries and those other countries with FTAs with the EU and the US (as appropriate).

With respect to domestic subsidies, it is unlikely that there will be much effort put into negotiating reductions. Strong support for seeking closure on the Doha Round constraints on Domestic Support may be all that is realistic in this area. However, the TTIP could include a ban on export subsidies on bilateral trade when tariffs reach zero, as well as an agreement on a common approach to state-trading enterprises and an attempt to converge on food aid policy.

The strengthening of disciplines on export restrictions and taxes, which has so far eluded negotiators in the WTO, could be possible in the TTIP. The TTIP discussions would seem to be an ideal locus for agreeing on a mutual ban on export restrictions and taxes on transatlantic trade in agricultural products.[26] Although this would not in itself prevent export restrictions on third-country trade, it would make it more difficult to administer such restrictions. And so the inclusion of a ban on US and EU export restrictions in the TTIP could pave the way for a similar undertaking by all exporters, either as a part of a WTO agreement in the Doha Round or as a plurilateral agreement among the major exporters.

---

[26] In any case, the US Constitution prohibits export taxes. The EU has the authority to tax exports but has not done so in recent years of high prices.

With respect to the regulations that have caused problems for the US and the EU, those involving animal and plant health are the least controversial. Both the EU and the US support the work of the international agencies – the OIE (Office International des Epizooties), which is concerned with animal health, and the IPPC (International Plant Protection Convention) – that have improved the transparency and scientific basis for trade regulations. There seems little reason not to harmonise some regulations where there are no critical differences in approach to trade. This could be true for many of the regulations relating to plant health. The TTIP talks should foster cooperation among agencies to take advantage of mutual interests in the area of animal and plant health. One focus should be on setting up a system for resolving future problems before they become trade conflicts.

Another set of problems are less likely to be resolved by the discussion of regulatory differences by Committees or agencies. These involve human diseases and risks as perceived by the importing country.[27] The issues relating to beef hormones, antibiotics, pathogen reduction techniques (PRTs) and zoonotic diseases also fall in this category, as explained below. The beef hormone ban may be the most politically visible and intractable: any move by the EU to weaken this ban in the short run seems unlikely. This may be one case where 'agreeing to differ' may be the best solution, with the political balance being kept by opening up the market for hormone-free beef and beef products. There seems to be some flexibility in the case of ractopamine, and a broader agreement that included third countries may be the way to defuse this as an EU-US conflict.

The potential conflicts over the use of antibiotics for growth purposes in animal rearing should certainly be addressed. But the issue here is not so much EU policy and US policy conflicting but rather that both the EU and the US face the same decisions. Non-therapeutic use of hormones is being restricted first in the EU, but US regulations are not far behind. So this is a case where the establishment of joint agencies to study the scientific issues would be advantageous. The public could conceivably come to respect the joint findings of such an agency and the recommendations could be made in such a way as to avoid serious conflicts.

---

[27] In the absence of any imports of a product the regulatory differences are unlikely to show up as trade problems. Of course, EU and US exporters could face different regulations in third-country export markets, but solving that problem is best left to other negotiations.

The seemingly minor regulatory issue of PRTs has been the cause of much controversy between the US and the EU in the past few years, and has so far eluded resolution. The US industry uses PRTs including chlorine wash, lactic acid and other antimicrobials to remove bacteria. The EU does not favour such PRTs and banned their use in poultry in 1997. As a result of these diverging approaches, imports of poultry from the US that would be legally sold in that country are banned from the EU market. In the EU, this issue is one of the more hotly debated matters in relation to TTIP which is sometimes portrayed by critics as potentially forcing 'chlorine chicken' on the table of reluctant EU consumers. The EU only allows water to be used to rinse pathogens in slaughter facilities. The argument is that PRTs act to cover up unsatisfactory practices at an earlier stage of the process. The US government regards the EU ban as unjustified by scientific evidence and hence out of line with obligations under the WTO SPS Agreement. Within the EU, there are differences of opinion: the European Commission has itself suggested in 2008 that PRTs be made legal for poultry processing in the EU, but this was rejected by the Council of Ministers. However, the EU has recently allowed the use of lactic acid as a wash in beef slaughter (as a good-faith measure at the start of the TTIP discussions), and there may be a chance for convergence over this issue in the negotiations.

The issue of zoonotic diseases is particularly problematic. Unlike hormones and antibiotics, which are used in livestock production but which under certain uncontrolled circumstances could pose a threat to human health, zoonotic diseases need to be addressed in the animal population in order to avoid the spread to humans. Concerns seem to be equally prevalent on either side of the Atlantic: the BSE outbreak was seen to be a UK problem until cases began to show up in other EU countries. Then when a small number of cases were found in the US and Canada it was no longer possible to ignore the impact. Export markets for beef have still not recovered. This is clearly a case where scientific opinion does not differ but the handling of the outbreak can vary. Avian flu is another such case. There needs to be a mechanism by which the best scientific evidence should be pooled and there should be consultation on the appropriate administrative action. As the objective of human health is shared on both sides of the Atlantic, it seems unfortunate to act in such a way that causes trade conflicts.

What about geographical indications (GIs)? This conflict has been around for many years, mainly as a result of the widespread use of European names by immigrants into the US, Canada, South Africa and Australasia. Attempts by the EU to repatriate such names, whether for wines, cheeses or meats, have met with resistance. But the issues are not insoluble. The agreement on lists of generic names in the US, backed up by evidence that the consumer does in fact regard these as common names, should not be impossible. Generic names cannot, under WTO rules, be protected as GIs. Only a handful of such true generics exist, and cause a disproportionate amount of concern: names such as "Parma ham" and "parmesan cheese" are commercially valuable to some North American firms. The producers in Europe should consider purchasing the rights to those names if they feel that their own market is being eroded. Regarding wine, the US-EU wine agreement of 2006 could be reaffirmed and it could be agreed to enter into its second phase where a number of outstanding issues could be discussed such as the further protection of all GIs for wine on both side, the use of semi-generic names, the process for acceptance of new wine-making practices, or certification requirements. For all other GIs the US should be willing to protect the names on the US market. And the question of extending the additional protection currently given to wines and spirits in the WTO TRIPS Agreement should be left to the multilateral negotiations.

A regulatory issue that has created major tensions between the US and the EU in the past is the treatment of GM products. In most EU member states there is strong resistance against 'green' (i.e. agricultural) GM products among the general public, or at least among powerful NGOs claiming to represent the public interest. In response to that popular aversion several national governments, for example in Austria, Germany and France, have refused to allow the planting of GM varieties in their territories even in cases where the European Commission, based on a positive assessment of the European Food Safety Authority (EFSA), had decided to authorise the respective GM seeds for planting in the EU.[28] For a long time the legal status of these national deviations from EU-wide decisions remained questionable, at both the EU and the WTO level. More recently, though, a new procedure was adopted that allows member states to ban cultivation of GM crops for reasons other than food safety or environmental concerns. The President of the new European Commission installed in November 2014, Jean-Claude Juncker, has already announced that he intends to confirm and strengthen the power of national governments to ban the

---

[28] For more detail on the respective legislative procedures in the EU, see Josling & Tangermann (forthcoming), Chapter 5.

planting of GM crops in their member states. In effect only one GM variety (maize MON810) can currently be planted commercially in the EU, most of which is grown in Spain.

A different matter is the approval of imports into the EU of GM products for commercial marketing as food and feed. For a while the EU was relatively liberal in allowing the marketing of GM varieties. But subsequent approvals of imports ran into opposition from those member states where the public resisted 'green' GM technology. Approvals on imports came to a halt, and in effect the EU instituted a moratorium. The approval process has been speeded up somewhat in recent years, and at present there are some 50 GM plant varieties whose product can be sold in the EU for use in food or animal feed. These products, however, have to be labelled. More than half of these crops are types of GM maize. Other crops include soybeans, rapeseed, sugar beets, cotton and potatoes.

One dimension of the growing public opposition to TTIP in Europe is fear that the EU might have to open up completely to the importation and cultivation of GM products. However, here again a distinction needs to be made between the approval of GM products for sale in the EU on the one hand and the question of licensing the planting of GM seed varieties in Europe on the other hand. It appears that US seed companies have for the time being essentially given up on hopes that resistance against cultivation of such seed varieties in Europe can be overcome in the near future. Hence US negotiators have understood that this is a matter that must be left to the EU and the member states, and therefore this is an issue that is unlikely to create major difficulties in the negotiations. The issue of labelling GM foods is also one that should not be a major point of contention in the TTIP talks. The US will have to grasp the nettle of public demands for labelling, no matter how shaky is the case for such action. Food products, like all other retail goods, will remain subject to local labelling and packaging regulations. So the main GM issue boils down to the speed at which the EU reviews and decides on the marketability of new types of GM products on the internal market. In exchange for the "live and let live" approach to GM plantings and labelling the EU should at the very least set up a more responsive approval process for commercial marketing of GM products as food and feed.

One significant aspect of the tension over GM approval is the possibility that it might spill over into future technology. One such example is the use of nanotechnology in food packaging.[29] One application that would appear to have consumer benefits is the development of a packaging material that will give a visual indication (e.g. a change in colour) if bacteria are present in significant quantities. The calls for regulation have come from concerned groups in the EU and in the US. The opportunity exists for the merits and hazards of this technology to be addressed by authorities working together, which might mean that the split between US and EU opinion apparent in the GM case can potentially be avoided.

Both sides will need some 'victories' in the regulatory area to demonstrate the value of the outcome. Though regulatory differences can persist for years and become major trade irritants, most can be resolved when political attention is sufficiently focused. Four cases of agreements in this area of food and agricultural regulations illustrate this possibility, and provide a basis of cooperation for the TTIP to build upon. In 1996 the US and the EU signed a Veterinary Equivalence Agreement (VEA) that aimed to facilitate the establishment of equivalence in SPS measures. Although this agreement has had limited scope so far, it represents a useful starting point for a broader agreement covering equivalence of testing and regulating in matters related to health and safety of animals.

In the area of food safety, the EU Food Hygiene Package of 2004 moved some way to dealing with transatlantic differences over sanitary standards by applying risk-based approval for US slaughterhouses. The EU has also negotiated a US-EU Wine Agreement (2006) that resolved several of the ongoing issues with respect to wine-making practices as well as some naming issues. This again created a useful basis for further resolution of the GI issue. And in 2012, the US and the EU reached agreement on an agreement on Organics that in effect made the two different organic certification systems in use mutually compatible. A product deemed organic by US officials can now bear the EU certification mark. Although each of these agreements may have had their own dynamic, they do give some hope that solutions can be found when the necessity arises.

---

[29] Nanotechnology refers to the alteration of the molecular structure of a material to alter its characteristics. In effect a new material is produced with features that are under the control of the developer. The use of the technology in medical and energy applications has been widely accepted, but its use in food packaging has raised questions of health and safety on both sides of the Atlantic.

Table 9.5 Potential landing zones for agriculture and food in the TTIP

Border Issues	US objective	EU objective	Landing zone
Market access	Access to EU cereals and vegetable markets	Access to US dairy markets	Free access for 95% of agricultural tariff lines with most sensitive items excluded: expanding TRQs for those items
Domestic subsidies	Lower EU farm-level subsidies	Keep lid on US spending on crop insurance	Agree to work for a solution in WTO Doha Round to achieve reduction of domestic support
Export subsidies	Phase out subsidies	Restrict US food "in kind" food aid and export credits	Agree to avoid intra export subsidies and to work toward WTO elimination of all export subsidies and similar measures
Export taxes, quotas	Avoid export restrictions on US-EU trade	Avoid export restrictions on US-EU trade	Agree to avoid export restrictions on US-EU trade and to work through WTO for multilateral disciplines on export restrictions
Regulations			
Animal health	Affirm SPS commitment	Affirm SPS commitment	Reaffirm SPS commitment to evidence-based rules and support work of OIE. Set up Committee to discuss SPS issues to avoid trade conflicts. Pre-notification of new regulations
Plant health	Affirm SPS commitment	Affirm SPS commitment	Reaffirm SPS commitment to evidence-based rules and support work of IPPC
Human health	Achieve coherence in	Achieve coherence in	Set up Committee to discuss SPS issues to avoid

(including PRTs, hormones, antibiotics and zoonotic diseases)	standards for PRTs; persuade EU to change hormone ban; avoid conflicts over antibiotics and zoonoses	standards for PRTs; avoid any change in hormone ban; avoid conflicts over antibiotics and zoonoses	trade conflicts. Pre-notification of new regulations. Joint scientific agencies to advise on PRTs; "agree to differ" on hormones; joint action on antibiotics and zoonoses
GIs	Avoid repatriation of European names	Register EU GIs for protection in US: expand "additional" protection beyond wines	Reaffirm US-EU wine agreement; agree on a list of "generics" that cannot be used as a GI; leave to TRIPS the issue of additional protection beyond wines
GM crops	Speed up EU approval process	Avoid weakening of GM planting rules and maintain labelling	Agreement to expedite approval for marketing GM crops; approval of GM plantings in EU left to EU and member states
Organic foods	Avoid trade problems	Avoid trade problems	Incorporate US-EU mutual recognition agreement for Organics
Animal welfare	Avoid trade problems	Avoid trade problems	Agree to build on OIE standards for animal welfare

Source: Authors' own compilation.

References

Donner Abreu, M.D. (2013), "Preferential Rules of Origin in Regional Trade Agreements", WTO Economic Research and Statistics Division, Staff Working Paper ERSD-2013-05, WTO, Geneva, 22 March.

Ecorys (2009), "Non-Tariff Measures in EU-US Trade and Investment – An Economic Analysis", Final Report of a study for the European Commission, DG Trade, Rotterdam, 11 December.

_____ (2012), "Study on 'EU-US High Level Working Group'", Final report of a study for the Ministry of Economic Affairs, Agriculture and Innovation of the Netherlands, Ecorys, 22 October.

European Commission (2013a), "Impact Assessment Report on the future of EU-US trade relations", Commission Staff Working Document, SWD(2013) 68 final, Strasbourg, 12 March.

_____ (2013b), "Transatlantic Trade and Investment Partnership – The Regulatory Part", Brussels.

European Parliament (2014), "Risks and Opportunities for the EU Agri-food Sector in a Possible EU-US Trade Agreement", Directorate for Internal Policies, European Parliament, Brussels.

Felbermayr, G. et al. (2013), "Dimensionen und Auswirkungen eines Freihandelsabkommens zwischen der EU und den USA", Studie im Auftrag des Bundesministeriums für Wirtschaft und Technologie, ifo-Institut, München.

Fontagné, L., J. Gourdon and S. Jean (2013), "Transatlantic Trade: Whither Partnership, Which Economic Consequences?", CEPII Policy Brief No. 1, CEPII, Paris.

Fulponi, L., M. Shearer and J. Almeida (2011), "Regional Trade Agreements – Treatment of Agriculture", OECD Food, Agriculture and Fisheries Paper No. 44, OECD, Paris, 31 March.

Francois, J., et al. (2013), "Reducing Transatlantic Barriers to Trade and Investment - An Economic Assessment", Final report of a project done for the European Commission, Centre for Economic Policy Research, London.

Grubel, Herbert G. and Peter J. Lloyd (1975), Intra-Industry Trade: The Theory and Measurement of International Trade in Differentiated Products, New York, NY: Wiley.

Grueff, James (2013), "Achieving a Successful Outcome for Agriculture in the US-EU Transatlantic Trade and Investment Partnership Agreement", IPC Discussion Paper, International Policy Council for Food and Agricultural Trade, Washington, D.C., February.

High Level Working Group on Jobs and Growth [HLWG] (2013), Final Report, 11 February (http://trade.ec.europa.eu/doclib/docs/2013/february/tradoc_150519.pdf).

Josling, T.E. (1993), "Agriculture in a World of Trading Blocs", Australian Journal of Agricultural Economics, Vol. 37, No. 3, December, pp. 155-179.

_____ (1997), "Implications of Regional Trade Arrangements for Agricultural Trade", Economic and Social Development Paper No. 133, Food and Agriculture Organization, Rome.

Josling, T.E. and S. Tangermann (forthcoming), Transatlantic Food and Agricultural Trade Policy: 50 Years of Conflict and Convergence, Cheltenham: Edward Elgar.

Kinnman, S. and T. Hagberg (2012), "Potential Effects from an EU–US Free Trade Agreement – Sweden in Focus", National Board of Trade, Stockholm.

Lejour, A., F. Mustilli, J. Pelkmans and J. Timini (2014), "Economic Incentives for Indirect TTIP Spillovers", CEPS Special Report No. 94 [TTIP Series No. 2], Centre for European Policy Studies, Brussels (www.ceps.eu/book/economic-incentives-indirect-ttip-spillovers).

McNulty, K. (2005), "EU-25 Trade Policy Monitoring – The US-EU Veterinary Equivalency Agreement: Content and Comparison 2005", USDA Foreign Agricultural Service, GAIN Report No. E35219, US Mission to the EU, Brussels.

Orden, D., D. Blandform and T. Josling (22011), WTO Disciplines on Agricultural Support: Seeking a fair basis for trade, Cambridge: Cambridge University Press.

Schott, Jeffrey J. and Cathleen Cimino (2013), "Crafting a Transatlantic Trade and Investment Partnership: What can be done?", PIIE Policy Brief PB13-8, Washington, D.C., March.

Trachtenberg, Eric (2012), "A Transatlantic Partnership – Agricultural Issues", Economic Policy Paper Series, German Marshall Fund of the United States, Washington, D.C., October.

WTO, ITC and UNCTAD (2013), "World Tariff Profiles 2013", WTO, Geneva (http://stat.wto.org/TariffProfile/WSDBTariffPF Home.aspx?Language=E).

10. TTIP AND PUBLIC PROCUREMENT
STEPHEN WOOLCOCK
AND JEAN HEILMAN GRIER

1. Introduction

For the past 35 years, the European Union and the United States have played leading roles in the development of international rules that apply to government procurement (or public procurement). They are parties to the WTO Government Procurement Agreement (GPA), which accounts for only a quarter of the membership of the WTO, as well as other bilateral and regional agreements with procurement commitments. Their interest in procurement obligations arises from the significant role that government procurement plays in most economies.

International agreements that provide disciplines for procurement have two elements: one is procurement rules and the second is the procurement that is subject to those rules. The EU and the US share similar views with regard to procurement rules, which are intended to ensure that procurement is conducted in a manner that is transparent, non-discriminatory, predictable and fair. But they have had differences with respect to the procurement that they open to one another. As a consequence, they have engaged in often contentious negotiations on government procurement for more than 20 years now. Their current procurement commitments and unresolved issues provide the basis for the TTIP negotiations.

Under the current state of affairs, the EU does not accord the US its most comprehensive coverage because it is dissatisfied with the level of procurement that the US has opened under the GPA. The US is constrained in responding to the EU's complaints by both its federal structure of government and its domestic purchasing requirements, only a few of which it has removed in international agreements. More often, the US has excluded procurement subject to such restrictions from its international obligations. In contrast to the EU's quest for access to more US procurement, American suppliers are more or less satisfied with their access to procurement in Europe.

This chapter aims to help the reader understand how the EU-US procurement relationship has reached its current state. It begins with an overview of the nature of government procurement markets, considering the size of the markets and penetration ratios of public procurement. It then examines the international procurement agreements that apply to the EU and the US, looking at both procurement rules and procurement commitments. It will detail the procurement that the EU and the US have agreed to open to one another, and the procurement that they exclude from their respective commitments.

The chapter then turns to how the EU and US might build on their existing commitments and defuse this long-contentious issue. Both sides have articulated objectives with respect to government procurement under the TTIP. The EU has placed a high priority on procurement in the TTIP and has specified a number of areas of interest. While the US has not singled out procurement as a priority, it has identified several objectives. The chapter proposes expansion of existing procurement commitments in several areas. At the same time, it points out some of the hurdles to an expansion of covered procurement, in particular with respect to US states. The report also considers how the TTIP might expand procurement rules that could have ramifications beyond the TTIP and set new international standards.

Given the likely difficulty in resolving all of their outstanding procurement issues in the TTIP negotiations, the chapter proposes ways for the parties to continue addressing these issues with the TTIP as a 'living agreement'. It focuses on the potential use of a forum that the EU and the US established at the end of 2011. The chapter also addresses the possibility of linking progress in the procurement negotiations to other sectors of the TTIP.

2. The nature of government procurement markets

2.1 The size of procurement markets

According to OECD Secretariat estimates, public procurement accounted for on average 13% of GDP in the OECD economies in 2011. If one adds state-owned enterprises (SOEs) this can mean an additional 2-12% of GDP, depending on the country. In all economies it is also the sector that has been least touched by the general liberalisation paradigm of the 1980s and 1990s. There are, therefore, significant potential economic and welfare gains to be achieved from more transparent, competitive and efficient procurement. At first glance, public procurement looks like an area of considerable promise, especially at a time of relatively slow growth and tight public finances. In practice, however, much less than 13% of GDP in procurement is likely to be open to international competition. If one assumes that public spending on health, social and education services, and core areas of defence will remain largely outside of competitive markets, this leaves 3-5% of GDP potentially open to international competition (European Commission (2011a, p. viii). Opening public procurement markets has also proved to be one of the most challenging areas of trade policy. Experience over the past 35 years shows that agreeing on the text of an agreement is only the first step in ensuring increased competition in public contracts. Competitive procurement also requires effective implementation of agreements, institutional and human resources and above all a commitment to open competition on the part of the purchasing entity/government.

Public procurement accounts for a larger share of GDP in the EU (with variations among member states) than in the US, for example. This is largely because the EU public sector is larger than that of the US. Most EU member states also have a state owned enterprises (SOEs) or parastatal sector (see Figure 10.1). In the EU internal procurement regime, central entities, sub-central entities and utilities are all covered by procurement rules and the EU has extended this approach to the plurilateral Government Procurement Agreements (GPA).

This means that the EU approach is more comprehensive than that of the US. As discussed above, not all procurement is subject to competition because large shares go to expenditures on health and social programmes, education, energy or defence. Figure 10.1 shows the total share of public procurement in other major markets.

Figure 10.1 The share of public procurement in GDP for general government and utilities

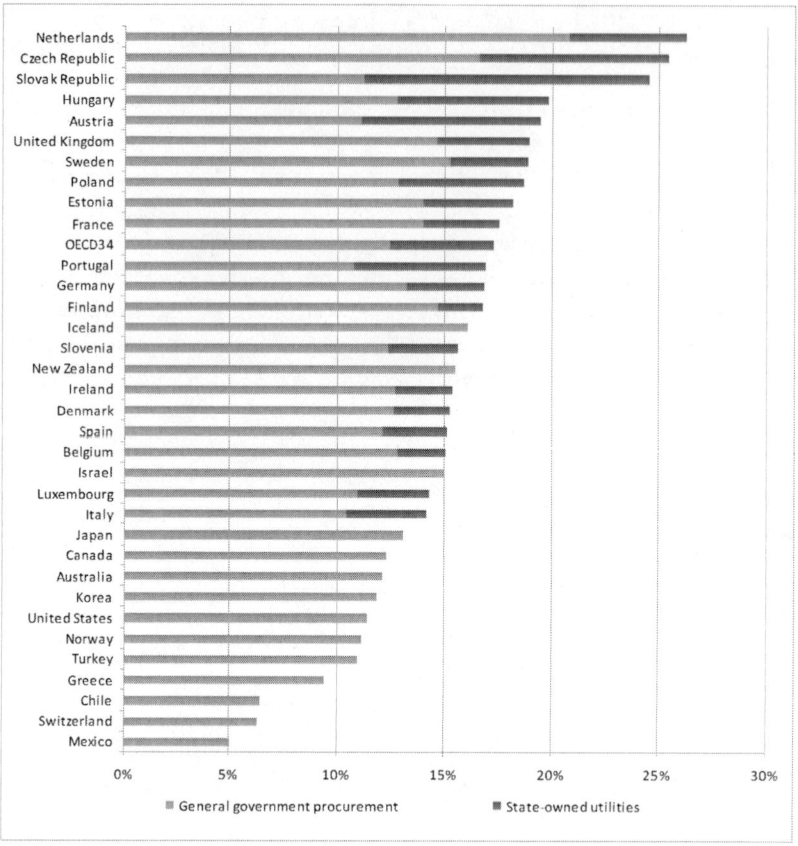

Data sources: OECD National Accounts Database and Eurostat. Data for Australia are based on a combination of Government Finance Statistics and National Accounts data provided by the Australian Bureau of Statistics.

2.2 The debate on the openness of procurement markets

2.2.1 The general picture

The relative size and openness of the EU and US procurement markets has been the subject of considerable debate. As in any trade negotiation, reciprocity has been an important factor in past and present discussions, so differences over the relative openness of markets have been a significant complicating factor and there are no unchallenged objective data with which to make a comparison. At a very general level, a recent study (Messerlin & Miroudot, 2012) takes the overall penetration ratios of public procurement based on imports. This appears to show the EU to have a lower penetration rate than China and India, but higher than that of the US (see Table 10.1). The penetration ratio here is based on direct imports as a share of the total public demand for goods and services, defined as the final consumption expenditure (government final consumption expenditure consists of expenditure, including imputed expenditure, incurred by general government on both individual consumption goods and services and collective consumption services). This definition of market opening therefore considers the general picture for the public sector as a whole.

Table 10.1 Penetration ratios of public procurement markets (selected countries and years)

Market	1995	2000	2005	2007
European Union	2.6	3.6	4.2	4.5
Brazil	2.1	3.1	3.1	3.0
China	3.8	3.4	5.6	5.2
India	4.2	4.4	5.8	6.3
Japan	1.9	2.3	3.2	4.2
Turkey	5.4	5.8	9.5	10.9
US	2.7	3.6	4.4	4.4

Source: Summary of data provided in Messerlin & Miroudot (2012).

As the data in Figure 10.2 show, small markets, including the small EU member states if these are taken as separate markets, tend to have a higher import-penetration ratio. This is to be expected given that smaller economies will not have the local/national capacity to supply all the goods and services required by their governments. If one takes the EU as a single market, one would clearly expect import penetration to be lower than in small markets and lower perhaps than developing-country markets as the EU possesses the capacity to supply the most advanced, high-value contracts, which some developing economies will be unable to do. Figure 10.2, indeed, shows a correlation between market size and 'openness' (in other words, imports to total public consumption) and shows the EU and US as roughly equivalent in terms of their degree of openness on this measure.

Figure 10.2 GDP and openness ratios, 2008

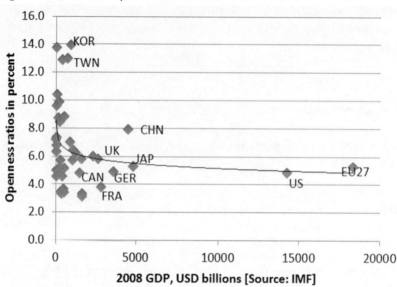

Source: Messerlin & Miroudot (2012).

2.3 Access via investment

The import penetration in Table 10.1 also relates to 'imports' or what the European Commission has termed direct imports, in other words goods and services crossing borders. It is, however, a feature of procurement markets that access is often achieved through foreign investment in the target market, which helps get around de facto preferences in that contracts awarded to local goods and services create local jobs and economic activity, even if the firm is foreign-owned. In the EU, cross-border supply of public procurement markets accounts for only 1.6% of public contracts and 3.5% of the value of public procurement. But indirect supply via an affiliate accounts for 11% of contracts and about 14% of the value of public procurement (European Commission, 2011b). This indirect access to EU markets appears to be focused on 'supplies' (goods) rather than services or works (construction). Indirect imports make up 25% of the value of EU supplies contracts, compared to just 6% for works and 12% for services. Access therefore clearly depends on the ease of establishment and whether inward foreign direct investment (FDI) is blocked or discouraged. This is seldom the case in transatlantic trade as both the EU and the US are open to foreign direct investment except in limited cases when the host state wishes to defend its national champion against such competition. But the option of setting up an affiliate will be less attractive to small- or medium-sized companies. Unfortunately, there does not seem to be equivalent data for indirect access to the US market, and so again it does not seem possible to conduct an objective comparison of how open markets are. But one can assume that larger EU suppliers wishing to access the US market will have considered doing so via affiliates.

2.4 Value of procurement covered under commitments in agreements

In the absence of comparable data, the European Commission has produced an estimate of relative market opening, summarised in Table 10.2 below. This appears to be based on commitments made in international agreements for contestable markets above the thresholds in the GPA. But the US has disputed the accuracy of these figures.

Table 10.2 Share of procurement covered by commitments

	EU	US	Japan	Canada	Brazil	India	China
Total procurement Above GPA threshold (€ bn)	370	559	96	59	25	42	20
% of GDP	3%	3%	3%	6%	3%	4%	2%
Percentage of procurement Internationally committed	95%	32%	28%	16%	65%	0	0

Source: European Commission (2012).

2.5 Strategic market access

These general figures for procurement and the degree of openness do not address the question of what might be called strategic market access. In certain sectors, large public contracts can make a significant difference between business success and failure. In other words winning a large public contract can have a significant effect on the relative competitive position of companies. This is especially the case in sectors such as aerospace where strategic trade policy conditions could be said to apply. The same features, however, are also present in other sectors such as rail transport, energy, non-lethal defence equipment and even construction. In these sectors, therefore, tacit support for national companies in the awarding of contracts is something that is very difficult to address and even governments that would otherwise follow liberal procurement policies have arguably found ways of awarding contracts to national suppliers. The recent EU debate on a Regulation to enhance the EU's negotiating leverage, which has not been adopted, drew on these kinds of strategic market access objectives.[1]

3. International procurement rules and EU and US commitments

3.1 International procurement agreements

When the international trading system was established in 1947 under the General Agreement on Tariffs and Trade (GATT), government procurement was explicitly excluded. As a consequence, there were no constraints on the adoption and application of *de jure* and *de facto* 'buy local' policies and practices. This unfettered use continued for more than three decades until procurement was brought under international trade disciplines. In 1981, the first international procurement agreement – the GATT Agreement on Government Procurement (GATT Code) – was implemented. As a plurilateral agreement, it only opened the procurement of the GATT members that accepted it and did not provide most-favoured-nation treatment (MFN) to non-Code parties.[2] It was also limited in scope, applying only to the procurement of goods by the central government entities listed by each party in the agreement. It did not apply to services or other types of entities. The GATT Code was replaced by the Government Procurement Agreement (GPA), which was established under the WTO in 1996.[3]

The GPA significantly expanded procurement subject to international disciplines to include services and construction services, as well as procurement by sub-central government entities, utilities and government enterprises. Currently, the GPA has 15 parties. Given that

---

[1] See Regulation on access to international procurement markets COM (2012) 124 final 21.3.2012.

[2] Those members included the US, the European Economic Community and its member states (Belgium, Denmark, Republic of Germany, France, Ireland, Italy, Luxembourg, the Netherlands and the United Kingdom), Austria, Finland and Sweden.

[3] Grier (2013b).

the EU and its 28 member states constitute one party, the GPA covers the procurement of 43 WTO members.

In December 2011, the GPA parties concluded a decade-long negotiation to revise the GPA.[4] The negotiations, which were led by the US and the EU, resulted in an expansion of the procurement covered by the Agreement[5] and an overhaul of its text.[6] In April 2014, the revision entered into force for two-thirds of the GPA parties, including the EU and the US.[7]

3.2   The elements of international procurement agreements

The negotiations on procurement in the TTIP are expected to follow the template that has been established over the years in international procurement agreements and is reflected in the GPA and bilateral FTAs. This template has two parts. One concerns coverage or market access commitments, often called 'liberalisation', which are based on negotiations aimed at achieving reciprocal commitments.

Neither the EU nor the US covers all of its procurement under any international procurement agreement. Instead, each specifies the procurement that it promises to conduct in accordance with the provisions of the agreement based on several elements, including lists of procuring entities. The second part of agreements is comprised of the principles such as national treatment and the procedural disciplines that apply to the procurement that is covered. See Box 10.1 for the elements of coverage commitments and the procurement rules.

Box 10.1 Elements of International Agreements on Public Procurement

Coverage

Rules in international agreements generally cover procurement of supplies (goods), works (construction) and services. Coverage is defined by several elements: 1) thresholds (monetary values at and above which the agreement applies to procurement), which are designed to ensure that the most valuable contracts are open to competition and avoid the significant compliance costs of imposing international disciplines on smaller contracts; 2) the entities covered, as specified in three categories

---

[4] World Trade Organization (2011).

[5] Grier (2014b and d).

[6] Grier (2013c).

[7] World Trade Organization (2014).

(central government, sub-central governments and other entities, such as utilities and SOEs); 3) negative list of goods, which means that the procurement of all goods is covered except those explicitly excluded; coverage of defence goods is generally based on a positive list; 4) services, including construction services, with coverage based on a positive list (only listed services are covered) or negative list (all services are covered except those listed); and 5) exclusions. [The coverage of the EU and US under the GPA is set out in Table 10.3 below.]

National treatment

A cornerstone of public procurement agreements is non-discrimination. Parties must provide national treatment for all covered procurement. This requires parties to treat the goods, services, and suppliers of other parties no less favourably than domestic goods, services and suppliers. They may not apply domestic preferences and other discriminatory purchasing provisions for procurement covered by an international agreement. National treatment obligations are the main means by which de jure preferences for specific categories of suppliers are tackled.

Transparency

Central to the aim of facilitating increased international competition, more efficient purchasing and reduced scope for corruption in public procurement is the provision of information. Transparency and procedural obligations are aimed at ensuring that procurement covered by an international agreement is conducted in a manner that is transparent, predictable, fair and non-discriminatory. This encompasses both information on the procurement system, as well as information on each stage of the specific procurement, including development of technical specifications, publication of notices of intended procurement and invitations to request participation in procurements, provision of tender documentation, tendering process, use of negotiations and contract awards. It also includes post-contract award transparency in which purchasing entities are obliged to explain contract award decisions and publish awards.

Contract award procedures

In order to ensure flexibility, procurement rules in international agreements tend to provide for open, selective and limited tendering. Open tendering allows all interested suppliers to participate and may be based on price or most advantageous tenders. Selective tendering is used when the procuring entity invites only suppliers that meet certain qualification requirements to submit tenders. It requires competition and transparent procedures for the selection of qualified suppliers. Limited tendering is when the procuring entity invites specific suppliers to submit tenders. Agreements include more or less detailed rules on how invitations for tender are issued, what information is provided, and what time limits are set for bidding and for awarding contracts. Short time limits may put foreign bidders at a disadvantage, while long time limits may be detrimental to the work of the procuring entity.

Technical specifications

Through specifications, a procuring entity can tailor the requirements for a procurement to match the capabilities of certain (local) suppliers. To avoid this outcome, rules encourage the use of international standards and performance standards over design (or prescriptive) standards. Where design standards are used, tenders of equivalent goods or services should be allowed.

Exemptions or exclusions

Agreements generally provide for exclusions of procurement from national treatment obligations for reasons of human health, national security and law enforcement.

Enforcement and compliance

Experience has shown that without effective compliance, rules on public procurement will have little effect. Given the thousands of contracts that are awarded every day, central compliance monitoring is impracticable. Rules therefore provide bidders who believe they have not been fairly treated with an opportunity to seek an independent review of a contract award decision. Penalties in the case of non-compliance may involve project cancellation, requirements to retender or financial penalties (limited to the costs of bids or exemplary damages). Rules requiring information on contracts awarded and reasons why bids failed can also facilitate compliance.

3.3   EU and US commitments under international agreements

The EU and the US have exchanged extensive procurement commitments under two international agreements, the GPA (see Table 10.3) and a 1995 exchange of letters (see Table 10.4).[8]

---

[8] Grier (2013a).

Table 10.3 EU and US coverage under GPA and relevance to TTIP

Elements of coverage	EU coverage	US coverage	Issue in TTIP?
Central government			
Thresholds: goods and services	130,000 Special Drawing Rights (SDRs)	130,000 SDRs	Not likely TTIP issue. EU Directives apply same threshold as GPA; EU has not applied lower thresholds in FTAs. But, US often applies lower thresholds in other FTAs. For example, it applies a $100,000 threshold in the US-Korea FTA. Since US reserves most federal procurement at and below $150,000 for small businesses, there would be little value in a threshold below that level.
Thresholds: Construction services	5,000,000 SDRs	5,000,000 SDRs	
Entities	Covers 3 EU-wide entities (Council, Commission and European External Action Service) and all central government entities of member states; withholds approximately 200 entities from access by US	85 federal entities, with several exclusions, including Federal Aviation Administration	Both could expand their coverage. US should be able to cover all federal agencies subject to the Federal Acquisition Regulation. The EU should be able to provide the US with comprehensive coverage of central government entities of member states and cover more EU-wide entities.

Sub-central government		
Thresholds: Goods and services	200,000 SDRs	355,000 SDRs	EU is seeking reduction. US likely to resist because of difficulty of obtaining necessary agreement of states.
Thresholds: Construction services	5,000,000 SDRs	5,000,000 SDRs	
Entities	All regional or local contracting authorities and all contracting authorities that are bodies governed by public law, as defined by EU public procurement directive. Includes indicative lists of entities covered.	37 states (see Table 10.4)	EU seeks expanded coverage of states, including the 13 states not covered by the GPA and greater access to the procurement of the 37-covered states.
Restrictions on coverage	EU denies rights to US suppliers to participate in services procured by its sub-central entities.	Exclusions include domestic content restrictions that apply to federally-funded highway and mass-transit projects and state-specific exclusions	EU seeks removal of the restrictions for mass transit projects.

Utilities and government enterprises			
Thresholds: Goods and services	400,000 SDRs	$250,000 for federal enterprises; 400,000 SDRs for other entities	
Thresholds: Construction services	5,000,000 SDRs	5,000,000 SDRs	
Entities	All contracting entities whose procurement is covered by EU utilities directive and which are contracting authorities covered by the GPA. It also covers public undertakings, which are engaged in activities in sectors that include drinking water, electricity, airports, maritime or inland ports and transportation (railways, urban railways, automated systems, tramway, trolley bus, bus and cable); Includes indicative lists of entities.	Federal electric utilities (Tennessee Valley Authority and four Power Administrations), St. Lawrence Seaway Development Corporation. 3 sub-central entities (Port Authority of New York and New Jersey, Port of Baltimore and New York Power Authority). Waives domestic content requirements for power generation and telecommunication projects financed by Rural Utilities Service.	

Restrictions	Excludes US from all utilities, except electric sector.	Excludes domestic content restrictions that apply to federal funds provided for airport projects.	
Goods	Covers all goods	Covers all goods with several exceptions	
Defence goods	Positive list of goods procured by defence and security entities.	Positive list of goods that are generally covered, subject to national security exception	
Services	Uses positive list which lists only the services that it covers, including most land and air transport services and all telecommunications services. EU does not give US rights to services procured by its sub-central entities. EU also provides US with access to a covered service only if US also covers that service.	Uses negative list to cover all services except transportation services; services associated with management and operation of government facilities, or privately owned facilities used for governmental purposes; public utilities services (except enhanced/value-added telecommunications services); and R&D services. Excludes printing for states. It provides EU with access to a covered service only if EU covers it.	EU could adopt negative list and US could consider expansion of telecommunications services.

Source: Grier (2013a).

Under those agreements, the US gives the EU the best access to its procurement that it offers any trading partner. In fact, it gives the EU better access than others because the 1995 agreement opens up procurement not provided to any other party. Under the GPA, the US does not withhold any of its procurement from the EU. But the EU does not reciprocate by providing the US with its best coverage. Instead, it denies the US the legal rights to participate in a significant portion of its GPA-covered procurement. This denial of *de jure access* applies to the procurement of services by its sub-central entities, procurement by EU utilities (except in the electric sector) and at least 200 central government entities of its member states. The EU withholds this procurement in response to US coverage. This disparity is less significant than it appears because US companies often have *de facto* access to the excluded procurement.[1]

Central government entities: Under the 1994 GPA, both the EU and the US used positive lists to specify their coverage of central government entities. The US continued that approach in the revised GPA, with the addition of 11 entities, to bring its total of covered entities to 85 – the most it offers in any agreement. However, in the negotiations on the revision of the GPA, the EU changed its approach and offered comprehensive coverage of the central government entities of its member states, that is, all existing entities, whether or not listed, as well as those created in the future. But it reserved this comprehensive coverage for members of the European Free Trade Association (Iceland, Norway, Liechtenstein and Switzerland) and the Netherlands with respect to Aruba. For the US and other GPA parties, the EU not only continued to use a positive list, but it also withheld some of the listed entities – more than 200 listed entities in the case of the US.[2]

Sub-central coverage: With regard to sub-central entity coverage, the EU provides comprehensive coverage of the sub-central entities of its member states, but withholds their purchases of services from the US. US sub-central coverage is not as comprehensive. Under the GPA, it covers 37 of its 50 states[3] and not all of the procurement of those

---

[1] Grier (2014k).

[2] Grier (2014f).

[3] The 13 states that are not covered by the GPA are: Alabama, Alaska, Georgia, Indiana, Nevada, New Jersey, New Mexico, North Carolina, North Dakota, Ohio, South Carolina, Virginia and West Virginia.

states. A variety of restrictions apply to the states.[4] For example, the US takes an exception for the domestic content restrictions that are attached to federal funds given to states for mass-transit and highway projects. In addition, the states open their procurement at a threshold that is almost twice that of the EU's sub-central entities (355,000 SDRs versus 200,000 SDRs). See Table 10.4 on US states covered under GPA and the 1995 exchange of letters.

Table 10.4 US states covered under GPA and 1995 Exchange of Letters

State	GPA	State-specific exclusions in GPA	1995 Exchange of Letters
Arizona	X	None	
Arkansas	X	Construction services	
California	X	None	
Colorado	X	None	
Connecticut	X	None	
Delaware	X	Construction-grade steel (including requirements on subcontracts), motor vehicles, coal	
Florida	X	Construction-grade steel (including requirements on subcontracts), motor vehicles, coal	
Hawaii	X	Construction services; software developed in state	
Idaho	X	None	
Illinois	X	Construction-grade steel (including requirements on subcontracts), motor vehicles, coal	X
Iowa	X	Construction-grade steel (including requirements on subcontracts), motor vehicles, coal	
Kansas	X	Construction services, automobiles, aircraft	
Kentucky	X	Construction services	

[4] Grier (2014n).

Louisiana	X	None	
Maine	X	Construction-grade steel (including requirements on subcontracts), motor vehicles, coal	
Maryland	X	Construction-grade steel (including requirements on subcontracts), motor vehicles, coal	
Massachusetts	X	None	
Michigan	X	Construction-grade steel (including requirements on subcontracts), motor vehicles, coal	
Minnesota	X	None	
Mississippi	X	Services	
Missouri	X	None	
Montana	X	Goods	
Nebraska	X	None	
New Hampshire	X	Construction-grade steel (including requirements on subcontracts), motor vehicles, coal	
New York	X	Construction-grade steel (including requirements on subcontracts), motor vehicles, coal; procurement by public authorities and public benefit corporations with multi-state mandates; transit cars, buses and related equipment	
North Dakota		None	X
Oklahoma	X	Construction services, construction-grade steel (including requirements on subcontracts), motor vehicles, coal	
Oregon	X	None	
Pennsylvania	X	Construction-grade steel (including requirements on subcontracts), motor vehicles, coal	

State			
Rhode Island	X	Boats, automobiles, buses, related equipment	
South Dakota	X	Beef	
Tennessee	X	Services, including construction services	
Texas	X	None	
Utah	X	None	
Vermont	X	None	
Washington	X	Fuel, paper products, boats, ships, vessels	
West Virginia		None	X
Wisconsin	X	None	
Wyoming	X	Construction-grade steel (including requirements on subcontracts, motor vehicles, coal	

Source: Grier (2014n).

In addition to the GPA, the US opens procurement of several sub-central entities under a 1995 US-European Communities Exchange of Letters.[5] That Agreement, which does not include any EU commitments, provides EU suppliers with access to the procurement of two states not covered by the GPA (North Dakota and West Virginia) and Illinois state procurement that is not covered under the GPA. The obligation in the Exchange of Letters is limited to best of out-of-state treatment for EU suppliers, but only if the state considers non-state suppliers in a procurement. It also commits to best of out-of-city treatment by seven cities (Boston, Chicago, Dallas, Detroit, Indianapolis, Nashville and San Antonio), if they consider bids from suppliers outside of their cities. Finally, that Agreement provides that the Massachusetts Port Authority will provide best of out-of-state treatment if it considers non-Massachusetts suppliers. That agreement does not include thresholds or any exclusions.[6]

---

[5] Office of the US Trade Representative (www.ustr.gov/trade-topics/government-procurement/us-european-communities-1995-exchange-letters).

[6] Grier (2014g).

Other entities (utilities and government enterprises): Under the GPA, the EU covers a broad spectrum of utilities in sectors that include drinking water, electricity, airports, maritime or inland ports and transportation (railways, urban railways, automated systems, tramway, trolley bus, bus and cable). But it withholds US access to all except the electric sector in response to the limitations in US coverage. The US covers only federal electric utilities plus several other entities in other sectors. In the revision of the GPA, the US expanded its coverage by extending its waiver of domestic content requirements that apply to funding by the Rural Utilities Services, a unit of the Department of Agriculture, to include telecommunications projects, (see Table 10.3).

Exclusions: Since its implementation of the GATT Code, the US has excluded procurement that it sets aside for its small and minority businesses from the GPA and FTAs. The federal government uses set-asides to help it meet the directive in the Small Business Act of 1953 to award a portion of its procurement to small and minority businesses. The current target is almost a quarter (23%) of federal procurement. The US Congress has explicitly prohibited waiver of the small business set-asides.[7]

3.4 EU and US commitments under bilateral and regional FTAs

In addition to their GPA membership, the EU and the US have undertaken procurement commitments with other trading partners in bilateral and regional free trade agreements (FTAs). The US is a party to 13 FTAs that cover the procurement of 19 countries on terms and conditions similar to those in the GPA. Several of those countries (Canada, Israel, Republic of Korea and Singapore) are also GPA parties. The only US FTA that does not include robust procurement commitments comparable to the GPA is its FTA with Jordan. That FTA's procurement provision is limited to a commitment that the parties engage in negotiations on Jordan's accession to the GPA. In addition to FTAs, in 2010, the United States and Canada negotiated a procurement agreement in which they exchanged sub-central coverage, and Canada opened up the procurement of its provinces and territories for the first time.[8]

---

[7] Grier (2014i).

[8] Grier (2013b).

The EU has included public procurement provisions in all of its comprehensive bilateral trade agreements. The agreements negotiated with GPA signatories such as the Republic of Korea, Canada and Singapore, simply apply the GPA rules but extend commitments. In the case of Canada in the CETA agreement, Canada extended its commitments to include its municipalities, municipal organisations, school boards and publicly funded academic, health and social service entities (MASH sector) for the first time. In preferential agreements signed with middle developing countries, such as those with Colombia and Peru and Central America, the EU has included procurement rules largely based on the GPA. With these partners the EU has accepted a degree of asymmetry in commitments in that it has offered more or less the same level of commitments to these countries as to GPA signatories but accepted more limited commitments from the countries concerned.

The EU–CARIFORUM agreement also includes rules very similar to those of the GPA, but it does not include coverage commitments, which are to be decided by the parties in the future. In its preferential agreements with developing countries such as the other ACP states procurement is envisaged for a later stage.[9]

4. Enhancing access to procurement markets

4.1 *De jure* and *de facto* barriers to access

The *de jure* preferences take the form of, for example, 'buy national' policies, which grant national suppliers a price preference as in the case of the US since the 1930s, in the case of the utilities Directive in the EU and in many other countries today. There are also *de jure* preferences for small- and medium-sized companies, used by developed as well as developing countries, such as US set-asides for its small and minority businesses. There is also a trend towards the use of public contracts to promote other policy objectives, such as through the use of 'green' procurement' that can constitute a potential barrier to access. Such *de jure* preferences can be targeted by national treatment commitments, such as in the GPA or a bilateral agreement such as the TTIP.

But experience suggests that the main barriers to public procurement markets are less obvious, *de facto* discrimination that exists as a result of the discretion available to contracting authorities or costs and other disincentives to bid. Such discretion is built into even

---

9 Woolcock (2013).

the most extensive rules as a result of the flexibility necessary to accommodate the diverse nature of public procurement. Cost effective means of addressing such *de facto* discrimination are not easy to develop, although the OECD has developed a set of Principles for Integrity in Public Procurement that begin to address some of the *de facto* barriers.[10] Requiring transparency is one approach, as is the specification of objective criteria for contract awards, the use of standard documentation and award procedures. The OECD Principles also include recommendations to ensure a proper cost-benefit analysis of the use of procurement in the pursuit of other policy objectives, better planning across the whole procurement cycle, promotion of procurement as a profession and tighter control of exceptional cases. Experience, including that with the EU internal market, suggests that much more than commitments to national treatment is required if there is to be increased competition. It may indeed, only come as a result of a paradigm shift in national policies towards acceptance of open, competitive markets and away from explicit or implicit policies of support for national champions and then usually as a result of indirect supply or exports, in other words via local affiliates.

4.2   *De jure* barriers to access

As described above, the EU and the US have exchanged extensive commitments under the GPA that provide substantial market opportunities in their respective government procurement markets. However, there are significant barriers to access in public procurement in both the EU and the US, and a tendency for such measures to grow, especially in the US, with the 'Buy American' provision in the American Recovery and Reinvestment Act of 2009 (ARRA) as a prominent example. The barriers are summarised in the following tables.

Table 10.5 Restrictions on market access in the US

Procurement Restriction	Description	Treatment in Trade Agreements
American Recovery and Reinvestment Act of 2009 (ARRA)	Required US-produced iron, steel and manufactured goods to be used in ARRA-funded projects	Did not apply to projects covered by trade agreements

[10] OECD (2009).

Berry Amendment	Requires DoD to purchase US-produced food and clothing, fabrics, specialty metals, stainless-steel flatware and hand- measuring tools.	Covered goods are excluded from trade agreements
Buy American Act of 1933	Requires federal agencies to purchase US goods unless a waiver applies	Waived for goods covered under trade agreements
Buy American Act	Requires use of US-produced iron, steel and manufactured products (with 100% domestic content) in highway, transit, railway and airport projects funded by DoT, unless a waiver applies.	Restriction is excluded from trade agreements
Small Business Act of 1953	Requires federal government to award a portion of federal procurement to US small and minority businesses	Set-asides for small and minority businesses are excluded from trade agreements
US-flag vessels requirements	Items procured by the military must be shipped in US-flagged vessels	Procurement of transportation services are excluded from trade agreements
Sub-central procurement not covered by trade agreements	Use of domestic content requirements and insufficient transparency	Not covered by trade agreements

Table 10.6 Barriers to market access in the EU

Cross-cutting NTM	Sectors where it applies	Other observations
Favouritism of EU firms	Construction	
Diverse national and local practices	All sectors	
Unavailability of procurement statistics (regarding foreign bidders)	All sectors	This NTM is decreasing in importance.
Local (domestic) content requirements in the bid (at least 50% European)	Water (production, transport, and distribution of drinking water), energy (gas and heat), urban transport (urban, railway, automated systems, tramway, bus, trolley bus, and cable), and postal services	
Excessive delays in finalising the contract and beginning of work	Infrastructure projects	
High level of bureaucracy and corruption	Public works	
Onerous qualification requirements	Government procurement	
Use of offsets in defence procurement	Defence	

Source: Authors' own compilation.

5.   Potential Expansion of Procurement under TTIP

5.1   Procurement objectives of the EU and US in TTIP

In the February 2013 final report of the United States-European Union High Level Working Group on Jobs and Growth (HLWG), the EU and US shared the goal to substantially improve access on the basis of national treatment.[11] Subsequently, each side has elaborated on their objectives for the TTIP. In March 2013, the US notified the Congress of its intention to launch negotiations of TTIP and its objectives.[12] It subsequently pointed to its interests in expanded access to procurement in construction, engineering and medical devices.[13] In July 2013, the European Commission published initial TTIP Position Papers, including one on public procurement.[14] See Table 10.7 for a comparison of the EU and US objectives in the negotiations.

Table 10.7 EU and US procurement objectives in the TTIP

Joint HLWG objectives	EU objectives	US objectives
Enhance business opportunities through substantially improved access to government procurement contracts at all levels of government on the basis of national treatment	*Central government entities* - Use negative list - Coverage of US federal government entities not covered under GPA - Access to procurement subject to specific policies, such as those related to small businesses (small business set-asides) *Sub-central entities* - Coverage of the 13 states not covered by the GPA; removal of restrictions maintained by the 37 states covered under the GPA - Coverage of municipalities, airports, ports, transit authorities and railway authorities	Expand market access opportunities for US goods, services and suppliers to procurement markets of the EU and its MSs Ensure that US suppliers are treated as favourably as domestic and other foreign goods, services, and suppliers in the EU and member states Ensure procurement is conducted in a fair, transparent & predictable manner

---

[11] See USTR (2013).

[12] See letter from Acting USTR Demetrios Marantis to Speaker of the US House of Representatives John Boehner, dated 20 March 2013 (Marantis, 2013).

[13] See USTR (2014).

[14] European Commission (2013).

	- Coverage of sub-central government entities "operating at the local, regional or municipal level, as well as any other entities whose procurement policies are substantially controlled by, dependent on, or influenced by sub-central, regional or local government and which are engaged in non-commercial or non-industrial activities"	Expand opportunities to bid on government contracts in areas that include construction, engineering and medical devices
	Other entities: coverage of "all entities governed by public law, state-owned companies and similar operating in particular in the field of utilities" (special interest in transit/railways, urban railways and urban transport)	
	Services: Coverage of all services, with specific interest in Information society services, particularly cloud-based services	
	Buy American restrictions	
	- Removal of existing domestic content requirements on mass-transit and highway projects	
	- Commitment to not impose any new Buy American requirements on federal funds given to states or other sub-central government entities, such as were imposed by the American Recovery and Reinvestment Act of 2009 (ARRA)	

	Procedural disciplines: GPA-plus disciplines, including access to procurement information, technical specifications, award criteria, qualification procedures, domestic challenge mechanisms	

Sources: Grier (2014a); USTR (2013 and 2014); European Commission (2013) and Marantis (2013).

In addition to its stated objectives, the US may be expected to seek access to the procurement that the EU covers under the revised GPA, but to which it does not provide access to the US. That includes the procurement of services by the EU's sub-central government entities, procurement by EU utilities, access to EU works concessions and procurement of more than 200 central government entities of member states.

Expanding procurement under the TTIP will be difficult since most of the easily covered procurement has already been offered. Moreover, the EU and the US have engaged in extensive negotiations over many of the remaining issues, most recently in the revision of the GPA. Nonetheless, there are some areas in which the two parties should be able to build on their existing commitments (see Table 10.3). The potential areas are explored in this section, along with the constraints.

5.2 Comprehensive central government coverage

In the TTIP, the EU and the US should exchange comprehensive coverage of central government entities, providing one another with the best coverage of central government entities that they offer any trading partner. This could be accomplished with the EU proposal to base TTIP coverage of central government coverage in the TTIP on a negative list. For the EU that would mean providing the US with the same comprehensive coverage of the central government entities of its member states that it provides to favoured parties under the revised GPA (see section 3.3). Comprehensive coverage could also extend beyond the three EU-wide entities that the EU covers under the GPA.[15]

---

[15] Grier (2014f).

The US may not be able to mirror the EU approach by offering coverage of *all* federal entities since there is no comprehensive list of federal agencies and, without such a list, the US could not ensure full compliance. Nonetheless, the US should be able to offer comprehensive coverage of all federal entities subject to the Federal Acquisition Regulation (FAR). The FAR is the primary federal regulation that applies to the procurement of most federal agencies and is intended to provide "uniform policies and procedures for acquisition by all executive agencies".[16] Basing US coverage on the entities subject to the FAR should address US uncertainty of ascertaining all the entities that would be captured by an overly broad category, while fulfilling the EU request for comprehensive coverage. If there are certain agencies that are subject to the FAR that the US is not able to cover for security or other reasons, they could be put on the negative list and excluded from the TTIP. It may be noted that the Federal Aviation Administration is not subject to the FAR, even though most of its regulations are consistent with the FAR.

The US approach should be acceptable to the EU as it is similar to central government coverage used by Japan and Armenia in the GPA. Both provide comprehensive coverage of all entities subject to a specified law. In Japan's case, it is covered by the Accounts Law and for Armenia, it is the Law on Procurement of the Republic of Armenia.

If the TTIP is to set a new standard for procurement obligations, one step that would contribute to that goal is for the EU and the US to exchange comprehensive coverage of central/federal entities and to offer one another their best coverage.

5.3 Constraints on broader sub-central entity coverage

Less promising for expansion of commitments is sub-central coverage. The EU has placed a high priority on coverage of the 13 states not covered by the GPA and access to more procurement of the states covered by the GPA. But it will likely be very difficult for the US to meet fully – or perhaps even partially – the expectations of the EU for several reasons.[17]

---

[16]   Federal Acquisition Regulation (FAR) 1.101 (http://www.acquisition.gov/far/loadmainre.html).

[17] Grier (2013d).

The first hurdle is the process for covering state procurement under trade agreements. As a consequence of the US federal system of government, the Administration only covers procurement of sub-central governments, including states and cities, with that government's authorisation.[18] In negotiations of prior agreements, the US Trade Representative has requested such authorisation from the state governors (or city mayors), on a state-by-state (or city-by-city) basis. Where a state has authorised coverage of its procurement, it has been allowed to limit its covered procurement to specific agencies and to exclude procurement of sensitive goods or services, such as those subject to domestic preferences.

A second hurdle is declining state interest in covering procurement under FTAs. The US covers state procurement under the GPA and eight FTAs, with the number of states covered varying by agreement. It lists 37 states under the GPA, and it covered those same states in the first two FTAs to cover state procurement – the US-Chile FTA[19] and the US-Singapore FTA,[20] without seeking additional authorisation from the states. However, in the subsequently negotiated FTAs, states were covered only with their authorization, and state participation declined. Thirty-one states were covered under the 2005 US-Australia FTA,[21] but the number dropped to 23 states in the 2006 US-Morocco FTA[22] and to 22 states (plus Puerto Rico) in the US-Central American-Dominican Republic FTA.[23]

In the latest FTAs – with Peru, Colombia and Panama, the US applied a reciprocity policy, which was aimed at encouraging state participation and avoiding the so-called 'free-rider' problem.[24] Under

---

[18] USTR (2011).

[19] US-Chile FTA, Annex 9.1, Section B, Schedule of the United States.

[20] US-Singapore FTA, Annex 13A, Schedule 1, For the United States, Section B.

[21] US-Australia FTA, Annex 15-A, Section B, Schedule of the United States.

[22] US-Morocco FTA, Annex 9-A-2, Schedule of the United States.

[23] US-DR-CAFTA, Annex 9.1.2(b)(i), Section B, Schedule of the United States, List A. The United States provides Honduras with access to only 16 states plus Puerto Rico. CAFTA, Annex 9.1.2(b)(i), Section B, Schedule of the United States, List A.

[24] The 'free rider' situation arises where states that do not authorise coverage of their procurement in an FTA nonetheless gain the same access to the procurement covered under an FTA as the states that agreed to cover their procurement under the FTA.

that policy, the FTA gave rights to a state's suppliers to participate in the FTA partner's sub-central procurement only if that state authorised its procurement to be covered under the FTA.[25] Unfortunately, the use of the reciprocity policy did not accomplish its aim, as only eight states and Puerto Rico agreed to bring their procurement under those FTAs.[26] (Subsequently, two more states were added to the FTA with Peru.[27])

Another hurdle exists in states that have enacted legislation transferring the authority to cover a state's procurement in a trade agreement from the governor to the legislature. Beginning in 2005, several states, including Hawaii, Maryland, Minnesota and Rhode Island, have enacted such legislation. Seeking the authorisation of states with this legislation is likely to result in a longer and more complicated process, and one that may be more politicised.

A fourth obstacle is the lack of a mechanism that would bring states together to develop a unified approach to covering state procurement under agreements, and perhaps lay a foundation for more comprehensive coverage.[28] Canada has such a mechanism under its Agreement on Internal Trade (AIT), an intergovernmental agreement among its federal government, provinces and territories. The AIT's chapter on procurement establishes a framework to ensure that all Canadian suppliers have equal access to the country's procurement above certain thresholds, and that such procurement is conducted in an open and transparent manner. The AIT even extends to Canada's so-called 'MASH sector', which includes all municipalities, municipal organisations, school boards and publicly funded academic, health and social service entities.

As a consequence of the AIT, Canada has been able to expeditiously develop negotiating positions on opening procurement by its provinces and territories. This was evident in two recent negotiations. First, in the negotiations of the US-Canada Agreement on Government Procurement in 2010, Canada was able to move quickly – in only six months – to reverse its long-standing refusal to open the procurement of its provinces to foreign firms. With the agreement of its

---

[25] See for example, Peru TPA, Annex 9.1, Section B, Schedule of Peru, Notes 7 and 8 to the Schedule of Peru and Notes 1 and 2 and Schedule of the United States.

[26] Colombia TPA, Annex 9.1, Section B, Schedule of the United States; Panama TPA, Annex 9.1, Section B, Schedule of the United States.

[27] US-Peru TPA, Annex 9.1, Section B, Schedule of the United States.

[28] Grier (2014c).

provinces, Canada offered permanent access to its provincial procurement, and to bind that coverage under the GPA, as well as temporary access to additional provincial and municipal construction projects. Canada undertook those commitments in exchange for access to the US states covered under the GPA and – most important – US agreement to not apply the Buy American requirement in the American Recovery and Reinvestment Act of 2009 (ARRA) to Canadian iron, steel and manufactured goods in a number of ARRA-funded programmes. More recently, in 2013, Canada was able to mobilise its provinces and MASH sector to open the procurement of both provincial utilities and the MASH sector under an agreement with the EU.[29]

The US does not have any similar means for developing common negotiating positions with its states. The US should consider setting up a forum for state consultations on covering procurement under international agreements. Such a mechanism could build on the US advisory committee system that the US Congress established 40 years ago to ensure that US trade policy and trade negotiation objectives adequately reflect US economic and commercial interests. That system includes an Intergovernmental Policy Advisory Committee (IGPAC), composed of state and local representatives from the three branches of government (executive, legislative and judicial), to provide advice on the impact of trade issues on state and local governments. While that Committee serves an important role, it is not sufficient for the type of consultations needed with respect to covering state procurement under trade agreements. Its broad membership includes only a few representatives from state governments.[30] A broader procurement consultation mechanism could be used for both the education of states on the consequences and benefits of coverage, and development of US positions. It would not be a panacea but it could facilitate discussions with the states.

But, whether or not the US develops a new consultative approach to the states, greater state participation in the TTIP will be possible only if states are convinced that there are substantial benefits in a commitment to open procurement to foreign suppliers and to refrain from adopting new measures that would favour local suppliers. From a state's perspective, it does not need a trade agreement in order to accept bids from foreign suppliers. For potential suppliers from the

---

[29] Grier (2014m).

[30] Grier (2014j).

EU however, the diversity of purchasing practices does not enhance transparency and could well discourage them from bidding.

A potentially more fruitful area of expansion of US sub-central procurement commitments is cities. The 1995 Exchange of Letters may be a model for coverage of more cities because it only imposes a national treatment obligation and does not impose any other procedural obligations. This approach could focus on cities of a certain size or cities of particular interest to EU suppliers.

5.4 Coverage of utilities and government enterprises

Of the three categories of entity coverage, the EU and the US have exchanged the narrowest coverage with regard to 'other entities', namely utilities and government enterprises. As described above, the EU has broad coverage of utilities under the EU's regime and in the GPA, but limits US access to just its electric utilities. This limited access reflects the EU aim of offering only reciprocal access to US suppliers given that US coverage extends only to its federal electric utilities and a handful of other entities. For example, it covers a few airports, most prominent of which are those under the jurisdiction of the Port Authority of New York and New Jersey (PANYNJ) (La Guardia, JFK and Newark) and three port authorities (PANYNJ, Port of Baltimore and the Port Authority of Massachusetts), as well as a scattering of transit entities under covered states.

With regard to other entities, the EU is particularly interested in coverage of transit and railway authorities, urban railways and urban transport entities. Unless they are transit agencies covered under states, their participation would have to be solicited. More importantly, even if authorised, their coverage would be limited as long as they are subject to Buy American requirements that apply to railway and transit projects funded by the federal government.[31] See section 5.5.

One of the possible approaches to expanding procurement obligations by utilities and government enterprises may be to limit the commitments to national treatment, and not require GPA-type procedures, as in the 1995 Exchange of Letters. The primary benefit of such an approach for the entities would be that they would not have to alter their procurement procedures. The requirement to adopt GPA-type procedures, in particular, the time periods for tendering, may serve as a deterrent to participation by such entities. For the EU, the

---

[31] Grier (2014k).

benefit would be access to the procurement of the entities. The fact that procedures do not conform to GPA rules would be less of an impediment for the kind of large companies that would supply railway or public transport equipment. The EU's identification of those entities of greatest interest should facilitate US engagement with a workable number of entities.

5.5 Buy American requirements attached to federal funding to states

A major aim of the EU in the TTIP negotiations is to remove the application of domestic content requirements that apply to state and local projects, especially transit projects, undertaken with federal funds. Those requirements, which are often referred to as Buy American[32] requirements, apply to iron and steel, as well as to manufactured products, used in non-federal infrastructure projects. European firms want to be able to participate in these projects without having to meet the Buy American requirements. The US has never waived these domestic content requirements in any agreement. Instead, it has consistently excluded them from its GPA and FTA obligations.[33] There would be strong opposition to any alteration of the US position on this issue from the iron and steel industry and their supporters in the Congress.

The US may be more amenable to a second EU aim – to obtain a US commitment that it will not impose any new Buy American requirement on EU suppliers when the federal government provides new funds to states and other sub-federal entities. In essence, the EU is seeking to avoid a repeat of the Buy American requirements in the American Recovery and Reinvestment Act of 2009 (ARRA). Even though the ARRA Buy American requirement did not apply to procurement covered by international agreements, its effect was wide-reaching as it disrupted EU and other country's participation in projects, such as water projects, not covered by agreements.

---

[32] The term "Buy America" is often used to refer to domestic content requirements in US federal government funding of state and local projects. This is in contrast to the term "Buy American," which generally refers to the Buy American Act that applies to US federal government procurement of goods. In this chapter, Buy American is used to refer to both situations.

[33] Grier (2014h).

A commitment to not impose any new Buy American requirements in legislation authorising funding to states and other sub-federal entities may be more than the US Congress could accept. However, such a commitment that was limited to EU goods, services and suppliers may be acceptable. As such a measure would constitute a significant US concession, the EU could be expected to reciprocate with an equally difficult concession in procurement, or some other element of the TTIP negotiations.[34]

5.6 Services coverage

The coverage of services provides another opportunity for the EU and US to expand their commitments. The US bases its coverage of services in the GPA and its FTAs on the use of a negative list. The EU has to date used a positive list. To align their commitments to the extent possible, they should consider basing their services coverage on a negative list.[35] That would provide an important foundation for them to seek similar services coverage in the next round of GPA negotiations.

Use of a negative list ensures more comprehensive coverage than a positive list, because it means that when new services, such as cloud computing, become available, they are automatically covered. By contrast, when a positive list is used, a new service is covered only if it fits within a category that is already covered. Since it is not always easy to fit a new service into existing categories, the issue of coverage of a new service can be subject to disputes.

In addition, the EU and the US should seek as comparable coverage of service categories as possible. One area that warrants close consideration is telecommunications. Until the revision of the GPA, the EU did not cover all telecommunications services. In the revision, the EU offers all such services, but conditions access on reciprocal coverage. The US continued its limited offering of telecommunications services, opening only enhanced or value-added services. The description of its covered telecommunications services has not changed since the GPA entered into force in 1996. Yet, there have been significant advances in telecommunications in the intervening two decades. Thus, the US should re-examine its coverage of such services with the aim of updating and broadening its coverage. It could exclude specific services as needed for national security or other purposes.

---

[34] Grier (2014l).

[35] Grier (2014k).

5.7 Exchange coverage of build-operate-transfer (BOT) contracts and works concessions

The EU and the US should also expand their commitments with respect to construction services. Currently, they open all construction services to one another, with two exceptions. The US excludes dredging and the EU does not extend its coverage of works concessions to the US. The latter would appear to be an area in which they could exchange commitments. While the US does not cover works concessions under the GPA, it covers build-operate-transfer (BOT) contracts and public works concessions under its FTAs, including in the US-Korea FTA (KORUS FTA). In its FTA with the EU, Korea provides that same BOT coverage. Since the EU has treated Korean coverage of BOT contracts as reciprocal to its coverage of public works concessions in both the GPA and their bilateral agreement, it should be able to accept US coverage of BOT contracts in the TTIP.[36]

6. Impact of broader procurement coverage

As discussed in the previous section, the prospects for government procurement in the TTIP are for relatively modest, incremental expansions of procurement commitments, but not a wholesale change in the EU-US procurement relationship or resolution of all the outstanding issues. While the sub-central level is of particular interest to the EU, it is also the most difficult for the US, as described above.

A challenge of the TTIP procurement negotiations is the fact that the United States has opened most of the procurement that is within the authority of the Administration. Many of the EU's requests are beyond the authority of the Administration, however, and would require changes in US laws or commitments by sub-central entities to bring their procurement in line with the discipline of the TTIP. For the US to undertake such a heavy burden, the EU would need to provide a strong incentive either in the procurement sector – or perhaps in other areas of the TTIP where the US is making demands on the EU.

While the EU imposes significant limitations on US rights to EU-covered procurement, those legal restrictions do not necessarily dictate what is happening on the ground. They do not prohibit EU entities from procuring US goods and services in the restricted areas, such as services purchased by EU sub-central entities. Even where purchasing entities retain the right to discriminate against foreign suppliers, this

[36] Grier (2014e).

does not mean that they do so. Purchasing entities are also interested in obtaining the best value for money and often find that this aim can best be achieved by purchasing from abroad. As a consequence, it would appear that US suppliers are relatively satisfied with their current access to EU procurement markets, notwithstanding their lack of legal rights.

Moreover, market access can also be achieved in the absence of any legal commitments to not discriminate against foreign suppliers. As noted above, access is very often indirect via affiliates established in the target market. EUROPEBUSINESS, a leading EU business organisation, has acknowledged that EU businesses have access to more procurement than is covered by agreements.[37]

The projections offered by the impact studies of welfare gains from the TTIP provisions on procurement are relatively small compared to the potential gains from measures addressing regulatory and technical barriers to trade. The estimates put welfare gains at €10.8 billion per year (in the long run) from the reduction of barriers in the field of public procurement. The benefits derived from economic changes are expected to be higher for the EU at €9.7 billion per year and the US €0.9 billion (Ecorys, 2009).

Trade flows are projected to grow slightly in procurement on both sides, but in percentage terms more growth will occur in the US. This is not unexpected; as discussed above, the nature of the procurement markets on both sides of the Atlantic is such that indirect supply is more the norm. The long-term household impact and wage-level effects range between 0.0% and 0.01% for the US and between 0.03% and 0.07% for the EU. With regard to the impact on the sectoral level, the motor vehicles, chemicals and food and beverages sectors in the EU are projected to benefit the most in percentage terms. In the US, electronics, metal production and machinery would gain the most (in line with the general results). In particular, construction is also expected to benefit in both the EU and US. These projections need to be treated with caution, however, as they may not have picked up some potential gains. Competition in procurement markets depends on potential suppliers bidding for contracts. When there are entrenched *de facto* preferences for local suppliers, this does not happen. International commitments such as an ambitious agreement on procurement in TTIP could provide potential suppliers with the confidence they need to bid for contracts they otherwise would not have. Nevertheless, in the field

---

[37] BUSINESSEUROPE (2013).

of procurement, we have a classic example of the political economy of liberalisation in which the benefits of liberalisation are widely diffused through society but the costs in terms of increased foreign competition are heavily concentrated.

7.   Impact of TTIP procurement provisions on third parties and the trading system

A second core aim of TTIP is to shape broad international trade rules. As in other policy areas, the US and the EU have been doing this for decades through the GPA (and its predecessor) as well as the OECD, including the work on integrity in public procurement discussed above. The comprehensive preferential trade agreements negotiated by the US and the EU have effectively exported the GPA framework of rules to many other countries. These norms have also shaped other more voluntary approaches such as the UNCITRAL Model Procurement Law. So in terms of the framework of rules governing the procurement process, such as transparency and due process, the US and the EU have effectively shaped the international rules. By pressing ahead with efforts to effectively apply best practice in public procurement at all levels of government, such as those set out in the OECD principles, bilateral efforts promoted through TTIP would then offer a means for the EU and the US to address *de facto* barriers to competition in public procurement and reduce corruption in procurement. Whilst estimates of corruption are inevitably very approximate, surveys by the World Economic Forum have shown that bribes are more prevalent in procurement than any other activity. It has been estimated that as much as 20-25% of the value of public contracts could be lost due to corrupt practices (OECD, 2013).

TTIP procurement commitments would not have a direct impact on multilateralism because there is no multilateral agreement that covers government procurement. Where there are government procurement agreements, commitments are made on a reciprocal basis. In so far as TTIP succeeds in extending liberalisation commitments, there could be some trade-diversion effects on third countries. These are likely to be incremental given the extended commitments under the revised GPA.

Extending transparency provisions, such as to more US states, and ensuring better implementation of existing transparency requirements by EU member states or applying best practice in procurement could well benefit third-country suppliers that participate in such procurement. Although third-country suppliers may not benefit from national treatment provisions, they would, for example, have the benefit of bidding for a contract from a US- or EU-based affiliate. In this sense there could well be positive externalities from TTIP provisions on procurement.

In terms of shaping international rules in the field of procurement, the EU and the US have effectively done so through their contributions to the development of the GPA and through the promotion of those agreed GPA rules in their respective FTAs. However, the TTIP could contribute to the international procurement arena by setting a new standard for procurement agreements. If the terms of the TTIP go beyond current procurement agreements, in particular, the GPA, it would likely provide the basis for the inclusion of its liberalisation of procurement in other agreements. If the US expands its sub-central coverage in the TTIP from its GPA coverage, it would set a baseline for future FTA and GPA negotiations. If the TTIP includes procurement rules that go beyond the revised GPA, they could provide the basis for incorporation in a subsequent revision of the GPA. Also, such new rules would likely be incorporated in any new FTAs that the EU and the US negotiate.

8. A living agreement

A Bilateral Procurement Forum, which the EU and the US established at the conclusion of the negotiations on the GPA revision, could provide the foundation for on-going dialogue, cooperation and collaboration on outstanding procurement issues. In December 2011, the EU and the US set up the Forum to continue work on procurement issues that were not resolved during the GPA negotiations. The Forum sets out three tracks: a dialogue on regulatory procurement issues, a dialogue on international procurement issues and exploration of possible expansion of their procurement commitments on a reciprocal basis.

The Forum's regulatory element provides an opportunity for an enhanced understanding of the respective procurement systems. It could also be used to address specific issues raised by either party's private sector with regard to their respective procurement markets. In this respect, bilateral efforts could support and draw on work carried out in the OECD. The OECD has developed a number of principles for integrity in public procurement, which could contribute to addressing de facto barriers to competitive procurement markets. The OECD principles include, for example, the provision of adequate transparency throughout the entire procurement cycle, so covering how contracts are managed as well as calls for tenders and contract award procedures. They also call for greater professionalism in procurement, proper auditing and the empowerment of civil society, the media and wider public opinion to scrutinise procurement (OECD, 2009).

Bilateral efforts could also promote common approaches to new challenges. For example, the increased tendency of governments to use public procurement as an instrument of environmental or other policies, such as promoting small- and medium-sized companies, could result in new distortions to competition if not adequately addressed. The increased use of public-private-partnerships (PPPs) could also pose a challenge and is another area where the development of agreed norms or codes could help to avoid the creation of new restrictions. The use of TTIP to promote compatibility between procurement systems such as in the use of e-procurement could enhance supplier confidence.[38] The furtherance of such principles by the EU and the US could then set a standard for wider international practice.

Under the international leg of the Forum, the EU and the US could also explore and coordinate positions on a variety of international procurement issues, such as China's accession to the GPA. Cooperation on preparing requests for improvements in China's offers (and for Russia when it begins its GPA accession in 2016) would strengthen their leverage. They could also develop a coordinated approach to encourage other countries, such as the other BRICS (Brazil, India and South Africa) to join the GPA.

The Forum's third part – exploration of expansion of procurement commitments – could be used to add new entities after the Agreement is concluded. The US has used this approach for states in several FTAs, in which it has a continuing obligation to add states after the FTA enters into force. For example, the US added five states to the US-Australia FTA after it entered into force and two states to its FTA with Peru after it was implemented.

9. Conclusion

Public procurement poses challenges when it comes to 'liberalisation'. Most of the low-hanging fruit has been picked, so that further progress will not be easy. As outlined above, there are several areas in which the US and EU could make, at least, modest expansions in their respective

---

[38] See OECD (2013).

procurement commitments and seek to accord one another with the best treatment that they provide under trade agreements.

But if the US and EU are unable in the TTIP negotiations to reach a level of commitments that sets a higher standard for international commitments, there would appear to be two broad options. The first option would be to continue to negotiate on procurement as part of a living agreement. Here reciprocal concessions would be within the procurement sector. As this chapter has illustrated, however, this is unlikely to be done quickly given the work required at the domestic level, such as to get US states or cities to authorise coverage. The second option would be to make further progress on liberalisation of procurement markets by linking with other policy areas under negotiation in the TTIP. If the TTIP aim of contributing to welfare gains and economic growth are to be achieved, this would be the option to follow.

In terms of the TTIP's second broad objective of shaping the rules for international trade, the US and the EU have effectively done this through the plurilateral GPA and the extension of GPA rules to other countries through their bilateral FTAs. At issue in the procurement field is less setting the rules that would be applied in national procurement laws, which has arguably already been achieved, but more promoting best practices in procurement by fully applying principles such as those developed by the OECD throughout all public procurement in the US and EU.

References

BUSINESSEUROPE (2013), "Public Procurement in the Transatlantic Trade and Economic Partnership", Position Paper, 11 December (www.businesseurope.eu/Content/ Default.asp?PageID=568&DocID=32446).

Ecorys (2009) Non-Tariff Measures in EU – US Trade and Investment – An Economic Analysis, Rotterdam.

European Commission (2011a) DG Internal Market and Services: Final Report. Cross Border Procurement above EU Thresholds, Ramboll Management Consulting (www.ramboll-management.com).

_____ (2011b) Commission Staff Working Paper. Evaluation Report, Impact and Effectiveness of EU Public Procurement Legislation. SEC (2011) 853.

_____ (2012) Proposal for a Regulation of the European Parliament and the Council on access of third-country goods and services to the Union's internal market in procurement and procedures supporting negotiations on access of Union goods and services to the public procurement markets of third countries COM (2012) 124 final, 21 March 2012.

_____ (2013), "EU-US Transatlantic Trade and Investment Partnership: Public Procurement", Initial EU Position Paper, July (http://trade.ec.eu`ropa.eu/doclib/docs/2013/july/tradoc_15162 3.pdf).

Grier, J.H. (2013a), "TTIP Negotiations: US-EU Procurement Commitments, Perspectives on Trade" (website posting), 25 October (http://trade.djaghe.com/?p=57).

_____ (2013b), "U.S. Agreements Open Foreign Procurement", Perspectives on Trade (website posting), 8 November (http://trade.djaghe.com/?p=121).

_____ (2013c), "Revising the GPA: Better Procedural Rules to Enhance Use", Perspectives on Trade (website posting), 11 November (http://trade.djaghe.com/?p=150).

_____ (2013d), "Challenges of Covering State Procurement in TPP and TTIP", Perspectives on Trade, (website posting), 16 December (http://trade.djaghe.com/?p=190 (Dec. 16, 2013).

_____ (2014a), "US and EU's Procurement Objectives in TTIP Negotiations", Perspectives on Trade, (website posting) 14 January (http://trade.djaghe.com/?p=334).

_____ (2014b), "U.S. Procurement Covered under Revised GPA", Perspectives on Trade (website posting), 10 February (http://trade.djaghe.com/?p=426).

_____ (2014c), "Can the U.S. Offer Comprehensive Coverage of States in TTIP?", Perspectives on Trade, (website posting), 3 March (http://trade.djaghe.com/?p=473).

_____ (2014d), "New Procurement Opportunities under Revised GPA", Perspectives on Trade (website posting), 17 March (http://trade.djaghe.com/?p=488).

_____ (2014e), "BOT Contracts and Works Concessions in TTIP", Perspectives on Trade (website posting), 24 March (http://trade.djaghe.com/?p=517).

_____ (2014f), "Comprehensive Coverage of Central Government Procurement in TTIP?", Perspectives on Trade (website posting) 12 May (http://trade.djaghe.com/?p=600).

_____ (2014g), "40 States Cover Procurement under International Agreements", Perspectives on Trade (website posting), 28 July (http://trade.djaghe.com/?p=771).

_____ (2014h), "Federal Domestic Content Restrictions on State and Local Projects", Perspectives on Trade (website posting), 4 August (http://trade.djaghe.com/?p=798).

_____ (2014i), "Opening Foreign Procurement Markets Amidst Domestic Preferences", America's Trade Policy (guest blog), Washington International Trade Association (WITA), 18 August (http://americastradepolicy.com/guest-blog-opening-foreign-procurement-markets-amid-domestic-preferences/#.U_fqIEs3Qds).

_____ (2014j), "Trade Advisory Committees: Eligibility Broadened", Trade Advisory Committees: Eligibility Broadened, Perspectives on Trade (website posting), 8 September (http://trade.djaghe.com/?p=837).

_____ (2014k), "TPP and TTIP Government Procurement Negotiations", America's Trade Policy (guest blog), Washington International Trade Association (WITA), 16 September http://americastradepolicy.com/guest-blog-tpp-and-ttip-government-procurement-negotiations/#.VEhB5ks3Qds).

_____ (2014l), "Freeze Buy American Requirements in TTIP?", Perspectives on Trade (website posting), 29 September (http://trade.djaghe.com/?p=880).

_____ (2014m), "UPDATE: EU-Canadian Trade Pact Now Public", Perspectives on Trade (website posting), 6 October (http://trade.djaghe.com/?p=890).

_____ (2014n), "State Procurement Restrictions in Agreements" (Backgrounder), Perspectives on Trade (website posting), 14 October (http://trade.djaghe.com/?p=906).

Marantis, D. (2013), Letter from Acting USTR to Speaker of the U.S. House of Representatives John Boehner, 20 March (http://www.ustr.gov/about-us/press-office/press-releases/2013/march/administration-notifies-congress-ttip

Messerlin, P.A. and S. Miroudot (2012), "Public procurement markets: Where are we?", VoxEU, 7 September (www.voxeu.org/article/public-procurement-markets-where-are-we).

OECD (2009), "Principles for Integrity in Public Procurement", Paris.

_____ (2013), "Implementing the OECD Principles for Integrity in Public Procurement: Progress since 2008", Paris.

US Trade Representative (USTR) (2011), "Benefits for the United States from the Revised WTO Government Procurement Agreement", 15 December (https://ustr.gov/about-us/policy-offices/press-office/fact-sheets/2011/december/benefits-united-states-revised-wto-government-procur).

_____ (2013), Final Report of the United States-European Union High Level Working Group on Jobs, 11 February (https://ustr.gov/about-us/policy-offices/press-office/reports-and-publications/2013/final-report-us-eu-hlwg).

_____ (2014), "U.S. Objectives, U.S. Benefits in the Transatlantic Trade and Investment Partnership: A Detailed View", March (www.ustr.gov/about-us/press-office/press-releases/2014/March/US-Objectives-US-Benefits-In-the-TTIP-a-Detailed-View).

Woolcock, S. (2013), "Policy diffusion in public procurement: The role of regional trade agreements", International Negotiations, Vol. 18 (1), pp. 153-173.

World Trade Organization (WTO) (2011), "Historic deal reached on government procurement", 15 December (www.wto.org/english/news_e/news11_e/gpro_15dec11_e.htm).

_____ (2014), "Revised WTO Agreement on Government Procurement enters into force", 7 April (www.wto.org/english/news_e/news14_e/gpro_07apr14_e.htm).

11. TTIP: THE SERVICES DIMENSION
PATRICK MESSERLIN

1. Introduction

The negotiations on the Transatlantic Trade and Investment Partnership (TTIP) are far from being the first attempt to establish a 'Transatlantic Market Place'. Indeed, the acronym 'NAFTA' was forged in the 1960s to designate the North Atlantic Free Trade Agreement among the US, Canada, the UK and the then European Community. This distant ancestor raises two interesting questions about the nature of TTIP.

- First, since their origin, the US-EU trade negotiations have had a geo-political dimension: the desire to shape world rules and governance, sometimes as a means of challenging other super-powers (the 1960s NAFTA initiative targeted the Soviet Union). Is this dimension still present when TTIP negotiators talk about "norms-setting" – a key question in the case of services, which are regulations (norms)-intense.

- Second, TTIP is the last 'mega-preferential trade agreement' (mega-PTA) to be launched by the world's largest economies – after the Trans-Pacific Partnership (TPP), the Economic Cooperation Framework Agreement between China Mainland and Taiwan, the China-Japan-Korea, the Regional Cooperative Economic Partnership (RCEP) in East Asia, the Japan-EU Free Trade Agreement. Why is TTIP the latest of these mega-PTAs, and not the first?

The TTIP 'negotiations' got off to a bad start. They were launched amid an explosive cocktail of unspecified 'grand' ambitions, excessive secrecy, unclear concepts (harmonisation, mutual recognition, careless mention of equivalence) and totally unrealistic deadlines. All this at a time when governments on both sides of the Atlantic are trying to play down just how hard it is to mobilise the necessary coalitions for such an endeavour – a problem not specific to trade issues, but one that prevails in many domains. Add a generous dose of spying among close friends and geopolitical turbulence in the wider world, and the cocktail was ready to create huge anxiety, fear and fury among EU and US public opinion, troubled by so much bad news since 2008. Both old and new opponents to the domestic reforms that TTIP was supposed to buttress have been very easy to mobilise.

All these mistakes are particularly costly in the area of services which, as argued below, should be run by 'talks' (rather than negotiations), well-defined (rather than unspecified) ambitions, trust (rather than secrecy) and realistic (not unrealistic) deadlines spread over time. The problem is that the economic significance of TTIP critically depends on services, which represent 73-79% of GDP on both sides of the Atlantic; 35% of EU exports to the US and 43% of US exports to the EU. Last but not least, the US accounts for 34% of the foreign direct investment stocks held by the EU in the rest of the world, and 44% of the foreign direct investment stocks held by the rest of the world in the EU.

The early months of 2015 have seen two serious attempts to correct these initial mistakes. First came the transparency initiative of the Commission (January 2015), which posted papers on its website to better explain the situation to stakeholders (see section 2). The second initiative (March 2015) is a paper on regulatory coherence and cooperation released by the US Chamber of Commerce – tackling the most crucial aspects of how to deal with services in the context of modern economies (see section 3).

The thrust of this chapter is as follows. The services dimension of TTIP will bring substantial welfare gains only if the two sides are convinced that, first, they need to undertake domestic reforms to improve the performance of their services sectors and, second, that TTIP is an essential instrument to buttress and boost these domestic reforms. In turn, such a use of TTIP requires a fundamental overhaul of the way 'talks' – not negotiations, as explained below – in services will be held.[1] Without such innovations, TTIP will only deliver welfare gains 'at the margins' of the services sectors, hence undermining its capacity to attract the strong political support it requires to be concluded successfully.

[1] The need for such innovations justifies abandoning the term 'negotiations' in services. This chapter uses the term 'talks' for reasons outlined in section 3. This point was also stressed by P. Lamy in his speech for the Third Jan Tumlir Lecture at ECIPE (9 March 2015).

The two last years have shown that it would be unwise to assume that such strong political support already exists. In fact, since mid-2014, TTIP has faced wide-ranging and vociferous opposition, including in EU member states that are traditionally free-trade supporters, such as Germany. In addition, services have considerable potential to be sources of toxic transatlantic disputes – be they old (audiovisual) or new (data protection); each of them capable of fuelling, at any time, emotional charges among public opinion of both sides of the Atlantic.

The chapter is organised in five sections. Section 2 looks at the broad political economy background, particularly at the strength of domestic political support as predicted by economic analysis. Section 3 examines market access issues in services, and the desirability of TTIP as an instrument to 'deepen' both the EU and US 'internal markets' in services. Section 4 turns to what 'talks' on services regulations means, arguing that the success of TTIP is highly dependent on its capacity to deal successfully with this set of issues. Section 5 briefly examines the relations between the TTIP countries and the rest of the world in the services area. Finally, a section concludes on the interactions between the TTIP and Trade in Services Agreement (TiSA) discussions.

2.   Political economy background

TTIP discussions in services are particularly sensitive to two key political economy issues. The first one has an international dimension: is TTIP a genuinely free-trade agreement or is it the eastern flank of the China-containing strategy that (at least some in) the US would like to see – the Trans-Pacific Partnership (TPP)? This question is particularly important since China is now realising the importance of services to a fully developed economy, hence will be increasingly ready to play an active role in the plurilateral discussions on TiSA in Geneva. The second political economy issue is the magnitude of the domestic political forces behind TTIP: what can economic analysis reveal about the strength and weakness of domestic political support for TTIP?

2.1   TTIP: A genuinely free-trade agreement?

The geopolitical background is particularly important for talks on services that focus on regulations, and hence require a huge amount of trust among partners. It is reasonable to posit that the necessary level of trust can only be achieved and sustained if both partners share a relatively similar geopolitical approach.

The presence of geopolitics in the EU and US PTAs is not new. But little attention was paid to it as long as the WTO negotiating forum was functioning well. Only a few EU and US PTAs were mostly driven by economic considerations: for instance, Canada and Mexico in NAFTA; the Korea-EU Free Trade Agreement (KOREU); and the Korea-US Free Trade Agreement (KORUS). These PTAs have two specific features. First, their economic impact on the EU and US economies is limited because their partners are (relatively) small economies. Second, the EU and US partners (particularly Mexico and Korea) have been deliberately using PTAs to shore up much-needed but politically painful domestic reforms – the best illustration of which being Korea's willingness to accept the liberalisation of its cinema market in KORUS (Parc, 2014).[2]

Neither of these features applies in the TTIP case. First, the impact of TTIP on each TTIP economy will be much greater than the impact of any other PTA because the economic size of the partner is much bigger and its range of produced goods and services much wider. Second, as of today, the largest EU member states (EUMS) and the US have not shown much willingness to undertake the deep structural domestic regulatory reforms that they need for their own good. Last year saw worrisome developments among the key EUMS in regulatory matters: Germany with a more regulated labour market (minimum wage) and a sudden attraction for some kind of industrial policy in services (internet operators); the UK is engulfed in constitutional debates that prevent it from exercising the great influence it once had on EU services liberalisation, hence to further expand it; a timid start to reform in France that most observers consider to be too limited to address France's challenges.

The current deadlock in the Doha Round adds its own heavy burden to this situation; these negotiations collapsed during the July 2008 mini-ministerial meeting. The then USTR Susan Schwab had the necessary authority to strike a deal during this meeting. Officially, the July 2008 failure was a conflict between the US and India over the level of safeguard measures in the Doha Agreement in agriculture. In fact, the breakdown reflected a much deeper problem: the collision course between the US and China on global governance in the WTO. The US argued that multilateral rules should be changed to significantly reduce the degree of freedom enjoyed by the emerging economies – above all China – thanks to the developing economy status in the WTO. China

---

[2] In sharp contrast to France in the TTIP.

disagreed, arguing that its several hundred million poor people and its very recent WTO membership still justified the remnants of its developing status in the WTO. Having lost all hope of changing the WTO game in July 2008, the US Administration swiftly 'pivoted' towards East Asia. In September 2008, it formally notified Congress of its willingness to be part of – de facto to lead – the TPP predecessor (P4 Agreement) (Gillson & Oliver, 2012). Since then, the US has seen the TPP as the blueprint of the 'WTO version 2.0' that it could not establish in the WTO forum.

In short, its origin has made the nature of TPP ambiguous: is it a free trade agreement or a China-containing strategy? Signals from Washington are still hard to decipher.[3] By the same token, the nature of TTIP is also ambiguous. Is the US looking essentially for economic benefits? Or is it thinking in terms of the 'West against the Rest (of the world)' by combining TPP (the Western flank) and TTIP (the Eastern flank), as echoed by the notion of 'norms setting'? (Rosecrance, 2013; Eizenstatt, 2013) (see section 4).

2.2 What domestic support for TTIP?

A successful TTIP requires robust domestic support. If adequately interpreted, the estimates of TTIP benefits and costs as provided by computable general equilibrium models (see Box 11.1) shed interesting light on the support to be expected from the two main groups of actors in these discussions: the top decision-makers (presidents, prime ministers and equivalents) and the other decision-makers involved in the negotiations (ministers, trade officials, business people, consumers and NGOs) (Messerlin, 2013).

---

[3] For instance, it is said that routine briefings are held on TPP by US negotiators in Beijing. In sharp contrast, no less than the US Defense Secretary has stepped into the debate on Trade Promotion Authority for TPP (International Wall Street Journal, April 8, 2015, p. 14) and a top ranking Democrat senator has declared that "the stated goal of this deal [TPP] is to lure [...] other countries away from China" (*International Wall Street Journal*, 18-19 April 2015, p. 10).

Box 11.1 Modelling TTIP

Several computable general equilibrium (CGE) studies on TTIP are available: Erixon and Bauer (2010), Francois et al. (hereafter CEPR) (2013), Febermayr et al. (2013), Kinman and Hogberg (2013) among others.[4]

For simplicity's sake, this chapter focuses on the CEPR and CEPII studies, which envisage roughly the same various levels of liberalisation: i) only tariff cuts focusing on goods; ii) a reduction of non-tariff measures covering goods and services; iii) a 'comprehensive' liberalisation combining tariff cuts and a reduction of non-tariff measures (NTMs).

Such estimates are subject to many limits, two of which are particularly important in the case of services. First, these estimates do not directly take into account foreign direct investment flows, which are the main channel of international competition for many services (CEPR, 2013, p. 22). Second, they aggregate all the economic activities into a very small number of sectors. This aggregation process leads to an average level of protection by sector. By construction, such a process underestimates the big welfare gains to be expected in the highly protected sectors because trade in relatively open activities is over-represented compared to trade in highly protected activities. This bias happens to be much more important for services (75% of EU/US GDP aggregated into 9 different sectors) than for manufacturing (22% of EU/US GDP aggregated into 8 different sectors) and agriculture (3% of EU/US GDP aggregated into 2 different sectors).

2.3   Top policy-makers

Top policy-makers (presidents, prime ministers, etc.) do not pay much attention to whether gains from a trade deal flow from agriculture, manufacturing or services. They are more interested in the expected impact of the agreement on the whole economy of their country because they see trade agreements only as an instrument to boost growth (Hamilton & Schwartz, 2012). Top policy-makers care about what happens to individual sectors only in 'crises' – big sectoral shocks, highly visible domestic vested interests; all cases that are more likely to occur in manufacturing and agriculture.

The results of the CEPR and CEPII studies are similar, and can be summarised as follows:

---

[4] For an in-depth review of the CEPR model, see Pelkmans et al. (2014).

- Gains from a comprehensive TTIP deal (tariff cuts, reductions in NTMs in goods and services) remain limited – roughly 0.4 to 0.7% of GDP.
- Most of these gains come from the reduction of NTMs in goods.
- Gains from the reduction of NTMs in services alone are small.

Before looking at their impact on top policy-makers, the last – surprising if one considers the size of the services sectors – result should be explained in more detail. In the CEPR and CEPII studies, gains from trade are a function of two main variables: the initial size of trade flows and the initial level of protection.

- In both studies, services are (much) less traded across borders than goods. But caution is needed here. Cross-border trade is not the main channel of international competition in services. In other words, the CEPR and CEPII studies underestimate the gains from more open US and EU services sectors to the extent that they do not directly capture FDI flows.
- The two studies differ on the level of protection in services because they have adopted two different ways to estimate the level of protection.

Indeed, Table 11.1 shows that CEPR and CEPII estimates of the level of protection differ much more in services than in goods. However, the higher protection level in the CEPII study does not generate a much larger impact on the estimated gains than the CEPR one because trade flows in services are relatively small.

Table 11.1 The level of protection in the EU and US (in %)

	CEPR estimates		CEPII estimates		Ratios	
	EU	US	EU	US	EU	US
Agriculture	56.8	73.3	48.2	51.3	0.8	0.7
Industry	19.3	23.4	42.8	32.3	2.2	1.4
Services	8.5	8.9	32.0	47.3	3.8	5.3

Notes: Ratios are defined as the CEPII estimates divided by the CEPR estimates.
Sources: CEPR 2013, Ecorys 2009, CEPII 2013, Fontagné et al. (2011).

Such modest results raise a key question for top policy-makers in the US and in the larger EUMS: why risk their limited political domestic capital to negotiate a deal with limited economic gains? The situation of the US and large EUMS' top policy-makers differs from the one faced by the top policy-makers in Canada or Korea when negotiating with the US and the EU (economic gains were much more sizeable for these relatively smaller economies).

If economic gains are not attractive enough, then the fate of the TTIP at the top political level will depend on geopolitical considerations. That makes TTIP volatile, as illustrated by two episodes: strong negative reactions in Europe (including in Germany – initially a staunch TTIP supporter) after leaks of US National Security Agency's phone-tapping; strong reactions in the US against the price agreement between the EU and China following the antidumping provisional measures on solar panel cells (*International Herald Tribune*, 29 July 2013).

2.4   The other decision-makers

If TTIP is unable to attract the attention of top politicians, its fate will be left to the many other decision-makers – officials (ministers of trade, agriculture, etc., trade negotiators and national regulators), business people, consumers, etc. involved in the day-to-day negotiations.

These actors have a much narrower scope of interest. It seems reasonable to suppose that they focus on the changes in trade balances that TTIP would generate in the sectors they are interested in. Economists do not see trade balances as a meaningful indicator, but business people, officials and journalists do. The next question is whether these decision-makers pay attention to changes in bilateral (US-EU) trade balances or to changes in global (world) trade balances generated by TTIP. What follows assumes that they pay attention to global trade balances because most of the firms involved in TTIP negotiations are multinationals (big and small) with worldwide interests and views.

Table 11.2 presents the (CEPR) predicted changes in such global trade balances. For simplicity's sake, it does so only for those sectors that would witness "substantial" trade changes – substantial being arbitrarily defined as changes in trade balances larger than US$ 1 billion in the comprehensive (tariff cuts and reduction of MTNS in goods and services) scenario. This threshold eliminates several service sectors from the TTIP political economy radar screen: water transport, air transport, communications, construction, personal services (for the EU) and other services (for the US).

For the remaining sectors, Table 11.2 assesses their position on the basis of changes in their import-export ratios:

- a sector with an import-export ratio lower than 1 (imports grow more than exports as a result of the TTIP agreement) is assumed to be hostile to the TTIP.
- a sector with an import-export ratio higher than 2 is assumed to be supportive of the TTIP;
- a sector with an import-export ratio of between 1 and 2 is assumed to be 'open' to a deal until the final days of negotiations.

Cells 1, 2 and 4 capture the hostile/hesitant sectors on both sides of the Atlantic, cells 6, 8 and 9 capture the supportive/hesitant sectors, cells 3, 5 and 7 the sectors likely to be open to a deal by the end of the negotiations, either because both sides are hesitant (cell 5) or because one side is supportive and the other side hostile (cells 3 and 7).

Table 11.2 suggests two main observations from a political economy perspective:

- The global *rapport de forces* based on all the goods and services that emerges from Table 11.2 looks very uncertain. Only one sector (cell 9) is strongly supportive in both partners, but it is a very heterogeneous (industrial) sector, hence unlikely to be the basis of a robust coalition. The same situation prevails for cells 6 and 8.
- The relatively homogeneous open sectors (chemicals and cars) are expected to play a key role in the negotiations. The same could be expected from business services, with the caveat that it is a very heterogeneous (huge) sector.
- No homogeneous services sector (finance, insurance) is ready to be strongly supportive of TTIP. Rather, these services reflect opposing views, depending on their side of the Atlantic.

Table 11.2 deserves a final caveat. As stated, most services in Table 11.2 are highly aggregated, heterogeneous sectors. As a result, some activities in a heterogeneous sector could strongly support TTIP while the other activities could strongly oppose it. That said, the long history of many PTAs negotiations shows that even tiny vested interests can poison negotiations, to the point of derailing them for years. Indeed, a small services sector – the French/EU audiovisual sector – has rapidly shown its trouble-making capacity in the TTIP context.

Table 11.2 TTIP political economy: A sectoral view

	US sectors		
EU sectors	Net ratio <1 (expected hostile)	Net ratio >1 and < 2 (expected open)	Net ratio > 2 (expected supportive)
Net ratio <1 (expected hostile)	**Cell 1** Other primary sectors Electrical machinery Wood & paper products Other services	**Cell 2** Metals & metal products	**Cell 3** Agriculture, forestry, fish Personal services
Net ratio >1 and < 2 (expected open)	**Cell 4** Processed foods	**Cell 5** Chemicals Motor vehicles Business services	**Cell 6** Other transport equip.
Net ratio > 2 (expected supportive)	**Cell 7** Finance Insurance	**Cell 8** Other manufactures	**Cell 9** Other machinery

Note: Sectors in bold are those with the largest weight in trade changes (more than US$ 10 billion US$ in the comprehensive scenario).

Source: Author's own configuration.

3.   Market access issues

In services, the High Level Working Group (HLWG) report states three objectives: "i) to bind the highest level of liberalisation that each side has achieved in trade agreements to date, ii) while seeking to achieve new market access by addressing remaining longstanding market access barriers, iii) recognising the sensitive nature of certain sectors".

This wording was not prudent enough. Binding is associated with the already reached 'highest' level of liberalisation, ignoring the massive differences among the existing level of liberalisation within the EU (see Tables 11.3 and 11.4, below) and probably within the US. Calls for new market access target the remaining longstanding market access barriers, that is, those successfully kept by the presumably strongest vested interests. The caveat for sensitive sectors was minimal ("recognition") – offering to the most aggressive vested interests a golden opportunity for fighting to set aside their services, such as French-EU audiovisuals and US maritime transport, despite the fact that these sectors are now much more divided about market opening than they used to be (for audiovisuals, see Messerlin, 2014).

3.1   The baseline: How are EU and US services protected?

As illustrated by the wide differences between the CEPR and CEPII estimates (Table 11.1), it is notoriously difficult to assess the current level of protection in services. That said, it is useful to have a sense of which are the most and the least protected services sectors – a sense of the ranking in terms of protection level that is provided by estimated *ad valorem* 'tariff equivalents' for the various services (CEPR, 2013). Table 11.3 suggests several observations in this respect:

- There are marked differences among sectoral tariff equivalents in the EU and US.

- The ranking of services sectors is not dissimilar on both sides of the Atlantic.

- There is a positive correlation between the level of tariff equivalents and the degree of 'actionability' (defined as the degree (according to the sectoral experts) to which non-tariff barriers can 'realistically' be reduced by 2018 if the political will to do so exists).

- The level of 'actionability' as assessed by the experts is relatively high. In other words, there is room to improve domestic regulatory quality, and by the same token market access.

Table 11.3 "Tariff equivalents" and actionability in services

	Tariff equivalents (%)		'Actionability'	
	US[a]	EU[b]	US[a]	EU[b]
	1	2	3	4
A. Sectors relatively more protected				
Financial services	31.7	11.3	55	49
Insurance services	19.1	10.8	48	52
Communication services	1.7	11.7	66	70
B. Sectors relatively less protected				
Other business services	3.9	14.9	49	51
Construction services	2.5	4.6	57	38
Personal, cultural & recreational services	2.5	4.4	47	37
C. Sectors with no estimated tariff equivalents				
Travel services	n.a.	n.a.	61	60
Air & water transport services	n.a.	n.a.	59	56

Notes: [a] US barriers to EU exports; [b] EU barriers to US exports.
Source: Ecorys (2009).

3.2   What does 'binding' mean in services?

The goal of 'binding', as stated by the HLWG is rather more difficult to interpret than it might seem at first glance (as is the case for goods). Table 11.4 illustrates this point on the EU side (for a detailed review of barriers in EU services, see Mustilli and Pelkmans (2013)). It provides the highest and lowest OECD-calculated "product market regulations" indicators for 18 EUMS, with the name of the corresponding EUMS for 2007, and for 2003, 2007 and 2013.[1] Naming the EUMS allows more light to be shed on the 'large' EUMS, which are likely to have more weight in the negotiations. It also gives a better sense of the two possible layers of the TTIP discussions: the one that is ongoing between the US and the EU, and the one that could be conducted among the EUMS and the various states of the US.

---

[1] The original range of the PMR indicators is 0 to 6, from the least to the most restrictive countries. A larger range (0 to 100) is used because it seems easier to read. But these PMR indicators should not be interpreted as tariff-equivalents since they only rank the existing level of protection associated with current services regulations in the services sectors covered. The services listed in Table 11.4 represent roughly two-thirds of the entire US and EU service sectors.

Table 11.4 Barriers to market access in selected services and EUMS, 2003-13

	Highest PMR		A: Highest PMR 2013		B: Highest PMR in large EUMS 2013		C: Lowest PMR 2013	
	2003	2008	PMR	EUMS	PMR	EUMS	PMR	EUMS
Electricity	68	67	54	Estonia	53	France	15	Spain
Gas	89	69	63	Greece	42	France	0	Britain
Post	78	72	56	Slovenia	56	Italy	11	Netherlands
Telecoms	52	38	33	Slovenia	19	Germany	5	Britain
Airlines	82	83	59	Slovenia	8	France	0	5 EUMS [b]
Rail	100	88	81	Ireland	67	Spain	4	Britain
Road	100	71	71	Italy	--	--	25	8 EUMS [c]
Retail	78	76	68	Belgium	53	Italy	10	Sweden
Prof. services [a]	59	50	48	Hungary	44	Germany	9	Sweden

Notes: [a] Accounting, Architect, Engineer, Legal. The 'large' EUMS are the UK, France, Germany, Italy and Spain. [b] Austria, Germany, Greece, Hungary, Slovakia. [b] Austria, Denmark, Finland, Germany, Ireland, Slovakia, Sweden and the UK.

Source: OECD (2014).

Table 11.4 helps to convey the elusiveness of the notion of "binding" as stressed by the HLWG report, and the huge differences in its various interpretations, such as:

- Would it consist of binding the autonomous liberalisation carried out between 2003 and 2013 by the most protected EUMS (the one having the highest PMR in 2013)? In this case, Table 11.3 shows that such binding would consist of limited additional market access.

- Or would it consist of binding the PMRs at the level of the second-highest PMR among the large EUMS in 2013? In this case, binding would generate rather better market access to most services sectors in the most protected EUMS.

- Or would it consist of binding the PMRs at the level of the most open large EUMS? This would create substantial (huge in some sectors, such as electricity, gas or airlines) new market access in the most protected EUMS.

Crucially, a complete assessment of the notion of 'binding' in TTIP would require equivalent information for the American states. There is some evidence that the American states also have regulatory differences in a significant number of service sectors. Unfortunately, there is no systematic evidence of such differences and providing such an assessment appears to be one of the most pressing tasks in the TTIP context. It would either dispel wrong expectations from the EU side if differences among American states happen to be small. Or it would make these states more conscious of the internal reforms they need to implement for their own good if differences happen to be large – illustrating the role of trade agreements as a boost for better domestic governance.

3.3 The state of play

Nothing in the TTIP will limit the ability of both sides to provide state support to public services, to designate public monopolies or to place limits on market access and national treatment regarding publicly funded education, health care or water services (Heydon, 2015). There is a long tradition in trade agreements of not dealing with such sectors. This situation is reinforced in the TTIP case by less polarised views on both sides of the Atlantic on these matters – the US and the EU are becoming more accommodating on these issues because their education, health and water services face problems that are different but severe in both economies. There now seems to be a willingness to learn lessons from others rather than impose any specific regime.

In January 2015, the EU Commission improved its website on the TTIP in order to give a better idea about what was going on. However, services are not as well covered by this effort as industrial goods. In its two-page 'Fact sheet' cover for services, the Commission lists five broad goals in a few words each:[2]

- tackle barriers in maritime services and in "other" (unspecified) services;
- improve mobility of qualified providers of professional services (such as architects or lawyers);
- make it faster and simpler to obtain licenses or formal approval in services like banking and insurance, accountancy, management consultancy and legal advice;
- agree on new rules in telecommunications, e-commerce, financial services, postal and courier services, and maritime transport;
- ensure protection for sensitive sectors such as audiovisual, public health and education, social services and water distribution.

The two other Commission papers that deal with services are devoted to "TTIP and culture" and "Protecting public services". But

---

[2] European Commission website (http://trade.ec.europa.eu/doclib/press/index.cfm?id=1230).

these papers simply restate the usual EU position on these topics – ranging from reluctance to outright opposition.

The US equivalent website is both more laconic and more vague. It states briefly that the US seeks:

- to obtain improved market access in the EU on a comprehensive basis;
- to address the operation of any designated monopolies and state-owned enterprises, as appropriate;
- to reinforce transparency, impartiality, and due process with regard to authorisations to supply services; and
- to obtain additional disciplines in certain services sectors, while improving regulatory cooperation where appropriate.

A better idea of the current situation may be provided by using non-official sources. In Europe, a recent communication from the European Services Forum (the most active coalition of EU service providers) lists six services where the EU believes to have strong export interests: professional services, maritime transport, aviation transport, financial services, mobility of services suppliers and public procurement in services (Kerneis, 2015). It also stresses the US reluctance to tackle the key issue of US-driven regulations and/or enforcement (particularly in professional services) and American unwillingness to discuss financial services, mobility of services suppliers and the Jones Act (maritime transport) in particular.[3] In the US, a forthcoming book adds three other recommendations for a TTIP compromise to the usual general desire for TTIP commitments to go beyond TiSA commitments: to target infrastructure, information communications technology and construction; to delay the application of TTIP obligations with regard to financial services regulatory policies until three years after the entry in force of TTIP; that is, once regulatory restructuring in each market is solidified. Finally, there is a desire to coordinate US and EU efforts to produce a successful TiSA in Geneva (Schott et al., forthcoming).

The last point to be examined is the fundamental choice among the two modalities available to the negotiators: would negotiators work on 'negative' or 'positive' lists of services to improve market access? The EU has traditionally relied on the positive list (only the sectors listed are liberalised, as in the KOREU agreement) while the US has

---

[3] The Jones Act requires that all goods transported by water between US ports be carried on US flagships, constructed in the US, owned by US citizens, and crewed by US citizens and US permanent residents.

traditionally relied on negative lists (every service is deemed to be liberalised except those listed, as in the KORUS agreement) – at least as long as US barriers are not imposed by American states (in some sectors, such as professional services, a US federal offer is of very limited interest since many American states have very specific regulations). Evidently, negative lists offer a much clearer view of what is effectively liberalised. By contrast, positive lists often require from the service providers a thorough knowledge of what has not been liberalised, which is crucial to take advantage of the agreed liberalisation provisions – a constraint that imposes high costs on foreign newcomers, and considerably weakens the pro-competitive impact of the liberalisation measures.

The EU seems ready to shift to a negative list approach. But, the full consequences of this shift on the whole TTIP architecture remain to be seen. First, the EU has to make its new negative list approach consistent with its previous positive list approach in its other PTAs, which means re-phrasing the many exceptions granted to EUMS. Second, such an exercise would logically require that the US starts to list its commitments at the American state level; an exercise it has rarely carried out before (the best illustration being public procurement) and may not be ready to do so.[4]

3.4 A 'static' vs. 'dynamic' negotiating structure

The current situation is thus problematic. It would greatly benefit from a table of 'enlarged' negotiations (in a form to be defined) to the EUMS and American states themselves. Why is the case? Table 11.4 suggests that the EU internal market is still very fragmented since PMRs vary considerably among EUMS (see also Miroudot and Shepherd (2011)). If it were possible for US or EU firms to export their services from a relatively open EUMS to a more protected EUMS, then efficient US and EU service providers would have established their activities in the most open EUMS and operate from there towards the rest of the EU. But if this were the case, then keeping high barriers at the EUMS level would make little sense for the most protected EUMS. In other words, the existence of high PMRs across EUMS is a robust indicator that the EU internal market remains fundamentally incomplete.

This lesson is essential because it suggests the adoption of a TTIP negotiating structure that is more conducive to a 'deep' liberalisation in

---

[4] For a detailed discussion of public procurement issues, see Woolcock and Grier (2015).

services than the current one. As of today, the structure of discussions is exclusively bilateral – that is, the US vs. the EU. By contrast, a more open structure of discussions that would involve (in ways to be found) individual EUMS and the US could develop interesting dynamics that would enlarge the frontiers of the available concessions in the direction of 'deeper' liberalisation. For instance, service providers from the most open EUMS and the most open American states in a given service would have an intrinsic interest in building an explicit transatlantic coalition in their sector in order to open the markets of the most protected EUMS and the US for the service in question. This approach is perfectly consistent with the need to involve regulators in talks on services, which is highlighted below (section 3).

4.   Regulatory issues

The first question when discussing services in a trade deal is whether these discussions should be limited to pure market access issues (allowing foreign firms to enter new markets without taking into account the impact of the existing regulations) or whether they should include 'talks' on regulations (examining whether some regulations constitute unjustified barriers to market access). The frequency and magnitude of NTMs in services explains why discussions in services very often boil down to 'talks' on regulations, as in the case of TTIP (Chase & Pelkmans, 2015).

This raises two challenges for a deal in services. The first is well known and occurs during the negotiation phase: it is hard to assess the level of 'unjustified' restrictions imposed on business in a given service by existing regulations. The second challenge is rarely mentioned although it is probably more important. It occurs after the conclusion of a deal: it is very difficult to monitor the faithful implementation of the liberalisation commitments of a trading partner. This is different from tariffs on goods where each country can easily monitor whether its trading partner is cutting its tariff as agreed. The post-agreement monitoring of commitments in services is particularly difficult when a partner modifies its regulations in order to improve the functioning of the service market at stake. By doing so, a partner may well make a foreign services provider's life more difficult, giving the impression of having reneged on its commitments.

All these challenges make it clear that 'talks' on services regulations should rely on innovative techniques or they will end up with pleasant but empty words.

4.1 How to 'talk' on services regulations? Innovation urgently required

The first step to defining innovative techniques is to be clear about words. The HLWG report is remarkably vague in this respect. It refers almost indiscriminately to "harmonization", "mutual recognition", "mutual equivalence", "regulatory convergence", "regulatory cooperation" and "regulatory coherence". This vagueness has fuelled suspicion and fear among public opinion that TTIP would boil down to a 'single transatlantic market' imposing changes in regulations on both partners that would inevitably lead to a general race to the bottom.

After months of confusion, a recent paper by the US Chamber (2015) is the first attempt in circles close to the TTIP discussions to clarify two of these terms: "regulatory cooperation" and "regulatory coherence":[5]

- regulatory coherence is *"about good regulatory practices, transparency and stakeholder engagement in the domestic regulatory process"*. Clearly, regulatory sovereignty cannot be limited by regulatory coherence, which is an entirely domestic matter. The only influence that TTIP could have on regulatory coherence is very indirect. It would consist of stimulating emulation among partners: the partner having the better practices in a given service is likely to emulate its partner in this service (and vice-versa for other services).

- regulatory cooperation *"is the process of interaction between US and EU regulators, founded on the benefits regulators can achieve through their partnership and greater regulatory interoperability"*. Here again, regulatory sovereignty is not limited by a regulatory cooperation process which puts the appropriate regulators (not the trade negotiators) explicitly in the driving seat of the TTIP talks, which are those in charge of the services at stake.

That said, adopting innovative techniques in the talks on services regulations requires clarification of the four remaining terms: harmonisation, mutual recognition, mutual equivalence, regulatory convergence (Messerlin, 2007, 2011, 2014).

---

[5] The Commission's website still illustrates this confusion with the title "Regulatory Cooperation" as its first paper under the "Regulatory Coherence" chapter.

4.2 Harmonisation (and regulatory convergence)

In their daily speeches, most TTIP trade negotiators and EU decision-makers refer to harmonisation (see Fabry et al. (2014)). This is rather paradoxical because the history of the EU internal market is a long history of failure to harmonise, especially in services. There is a good reason for such a poor outcome. As modern economies are characterised by a huge variety of differentiated services, a regulation can work well in one country, and badly in another. The OECD database on regulations in services shows that, in most services, only a few regulations have a systematically detrimental impact in all member states on the efficient provision of the service at stake. Moreover, the simultaneous but uncoordinated negotiations of several mega-PTA add another reason to doubt the usefulness of the harmonisation instrument in such a context: how could it be possible to harmonise at the same time and in a consistent way within TTIP, within TPP and within EU-Japan?

Regulatory convergence is a weak variant of harmonisation. It consists of a belief that, although harmonisation is not possible now, it will occur over time. Such a belief relies on an unfounded assumption: the existence of an ideal regulation in a given service that would be better than all the other alternatives for all the partners – an assumption very unlikely to be met for reasons mentioned above on the dominant role of differentiation in modern economies. Indeed, such a belief is not supported by evidence in the EU case. It would suggest that over time the EUMS regulatory performance would have become increasingly similar – an observation that is not supported by the available indicators such as those of Doing Business or the World Economic Forum. These indicators do not suggest that the EUMS converge to the same level of regulatory quality. Rather, they suggest complex trajectories over time, with some EU-founding EUMS having slipped behind some recently acceded EUMS in terms of regulatory quality.

4.3 Mutual recognition

Mutual recognition (MR) means that each party accepts the regulations of its partner for the services at stake. But this recognition is conditional upon the adoption of a 'core' of common provisions ("essential requirements" in EU legal jargon). MR is thus a hybrid instrument: there is a harmonised "core" of provisions, and only the remaining provisions are subject to mutual recognition. As the core is harmonised, the whole MR approach suffers from the same limits as harmonisation

– pressures from firms and their backing EUMS for limiting the pro-competition impact of MR by imposing core provisions making costly entry to market. Over time, as core provisions have often been more numerous and costly, MR has increasingly drifted towards harmonisation – hence today a very imperfect "internal market" in many services.

4.4 Mutual equivalence

Mutual equivalence (ME) means that each party considers the partner's regulatory package – the regulations *per se*, the certification or licensing procedures, or both – in a given service as "different but equivalent" to its own.[6] To be politically acceptable, ME requires a systematic crucial step: a joint process of "mutual evaluation" of existing regulations (and their certification or licensing procedures) by the regulating bodies of the partners. The aim of this joint evaluation process is for each partner to decide whether the regulations at stake could be accepted as equivalent or not. (Such an involvement of the national regulatory bodies fits the definition of regulatory cooperation in the US Chamber's paper perfectly.)

At first glance, ME seems a bold move into the unknown. The EU's perspective is somewhat different, however. In sharp contrast to the case of goods, the EU has drawn its conclusions about the poor performance of harmonisation and MR in services by adopting the ME approach when designing its 2006 Services Directive (Article 15 of this Directive provides a fine description of what should constitute 'talks' in services).

The joint process of mutual evaluation of their respective regulations by the two TTIP partners has two interesting features. First, it reinforces the good regulatory practices required by domestic good regulatory coherence. As it requires the involvement of the partner's regulating bodies in the negotiating process, it suggests some kind of division of labour between TTIP trade negotiators and national services regulators. Trade negotiators could suggest broad areas of services they consider as promising candidates for the ME approach in the TTIP. Then, national regulators in charge of these services should confirm

---

[6] Of course, there is the option of "unilateral equivalence": one partner considers the partner's laws and/or processes as equivalent to its own regulations, while the other partner does not do the same.

these opportunities and undertake the mutual evaluation process consisting of:

- Examining the partner's regulations;
- Asking for clarifications and possibly changes in the partner's regulations as pre-requisites for granting the ME status;
- Defining exceptions (if any) for some sub-sectors of the services examined and,
- Requesting reviews to be performed after a few years.

The joint evaluation process offers a unique opportunity to build, restore and/or improve trust within each signatory and among them. First, within each signatory. Among the most interesting documents on the Commission's website on TTIP are those on the joint evaluation of seatbelts and lighting and visibility for cars.[7] These documents offer a very careful technical review of each element of these two essential components of car safety. The EU public has thus the best available assessment of EU regulations by the US and EU regulators, and vice-versa. Second, trust is built among the signatories. It would be unwise to assume that the US and the EU have little need to build trust. Paradoxically, the long history of the transatlantic trade tends to highlight cases where mistrust has flourished. In this respect, mutual evaluation offers an appropriate solution to such situations.

4.5 A realistic bundle of techniques

Of course, it would be unwise to assume that TTIP negotiators could shift entirely to the ME approach. First, it cannot be excluded that harmonisation could remain the best solution in rare cases. Second, the ME approach requires a serious change of mind from regulators, trade negotiators, the public and, last but not least, by politicians since, at least in some TTIP countries, regulators are closely monitored by parliaments. As a result, the TTIP negotiators may have to stick to the traditional MR approach in a substantial number of cases for some time in the future.

Such a situation is not a serious problem as long as TTIP is conceived as a living agreement – meaning that the EU and the US agree to return to the table of negotiations within a few years after the conclusion of this first episode of TTIP negotiations in order to further deepen and/or expand their market opening. Indeed, the joint process

---

[7] European Commission website (http://trade.ec.europa.eu/doclib/press/index.cfm?id=1230).

of mutual evaluation itself requires time to be appropriately conducted, and also a living agreement in order to review the previous evaluations, if needed.

5.   TTIP and the world

Almost any PTA is doomed to generate discrimination against non-PTA members. This discrimination is costly for efficient non-PTA producers that are excluded from the PTA markets, and by the same token for the PTA consumers who buy goods produced in the PTA which happen to be less expensive than those produced in the rest of the world only because efficient foreign producers have still to face trade barriers on their products. These general remarks raise four specific issues in the TTIP case: the likelihood and magnitude of its discriminatory impact, the case for compensating spill-over effects, preference erosion of previous EU and US PTAs, and the beneficial impact of mutual equivalence in this worldwide context.

5.1   TTIP discriminatory impact

The TTIP is the PTA between the current two largest world economies. It may thus be a source of discriminations on an unprecedented scale (for a more detailed examination of the risks of discrimination, see Akman et al., 2015). In a nutshell, the risks and costs of discrimination depend on three key elements:

*   the higher the initial (pre-TTIP) MFN protection of the TTIP countries,
*   the deeper the intra-TTIP liberalisation and
*   the stronger the intra-TTIP emulation long-term dynamics (the capacity to 'deepen' further the transatlantic market access as time flows.

The higher the risks and magnitude of discriminatory impacts on non-TTIP economies. For instance, a 'deep' TTIP agreement in agricultural products would open wide the highly protected EU markets to US products to the detriment of similar goods produced in the rest of the world at a much lower cost, since the EU MFN barriers are high in agricultural products. Similarly, the high *ad valorem* equivalents shown in Table 11.3 clearly set out the risks of strong discriminatory impact in the most protected services.

That said, it is often stated that the risks of discrimination are much lower in services than in goods because it is difficult to open markets in services in a discriminatory way. However, there is no systematic evidence of such an intrinsically 'non-discriminatory' nature of services regulations. Rather, Table 11.4 supports the opposite view: the remaining range and magnitude of intra-EUMS barriers in services suggests strong possibilities of substantial discriminatory protection.

5.2 Spill-over effects

The potential discriminatory impact of TTIP on non-TTIP economies could be mitigated by the fact that dismantling barriers between US and EU markets would generate positive 'spill-over' effects for the rest of the world. There are two kinds of spill-over effects. Direct spill-over effects would occur if post-TTIP regulations in the US and the EU would decrease trade costs, not only among the US and the EU services providers, but also those of the third countries exporting to the US and to the EU. Indirect spill-over effects would occur if third countries adopted 'better' regulations that TTIP partners would adopt in the emulation context examined in section 3.

Spill-over effects are mere possibilities. Their likelihood and magnitude are unknown. From a policy perspective, it is important to stress the fact that the nature of these two spill-over effects is very different.

- Direct spill-over effects do not require action by third countries. They are provided somewhat 'automatically' by post-TTIP regulations, which are assumed to be cost-improving for non-TTIP and TTIP service providers. It is crucial to stress that such situations depend, at least partly, on the instruments used in the 'talks' on services regulations. Under harmonisation and mutual recognition, post-TTIP regulations are entirely (harmonisation) or partly (mutual recognition) negotiated. As experience shows, it is far from certain that negotiated regulations are necessarily better than the pre-existing ones: this is because they are the outcomes of political compromises that may ignore important economic and technological aspects. By contrast, because it introduces emulation among regulators, mutual equivalence (ME) is more amenable to the possibility of post-TTIP regulations being truly better than the pre-TTIP ones.

- Indirect spill-over effects require appropriate action by third-countries which choose to align their national regulations to the post-TTIP regulations. Hence, such spill-over effects should rather be interpreted as autonomous (unilateral) liberalisations undertaken by third countries. It seems quite inappropriate to interpret them as a TTIP result. Once again, such unilateral liberalisations are likely to occur more often in a context of ME-engineered regulatory emulation among TTIP regulators eager to deliver better regulations.

5.3   Preferences erosion

The non-TTIP economies are not 'equal' with respect to the TTIP discriminatory potential.[8] Non-TTIP countries with a PTA with the US and/or the EU already in place have a kind of 'insurance' scheme against TTIP discriminatory impact. (The case of non-TTIP economies without a PTA with the EU and the US is examined in the concluding section.) EU and US PTAs with a substantial services dimension are rare: Canada, Chile, Korea and Singapore with both the EU and the US, Australia and Mexico with the US. The deeper the existing PTAs with the EU and/or the US, the better the 'insurance' scheme of the non-TTIP country.

That said, the preferences that the non-TTIP countries listed above could have enjoyed under their PTAs with the EU or the US will be eroded or eliminated by TTIP to an extent that depends on the TTIP's own 'depth'. From these non-TTIP countries, such a turn of events may be painful for their service providers that will face increased competition from additional TTIP services providers. But, viewed from a world welfare perspective, this evolution should be seen as positive: preference 'erosion' is a systemic, inevitable and indeed desirable down-side effect of PTAs in a world subject to the permanent forces of further liberalisation.

5.4   Mutual equivalence and world welfare: From 'norm setting' to 'norm attracting'

Finally, the impact of TTIP on the rest of the world's economies depends on the 'basic philosophy' of TTIP negotiations. TTIP negotiators have often made reference to TTIP as a 'norm-setting'

---

[8] Of course, there are the options of 'opening' TTIP to other countries on an *ex post* basis and the option to design it as an open agreement. Such options will substantially reduce the TTIP's discriminatory impact and the risks of preference erosion. Despite their intellectual attraction, it is fair to say that such options have rarely been used in the past and, more decisively, that they do not fit today's mood in trade matters. That said, the mutual equivalent approach can easily be adapted to such options on a case by case basis.

endeavour for the rest of the world, particularly in the context of regulations. This notion conveys a sense of TTIP as a duopoly of (shrinking in relative terms) economies trying to impose their regulations on the rest of the world while there is still time. This is not a very convincing approach, for two reasons. From an international relations perspective, it is hard to believe that the large non-TTIP economies will accept such a set of '*diktat*'. From an economic perspective, such an approach increases the risks and magnitude of TTIP discriminatory impact because the EU and the US, being very similar economies and societies, inevitably have intrinsic difficulties to take into account the wide range of regulatory capacities and objectives in the rest of the world.

That said, once again the choice of the techniques used for talks in services plays a key role. Harmonisation and mutual recognition have an intrinsic bias in favour of 'norm setting'. By contrast, mutual equivalence offers the alternative of a dynamic 'norm-attracting' approach because it generates *de facto* emulation among the regulatory bodies of TTIP members, hence giving incentives to each regulator to provide the best regulations to its domestic firms.

- The more innovative a TTIP regulator member is, the more attractive the regulations it designs may be for its own domestic firms and possibly for the TTIP partner's firms.

- The more innovative a TTIP regulator is, the more attractive it may also be for third-countries' service providers. As a result, third-country service providers may be induced to enter TTIP markets via the most innovative TTIP member (a case of direct spill-over effects) and/or to adopt regulations similar to those of the most innovative TTIP member (a case of indirect spill-over effects). Of course, all these dynamic effects are conditional on the fact that TTIP has no restrictive rules of origin on foreign services or services providers.

Last but not least, mutual equivalence is the best protection against regulatory reforms that would diminish the country's welfare – the much feared 'race to the bottom'. Not only is such an attempt the last thing to expect from a regulator (it would be suicidal), but promoting welfare-diminishing reform would also immediately trigger the partners' regulators withdrawing their agreement for mutual equivalence for the regulation at stake.

In short, by inducing TTIP to shift from a 'norm-setting' to a 'norm-attracting' perspective, mutual equivalence largely blurs the frontiers between multilateral and bilateral negotiations by creating permanent incentives among the TTIP members to take into account the rest of the world – the multilateral dimension – when reforming their domestic regulations.

6. Concluding remarks: TTIP, the WTO and TISA

In order to eliminate the risks of discrimination generated by TTIP, non-TTIP countries with shallow or no PTAs in services with the EU or the US could apply some collective pressure to re-launch the WTO negotiations in services or to focus on the Trade in Services Agreement (TiSA) discussions.

Re-launching (it would probably be more accurate to say launching) the services negotiations in the WTO forum is highly unlikely. The chapter has provided ample explanation that talks on services regulations require a level of trust among negotiating countries to a point never before needed in the case of negotiations in goods. Trust is necessary to assess regulations that are hard to compare. It is needed to monitor the implementation of the agreed commitments in an economically sound way. And it is needed to use the mutual equivalence instrument – both at the preliminary stage of the joint mutual evaluation and during the regulatory emulation process that mutual equivalence nurtures. The WTO cannot provide the sufficient level of trust needed: each member cannot trust all its (current) 159 partners.

The trust factor can be (much) better handled by plurilateral negotiations, such as TiSA, because of their limited number of like-minded participants. Indeed, today TiSA negotiators are testing the level of trust that could exist in TiSA, including if China or other large emerging economies enter into these negotiations.

In this context, the fates of TTIP and TiSA appear largely interdependent – more precisely the mirror image of each other. If the TTIP negotiations do not see the necessary innovations in services 'talks', they are unlikely to deliver more than improved market access at the margin. Political support is then doomed to be low and the whole fate of TTIP becomes volatile and highly subject to political turbulence and/or on small but aggressive vested interests.

In such a case, TiSA becomes an attractive alternative to TTIP. The reason is not that TiSA will deliver significantly deeper results than those of TTIP. In fact, TiSA is unlikely to be friendly to a mutual equivalence process – the only one that is promising in terms of substantial economic benefits. But it will deliver (very) limited additional market access on a wider range of countries – hence possibly on a wider range of services. As a result, it is quite possible that the global outcome to TiSA would be (notably) higher than the TTIP outcome if TTIP negotiators are unable or unwilling to use innovative ways to hold 'talks' on services regulations.

If correct, this analysis suggests that a good yardstick to measure true progress in TTIP talks in services is not TTIP negotiators' declarations or the number of TTIP negotiating rounds, but the intensity of TiSA negotiations.

References

Akman, S., S. Evenett, and P. Low (eds) (2015), *Catalyst? TTIP's impact on the Rest*, CEPR and Tepav, A VoxEU.org eBook.

Chase, P. and J. Pelkmans (2015), "This time it's different: turbo-charging regulatory cooperation in TTIP", chapter 2 in this volume.

Ecorys (2009), "Non-tariff measures in the EU-US trade and investment: An economic analysis", Ref., OJ 2007/S 180-219493.

Eizenstat, S. (2013), "A new Transatlantic partnership", essay based on a speech delivered at the Wilson International Center for Scholars.

Erixon, F. and M. Bauer (2010), "A Transatlantic zero agreement: Estimating the gains from transatlantic free trade in goods", ECIPE, Brussels.

Fabry, E., G. Garbasso and R. Pardo (2014), "TTIP: A Negotiation a la Pirandello", Notre Europe, Brussels.

Felbermayr, G., B. Heid and S. Lehwald (2013), "Transatlantic Trade and Investment Partnership (PTCI) – Who benefits from a free trade deal? Part 1: Macroeconomic Effects", Bertelsmann Stiftung-GED, Gütersloh.

Francois, Joseph, Miriam Manchin, Hanna Norberg, Olga Pindyuk and Patrick Tomberger (2013), Reducing Trans-Atlantic Barriers to Trade and Investment, CEPR (a study for the European Commission, TRADE10/A2/A16).

Hamilton, D. and P. Schwartz (2012), A Transatlantic Free Trade Area: A Boost to Economic Growth, Center for Transatlantic Relations and New Direction – The Foundation for European Reform, Washington and Brussels, January.

Heydon, Ken (2015), The TTIP: Challenges and opportunities for the Internal Market and consumer protection in the area of services.

High Level Working Group on Jobs and Growth (2013), Final report (http://trade.ec.europa.eu/doclib/docs/2013/february/tradoc_15 0519.pdf).

Kerneis, Pascal (2015), "Why services are critical in TTIP", ESF/CEPR Luncheon Meeting, 25 March.

Kinman S. and T. Hagberd (2012), "Potential effects from an EU-US free trade agreement – Sweden in Focus", Sweden National Board of Trade (Kommers Kollegium), Stockholm.

Messerlin, Patrick (2007), Economic and regulatory reforms in Europe: Past experiences and future challenges, Productivity Commission, Richard Snape Lectures, Australian Government, Melbourne.

_____ (2011), "The EU Single Market in goods: between mutual recognition and harmonization", *Australian Journal of International Affairs*, Vol. 65, No. 4, pp. 410-435.

_____ (2013), "The domestic political economy of preferential trade agreements", in David Kleimann, *EU preferential trade agreements: Commerce, foreign policy and development*, European University Institute.

_____ (2014a), "Negotiating mega-agreements: Lessons from the EU", Working Paper RSCAS 2014/112, European University Institute, Florence.

_____ (2014b), "The French Audiovisual Policies: *"A bout de souffle""*, mimeo, Groupe d'Economie Mondiale at Sciences Po, September (http://gem.sciences-po.fr).

Messerlin P. and E. van der Marel (2012), "The dynamics of Transatlantic negotiations in services", German Marshall Fund. Economic Policy Paper Series.

Miroudot S. and B. Shepherd (2012), "The paradox of references: regional trade agreements and trade costs in services", Munich, Personal RePEc Archives 41090.

Mustilli, Federica and Jacques Pelkmans (2013), "Access Barriers to Services Markets: Mapping, tracing, understanding and measuring", CEPS Special Report No. 77, June.

OECD (2014) *Indicators of Product Market Regulation*, OECD Statistics, OECD, Paris.

Rosecrance, Richard (2013), "Wants world domination? Size matters", *New York Times*, 28 July.

Parc, Jimmyn (2014), "A Retrospective on the Korean Film Policies: Return of the Jedi", Groupe d'Economie Mondiale, Paris (http://gem.sciences-po.fr).

Pelkmans, Jacques, Arjan Lejour, Lorna Schrefler, Federica Mustilli and Jacopo Timini (2014), "The impact of TTIP: The underlying economic model and comparisons", CEPS Special Report No. 93, June.

Schott, J. and V. Cimino (2013), "Crafting a TTIP: What can be done", Peterson Institute of International Economics, Policy Brief No. 13-8.

Schott, J., V. Cimino, S. Miner and T. Moran (2014), "Does the Transatlantic Trade and Investment Partnership need a mid-course correction?", mimeo, Peterson Institute for International Economics, Washington, D.C., December.

US Chamber of Commerce (2015), "Regulatory coherence and cooperation in the Transatlantic Trade and Investment Partnership", mimeo, US Chamber of Commerce. Washington, D.C.

Woolcock, S. and J.H. Grier (2015), "Public procurement in the TTIP negotiations", chapter 10 in this volume.

12. TELECOMMUNICATIONS AND THE INTERNET: TTIP'S DIGITAL DIMENSION
ANDREA RENDA
AND CHRISTOPHER S. YOO

1. Introduction

As negotiations on the Transatlantic Trade and Investment Partnership (TTIP) have progressed, the digital component appears to be growing in importance. This is due to a number of recent events that have led digital issues to increasingly occupy the spotlight in the negotiations. First, the Datagate scandal, spurred by the revelations of Edward Snowden, has seriously undermined trust between US and EU authorities, leading the European Parliament to call for the suspension of the Safe Harbour Agreement, which allows smooth flows of data between the two sides of the Atlantic. Tensions between the parties at the table are so heightened now that it is widely thought that there can be no TTIP agreement without an agreement on data protection (possibly outside the TTIP and before its conclusion). Second, the growing importance of the data economy and the enabling nature of ICT as a driver of productivity and innovation in many other sectors makes the Digital TTIP a key complement, if not a precondition, to a successful and comprehensive agreement between the US and the EU. Third, the evolution of the debate over network neutrality in both legal systems has led the general public to focus on the possibility for the two superpowers to achieve some consistency in the regulation of traffic management practices on the Internet. Last but not least, all of this is occurring as the stalemate in other chapters (e.g. agriculture, financial services, and others) is motivating the parties to revert to the digital transatlantic economy as a natural candidate for a resounding agreement.

To date, however, the evidence on convergence between the two major blocs is mixed at best. In fact, while there have been some timid attempts to reach agreement on delicate issues such as data protection and cybersecurity, differences in the application of competition law and regulation in a number of crucial policy areas (such as online search, e-commerce and copyright) seem to be growing, rather than shrinking, undercutting the preconditions for creating a vibrant transatlantic digital economy. One easy example is the evolution of the European Commission's antitrust investigation against Google, now coupled with the launch of an extensive sectoral inquiry into e-commerce and a pompous campaign against geo-blocking practices, both likely to target US-based IT giants such as Amazon. More generally, the European Parliament and some national authorities (primarily France and Germany) are extensively campaigning against the so-called 'GAFA' (Google, Amazon, Facebook, Apple), or even the 'GAFTAM' (Google, Amazon, Facebook, Twitter, Apple, Microsoft), all companies headquartered in the US. And to some extent, similar signals are also sent by large-scale government policies on advanced manufacturing, which seem to be developing incompatible standards in essential fields such as the Internet of Things and cloud computing.

Many of these initiatives are now included in the new Digital Single Market Strategy adopted by the European Commission on 6 May 2015. The strategy, expected to contribute €415 billion per year to the EU economy, includes 16 targeted actions based on three pillars: i) better access for consumers and businesses to digital goods and services across Europe, ii) creating the right conditions and a level playing field for digital networks and innovative services and iii) maximising the growth potential of the digital economy. The Commission wants to complete the package by 2016, noting that all proposals have to go through the European Parliament and the Council: the first initiatives have mostly focused on copyright reform (see below).

Against this background, what are the prospects for a comprehensive Digital TTIP? In an unprecedented effort to increase the transparency of the ongoing negotiations, the European Commission has recently stated that its primary objectives in the negotiations on the ICT chapter are to improve enforcement of regulations and consumer protection, to make it easier for EU firms to export to the US and to cut unnecessary costs. It also stated that the agreement will not lead to any lowering of safety and security standards for EU citizens, an outcome that some commentators and advocacy groups had otherwise considered likely. Current documents released by the European Commission suggest that the parties may be able to reach agreement on an initial set of important issues.[1] These include:

- *e-labelling*: setting standards for providing product information to consumers in electronic format, replacing labels and stickers;

- *e-accessibility*: making ICT easier to use for people with disabilities and

- *cryptography*: setting common principles for certifying ICT products, especially for encoding and decoding information.

However, the Digital TTIP has the potential to become much more ambitious, covering issues such as network neutrality and data protection, if not also intermediary liability, cybersecurity and copyright. Already in its first document released in early 2015, the European Commission mentions one issue that appears simple, but can prove very controversial in practice: the potential for an agreement on data interoperability, which would enable users to exchange data easily between different products or platforms. In addition, a 'non-paper' presented at the EU Council Trade Policy Committee by the French and Austrian delegations in October 2014 contained a much more comprehensive list of issues, including an adaptation of the concepts of 'essential facilities' and 'major suppliers' to the digital environment, an agreement on the treatment of digital platforms concerning privacy, interoperability and competition, and agreement on network neutrality principles.

In this chapter, we explore the current divergence between the US and the EU on a number of issues and comment on potential consequences for the TTIP. Section 2 below discusses rules on infrastructure-sharing and network neutrality and the prospects for convergence between the two legal systems on these crucial issues. Section 3 contains an illustration of the divergence between the US and the EU on antitrust rules. Section 4 compares the approach followed by the two jurisdictions in the online search market and in e-commerce, in what has been termed the 'platform regulation' debate. Section 5 addresses issues related to user information and in particular e-labelling and e-accessibility. Section 6 compares US and EU public-policy initiatives for the transition towards the Internet of Things.

---

[1] The European Commission published in February 2015 a series of 2-page factsheets and EU textual proposals on parts 2 and 3 of the TTIP (see http://trade.ec.europa.eu/doclib/press/index.cfm?id=1230).

Section 7 compares data protection legislation in the US and the EU and comments on possible scenarios for transatlantic data flows, including the possible suspension of the Safe Harbour.

2. Broadband infrastructure and net neutrality

2.1 Infrastructure-sharing: Between competition and investment

Over the past decade, the regulatory approach to broadband telecommunications in the US and the EU has diverged widely. On the one hand, the US Federal Communications Commission (FCC) has actively pursued a deregulatory approach in order to stimulate the deployment of high-speed broadband networks, which resulted in the lifting of infrastructure-sharing obligations on high-speed broadband networks since 2003. The presence of a pervasive legacy cable infrastructure, which itself could be upgraded to high-speed networks thanks to new technologies and standards such as DOCSIS 3.0, has led to the emergence of vibrant facilities-based competition throughout the US.[2]

On the other hand, the absence (in many countries) of a legacy cable infrastructure in Europe has led regulators to opt for infrastructure-sharing, which was made even more extensive and invasive after 2003, exactly as the US was going in the opposite direction. The application of the so-called 'ladder of investment' model to encourage the entry of new players in each of the EU member states has led to a significant fragmentation of the market, with hundreds of telecoms operators now populating the continent.[3] While offering consumers a variety of alternative providers, in many countries this fragmentation has led to a catch-22 situation, in which the obligation to share any improvements at regulated prices deters incumbent players from upgrading their infrastructure and the ability to access the existing infrastructure on quite favourable terms discourages new entrants from investing as well. European regulators once placed great hopes in the so-called 'ladder of investment' model, under which infrastructure-sharing served as a stepping stone to full facilities-based competition. Empirical studies have shown that although existing

---

[2] See Renda (2007, 2009) and Yoo (2014).

[3] For a description, see Renda (2009) and Pelkmans & Renda (2011).

policies have encouraged entrants to shift from resale to bitstream access to accessing unbundled local loops, they have failed to encourage them to make the final step to full facilities-based competition.[4] The result is new entrants compete only by squeezing margins ever closer to the wholesale price rather than by investing in improved services. Against this background, the only (limited) investment in ultra-fast broadband in Europe has come from cable operators and electric companies or from municipalities, often using EU cohesion funds.[5]

The impact of these policies is most visible in the availability of Next Generation Networks (NGNs) capable of providing service of 30 Mbps. Studies commissioned by the US and the EU on broadband coverage in 2011, 2012 and 2013 reveal that the US has consistently outpaced Europe in NGN coverage (see Figure 12.1).[6]

Figure 12.1 Next generation coverage in the US and EU, 2011-13

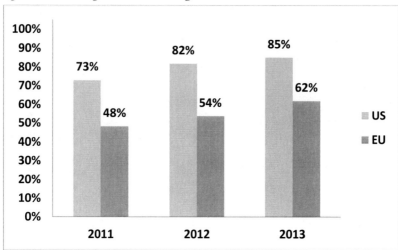

Source: Yoo (2014).

Data on investment levels reveal the same pattern. From 2007 to 2012, US providers invested on average more than twice as much per

---

[4] See e.g. Bourreau et al. (2010).

[5] Yoo (2014).

[6] Note that although the European Commission defines NGN as 30 Mbps service, it collects data on 25 Mbps service.

household as their European counterparts. Since 2008, European investment levels have languished at 35% below their pre-2008 peak, while the drop-off in the US has been more modest 7% (see Figure 12.2).[7]

Figure 12.2 Electronic communications sector investment per household in the US and EU, 2007-12

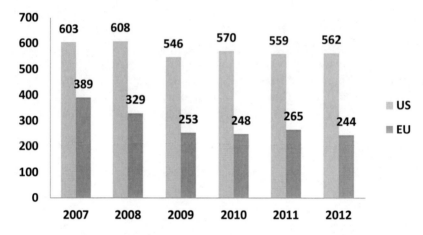

Source: Yoo (2014).

At the same time, a proactive spectrum policy by the FCC has led to the early auctioning of the digital dividend spectrum (e.g. the 700 Mhz band), which enabled the early deployment of very high-speed mobile broadband networks such as 4G (Long-Term Evolution, LTE). Likewise, difficulties in achieving the needed coordination between national authorities have led to significant delays in the reallocation of spectrum to mobile operators in key bands such as 800Mhz and 700Mhz. The absence of a timely, coordinated EU spectrum policy has made Europe a laggard in the deployment of 4G broadband (see Figure 12.3). The US market has also become quite competitive. As of December 2014, AT&T served 99% of the US population with LTE, with Verizon serving 96%, Sprint serving 78% and T-Mobile serving 72% (FCC, 2014b). This makes it quite likely that more than 70% of the population can choose from among three, if not four, LTE providers.

---

[7] Yoo (2014).

Figure 12.3 4G LTE coverage in the US and EU, 2011-13

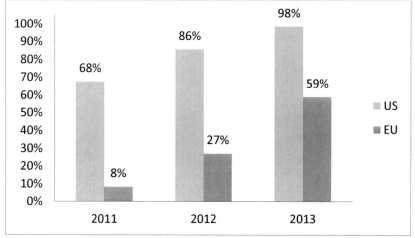

Source: Yoo (2014).

This stark divergence of regulatory approaches has led to the exact result one would expect: while in the US the FCC has started to worry about vertical exclusion, in Europe the priority is now stimulating investment and possibly achieving a degree of industry consolidation. Both stances bear important consequences for the current debate on network neutrality, since recent initiatives in the two jurisdictions on this issue have been grounded in (or heavily affected by) the current state of the telecommunications infrastructure.

2.2 Network neutrality

One of the policy areas in which the divergence between the US and the EU has been most evident over the past decade is network neutrality, defined as a rule prohibiting network operators from discriminating between types of Internet traffic and thus obliging them to treat all bits in the same manner. Companies operating at the application and content layers of the Internet ecosystem have advocated such a rule since the mid-2000s. Their efforts have triggered a furious debate first in the United States and later in the EU and globally. Arguments in favour of regulatory intervention to mandate network neutrality and to keep telecoms networks as 'dumb pipes' developed mostly with reference to the infrastructure and logical layers of the Internet value chain. On the one hand, telecoms operators claim that disabling them from managing traffic on their networks would jeopardise the quality of the user experience, deny the possibility of a more efficient and effective provision of the Internet service and leave the whole Web prey to spam and illegal peer-to-peer file-sharing, which – despite its illegality – has continued for many years to represent roughly half of all Internet traffic. On the other hand, 'neutralists' challenged this view by stating that the end-to-end nature of the Internet should not be contaminated by intelligence in the core of the network, which would reduce the value of the network due to filtering of content and speech and the narrowing down of spaces for creativity at the edges.

The network neutrality debate can be approached from several angles. From a competition policy perspective, network neutrality is more needed if consumers do not have sufficient choice between alternative Internet Service Providers (ISPs): the existence of a single ISP with significant market power could lead to situations in which blocking or throttling of competing applications or 'unwanted' content could be the equivalent of discrimination or refusal to deal (see below, section 2). From a dynamic efficiency perspective, a relaxation of network neutrality rules could allow ISPs to monetise investment in new networks by charging 'bandwidth hogs', such as Netflix, a fee for the occupying their networks or by offering certain application providers a 'toll lane' over the public Internet, where quality of service would be guaranteed. Moreover, the neutrality debate has been approached from the standpoint of data protection (Should ISPs inspect the traffic that flows over their networks?), innovation (Will the new Google be forced to bribe an ISP to be visible on the Internet?), and even freedom of expression and media pluralism (Will ISPs decide which content should be prioritised, and which one should be delayed? or Should ISPs be free to decide which content to prioritise, in the name of freedom of expression?). While a full account of all these positions would fall outside the scope of this chapter, appreciating the complexity of the debate is critical for anyone seeking to assess the likelihood that the US and the EU will find common ground.

2.2.1   Network neutrality in the United States

Although the controversy over network neutrality can trace its roots to disputes over open access to cable modem systems that took place during the late 1990s, the debate began in earnest in 2002, when the FCC issued a ruling to classify cable modem systems as 'information services' instead of 'telecommunications services', which exempted them from Title II regulation, including, inter alia, network-sharing obligations (FCC, 2002b).[8] The US Supreme Court eventually upheld the FCC's action in *Brand X Internet Services v. FCC* (2005).

In response to concerns raised in the aftermath of this ruling, then-FCC Chairman Michael Powell (2004) called upon the industry to voluntarily embrace a series of Internet freedoms that would ensure end users' ability to access content, run applications and attach personal devices as they saw fit, subject only to restrictions needed to manage networks, ensure quality experiences, prevent disruption of the network and prevent theft of service. Powell also called for the industry to provide consumers with clear and meaningful information regarding the terms of their broadband service plans.

Concerns about blocking were heightened when a small local telephone company known as Madison River Communications prevented its DSL (digital subscriber line) customers from using the ports needed to access Internet telephony (also known as Voice over Internet protocol or VoIP) The FCC (2005a) invoked Title II when approving a consent decree settling this matter. The FCC (2005b) reversed course after the US Supreme Court's decision in *Brand X*, classifying DSL and other wireline forms of broadband Internet access constituted an information service. Shortly thereafter, the FCC also classified broadband over powerline and wireless broadband as information services as well (FCC, 2006 and 2007).

Since then, the FCC has constantly been under pressure to strengthen network neutrality rules. For example, at the same time that the FCC classified DSL as an information service, it issued a Policy Statement recognising the agency's intent to preserve consumers' rights to access content, run applications and attach devices as they saw fit. As such, the rule prohibited the blocking of content, but did not explicitly prohibit non-discrimination and even acknowledged the need for exceptions to the no-blocking principle for the needs of law enforcement and for "reasonable network management" (FCC, 2005c). But the Policy Statement did not formally adopt any regulatory mandates, and network neutrality proponents began to regard non-

---

[8] As the cable modem declaratory ruling noted, the federal government had never subjected cable systems to common carriage regulation (FCC, 2002b). Just the FCC concluded that broadband was an information service did not necessarily mean it would not be regulated. With respect to both DSL and cable modem service, the FCC sought comment on what regulations, if any, the FCC should impose under its general rulemaking authority (FCC, 2002a, pp. 3040-3048; 2002b, pp. 4839-4854).

blocking obligations as insufficient. Also the US Congress began to debate the issue during its consideration of major telecommunications reform legislation in 2006.[9] Although attempts to introduce network neutrality into the legislation were rejected by wide margins in the House of Representatives, the issue proved more controversial in the Senate, where an evenly divided Commerce Committee rejected a network neutrality amendment by a vote of 11 to 11. The underlying bill was never brought to the floor of the Senate.

During the Obama Administration, calls for stronger network neutrality have become even more frequent.[10] After taking office, the Obama Administration included provisions in the stimulus package that required that that broadband infrastructure grants made by the National Telecommunications and Information Administration comply with the 2005 policy statement on network neutrality (American Recovery and Reinvestment Act of 2009). This new momentum led the FCC to issue a notice of proposed rule-making recommending the adoption of formal network neutrality rules for the first time in 2009: the proposed rule also included provisions on non-discrimination, while maintaining exceptions for reasonable network management and law enforcement/public safety and applying a lower standard to wireless networks. At that time, the FCC decided against reclassifying broadband as a Title II telecommunications service. Although the FCC's first Open Internet Order was adopted at the end of 2010, it was not published in the *Federal Register* until 23 September 2011. Shortly thereafter, Verizon challenged the 2010 order in court, with the court resolving the matter in January 2014 (*Verizon v. FCC* 2014). The court ruled that the FCC has ancillary authority over the broadband Internet as a general matter, but struck down the FCC's non-discrimination and non-blocking rules as improper exercises of that authority, while providing guidance on how to reframe those rules so that they would comply with the statute.[11]

---

[9] For a review of the history of this legislative debate, see Yoo (2006).

[10] Barack Obama endorsed network neutrality both as a Senator and a candidate during the 2008 presidential campaign (http://change.gov/agenda/technology_agenda/).

[11] Specific exercises of ancillary authority under Title I are subject to the constraint that they not contravene any other specific statutory provision. The statute provides that the FCC can impose common carriage obligations only on providers of telecommunications services, not on providers of information services. Because the prohibition of unjust and unreasonable non-

In May 2014, four months after the court's opinion in *Verizon v. FCC*, the agency proposed new rules that followed the approach described by the court (FCC, 2014a). But while the FCC seemed to favour a compromise solution in which non-blocking rules would be coupled with exceptions for specialised services and reasonable traffic management, the political landscape changed abruptly in November 2014, when the President endorsed Title II as the basis for network neutrality in a public speech. This speech heavily influenced the content of the new Open Internet Order adopted by the FCC on 26 February 2015, and released on 12 March 2015.

The new Open Internet Order reclassified broadband Internet access services (BIAS) as a telecommunications service governed by Title II of the Communications Act of 1934, completing what can only be seen as a U-turn from the direction the FCC had taken since 2002.[12] The Order establishes three 'bright-line rules' prohibiting blocking, throttling and paid prioritisation, with all other conduct being governed by a general standard prohibiting unreasonably interfering with disadvantaging consumers' ability to reach the content, applications, services or devices of their choice or edge providers' ability to access consumers using the Internet. The order created exceptions for reasonable network management, defined as practices primarily used for and tailored to achieving a legitimate network management purpose as opposed to a business purpose. Another new feature of the Order is that it extends full network neutrality protection to wireless networks.[13] With respect to specialised services, which the order renamed non-Broadband Internet Access Services (non-BIAS) data services, the FCC continued to permit providers to offer these services while continuing to monitor their development and use. But

---

discrimination is the quintessential obligation borne by common carriers, mandating non-discrimination would represent an improper imposition of common carriage obligations onto an information service. The court similarly concluded that the anti-blocking rule combined with prohibition of charging edge providers any fee for providing connectivity essentially imposed common carriage obligations with a price of zero. The court did uphold the transparency rules as a valid exercise of the FCC's ancillary authority under Section 706.

[12] The FCC has also stated it will refrain from applying as many as 27 provisions of Title II, and as many as 700 codified rules, resulting in what the Commission calls a "light-touch" approach for the use of Title II" See FCC (2015, p. 12).

[13] Instead of a separate rule for wireless, the FCC ruled that it would instead simply take engineering attributes into account when assessing reasonable network management.

perhaps the biggest change in the scope of the order is the inclusion of interconnection in its regulatory purview. Until the adoption of the 2015 order, network neutrality sought to equalise how traffic is handled within a broadband network. Regulating interconnection, in contrast, seeks to equalise the terms under which how traffic arrives at a network.

What is most striking is the extent to which network neutrality has represented a moving target. What began in 2005 as a prohibition on blocking also became in 2010 a prohibition on discrimination and in 2015 direct regulation of interconnection as well. At the same time, the jurisdictional foundation for network neutrality has shifted from the general, more flexible provisions of Title I to the more intrusive framework of Title II. What will happen next is anyone's guess, since (as occurred in 2010 after the adoption of the first Open Internet Order) network providers have brought a judicial challenge to reclassification of broadband as a Title II service.

2.2.2 Network neutrality in Europe

Back in 2005, when the *Madison River* case was intensifying the network neutrality debate in the US, the European Commission was deeply convinced that the debate would never gain traction in Europe. Ten years later, it is clear that these early predictions were wrong: since 2009, Europe has been trapped in a fierce discussion, which – as will be clarified at the end of this section – seems to have been recently affected also by the resurgence of protectionism and industrial policy at the EU and at the national level and is likely to reach new policy areas, such as platform neutrality and search neutrality.

The first EU rules on network neutrality were adopted in 2009 and included in Articles 20 and 22 of the then-amended Universal Service Obligations (USO) Directive. Article 20 of the USO Directive mandates that network operators that manage traffic should inform end users in a transparent way of the practices they adopt so that users can make an informed choice when deciding whether to subscribe. Article 22 of the USO Directive introduced the possibility for national regulators to intervene and impose a minimum quality-of-service level in case the quality of certain applications became unacceptable for end users, arguably due to traffic management practices.

Despite difficulties faced by national regulators in applying this rule, in late 2013 the 'Connected Continent' proposal presented by the European Commission contained a very similar approach. On the one hand, the proposed package recognised that network neutrality is what keeps the Internet open and as such should be the default principle for all ISPs (Internet service providers) in the EU-28. On the other hand, the proposed rule left the door open to the creation of specialised services through agreements between ISPs and application/content providers, under the condition that such services do not disrupt the open Internet. However, in April 2014, the proposal was significantly modified by the European Parliament, which basically rejected the possibility of specialised services and reinstated network neutrality as an almost insuperable principle for ISPs.

The text of the Connected Continent package is currently under trilogue (negotiations between the European Commission, the European Parliament, and the Council), but a political agreement was announced by the European Commission on 30 June 2015. Under the new agreement, the principle of net neutrality will for the first time be enshrined into EU law: users will be free to access the content of their choice, they will not be unfairly blocked or slowed down anymore and paid prioritisation will not be allowed. In parallel, Internet access providers will still be able to offer specialised services of higher quality, such as Internet TV and new innovative applications, so long as these services are not supplied at the expense of the quality of the open Internet. These rules will be a reality across all member states as soon as the text officially applies on 30 April 2016.[14] Accordingly, the final compromise is closer to the original position of the European Commission and, as such, contemplates the possibility of specialised services and reasonable traffic management. More specifically, the Commission explains that "all traffic will be treated equally, subject to strict and clearly identified public-interest exceptions, such as network security or combating child pornography, and subject to efficient day-to-day network management by Internet service providers".[15]

In summary, the EU position on network neutrality is likely to remain controversial in the coming years: despite the recent political agreement, which will take effect in April 2016, implementation issues are still far from settled.[16] Meanwhile, a number of member states have taken the initiative to regulate the issue, leading to remarkable inconsistencies across the EU. While countries like the Netherlands,

---

[14] http://europa.eu/rapid/press-release_IP-15-5265_en.htm.

[15] Ibid.

[16] See Renda (2013) on the lack of detail on the implementation of a rule based on the co-existence of best effort Internet and specialised services.

Finland and Slovenia have enacted very strict neutrality rules, France has explicitly allowed traffic management practices, and the United Kingdom regards the possibility to charge quality of service fees as a much-needed opportunity for ISPs to monetise their investments in broadband networks.

2.2.3   Will there be convergence on network neutrality rules in the TTIP?

Despite the similarities of the terms of the debate on both sides of the Atlantic, there are many reasons to doubt that there will be explicit convergence on network neutrality in the Digital TTIP, even if – as seems straightforward – such a result would be greatly beneficial for all the players in the Internet ecosystem. First, the state of competition and investment in broadband networks is very different, and accordingly the rationale for intervening on network neutrality (and the likely impact of neutrality rules on the market) is also likely to be very different. Not surprisingly, the FCC has mentioned the lack of real alternatives (beyond one fibre, one cable and wireless network) for consumers in many parts of the United States as the basis for mandating network neutrality in the 2015 Open Internet Order. In Europe, if anything, there is a growing concern that there might be too many telecommunications operators, hence the calls for industry consolidation and the need to foster investment.

Second, the recent ruling of the FCC and the upcoming Connected Continent package in the EU incorporate slightly different rules on network neutrality. A deeper look at the text of the two rules reveals a remarkable degree of uncertainty, both due to the threat of extensive litigation in the United States and to the implementation challenges that the rules will pose on both sides of the Atlantic. As these uncertainties are unlikely to be solved in the coming months, a meaningful agreement on network neutrality seems incompatible with the timing of the first version of the TTIP.

To be sure, finding an agreement on specific issues would be advisable and would add to legal certainty and overall market performance both in the United States and in the increasingly fragmented European Union. Examples include a black list of practices that are always to be considered prohibited (regardless of the market power of the ISP); a grey list of practices that are to be prohibited under well-detailed circumstances; and a white list of allowed practices, to be consistently interpreted and regularly updated in what could become a very useful living agreement.

Finally, the prospects for an agreement on network neutrality chiefly depend on the position that the EU will take in related fields, and most notably in its regulatory reforms on e-commerce and copyright and in the antitrust investigations against Google. All these dossiers are deeply intertwined with network neutrality, not only because they call into question the potential introduction of platform-neutrality obligations; but also since they all directly or indirectly refer to the conduct of US companies in the European territory. We deal with these issues in the sections 3 and 4 below.

3. Antitrust and cyberspace

3.1 How similar are antitrust rules in the US and the EU?

Nowhere have the United States and Europe shown signs of convergence in the past century as they have in the area of antitrust. As a matter of fact, the introduction of rules on competition in the Treaty of Rome in 1957 is seen as largely inspired by the US tradition, starting with the 1890 Sherman Act and the 1914 Clayton Act. And indeed, the rules contained in the antitrust legislation of the two blocs are quite similar. When it comes to antitrust, however, the devil is the details, and the details are numerous. Without pretending to provide an exhaustive explanation, this section explores existing differences with a specific focus on digital markets and the Internet ecosystem.

First, even if the wording of sections 1 and 2 of the Sherman Act and Arts 101 and 102 TFEU is comparable, the two jurisdictions have taken divergent approaches to single-firm conduct ('abuse of dominance' in the EU jargon), due to the prevalence of the Chicago School of economics in the United States and the influence of the more structuralist 'Ordoliberal school' in Europe, starting from the early days of the debate on the Treaty of Rome.[17] This is not only a matter for historians or a subject for academic writings: the different approach has resulted in starkly divergent positions being adopted in merger control (e.g. the *GE/Honeywell* merger cleared in the US but was rejected in the EU in 2001) and also most notably in the area of single-firm conduct (e.g. the US and EU *Microsoft* cases).[18]

Second, some of the most notable differences between the two legal systems on the treatment of single-firm conduct are highly

---

[17] See Gerber (1994) and Akman (2009).

[18] Renda (2001 and 2004).

relevant for the electronic communications sector. For example, EU antitrust rules (and consequently, also the 2003 e-communications package) rely heavily on the so-called 'essential facilities' doctrine, whereas the US Supreme Court has never embraced that doctrine. In practice, this means that EU authorities are more likely to mandate asset sharing or compulsory licensing in 'refusal to deal' cases than US authorities. Cases like *Trinko* in the United States contrast sharply with the interoperability stance taken by the European Commission and the Court of First Instance (now the General Tribunal) in their *Microsoft* decisions in 2004 and 2007, respectively. Moreover, the rulings of the Court of Justice of the European Union (CJEU) on issues of predation and margin squeeze (especially the *Telia Sonera* case) have confirmed that EU antitrust dances to a different drummer than the US. In particular, in Europe large companies are explicitly attributed a special responsibility vis-à-vis their market, which has recently led the Court to theorise that large firms should ensure, besides the survival, also the profitability of their smaller rivals.[19] By contrast, the US antitrust law has rejected price squeezes (*linkLine*) and is more equivocal than European law with respect to loyalty rebates (compare *LePage's* with *PeaceHealth*).

Third, differences in the way in which antitrust economics are applied in the two jurisdictions becomes even more acute when it comes to high-tech markets and in particular on the Internet, due to the prevalence of network externalities and multi-sided platforms. Many of these settings tend to be characterised by competition 'for' rather than 'in' the market, as firms compete in a high-risk, high-reward game that produces only one winner. The structuralist view of competition prevailing in the European Union reverberates on the authorities' distrust of this dynamic form of competition (regarding it as a 'sequence of monopolies', rather than a static situation of pluralism), despite the fact that in Europe, just as in the US, market power is not equated with market share, but in principle requires a finding of independence of behaviour.[20] The consequence is that the European

---

[19] See Petit (2014).

[20] Thus, as the European Commission explains on its website: "Market shares are a useful first indication of the importance of each firm on the market in comparison to the others. The Commission's view is that the higher the market share, and the longer the period of time over which it is held, the more likely it is to be a preliminary indication of dominance. If a company has a market share of less than 40%, it is unlikely to be dominant" (see http://ec.europa.eu/competition/antitrust/procedures_102_en.html).

Commission can regard certain companies as dominant companies even when they have a high chance of being displaced by market competitors in the generation of their product in what is an ever-changing competitive landscape.

The continental drift in antitrust, exacerbated by the peculiar economics of high-tech markets, lies at the roots of many differences between regulatory practices in the two legal systems, particularly regarding infrastructure regulation and network neutrality. It underlies the US relatively hands-off approach to both merger regulation and single-firm conduct in cyberspace, which contrasts sharply with the EU interventionist approach. And while the numerous antitrust investigations against Microsoft in both jurisdictions over the past 15 years are probably the clearest illustration of the existing divergence, the current European Commission's case against Google is a good example of a case dismissed by the FTC in the United States and currently being re-proposed, with remarkable emphasis, in the European Union. The new European Commissioner for Competition Margarethe Vestager announced on 15 April 2015 that the Commission had sent a Statement of Objections to Google, arguing that the giant IT company abused its dominant position in the "general Internet search" market. The Commission has also launched a similar investigation with respect to the market for mobile operating systems, apps and services. Most importantly, Ms Vestager is accusing Google of having awarded preferential treatment to its own online comparison-shopping service to the detriment of competing services. In so doing, Google has allegedly leveraged its market power in searching into a neighbouring market, thereby foreclosing competitors from that market and thwarting competition on the merits.

3.2   Is an agreement on antitrust principles in cyberspace possible, and desirable?

In the case of antitrust rules, a full agreement between the two parties in the Digital TTIP (and on pending cases) is unlikely for a variety of reasons. First, full alignment of antitrust rules would neither be possible, nor advisable, particularly given that enforcement of antitrust rules is completely different in the two legal systems. The prevalence of private enforcement (i.e. actions before the court aimed at seeking injunctions and damage compensation) in the US contrasts with the almost-exclusive reliance on public enforcement in the European Union, which significantly limits the effectiveness of antitrust rules. To some extent, antitrust rules in the US that appear more light-handed may be more effectively enforced compared with the EU's stricter rules that omit such formidable tools as 'opt-out' class actions, criminal sanctions, punitive damages and contingent fees between lawyers and clients.[21]

Second, the Google investigation is a good example of the attempt to extend the net neutrality debate into the higher layers of the Internet. The main allegation against Google is indeed one of 'non-neutrality': Google is charged with unduly discriminating among Internet content by providing a non-neutral, non-objective view of the Internet. Without entering into the merits of the Google search investigation, which would exceed the scope of this chapter, it is clear that advocating neutrality for search engines raises a range of complex issues. And it is also clear that in the United States, any attempt to compel a re-design of Google's home page or the disclosure of Google's algorithm would be seen as contrary to the narrow and deferential approach towards product design that US courts have followed since the antitrust cases against IBM in the 1970s.[22]

Third, any convergence on antitrust rules would have to dispel the suspicion that some of the most far-reaching antitrust investigations of the past years have been motivated by a combination of competition policy and industrial policy concerns. On the one hand, recent rumours have hinted at possible White House involvement in the FTC decision not to proceed against Google for anti-competitive conduct.[23] On the other hand, the European Commission's current investigation against Google is difficult to disentangle from the calls for enhanced regulation of online intermediaries launched by several institutions, including the European Parliament and the legislatures of France and Germany. If the Google antitrust investigation is part and parcel of a more general tendency towards platform regulation and neutrality, the United States is unlikely to follow Europe. This would not only go against the interests of many US-based companies; it would also contradict the way in which competition policy has been framed and applied in the United States for more than a century.

---

[21] See Renda et al. (2006).

[22] See e.g. *Telex Corp. v. IBM* (1973); *Innovation Data Processing v. IBM* (1984).

[23] See "Inside the US Antitrust Probe of Google", *Wall Street Journal*, 19 March 2015 (www.wsj.com/articles/inside-the-u-s-antitrust-probe-of-google-1426793274).

4. The EU's platform regulation debate: Towards the end of the 'mere conduit' principle?

As briefly mentioned in the previous section, while the network neutrality debate still looms, the Juncker Commission has also launched a new initiative to extend the neutrality principle to Internet platforms. Many official documents published by the European Commission and the European Parliament in the past months allude to the pressing need to limit US-headquartered companies' dominance over the value of the Internet. Since last year, French and German institutions have repeatedly called on the European Commission to split Google into two companies, a recommendation endorsed by the European Parliament in November 2014. The French Digital Council has vigorously called for legislation that would impose neutrality obligations on large Internet platforms, starting obviously from Google but then reaching all of the so-called GAFTAM companies.[24] And the first weeks of the Juncker Commission seem to have emphasised the need to go beyond a 'silo' approach in telecoms and media regulation to address the problem of the rising power of over-the-top (OTT) platforms through a consistent set of legal documents covering competition, copyright, privacy and security issues. What might emerge is an additional layer of regulation and responsibilities for Internet intermediaries, which would be a complete U-turn compared to the early days of the Internet, when legislation such as the EU e-commerce Directive and the US Digital Millennium Copyright Act provided for intermediary immunity to preserve the 'mere conduit' role of network operators as well as the neutrality of the Internet itself.

The most relevant issues currently being examined by EU policy-makers in this context (and most notably included in the Digital Single Market strategy presented by the European Commission on 6 May 2015) are the reform of copyright and e-commerce rules, in particular regarding the liability of online intermediaries. The two must be analysed together, since such reform would represent the revision of a concept that has governed the relationship between both areas of legislation since the birth of the Internet, namely the 'mere conduit' principle.

Regarding copyright, the Commission plans to propose revisions by the end of 2015. The increasingly poor fit between the 2001 Information Society Directive and the features of the evolving Internet

---

[24] See Conseil National du Numérique (2014).

ecosystem make the need for such reforms particularly urgent.[25] In particular, the 2001 Directive was adopted at a time when the key principle of Internet regulation was immunising ISPs from liability for the conduct of their subscribers. The US Digital Millennium Copyright Act follows the same approach. Both enactments are strongly linked to the 1996 WIPO Copyright Treaty, which sought to strengthen technological protection measures while preserving the 'dumb pipe' nature of ISPs.[26] Moreover, the 2001 Directive clearly reflects the assumption that digital rights management technologies would become the dominant mechanism for protecting content online, an assumption that has proven wrong in many media sectors. Since then, many member states (with France often being the most vocal) have called for giving ISPs greater responsibility for detecting and even penalising copyright infringements, which would represent a sea change in EU copyright legislation and enforcement.[27] This issue has already proven extremely controversial in the negotiations over the copyright package: during the hectic debate that led to the European Parliament's rejection of the Anti-Counterfeiting Trade Agreement (ACTA) in 2012, ISP liability proved to be a sticking point for both IT companies and civil society.

Reforming the Information Society Directive to introduce ISP liability would also clash with the 'mere conduit' principle introduced in the 2000 e-commerce Directive.[28] This means that any reform of copyright reform necessarily requires reform of EU e-commerce rules as well. In this respect, the European Commission has recently announced a "comprehensive assessment of the role of platforms before the end of 2015 that will examine both the sharing economy, and online intermediaries. Issues will include such as (i) transparency, e.g., in search results (involving paid for links and/or advertisement), (ii) platforms' usage of the information they collect, (iii) relations between platforms and suppliers, (iv) constraints on the ability of individuals

---

[25] See Renda et al. (2015).

[26] See WIPO Copyright Treaty and WIPO Performances and Phonograms Treaty, adopted in Geneva, 20 December 1996 (www.wipo.int/treaties).

[27] See France's HADOPI law (Haute Autorité pour la Diffusion des œuvres et la Protection des droits d'auteur sur Internet), which was introduced in 2009 to promote the distribution and protection of creative works on the internet.

[28] Directive 2000/31/EC of the European Parliament and of the Council of 8 June 2000 on certain legal aspects of information society services, in particular electronic commerce, in the Internal Market, OJ L 178, 17 July 2000.

and businesses to move from one platform to another, (v) the best way to tackle illegal content on the Internet."[29] The underlying position of the Commission is that while the 'mere conduit' principle enshrined in the e-Commerce Directive has underpinned the development of the Internet in Europe, today blocking access to and removing illegal content by providers of hosting services can be slow and complicated, and "it is not always easy to define the limits on what intermediaries can do with the content that they transmit, store or host before losing the possibility to benefit from the exemptions from liability set out in the e-Commerce Directive".[30] In other words, the more ISPs manage and inspect traffic and use data generated by user behaviour, the weaker the justification for exempting intermediaries from liability becomes.

Just like the net neutrality debate, the war on copyright and the 'mere conduit' principle is extending from ISPs into the higher layers of the Internet ecosystem. After large EU countries like Germany, France and Spain have taken action to expand Google's liability for copyright infringement, the European Commissioner for the Digital Single Market Günther Oettinger recently stated that in future EU legislation, "when Google takes intellectual works from within the EU and works with them, then the EU can protect those works and demand a levy from Google." However, recent history about the likely impact of current plans to strengthen copyright liability are not encouraging: the two existing examples of ancillary copyright being rolled out nationally, in Germany and in Spain, seem to have largely backfired.[31]

Finally, one critical component of the current debate on copyright and e-commerce reform is the aggressive stance adopted by the European Commission against so-called 'geo-blocking' practices, now being considered as one of the worst obstacles on the way to market integration, and accordingly included in the new EU Digital

---

[29] See the European Commission's Communication on "A Digital Single Market Strategy for Europe", COM(2015) 192 final, Brussels, 6.5.2015.

[30] Ibid.

[31] In Germany, local publishers were forced to grant Google free use of their text snippets and thumbnails after the company delisted them from Google News, and traffic to their websites predictably plummeted. In Spain, the severity of the local ancillary copyright law has created an even-worse situation – the publishers, who lobbied for the law, cannot grant Google free access even if they want to do so, and now Google has axed Google News in Spain altogether, again causing a precipitous drop in traffic to publishers' websites.

Single Market strategy.[32] Geo-blocking refer to commercial practices that either prevent online customers from accessing and purchasing products and services from a website based in other member states or automatically re-route requests to a domestically located store. As a result of these practices, consumers are often charged more for products or services (particularly music or audio-visual) purchased online on the basis of their IP address, their postal address, or the credit card used to make the purchase. Again, practices adopted by US-based e-commerce giants like Amazon are often quoted as the real target of initiatives of this kind. This suspicion was strengthened by the launch, on 6 May 2015, of a Competition Sector Inquiry to assess whether geo-blocking restrictions (often embodied in contractual and distribution agreements for online trade of tangible goods but also in the licensing of audio-visual and content online services) constitute undue barriers to cross-border online shopping;[33] and finally confirmed by the subsequent opening, on 11 June 2015, of an antitrust investigation against Amazon for certain business practices adopted in the distribution of electronic books.[34]

In conclusion, the EU seems to have opened a debate on issues that are largely underexplored in the United States. This is partly justified by the greater integration of the US internal market (at least in terms of geo-blocking practices). But at the same time, it also reflects the fact that Europe is increasingly considering policies to re-distribute revenues along the Internet value chain, away from large IT intermediaries and towards content producers (in copyright legislation) and infrastructure operators (deviations from net neutrality). We consider it quite unlikely that any measure on intermediary liability and deviations from the mere conduit principle, if actively pursued by the European Commission within a Digital TTIP, would be subject of an agreement. Moreover, an agreement on platform liability based on the emerging EU approach would likely be unfortunate in economic and legal terms. Imposing heavy obligations on emerging Internet intermediaries both in terms of neutrality and liability for copyright and privacy would amount to a true oxymoron: treating them as dumb pipes on the one hand and as editors of content on the other.

---

[32] European Commission's Communication, "A Digital Single Market Strategy for Europe", COM(2015) 192 final, Brussels, 6.5.2015.

[33] http://europa.eu/rapid/press-release_IP-15-4921_en.htm.

[34] http://europa.eu/rapid/press-release_IP-15-5166_en.htm.

5.   End user information and accessibility issues

Among the many issues that are under discussion in the final TTIP agreement, one of the most promising relates to consumer protection issues, particularly e-labelling and e-accessibility. The first issue relates to the possibility of displaying some of the required and voluntary product information via a product's screen instead of physically affixing a permanent label to the product. Electronic marking would ensure that any changes to any labelling mandated by regulation can be updated more easily and therefore be more likely to remain current. In addition, the use of electronic marking would enhance consumers' ability to access and understand the regulatory information as well as facilitate access by disabled users. It would reduce costs and reduce time to market.

On the specific issue of e-labelling, legislation has already been enacted in both legal systems. However, the EU legislation was adopted specifically for medical devices and limited to the provision of instructions for use. In particular, Regulation 207/2012 on electronic instructions for use of medical devices specifies how to build the instructions for use in a medical device's label in an electronic format and the devices for which they may be used.

In the United States, the Enhance Labelling, Accessing, and Branding of Electronic Licenses Act of 2014 (E-LABEL Act) was signed by President Obama at the end of November 2014. The Act requires the FCC to allow manufacturers of radio-frequency devices to use electronic labelling for the equipment instead of affixing physical labels to the equipment. The statute defines "radio-frequency device with display" as any equipment or device that 1) requires the FCC's authorisation before the equipment or device may be marketed or sold within the United States and 2) is capable of digitally displaying required labelling and regulatory information. On 10 July 2014, the FCC also issued guidance describing how devices with integrated displays can present label information electronically.

Despite the differences in the frameworks adopted by the two legal systems, there should be no significant obstacle to the adoption of common solutions on e-labelling in the Digital TTIP. The starting point could be the US guidance on how to present information, with further discussions focusing on issues such as the clarity and user-friendliness of the message to be displayed, as well as the modalities of the transmission.

In contrast, e-accessibility has been one of the core issues discussed by the Transatlantic Economic Council throughout the past decade. Back in December 2005, the European Commission issued standards mandate n. 376 (M376) to harmonise and facilitate the public procurement of accessible ICT products and services and to enable public procurers to make use of these harmonised requirements in the procurement process. The intention of M376 was already aimed at achieving a degree of similarity with section 508 of the US Rehabilitation Act of 1973 (S508), but the industry has long criticised the two standards as needlessly different, and has been long calling for further harmonisation.[35] Since then, the M376 and S508 teams have been working without frequent technical exchanges and on different schedules at a time when close cooperation is vital for success. Work is underway to ensure better coordination, and the S508 standard is being revised following a proposal by the US Access Board, which aims to merge them with its guidelines for telecommunications equipment and customer premises equipment covered by section 255 of the Communications Act of 1934. The proposed revisions and updates to the section 508-based standards and section 255-based guidelines are intended to ensure that ICT covered by the respective statutes is accessible to and usable by individuals with disabilities. Both parties in the TTIP can use as a reference the Web Content Accessibility Guidelines (WCAG) 2.0, an international standard prepared by a working group composed of academics and corporate representatives within the World Wide Web Consortium (W3C).

Agreements on both e-labelling and e-accessibility appear to be attainable for the Digital TTIP chapter. The European Commission's TTIP factsheet on the information society concurs, and there is no reason to expect negotiations to fail on these issues.

In addition to these matters, which have been part of the transatlantic dialogue for quite some time, other related topics might also find their way into an initial agreement. These include consumer protection standards or rules for e-health and in particular M-health applications, on which the industry has been quite vocal over the past months.

---

[35] The problems are exemplified by the delay in the publication of the latest US Advanced Notice of Proposed Rule-making (ANPRM) version of S508 that was announced by the US Access Board in early October 2011. Because of the lack of exchange of information, this delay has caused a problem for the EU M376 team that could lead to a harmonisation failure.

6.   The Internet of Things and smart manufacturing

One of the most important current developments in the digital sector is the advent of the Internet of Things (IoT). According to major IT companies such as Cisco and Huawei, the number of devices connected to the network globally is projected to grow from fewer than 10 billion to more than 50 billion devices by 2020. The quest for connecting the "remaining 99% of things" that have not been connected to date and for capturing market share in the run-up to the IoT age is one of the most vibrant competitive races of our time. Like all network-based phenomena, IoT is a natural candidate for global standards in order to allow market participants to fully realise the benefits of scale economies and network economic effects. As a result, one would expect the many industrial sectors involved to share an interest in developing standards and rules that will be adopted worldwide. Indeed, a number of industry players have called for including harmonised rules for IOT within the TTIP, especially on the manufacturing side. However, the temptation to develop incompatible standards as a way to protect domestic industry is reportedly emerging, in particular on the EU side.

In the US, since February 2010, manufacturing has added more than 700,000 jobs, the fastest pace of job growth since the 1990s. In order to continue this extraordinary momentum, the Obama Administration launched an Advanced Manufacturing Partnership (AMP) within the President's Council of Advisors in Science and Technology. President Obama then launched four manufacturing innovation institutes with four more on the way; invested nearly $1 billion to upgrade our community colleges to train workers for advanced manufacturing jobs; expanded investments in applied research for emerging, cross-cutting manufacturing technologies; and launched a new initiative to deploy the talent of returning veterans to in-demand jobs, including advanced manufacturing. The AMP delivered its final report in November 2014, making recommendations addressing three key pillars that support American manufacturing: 1) enabling innovation, 2) securing the talent pipeline and 3) improving the business climate. These recommendations are now being followed up by executive actions in all three areas.

In Europe, work on advanced manufacturing has been underway, especially since the launch of the 7th Framework Programme for Research (followed in 2014 by the Horizon 2020 program) and the Europe 2020 strategy announced in 2010, which contained a flagship initiative dedicated to an Industrial Policy for the Globalisation Era. However, the March 2014 report of the European

Commission's Task Force on Advanced Manufacturing for Clean Production acknowledged that initiatives so far have remained mostly patchy and isolated.[36] But the new European Commission seems willing to shift gears and is reportedly ready to adopt a non-legislative initiative that will expand the *Industrie 4.0* already launched by the German government in cooperation with industry and academia in 2011 to the pan-European level. The use of cyber-physical objects and equipment in the factories of the future is often described as the 'fourth industrial revolution', which might prove so disruptive that it is expected to bring about paradigm shifts in modes of production and distribution.

Industry 4.0 is indeed powered by a mix of technologies, which include nano-technologies and IoT technologies that design and realise smart objects, cloud computing technologies for the low-cost storage of data and applications, a mix of wireless technologies for always-on connectivity (including 5G), advanced robotics, 3D printing, and big-data analytics for optimised management of the supply chain. A report by PwC for the German government estimated that over the next five years, a yearly investment of as much as €40 billion might bring an 18% increase in the productivity of German industry and a 12% increase in the industry's turnover[37].

However, the Europeanisation of the German *Industrie 4.0* strategy will not come without consequences. First, it is to be anticipated that all other member states will find the initiative less attractive, since they do not feature the same industry leadership that Germany still enjoys in some sectors. Germany's market for embedded systems, i.e. computer *systems* with a dedicated function within a larger mechanical or electrical *system*, generates €20 billion annually (expected to reach €40 billion by 2020) and ranks third in the world behind the US and Japan. Other countries do not reach anywhere near these figures and thus have much lower chances to develop industrial leadership in most of the technologies involved. At the same time, countries like Italy (second only to Germany in terms of industry size in Europe) feature a completely different industry structure, with a myriad of micro-enterprises that would lack the scale to fully capitalise on a pan-European initiative of this size.

---

[36] See http://ec.europa.eu/growth/industry/innovation/advanced-manufacturing/index_en.htm

[37] See PwC, Opportunities and challenges for the Industrial Internet, 2014, available at http://www.pwc.nl/en/publicaties/industrie-4-0.jhtml.

But perhaps the most worrying aspect of the European side of the debate is the possibility that some of the key industry players involved in *Industrie 4.0* might decide to develop standards that are incompatible with those being developed in the US, in particular when it comes to cloud computing, but also with respect to supply chain management. One possible example is the recent joint initiative launched by Deutsche Telekom and SAP to merge production technology with IT and telecommunications. The CEO of Deutsche Telekom recently observed: "We don't need to fear standards from the United States. We want Germany's voice to be heard as well on such an important issue."[38] The emergence of national standards in such a globalised industry is apparently motivated by industrial policy, such as the need to counter the current leadership of US-based companies, such as AT&T, Cisco, IBM, Intel and General Electric, which dominate the top standards alliances in this field, including the Industrial Internet Consortium, the Open Interconnected Consortium and the AllSeenAlliance. But an additional motivating factor is the desire to respond to the Snowden revelations by creating a national environment in which data will be preserved within German territory – the so-called 'German cloud' (or, at least, a European cloud), already invoked a few times by Chancellor Angela Merkel.[39]

In summary, an agreement on IoT standards would be highly desirable in the Digital TTIP and would likely speed up the deployment of *Industrie 4.0* technologies. However, such an agreement is unlikely to occur, since both parties are deploying advanced manufacturing strategies as part of their industrial policy initiatives and are therefore acting more as competitors than as allies. In addition, the NSA scandal seems to be making an agreement in this field harder to reach and appears to be spurring the development of incompatible standards.

7.   A continental drift in data protection?

No other issue related to the online world has been as prominent in the debate over the TTIP as data protection. Even before the Snowden revelations, the issue was almost intractable in transatlantic regulatory cooperation. Against this background, the emergence of the Internet, and even more of cloud computing, creates significant legal challenges

---

[38] https://www.telekom.com/media/company/271966.

[39] See, inter alia, Hilmar Schmundt and Gerald Traufetter, "Digital Independence: NSA Scandal Boosts German Tech Industry", *Der Spiegel*, 4 February 2014.

alongside undoubted potential benefits. Cloud computing permits a degree of flexibility that makes it increasingly difficult to identify who should be held accountable vis-à-vis cloud customers for the handling and processing of personal data and on the legal regime that should govern data transfers outside the US and EU jurisdictions (Hon et al., 2011a, 2011b, 2012; Schwartz, 2013; Schwartz & Solove, 2013). This section briefly describes the existing legislation on privacy in the US and the EU and the current debate on the regulation of transatlantic data flows. Section 6.1 introduces the main privacy laws (along with case law and enforcement practice) in the United States and the EU. Section 6.2 discusses the Safe Harbour regime and the Binding Corporate Rules. Section 6.3 briefly concludes by illustrating possible 'landing zones' in current TTIP negotiations or in separate deals.

7.1 Privacy law in the United States and in the EU

The United States and the European Union have always followed different legal approaches to privacy and data protection (Schwartz & Solove, 2013). First, the US has traditionally relied on piecemeal, sectoral regulation and private ordering to address privacy issues. The European Union, in contrast, enacted the first horizontal, omnibus data protection laws in the 1970s followed by the adoption of the Convention for the Protection of Individuals with regard to Automatic Processing of Personal Data in 1981 and the enactment of the EU Data Protection Directive 95/46 in 1995. Moreover, in Europe privacy is explicitly considered as a fundamental right, whereas the US Constitution contains no explicit reference to privacy.[40] Many prominent US scholars consider privacy as amounting to a property right, i.e., an alienable commodity that can be traded in exchange for customised service. Finally, in the US privacy legislation and case law traditionally focused on the protection of the citizen against violations and misbehaviour of public authorities (also due to the scope of the Fourth Amendment), whereas in the EU the focus is rather on the private sector. In a widely cited article published in the *Yale Law Journal*, James Whitman (2004) interpreted the fundamental divergence between the legal approaches to privacy in the US and the EU as rooted

---

[40] The term 'privacy' does not appear explicitly in the US Constitution or the Bill of Rights. However, the US Supreme Court has ruled in favour of various privacy interests, deriving the right to privacy from the First, Third, Fourth, Fifth, Ninth, and Fourteenth Amendments to the Constitution.

in a cultural difference between those who view privacy as an aspect of liberty and those who regard privacy as an aspect of dignity.[41]

7.1.1   Privacy laws in the United States

In the United States, the right to privacy is historically and legally rooted in the Fourth Amendment, which provides: "The right of the people to be secure in their persons, houses, papers, and effects, against unreasonable searches and seizures, shall not be violated, and no Warrants shall issue, but upon probable cause, supported by Oath or affirmation, and particularly describing the place to be searched, and the persons or things to be seized." The Supreme Court initially framed such a right with respect to the confidentiality of personal postal correspondence such as letters and sealed packages.[42] Over the past few decades, various scholarly approaches to privacy have emerged, mostly viewing privacy as control over data and framing it as a commodity rather than a fundamental right, with important consequences in terms of its alienability (Solove, 2006).

Regarding statutory law, early attempts to regulate privacy include the Fair Credit Reporting Act (FCRA) of 1970 and the Family Educational Rights and Privacy Act (FERPA) of 1974. Other federal statutes addressing specific privacy issues include the Children's Online Privacy Protection Act (COPPA), the Health Information Portability and Accessibility Act (HIPAA), the Electronic Communications Privacy Act (ECPA), and the Gramm-Leach-Bliley Act (GLBA). Several of these federal statutes focused on the presence

---

[41] See Whitman (2004, p.161) quoting Post (2001), and arguing: "Continental privacy protections are, at their core, a form of protection of a right to respect and personal dignity ...By contrast, America, in this as in so many things, is much more oriented toward values of liberty, and especially liberty against the state."

[42] See *Ex parte Jackson* (1878) in which the US Supreme Court ruled: "The constitutional guaranty of the right of the people to be secure in their papers against unreasonable searches and seizures extends to their papers, thus closed against inspection, wherever they may be ... No law of Congress can place in the hands of officials connected with the postal service any authority to invade the secrecy of letters and such sealed packages in the mail; and all regulations adopted as to mail matter of this kind must be in subordination to the great principle embodied in the fourth amendment of the Constitution." Later, the US Supreme Court has ruled in favour of various privacy interests – deriving the right to privacy from the First, Third, Fourth, Fifth, Ninth and Fourteenth Amendments to the Constitution.

of 'personally identifiable information' while others focus on transparency and access to information, on protecting consumers from inappropriate use of their personal data or on imposing duties of confidentiality. Of these statutes, the most relevant are certainly ECPA (in particular its Title II, also known as the Stored Communications Act), the US PATRIOT Act and the FAA. All these statutes have received criticism over the past few years: while ECPA (and its Title II in particular) has been criticised for having been largely outpaced by technological innovation, and in particular by cloud computing, the *Uniting and Strengthening America Provide Appropriate Tools Required to Intercept and Obstruct Terrorism* (US PATRIOT) Act of 2001 was criticised for provisions that can lead companies to turn over data to the US government even without notice to the customer. Data stored outside US borders, if held in servers owned by a US company, are potentially covered by this provision: even contract provisions specifying that data will be governed by foreign law can be ignored by the US government.[43] But the most heavily criticised provision is certainly the Foreign Intelligence Surveillance Amendment Act (FAA), which amended the 1978 Foreign Intelligence Surveillance Act. Section 1881a of the FAA introduces the possibility for the US government to monitor foreign communications and access data of foreign citizens located outside of the US without a warrant (a requirement that, by virtue of the Fourth amendment, would apply only to US citizens). A recent report for the European Parliament observed that "while there has been a great deal of concern at the international level over the US PATRIOT Act, there has been virtually no discussion of the implications of ... § 1881a of FAA," which "for the first time created a power of mass-surveillance specifically targeted at the data of non-US persons located outside the US, which applies to cloud computing" (Bigo et al., 2013).

Beyond privacy legislation and case law, which mostly focuses on the possibility for government institutions to inspect personal data and communications, an increasingly important player in the privacy domain is the Federal Trade Commission in its role of consumer protection enforcer. The number of investigations and sanctions accumulated by the FTC over the past few years is remarkable (Cline, 2014). To be sure, the FTC has filled an important gap in US privacy law

[43] Specifically, section 215 of the Patriot Act allows the FBI to access data related to investigations in an *ex-parte* proceeding with the requirement that "no person shall disclose to any other person ... that the [FBI] has sought beyond privacy legislation and case law ... or obtained things under this section."

by protecting customers against privacy- and security-reducing practices adopted by their providers. However, there seems to be significant space for a clarification of the FTC powers, as well as of the criteria and definitions used by the FTC in enforcing legislation to protect consumer privacy and data security.

All entities that store consumer information on the Internet face the threat of FTC enforcement if the way they store and secure information does not match their declarations to their customers. This unfair behaviour amounts to a deceptive or unfair practice under Section 5 of the FTC Act. In addition, the FTC enforces a handful of sector-specific privacy laws, including COPPA, GLBA, FCRA, TCPA and the Telecommunications Act, as well as the EU-US Safe Harbour (see below).[44]

7.1.2 The EU legal framework for data protection

The first European data protection laws were enacted in the 1970s, followed by the adoption of the Convention for the Protection of Individuals with regard to Automatic Processing of Personal Data in 1981. At the EU level, the right to privacy has been so far regulated by Data Protection Directive 95/46 (1995) (DPD), which, however, does not cover judicial and police cooperation.[45] Other relevant legislation in force include the 2002 and 2009 e-Privacy Directives and the data retention Directive, which has however been declared invalid by the Court of Justice in a recent decision. The EU data protection Directive applies to data held both by the public sector and the private sector. There are, however, important exemptions that give government the possibility to access and process data for tax and criminal law purposes. As a result, it is fair to state that, contrary to what occurs under US statutory law, the main EU Directive applies far more stringently to the private sector than to the public sector.

---

[44] Under Section 5, a trade practice is:

- Deceptive, if it involves a "material representation, omission or practice that is likely to mislead a consumer acting reasonably in the circumstances, to the consumer's detriment";
- Unfair, if it "causes or is likely to cause substantial injury to consumers which is not reasonably avoidable by consumers themselves and is not outweighed by countervailing benefits to consumers or competition" (the so called 'three-part test' of Section 5(n) of the FTC Act).

[45] Such area is currently covered by the Council of the European Union's 2008 Framework Decision on the protection of personal data processed in the framework of police and judicial cooperation in criminal matters.

In terms of scope, the DPD focuses on the protection of personal data, which it defines as "information relating to an identified or identifiable natural person". No data protection rules will apply at all where data are not personal but are instead anonymous, i.e. "data rendered anonymous in such a way that the data subject is no longer identifiable" (Recital 26). The DPD identifies three main classes of persons to whom EU data protection law applies:

- Data controllers, who are those persons who determine the purposes for which and the means whereby personal data are collected and processed;

- Data processors, who act under the instruction of controllers and do not themselves decide the processing purposes and

- Data subjects, the individuals whose personal data is being processed.

The DPD directed member states to impose legal obligations on controllers to protect personal data by complying with certain principles when processing personal data, including transparency, purpose specification and limitation and erasure, meaning that personal data that are not necessary anymore must be erased or truly anonymised.

Besides the DPD, privacy laws in the EU also include the e-Privacy Directive (as amended in 2009), which forms part of the regulatory framework for electronic communications and introduces obligations of security and confidentiality for providers of e-communications only. It deals with a number of important issues, such as confidentiality of information, treatment of traffic data, spam and cookies. Security of services includes the duty to inform the subscribers whenever there is a particular risk, such as a virus or other malware attack. Confidentiality obligations are addressed at member states, who should prohibit listening, tapping, storage, or other kinds of interception or surveillance of communication and related traffic, unless the users have given their consent or conditions of Article 15(1) have been fulfilled.

Finally, the data retention Directive (2006/24/EC) was adopted to amend the e-Privacy Directive to provide a more effective response to the terrorist attacks in New York 2001 and Madrid in 2004. It focused on the regulation of data retention to permit access by law enforcement authorities for a certain period if necessary as a means for prevention, investigation and prosecution of serious crime as defined by each of the member states in its national law. In April 2014, a judgment of the CJEU held that the directive was invalid as it "interferes in a particularly serious manner with the fundamental rights to respect for private life and to the protection of personal data". Hence, "by adopting the Data Retention Directive, the EU legislature has exceeded the limits imposed by compliance with the principle of proportionality". This judgment might constitute an important precedent for the interpretation of the validity of existing US legislation (e.g. the FAA) in the EU context and shows that even security issues are unlikely to trump privacy when it comes to EU legislation and CJEU case law.

Recently, in evaluating the data protection Directive and related legislation, the European Commission acknowledged that the legal framework needs an update, both in light of the new challenges posed by technological developments and differences in the ways that member states have transposed and enforced the DPD. Moreover, the application of the EU data protection *acquis* in the area of police cooperation and judicial cooperation in criminal matters, in particular the 2008 Framework Decision, resulted in gaps and inconsistencies (European Commission, 2012). Accordingly, the Commission proposed a strong and consistent legislative reform, which consists of a Regulation (replacing Directive 95/46/EC) setting out a general EU framework for data protection[46] and a Directive replacing the 2008 Framework Decision setting out rules on the protection of personal data processed for the purposes of prevention, detection, investigation or prosecution of criminal offences and related judicial activities.

The new proposed rules aim to improve individuals' ability to control their data by ensuring that when their consent is required, it is given explicitly, meaning that it is based either on a statement or on a clear affirmative action by the person concerned, and is freely given; equipping internet users with an effective 'right to be forgotten' in the online environment;[47] guaranteeing easy access to one's own data and a right to data portability; and reinforcing the right to information so that individuals fully understand how their personal data are handled, particularly when the processing activities concern children. The rules

---

[46] It should be noted that the choice of a Regulation replacing the DPD implies much less discretion in the implementation of the text at national level, as the Regulation is directly applicable and requires no transposition measure by EU member states.

[47] The right to be forgotten is described as the right to have one's data deleted if the owner withdraws his/her consent and if there are no other legitimate grounds for retaining the data (see European Commission, 2012).

also seek to improve the means for individuals to exercise their rights by strengthening national data protection authorities' independence and powers and enhancing administrative and judicial remedies when data protection rights are violated. In particular, qualified associations will be able to bring actions to court on behalf of the individual. Finally, the new rules aim at reinforcing data security by encouraging the use of privacy-enhancing technologies, privacy-friendly default settings and privacy certification schemes and introducing a general obligation for data controllers to notify both data protection authorities and data subjects about data breaches without undue delay. This implies measures aimed at enhancing the accountability of those processing data: companies with more than 250 employees and in firms that are involved in processing operations which, by virtue of their nature, their scope or their purposes, present specific risks to the rights and freedoms of individuals will be asked to designate a Data Protection Officer. The proposed regulation also foresees very harsh sanctions for non-compliance.

In a recent commentary, Berkeley Professor Paul Schwartz (2013) observed that the proposed new rules would significantly affect US companies' daily practice of authorising the sharing of personal information through simple 'notice and consent'. As mentioned, the Proposed Regulation lists 'consent' as one of the legal justifications for the processing of personal data, but requires that written consent for personal information processing be presented in a form 'distinguishable' from any other matter. More importantly, Article 7 of the proposed text places the burden of proof of demonstrating consent on the controller. This requirement "heightens the risk that a user's consent will not stand up if a data protection commissioner or the user herself challenges the assent after the fact."

Finally, and most problematically, the proposed Regulation states that consent "shall not provide a legal basis for the processing" when "there is a significant imbalance between the position" of the controller and the party to whom the data refers. Thus, Internet companies would not be able to justify processing by a party's consent if they offer take-it-or-leave-it terms for the processing of personal data or provide services for employees or other parties that lack effective bargaining power. As a consequence, Schwartz concludes that US IT companies will not be able to rely on one-sided click-through agreements. The new rules are far-reaching also in terms of jurisdiction, since the proposed Regulation potentially subjects all cloud services to EU privacy law.

The effect of the expansion of the remit of EU data protection rules is already being felt while the general Data Protection Regulation is still pending final approval by EU institutions. In May 2014, the European Court of Justice (CJEU) ruled against Google in *Google Spain SL, Google Inc. v Agencia Española de Protección de Datos, Mario Costeja González*, a case brought by a Spanish individual who requested the removal of a link to a digitised 1998 article in *La Vanguardia* newspaper about an auction for his foreclosed home for a debt that he had subsequently paid.[48] The court ruled in *Costeja* that search engines are 'data controllers' and, as such, are responsible for the content to which they point. Thus, Google was required to comply with EU data privacy laws. In so ruling, the Court also clarified that even if the physical server of the search engine operator processing the data is located outside Europe, EU rules apply if the operator has a branch or a subsidiary in a member state that promotes the selling of advertising space offered by the search engine. Moreover, search engines are to be considered controllers of personal data. Google can therefore not escape its responsibilities under European law when handling personal data by saying it is a search engine. EU data protection law applies, and so does the right to be forgotten. Furthermore, the CJEU ruled that individuals have the right – under certain conditions – to ask search engines to remove links with personal information about them. This applies where the information is inaccurate, inadequate or excessive and is subject to a balancing test with other fundamental rights such as freedom of expression. The responsibility for performing this test rests with the data controller in the first instance.

The *Costeja* case is a good example of the tendency, increasingly evident in Europe, to expand the territorial scope of EU data protection rules to avoid their circumvention by the locating of servers outside the territory of the EU and to increasingly ask online intermediaries to cooperate in the enforcement of the EU rules. The latter tendency is, indeed, consistent with other reforms currently being discussed in the EU, including the proposed reform of the 2001 Information Society Directive and the 2000 e-Commerce Directive.

---

[48] Costeja initially attempted to have the article removed by complaining to Spain's data protection agency, which rejected the claim on the grounds that it was lawful and accurate, but accepted a complaint against Google and asked Google to remove the results. Google sued in the Spanish *Audiencia Nacional*, which referred a series of questions to the CJEU.

7.2 Cross-border data flows: What future for the US-EU Safe Harbour?

The EU data protection Directive also governs the transfer of data, permitting data transfers only to other countries with an 'adequate' level of protection. The US does not appear on the list of countries with 'adequate' protection. However, the US Department of Commerce (DoC) in consultation with the EU developed a Safe Harbour Agreement so that that US companies can transfer European data to the United States if the company handling the transfer essentially complies with the DPD in handling and processing the data. Today, almost 5,000 organisations are reportedly certified under the Safe Harbour framework.

Safe Harbour principles include the following:

- *Notice*: Individuals must be informed that their data are being collected and about how it will be used.
- *Choice*: Individuals must have the option to opt-out of the collection and forward transfer of the data to third parties.
- *Onward transfer*: Transfers of data to third parties may only occur to other organisations that follow adequate data protection principles.
- *Security*: Reasonable efforts must be made to prevent loss of collected information.
- *Data integrity*: Data must be relevant and reliable for the purpose for which it was collected.
- *Access*: Individuals must be able to access information held about them and correct or delete it if it is inaccurate.
- *Enforcement*: There must be effective means of enforcing these rules.

The Safe Harbour has always been controversial: in Germany, data protection authorities have voiced their concerns since 2010.[49] After the Snowden revelations, some member states, the European

---

[49] In 2010, the Dusseldorf Kreis, a working group comprised of 16 German state DPAs that are responsible for the private sector, issued a resolution requiring German data exporters to exercise additional diligence when transferring data to Safe Harbour-certified organisations, and prohibited German data exporters from relying solely on Safe Harbour in order to transfer data to the US, By requiring additional diligence, the resolution appeared to question Safe Harbour, and whether the system was sufficient to demonstrate an adequate level of protection for personal data.

Commission and, in March 2014, the European Parliament called for a suspension and a thorough revision of the Safe Harbour.[50] Meanwhile, on the basis of a thorough analysis and consultations with companies, the European Commission made 13 recommendations to improve the functioning of the Safe Harbour scheme. The Commission called on US authorities to identify remedies by summer 2014 (but the deadline was not met). The Commission would then review the functioning of the Safe Harbour scheme based on the implementation of these 13 recommendations.

The Commission's recommendations address four key areas.

- First, in terms of *transparency*, the Commission recommended that self-certified companies should publicly disclose their privacy policies, that online Safe Harbour privacy policies should include a link to the Department of Commerce's Safe Harbour list of current Safe Harbour members, that self-certified companies publish privacy conditions of any contracts they conclude with subcontractors, and that the DoC's Safe Harbour list clearly flags those companies that are not current members.

- Second, on *redress*, the Commission stated that online Safe Harbour privacy policies should include a link to the chosen Alternative Dispute Resolution (ADR) provider, that the ADR choice should be readily available and affordable, and that the DoC should systematically monitor ADR providers, specifically in relation to the transparency and accessibility of their procedures and how they follow up complaints.

- Third, concerning *enforcement*, Safe Harbour members should be subject to spot check *ex-officio* investigations in order to verify the substantive compliance of their privacy policies. In addition, where there has been a finding of non-compliance, follow-up investigations should be implemented after one year. The DoC

---

[50] In July 2013, the Conference of the German Data Protection Commissioners, including both federal and state Commissioners, issued a press release stating that surveillance activities by foreign intelligence and security agencies threaten international data traffic between Germany and countries outside the EEA. In light of these recent developments, the German Commissioners decided to stop issuing approvals for international data transfers until the German government can demonstrate that unlimited access to German citizens' personal data by foreign national intelligence services complies with fundamental principles of data protection law (namely, necessity, proportionality and purpose limitation).

should inform the competent EU DPA of pending complaints and suspected non-compliance. Finally, allegations of false claims of Safe Harbour adherence should be investigated thoroughly.

- Finally, on the issue of *access to data* by US authorities, the Commission stated that Safe Harbour privacy policies should specify the extent to which US law allows public authorities to collect and process data transferred under Safe Harbour and that the national security exception under Safe Harbour should be used only to the extent strictly necessary or proportionate.

In addition to the recommendations, new developments have created even more tensions between the two blocs. The concerns, initially voiced mostly with respect to existing legislation, have also gradually moved towards questioning the conduct of giant online intermediaries, accused of infringing even the principles of the Safe Harbour. Most notably, Austrian privacy activist Max Schrems argued that the National Security Agency's PRISM programme has shown that no meaningful data protection for Europeans exists under US law and that Facebook Ireland was "facilitating the processing of such data."[51] In a letter dated 26 July 2013, the Irish Data Protection Commissioner refused to investigate Facebook because the Irish branch of the company was registered under the Safe Harbour arrangement and provided access to US law enforcement. Following these considerations, the Irish High Court decided on 18 June 2014 to refer the case to the CJEU. While the ruling is expected by the end of 2015, various committees of the European Parliament have called for an official intervention in the case. The opinion of the CJEU's Advocate General on this case, originally expected on 24 June 2015, has meanwhile been delayed. At the same time, a coordinated series of investigations into Facebook's privacy practices is being carried out by privacy regulators in the Netherlands, Spain, France and Germany. On 15 May 2015, Belgium's Privacy Commission released a report examining the new privacy policies that Facebook implemented this year for use of data from its services, which include Instagram and WhatsApp, to target advertising. The report observes that Facebook processes the personal data of its members as well as other Internet

---

[51] *Schrems v Data Protection Commissioner* [2014] IEHC 310; [2014] 3 CMLR 37 (text freely available at <www.europe-v-facebook.org/hcj.pdf> accessed 14 November 2014).

users "in secret", without asking for consent or adequately explaining how the data would be used; and the president of the Belgian authority publicly stated: "The way in which [Facebook] is contemptuous of the private lives of its members and of all Internet users demands action."[52]

As tensions mount in the EU, the US has shown signs of reaction. In 2014, the FTC brought several instances of enforcement, including high-profile actions against MySpace, Facebook, and Google.[53] In 2015, actions were brought against companies that were falsely claiming to be under Safe Harbour certification in an attempt to show more concern for the adequacy of the Safe Harbour's self-certification procedure.[54] Similarly, the Department of Commerce, which is responsible for administering the programme, is likely to increase the rigor with which it oversees the programme. While the certification process is a self-certification programme and not subject to formal regulatory approval, an increase in substantive focus from the Department of Commerce during the certification phase and thereafter is likely as a result of the pressure from Europe.

---

[52] See "Belgian Watchdog Raps Facebook for Treating Personal Data 'with Contempt'", Lisa Fleischer and Tom Fairless, *Wall Street Journal*, 15 May 2015 (www.wsj.com/articles/belgian-watchdog-slams-facebooks-privacy-controls-1431685985).

[53] See e.g. "Google, Facebook, MySpace: Privacy rule breakers or trend makers?", John Fontana, ZDNet (www.zdnet.com/article/google-facebook-myspace-privacy-rule-breakers-or-trend-makers/).

[54] In January 2014, the FTC announced settlements with 12 companies that allegedly falsely claimed they complied with Safe Harbour, even though there were no substantive violations of the Safe Harbour privacy principles. In February, the Commission announced a proposed settlement with Fantage.com for allegedly deceptively claiming in its privacy policy that it held a current Safe Harbour certification, when in fact its certification had lapsed in June 2012. In May 2014, the FTC announced a settlement with the clothing manufacturer American Apparel related to charges that the company falsely claimed to comply with Safe Harbour, even though it had allowed the certification to expire. In November 2014, the FTC announced that data privacy certifier True Ultimate Standards Everywhere, Inc. ('TRUSTe') agreed to settle charges that the company deceived consumers about its Safe Harbour recertification programme (see Press Release, "FTC Settles with Two Companies Falsely Claiming to Comply with International Safe Harbour Privacy Framework", 7 April 2015 at www.ftc.gov/news-events/press-releases/2015/04/ftc-settles-two-companies-falsely-claiming-comply-international).

Moreover, both courts and legislators have taken action to address the problem of bulk collection of metadata. An important legal clarification came recently from the US Court of Appeals for the Second Circuit in *ACLU v. Clapper*, in which the Court ruled that the NSA's bulk collection of phone and other records was never authorised under section 215 of the US PATRIOT Act. The appellate court's decision in *ACLU v. Clapper* is the culmination of a series of lawsuits by activists and the civil liberties community aimed at putting an end to the NSA's mass surveillance programmes.

This decision arrived just as the US PATRIOT Act (set to expire at the end of May 2015) was being replaced by the US Freedom Act, approved by the House Judiciary Committee on 19 May 2015, and now finally signed into law on 2 June 2015.[55] The new Act explicitly bans the limitless collection of telephone data by forcing the government to use a 'specific selection term' (SST) in any surveillance warrant and replaces the centralised bulk-data collection system with an obligation for network providers to store data and, upon request, deliver it to the government. More specifically, the Act requires the FBI, in applications for ongoing production of call detail records for investigations to protect against international terrorism, to show reasonable grounds to believe that the call detail records are relevant to such investigation; and a reasonable, articulable suspicion that the SST is associated with a foreign power or an agent of a foreign power engaged in international terrorism or activities in preparation for such terrorism.

The Act also requires a judge approving such an ongoing release of call detail records for an investigation to protect against international terrorism to limit such production to a period not to exceed 180 days but allow such orders to be extended upon application, subject to approval by the FISA Court. The Act will allow the government to require the production of an initial set of call records using the reasonable, articulable suspicion standard that the term is associated with a foreign power or an agent of a foreign power and then a subsequent set of call records using session-identifying information or a telephone calling-card number identified by the specific selection term that was used to produce the initial set of records (thus limiting the government to what is commonly referred to as two 'hops' of call records). The government should however adopt minimisation

---

[55] Uniting and Strengthening America by Fulfilling Rights and Ensuring Effective Discipline Over Monitoring Act of 2015 or the USA FREEDOM Act of 2015.

procedures requiring prompt destruction of produced call records that are not foreign intelligence information.

This new system has been criticised for failing to remove massive data collection (which, critics say, is only delegated to private corporations), and at the same time reducing the efficiency and effectiveness of government surveillance action. Criticisms have also been raised since a few hours after signing the act into law, the Obama administration reportedly asked the FISA court to restore the mass data collection at least for a transitional period of six months, even clarifying that the *ACLU v. Clapper* decision, being a second circuit ruling, does not constitute controlling precedent for the FISA court.[56] The Act also re-authorises Section 215 of the US PATRIOT Act and Section 702 of the FISA Amendments Act (see above) through to the end of 2017. Against this background, the new Freedom Act seems unlikely to achieve all the steps forward that EU authorities were expecting, and its actual impact on mass surveillance activities seems obscure at best at the time of writing.

Finally, another development in the United States is the introduction in the House of a proposed Judicial Redress Act of 2015 by Representatives from both of the leading parties. The Act aims at extending to citizens of designated countries (including EU member states) the right to challenge possible misuse of their data by the US government in US courts. The proposed Act would allow the Attorney General to extend US judicial redress protections to citizens of selected third countries. If eventually passed by Congress, the Act would address some of the key concerns expressed over the past few years by EU institutions with respect to US privacy laws. For example, former EU Vice-President and Commissioner for Justice Viviane Reding observed: "When Americans come to Europe and they think the authorities have not handled their case correctly, they can go to a European court. However an EU citizen cannot do the same in the US and go to an American court. There is no reciprocity; we do not have the basis for judicial redress ... The US has recognised the importance of this request on several occasions – but they need to have a law. I have

---

[56] See, inter alia, S. Ackerman, "Obama lawyers asked secret court to ignore public court's decision on spying", *The Guardian*, 9 June (www.theguardian.com/world/2015/jun/09/obama-fisa-court-surveillance-phone-records).

not yet seen it."[57] Also the new European Commission President Juncker wrote in his mission letter to Věra Jourová, the new Commissioner for Justice, Consumers and Gender Equality, that one of her tasks will be to "conclude negotiations on a comprehensive EU-US data protection agreement which provides justiciable rights for all EU citizens, regardless of where they reside, as well as reviewing the Safe Harbour arrangement".

Will these initiatives be enough to avoid the suspension of the Safe Harbour? As things stand, it is still unclear whether or not the US will implement the entirety of the EU's recommendations, such as empowering the FTC to conduct *ex-officio* investigations to assure that US companies are in compliance with their privacy policies and that any false claims would eventually be further investigated. At the end of 2014, when taking office, Ms Jourová already expressed strong doubts that Safe Harbour can be considered as really secure for EU citizens and called for a 'plan B'. Vice President Andrus Ansip was even more aggressive and specified that if there are no satisfying results from negotiations with the US, "the suspension of the agreement might then be the option".[58] Some commentators have reported that the negotiation pendulum is shifting between calls for interoperability of EU and US legislation; proposals to suspend the Safe Harbour and take it out of the TTIP, also due to the European Commission's uncertain mandate;[59] and more aggressive calls for 'data localisation'

---

[57] See Vivian Reding's speech at http://europa.eu/rapid/press-release_ SPEECH-14-431_en.htm.

[58] See the initial hearing of Andrus Ansip in the European Parliament (www.europarl.europa.eu/hearings-2014/resources/library/media/ 20141022RES75838/20141022RES75838.pdf).

[59] The negotiation mandate for the European Commission instead refers to Article XIV of the General Agreement on Trade in Services (GATS) of the World Trade Organization. Article XIV contains a general exception clause stipulating that "nothing in the agreement may be construed to prevent the adoption or enforcement by any member of measures [...] necessary to secure compliance with laws or regulations [...] relating to [...] the protection of the privacy of individuals in relation to the processing and dissemination of personal data." The Commission's negotiation mandate states in Article 18: "The Agreement will not preclude the enforcement of exceptions on the supply of services justifiable under the relevant WTO rules (Articles XIV and XIVbis GATS)." Article XIV of GATS was indeed copied verbatim into a draft text of the TTIP agreement proposed by the Commission negotiators in July 2013 and leaked in February 2014.

requirements, with localisation even being presented as a fundamental right. This is even more worrying since on the US side, drafts from the e-commerce section of TTIP include completely opposite stances: the principle of 'interoperability' of European and US data protection rules, and a ban on 'localisation.' In October 2014, the US negotiators placed a concrete text proposal on 'data flows' on the table. But the papers published in January 2015 by the European Commission clearly state: "Data protection standards won't be part of TTIP negotiations. TTIP will make sure that the EU's data protection laws prevail over any commitments."[60]

7.3   What landing zones for data protection in the TTIP?

In an age of convergence, globalisation, and the data-driven economy, the US and the EU do not seem to be converging fast enough in their approaches to data protection. First, existing legislation confirms the existence of key differences in the main approaches followed by the two legal systems, with a clear focus on government intrusion into the private sphere in the US and significant emphasis on the relationship between data controllers and data subjects in the EU. Second, and relatedly, while in the United States privacy law focuses on redressing consumer harm and balancing privacy with efficient commercial transactions, in the EU privacy is considered as a fundamental right that prevails over competing interests (Hartzog and Solove 2014). Third, privacy protection is essentially triggered by the existence of 'personal data' or 'personally identifiable information' (PII): however, the definition of PII on the two sides of the Atlantic diverges significantly, with the US featuring a patchwork or partly inconsistent definitions and the EU relying on a single definition that broadly defines PII to encompass all information that is identifiable to a person.[61] Fourth, coverage of both personal *identified* and *identifiable* information seems to be more consistent in Europe than in the US: however, the EU seems too expansionist in its coverage of PII, whereas the US might err at the opposite extreme.

In addition, frictions between the US and EU authorities have mounted in the months following the Datagate scandal, such that even

---

[60]   http://trade.ec.europa.eu/doclib/docs/2015/january/tradoc_152999.2% 20Services.pdf

[61] Hartzog & Solove (2014, p. 888) explain that there are three predominant approaches to defining personal information in the US: 1) the tautological approach, 2) the non-public approach and 3) the specific-types approach.

established cooperation and recognition frameworks such as the Safe Harbour regime are now being reconsidered. Calls for a European cloud or even clouds limited to national territory (e.g. in Germany) have become common in the debate over cloud privacy and security. The European Parliament has expressed its intention to reconsider the Safe Harbour as well as the Data Protection Umbrella Agreement that has been under discussion between the two parties since 2011. Reforms underway in the United States, including the US Freedom Act, do not seem to fully address the concerns expressed by the EU authorities, and the negotiations on the Safe Harbour seems still likely to face problems: on the one hand, EU authorities deem US privacy laws inadequate in terms of the level of protection they achieve for European citizens and increasingly consider data localisation as a fundamental right; on the other hand, US authorities seek to obtain a recognition of interoperability and a ban on data localisation in the TTIP negotiations. In short, the parties are almost as far from an agreement as they were a year ago, and despite some signs of good will the tensions are unlikely to be put to rest any time soon: on the contrary, the situation is even worsening as some EU member states are now taking action to create massive surveillance programmes, as in the case of France, which (after the terrorist attacks of January 2015) is considering the instruction of a *Loi de renseignement* (Intelligence Bill) that would go further than the US PATRIOT Act and the already annulled EU Data Retention Directive in providing authorities with new technologies of mass surveillance of electronic communications.[62]

Needless to say, the persistence of divergent approaches can become an obstacle (or, at a minimum, a source of unnecessary compliance burdens) for companies wishing to provide Internet-based services on both sides of the Atlantic. This is especially the case for world-leading US-based Internet companies, which would profit enormously from a streamlining, update, and harmonisation of the definition of PII and, more generally, of the rules that apply to online data protection. To be sure, the Internet is challenging both legal

---

[62] These new technologies include so-called 'black boxes' or source code injected by French intelligence services on ISPs' infrastructure to detect suspicious user behaviour in real time. This would bring all residents in France under surveillance and expand monitoring to include private pictures, company trade secrets, medical records, etc. The authorities are expected shortly to propose a new register for suspected persons and new measures to record phone calls without authorisation from a judge, thus undermining data privacy protections.

regimes in a way that might end up requiring a thorough reform process. As of now, what seems likely is that the US will keep under-protecting privacy in the name of efficient commercial transactions (with a great responsibility being placed on the FTC to monitor abuses of bargaining power and other deceptive/abusive practices), whereas in the EU, Internet services might end up caught in the net of an overly formalistic, overly comprehensive legal framework, which leaves little room for trade-offs between privacy and welfare-enhancing customised service for data subjects.

8. Conclusions: What should the Digital TTIP achieve and what will it achieve?

Notwithstanding the strong political commitment shown by both the US and EU negotiators to speed up the conclusion of the TTIP agreement, the overall environment does not seem favourable to a comprehensive agreement in the digital sphere. Suffice it to recall that in a recent interview, President Barack Obama accused European corporations and regulators to be strategically hampering the position of US Internet companies.[63] The underlying reason, according to the American President, is that European companies "can't compete with us" and thus need to alter the level playing field to be able to survive. The reference is not only to the ongoing antitrust investigation into Google, but also to recent calls by the European Parliament to unbundle search engines (read: Google) from other commercial services, the current uprising of taxi drivers against Uber in many cities, the mounting debate on tax avoidance practices by several IT companies, the wave of 'Google taxes' imposed to remunerate publishers and the repeated calls to suspend the US-EU Safe Harbour Agreement on data protection due to the alleged unreliability of US companies' privacy policies. Obama's statements triggered a blunt reaction: a European Commission's spokesperson called these comments "out of line".[64]

Is Obama right or wrong? To be sure, much of the EU regulation that applies to the Internet is stricter than US regulation, but these rules apply regardless of nationality. In the EU, network operators have to share their networks even when they invest in high-speed broadband,

---

[63] See "Obama attacks Europe over technology protectionism", by Murad Ahmed, Duncan Robinson and Richard Waters, *Financial Times*, 16 February 2015 (www.ft.com/cms/s/0/41d968d6-b5d2-11e4-b58d-00144feab7de.html#axzz3ejxpiSNf).

[64] Ibid.

while in the US such obligation was lifted a decade ago. In the EU, privacy is a fundamental right, whereas in the US it is treated as a tradable right. In the EU, antitrust follows a different approach than the US, and this usually results in stricter remedies imposed on companies with market power. Other fields, such as cybersecurity and consumer protection are more regulated in the EU than they are in the US. These rules have been applied more often to US companies since these companies have come to dominate the Internet ecosystem since the early days. In some cases, an aggravating factor was that EU rules were largely unfit for the Internet age, and this created significant problems when it came to their application to the Internet. That said, there is reason to believe that it is mostly the inadequate and obsolete features of EU law, rather than a design to hamper US companies, that inspired the Commission in these actions. Otherwise, important merger cases such as Google/DoubleClick, Google/ITA, Facebook/WhatsApp, Microsoft/Nokia, Microsoft/Skype and others would have been handled differently by the Brussels trustbusters.

The past months, however, have marked a change of direction. Many recent documents of the European Commission and European Parliament speak clearly of the need to revive industrial policy in a way that protects EU champions against the current domination of US Internet companies. The Commissioner for the digital agenda Günther Oettinger claims that EU telecom companies should become more profitable. Conferences are being organised in the Parliament with titles such as "How can we stop Internet giants?". Google and Facebook are constantly demonised in the public debate, not to mention Uber (but this would probably occur even if Uber were European) and Amazon (recently accused of unfair tax deals in, and with, Luxembourg). The Digital Single Market debate is mostly centred around industry consolidation and the creation of large mobile operators that would negotiate on a more equal footing with the Googles and the Apples. In Germany and France, pressure from content providers and publishers even led institutions to think that splitting Google could be reasonable. The European Parliament followed this trend by advocating such a structural remedy in the belief that "indexation, evaluation, presentation and ranking by search engines must be unbiased and transparent" (although an in-depth discussion of effects on users has never occurred to date). And most importantly, the European Commission is reportedly considering the extension of regulation from telecoms infrastructure to Internet platforms, in the name of so-called 'platform neutrality'. Such move would impose interoperability obligations on all leading platforms, in the attempt to create a neutral Internet. And again, it would likely damage consumers.

Getting out of this impasse and inverting the current trend of divergence requires an effort on both sides, and TTIP talks could become a viable setting to this end. The EU should understand that economic recovery would be hampered, not helped, by a revival of protectionism, and that the word "neutrality" is not a panacea for all the evils of the Internet, but rather a double-edged sword to be handled with care. Not surprisingly, but also not fully convincingly, the European Commission has taken great pains to reassure the United States that the DSM is not a protectionist strategy. The US should do its homework on data protection, settle the network neutrality debate with a convincing compromise, and avoid that the urge to claim US leadership in global Internet talks ends up bringing the Internet under an unprecedented, ill-advised wave of regulatory interventionism. Should the TTIP take the form of a 'living agreement,' as seems likely, then obvious starting points would be the easy-to-reach agreements on e-labelling and e-accessibility, plus (if possible) an agreement to cooperate on standards related to cloud computing and the Internet of Things. In the coming years, however, it would be of utmost importance that such agreement encompasses network neutrality rules, data protection rules, intermediary liability, online copyright protection and related exceptions and limitations, and gradual convergence of competition law and policy in a field that is increasingly thirsty for legal certainty and streamlined, converging regulatory requirements on both sides of the Atlantic.

References

Akman, Pinar, (2009), "Searching for the Long-Lost Soul of Article 82", *Oxford Journal of Legal Studies*, Vol. 29, No. 2, pp. 267-303.

Bigo, Didier, Sergio Carrera, Nicholas Hernanz, Julien Jeandesboz, Joanna Parkin, Francesco Ragazzi, and Amandine Scherrer (2013), "National Programmes for Mass Surveillance of Personal Data in EU Member States and Their Compatibility with EU Law", European Parliament, Brussels.

Bourreau, Marc, Pinar Doğan and Mathieu Manant (2010), "A Critical Review of the 'Ladder of Investment' Approach", *Telecommunications Policy*, Vol. 34, No. 11, pp. 683–696.

Cline, Jay (2014), "U.S. Takes the Gold in Doling out Privacy Fines. Computerworld 17", 17 February (www.computerworld.com/s/

article/9246393/Jay_Cline_U.S._takes_the_gold_in_doling_out_pri vacy_fines?taxonomyId=84&pageNumber=3).

Conseil National du Numérique (2014), "Platform Neutrality: Building an open and sustainable digital environment", Opinion No. 2014-2, of the French Digital Council, Paris (www.cnnumerique.fr/wp-content/uploads/2014/06/PlatformNeutrality_VA.pdf).

Directive 2000/31/EC of the European Parliament and of the Council of 8 June 2000 on certain legal aspects of information society services, in particular electronic commerce, in the Internal Market, OJ L 178, 17 July 2000.

European Commission (nd), Factsheets and EU textual proposals on parts 2 and 3 of the TTIP (http://trade.ec.europa.eu/doclib/press/index.cfm?id=1230).

_____ (2012), Communication from the Commission to the European Parliament, the Council, the European Economic and Social Committee, and the Committee of the Regions — Unleashing the Potential of Cloud Computing in Europe, COM(2012) 529 final (September 27, 2012).

_____ (2015), Communication on "A Digital Single Market Strategy for Europe", COM(2015) 192 final, Brussels, 6.5.2015.

Federal Communications Commission (FCC) (2002a), "Appropriate Framework for Broadband Access to the Internet over Wireline Facilities", Notice of Proposed Rulemaking, *Federal Communications Commission Record*, Vol. 17, No. 4, pp. 3019–3076.

_____ (2002b), "Inquiry Concerning High-Speed Access to the Internet over Cable and Other Facilities", Declaratory Ruling and Notice of Proposed Rulemaking, *Federal Communications Commission Record*, Vol. 17, No. 7, pp. 4798–4872.

_____ (2005a), "Madison River Communications, LLC", Order, *Federal Communications Commission Record*, Vol. 20, No. 6, pp. 4295–4300.

_____ (2005b), "Appropriate Framework for Broadband Access to the Internet over Wireline Facilities", Report and Order and Notice of Proposed Rulemaking, *Federal Communications Commission Record*, Vol. 20, No. 17, pp. 14853–14985.

_____ (2005c), "Appropriate Framework for Broadband Access to the Internet over Wireline Facilities", Policy Statement, *Federal Communications Commission Record*, Vol. 20, No. 17, pp. 14986–14988.

_____ (2006), "United Power Line Council's Petition for Declaratory Ruling Regarding the Classification of Broadband over Power Line Internet Access Service as an Information Service", Memorandum

Opinion and Order, *Federal Communications Commission Record*, Vol. 21, No. 17, pp. 13281–13298.

_____ (2007), "Appropriate Regulatory Treatment for Broadband Access to the Internet over Wireless Networks", Declaratory Ruling, *Federal Communications Commission Record* Vol. 22, No. 8, pp. 5901–5934.

_____ (2010), "Preserving the Open Internet", Report and Order, *Federal Communications Commission Record*, Vol. 25, No. 21, pp. 17905–18098.

_____ (2014a), "Protecting and Promoting the Open Internet", Notice of Proposed Rulemaking, *Federal Communications Commission Record*, Vol. 29, No. 7, pp. 5561–5659.

_____ (2014b), "Implementation of Section 6002(b) of the Omnibus Budget Reconciliation Act of 1993", Seventeenth Report, *Federal Communications Commission Record*, Vol. 29, No. 19, pp. 15311–15478.

_____ (2015), "Protecting and Promoting the Open Internet", Report and Order on Remand, Declaratory Ruling, and Order (https://apps.fcc.gov/edocs_public/attachmatch/FCC-15-24A1.pdf).

Gerber, David (1994), "Constitutionalizing the Economy: German Neo-liberalism, Competition Law and the 'New' Europe", *American Journal of Comparative Law*, Vol. 42, pp. 25-84.

Hartzog, Woodrow and Daniel J. Solove (2014), "The FTC as data security regulator: *FTC v. Wyndham* and its implications", *BNA Privacy and Security Law Report* 13 (xx).

Hon, W. Kuan, Julia Hörnle and Christopher Millard (2011a), "The Problem of 'Personal Data' in Cloud Computing: What Information Is Regulated? – The Cloud of Unknowing", *International Data Privacy Law*, Vol. 1, No. 4, pp. 211–228.

_____ (2011b), "Who Is Responsible for 'Personal Data' in Cloud Computing?", *International Data Privacy Law*, Vol. 2, No. 1, pp. 3–18.

_____ (2012), "Data Protection Jurisdic tion and Cloud Computing – When Are Cloud Users and Providers Subject to EU Data Protection Law? The Cloud of Unknowing", *International Review of Law Computers & Technology*, Vol. 26, Nos. 2–3, pp. 129–164.

Pelkmans, Jacques and Andrea Renda (2011), "Single eComms market? No such thing", *Communications & Strategies*, 2nd quarter.

Petit, Nicolas (2014), "Price Squeezes with Positive Margins in EU Competition Law: Economic and Legal Anatomy of a Zombie" (http://ssrn.com/abstract=2506521   or http://dx.doi.org/10.2139/ssrn.2506521).

Post, Robert C. (2001), "Three concepts of privacy," *Georgetown Law Journal*, Vol. 89, No. 6, pp. 2087-2098.

Powell, Michael K. (2004), "Preserving Internet Freedom: Guiding Principles for the Industry", *Journal on Telecommunications and High Technology Law*, Vol. 3, No. 1, pp. 5–21.

Renda, Andrea (2005), "Telecom Services: a Transatlantic Perspective", in D.S. Hamilton and J.P. Quinlan (eds), *Deep Integration. How Transatlantic Markets are Leading Globalization*, CEPS Paperbacks, Chapter 11.

_____ (2007), "The Costs and Benefits of Transatlantic Convergence in Telecom Services, in Dan Hamilton and Joseph Quinlan (eds), *Sleeping Giant: Awakening the Transatlantic Services Economy*, Johns Hopkins University and Brookings Institution, Washington, D.C., November.

_____ (2009), "The review of the telecoms framework: a tale of the anti-commons, paper for the first report of the "Monitoring ICT European Regulation" initiative, NEREC, Madrid.

_____ (2010), "Competition-regulation Interface in Telecommunications. What's left of the Essential Facilities Doctrine", *Telecommunications Policy*, Vol. 34, Nos. 1-2, February-March, pp. 23-35.

_____ (2013), "Net Neutrality and Mandatory Network-Sharing: How to disconnect the continent", CEPS Policy Briefs, 18 December, CEPS, Brussels (www.ceps.eu/system/files/ PB309%20AR%20Net%20Neutrality_0.pdf).

_____ (2015a), "Antitrust, regulation and the 'neutrality trap'", CEPS Special Report No. 104, CEPS, Brussels, April.

_____ (forthcoming 2015b), "Cloud Privacy law in the United States and the European Union", in Christopher S. Yoo and Jean-Francois Blanchette (eds), *Regulating the Cloud: Policy for Computing Infrastructure*, Cambridge, MA: MIT Press, August.

Renda, Andrea et al. (2006), "Making Antitrust Damages Actions More Effective in Europe", Study for the European Commission, DG COMP, available online at http://ec.europa.eu/competition/ antitrust/actionsdamages/files_white_paper/impact_study.pdf.

Renda, Andrea et al. (2015), Study on the implementation, application and effects of Directive 2001/29/EC on the harmonisation of certain aspects of copyright and related rights in the information society (InfoSoc) Directive and of its related instruments, Study for the European Parliament Research Service, forthcoming July 2015, to be published on the European Parliament's website.

Solove, Daniel J. (2006), "A Taxonomy of Privacy", *University of Pennsylvania Law Review*, Vol. 154, No. 3, pp. 477–560.

Schwartz, Paul M. (2013), "EU Privacy and the Cloud: Consent and Jurisdiction under the Proposed Regulation", BNA Privacy and Security Law Report 12 (April 29): 1-3.

Schwartz, Paul M. and Daniel J. Solove (2013), "Reconciling Personal Information in the United States and European Union", UC Berkeley Public Law Research Paper No. 2271442.

Whitman, James Q. (2004), "The Two Western Cultures of Privacy: Dignity versus Liberty", Faculty Scholarship Series. Paper 649, Yale Law School, Yale University, New Haven, CT (http://digitalcommons.law.yale.edu/fss_papers/649).

WIPO Copyright Treaty and WIPO Performances and Phonograms Treaty, adopted in Geneva in December 20, 1996 (http://www.wipo.int/treaties).

Yoo, Christopher S. (2006), "Network Neutrality and the Economics of Congestion", *Georgetown Law Journal*, Vol. 94, No. 6, pp. 1847-1908.

_____ (2014), "US vs. European Broadband Deployment: What Do the Data Say?", Institute for Law and Economics Research Paper No. 14-35, University of Pennsylvania, Philadelphia, PA.

US Case Law

American Civil Liberties Union v. James Clapper, No. 13-3994 (S.D. New York December 28, 2013)

Brand X Internet Services et al., 545 U.S. 967 (2005).

Cascade Health Solutions v. PeaceHealth, 515 F.3d 883 (9th Cir. 2008).

Innovation Data Processing v. IBM, 585 F. Supp. 1470 (D.N.J. 1984).

LePage's Inc. v. 3M, 324 F.3d 141 (3d Cir. 2003) (en banc).

National Cable & Telecommunications Association v. Brand X Internet Services, 545 US 967 (2005).

Pacific Bell Telephone Co. v. Linkline Communications, Inc., 555 US 438 (2009).

Telex Corp. v. IBM, 367 F. Supp. 258 (N.D. Okla. 1973), *aff'd in relevant part & rev'd on other grounds*, 510 F.2d 894 (10th Cir. 1975).

Verizon Communications, Inc. v. Law Offices of Curtis V. Trinko, L.L.P., 540 US 398 (2004).

Verizon v. FCC, 740 F.3d 623 (D.C. Cir. 2014).

13. GREATER TTIP AMBITION IN CHEMICALS: WHY AND HOW
E. DONALD ELLIOTT
AND JACQUES PELKMANS

> *Politics is the art of the possible.*
> Otto Von Bismarck (1867).

1.   Introduction and purpose

This chapter discusses the chemicals chapter of the Transatlantic Trade and Investment Partnership (TTIP), in particular the regulatory part. The flaw we see in US-EU chemical regulatory cooperation is that the focus has been far too much on the differences in procedures between the two regulatory systems rather than on what ultimately matters: the actual *level* of SHEC (safety, health, environment and consumer) protection provided for substances that are regulated by both the EU and the US. This flaw is still valid today in TTIP. The only difference is that the TTIP initiative is being sold as far more ambitious in terms of regulatory cooperation for the North Atlantic than ever before, and that it might also influence regulatory ambitions of other WTO partners. But this prospect seems not to apply to chemicals, which is precisely one motivation of the chapter. To date, the TTIP talks over chemicals have not been ambitious enough in our view and there is no chance whatsoever that a TTIP chemical regime will emerge as a shining example for the rest of the world. Within the confines of this chapter, we shall attempt to demonstrate that it is far more productive to focus on the identification of equivalent levels of protection against risky chemical substances than to harp on the 'systemic' divergences.

So far, the political and societal debates on the chemical aspects of TTIP have been neither productive nor constructive. They are stuck in stereotypes that are believed simply because certain forces keep on repeating them endlessly, rather than systematically scrutinising the various arguments. Outside industry (but in the present climate, industry suffers from a credibility problem, rightly or wrongly), few, if any, experts or independent analysts take the trouble to publish careful assessments and steer the public debate into fact-finding and constructive analyses. Assertions about a lowering of levels of protection are repeated, although such lowering was neither explicit nor implicit in the mandate; indeed, the opposite is found in writings and in numerous statements of the EU and by the negotiators on both sides. Discussions tend to be elusive or highly principled, complemented by plenty of accusations, misunderstandings, caricatures, recriminations or indeed outright suspicion. In such a political climate for the case of chemicals, the original ideas behind TTIP tend to be forgotten or dismissed without any search for the facts or for solid ideas. Such a style of 'debating' and the creation of a climate of profound suspicion, despite the distinct separation between the untouchable level(s) of protection and having a focus on the instruments (as indeed is done for other TTIP sectoral annexes), is not in keeping with the aim and spirit of TTIP. It cannot be in the EU and/or US public interest either.

The aim of our chapter is to introduce at least the beginnings of a fruitful factual analysis of what can and cannot be done in chemicals in TTIP and why. Our chapter will not deeply discuss the differences between the two systems, as this has been done before: this divergence is, for now, far too great. Nevertheless, the knowledge and understanding of how the US regulates chemicals are poor in Europe and therefore we do offer a concise 'primer' on it (see Box 13.1 in section 4). However, agreeing that 'the systems' are different is not the end of the story but precisely the beginning! Protecting citizens and workers against risky chemicals is less a matter of systems and much more, if not decisively, a matter of checking the protection in terms of results for each and every substance. When focusing on the level of protection against risky chemicals – and *not* on 'the systems' or their equivalence – we shall focus on two possibilities: one is TTIP action when, for individual substances, the level of protection is found to be equivalent in the US and EU, and the other is an opt-in choice for companies to the more stringent regime for substances that are regulated on both sides, automatically allowing access to the market with the less-stringent regime but at the price of following the more-restrictive standard in both markets. The EU and the US can act together in TTIP and in its living agreement in all cases where the level of protection is adequate, despite the systemic differences of how this came about. However, where equivalence of protection levels is found, it is far from easy to appreciate what *can* be done and requires innovative policy thinking. This is what our chapter attempts to do, in the spirit of TTIP as first formulated in the US-EU High Level Group (2013) and later in the TTIP mandates.

The structure of the chapter is as follows. We begin by querying whether the often-mentioned 'systemic' divergences in chemical regulation of the US and the EU are a justifiable reason to remain unambitious in TTIP. The present authors do not think so. Instead, the ultimate goals of chemical regulation should be the main focus of TTIP: where exactly are the levels of protection similar and where not, and when similar, can the trading costs, in particular duplications of many costly obligations, be addressed? In section 3 we observe that the TTIP chemicals discussions are modest, in sharp contrast with suggestions, at high transatlantic level, nearly two decades ago. Have all such efforts come to nothing at all? This is elaborated in section 4, recalling US-EU chemical regulatory cooperation since the mid-1990s. In the late 1990s, proposals were far more ambitious than even TTIP is today! It is no exaggeration to characterise the intervening period as an era of missed opportunities, whether selective harmonisation, carefully crafted mutual recognition or targeted equivalence agreements. Section 5 explains in some detail how modestly TTIP is now pursued in chemicals. Unfortunately, the information on the US position is scant, and no transparency has been provided so far. Therefore, we mainly rely on the EU positioning. The EU proposals, as published in November 2014, are summarised in Box 13.3. However, we have also inserted a Box 13.2 on the OECD's accomplishments in chemicals regulatory cooperation; this begs the question of how much more ambitious TTIP in chemicals really is. Some highly tentative discussion of the unspoken background to the proposals in Box 13.3 is provided as well.

This discussion is followed by two sections: one (section 6) about perceptions and criticism when contrasting the EU's Regulation on Registration, Evaluation, Authorisation and Restriction of Chemicals (REACH)) and the US Toxic Subtances Control Act (TSCA,) and section 7 about 'frozen' policy attitudes in Brussels and Washington, under the heading 'carved in stone'. A brief and inevitably incomplete discussion of the links with a global regime, so important now that the share of non-TTIP chemical production in the world is increasing steadily, is provided in section 8. It deals with potential positive spill-overs and US objections against REACH as the basis for a world regime. Our approach to eventually faciliate mutual market access between the US and the EU, highly tentative to be sure, is spelled out in section 9. As noted, it focuses on SHEC (safety, health, environment and consumer) objectives and functional equivalence of protection against risky substances, in areas where the level of legal regulation is similar or allowing companies to opt into abiding by the more stringent system everywhere. The latter can improve market access immediately, as an early harvest in TTIP, and is spelled out in section 10. The final section 11 concludes.

2.   Divergences in regulatory systems are not the right focus in TTIP

A quarter century ago, during the heyday of rational actor models derived from neo-classical economics, UC Berkeley political scientist and business professor David Vogel made a powerful prediction that trade negotiations would result in 'harmonising up'. By that term, he meant adopting the more stringent or precautionary environmental or consumer standards in order to obtain the efficiency gains that come from eliminating inconsistencies that impede trade for mutual gain.

> Trade liberalization is most likely to *strengthen* consumer and environmental protection when a group of nations has agreed to reduce the role of regulations as trade barriers and the most powerful among them has influential domestic constituencies that support stronger regulatory standards.[1]

As book goes to press, it seems highly unlikely that Vogel's prediction for 'harmonising up' will come to pass in the TTIP negotiations for chemicals. NGOs and mass publics on both sides of the Atlantic are concerned that TTIP will become an excuse for 'rolling back' regulatory protections.[2] Both negotiating parties seem wedded to

---

[1] See Vogel (2012, p. 8). In fairness, Vogel did include a number of caveats, including that there must be powerful support for the tougher standards in the domestic politics of the "most powerful" nation in the trade talks. Unlike NAFTA, which was the model uppermost in Vogel's mind, the EU-US negotiations are taking place between two relative equals in economic power.

[2] See Matthew Dalton, "TTIP Could Weaken Chemical Rules, Environmental Groups Say", Wall Street Journal Real Time Brussels Blog, 7 October 2014 (http://blogs.wsj.com/brussels/2014/10/07/ttip-could-weaken-chemical-rules-environmental-groups-say/). On both sides of the Atlantic, NGOs, often jointly, keep repeating these types of messages of doubt, if not suspicion. On 10 July 2014, no less than 111 (!!) NGOs – 30 of which were EU organisations and 78 US – wrote a letter to top TTIP negotiators Michael Froman and Karel De

sticking with their own systems for regulating the health and safety issues relating to chemical usage.

The goal of this chapter is to explain why the current negotiations seem unlikely to result in mutually-beneficial 'harmonising up', as suggested by Vogel's logic, and to recommend ways in which we can eventually achieve more North Atlantic regulatory cooperation in chemicals, in particular, by reducing the costs and instances of pointless duplication in the future. We consider several possible explanations for why the current negotiations did not set more ambitious goals for the chemicals sector, but in the final analysis, we conclude that the two sides cannot yet agree on what constitutes 'up': European governments, industry trade associations and the general public generally perceive their recently-enacted Regulation on registration, evaluation, authorisation and restriction of chemicals (REACH) as providing better protection than does the US system,[3] as also do some US academics and NGOs. US companies and negotiators, however, are loathe to adopt the REACH system, which they perceive as being overly 'precautionary' and unduly burdensome.[4] This problem of

---

Gucht, with an annex spelling out seven types of concerns. A return letter from Commissioner De Gucht dated 2 October 2014, firmly dismissed all seven concerns in clear terms. For reasons that are hard to understand, however, this clear rebuttal seems almost irrelevant for (at least) some NGOs, because statements of doubt and fear are still reiterated. Just one more recent example is BUND (2015). It would take a separate paper to try to understand this NGO's tendency to make long-rejected allegations on TTIP all the time. One wonders, for instance, whether European NGOs and some sceptical MEPs do not believe that the European Commission is capable of sticking to the levels of protection in the TTIP negotiations and would not be lured into 'issue linkages' or trade-offs on this question.

[3] Of course, it will be remembered that the enactment of the REACH Regulation late in 2006 took place amidst enormous controversy. Now that REACH is EU law, there seems little point in continuing the debate, but this does not mean that REACH is well accepted. What is accepted are the objectives of REACH, much less (or rejected) the high costs.

[4] As this book goes to press, long-pending legislation in the US Congress to adopt a somewhat more 'REACH-like' system of national chemical regulation has cleared some important hurdles but still faces others (Kollipara, 2015). TSCA Reform has been passed by the House, and it now seems that the US Senate may pass it in early August, and a merged version of the two (House and Senate bills) might well go to the US President for signature in September 2015. Even if TSCA reform is eventually enacted, it will take many years to be

divergent perceptions of the effectiveness of the other sides' regulatory system is not limited to chemicals. These perceptions (or misperceptions) are inverted for other sectors: some Americans perceive European regulation of automobiles as 'weaker' than theirs,[5] and they, like Europeans regarding chemicals, are so far unwilling to 'roll back' existing protections in order to strike a trade deal.

These perceptions are probably at least in part caricatures. The most amazing are the perceptions of some (mostly European) NGOs and indeed citizens (e.g. in social media and in advocacy activities) about how Americans seem to live with woefully inadequate protection against risky chemicals. The caricature amounts to the notion that Americans are swimming in a toxic soup of dangerous chemicals every day! Few if any in Europe appear to have second thoughts about such caricatures, as if American citizens and workers would easily accept such a predicament, as if liability would not undo this at least in part, as if many other laws than TSCA do not exist (which actually have the effect of regulating many substances). If it were so bad, have Americans (and especially workers) contracted many diseases associated with such unregulated risky chemicals to an extent not found[6] in Europe? The surprising fact remains that there is very little objective data that would allow a neutral observer to assess whether it is so bad in the US, or, more generally, which side is 'right'. In addition, the actual situation

---

implemented through regulations and enforcement and to gain credibility in Europe.

[5] See Brad Berman, "Lusting for Europe's Illegal 60-MPG Cars", 8 December 2008 (www.hybridcars.com/lusting-europe-illegal-high-mpg-cars-25323/).

[6] There are some instances where a substance, prohibited in the EU, may cause adverse health effects in the US, e.g. electronic devices with nickel in their cases, but is this product-specific or a general pattern? And are people actually being exposed to the nickel? Europe often regulates based on 'hazard', the presence of a potentially toxic substance, whereas the US tends to consider 'risk', which also weighs in the balance exposure and the seriousness of the harm. The seriousness of the adverse health effect might also be weighed in considering whether a ban or some other form of regulation such as a notice to susceptible populations makes sense. In the case of nickel in electronic devices, the main adverse health effect seems to be a skin rash in a small proportion of the population who are allergic to nickel. One proposed solution is to cover the nickel with a case or a lacquer to avoid skin contact (see Rita Arrup, "Electronic Devices and Nickel Allergic Reactions", Nickel Allergy Information News and Solutions, 14 July 2014 (www.nickelallergyinformation.com/2014/07/electronic_devices_and_nickel.htm).

may be a mixed bag, in which one side regulates more stringently in some areas, and the other more stringently in others. The fact is we just don't know, although this is rarely acknowledged. Most of the literature comparing the two regimes[7] is anecdotal and evidently not sufficient to persuade governments and their publics that the differences in actual outcomes are not as great as they are often perceived to be. That in itself is a puzzle: those who think the world is efficient would predict that both sides would invest in developing better information about how the two systems of chemicals regulation actually function so that they could make rational decisions for their mutual benefit.

That the two largest trading blocs are making important decisions about one of their largest market segments without good data about how chemicals regulation *actually* works (in terms of what is regulated and how well for SHEC protection) on the two sides of the Atlantic suggests there may well be something to a tradition older than rational actor models such as Vogel's. This alternative vision of how human beings behave emphasises the role of error and misperception, in addition to rational calculation in human affairs, and it is now experiencing a rebirth under the rubric 'behavioral law and economics'.[8] Its essence is aptly captured in former Israeli foreign minister Abba Eban's line: "History teaches us that men and nations behave wisely once they have exhausted all other alternatives."[9]

The assumption that people are often guided by errors and misperceptions[10] leads us to conclude that the negotiators on both sides of the Atlantic may not be unwise in setting modest goals after all. Greater harmonisation of chemical regulatory systems across the Atlantic may be premature. We may have to go through a period of mutual confidence-building to overcome the stereotypes and misperceptions that currently limit progress; in Abba Eban's words, we

---

[7] The best work comparing risk regulation in the US and the EU concludes there is actually very little difference, but one sector or another may be more 'precautionary' on one side or the other (see Renn & Elliott, 2011). Most of the literature comparing TSCA and REACH focuses on the procedural and systemic aspects, often with a view to reforming TSCA. Examples include GAO (2007) and Applegate (2008).

[8] See Thaler & Sunstein (2008).

[9] Speech delivered in London, 16 December 1970, as quoted in *The Times* [London], 17 December 1970 and in *Great Jewish Quotations* (1996) by Alfred J. Kolatch, p. 115 (http://en.wikiquote.org/wiki/Abba_Eban).

[10] See generally Kahneman (2011).

have to "exhaust all the other alternatives" before we can move to a more rational, more efficient system that would benefit both sides by eliminating needless duplication and inconsistency. The negotiators appear to be setting only modest goals to promote greater data-sharing and collaboration at the technical level. This might eventually lead both sides to greater convergence in regulatory outcomes and to increasing the perception that the actual substantive *results* of the two systems of chemical regulation in many areas are not that different, despite major differences in legal structure and procedure.

Our assessment of the current situation leads us to make two practical recommendations, which will be elaborated later in this chapter.

1) *Optional asymmetric harmonisation.* We recommend that the TTIP should include an optional process for 'harmonising up' by gradually voluntarily opting into what are perceived to be more stringent regulations on one side or the other. This would be achieved by maintaining an official list of regulations that are deemed to be more stringent by both sides and allowing companies to opt in to be governed by the concededly more stringent rules. This option would promote efficiency by eliminating duplication where the benefits of eliminating duplicative regulation are greater than the costs of over-compliance. Opting in to more stringent regulation where the costs of doing so are low also may begin a bottom-up process of creating de facto internationally harmonised regulations worldwide.

2) *Ongoing expert assessment of comparative effectiveness of regulation.* We also recommend that the TTIP should include a new institution for developing mutually credible assessments and data about the actual performance of chemicals regulation on both sides of the Atlantic. Future negotiators should not be working from the stereotypes and caricatures that currently define mutual misperceptions of the other's system of chemicals regulation. Joint panels of experts should be convened to assess and report on where actual regulatory outcomes differ and where they are either 'essentially equivalent' or at least good enough to protect the public as intended.

An interesting model for such an institution was recently provided by the automobile industry. The European Automobile Manufacturers' Association, the American Automotive Policy Council and the Alliance of Automobile Manufacturers together commissioned a recent study by two leading engineering think tanks, one American – the University of Michigan Transportation Research Institute – and one European – SAFER, a transportation research centre at Chalmers

University in Gothenburg, Sweden – to evaluate whether motor vehicles manufactured in compliance with EU and US regulatory requirements provide essentially equivalent real-world safety performance.[11] Although one might debate whether 'essential (or functional) equivalence', as opposed to 'adequate to protect the public',[12] is the right standard for evaluation, the model of neutral evaluation by experts on both sides of the Atlantic is a promising one. We recommend that something like this should be embodied in a permanent institution under TTIP, which would be mandated to carry out comparative studies of the effectiveness of regulation in the two trading partners and make consensus recommendations for areas where greater harmonisation would not reduce the practical level of protection on either side.[13]

3. Why did so much effort and prospective gains produce so little?

Why did so much effort produce so little convergence of regulatory systems is the over-riding question about the TTIP negotiations for the chemicals sector. In fact, a lot of effort in chemicals preceded the TTIP negotiations under the Transatlantic Market Place since 1996 and the

[11] See European Automobile Manufacturers' Association Press Release, "TTIP: Study examines EU & US vehicle safety equivalence", 21 May 2014 (www.acea.be/press-releases/article/ttip-study-examines-eu-us-vehicle-safety-equivalence). The results of this highly technical study were not yet available when the present book went to press. However, the European Commission published two practical examples of testing for equivalence, one on seat belt anchorages and one on lighting and vision standards, both of which were found functionally equivalent, despite diverging technical requirements. See http://trade.ec.europa.eu/doclib/docs/2015/january/tradoc_153023.pdf and
http://trade.ec.europa.eu/doclib/docs/2015/february/tradoc_153168.pdf

[12] See US Administrative Conference Recommendation 2011-6 on International Regulatory Cooperation, Paragraph 4, adopted 8 December 2011: "To deploy limited resources more effectively, agencies should, where appropriate and practicable, identify foreign authorities that maintain high quality and effective standards and practices and identify areas in which the tests, inspections, or certifications by agencies and such foreign agencies overlap." (www.acus.gov/recommendation/international-regulatory-cooperation)

[13] For an analysis of the political economy of recommendations by expert consensus bodies, and why they are often adopted by politicians without controversy, see Elliott (2008).

proposals of the Transatlantic Business Dialogue (TABD). As we shall remind the reader, the common chemical TABD proposals of one and a half decades ago were much bolder than what is on the table in TTIP. In chemicals, TTIP as it stands today, is anything but bold. Although the terms of a final agreement are still to be agreed, the negotiators (particularly those for the EU) have taken pains in public statements to reassure an anxious public and NGO community that "joint chemicals regulation is absolutely off the table".[14] As reported in ENDS Europe DAILY, "both [US chief negotiator Dan] Mullaney and the EU's [chief negotiator Ignacio] Garcia Bercero emphasised that they are not considering 'harmonising or mutually recognising' the two regulatory systems."[15] Of course, some two decades ago, REACH did not exist. One can argue with some justification that the emergence of REACH itself has killed the ambitious proposals emerging from the TABD. However (as far as we know), no alternative approaches have been suggested by the negotiators to reduce significantly technical barriers to trade (TBTs) in chemicals trade, without reducing SI IEC -protection on either side. Looking at the EU negotiation position on chemicals,[16] the proposals are modest and will hardly address the high costs of TBTs in the sector.

And it is lowering TBTs that is the prime economic justification of TTIP. The present chapter is not the right place to elaborate on TBTs in chemicals trade. The most respectable study on the overall costs of TBTs and their partial removal under TTIP is Francois et al. (2013) for the Commission's Impact Assessment. A non-technical assessment of the study and alternatives can be found in Pelkmans et al. (2014) for the European Parliament. The simulations by Francois et al. are the only ones with specific sectoral TBT estimates: for chemicals, TBT costs of EU exports to the US amount to 19.1%; for US exports to the EU, some 13.6%. These compare with chemical tariffs in the 3%-6% range, with quite a few actually being zero. This is not to suggest that these TBT estimates are rock-solid – it is exceedingly difficult to come to such estimates (which is why sectoral TBT estimates are so very rare). Moreover, in discussions with the chemicals industry, it was indicated that TBTs due to regulatory (systems) divergence are costly, no doubt,

---

[14] "Shared Chemicals Assessment on TTIP Table", ENDS Europe DAILY, 3 October 2014.

[15] Ibid.

[16] See the EU's position on chemicals on the European Commission's website (http://trade.ec.europa.eu/doclib/docs/2014/may/tradoc_152468.pdf).

and should be reduced significantly, but these fairly high costs are not seen as a true trade barrier by the larger chemicals firms, only by the many SMEs. Still, going by the best study available (Francois et al., 2013), a halving of the TBT costs in chemicals would give a boost in mutual exports of respectively €29.9 billion (36%) for the EU and €27.3 billion (34%) for the US, which are impressive statistics by any account. It ought to be noted that these effects incorporate general equilibrium effects (e.g. also of other TTIP sectors and their relations with the chemical industry) and, moreover, are calculated on the assumption of positive spill-overs to third countries.[17] However, if SMEs would find it feasible, once TTIP would have reduced TBTs significantly, to enter transatlantic trade, the economic effects would become larger still. This SME effect cannot be modelled in CGE approaches. Thus, the case for tackling TBTs in chemicals in TTIP is powerful.

This is not to say, however, that a TTIP agreement on chemicals, without lowering TBTs significantly at first, would be unimportant. An agreement, if one is eventually reached, will undoubtedly result in progress towards reducing certain trade barriers, including the elimination of (relatively low) tariffs on chemicals, as well as increased collaboration at the scientific and technical level and probably also to greater standardisation of testing methods, labelling and sharing of datasets. According to reports in the trade press, "EU and US negotiators are examining how regulators can share the work of assessing priority chemicals as part of the TTIP trade deal ...."[18] These could lead to substantial accomplishments. Moreover, eliminating tariffs alone is estimated to save €1.5 billion annually,[19] and this tariff-cutting would also avoid distorting trade by deterring transactions that

---

[17] A spill-over of 20% has been assumed. This also has a positive effect on EU and US exports of chemicals to the rest of the world, up by some 9%. It is also good to re-emphasise that TBTs have nothing to do with SHEC objectives (or, the 'level of protection'). TTIP discussions painfully demonstrate that many commentators are hardly or not at all aware of the WTO TBT agreement, which assumes SHEC objectives of national governments as given. It is all about instruments or red tape or avoidable duplications of tests, etc.

[18] ENDS Europe DAILY (3 October 2014). See also Box 13.2.

[19] "US-EU trade pact can cut import duties on €48 billion in chemical trade: Cefic", *Platts*, 18 June 2013 (www.platts.com/latest-news/petrochemicals/london/us-eu-trade-pact-can-cut-import-duties-on-eur48-26030822).

might otherwise occur in their absence.[20] Greater collaboration and familiarity at the scientific level may eventually lead to building greater confidence in one another's regulatory approaches and that in turn could lead to further progress to reduce regulatory differences.[21]

4. Two decades lost? Missed opportunities for harmonisation?

Proponents of regulatory convergence in the chemical sector had higher hopes[22] when the US and the EU announced that chemicals regulation would be a focus of the TTIP negotiations. TTIP came on the heels of nearly two decades of attempts to reduce the costs of mutual market access in chemicals through the Transatlantic Business Dialogue, as well as increased regulatory cooperation between the European Commission and the US Environmental Protection Agency,[23] and also broad-based efforts to harmonise chemical regulatory systems in developed countries more generally through the OECD.[24] The rationale behind all these efforts to reduce regulatory divergences was

---

[20] One study (Erixon & Bauer, 2010) estimates that eliminating tariffs on all products would boost EU exports by 7% and US exports by 8%. See also the comments of E.I. du Pont de Nemours and Company (2013): "Elimination of the remaining import duties on chemicals, currently averaging between 3-6%, would result in considerable savings to our company and remove many economic barriers to shipping technical and chemical intermediates.". Francois et al. (2013) estimate that tariff removal only would boost EU chemical exports to the US by 5.4%; for US exports, it is no less than 12.4% (again, under the assumption of a 20% spill-over to 3rd countries).

[21] Remarks of Jim Jones, Acting Assistant Administrator for the Office of Chemicals Safety and Pollution Prevention, US Environmental Protection Agency, "Towards a Transatlantic Market for Trade in Chemicals", 17 July 2013, Washington, D.C.

[22] See remarks e.g. of Stuart E. Eizenstat (2013) in E!Sharp: "In fact, we should have confidence in the 21st century that the regulatory standards in both the EU and US are adequate to protect our publics and should be accepted, ... Mutual recognition is a sounder basis for regulatory cooperation than actual harmonization."

[23] For summaries of these precursors, see Quick (2007) and Shaffer & Pollack (2005, pp. 220-221).

[24] For example, see Box 13.1 and OECD Guidelines for the Testing of Chemicals (www.oecd.org/env/ehs/testing/oecdguidelinesforthetestingofchemicals.htm).

succinctly summarised in a 2008 Congressional Research Service (CRS) report to the US Congress:

> Since the mid-1990s, both US and European multinational companies have viewed divergent ways of regulating markets for both goods and services as the most serious barriers to transatlantic commerce. The primary reason why these companies seek to achieve greater harmonization in standards and regulatory procedures is to reduce costs imposed by complying with two different sets of regulations and standards.[25]

The CRS report went on to opine: "Redundant standards, testing, and certification procedures are seen by [multinational] companies as far more costly and harmful than any trade barriers imposed at the border, such as tariffs or quotas" and that "[i]n no area has [regulatory divergence] been a greater problem than in chemicals".[26]

Hopes for progress on regulatory convergence received a boost in May 2012, when President Obama signed Executive Order 13609, Promoting International Regulatory Cooperation,[27] which declared the following as official US policy:

> In some cases, the differences between the regulatory approaches of US agencies and those of their foreign counterparts might not be necessary and might impair the ability of American businesses to export and compete internationally. In meeting shared challenges involving health, safety, labor, security, environmental, and other issues, international regulatory cooperation can identify approaches that are at least as protective as those that are or would be adopted in the absence of such cooperation. International regulatory cooperation can also reduce, eliminate, or prevent unnecessary differences in regulatory requirements.[28]

---

[25] Raymond J. Ahearn, "Transatlantic Regulatory Cooperation and Analysis: Background and Analysis", Congressional Research Service Report for Congress, 22 October 2008 (http://fpc.state.gov/documents/organization/112019.pdf).

[26] Ibid., pp. 2-3. This is consistent with the economic study conducted by Francois et al. (2013) for the Commission's Impact Assessment of TTIP, finding that the costs of chemical TBTs are the second-highest (after automotive).

[27] www.gpo.gov/fdsys/pkg/DCPD-201200327/pdf/DCPD-201200327.pdf

[28] Executive Order 13609, §1.

Nevertheless, it is useful to recall that chemical regulatory cooperation was agreed to be reinforced following the New Transatlantic Marketplace in Madrid in 1995. As the survey by Quick (2007) describes in painstaking detail, *joint* US-EU business proposals by TABD were made, some of which were innovative. One might even call them bold! Without rehearsing the history in all its aspects, already in 1996 in Chicago, proposals were launched to follow up the OECD GLP and MAD agreements (see Box 13.2 in section 5) and negotiate Conditional Equivalence Agreements in a) risk assessment, b) notification of new chemicals, c) application and use and d) classification and labelling. Interestingly, the end point would be 'unconditional equivalence agreements' by 2000! Knowing that harmonisation was pointless, the TABD made a strong plea for forms of mutual recognition or acceptance as feasible alternatives. For instance, enhancing understanding and acceptance of methods used for hazard assessment and risk assessment was seen as a priority; exceptions for low-risk chemicals, polymers and R&D chemicals were favoured when registering new chemicals substances (to be fair, these suggestions were later echoed in REACH to some degree). For new polymers, an equivalence agreement (like mutual recognition) was proposed: once allowed to be sold in the US (EU), it could also be marketed in the EU (US). But Quick (2007, p. 255), complains that the "biggest obstacle to progress is the lack of understanding among the authorities concerning the other regulatory system". And, not to forget, REACH was in the early preparatory stages, which undoubtedly widened systemic divergence.[29]

While misunderstanding of one another's systems is certainly an important factor, we also suggest an additional reason: the perception by key players that Atlantic regulatory cooperation is but an interim step towards developing chemical regulatory systems worldwide. Since REACH was proposed in 2003, if not before with the Chemicals White Paper in 2001 proposing the precautionary principle, Atlantic regulatory cooperation was throttled, if not in coma (except for very specific practical issues, case by case). Staking out positions for this larger game of defining the rules for trade in chemicals worldwide was more important to participants on both sides than the immediate gains that could be made by reducing differences in regulatory systems between the US and the EU.

---

[29] See Pelkmans (2005).

However, other factors also contributed to the failure of chemical regulatory cooperation between the EU and the US, including the politics of chemical regulation. As a practical, political matter in the current environment, making changes to REACH in Europe would have been extremely difficult and reform of TSCA has long been stalled in Congress. As this book goes to press, there is renewed hope that a bipartisan compromise may finally be reached in Congress to overhaul the outdated US Toxic Substances Control Act (TSCA), first enacted in 1976 and not significantly amended in the ensuing 40 years. However, from the EU end, the proposed changes are regarded as incremental: easier to regulate 'restrictions' but no comprehensive requirement for 'registration' (testing) of all chemicals before bringing them to the market [30] and no 'authorisations' regime for SVHCs on a company basis, and hence, only a little bit more 'REACH-like'.[31]

There is a broad consensus in Europe and among academics in the United States that Section 6 of TSCA, which gives EPA authority to regulate chemicals analogous to 'restriction' under REACH, is currently ineffective. However, it is not always appreciated, particularly in Europe, that TSCA Section 6 is by its terms *only one* tool available to the federal and state governments in the US to regulate chemicals; indeed, by law EPA is supposed to regulate under (many) other statutes than TSCA if it can. [32] Thus, the TSCA-REACH

---

[30] This should not be misread: for new chemicals, a PMN (= pre-manufacture notification) is required, but testing is not necessarily comprehensive (and not standardised a priori, as in REACH), dependingt e.g. on whether the substance is very similar to other ones known to be safe. Around one-third of the chemicals, for which a PMN is submitted, are *not* approved. For existing chemicals, no registration or testing is required and the burden of proof is on the EPA; here, the gap with REACH is wide.

[31] See Kollipara (2015).

[32] TSCA Sec 6, which is similar to 'restrictions' under REACH, only applies if the EPA lacks authority to address the risk under another statute. This limitation is explicit in the statutory language:

If the Administrator [of EPA] determines that a risk of injury to health or the environment could be eliminated or reduced to a sufficient extent by actions taken under another Federal law (or laws) administered in whole or in part by the Administrator, the Administrator may not promulgate a rule under subsection (a) to protect against such risk of injury unless the Administrator finds, in the Administrator's discretion, that it is in the public interest to protect against such risk under this Act. In making such a finding the Administrator shall consider (i) all relevant aspects of the risk, as determined by the

comparison is far from a complete comparison of the effectiveness of chemical regulation as a whole. For this reason, Box 13.1 provides a primer on how the US regulates chemicals, as this seems too little known in Europe, and perhaps even in the US.

Box 13.1 A primer on how the US regulates chemicals

The US system for regulating chemical exposures is much more complex and multi-faceted than the one followed in Europe. This complexity is not necessarily desirable but instead reflects aspects of the US constitutional system and the incentives for US politicians to pass new laws for which they can claim credit rather than to amend or codify old ones.[33] In addition, US legal culture and traditions are more skeptical of government, resulting in the construction of multiple, redundant programmes.[34] The multiplicity of US laws and institutions does mean, however, that a simple-minded comparison between TSCA and REACH is misleading. TSCA is merely a last line of defence; by law, TSCA Section 6 authority can only be used if regulation under another statute would not be effective.[35]

Administrator in the Administrator's discretion, (ii) a comparison of the estimated costs of complying with actions taken under this Act and under such law (or laws), and (iii) the relative efficiency of actions under this Act and under such law (or laws) to protect against such risk of injury.
15 USC. §2605(c), http://www.law.cornell.edu/uscode/text/15/2605

The EPA has generally found that addressing particular uses of a substance, e.g. in pesticides, foods, consumer products or releases to water, etc., is more effective than addressing it across the board under TSCA.

[33] For an account of 'competitive credit claiming' by politicians in creating US environmental laws, see Elliott, Ackerman & Millian (1985).

[34] This fundamental difference between the prevailing legal strategies in Europe and the US was noted by the sagacious European observer Walter Bagehot (1901) over a century ago: "The English constitution, in a word, is framed on the principle of choosing a single sovereign authority, and making it good; the American, upon the principle of having many sovereign authorities, and hoping that their multitude will atone for their inferiority."

[35] TSCA Sec 6, which is somewhat similar to banning or 'restriction' for particular uses under REACH, only applies if EPA lacks authority to address the risk under another statute. This limitation is explicit in the statutory language. If the Administrator [of EPA] determines that a risk of injury to health or the environment could be eliminated or reduced to a sufficient extent by actions taken under another Federal law (or laws) administered in whole or in part by the Administrator, the Administrator may not promulgate a rule

Numerous other statutory authorities and common law principles would have to be considered in order to assess the overall effectiveness of chemical regulation in the US versus Europe, and so far as we are aware, this has never been done.[36] For example, the standard West Publishing Company pamphlet of *Federal Environmental Statutes* lists 59 federal environmental laws alphabetically from the Acid Precipitation Act of 1980 through the Wood Residue Utilization Act of 1980, running to a total of 1,842 pages of small, 10-point type. About half of them apply to chemicals in various contexts. Add to these the administrative regulations in the *Code of Federal Regulations* (CFR) which are much more voluminous and detailed than the statutes themselves and the laws of the 50 states, which are generally allowed to add legal restrictions in addition to the federal ones in most fields.[37] And in addition, there are many other federal laws that regulate chemicals in various contexts that Americans do not consider 'environmental'. For example, the Occupational Safety and Health Act (OSHA)[38] regulates permissible exposure limits (PELs) for several hundred chemicals in the workplace.[39] Under the Federal Food Drug and Cosmetic Act, the Food and Drug Administration (FDA) has promulgated several short lists of chemical additives that are permitted for use in cosmetics, medicines and foods but bans all others unless they obtain special approval on a

---

under subsection a) to protect against such risk of injury unless the Administrator finds, in the Administrator's discretion, that it is in the public interest to protect against such risk under this Act. In making such a finding the Administrator shall consider: i) all relevant aspects of the risk, as determined by the Administrator in the Administrator's discretion, ii) a comparison of the estimated costs of complying with actions taken under this Act and under such law (or laws) and iii) the relative efficiency of actions under this Act and under such law (or laws) to protect against such risk of injury. See 15 C. §2605(c) www.law.cornell.edu/uscode/text/15/2605 and www.law.cornell.edu/uscode/text/42/7416.

[36] In the 1990s, one of the co-authors published a 97-page chapter in a treatise merely cataloguing the various federal environmental laws affecting the chemical industry, but did not purport to assess their effectiveness (see Elliott & Thomas, 1993).

[37] See e.g. Clean Air Act, §116, 42 U.S.C. §7416.

[38] 29 U.S.C. ch. 15 § 651 et seq.

[39] See 29 CFR 1910.1000, Tables Z-1, Z-2 and Z-3 (www.osha.gov/pls/oshaweb/owadisp.show_document?p_table=STANDARDS&p_id=9992).

case-by-case basis based on test data.[40] The Consumer Product Safety Act (CPSA) regulates toxics in articles to which consumers may be exposed such as toys.[41]

Thus, the frequently quoted nostrum that REACH regulates 'articles' but TSCA does not, while literally true, is inherently misleading; TSCA does not regulate chemical usage in articles, but another federal statute does. Finally, one should not forget that the US is a common-law country. One of the reasons that TSCA has not been amended in 40 years is that many adaptations have been accomplished by judicial and administrative interpretation and practice, without ever codifying them in changes of the statute. Thus, the 'endangered species act' was converted from a statute protecting individual animals into one that protects biodiversity and critical habitat, without ever modifying the words of the statute. A somewhat analoguous example of adaptation by administrative interpretation is the EPA's standard 'consent decree' for new chemicals (which comes closer to specific 'authorisation' under REACH) that a company agrees to restrict production, distribution and disposal of a new – presumably risky - substance until more knowledge becomes available.[42] Its application is quite different from what the statute's drafters originally contemplated.

Yet another very different example is POPs (Persistent Organic Pollutants), which are chemical substances that persist in the environment, bioaccumulate through the food web and pose a risk of causing adverse effects to human health and the environment. Although the US signed, but never ratified, the Stockholm Convention, POPs are forbidden in the US in domestic legislation. In summary, the legal systems in the US and Europe are very different in their structure, which makes comprehensive comparisons difficult, but one thing is sure: counting the number of chemicals banned under REACH versus the number banned under TSCA is not an accurate measure of their differences.

---

[40] 21 CFR Parts 73, 74, 81 and 82 (www.fda.gov/ForIndustry/ColorAdditives/ColorAdditiveInventories/ucm115641.htm).

[41] See Ed Loewenton, "CPSC Toughens Lead Regulations in Toys", 28 October 2008, describing provisions of the US Consumer Product Safety Improvement Act of 2008, §101 (http://turnertoys.com/CPSC-Toughens-Lead-Regulations-in-Toys.html).

[42] See Renn & Elliott (2011, p. 237) describing "EPA's standard consent decree [under TSCA §5], which allows limited production and use of substances in specified uses with limited potential to cause harm while further information is developed".

One paper found that only a few substances had been regulated under TSCA, but conceded that at least 1,134 chemicals had been regulated under other US statutes as of 2011 (Schwarzman & Wilson, 2011, p. 109, Table 5.1). These statistics are old,[43] however, and do not even include de facto restrictive or chilling effects caused by tough US liability cases or voluntary withdrawals under EPA pressure. Schwarzman and Wilson went on to declare TSCA's ineffectiveness had created a 'data gap' and a 'safety gap' between the US and Europe. It is easy to count how many substances have been regulated under TSCA. It is much more difficult to assess the overall effectiveness of the US chemical control programme[44] and incentives created by common-law liability cases (see Box 13.1). In other words, there seems to be no ready, comprehensive and accessible information about the extent and level of protection against risky chemicals in the US, a remarkable circumstance to say the least.

There is very little literature comparing the actual breadth and stringency of regulation of chemicals in the US versus Europe on a systematic basis. There is, however, a widespread perception that REACH is more effective than TSCA and even if Congress ultimately does strengthen TSCA, it will require many years of implementation to build confidence in Europe that US regulation of chemicals is comparable to that in Europe.

The perceived differences between the effectiveness of regulation under TSCA and REACH may have been uppermost in the minds of the industry and the negotiators when drafting TTIP negotiation positions and we do not wish to be misperceived as discounting the importance of this factor. But in the long run, describing the politics of chemical regulation in the US and the EU at a particular point in time is less important than understanding the

---

[43] Note that Table 5.1 is based on rather old evidence by Dernbach (1997).

[44] Schwarzman & Wilson (2011) mention five such statutes: Clean Water Act, Resource Conservation and Recovery Act, Clean Air Act, Occupational Health and Safety Act and the Toxics Release Inventory of the Community Right-to-Know Act. As noted in Box 13.1, this is a painfully incomplete view of chemical protection in the US. At the same time, both the EU and the US have a lot of product-specific regulation of chemicals; in other words, also for the EU, there is much more than REACH (e.g. hazardous chemicals in electronic goods, end-of-life-vehicles, POPs, toys, food contact materials, etc.) A survey of 155 pieces of EU legislation, outside REACH, which may affect chemicals is in Milieu (2012).

dynamics of bilateral trade negotiations in the new era of globalisation of trade, and it is on that larger lesson that we focus.

5.   Setting modest goals for TTIP

5.1   The joint position of the chemical industry and EU suggestions

Despite high hopes for greater regulatory convergence in the run-up to TTIP, substantive changes to the divergent regulatory systems for regulating chemicals on the two sides of the Atlantic were taken off the table even before the TTIP talks began, according to the position of the European negotiators that were leaked early in the process:

> Industry associations, civil society and governments are aware that neither full harmonisation nor mutual recognition seems feasible on the basis of the existing framework legislations in the US and EU: REACH (Regulation (EC) 1907/2006) and TSCA (Toxic Substances Control Act) are too different with regard to some fundamental principles.
>
> The recently completed REACH Review concluded that REACH should not be amended, while in the US a bipartisan proposal to amend TSCA has been introduced into Congress in May 2013.
>
> However, the draft TSCA reform legislation does not foresee any general registration obligation for substances as a condition for their marketing (a fundamental requirement under REACH), nor elements comparable to authorisation, while it would give the EPA (Environmental Protection Agency) new and easier possibilities to conduct chemical assessments and adopt risk management measures such as restrictions.[45]

This positioning rings true because, remarkably, the trade associations representing the chemicals industry on both sides of the Atlantic proposed a limited (joint) agenda that did not include making progress towards reducing non-tariff trade barriers in the form of duplicative regulatory reviews. A joint paper drafted by the European Chemical Industry Council (CEFIC), "with the cooperation of ACC," the American Chemistry Council representing the US chemical

---

[45] These quotations are literally found in the EU's position on chemicals, published a little later on the European Commission's website (http://trade.ec.europa.eu/doclib/docs/2014/may/tradoc_152468.pdf).

industry, outlined very limited "joint ACC-CEFIC proposals for enhanced cooperation in chemicals":

- Common prioritisation principles and burden-sharing for assessments of high-priority chemicals and, where appropriate, categories of substances (e.g. substance evaluation under REACH and high-priority targeted risk assessments under the current TSCA and safety determinations under a modernised TSCA).

- Recognition of each other's data and studies and harmonised standards and methodologies for hazard and risk assessment are necessary for effective burden-sharing.[46]

The chemical industry's joint position was that:

> Closer cooperation on prioritisation of substances for further assessment would lead to cost reductions for both authorities and companies by creating opportunities for burden-sharing. That would also contribute to narrowing the difference in outcomes of assessments by fostering coherence and building confidence in each other's assessments. *In the long run that could also result in greater coherence in regulatory outcomes including down-stream legislation which would further reduce regulatory divergence.*[47]

Box 13.2 OECD accomplishments in chemicals regulatory cooperation

The OECD is usually regarded as fostering policy research in many domains, ensuring the quality of statistical series and economic studies in many fields and stimulating a wide range of cooperative and exchange activities amongst policy-makers. But it is not typically referred to as an agenda-setter or rule-maker. Yet, that is exactly what it has accomplished in chemicals, after decades of low-key technical work. Interestingly, the US and the EU have been leading in this work. When discussing regulatory convergence in chemicals over the North Atlantic, and even more so when suggesting that a gradual move to a common minimum of world regulatory requirements and methods in chemical risk management is so important for the EU and the US, one should first

---

[46] See CEFIC's response to the European Commission's request for further details on joint ACC-CEFIC proposals for enhanced cooperation on chemicals under TTIP, 7 March 2014 (www.cefic.org/Documents/PolicyCentre/TTIP/%5bTTIP%5d%20Cefic%20response%20to%20Commission%20ACC-efic%20proposal%20on%20TTIP%207%20March%202014%20(web%20and%20click-in).pdf).

[47] Ibid. (emphasis supplied).

be aware of the achievements by the OECD. Alternatively, when assessing the current ideas of the negotiators in TTIP or, for that matter, of the chemical industry in their joint paper, the accomplishments of the OECD so far prompt the query: What value-added can the TTIP proposals really bring beyond the results of the OECD, quite apart from other – indeed higher - ambitions on chemical cooperation?

The OECD has generated three significant accomplishments. The most important one is the MAD system (MAD = Mutual Acceptance of Data). This is a *binding* agreement for member states based on an OECD Council Act from 1981.* The obligation is to accept chemical safety data from other OECD countries, plus seven other signatories (e.g. India, Brazil, South Africa, Singapore), if and only if these data have been generated using OECD Test Guidelines and OECD Good Laboratory Practices (GLP). The objectives of the MAD system is i) to save resources by avoiding duplication, ii) reduce NTBs, iii) reduce animal testing by acceptance of earlier testing and iv) arrive at a level-playing field for industry in if not beyond the OECD. The second accomplishment consists of agenda-setting for and follow-up actions in four types of OECD activity, all building on MAD: burden-sharing between countries on actual assessments of chemicals, such as the evaluation of safety of high-production-volume (HPV) chemicals; harmonisation of industry dossiers for chemicals and review reports for pesticides; exchanging technical and policy information; and outreach to non-OECD countries, crucial as the weight of chemical output in non-OECD countries rapidly increases. For instance, the 'guidance documents' for industry dossiers and reviews for pesticides (sometimes called a 'monograph') formulated ever since 1998 can be found in areas such as biocides, chemical accidents, regulatory oversight of biotech, safety of novel food and feed, and manufactured nanomaterials.

----

* There are two other OECD Council texts relevant for MAD. One is a Recommendation in 1989 on a range of practical implementation and enforcement issues of GLP. The other is a Decision of 1997 providing a step-wise procedure for allowing non-OECD countries to take part.
Source: Sigman (2013).

Conspicuous by its absence from the chemical industry's 'wish list' is any mention of regulatory convergence or recognition of regulatory outcomes on either side. On the contrary, according to the chemical industry's joint position, reducing regulatory divergence will have to await downstream legislation, because of differences in current legislation. The joint paper continues:

REACH and TSCA are very different with regard to prioritisation of substances for assessment and further risk management actions. Whilst TSCA applies risk-based prioritisation, REACH includes prioritisation based on production volume or hazard and, in several procedures, risk.

There are also substantial differences at later stages of the regulatory process, including 'authorisation' and whether government or the industry has the burden of producing safety information. It is interesting, and perhaps significant, however, that the joint industry paper emphasises the differences in the front end of the process, setting priorities. One even wonders how far beyond the useful but modest OECD chemical programme can TTIP move, with such a timid mandate (see Box 13.3). With the UN GHS being partly adopted inside the US (e.g. by OSHA) and the OECD programme working more or less reasonably well, should TTIP not go far beyond the mild aspirations of these intergovernmental organisations?

Box 13.3 Edging towards a draft text of the chemicals annex, EU suggestions

Following the EU position on chemicals (May 2014), the Commission published two so-called 'non-papers' in November 2014. In May 2014, it proposed 'enhanced cooperation' in four areas: i) prioritisation of chemicals for assessment and assessment methodologies; ii) promoting alignment in classification and labelling of chemicals, i.e. a full implementation of GHS in the US, which is a binding obligation – although without sanctions; iii) new and emerging issues, e.g. endocrine disruptors and nanomaterials; and iv) enhanced information-sharing, while protecting CBI (confidential business information). All these are useful but low-key approaches (in the words of the Commission, they "seek opportunities for cooperation exclusively in specific areas which do not require or imply any change in the regulatory systems of each side"). However, when no change in the systems and/or objectives is implied, one can do so much more to lower TBT costs. One 'non-paper' (http://trade.ec.europa.eu/doclib/docs/2014/november/tradoc_1529 12.pdf) is a first outline of how the Annex on chemicals in TTIP would look like. It repeats most of what is in the Position Paper, but adds a series of objectives, which do include (for the 'living agreement', one supposes) i) to "avoid unnecessary duplicative requirements" and ii) "to identify and implement actions that can lead to reduction of unnecessary costs to transatlantic trade". Thus, in the longer run, a reduction of TBTs remains possible within the living agreement of TTIP.

Also, a Chemicals Working Group would be established, consisting of regulators. The second 'non-paper' (http://trade.ec.europa.eu/doclib/docs/2014/november/tradoc_1529 13.pdf) provides considerable practical detail on six areas of cooperation and how the US (usually, EPA) would be involved, step by step, in notice & comments and information (with an explicit call on the US to draft a similar non-paper for three of the six areas). These areas are: prioritisation of chemicals, i.e. updates of CoRAP under REACH, process for harmonised classification and labelling (which is already a UN standard, called GHS, but implemented in the US only by OSHA, so far; call on the US to develop a similar scheme for their NTP activities), nomination of SVHCs (very risky chemicals) for the candidate list of authorisation, prioritisation of SVHCs to be moved from candidate list to authorisation (Annex XIV REACH), involving the US when a restriction proposal (by ECHA or a member state) is listed in the Registry of Intent, and finally when companies (or consortia) submit applications for authorisation (e.g. link with alternatives based on EPA's Design for Environment Program).

These options cannot be belittled: no less than 22 different steps involving the US are identified for the six areas, implying numerous consultations, exchanges, comments and follow-ups between US and EU regulators. However, in TTIP one would assume the US to offer similar options, which would perhaps double the number of optional or obligatory interchanges between the two authorities. Where SHEC objectives are not that different over the North Atlantic, one should expect that quite often convergence or similar outcomes might finally be found. Although all this does not amount to a direct assault on TBTs, it is essential for building trust.

5.2 Backtracking by the European Parliament: 'Angst' or a sound case?

In July 2015 and without referring to the detailed proposals in Box 13.3, the European Parliament adopted a TTIP resolution which seems to turn against, or at least minimises, the chemicals negotiations in TTIP. The rationale of the negative attitude on chemicals is problematic. For this reason, we offer some further considerations on the hesitations of some European political actors. These considerations, however, are only partially based on public documents, as some actors are careful not to go public with their views. Therefore, the authors have weighed the drawbacks of relying on informal information obtained from various discussions in the US and EU policy circuits, against the benefits for the readers of additional insights about the implications of these positions or interests. We have decided that the insights matter more, but the reader should judge.

A good deal of the nervousness or mistrust amongst some EU member state governments as well as some political forces in Europe, not to speak of some NGOs, is caused by the conviction that the US is suspected to have (hidden) hopes to be able to soften REACH or, seen as more likely, exercise 'regulatory chill' in the TTIP living agreement in subtle ways for future issues. This conviction may be right or wrong – there is no way of verifying[48] – but it is prompting a fairly defensive stance by the Greens and others in the EP, but also by some EU national governments (including, apparently, Germany). Asserting that, in future, TTIP might lead to 'regulatory chill' is a very poor 'argument'; in fact, it is not really an argument at all, it is a conviction driven by mistrust. In numerous trade and regulatory negotiations, all kinds of suspicions might be uttered, but should that be a reason not to negotiate?

More logically, the fear might be a reason to carefully draft agreements and rules, presumably. Moreover, what is 'regulatory chill' actually? Regulation has to be based on scientific risk assessment and subsequently solid impact assessment, as the Guidelines of the Commission help to do. If, and only if, risk assessment is not fully possible, as science cannot (yet) establish risks with acceptable degrees of probabilities, is there a choice of opting for the application of the precautionary principle. Is 'regulatory chill' meant to refer to TTIP possibly limiting the freedom to exercise this choice? Or is it a concern that joint work on the science might eventually persuade Europeans that their present approach is overly precautionary? But that is exactly what has to be specified in both horizontal and sectoral TTIP regulatory cooperation. Why would that be different for chemicals to such a degree that the EP should be so negative about it?

The present authors have difficulty understanding the logic of this defensive stance. Even if 'regulatory chill' might be regarded as a possibility, why would that be a problem for EU negotiators in TTIP now, or, later, in the living agreement? If US suggestions would be made having this effect, they would simply be dismissed and this is not

---

[48] US negotiators or involved officials have been tightlipped and no detailed documents, let alone proposals or positions, have been published by US Trade Representative.

new. Discussions with the US on REACH have been conducted for a decade or longer, in Brussels, Washington and indeed in Geneva (WTO) as well. Why would the Commission suddenly be incapable of properly pursuing a well-defined EU mandate or its specific manifestations? Can it be traced back to a simmering tension or distrust between those (more?) preoccupied with environmental and health matters and those primarily working on chemicals with industry and other chemicals found downstream in value-chains? The 'angst' for regulatory chill is found frequently amongst advocacy groups in Europe – it is a most convenient plank on which to campaign but it is purely assertive. It seems to reflect a sentiment that EU regulators and negotiators are too 'malleable' due to business pressures or simply soft negotiators. Given the record of the EU in many FTAs and in EU trade policy more generally, as well as in the international debate on REACH (including with the US), there is no rationale whatsoever to support this defensiveness.

Nevertheless, the European Parliament has, in its TTIP resolution of 8 July 2015,[49] stipulated that negotiators, when it comes to regulatory cooperation, should "recognise that, where the EU and the US have very different rules, there will be no agreement, such as on ... REACH and its implementation ... and therefore not to negotiate on these issues". The possible problem of this formulation is not that REACH cannot be negotiated, as noted before: this was always clear and explicit, too. The additional words "and its implementation" constitute an attempt to exercise 'cooperative chill' due to plain mistrust. The 'cooperative chill' in TTIP on the 'implementation' of REACH imposed by the EP is of course a heavily-fought political compromise, or reflects an 'exchange' of give-and-take, in an already rather fragmented EP (with many parties) exhibiting several severe sensivities with respect to TTIP. Moreover, it would appear to be inconsistent with several other paragraphs in the same resolution, also a regular phenomenon in EP resolutions. One can also query what the 'implementation' of REACH really refers to. The present chapter is not the place to analyse this question in-depth, but the giant REACH regulation cannot possibly be made to work satisfactorily by mechanical and pure 'implementation', as the resolution seems to suggest. REACH has and must have many processes which are governed by the overall objectives of REACH and disciplined by strict criteria, science for risk assessment and many other features, exercised e.g. by the Commission, ECHA, the member states and expert

---

[49] Under P8_TA-PROV(2015)0252 of 8 July 2015, para. 2. (c) (iii).

committees. The four elements in the EU's suggestions for chemicals in TTIP (Box 13.3) would not 'undermine' or negatively affect these processes. As noted, all four, in different ways, are discussed in international organisations, too. Does the EP fear that TTIP regulatory cooperation amounts to a duty-to-agree? This would be absurd. Does it fear that the involvement (mostly by comments and consultation more broadly) of the US will a priori exercise a chilling effect, or, lead to compromises that would be less ambitious than what the EU on its own would have decided (apparently this is what German government circles are afraid of)? But is it not true as well that, if TTIP would come into being, the EU could then exercise a similar influence in the US where chemicals are hardly less controversial than in the EU?

It is also worthwhile to discuss briefly three of the four suggestions in Box 13.3 (ignoring data-sharing). First on classification and labelling where the UN GHS has long been accepted by both the US and the EU (and many other countries). However, whereas OSHA in the US applies GHS, EPA does not. What is holding back the EPA from implementing a binding agreement that has the advantageous effect of lowering trading costs over the Atlantic and worldwide? It is said that this is due to pressures from leading pesticides companies (which include three European firms as well). Moreover, when applying GHS, one might attempt to harmonise further (e.g. in choosing the same classification for any given substance), but here the intricacies become greater. Why and when does the EU or US classify substance x as carcinogenic or not (and subsequently apply GHS)? Let us suppose that one would agree to apply a Vogel-type harmonisation-up and decide to always go for the highest classification on either side. On the face of it, this would rule out controversy. But there is a snag: the EU identifying x as a SVHC thereby automatically blocks its use in pesticides. Second, the prioritisation for the evaluation of chemicals (and methodologies) does not affect the decision how and how stringently one protects, in case the substance turns out to be risky. This cooperation is meant to cut costs for the two parties by sharing the burden. Of course, this does require regulatory cooperation and precise agreement, case by case or in agreed programmes, presumably based on the chemical annex in TTIP. To block such useful cooperation (aiming precisely at cutting needless duplication), on the basis of the EP resolution, is simply not sensible.[50] These are REACH processes that have to be pursued anyway.

---

[50] Paragraphs 2.(c)(v), (vi) and (viii) of the EP Resolution acknowledge this.

What one might suggest doing is that such (TTIP) programmes are first justified by scientific analysis in a report and discussed in the EP, so that trust is created. Third, 'new and emerging issues' such as endocrine disruptors (EDs) and nanomaterials has a scientific and a more judgmental or 'political' aspect. On the former, cooperation and burden-sharing seems eminently sensible in TTIP, OECD, WHO or indeed in all of them. On the latter, the EU has become quite prudent. For example, Commission Vice-President Frans Timmermans has decided to subject the draft delegated act on EDs, biocides and pesticides, which has passed its deadline for publication, to impact assessment, a sound decision in itself but mistrusted, by the same forces that are so sceptical in the EP, as a sign of unwillingness to extend the EDs list. For them it is a small step to suggest that this is 'due' to TTIP. These sensitivities are not a good reason to reject the option of regulatory cooperation on 'new and emerging issues' – not least because chemicals is a world market and derivatives in value chains can simply not be ignored. Nevertheless, one should exercise utmost prudence and make every attempt to build confidence-building measures rather than turn a blind eye to the problem. One may also want this issue to be shifted from horizontal regulatory cooperation to the specific chemicals annex where chemicals regulators govern the process.

The chemicals section of TTIP has been much less controversial in the US, with most of the concern focusing instead on the 12-nation Trans-Pacific Partnership (TPP), which has been characterised as America's "most ambitious trade deal since the North American Free Trade Agreement in the 1990's".[51] Much of the political dialogue in the US does not distinguish between TTIP and TPP, but is opposed to free trade agreements more generally as weakening US regulatory protections.[52]

---

[51] Writing in the *New York Times,* Granville (2015) observes: "Opponents in the United States see the pact as mostly a giveaway to business, encouraging further export of manufacturing jobs to low-wage nations while limiting competition and encouraging higher prices for pharmaceuticals and other high-value products by spreading American standards for patent protections to other countries. A provision allowing multinational corporations to challenge regulations and court rulings before special tribunals is drawing intense opposition."

[52] In a posting on techdirt.com, a blogger quotes from a press release from the Sierra Club: "Governments must take a page out of the history books and stop

6. Contrasting REACH and TSCA: Perceptions and critical assessment

6.1 Why both are criticised?

Curiously, there is resistance against TTIP chemicals negotiations going deeper both from the two sides in the negotiations *and* from NGOs. The position of business (CEFIC and ACC together) is accommodating this resistance by not offering an alternative view, but merely a useful, yet cautious preparatory route. From a trade-policy point of view, this is peculiar because the costs of TBTs in chemicals trade over the North Atlantic are amongst the highest of all industrial sectors. Lowering these TBT costs drastically would probably yield large economic gains. It is thus disappointing that the chemicals TTIP chapter does not reflect the original spirit of the partnership and is not more ambitious in focusing on removing or minimising TBTs.

Can one understand this resistance from a regulatory point of view? Yes and no. No, one cannot, once one is willing and capable to assume a more rational and detached analytical view of how EU-US chemical regulation *should* be designed. Yes, one can, if one joins the many stakeholders and officials of the chemical policy-making communities on both sides, repeating all the time that the two regulatory regimes are too divergent. Nobody seems to ask the more relevant question whether the one or the other regime, or both, embody '*good regulation*', applying GRPs (Good Regulatory Practices). And, as a corollary, whether, if GRPs were applied on both sides, the 'divergence' would shrink with it. 'Better regulation' would yield additional economic welfare, and if its application would indeed also shrink the divergence, TBTs would be much lower, too: a clear *win-win*. It is fairly obvious that both chemical regulatory regimes can be improved and a mutually compatible and sound way of doing that is to employ 'Better Regulation' principles, most of which have long been agreed transatlantically![53] Since the very purpose of TTIP is to reap economic

---

negotiating trade pacts that cut protections for our air, water, land, workers, and communities" and adds: "That last comment is a clear reference to TPP, but applies equally to TAFTA/TTIP" (see "US Free Trade Agreements Are Bad Not Just For The Economy, But For The Environment" at: https://www.techdirt.com/articles/20131022/10231424967/us-free-trade-agreements-are-not-just-bad-economy-environment-too.shtml).

[53] See e.g. Quick (2008a). See also US-EU High Level Regulatory Forum (2011) and Chase & Pelkmans, ch 2 in the volume.

gains and, as a subsidiary goal, to set proper world standards for good regulation benefitting everybody, why is such beneficial regulatory reform not embraced and pursued?

Both chemical regimes are criticised, but for very different reasons. Rightly or wrongly, the TSCA is mainly criticised for not addressing existing hazardous chemical substances that meanwhile are asserted, feared or found to be of 'serious concern' and are or may soon be forbidden or restricted in other countries, including EU member states. In short, the TSCA is said to suffer from '*under-regulation*': a number of sensitive, risky substances are said not to be tackled and the tools and intervention options for the EPA are too restrained. As Schwarzman & Wilson (2011) call it: TSCA generates a 'data gap' and a 'safety gap'.[54] How true this is remains unclear. There are isolated examples like asbestos,[55] but can one generalise?

REACH, on the contrary, is said by many to suffer from '*over-regulation*': it supposedly imposes unreasonably heavy and costly means in order to ensure the availability of quite demanding data on the possible hazards of each and every substance above 1 tonne per year, for presumably some 30,000 substances, including complicated information and interaction flows up and down the value chains. There is no clarity at all whether or not all this data is 'needed' or even 'read' by regulators (despite their high costs) except in a limited number of instances. None of this directly supports health, safety and the environment, but some of it might, later on; the latter is all to be ensured in a lengthy second set of procedures of REACH, to wit, evaluation, authorisation and (new?) restrictions. The costs of the first stage (registration) now begin to be better estimated and they seem to be roughly double what was already seen as very high upfront costs in the constitutive days of the Regulation. This would imply some €4-5 billion costs for registration and what it takes, alone.[56] Nobody has any clue

---

[54] They also mention a technology gap, the lack of incentives under the TSCA to invest in 'green chemistry'.

[55] Note, however, that the EPA banned asbestos in 1989 (54 Fed. Reg. 29,460), but this regulation was set aside by the courts in *Corrosion Proof Fittings v. EPA*, 947 F.2d 1201 (5th Cir., 1991). Later, under pressure from EPA to re-regulate, manufacturers in the US entered into an agreement to take asbestos-containing products off the market.

[56] The 2003 Impact Assessment of REACH estimated some €2.3 billion of upfront costs (direct costs for registration, mainly testing), some €1.1 billion of which would materialise in the early stage. The CSES (2012) review report of

about the eventual benefits later on.[57] By definition, these direct costs are not justified by the benefits because the latter cannot possibly be known even in a very crude estimate. The costs are only 'justified' by a *wholesale* application of the precautionary principle (PP) to *all* chemical substances known (above 1 tonne). Note that these costly testing and registration requirements are not just applied to several thousands of substances about which a suspicion might exist but not 'enough' scientific evidence has been generated – then pre-caution makes sense and testing and research seem justified (if possible, proportionately).

However, the idea is that one applies the (often-costly) PP to many thousands, indeed tens of thousands, of chemical substances, without having a clue whether that application is in any way justifiable in most of these tens of thousands of cases. This is surely *not* in keeping with the avowed notion of that principle, as elaborated e.g. in the famous European Commission (2000) paper on the Precautionary Principle. Application of PP requires there to be 'insufficient' knowledge about risks, in other words, there have to be *some* compelling but as yet 'insufficiently' certain or clear risk indicators. If the PP requires a recognition of 'insufficient knowledge', it follows directly that it cannot be applicable when there is no risk by any sign or indication. The PP may be justified, as historical examples of instances in which governments failed to act upon early signs of trouble may suggest,[58] in instances where there are indications via victims and other possible evidence of harm as well as early signals in research, without being sure. However, severe and irreversible damage might be caused and a temporary PP application can be defended (e.g. BSE should have been dealt with PP at an earlier stage).

The PP may 'be better safe than sorry', but it also brings with it the risk of false positives and excessively heavy intervention. Assume,

---

REACH (for the Commission) reports instead a 'mid-range' amount of €2.1 billion. With the big wave of numerous small-volumes registrations driven by SMEs in 2018 still ahead, and assuming a similar underestimation in 2003 for this wave, it further estimates that one would arrive at direct costs of some €4.5 billion.

[57] Note that, even if some benefits would be identified under 'better regulation' principles, this is not necessarily convincing, as – possibly - the same benefits might have been found with a far less-imposing system. As in impact assessment, one always has to think in terms of alternatives.

[58] See EEA (2001); a second report ("Late lessons from early warnings: Science, precaution, innovation", was published by the EEA in 2013: www.eea.europa.eu/publications/late-lessons-2).

454 | ELLIOTT & PELKMANS

for example, that of the 30,000 existing substances (from 1981), there are no signs of hazard in 25,000 instances, perhaps even more; some others suggest that a 40% benchmark would be safe, implying that 18,000 need not be investigated at all. The point is that one cannot credibly assert that all or nearly all substances pose dangers for inflicting harm on consumers or workers. Many of these substances have been around for a long time and, in many cases, there are no suspicions whatsoever. Why the PP would have to be applied in a heavy way, or at all, for all *other* substances as well, merely on the criterion of tonnage, is still in need of justification. One may call this objection 'risk-based' – and indeed, it is – but it is just as much a *proper* application of PP. In the absence of any sign or indicator of risk, why impose such costs?

It is, however, possible to assume a slightly more cautious position, with some justification, when observing that the C&L (classification and labelling) Inventory does comprise many substances with hazards (not necessarily risks, as exposures might be minimal). The authors have been informed that some 120,000 substances in the inventory have been classified with at least one hazard. Thus, it should be possible to develop a proportionate system, where substances (not known to carry a risk) could be subject to an alert system followed by testing, when there would be any reportable sign of this hazard having turned into a risk. That would reflect the spirit of PP.

In all likelihood, there are now huge costs to registration in REACH, especially for SMEs,[59] and no or next to no societal benefits anywhere on the horizon for the very large majority of substances. That is 'over-regulation', indeed, uniquely costly over-regulation, because of the wholesale application of PP to registration via tonnage (rather than risks or even a sign of it) and the separation of a lengthy trajectory of incurring costs (costly testing and data collection) from the search of societal benefits. There is a better case for demanding data collection for the registration of 'new' substances, but even here sophisticated forms of pre-selection of what might constitute hazardous chemicals would seem to be possible, underpinning a more targeted approach (as noted, some exceptions accepted by REACH do reflect this approach). These considerations carry over to different perspectives on priority setting for new chemicals, discussed in section 9.

---

[59] See Pelkmans, Schrefler & Gubbels (2013) for worrying mid-range evidence.

6.2   What we do not know about 'divergence'?

One can also argue, that in the final analysis, what matters for improving safety, health and the environment – the societal benefits - is the overall effect of the legal system as a whole in banning, restricting or (targeted and restrictedly) authorising specific substances, or their uses. The critical question in TTIP is not whether the legal procedures of the two regimes are so divergent, but whether they are good (enough) *in delivering the desired societal benefits*. To be more precise, how comparable are the bans, restrictions and (what in REACH is called) authorisations referring to the same substances on both sides of the North Atlantic? One would expect some divergence there because the TSCA (combined with other US federal laws on food, pesticides, etc.) might be 'under-regulating' (i.e. not all market failures are overcome), but it seems not so easy to establish firmly how severe that 'divergence' is. Moreover, the effects are not uniform in all areas. In some areas (such as suspect carcinogens in diesel exhaust, e.g.), the US tends to regulate more stringently than in Europe, whereas in others (such as suspected endocrine disruptors), Europe regulates more stringently. The authors have not been able to find authoritative evidence on the specifics of this divergence, let alone on how 'wide' it really is. Adding up REACH (where four authorisations have been made so far[60] and several hundreds or more restrictions[61] exist at the moment), some remaining chemical directives, pesticides and cosmetics regulation (prohibiting animal testing, unlike the US), the EU has probably banned or restricted more substances than the US, but that remains a conjecture. Ultimately, it is this *factual* divergence in some sensitive substances regulation, but

---

[60] On 5 July 2015, the REACH Commission website listed four substances with an authorisation decision having appeared in the EU Official Journal, and a total of eight substances, with a range of applications, "pending adoption". There are 166 substances on the candidates list.

[61] On 11 July 2015, the ECHA list of restrictions (http://echa.europa.eu/ addressing-chemicals-of-concern/restrictions/list-of-restrictions) identifies 64 restrictions in categories of substances, with subdivisions, totalling altogether 105 entries. Note that this list includes Annex XVII of REACH and 'old' restrictions under the former Directive 76/769/EEC. Another five restrictions are under consideration. However, the total of 105 does not relate to individual substances only; thus, entries no. 3, 28, 29, 30 and 40 refer to classes of substances (e.g. carcinogens, mutagen categories, flammable gases, liquids, solids, etc.). Moreover, quite a few entries refer to families of substances with the same name (e.g. azocolourants and azodyes). Any comparison with the US would thus have to carefully specify the individual restrictions on both sides.

more importantly the *overlap* of substances regulated both by the US and the EU, that matters for SHEC regulation and society. And it is this area of overlap where much more constructive and innovative transatlantic approaches could be proposed and scrutinised. Even if the overlaps were few and far between, say 'mere islands of convergence in a vast sea of divergence', the places where the two parties can come together are what is important for trade agreements. Later we propose a system whereby such areas of similar or mutually acceptable levels of regulation can be identified and unnecessary trade barriers gradually eliminated over time.

7. Carved in stone: REACH and TSCA suffer from excessive rigidity

7.1 REACH immobilises

In order to conduct fruitful TTIP negotiations in chemical regulation and trade, reform of both regulatory regimes would be very helpful. However, these reforms do not 'need' TTIP; such reforms are justified in their own right. Reforms have a double rationale: i) both systems would be much improved if subjected to 'better regulation' principles, and ii) reforms should facilitate TTIP to generate major economic gains. This recognition has emerged in the US, but until recently, it has been hard to organise a winning, bipartisan coalition in Congress, leading to repeated delays up until today in reforming TSCA. One might also wonder how 'deep' the reform would be. But such a recognition is lacking in the EU. REACH has become a sacred cow! Alas, for the wrong reasons. Although the design of REACH is heavy and overly costly, especially in its processes, mainly due to the wholesale application of PP to registration (with demanding data) of all chemical substances, it is treated as 'untouchable'. A steady flow of criticism from e.g. SMEs among others, is answered either with marginal or symbolic responses or neglect, or legal defences are formulated without ever reacting to the core of the issue.

There would seem to be two reasons why REACH has become a sacred cow, thereby incurring unnecessary burdens for EU industry and ultimately the supply chain and possibly consumers, and, in addition, making meaningful TTIP negotiations more difficult or reducing them to modest features. First and foremost, it is about the very long duration of the implementation process. The official position is that the process will take 11 years, until 2018 inclusive, when small-volumes registration will take place. That is an extremely long period during which EU bodies are in the frustrating position of having to implement, process and enforce numerous measures, without being able to change the legislation (only some annexes in modest or purely technical ways). This is a direct consequence of the design of the REACH Regulation, with its highly principled and wholesale approach of requiring very demanding data for all chemical substances and uses, as discussed before. But now that the REACH obligations are enshrined in EU law, SMEs cannot be treated on a more sensible and far less-costly risk-basis for (say) 2018, as this would be regarded as discriminatory for all earlier registrations. REACH has stifled any initiative or even any serious debate on switching REACH towards a more risk-based approach, which need not and should *not affect any eventual societal benefit* but greatly reduce private costs (and to some extent public costs).

As a result, a 'deep' TTIP approach in chemicals is doomed not to touch the instrumentalities of registration (no data, no market), which constitutes a big TBT where substances do not have any risk indication. Also, the communication over the value chain, often two-ways and costly,[62] is just as valid for US exporters as for EU-based producers and users, irrespective of whether the substances are suspect or not. The REACH system now governs the TBTs as given, indeed, carved in stone, even though precisely this instrument – not a 'level of protection'- should be at issue! In other words, the very long duration of REACH implementation creates an excessive form of rigidity that is immune to sensible calls for flexibility or amendments made in Europe, let alone, for reasons of 'deeper' TTIP negotiations or sensible REACH reform.

One might perhaps entertain some hope that TTIP, as a 'living' agreement, might be able to address such issues after 2018. However, and this is the second reason, by 2018, REACH will only be relatively early in the complementary stage of going through heavy and time-consuming authorisation procedures, and possibly new restrictions. The original idea behind authorisations was that SVHCs would be identified – and not known before or now better understood – so that substitution could be stimulated and 'temporary permissions' be given to companies using the SVHC. An outer bound of the expectation is the infamous SIN (Substitute It Now) list put together by the NGO community. As is well known, the candidate list of SVHCs, being continuously filled up with substances for authorisation, has an immediate chilling effect in markets (including value chains), although

---

[62] See CSES (2012) and Pelkmans, Schrefler & Gubbels, (2013).

the whole point of the authorisation procedure is precisely to verify risk in-depth and subject the production and use to a careful societal balancing procedure.

In any event, an outer bound would be that the EU would end up with the SIN list of 300-minus substances. Yet, this would then have taken a decade or more of authorisation procedures. And the SIN list is a mere 1% of existing substances under REACH (if the 1981 inventory is taken). However, that list was already made up in 2007,[63] when REACH had not even begun. If the SIN list were so clear, and if market players do regard it as critical for their reputation, why the huge data requirements for *all* substances over no less than 11 years? And why all these heavy procedures for many years more? Most restrictions actually pre-date REACH. However, these expectations are now in doubt. It is suggested in REACH circles that authorisations will be generated for decades to come, as data (including new data) may well prompt demands from member states to verify the SVHC nature of ever-more substances. Clearly, if this is true, it is of utmost importance that the US and the EU cooperate on the prioritisation of substances and try to reach convergence on when, and based on what criteria, a risk renders a substance a SVHC.

TTIP in chemicals is perhaps doomed to stick to negotiating the forms of 'regulatory cooperation', as mentioned in Box 13.3. The 'frozen' attitudes on both sides, working from two instances of regulation subject to improvement (that is, not applying Good Regulatory Practices), and with regulators not in a position to question the instruments of the regimes – the objectives are not at issue - even when the arguments are convincing, are inconsistent with the very aims of TTIP: higher economic welfare, that is, ensuring societal benefits (overcoming SHEC market failures) with the lowest costs possible. The high TBTs in chemicals trade are a direct consequence of two regimes being subject to significant improvement; their 'divergence' is largely a consequence of their absolute immobility.

---

[63] The SIN list is a collection of SVHCs as identified by the NGO Chemsec (see http://chemsec.org/what-we-do/sin-list). Last updated 8 October 2014, the total list includes some 800 possibly harmful chemical substances, but some 300 are now claimed to be SVHCs (by Chemsec). The list is not considered fully reliable from a scientific point of view.

7.2   Is the US incapable of 'harmonising up'?

One could also argue that the challenging question is not why Europeans would want to hang on to the perceived benefits of REACH, but why Americans would not want to use TTIP as an opportunity to 'harmonise up' to the system that the EU and many US academics and NGOs perceive as superior.

The prevailing academic understanding of bilateral trade talks was defined in the mid-1990s by David Vogel in his influential book *Trading Up*.[64] Professor Vogel studied a series of trade negotiations in the 1980s and early 1990s, including the North American Free Trade Agreement (NAFTA) between the United States, Mexico and Canada and concluded that 'harmonisation up', adopting the more stringent standard for mutual gain, was nearly inevitable in trade talks, provided that certain minimal conditions were satisfied. Vogel called this the 'California effect', a term that seems somehow quaintly parochial by the standards of today's more international discourse,[65] but by which he meant a race to the top rather than a race to the bottom:

> Trade liberalization is most likely to *strengthen* consumer and environmental protection when a group of nations has agreed to reduce the role of regulations as trade barriers and the most powerful among them has influential domestic constituencies that support stronger regulatory standards. Thus, the stronger the commitment of nations to coordinate their regulatory policies, the more powerful is the California effect [i.e. race to the top rather than the bottom]. Likewise, the weaker the institutions created by regional or international trade agreements on treaties, the weaker the California effect.[66]

Vogel's model is a simple one: each trade negotiation is imagined as a discrete single-play game between two players about a single regulatory issue; each side believes that it will benefit to some extent from the increased exchange that comes from reducing trade barriers, including non-tariff barriers from divergent regulatory systems. If more stringent regulations on one side are sufficiently supported by a

---

[64] See Vogel (1995).

[65] However, an interesting elaboration of the interaction between Californian regulation and EU regulatory thinking is found in Vogel & Swinnen (eds) (2007); in Vogel's later work, he demonstrates a U-turn for the EU becoming more and the US less precautionary. See Vogel (2012).

[66] Ibid., p. 8.

domestic political constituency so that adopting them is a condition for obtaining the benefits from greater exchange, the more stringent regulation will be adopted by the other side, Vogel argues, provided that the costs of doing so do not exceed the anticipated benefits of getting a deal. Thus, according to Vogel, the greater the perceived benefits from reaching agreement, the greater the 'California effect' of inducing regulatory laggards to come up to the higher standards of their trading partners. The game becomes more complicated, and more realistic, if more than a single regulatory issue is subject to negotiation, so that trading one issue off against another becomes possible, but the logic is essentially the same: parties will agree to more stringent regulatory standards where the benefits from increased trade are greater than the costs from more stringent instruments of regulation.

From the standpoint of Vogel's model, harmonisation of chemical regulation through TTIP should have been an easy case: Europe's REACH programme is generally perceived as more stringent than US regulation under TSCA, at least in the sense of having higher compliance costs.[67] As described in more detail later, most of these extra costs are not a result of setting more constraining standards for exposure to substances that are regulated. Indeed, indications suggest that *actual* regulatory levels are remarkably similar in both systems, although far more precision on this point is desirable. Rather, the higher costs of compliance with REACH are due primarily to two factors: i) higher costs of compliance for preparing dossiers of health and safety data for all chemicals above certain production limits, whereas TSCA uses a much more targeted approach in which health and safety data are required for only a very small subset of chemicals, and until recently, none for *existing* chemicals that were already on the market when the law was enacted in 1976; and ii) some substances that are regulated in Europe are not regulated in the US, and vice-versa.

---

[67] For an argument that a regulatory system is not necessarily better merely because it imposes higher costs of compliance, see Renn & Elliott (2011). Moreover, according to Elliott & Elliott (2009), "a legal system is not necessarily 'ahead' merely because it stimulates a greater degree of precautionary behavior by those it regulates. Rather, the proper question is whether a legal system is achieving the degree of precaution that is deemed appropriate under the circumstances. Too much precaution, as well as too little, may have both costs and benefits, in terms of useful products or innovations that are needlessly not marketed."

Why didn't the US side simply agree to adopt a more REACH-like system, at least for those substances that are already regulated by both the US and the EU, as predicted by Vogel's model? One obvious answer endogenous to Vogel's model could be that the perceived costs of adopting REACH on the US side were greater than the expected benefits from harmonisation. In a sense, the conclusion that perceived costs were greater than perceived benefits is tautological: there must be some rational reason why the negotiators were unwilling to 'trade up', as Vogel predicts they would.[68] But exactly what were the perceived costs of adopting REACH (or a more REACH-like compromise) on both sides of the Atlantic, and why were these costs thought to be greater than the benefits of harmonisation?

The puzzle becomes even more interesting when one realises that virtually all of the extra costs of complying with REACH are (once and for all) 'sunk costs' that have already been paid by many US-based chemical companies, because many of the chemical companies operating in the US also either sell some of their products in Europe or someone else who does sell that substance in Europe has already registered it under REACH and hence they have already been required to comply with REACH, at least for existing substances. Rational economic actors are not supposed to consider sunk costs, that are behind them, in making decisions about what is best for the future, although we know that sometimes people (and possibly even companies and nations) do not always behave 'rationally', as predicted by neo-classical economic models.[69] It is also theoretically possible that the additional economic costs of complying with a REACH-like system in the US for new substances not already regulated under REACH were perceived to be greater than the perceived trade benefits from harmonisation, although we think that is unlikely, in part because US chemical companies frequently supply to the large European market. Even for substances that will be developed in the future, they must anticipate that they are going to have to comply with REACH.

---

[68] See generally Leff (1974), who points out that the 'discovery' that the people often act to maximise perceived benefits and reduce costs is nominalism.

[69] "Behavioral economics recognizes that sunk costs often affect economic decisions due to loss aversion: the price paid becomes a benchmark for the value, whereas the price paid should be irrelevant. ... Economic experiments have shown that the sunk cost fallacy and loss aversion are common, and hence economic rationality — as assumed by much of economics — is limited. ...."
"Prospect Theory" Kahneman & Tversky; For an accessible summary, see http://youarenotsosmart.com/2011/03/25/the-sunk-cost-fallacy/

A simpler answer to why the US is not capable of 'harmonising up' might be the pressure from US industry not to accept REACH's costly general registration requirements (with demanding data-development obligations) for existing chemicals and instead to accept – but also limit – new powers for restrictions in a reformed TSCA.

8. Spill-overs and a world regime?

8.1 Positive spill-overs with or without TTIP

Our off-the-record interviews with participants lead us to conclude that regulatory convergence was taken off the table early because both sides perceived TTIP not as an isolated single-play game (as Vogel's model implicitly assumes) *but rather as a step in a larger process of defining the rules for commerce in chemicals in a rapidly-globalising economy*. Neither side was willing to give up its position on what should be the emerging worldwide system of chemical regulation in order to obtain the immediate benefits of harmonisation through TTIP. The important, and generally overlooked spill-overs from the TTIP negotiations, are described by Lejour et al. (2014) as follows:

> The CEPR study [Francois et al., 2013] on the TTIP briefly deals with the spill-over effect to third countries, following the lowering of regulatory barriers between the US and the EU. These spill-over effects would not emerge if two small countries form a FTA, but this is different once the two largest economies in the world cooperate on regulatory issues. Direct and indirect spill-over effects are positive for 3rd countries and can be modelled. Direct spill-overs improve the trade possibilities of third countries with the EU and US without any further action on the part of 3rd countries – they are automatic. If the EU and the US streamline their regulatory procedures, this is subject to most-favoured-nation treatment (MFN) under the WTO and it becomes also easier for firms from other countries to export to the US or the EU. ... It makes sense that firms in other countries adopt the regulatory standards of large countries, when the former are closely linked to the EU, the US or both. This would also improve market opportunities for American and European firms in these third countries. ...
>
> Of course, the greater the spill-overs to 3rd countries, the more TTIP outcomes begin to look like multilateral or plurilateral - rather than bilateral - results benefitting all. This important significance is further enhanced by the

consequence that also TTIP itself would see its gains enlarge due to such spill-overs. [70]

This type of argument focuses primarily on the optimistic case in which the US and the EU reach agreement on a harmonisation approach, where "the two largest economies in the world cooperate on regulatory issues". What they did not analyse until now is the other side of the decision tree of how spill-overs from TTIP may play out if the two sides do NOT agree on regulatory convergence.

Many countries around the world are now developing their own national system for regulating chemicals. In October 2010, REACH-style legislation came into effect in China to regulate the environmental risk and hazard of China's new chemical substances, under the Ministry of Environmental Protection (MEP) Order No. 7. Called Measures for the Environmental Management of New Chemical Substances, this regulation comprises notification requirements for new chemicals and catalogues hazardous chemicals among existing ones, but it hardly follows REACH principles despite elusive suggestions to the contrary (leading to the nickname 'China REACH').

South Korea has also developed its own regulatory system, called K-REACH, which went into effect 1 January 2015.[71] K-REACH was more explicitly "designed to closely mirror REACH"[72] (in a more risk-based and proportionate form). Other countries such as India, Thailand, Australia, Malaysia and Turkey are also reportedly developing their own national systems. Indeed, if the EU and the US were to reach agreement on a common approach to regulating chemicals, it would be hard for other countries to ignore their shared approach, as the combined EU-US market is the largest in the world,

---

[70] Much the same point was also made by Daniel Hamilton, co-director of the CEPS/CTR project on TTIP, in his public remarks in Brussels on 9 April 2014, when the present project was announced. Hamilton observed that if the EU and the US were able to agree on their higher standards for protecting environment, safety and workers, these standards would become the de facto international standards going forward as opposed to lower "Asian standards." Hamilton argued that the benefits to the EU and US of setting the bar higher far outweighed the small differences between the two.

[71] See the website dedicated to Korea's own regulatory system for chemicals (www.thereachcentre.com/site/content_south_korean_chemicals_info.php).

[72] Ibid.

particularly for chemicals.[73] But what happens if the US and EU do *not* agree, but instead maintain their divergent approaches?

From the European side, Europe might well gain a trade advantage vis-à-vis the US if other countries adopt REACH-like systems, because European companies would be more familiar with REACH requirements in Europe and would not have to bear the costs of duplicative regulation in other countries. The European Union is quietly promoting the REACH model to other countries. On the US side, US chemical companies maintain that they are not yet ready to concede that REACH represents the future of chemical management worldwide. They still hold out hope that more targeted approaches, represented by the Canadian Chemicals Management Plan (CMP),[74] and pending TSCA Reform legislation may prevail over the long run as the model for a harmonised international system.

8.2   US industry objections against REACH

The essential difference between the Canadian Chemicals Management Plan (CMP) and REACH is that under the CMP, experts agree in advance on high-priority substances and only require submission of test data for those substances. Proposed bipartisan amendments to TSCA that are supported by industry in the US adopt a similar approach, in which the Environmental Protection Agency (EPA) would conduct rule-making to categorise substances are either 'high risk' requiring further analysis, or 'low risk' so that they can be marketed without further studies.[75] This carries forward to *existing* substances in the current approach of the TSCA 'pre-manufacture notification' programme, under which EPA uses predictive techniques, such as computer models and 'structure activity relationships' (SARs) or

---

[73] According to Eizenstat (2013), "The EU and US together account for almost half of global output of goods and services and almost a third of global trade – almost $1 trillion annually." Specifically for chemicals, the 2012 domestic sales in chemicals of the US and the EU amounts to one-third of total global sales, with China alone having another one-third. In terms of world exports of chemicals, the US and the EU hold 40.5%, with China enjoying 14.3%.

[74] For a description, see
http://chemicalsubstanceschimiques.gc.ca/plan/index-eng.php

[75] §4(a), Chemical Safety Improvement Act, S. 1009, 113th Congress, 1st Session, (https://beta.congress.gov/bill/113th-congress/senate-bill/1009/text).

'quantitative structure activity relationships' ((Q)SARs[76]) to predict whether substances are likely to be hazardous *in silico* (i.e. through computer simulations) rather than requiring animal or other test data. Moreover, pathway-based toxicological testing in cell lines is thought by many to be the future of toxicology.[77]

Many US companies believe it is unnecessarily wasteful to require comprehensive testing for all substances if science can target limited resources on substances that are most likely to cause problems. There are also independent critical voices. One of the present co-authors has written:

> The new REACH program in Europe requires private parties to submit enormous reams of data about the safety of chemicals to a new government agency. In our view, one fatal flaw in programs such as REACH is that its drafters appear to imagine that sufficient analytical resources can be marshaled at the governmental level to conduct all of the risk assessments that need to be conducted in a complex industrial society. We believe that this assumption is incorrect, and that the overwhelming majority of the data assembled at great cost by industry in response to the REACH program will remain unread in government files.[78]

One key difference between REACH and the US/Canadian approach is that under REACH, prioritisation occurs *after* data submission in terms of what dossiers will actually be reviewed by government as opposed to prioritisation in the US and Canada *before* requiring data to be generated and submitted. But it should be noted

---

[76] For an explanation, see http://ihcp.jrc.ec.europa.eu/glossary/q-sars-quantitative-structure-activity-relationships

[77] See generally Committee on Toxicity Testing and Assessment of Environmental Agents (2007), National Research Council, "Toxicity Testing in the Twenty-First Century: A Vision and a Strategy". In a brief accessible summary, the US National Academy of Sciences (http://dels.nas.edu/dels/rpt_briefs/Toxicity_Testing_final.pdf) writes: "The report envisions a new toxicity-testing system that relies mainly on understanding 'toxicity pathways' – the cellular response pathways that can result in adverse health effects when sufficiently perturbed. Such a system would evaluate biologically significant alterations without relying on studies of whole animals." See also "Toxicity Testing in the 21st Century: Better Results, Less Use of Animals", 25 *The Environmental Forum* 46, Mar/Apr 2008.

[78] See Elliott & Elliott (2009, p. 74).

that REACH proponents in Europe believe that requiring the data to be generated is good in and of itself (especially in terms of increasing awareness in industry), whether or not government considers it for purposes of regulating.

If it were correct that current and emerging science allows us to predict in advance with a higher degree of confidence than in the past which chemical substances are likely to be 'bad actors', and to focus greater regulatory scrutiny on those, then the extensive efforts to test all substances, even those that are highly unlikely to prove hazardous, could be seen as costly 'dead-weight losses' unnecessary expenses that do not contribute to protecting health and safety. In Europe, views are mixed. Defenders of REACH assert that compiling and submitting comprehensive test data on the safety of substances promotes public confidence,[79] even if government resources are insufficient to actually review all the dossiers that have been submitted.

Spill-over effects not only multiply the benefits of harmonisation; they also multiply the costs of agreeing to an inefficient duplicative system. Thus, for industry on both sides of the Atlantic, the calculus was not merely whether the benefits of harmonisation in TTIP were greater than the extra costs of trading up, as envisioned by Vogel, but whether the benefits exceed costs when both positive and negative spill-overs from TTIP to anticipated future regulatory systems around the world are taken into account.

9. What really matters: SHEC equivalence and market access

The stated rationale for giving up on the possibilities of incremental harmonisation or regulatory convergence before the negotiations even began, boils down to the idea that REACH and TSCA are "very different" (in the words of the industry joint position paper) or "too different with regard to some fundamental principles" (in the words of the EU negotiation position).

But that observation, while true, avoids or by-passes the relevant question. Negotiations over a free trade agreement always begin from the starting point that regulatory systems on the two sides are different. The proper question is whether the differences in regulatory processes

---

[79] The mid-term review of REACH (CSES, 2012) finds practically no empirical support for this greater confidence. Pelkmans, Schrefler & Gubbels (2013) reach the same conclusion.

are so 'fundamental' that they cannot reasonably be bridged. It seems never to have occurred to the TTIP negotiators that, even though processes and 'fundamental principles' of regulation may differ, the actual *outcomes* of these divergent processes are substantially similar in some areas, or at the very least 'adequate' to protect the public, in cases when substances ARE regulated by both sides. The main difference between the US and Europe seems to be that Europe often regulates on a precautionary basis but the US holds off for more definitive science that will stand up in court if challenged.[80]

Empirical studies of the actual results of chemical regulation in the US and the EU suggest that despite assertions about ideological and rhetorical differences, such as the precautionary principle versus risk assessment as philosophies for regulating chemicals, the actual results of regulation in some area are not very different between the US and EU,[81] at least for many substances that are regulated in both. Merely as an illustration of this similarity, we compared the chronic oral and drinking water limits for the top 30 chemicals by volume released to the environment in EPA's Toxic Release Inventory. Table 13.1 below shows that for those substances for which both the EU and US had exposure limits, 75% (12 of 16) differed by less than a factor of 3. Only one (xylenes) differed by more than a single order of magnitude (10x). From a toxicological standpoint, differences this small at low levels such as those involved here are insignificant.

In every case, differences in the actual stringency of regulation were inconsequential, despite the fundamental differences in the processes, systems and philosophies that had been used to reach the results. It is important to note, however, that only about half of the substances (16 of 30) were regulated by both sides; in some instances the US regulated but the EU did not, but in more cases in this small sample, the EU regulated but the US did not. Of course, we are reluctant to draw any broad general conclusions from this small sample. What is important for our purposes is that there were *some* areas of overlap where duplication could be eliminated.

---

[80] For criticism and suggestions for improvement of the current European approach to the use of science in risk regulation, see Schrefler & Pelkmans (2014). See also Charnley & Elliott (2002), who argue that broader availability of judicial review by private parties challenging government regulation makes regulating based on suggestive but not yet definitive science more difficult in the US.

[81] See Renn & Elliott (2011).

Table 13.1 Exposure limits of chemicals: US-EU regulatory comparison

Substance[a]	Difference < 3x		
	US	EU	value
Zinc	3E-1	5E-1	CR[b]
Arsenic	0.01	0.01	DW[c]
Lead	0.015	0.01	DW
Copper	1.3	2	DW
Nitrate	10 (as N)	50 (as NO₃)	DW
Barium	2	0.7	DW
Toluene	8E-2	2.23E-1	CR
Toluene	1	0.7	DW
Chromium VI	3.E-3	5E-3	CR
Total chomium	0.1	0.05	DW
Nickel	2E-2	5E-2	CR
Chlorine	4	5	DW
	Difference > 3x		
Substance	US	EU	value
Arsenic	3E-4	1E-3	CR
Barium	2E-1	2E-2	CR
Styrene	0.1	0.02	DW
Xylenes	10	0.5	DW

a. Listed in order of total volume released to the environment in the US reported in EPA's Toxic Release Inventory (highest to lowest) for which comparisons were possible because regulated in both the US and the EU.
b. CR = chronic oral exposure limit in mg/kg-day.
c. DW = drinking water limit in mg/L.
Source: Authors' own compilation.

It is true that drinking water is not typically shipped across the Atlantic, but what these examples suggest is that despite differences in legal procedures, when the two sides regulate a chemical, sometimes they regulate it with similar stringency. On reflection, these conclusions are not surprising. The science is the same on both sides of the Atlantic, and regulators in the US and the EU are both trying conscientiously to protect public health and the environment with an adequate margin of safety to the best of their ability and judgment. It is not surprising that sometimes they would reach similar outcomes.

Admittedly, this is not the whole story, as some substances may be regulated in the EU but not the US or vice versa. European opposition to TSCA centres around the perception that many risky substances are not tackled in the US (but this does require a much broader inspection than TSCA alone; see Box 13.1). As noted, a precise and verifiable survey of these divergences seems not to be available and is much needed. But where both sides have 'tackled' a high-volume substance, regulatory limits in this small sample turn out to be remarkably similar. This suggests that the TTIP negotiators were wise to focus on expanding technical and scientific assessments, which have tended to come out very close to one another in the past.

The relevant case for trade negotiations, however, is whether, when one side has regulated something, the other partner should have enough confidence that it is willing to accept those results *without* duplicating its own regulatory processes. The absence of significant differences in this example where both sides have addressed high-volume substances, should give confidence that in at least some instances, as former Ambassador Eizenstat (2103) put it, "we should have confidence in the 21st century that the regulatory standards in both the EU and US are adequate to protect our publics and should be accepted ..."

International negotiations often begin this way with each side insisting that its system is best. The more productive question is whether the other side's system is good enough, given one's SHEC objectives.[82] For trade negotiations such as TTIP to succeed, both sides must move beyond familiar national legal *procedures* for regulating chemicals, to ask whether the actual *results* are comparable and acceptable in terms of protecting against risky chemicals, despite differences in the legal procedures that lead up to them. Ultimately, this is about the SHEC objectives, the societal benefits the citizens and workers care about. Comparability includes, however, both what substances need to be regulated and how stringently they are regulated once regulation is put in place.

---

[82] See Executive Order 13609, Promoting International Regulatory Cooperation, 1 May 2012, §1 www.gpo.gov/fdsys/pkg/DCPD-201200327/pdf/DCPD-201200327.pdf: "[i]n meeting shared challenges involving health, safety, ... environmental, and other issues, international regulatory cooperation can identify approaches that are *at least as protective as those that are or would be adopted in the absence of such cooperation.*"

Perhaps the particular high-volume chemicals in water in Table 13.1 are an exception. We really don't know objectively how much convergence in outcomes actually exists despite differences in regulatory processes. But even if areas of similar regulatory outcomes are 'islands of convergence in a vast sea of difference', they show that in some areas greater harmonisation for mutual benefit should be possible. Plus the size of the islands of convergence would be expected to grow over time as TSCA reform is implemented and greater collaboration occurs between the US and the EU at the scientific and technical level.

The challenge for a 'living' TTIP is to create a process that will i) gradually identify other islands in which regulatory outcomes are similar, or at least, 'good enough' to protect the public, and ii) provide a mechanism to eliminate needless duplication and inconsistency in those islands, however large or narrow they may be.

10. A proposal: Unilateral recognition under TTIP

To date, those seeking convergence of regulatory systems have tended to focus on 'mutual recognition', the idea that each side will accept the other's regulation as adequate.[83] This approach is particularly problematic when one side has regulated a substance but the other has not. Would the European side be required to accept a US EPA decision *not* to regulate because risks were assessed to be very low? That is not likely to happen, at least not any time soon, as many Europeans apparently still perceive Americans as swimming 'in a toxic soup of poisonous chemicals' (as Europe itself presumably also must have been before REACH was enacted in 2006). It remains surprising why so few Europeans seem to wonder why US citizens would accept that, not to speak of workers, but we refer to the discussion in section 4.

There are, however, other approaches to achieving greater regulatory convergence that may be more promising, particularly

---

[83] For a classic statement of the case for mutual recognition, see Eizenstat, *supra* note 42. For the many forms of mutual recognition, including MRAs, see Jacques Pelkmans & Anabela Correia de Brito, *Study on Mutual Recognition Agreements*, OECD, Paris, forthcoming (2015). A survey of how mutual recognition works in the goods and services markets in the EU is found in Jacques Pelkmans (2012), "Mutual recognition: economic and regulatory logic in goods and services", in T. Eger and H-B. Schaefer (eds), *Research Handbook on the economics of EU law*, Cheltenham: E. Elgar.

when one side or the other is particularly 'dug in' about the superiority of its system, as some groups and some governments in Europe appear to be about REACH, and the US appears to be about risk-based regulation.

An option that one of us has proposed is called 'optional asymmetric recognition'[84] Under such a system, a regulated party would be given the option to opt-into the regulatory system for a chemical that is perceived by the TTIP negotiating parties as more stringent, such as REACH. Thereby, the costs of duplicative regulatory processes in the second country could be avoided in at least some instances in which "the game was not worth the candle". It is even possible to trade asymmetric recognition in one area, where one side is perceived as more stringent, for asymmetric recognition in another area, where the other sides' regulations are perceived as more stringent. (This is actually the usual situation in negotiations, in which it is rare to trade like for like; rather, the path to a successful negotiation generally involves trading away something that one values less but the other sides values more.)

If a company decided that the potential 'over-regulation' under REACH was not worth arguing about, the company could decide to have the REACH restrictions become legally binding in the US, and thereby avoid the costs of going through a duplicative regulatory process in the US. These conditions are most likely to be satisfied when (1) the costs of going through duplicative regulation are relatively high, but (2) the marginal costs of accepting over-regulation are relatively low, such as because the company expects to sell the same product everywhere anyway. For example, assume that a pesticide is already registered in the EU, and the producer intends to sell exactly the same formulation in the US. If we know that EU regulation is more stringent, what is the value in requiring the company to re-register the product in the US? The same would be true for anti-microbials, or additives for cosmetics. Companies should have the option of accepting a more stringent regulatory result as the *de facto* international standard. In this way, a *de facto* harmonised standard may develop internationally from the bottom up, rather than top down, as many countries gradually defer to a single regulation as adequate to protect their publics. In practice, many companies selling products internationally already, adopt a

---

[84] The discussion of "optional asymmetric recognition" is based on a presentation by Donald Elliott to the European Risk Forum in Brussels, 11 June 2013.

single design standard for their products worldwide rather than making different products for different markets depending on vagaries of local regulations.

But optional asymmetric recognition would not work in the other direction: EPA's failure to regulate something, or having less stringent regulation than under REACH, would have no legal consequences. Thus, optional *asymmetric* (or, unilateral) recognition differs from *mutual* recognition in that it is a one-way street, and that it is optional, not automatic. But optional asymmetric recognition has the advantage that some of the gains from eliminating duplicative regulatory burdens can be achieved in a situation where only one side trusts the other to regulate adequately albeit perhaps too stringently. Thus, if the US side believes that EU regulation under REACH may be too stringent in some instances, but the EU believes that US regulation is not stringent enough in some instances, mutual recognition is a non-starter. Yet, there still may be some situations in which some gains are still possible through asymmetric (*i.e.* unilateral) recognition of the other side's regulation as adequate and these potential gains should not be left on the table in TTIP negotiations. Gains from optional asymmetric recognition would generally occur when the costs of duplicative regulation are greater than the excess costs of what is perceived to be 'more stringent than necessary' regulation. It may seem intuitive that there would be few such situations, but that is not necessarily the case if companies are manufacturing and selling into multi-national markets, as they often are for chemicals. If a company is selling in both the US and the EU, and is already regulated in the EU, requiring the company to go through a duplicative regulatory process in the US when it would be willing to carry over EU regulation into the US, is a pure and costly deadweight loss. Moreover, to maintain public confidence, the most stringent standard by a major trading partner may well become the *de facto* regulatory standard worldwide. Why not negotiate an agreement that US companies may opt in to REACH regulation in the US when they do not object to doing so?

11. Conclusions

As Otto von Bismarck famously stated in the remark that we quote in the epigraph at the beginning of this chapter, "Politics is the art of the possible." From that standpoint, the TTIP negotiators were probably wise to focus on the modest but important goals of eliminating tariffs, sharing datasets, standardising labelling and expanding sharing the technical work of assessing priority chemicals at the scientific level.

While proponents of harmonisation of regulatory systems, such as Ambassador Stuart Eizenstat, admonish us that "we *should* have confidence in the 21st century that the regulatory standards in both the EU and US are adequate to protect our publics and should be accepted",[85] regrettably, that mutual confidence that he asserts "should" be taken for granted, does not yet exist. The difference between the EU and the US over whether regulation should be precautionary, or based on more mature, demonstrated science continues to be a fundamental divide at this time. Perhaps greater confidence will come later in the 21st century after a period of working together at the technical and scientific level.

One critical focus we strongly advocate is to establish authoritatively in what areas the level of SHEC protection for substances which are regulated on both sides is similar. Establishing this is, as we have shown, a major task in and by itself. In areas where that similarity is found, it would open possibilities for much greater ambition in TTIP for chemicals. Unfortunately, but also surprisingly, the knowledge about the areas and substances which are regulated in some form (be it by precisely identified regulation by agencies or in annexes of a range of laws, or otherwise, including judicial review and the chilling effect of liability suits) is rather imperfect, in particular in the US. Knowing the possibilities for liability cases in the US and realising that chemical substances are regulated outside TSCA (under other laws and statutes, and by federal agencies) far more often than under TSCA, the European perception that protection against risky chemicals in the US is often lousy or even absent, is almost certainly profoundly mistaken. We recommend that TTIP should include a trans-Atlantic body that is assigned with assessing objectively the actual outcomes (i.e. levels of protection against risky chemicals) of divergent regulatory processes and identifying those areas where differences in the level of protection are not material, that means, equivalent. These findings should lay the foundation for greater but well-targeted ambition in lowering the costs of TBTs, so high in transatlantic chemicals trade. Getting US and EU negotiators (and the governments behind them) out of their trenches may well hold significant promises for economic gains, without affecting in any way the achieved protection against risky chemicals.

---

[85] Stuart E. Eizenstat, A new transatlantic partnership (April 2013) (italics supplied), http://esharp.eu/essay/23-a-new-transatlantic-partnership/, *quoted supra* page 26.

However, apart from this very long run perspective, we also discuss at some length the EU suggestions done in November 2014 and some of the background issues behind those. We regard them as modest, given what TTIP stands for from its start, but useful. However, chemicals trade suffering from the second-highest TBTs over the North Atlantic, the EU suggestions are expected to do little in reducing TBT costs in the short to medium run. Nevertheless, the EU suggestions, modest as they are, might have become more problematic because of the somewhat defensive EP TTIP resolution of 8 July 2015 although the authors are not convinced that this is necessarily the case. Seen in this political climate, what might be regarded (e.g. by the authors) as a modest proposal for chemicals in TTIP – never mind, the US position on chemicals about which little is known - may well be the maximum possible for a while to come. This is regrettable but a political fact of life. It renders the main message in our chapter even more crucial: in the final analysis, what really matters is where the US and the US do protect citizens and workers against risky chemicals and, if both do this in an equivalent manner, how can trading costs be sliced without ever touching SHEC objectives? Finally, we suggest an easy and relatively simple solution to facilitate market access and reduce the costs of duplication for companies selling in both the EU and US markets, in case the substance is regulated on both sides. Called (asymmetric) unilateral recognition, it would allow a company to opt-in into the most stringent of the two regulatory regimes for substance z, thereby having to comply only once, and get automatic recognition, hence market access, in the less stringently regulated market (for this substance). For those substances, costs could be cut considerably. Many chemical companies including SMEs do indeed sell in both Europe and the US and would benefit directly without setting up TTIP harmonisation. By definition, it would imply a race-to-the-top for these substances.

References

Ahearn, Raymond J. (2008), "Transatlantic Regulatory Cooperation and Analysis: Background and Analysis", CRS Report for Congress, 22 October (http://fpc.state.gov/documents/organization/112019.pdf).

Applegate, John (2008), "Synthesizing TSCA and REACH: practical principles for chemical regulation reform" (http://works.bepress.com/john_applegate/1).

Bagehot, W. (1901), *The English Constitution and Other Political Essays* (rev. ed.).

Berman, B. (2008), "Lusting for Europe's Illegal 60-MPG Cars", 8 December (www.hybridcars.com/lusting-europe-illegal-high-mpg-cars-25323/).

BUND (2015), "TTIP und die Chemikalienpolitik in der EU" ("TTIP and chemicals policy in the EU"), June (www.bund.et/fileadmin/bundnet/pdfs/sonstiges/150623_bund_son stiges_ttip_chemie_hintergrund.pdf).

Cefic (2014), response to Commission's request for further details on joint ACC-Cefic proposals for enhanced cooperation on chemicals under TTIP, 7 March (www.cefic.org/Documents/PolicyCentre/TTIP/%5bTTIP%5d%20Ce fic%20response%20to%20Commission%20ACC-Cefic%20proposal%20on%20TTIP%207%20March%202014%20(web%2 0and%20click-in).pdf).

Charnley, Gail and E. Donald Elliott (2002), "Risk Versus Precaution: Environmental Law and Public Health Protection", *Environmental Law Reporter*, Vol. 32, No. 3, 10363, March.

Chase, Peter and Jacques Pelkmans (2015), "This time it's different: Turbo-charging regulatory cooperation in TTIP", CEPS Special Report No. 110, Centre for European Policy Studies, Brussels and chapter 2 in this volume.

CSES (2012), "Interim evaluation: functioning of the European chemical market after the introduction of REACH", study for the European Commission, London, 30 March (www.cses.co.uk).

Dernbach, J.C. (1997), "The Unfocused Regulation of Toxic and Hazardous Pollutants", *Harvard Environmental Law Review*, Vol. 21, No. 1, 1997

du Pont de Nemours, E.I. and Company (2013), "Comments", Docket number: USTR-2013-0019 - Request for Comments Concerning Proposed Transatlantic Trade and Investment Agreement (TTIP), 10 May.

EEA (2001), "Late lessons from early warnings, the precautionary principle 1896 – 2000", Environmental Issues Report No. 22, Copenhagen (www.eea.europa.eu).

_____ (2013), "Late lessons from early warnings: science, precaution, innovation" (www.eea.europa.eu/publications/late-lessons-2).

Eizenstat, Stuart E. (2013), "A new transatlantic partnership", April (http://esharp.eu/essay/23-a-new-transatlantic-partnership/).

Elliott, E. Donald (2008), "Portage Strategies for Adapting Environmental Law and Policy During a Logjam Era", *New York University Environmental Law Journal*, Vol. 17, p. 24.

Elliott, E. Donald and E. Michael Thomas (1993), "Chemicals", Chapter 17 in C. Campbell-Mohn, W. Futrell and B. Breen (eds), Sustainable Environmental Law pp. 1257-1354 (West Pub. Co.).

Elliott, E. Donald, Bruce A. Ackerman and John C. Millian (1985), "Toward a Theory of Statutory Evolution: The Federalization of Environmental Law", *Journal of Law, Economics, Organization*, Vol. 1, pp. 313-340.

Elliott, E. Donald and Gail Charnley Elliott (2009), "Private Product-Risk Assessment and the Role of Government", *John Liner Review*, Vol. 23, p. 72.

European Commission (2000), "On the precautionary principle", COM(2000)1 of 2 February.

Erixon, Frederik and Matthias Bauer (2010), "A Transatlantic Zero Agreement: Estimating the Gains from Transatlantic Free Trade in Goods", ECIPE Occasional Paper No. 4, European Centre for International Political Economy, Brussels (www.ecipe.org).

Francois, J., M. Manchin, H. Norberg, O. Pindyuk and P. Tomberger (2013), "Reducing Transatlantic barriers to trade and investment, an economic assessment", study prepared for DG Trade of the European Commission (http://trade.ec.europe.eu/doclib/docs/2013/march/tradoc_150737. pdf).

GAO (2007), "Chemical regulation, comparison of US and recently enacted EU approaches to protect against the risks of toxic chemicals" (www.gao.gov/cgi-bin/getrpt?GAO-07-825).

Granville, Kevin (2015), "The Trans-Pacific Partnership Trade Deal Explained", *New York Times*, 11 May (www.nytimes.com/2015/05/12/business/unpacking-the-trans-pacific-partnership-trade-deal.html?_r=0).

Greenberg, Michael and Karen Lowrie (2008), "Toxicity Testing in the 21st Century: Better Results, Less Use of Animals, Editorial", *The Environmental Forum*, Vol. 25, pp. 46-51.

Jones, Jim, Acting Assistant Administrator for the Office of Chemicals Safety and Pollution Prevention, US Environmental Protection Agency (2013), "Towards a Transatlantic Market for Trade in Chemicals", 17 July, Washington, D.C.

Kahneman, Daniel (2011), *Thinking, Fast and Slow*, New York: Farrar, Straus and Giroux.

Kahneman, D. and A. Tversky (1979), "Prospect Theory: An Analysis of Decision under Risk", *Econometrica*, Vol. 47, No. 2, pp. 263-291, March (for an accessible summary, see http://youarenotsosmart.com/2011/03/25/the-sunk-cost-fallacy/).

Kollipara, K. (2015), "US Senate makes progress on chemical regulation reform, but obstacles await", *Science*, 6 May (http://news.sciencemag.org/chemistry/2015/05/u-s-senate-makes-progress-chemical-regulation-reform-obstacles-await).

Leff, Arthur (1974), "Economic Analysis of Law: Some Realism About Nominalism", *Virginia Law Review*, Vol. 60, pp. 451-482.

Lejour, Arjan, Federica Mustilli, Jacques Pelkmans and Jacopo Timini (2014), "Economic incentives for indirect TTIP spill-overs", CEPS Research Report No. 94, Centre for European Policy Studies, Brussels, October.

Loewenton, Ed (2008), "CPSC Toughens Lead Regulations in Toys", 28 October (http://turnertoys.com/CPSC-Toughens-Lead-Regulations-in-Toys.html).

Milieu (2012), "Technical assistance related to the scope of REACH legislation to assess overlaps", report prepared for DG Environment, European Commission, 12 March (http://ec.europa.eu/enterprise/sectors/chemicals/files/reach/revie w2012/scope-final-report_en.pdf).

National Research Council, Committee on Toxicity Testing and Assessment of Environmental Agents, (2007), "Toxicity Testing in the Twenty-First Century: A Vision and a Strategy", report commissioned by the US Environmental Protection Agency (http://www.nap.edu/catalog/11970/toxicity-testing-in-the-21st-century-a-vision-and-a).

Pelkmans, Jacques (2005), "REACH: getting the chemistry right in Europe", in Daniel Hamilton and Joseph Quinlan (eds), *Deep integration, how transatlantic markets are leading globalization*, CEPS, Brussels and CTR at SAIS, Johns Hopkins, Washington, D.C.

_____ (2012), "Mutual recognition: economic and regulatory logic in goods and services", in T. Eger and H-B. Schaefer (eds), *Research Handbook on the economics of EU law*, Cheltenham: E. Elgar.

Pelkmans, Jacques and Anabela Correia de Brito (2015), "Study on Mutual Recognition Agreements", OECD, Paris, forthcoming.

Pelkmans, Jacques, Lorna Schrefler and Ineke Gubbels (2013), "The consequences of REACH for SMEs", study PE 507 486 in 2013 for the European Parliament (www.europarl.europa.eu/studies); also published as "REACH: a killer whale for SMEs?", CEPS Policy Brief No. 307, Centre for European Policy Studies, Brussels, December.

Pelkmans, J., A. Lejour, L. Schrefler, F. Mustilli and J. Timini (2014), "The Impact of TTIP, the underlying economic model and comparisons", CEPS Special Report No. 93, Centre for European Policy Studies, Brussels, October (www.ceps.eu).

Quick, Reinhard (2008a), "Regulatory cooperation – a subject of bilateral negotiations or even for the WTO", *Journal of World Trade*, Vol. 42, pp. 391-406.

_____ (2008b), "Transatlantic Regulatory Cooperation on Chemicals — An Idealist's Dream?," German Marshall Fund Academic Research Conference, Ford School, University of Michigan (http:fordschool.umich.edu/news/events_details/re_coop_and-comp_08/).

Renn, O. and E.D. Elliott (2011), "Chemicals", in J.B. Wiener, M.D. Rogers, J.K. Hammitt and P.H. Sand (eds), *The Reality of Precaution: Comparing Risk Regulation in the United States and Europe*, Abingdon: RFF Press, pp. 223-256.

Schrefler, Lorna and Jacques Pelkmans (2014), "Better Use of Science for Better EU Regulation", *European Journal of Risk Regulation*, Vol. 5, No. 3, pp. 314-323, March.

Shaffer, Gregory C. and Mark A. Pollack (2005), "Reconciling Regulatory Differences: The Ongoing Transatlantic Dispute over the Regulation of Biotechnology", in David M. Andrews, Mark A. Pollack, Gregory C. Shaffer and Helen Wallace (eds), *The Future of Transatlantic Economic Relations*, Robert Schuman Centre for Advanced Studies, pp. 220-221.

Schwarzman, Megan and Michael Wilson (2011), "Reshaping chemicals policy on two sides of the Atlantic: the promise of improved sustainability through international collaboration", in David Vogel and Johan Swinnen (eds), *Transatlantic regulatory cooperation, shifting roles of the EU, the US and California*, Cheltenham/Northhampton: E. Elgar.

Sigman, R. (2013), "Chemical safety", in OECD, *International Regulatory Cooperation: Case Studies*, Vol. 1., pp. 9-26, Paris.

Thaler, Richard H. and Cass R. Sunstein (2008), *Nudge: Improving Decisions about Health, Wealth, and Happiness*, New Haven, CT: Yale University Press.

US-EU High Level Regulatory Forum (2011), "Common Understanding on Regulatory Principles and Best Practices" (http://trade.ec.europa.eu/doclib/docs/2011/december/tradoc_148392.pdf).

US-EU High Level Working Group on Jobs and Growth (2013), Final Report, 11 February (https://ustr.gov/about-us/policy-offices/press-office/reports-and-publications/2013/final-report-us-eu-hlwg).

Vogel, D. (1995), *Trading Up: Consumer And Environmental Regulation In A Global Economy*, Cambridge. MA: Harvard University Press.

——— (2012), *The politics of precaution: Regulating Health, Safety, and Environmental Risks in Europe and the United States*, Princeton, NJ: Princeton University Press.

Vogel, D. and J. Swinnen (eds) (2011), *Transatlantic regulatory cooperation – the shifting roles of the EU, the US and California*, Cheltenham: E. Elgar.

Wiener, J.B., M.D. Rogers, J.K. Hammitt and P.H. Sand (eds) (2011), *The Reality of Precaution: Comparing Risk Regulation in the United States and Europe*, Abingdon: RFF Press.

14. TTIP AND ENERGY
PAOLO NATALI, CHRISTIAN EGENHOFER AND GERGELY MOLNAR

1. Introduction

Despite accounting for a significant share of global trade[1] and the resulting interdependencies from it, energy governance remains largely fragmented and there is no global framework or agreement defining the rules of energy trade. While the GATT/WTO Agreements do not specifically deal with energy trade and the Energy Charter Treaty (Box 14.1) failed to establish an effective agreement on cross-border trade, countries tend to frame energy trade into bilateral cooperation schemes – as energy is considered an area of high strategic relevance, having a strong impact on national security and sovereignty, which can also open the door to protectionism.

Box 14.1 Energy Charter Treaty

The Energy Charter Treaty aims to promote international cooperation in the energy sector. Entering into force in April 1998, the Treaty's provisions focus on four broad areas: 1) the protection of foreign investment, based on the extension of national treatment, or most-favoured nation treatment and protection against key non-commercial risks; 2) non-discriminatory conditions for trade in energy materials, products and energy-related equipment based on WTO rules, and provisions to ensure reliable cross-border energy transit flows through pipelines, grids and other means of transportation; 3) the resolution of disputes between participating states, and – in the case of investment – between investors and host states; and 4) the promotion of energy efficiency.

---

[1] According to the World Bank the trade value in fuels is about 14.33% of global trade: (http://wits.worldbank.org/CountryProfile/Country/WLD/Year/ LTST/Summary).

Members of the Energy Charter Conference, i.e. the ECT's membership base, are from the European Economic Area, EU candidate and Neighbourhood countries, the Russian Federation and other countries from the former Soviet Union as well as Japan, Australia, Mongolia and Afghanistan. The Russian Parliament refused the ratification of the ECT, as the ECT's Transit Protocol would require Russia to apply the principles of freedom of transit and non-discriminatory pricing to its oil and gas pipeline systems. In April 2004, the Russian Duma decided to remove the Transit Protocol from its agenda.

The Treaty remains open for accession by all countries committed to the Charter's principles. In an effort to enlarge its geographical scope, the International Energy Charter initiative has been launched in May 2015 in The Hague.

It is often suggested that the emergence of the US as a new energy superpower as a consequence of the shale revolution and the EU's desire to reduce its energy import dependence on Russia in the wake of deteriorating EU-Russia relations, would not only increase the value of transatlantic energy trade but also deepen EU-US cooperation in this field, and possibly in foreign and security policy. Therefore, perhaps not surprisingly, the EU would like to include a distinct 'energy and raw materials' chapter into the TTIP (European Commission, 2013a; European Commission, 2015).

On the other hand, to date, the US has pursued its 'energy security' or 'oil independence' approach since the mid-1970s. Oil and gas policy has been a result of the US fear of oil dependence, mainly on the Persian Gulf, and later of the fear of similar dependence on imported gas (see, for example, Yergin (2006)). Seen from this perspective, it is not obvious why energy should be included in TTIP. Energy is indeed rather special and faces rather uncommon trade and other barriers, some of which in the past seem to have served rather well the national interest of the US. Such US barriers include an export ban on US crude oil and a licencing regime for Liquefied Natural Gas (LNG) trade for those countries with which the US does not have a free trade agreement. To date US negotiators seem unconvinced of the value of an energy chapter and argue that energy is already sufficiently covered in other chapters of the TTIP. Notably, they hold that once TTIP is concluded, natural gas exports from the US to the EU would be sufficiently facilitated, should there be a market in Europe. This is because under the Natural Gas Act, LNG exports to countries with which the US has free trade agreements that require "national treatment" for trade in natural gas are automatically considered in the public interest. Applications to export gas to such countries must be approved without modification or delay. However, LNG exports destined to non-FTA countries, with which the US does not have a free trade agreement, are subject to a project-based licencing system. Hence, they need the approval not only of the FERC (for environmental issues) but also of the Department of Energy (to ensure that these exports do not harm 'the public interest') (Chadbourne, 2014; Energy.gov, n.d.).

The primary motivation for the EU to include a chapter on energy into the TTIP seems to be to set a benchmark not only in terms of transparency, non-discrimination and competition rules but also of an open international market for trade of 'environmental goods and services and climate-friendly products and technologies'. At first sight, one might think this is the predictable EU reflex on spreading its rules, often referred to as 'Europeanisation'. This tactical move to make TTIP more palatable inside the EU given the concessions that it might need to make might play a role. But when reading the "Initial EU position paper" (European Commission, 2013a), it is easy to see that the target is not so much the TTIP in itself but other trade agreements that might appear as spin-offs. The EU would like to anchor energy in what might become a template or part of the template for future agreements.

This chapter will analyse how the market dynamics unleashed by the US energy revolutions might shape the transatlantic energy agenda, in particular in TTIP, and what potential economic and political benefits it could yield. The concluding section will identify the future transatlantic energy agenda.

2. The TTIP energy market context

2.1 The US shale revolution

For many years there has been transatlantic trade of coal and oil products. This trade has been stable, i.e. diesel and petrol with a value amounting to around €298 billion between 2004 and 2014.[2] There was no export of crude oil from the US, to a large extent because of the 1975 export ban, although the type of crude which could have been exported, i.e. light sweet, would not have been available in sufficient quantity to do so. With the shale revolution this has changed. In the

---

[2] Eurostat, International trade, EU trade since 1988 by SITC [DS-018995].

aftermath of the 1973 Arab oil embargo, in December 1975 the US passed the Energy Policy and Energy Conservation Act, a ban on most US oil exports. A few exceptions exist such as crude from Alaska's Cook Inlet and North Slope and heavy oil from certain California fields. Article 605 of NAFTA restricts the US ability to limit its crude oil and petrochemical exports to Canada (and vice versa). While Mexico is not part of Article 605, there are also exceptions for re-exporting foreign oil and for small swaps with Mexico.

Similarly, all US natural gas exports are subject to certain limitations. Those destined to non-FTA countries, with which the US does not have a free trade agreement, are subject to a project-based licencing system and need the approval of both FERC (for environmental issues) and the Department of Energy (to ensure that these exports do not harm 'the public interest').

This situation remained relatively stable as long as the US was facing increasing import dependency for both oil and natural gas. The US shale gas and shale oil revolution has fundamentally reversed this situation. Coupling hydraulic fracturing with horizontal drilling resulted in a tremendous increase in shale gas production in the US. The same techniques have also generated a comparable revolution in oil. As a result, the US became the world's largest natural gas producer in 2012 and the largest oil producer in 2013. As shown in Figure 14.1, both crude oil and natural gas imports into the US declined over the last decade, and this trend is more than likely to continue in the future.

This technological breakthrough in the North American upstream energy, i.e. production, sector over the last decade has affected almost all segments of the energy markets, not only in North America but globally. The sudden abundance of natural gas within North America transformed the continent from a net importer to a one in need of finding export markets. Export markets are seen as potentially constituting a safety valve, in order to release domestic production internationally, thus reducing oversupply and the subsequent severely depressed domestic price. Natural gas is literally 'trapped inside' the region until export licences are granted and LNG export terminals are built.

Figure 14.1 US oil and gas imports (2004-14)

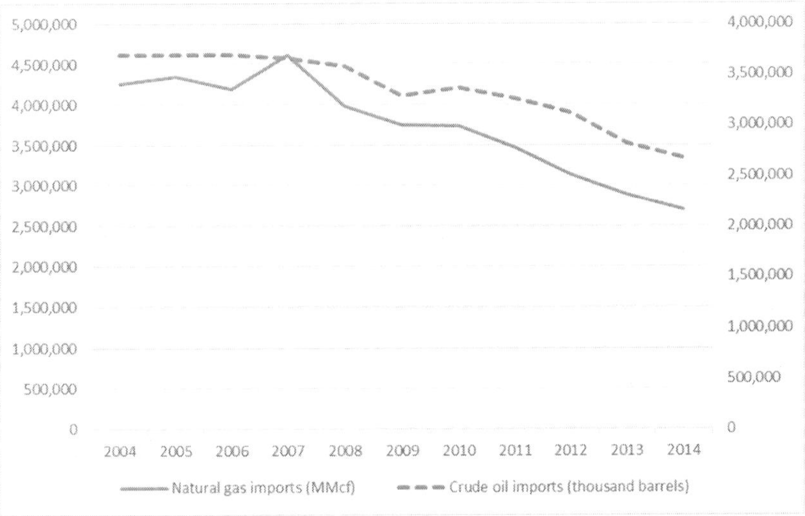

Source: Authors' own configuration based on data from US Energy Information Agency.

With production increasing from 0.6 mb/d in 2008 to 4.7 mb/d in 2014, the situation for shale oil is shaping up in a similar fashion, despite it being more complicated owing to crude quality issues. Crude oil is legally 'trapped' until the long-lasting export ban is lifted. Legislation hindering the free flow of oil, the world's most easily transportable energy source, widens the gap between the US oil prices and other international oil price benchmarks. For instance, in 2014 the spread between Brent and WTI (West Texas Intermediate) reached $12/barrel (Reuters, 2015). Hence, the US refining sector is experiencing high margins and utilisation rates thanks to the cheaper feedstock and whilst European refining is losing ground in a more and more severe way. According to the International Energy Agency (IEA), since 2008 crude processing capacity in the EU has contracted by around 8% with 15 refineries closing and three reducing their output (IEA, 2014). While the recent fall in crude oil prices improved the competitiveness of the European refinery sector, the longer-term outlook remains less optimistic, not least because of tightening regulations in the EU and the rising competitiveness of the US refinery complex ICIS (2015). Moreover, one should note that the US is facing an oversupply of light sweet crude oil (particularly desirable as a feedstock for gasoline refining) as US refineries are more suitable to heavy crude oil (EIA, 2015c).

In addition, coal consumption for electricity generation in the US has fallen significantly as natural gas has become more cost competitive. US coal can freely move out of North America to flood other regions and in particular Europe (see Figure 14.2). This trend is reinforced by the fact that US coal prices dropped to their lowest level in six years in the first quarter of 2015.[3]

Figure 14.2 EU-28 solid fuel imports from the US (thousand tonnes)

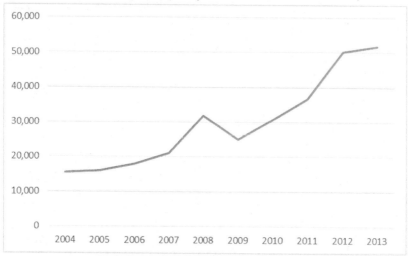

Source: Authors' own configuration based on data from Eurostat.

In order to understand the energy politics of TTIP, one must understand the changes in market dynamics in the US. The result of the interplay of technological breakthroughs, regulation and market dynamics has had enormous implications within the US and worldwide (Morse, 2014). For the US and its North American neighbours the shale gas revolution has indisputably been the main energy event of the last decade. Since 2008, it has changed the original shape of natural gas flows within the domestic pipeline system. The system was originally intended to bring gas from the production/import centres of the Gulf of Mexico and Canada into the main consumption areas, especially the north-east. The emergence of the main shale geographic areas – referred to as 'plays' – has somewhat reversed this picture: while Eagle Ford, in Texas, is relatively close to

---

[3] Central Appalachian coal prices, the benchmark dropped to $52.75/short tonne; see EIA (2015b).

Henry Hub and thus still pushes gas in the same original directions, the Marcellus shale play stretches from Maryland to upstate New York, thus sitting right in the backyard of the big cities of the north-east, which are the main consumption centres. Such is the abundance of gas that reverse flows from Marcellus to the south-east are becoming a reality.

The physical change in flows has brought about a corresponding change in local pricing, and hereof positioning by all players in order to secure transportation capacities in different and previously ancillary pipelines, reverse flows and the like (Hamilton & Santa Maria, 2014). The traditional domestic price differentials, measured in terms of a positive "basis" from the reference Henry Hub, have reduced dramatically[4] and no longer justify transport from Texas, hence effectively becoming negative (EIA, 2013b).

The abundance of gas traded at Henry Hub itself has brought down the price by around four times, i.e. from $11.27/MMBtu[5] in May 2008 to $2.85/MMBtu in May 2015. Many early entrants in domestic shale gas production have been struggling with financing their projects due to this depressed price situation. LNG imports have become virtually non-existent[6] and the low prices are here to stay until LNG export terminals come on stream to work as a safety valve to the system. The first LNG exports from the contiguous US are scheduled for the end of 2015. However, exports might impact domestic gas prices only when they reach a more significant level, but this is not going to happen at least for two or three years.[7]

---

[4] Spot prices, in $/MMBtu, on 27 August 2014: Henry Hub 3.99, New York 2.79. NGI Daily Gas Price Index.

[5] Millions of British thermal units.

[6] LNG imports into the US are expected to be 0.17 Bcf/d in both 2014 and 2015, a very tiny volume when compared to a domestic consumption expected to average 72.6 Bcf/d during 2014. See EIA (2014), section on "Natural Gas".

[7] "Many of the latecomers frantically snatched up shale leases during the buying spree of 2009-12. But lots of these parcels of land have proved disappointing and now look to have been overpriced. The influx of the supermajors has contributed to another problem, too: a gas glut, exacerbated by inadequate pipeline infrastructure, that has kept US benchmark Henry Hub spot prices largely below $4 per MMBtu since 2011. Companies are being forced to redirect their efforts to areas rich in more profitable crude oil and natural gas liquids (NGLs)." See Economist Intelligence Unit (2013).

Moreover, in recent years the global LNG market has experienced two phases: with European[8] NBP (National Balancing Point) prices typically hovering around the $8-10/MMBtu mark, and US (Henry Hub)[9] prices plunging below $5/MMBtu after the first batches of shale gas production came to market, there has been a period, roughly corresponding with 2013, during which Asian prices above $15/MMBtu would certainly justify US exports to Asia. Note that during that period and up to now, not a single load of LNG landed from the contiguous US in Asia, because the pre-shale gas revolution market did not need export capacity, and building new LNG export terminals takes time.

Several changes in market fundamentals in 2014 have brought Asian prices down and in the first months of 2015 even below those of Europe's average import price) (see Figure 14.3).

Figure 14.3 Regional gas price dynamics: The disappearing 'Asian premium'

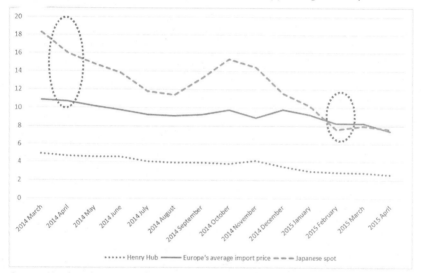

Source: Authors' own configuration based on data from Japan's Ministry of Economy, Trade and Industry (METI), World Bank and EIA.

The main reasons behind this are slowing Chinese economic growth and its increasing interest in piped gas, weather conditions in the Pacific-Asian region (cold summer followed by a mild winter),

---

[8] UK National Balancing Point, i.e. UK import price.

[9] US hub price.

nuclear restarts in South Korea, Japan's drive for energy efficiency to diminish the Fukushima effect, the appearance of new supply sources (start of the PNG LNG[10] export plant in May 2014) and finally the new low-price oil era.

All in all, this means that we are entering uncharted territory in a second phase in which, theoretically at least, a hypothetical US LNG tanker could be better off in Europe than in Asia, especially if liquefied in the Gulf of Mexico or the East Coast, thanks to the lower cost of logistics.

Whatever the views on future fundamentals and therefore on possible LNG flows, it is safe to say that they will swing between one and the other of these two phases. At current technology and logistics levels, US exports to Europe are commercially viable roughly when the NBP-Henry Hub spread is higher than $5/MMBtu. A spread of $7-8/MMBtu would be required to justify exports from the Gulf of Mexico or East Coast to Asia. It is straightforward to observe that if US export terminals had been in operation, in the first phase Asia would have competed with Europe as a destination for LNG, while in the second (current) phase, export volumes would have reached European shores. Hence, flows will be directed by commercial logic, regardless of the TTIP or the Trans-Pacific Partnership (TPP). But these agreements send a strong signal to the main market players and project investors that there is political will to ease LNG flows, if they are commercially viable.

Hence, Europe could secure transatlantic trade. However, in the US this would require US LNG export terminals to be in put place along with legislation providing clarity about the expected or maximum export capacity. For that matter, to allow the EU to fully benefit from the global LNG market, the interconnectivity of Europe's internal gas market would need to be improved and regasification capacity in north-east and south-east Europe increased (see Figure 14.4).

If this happens, the TTIP commitment to market-opening as well as discipline on restrictions such as the lifting of licencing regimes or export bans (in the case of oil) will facilitate the flow of goods and services. This will be facilitated if common rules can be agreed upon. Whether LNG flows towards the EU will become commercially viable is a different matter, and much will depend on whether European gas prices will be able to compete with those proposed by Asian buyers.

---

[10] Papua New Guinea LNG plant, with a 6.9 MTPA capacity. The plant started its first LNG shipments in May 2014.

Figure 14.4 Existing, constructed and planned LNG import plants in Europe

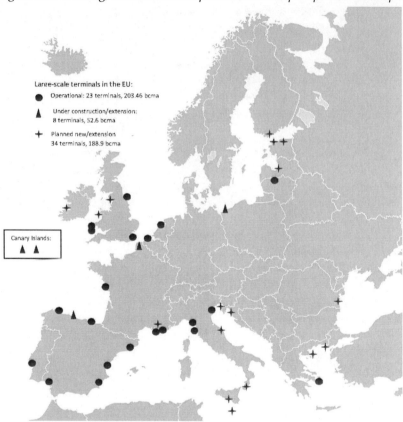

Note: bcma = billion cubic metres/annum.
Source: Authors' own configuration based on data from Gas Infrastructure Europe (GIE).

All in all, the picture looks favourable on a systemic level, but with a number of specific unsolved issues related to market dynamics and, most notably, the consolidation of the shale industry over time. The main player, the US government, needs to decide whether to grant export licences and, if so, how many, and whether to let the market decide or to try to control the flows and therefore domestic prices and production levels. This choice will be more political than economic, not because there will not be an economic gain or loss from it, but because such gain or loss will be due to the interplay of too many actors on a systemic level to be foreseen today. In broad terms, opinions in the US are divided between the supporters of the protectionist view, that is, modulating the newly found reserves so that they, in a protectionist manner, power the domestic economy for the longest possible time; and those who instead argue that maximising US exports would act as a multiplier through the overall economy, hence generating more wealth over time than simply earmarking indigenous reserves for domestic use. It is easy to see how the two camps advocate opposite trade measures: the former supports protectionism, the latter free trade. But the choice cannot ignore the systemic dynamics, including those at the global level.

2.2 The EU's quest for energy diversification

Europe is in a different position than the US. The energy mix is not radically different from that of its transatlantic counterpart, but the forces at play suggest a likely divergence in the foreseeable future. Europe is import dependent and will remain so in the future, even if there is a question of how great this import dependence will be. Rapidly depleting domestic gas reserves and sustained gas demand (highly dependent on the effectiveness of measures taken to phase out coal) suggest that the EU's gas import dependence will further increase in the future, although there is controversy on how much.[11]

Prior to the shale revolution, the shape of Europe's import patterns for natural gas would have looked different to those of North America, which would have increased its reliance primarily on LNG. But the geological and political situation is now such that even if indigenous European shale gas might end up being produced, it is unlikely to trigger a proper revolution of the energy sector as was the case in North America.[12] And if anything, the relationship with its main supplier, Russia, is evolving in a way that suggests diversification out of gas might be in order (Egenhofer, Genoese & Dimitrova, 2014). Currently, the EU produces about 34% of its internal natural gas demand, and it imports the balance from a handful of countries: Russia, Norway, Algeria and (LNG from) Qatar. Most natural gas supply is entrenched in long-term contracts, often indexed to oil. The majority of

---

[11] For instance, according to BP (2014) the EU will need to import 49% more natural gas by 2035. Similarly, European Commission (2013b) considers that the EU will import by 32 more Mtoe of natural gas by 2030 than it did in 2005. Honoré (2014) also suggests an increase of EU gas imports during this period.

[12] For a comprehensive analysis of the reasons for arguing a different trajectory in European shale gas compared to North America, see Sandrea (2014).

these contracts will be due for renegotiation or renewal within the next 10-15 years, and increased liquidity at the hubs suggests that more and more gas is being traded on a short-term basis.[13]

2.3   Cheap coal

Another aspect of the transatlantic relationship when it comes to energy is the effect of cheap US natural gas on global coal flows. As a consequence of low natural gas prices, the US is experiencing a significant switch from coal to gas in power generation, and a very limited switch from fuel oil to gas in home heating. The diminishing need for coal, heightened by the planned phase-out of older coal plants through performance regulation, has generated an export trend of cheap coal to Asia and Europe.

The share of coal used for electricity generation has been shrinking in the US for the last few years – even if it still accounts for 39% of the country's power mix in 2014. The European Union, however, experienced a sort of 'coal renaissance' between 2010 and 2012 as the share of coal increased in the EU's power mix from 24% to almost 28%, although in 2013 the share of coal started to decrease in Europe (Eurostat data).

Indeed, due to structural design problems and their exacerbation by the world financial crisis and the so-called 'euro crisis', the Emissions Trading System (ETS) as the EU's main climate policy instrument has not been able to drive the phase-out of coal in Europe. The severity of the recession has led to a fall in economic activity and therefore to large emissions reductions. In addition, world coal prices have fallen so that the relative competitiveness of coal has increased. Without introducing a supply mechanism in the EU ETS, such as the proposed Market Stability Reserve, it might take until the mid-2020s at the earliest before a high enough carbon price would re-emerge to make gas more competitive. Many doubt, however, whether the ETS will be a suitable tool for supporting investment signals for low-carbon generation capacity. On top of this, the present coal oversupply in the US makes this fuel even cheaper than it used to be, providing a competitive substitute to gas in power generation.

However, there is a range of other policy measures on both sides influencing the electricity mix, in particular pollutants emissions control policies such as the EU ETS and the EU Industrial Emissions

---

[13] For a comprehensive analysis, see Stern (2014).

Directive (IED) and the U.S. Clean Power Plan. Inside the EU, other such measures have been initiated by EU member states, such as the withdrawal of the German nuclear programme after the Fukushima accident in March 2011, and the renewables support measures to phase out coal-fired plants in the UK, the Netherlands and possibly in Germany.[14] These EU, US and national regulatory developments influence the power mix and are supplemented by exogenous changes, which markets have experienced as a result of other factors: among these are Asian economic growth, the 2008-09 financial crisis and subsequent economic downturn (which took place at different paces in different parts of the world economy), and resource developments across the globe. All of these elements influence the natural gas market to a great extent.

Nevertheless, the reality in Europe is that coal is still a strategic resource in a number of EU member states for an array of reasons: it was the only source of power for the Polish economy until very recently; it is needed to complete the German power mix after the government's decision to phase out its nuclear power generation; it is defended by trade unions in Spain on employment grounds. Hence, a phase-out will be uneven across member states at best.

3. The opportunities the TTIP could unlock in the long run

Like the other sectors included in TTIP, the potential for improvement in energy trade lies in the area of non-tariff barriers (NTBs), which would lead to immediate mutual benefits. The removal of barriers to LNG exports from the US would benefit the sector, with LNG exports opening an alternative source of supply to develop over time in order to find an alternative to the cheaper, potentially less secure, Russian gas.

The impact of the removal of barriers can be increased further by common rules. For example, harmonising regulation related to the

---

[14] The UK introduced a carbon price to bolster the existing (too low) EU carbon price and is developing the legislative framework for the implementation of the Emissions Performance Standard for new fossil fuel plants as an annual limit on carbon emissions from new fossil fuel plants equivalent to 450g/kWh. The Netherlands under its national Energy Agreement of 2013, a settlement negotiated by the stakeholders, will phase out the technically least efficient capacity, which typically is coal. The German government is also considering additional regulation to deal with least efficient generation.

limitation of carbon emissions – even if not a realistic proposition at the moment and possibly for the foreseeable future – would create a level playing field that could at least partially create some clarity in a complicated field, which is currently being tackled in very different ways such as cap-and-trade, emissions standards or subsidies. Transatlantic coordination could prove useful in the long run in this respect, especially now that an alignment seems possible on the need for binding carbon reduction commitments, which the US had resisted for a long time. One could imagine the gradual linking of transatlantic cap-and-trade systems (Egenhofer, 2005) building on the experiences of existing systems such as the ETS or the one in California (and which is now gradually linked with the systems of the Canadian provinces of Quebec and Ontario). This would not only send a signal that the transatlantic region is ready to factor a high CO_2 price into its value chains but could also address sensitive issues such as 'carbon leakage' (Gros & Egenhofer, 2011) towards Asia. A high price of carbon in Europe would mean fewer outlets for its outflow of unused coal while a high carbon price in the US would mean a higher price of energy, which is actually going counter to the centrepiece of the shale revolution. Whether this happens will depend on many factors, not least the politics in the two regions, and currently there seems to be little immediate prospect. But the issue will not only not go away but become more important.

3.1 US authorisation of LNG export terminals

Although market projections suggest that American LNG will flow towards Europe and Asia, the current geopolitical situation suggests that non-economic factors might arise, if not dominate and justify some form of eastbound flow towards European LNG regasification terminals. In absence of a TTIP section providing energy cooperation and disciplines, the issue is left with the US regulator having to decide how many export terminals, and therefore how much export capacity, will be available. Moreover, leaving aside LNG could be interpreted by certain market players and project investors as a sign of lacking political will to ease LNG flows.

3.2 Regulatory harmonisation over the longer term

A further range of NTBs is caused by environmental regulations on both shores, especially where regulatory divergence results in certain plant or fuels being allowed in one region and not in the other. In this respect the most relevant area is pollutants emissions, and their indirect impact on fuels through regulation that implies the phase-out of some types of electricity generation plants. In 2011 the US Environmental Protection Agency (EPA) introduced emissions standards for toxic air pollutants such as mercury, acid gases and sulphur dioxide.

In September 2013 the EPA reintroduced CO_2 performance standards for new power stations and in June 2014 it issued a proposal on the performance standards for existing power plants. In the proposed framework, the EPA would issue guidelines about the appropriate standards, but US states would be responsible for establishing and eventually implementing the performance standards once they have been approved by the EPA. Each state will have individual goals set by the EPA (a state-specific future carbon intensity of covered existing fossil-fuel-fired power plants in that state) and they will be free to choose the means to achieve the interim and then the final goal. All in all, the EPA expects that the Clean Power Plan would reduce nationwide CO_2 emissions from the power sector by around 30% from 2005 levels by 2030 (EPA, 2014).

In the EU, the Industrial Emissions Directive sets out a pathway for the reduction of pollutants emissions, but the carbon emissions are only regulated through the 2007-09 Climate Package, which sets a 20% overall emissions reduction target. Industrial and power sector emissions are regulated by the EU ETS (Ellerman, Convery & de Perthuis, 2010). On 23-24 October 2014 the European Council decided on a new set of targets for 2030 ("2030 Framework for climate and energy policy"), including a 40% greenhouse gas reduction, a minimum 27% renewables and a minimum 27% efficiency target. The EU ETS is also set to be strengthened, as the linear reduction factor of the EU-wide carbon cap will increase from the current 1.74% per year to 2.2% from 2021. In addition, the European Commission is trying to address the oversupply of carbon allowances, which has led to a fall of the allowances to less than €10/tonne of CO_2. One strategy is changing the allocation time path. The other is establishing a supply side mechanism, e.g. the so-called 'Market Stability Reserve' (MSR) to adjust the auctioning volume by 'parking' allowances intended to be auctioned in a reserve and releasing them from the reserve to the market to maintain the total amount of allowances in circulation in a given year within a prescribed band.

Should the US Clean Power Plan go ahead and the EU ETS not quickly manage to effectively address the current glut in emission allowances, an imbalance could be created whereby coal power plants would be forced to shut down faster in the US than in the EU, hence reinforcing the existing 'coal leakage'. Whether this will be the case or will also depend on member states' policies, such as those in the UK or the Netherlands, which are considering national measures emissions performance standards similar to those of the US, could potentially polarise the coal leakage problem towards some European countries and not others.

Hence, regulatory cooperation between the EU and the US in the elaboration of emissions performance standards could effectively address the issue of coal leakage. On the other hand, the US could ask the EU to put its house in order. If not, the lack of a cap-and-trade carbon emissions system in the US, combined with the lower natural gas prices, will favour a sizeable medium-term switch from coal to gas in power generation, which will not be matched in Europe. Currently, there is no short-term scenario where the ratio between gas and coal prices would change so that gas increases market share in the EU power sector.

4.   Bringing it all together

Several changes in the structure of trade across the Atlantic might either benefit or harm various aspects of energy policy on both shores, typically enshrined in the triangular model for energy policy that combines the objectives of security of supply, competitiveness and sustainability.

4.1   Security of supply

North American LNG could serve European interests in starting, or at the very least introducing, diversification away from Russian imports of piped natural gas, not least because of supply security reasons. Whether this is an economically viable proposition depends on both the kind of security premium Europe is willing to pay and relative prices. As pointed out earlier, the 2013 scenario of prices of $18/MMBtu in Asia and $10/MMBtu in Europe would not justify Europe-bound flows (unless locked in long-term agreements); but the current scenario, where these prices are roughly equal and the spread with Henry Hub is around $5/MMBtu would create a strong case for it.[15] The

---

[15] It should be noted that the reason is not absolute cost, but arbitrage. The estimated cost of liquefaction and transport for US LNG to Europe is around $4/MMBtu, to Asia $5/MMBtu. Spot price differentials of more than $4/MMBtu between Henry Hub and NBP are not infrequent, and in a two-

fundamentals of this market strongly suggest that prices in the next decade will reflect one of these two scenarios, perhaps switching several times between the two. European policy-makers might want to stop looking only to the east and to the south and perhaps turn their eye to the west as well. The politics and transatlantic commitments between authorities will need to be right in order to convince the market to create binding transatlantic ties. LNG imports from the US have the potential of being much more than the odd spot cargo. In the longer run, exports may well reduce the Asia/Europe price disparity.

The other side of the coin is that for North America, shale gas can have the same security value as it would have for Europe – in fact, as has been seen, there is advocacy in favour of protectionism. Moreover, and in this case joined with oil, energy independence for the US means having more options in foreign policy, as dependence eases. This is also true for Europe. Commercial links grow fastest once they are embedded in an agreement such as TTIP. However, one should note that the extent to which such an agreement would facilitate natural gas trade will depend on two aspects. First, it will depend on the exact wording of the agreement, i.e. whether it would be fully inclusive or whether exclusions exist. The second aspect is how the LNG export licensing system will evolve in the US, i.e. the regime of planning permission for the export terminals (issued by the Federal Energy Regulatory Commission). This is not a TTIP issue, however. The value of the aforementioned optionality is increasing the more the geopolitical situation gets complicated around the regions, which have traditionally exported to the EU.

4.2   Competitiveness

America is enjoying low natural gas and electricity prices that are at least in part enabled by the absence of LNG export capacity, while Europe struggles with higher gas prices and uncertainties from some of its traditional external suppliers. The argument for enabling transatlantic trade in natural gas is therefore in some respect similar to the arguments related to crude oil. But this also means that, inside the US, there are vested interests in industry and the energy sector pushing against it. While Russian gas is cheaper than LNG in monetary terms, member states seem to place different values on enhanced

---

country, NTB-free model that would suffice to justify Europe-bound flows. But as long as the Asian price remains much higher, markets will choose it as preferred destination. See Medlock III (2012).

diversification and having more supply options. Ultimately, the political choice for Europe is what price it is willing to pay for diversification and to increase optionality (such in the case of Poland and Lithuania, which opted for regasification facilities, or the EU's push to establish a Southern Gas Corridor). This political choice may well cause controversy: some member states are keener to diversify energy sources away from Russia than others.

4.3   Sustainability

When it comes to environmental policy, transatlantic cooperation is virtually non-existent despite the huge impact it could have on global climate change policy. Cooperation could range from a common ETS to the regulation of product standards and elaboration of support schemes for renewables subsidies. Each partner has its own environmental policies; carbon emissions reduction, the phasing out of polluting plants, steering the electricity mix, cleaning the transport sector, promoting greener 'infant industries'. Of all these policies, the ones that the TTIP might potentially address would possibly be a common emissions performance standard, carbon tax or trading system.

5.   Towards a future agenda: Include other energy commodities

While the debate seems mature for the inclusion of natural gas as part of transatlantic trade talks, other energy commodities and policies would equally benefit from becoming part of the transatlantic trade agenda.

5.1   Oil independence in a single country

Oil is the foremost of these. As has been mentioned before, in the US, the shale oil revolution is expected to follow a very similar pattern as that of gas a few years before, with the main reserves located between Canada, North Dakota and Texas. Gas is dependent on the availability of pipelines for its transport, like water flows from the aqueduct under the streets of a town and finally into the pipes of a household, and this structure defines the volumes that can be shipped and the route options that can be chosen. Oil incurs fewer such issues, as it is ultimately more easily transportable than gas. Yet the debate over the proposed Keystone XL pipeline is a relevant example of how the old pipeline system is called to task: by making more oil transportable via pipeline, many argue Keystone XL would reduce the need for oil to find alternative and less secure means of transportation, and more specifically limit the scope for railway congestion and accidents involving cargo trains bringing crude and products to market from North Dakota and Canada.

Availability of indigenous shale oil in North America means that the US, which used to be a net importer, is now becoming less and less dependent on external suppliers. However, the export ban on crude oil means all domestically produced crude has to be processed in the US refining system. From a transatlantic perspective, there would be scope for lifting such a ban and opening an eastbound trade route towards Europe. The crude export ban creates a domestic glut, with downward pressure on pricing, which on the one hand represents a disincentive for producers, and on the other hand marks domestic crude for exclusive use as feedstock for domestic refineries, boosting the latter's profitability, thus making American oil products, e.g. in the petrochemical industry, more competitive abroad and reinforcing the US's position as the world largest petroleum product exporter.

For this reason, the US refining industry is resisting this potential change: not only has it reinforced its traditional export route for diesel, but it has also contributed to the inversion of a traditional gasoline import trend from Europe into the US. Losing the competitive advantage in producing gasoline, which somewhat balanced the US supremacy in diesel, Europe remains a net importer of all energy commodities, and is left with a struggling refining industry. Swamped with refined products and having lost its supremacy on the gasoline side, many European majors are now facing increasing pressure to downsize their refining and retail business as a result.

With some small exceptions, the bulk of crude will still have to be processed in the US, whose policy-makers worry that the newly found advantage of increasing self-sufficiency could be threatened if the ban were lifted.[16] But holding that lifting the ban would automatically realign refining margins across the Atlantic is not correct: transportation costs and current contractual structures would still be such that the region where crude is produced would retain a competitive advantage over the relatively resource-scarce region, in this case Europe. But modest trade flows, and therefore realignment in margins, might occur. How this will occur is a crude quality issue and

---

[16] This reluctance on the US side is also the gist of the most recent debate on inserting an energy chapter in the TTIP. See EUobserver (2014).

uncertainty on crude exports is freezing US refining investment. There will be winners and losers inside the US refining system, given the distorted light/heavy crude differential and depending on whether one is running a complex or simple refinery, which differs by region in the US. This is why the US debate on the ban is difficult.

5.2 Biofuels

Global trade in biofuels has expanded in recent years, the two main commodities traded being ethanol and biodiesel. The US has been the world's largest producer of ethanol since the early 2000s but, being also the largest consumer, it has only become a net exporter in 2011. In 2014 US ethanol exports amounted to around 20 million barrels (EIA, 2015d). Brazil, Jamaica and El Salvador are its main import sources. The US was a net exporter of biodiesel between 2007 and 2012, only to become a net importer in 2013, with imports amounting to 8.152 and 5.059 millions of barrels in 2013 and 2014 respectively (EIA, 2015a).

These trends for both fuels are mainly steered by government policy, in particular subsidies on domestic ethanol production (in the form of tax credits) as well as the price support for sugar production. On the other hand, to some extent the ethanol demand faces a technical ceiling in the amount of ethanol that can be blended with gasoline. The current US biofuel policy is based on the Renewable Fuels Standards. Enacted by the Energy Policy Act in 2005 and expanded by the 2007 *Energy Independence and Security Act (EISA)*, the Renewable Fuels Standards requires adding continually increasing volumes of renewable sources into the country's fuel supply – growing from nearly 13 billion gallons in 2011 to 36 billion gallons by 2022 (EIA, 2013a). In addition, the EISA authorised $500 million annually for the 2008-15 fiscal years for the production of advanced biofuels with at least an 80% reduction in life-cycle greenhouse gas emissions relative to current fuels. The use of biofuels is also encouraged through tax benefits. For instance, on 1 January 2012 the US eliminated the $0.54-per-gallon import tariff it used to impose on ethanol imports. The $0.45-per-gallon tax credit to blenders has also been removed.

In the EU, on the other hand, demand for biofuels is growing strongly, due to organic demand growth, as well as to the fact that the 2007-09 Climate and Energy Package includes a 10% renewable target for the transport sector by 2020, and the Fuel Quality Directive implies a 6% reduction in GHG emissions in the sector. The former obviously implies the introduction of liquid biofuels, while the latter is an additional incentive in that direction. According to the National

Renewable Energy Action Plans (NREAPs) submitted to the European Commission, member states intend to collectively exceed the 10% target. The NREAPs also indicated that the 10% target would be met by 8.5% conventional biofuels, 1% second generation biofuels and 1% renewable electricity, most of which would be used in rail. The contribution of hydrogen is expected to be negligible (ePURE, 2014). There is no biofuel target agreed within the 2030 Framework for Climate and Energy Policies (European Commission, 2014a).

Europe does not produce enough biofuels to satisfy demand and therefore large volumes are imported, especially biodiesel. The source of these imports depends mainly on technical requirements for compliance with the fuel quality Directive (see below). Indeed, to qualify for both the renewables energy and fuel quality Directives, biofuels consumed in the EU must comply and demonstrate compliance with strict sustainability criteria. They set rigorous requirements on the minimum level of greenhouse gas emissions savings (provide at least 35% GHG emissions savings compared to fossil fuels, a threshold set to rise to 50% as of 2017, and to 60% as of 2018), appropriate land use (raw material must not be grown on land with high-carbon stocks) as well as monitoring requirements for any potential adverse effect. Moreover, the European Commission is duty-bound to report on food availability, compliance with land-use rights and with international labour conventions. The technical requirements for compliance amount to 'methods of production' and not to 'like products' (the fuels themselves), the basis for trade liberalisation in the WTO ever since GATT was started. They therefore qualify as technical barriers to trade, and for many WTO partners these are very sensitive, if not regarded as quasi-protectionism. The TTIP could address this.

5.3 The EU's fuel quality Directive

A third area for potential barriers to be removed relates to the text of the EU's fuel quality Directive of 2009. In particular, the fuel quality Directive ranks transport fuels by carbon intensity and is intended to put the more carbon intensive at a disadvantage, hence promoting the 'cleaner' ones, in particular by discriminating between the qualities of the source crudes. This implies that fuels produced from Canadian tar sands or US unconventional oil would face entry barriers into the EU's transport fuel market. In practice, however, the text has never been translated into enforceable standards. Furthermore, not having been included in the EU discussions on the renewal of the climate targets to

2030, the scope of the fuel quality Directive expires in 2020, while it is not clear what regime will be in place from 2020 onwards.

A similar argument exists in relation to biofuels trade, but in this case the US and the EU are playing on the same side, using technical standards to discriminate against imports, mainly from Latin America, and thereby indirectly supporting domestic production. However, such technical barriers also limit the possibility of trading between each other, and in particular hamper the potential for US ethanol and biodiesel exports to the EU. Even inside the EU, however, the camps are divided between those who would prefer the fuel quality Directive to effectively become a barrier, hence promoting domestic production of biofuels (a segment which has a lot in common with agriculture, traditionally a protectionist stronghold) as opposed to their penetration into the fuel mix if there is a positive environmental effect. The TTIP could start that debate.

6.   Conclusions

There are potential gains in facilitating trade in energy products across the Atlantic, possibly to an even larger extent than there is in sectors currently included in the scope of the TTIP. The benefits can be divided into direct gains and policy gains, and the action required to unlock these benefits relates to NTBs, in line with the nature and hard core of the TTIP itself.

It is fair to say that LNG exports to Europe will depend on regional pricing, which however is in flux right now. Europe would have to want LNG for this pattern to be put in place. Quite the opposite could be said of crude oil flows, as US grades would likely flow to Europe in the event the 1975 export ban were lifted,[17] thus improving EU refining margins and perhaps reducing the new westbound gasoline trend, possibly to the point of restoring the traditional pattern of European exports to the US. New players entering the distressed EU refining industry with different goals than the vertically integrated incumbents might also change the picture in favour of a resurrection of European refining and possibly, in the end, even eroding the US advantage in the diesel segment, and the corresponding trade flows.

---

[17] To a small extent, they already are: since 2014, some US Gulf Coast producers have been able to sell Eagle Ford light crude for export to European buyers, bypassing it through a splitter and self-classifying it as a product, thus circumventing the ban.

A gradual convergence in regulatory norms and practice would accelerate this trend. For example, successful conclusion of the debate over the fuel quality Directive, with the adoption of European limitations, would also impact this trend. The failure of this piece of legislation, or the more unlikely adoption of something similar in North America, could maintain the status quo. That aside, the fuel quality Directive could represent a piece of a broader process of regulatory harmonisation that has the potential to create mutual advantages; the introduction of a common framework for the limitation of pollutants, including greenhouse gases, could be another one, even if prospects seems remote. The fuel quality Directive is also a double-edged sword in that it works as a protectionist measure against EU imports of biofuels from the US. It seems fair to suggest that the effectiveness of this Directive is sacrificed as a bargaining chip for the EU, in order to achieve the inclusion of energy in the TTIP in the form of an opening for export of oil and gas from the US.

Most of these policy improvements are more grounded in politics than they are in trade: improving transatlantic security and tackling environmental issues together, if not sharing the burden on the competitiveness of the energy sector at large, would be an undisputable improvement. Granted, the US cannot be asked to give up its competitive advantage for the sake of transatlantic cooperation. But the US should not fear removing NTBs in the refining and biofuels sectors, although losers would need to be addressed. On a systemic level, trade in a commodity benefits the factor that is specific to the export sector; it triggers a shift of all other factors towards production that is intensive in that factor; and therefore, it ultimately works to the benefit of the economy which is most abundant in that factor. The US, now rich in hydrocarbons, has no reason to fear for its competitiveness in a free trade Atlantic community.

References

BP (2014), "BP Energy Outlook 2035: the European Union" (www.bp.com/content/dam/bp/pdf/Energy-economics/Energy-Outlook/Regional_insights_European_Union_2035.pdf).

Chadbourne (2014), "US Takes Steps to Advance LNG Exports – DOE, Export License, Applications" (www.chadbourne.com/us_advance_lng_exports_june2014_projectfinance/).

Chase, P. and J. Pelkmans (2015), "This time it's different: Turbo-charging regulatory cooperation in TTIP", Paper No. 7 in the CEPS-CTR project "TTIP in the Balance" and CEPS Special Report No. 110, June (www.ceps.eu/system/files/SR110%20Regulatory%20Cooperation%2 0in%20TTIP.pdf).

Economist Intelligence Unit (2013), "US: Failing in Shale" (www.eiu.com/ industry/article/921249876/us-failing-in-shale/2013-11-20).

Egenhofer, C. (2005), "Climate Change: Could a transatlantic greenhouse gas emissions market work?", in D.S. Hamilton and J.P. Quinlan (eds), *Deep Integration: How Transatlantic Markets Are Leading Globalization*, CEPS-CTR Paperback, Centre for European Policy Studies, Brussels, and Center for Transatlantic Relations, John Hopkins University SAIS, Washington, D.C.

Egenhofer, C., F. Genoese and A. Dimitrova (2014), "Making the most of Energy Union", CEPS Commentary, 16 December (www.ceps.be/system/files/Energy%20Union.pdf).

EIA (2013a), "Biofuels in the United States: Context and Outlook" (www.eia.gov/pressroom/presentations/howard_01242013.pdf).

_____ (2013b), "Markets expect Marcellus growth to drive Appalachian natural gas prices below Henry Hub" (www.eia.gov/todayinenergy/detail.cfm?id=13331).

_____ (2014), "Short-Term Energy Outlook" (www.eia.gov/forecasts/steo/archives/aug14.pdf).

_____ (2015a), "Biodiesel Overview" (www.eia.gov/totalenergy/data/ monthly/pdf/sec10_8.pdf).

_____ (2015b), "Historical coal prices by region, 2010-2015" (www.eia.gov/coal/news_markets/archive/).

_____ (2015c), "Increases in U.S. crude oil production are predominantly light, sweet crude" (www.eia.gov/todayinenergy/detail.cfm?id=21512).

_____ (2015d), "U.S. ethanol exports in 2014 reach highest level since 2011" (www.eia.gov/todayinenergy/detail.cfm?id=20532).

Ellerman, A.D., F. Convery and C. de Perthuis (2010), *Pricing Carbon: The European Union Emissions Trading Scheme*, Cambridge: Cambridge University Press.

Energy.gov (n.d.), "How to obtain authorization to import and/or export natural gas and LNG" (http://energy.gov/fe/services/natural-gas-regulation/how-obtain-authorization-import-andor-export-natural-gas-and-lng#LNG).

EPA (2014), "Clean Power Plan: Reducing Carbon Pollution From Existing Power Plants" (www2.epa.gov/cleanpowerplan/clean-power-plan-existing-power-plants).

ePURE (2014), "The EU Biofuels Policy" (www.epure.org/policy-areas/the-eu-biofuels-policy).

EUobserver (2014), "EU repeats demand for energy chapter in US trade treaty" (http://euobserver.com/news/125544).

European Commission (2013a), "TTIP Initial EU position paper on Raw materials and energy" (http://trade.ec.europa.eu/doclib/docs/ 2013/july/tradoc_151624.pdf).

_____ (2013b), "EU Energy, Transport and GHG Emissions Trends to 2050 Reference Scenario" (http://ec.europa.eu/transport/media/publications/doc/trends-to-2050-update-2013.pdf).

_____ (2014a), "2030 framework for climate and energy policies" (http://ec.europa.eu/clima/policies/2030/index_en.htm).

_____ 2014b), "The Transatlantic Trade and Investment Partnership (TTIP) Explained" (http://trade.ec.europa.eu/doclib/docs/2014/may/tradoc_152462.pdf).

_____ (2015), "Factsheet on Energy and Raw Materials (ERMs)" (http://trade.ec.europa.eu/doclib/docs/2015/january/tradoc_153015.2%20Energy%20and%20raw%20materials.pdf).

Gros, D. and C. Egenhofer (2011), "The case for taxing carbon at the border", *Climate Policy*, 11 (5), Special Issue, 2011, pp. 1212-1225.

Hamilton, T.L. and S. Santa Maria (2014), "US gas pipelines reverse course" (www.platts.com/news-feature/2014/naturalgas/us-pipeline-reversals/index).

Honoré, A. (2014), "The Outlook for Natural Gas Demand in Europe", Oxford Institute for Energy Studies (www.oxfordenergy.org/wpcms/wp-content/uploads/2014/06/NG-87.pdf).

ICIS (2015), "Europe faces 40 refinery closures on 'major obstacles, regulation'" (www.icis.com/resources/news/2015/04/21/9877982/europe-faces-40-refinery-closures-on-major-obstacles-regulation-/).

IEA (2014), *Energy Policies of IEA Countries European Union 2014 Review*, Paris: IEA.

Medlock III, K.B. (2012), "US LNG Exports: Truth and Consequence", Working Paper, James A. Baker III Institute for Public Policy, Rice University, Houston, TX, 10 August (http://bakerinstitute.org/files/842/).

Morse, E.L. (2014), "Welcome to the Revolution", *Foreign Affairs*, May/June.

Reuters (2015), "Watch the shale spread: Brent vs WTI crude oil prices", 27 February (www.reuters.com/article/2015/02/27/oil-wti-brent-spread-idUSL4N0W120120150227).

Sandrea, I. (2014), "US shale gas and tight oil industry performance: challenges and opportunities", Oxford Energy Comment, Oxford Institute for Energy Studies, Oxford (www.oxfordenergy.org/2014/03/us-shale-gas-and-tight-oil-industry-performance-challenges-and-opportunities/).

Stern, J. (2014), "Russian responses to changes in the European gas market: exports, pricing and pipelines", in J. Henderson and S. Pirani, (eds), *The Russian Gas Matrix: How Markets Are Driving Change*, Oxford: OIES/Oxford University Press.

Yergin, D. (2006), "Ensuring Energy Security", *Foreign Affairs*, No. 2, pp. 69-82.

15. Gains from Convergence in US and EU Auto Regulations under TTIP[*]

Caroline Freund and Sarah Oliver[**]

1. Introduction

The Transatlantic Trade and Investment Partnership (TTIP) aims at harmonising regulations across the European Union and the United States. The European Commission states TTIP's objective as achieving "greater regulatory compatibility between the EU and the US, and paving the way for setting global standards". The US Trade Representative says: "T-TIP can set high standards and pioneer new rules for the global trading system."[1]

This chapter focuses on the gains that both partners could reap from regulatory coherence in the automobile industry, using the trade effects of the 1958 Agreement – the most comprehensive agreement on technical prescriptions for automobiles to date – as an event study. The 1958 Agreement establishes a set of uniform standards for vehicles and

[*] The editors are grateful to the Peterson Institute for International Economics for permission to republish this paper, which was originally published as Freund & Oliver (2015).

[**] We are grateful to Lucian Cernat, Bill Cline, Bernard Hoekman, Gary Hufbauer, Brad Jensen, Robert Lawrence, Jeff Schott, Jennifer Thomas, Charles Ulthus, and participants at the Standards, Regulation and Trans-Atlantic Trade Conference at the European University Institute, Florence, 10 October 2014, for helpful comments. Partial support for this study was provided by the Italian Trade Commission.

[1] "Member States Endorse EU-US Trade and Investment Negotiations", European Commission Memo, 14 June 2013; Dan Mullaney, "Five Things You Should Know about the Transatlantic Trade and Investment Partnership," USTR Tradewinds Blog, November 2013.

their components relating to safety, environment, energy and anti-theft requirements. The European Union, as well as Japan and Korea among others, are parties to the agreement. The United States, however, has its own safety standards and is not a contracting party to the 1958 Agreement.

Given the feasibility of regulatory harmonisation (as evidenced by the 1958 Agreement), the auto industry stands out as a critical test case in the TTIP for improving regulatory coherence between the United States and the European Union. Both maintain vastly different regulations as well as different ways of administering them. Despite disparities in regulations and hence production requirements, we show that these regulatory regimes are not significantly different in terms of the safety outcomes they deliver.

The regulatory divergence distorts the market, raising production costs, encouraging price discrimination across markets and limiting the available import varieties. To measure the trade loss from having two sets of regulations, the chapter examines how the 1958 Agreement affects trade, using a difference-in-differences approach. The advantage of our methodology is that it uses an actual case of regulatory harmonisation (accession to the 1958 Agreement) in the same industry to estimate the effect of regulatory convergence. Because of variation in dates of members' accession, we can control for exporter-year specific effects, importer-year effects, country-pair effects, as well as other bilateral time-varying events such as EU accession or voluntary export restraints. In contrast, other studies have estimated trade gains from regulatory harmonisation using an ad-valorem tariff equivalent of regulatory differences. Regulatory convergence could have very different effects from tariffs because adhering to two distinct regulatory frameworks affects a company's production structure, lowering both variable and fixed costs.

We find that joining the 1958 Agreement boosts auto trade by more than 20%. This effect is significantly higher than effects estimated using tariff equivalents and almost as large as the additional increase from joining the European Union. The results are robust to different periods, different samples, and controlling for EU accession, high market share exporters, and for voluntary export restraints that were in effect over the period, as well as potential endogeneity of the agreement. We further show that foreign direct investment has not already segmented markets to such a degree that it would limit the medium-run trade gains from regulatory convergence.

Achieving regulatory harmonisation or mutual recognition of regulations now would help US and EU producers benefit from scale economies and compete in the global marketplace, while providing consumers with more varieties within a market and equivalent safety at lower prices. More broadly, the TTIP agreement is about both market integration and first-mover advantage. Simply put, by harmonising regulations in some industries or agreeing to recognise each other's regulations, replication in production could be avoided, generating real productivity gains. Moreover, as the largest combined market for many products, the rest of the world will be very likely to follow similar rules.

2.   The equivalence of regulations

Regulatory standards ensure that products are safe for consumers and do not excessively damage the environment. The EU and US safety and environmental regulations are both relatively high and well enforced, but have different requirements. This section focuses on safety regulations because although environmental standards also differ, they are less distortionary from an economic perspective. While there are barriers to harmonising environmental regulations, notably in the driving pattern required during testing (including distance, speed, and whether the car is allowed to warm up before testing begins), there is also room from a manufacturing perspective to create one model for both markets that adheres to the most stringent emissions regulation. For example, the European Union is moving toward a greenhouse gas emissions standard of 95 grams/kilometre (60.6 miles per gallon equivalent) for 95% of vehicles by 2020 and the United States is moving toward an average level of 163 grams/mile (54.5 miles per gallon equivalent) by 2025. It may be in the producer's interest to make one car for both markets that meets the 60.6 miles per gallon threshold.[2] A clear hierarchy in these regulations favours low emissions. As a result, environmental regulations can create a race to the top, where an automobile that meets the highest standard on various emissions tests is marketable in both economies. In contrast, safety requirements are more complex and often incompatible in the sense that one car cannot meet both regulations simultaneously.

The US and EU models of the 2014 Ford Fusion have 80% of the same parts, which is higher than the industry average for overlapping

[2] See Canis & Lattanzio (2014) for a detailed analysis of the differences between US and EU emissions standards.

parts,[3] yet a fifth of the Fusion's parts need to be manufactured separately for the two markets. Some of the parts are different because of testing regulations, while other differences lie in specific parts. For example, both markets require crash testing but the tests are distinct, in both speed of the car and rigidness of the barrier. US standards are tougher because cars must satisfy certain criteria even accounting for passengers not wearing seatbelts. Other parts that are different are individually small, such as the colour of the tail light or the presence of side lights (only the United States requires them) – but these add up.

To demonstrate the technical differences in a single part, Table 15.1 shows the differences in regulatory standards between US and EU lighting systems for automobiles, in particular side turn signal lamps. The first column lists the technical regulation in the European Union, column 2 is the corresponding US regulation, and column 3 explains the differences, if any, between the two regulations. In many cases, an EU manufacturer can clearly comply with US regulations, such as the height of the front lights, which has a lower minimum in the European Union. In other cases, there is no overlap, such as the front light colour. This extensive table only addresses one specific light system.

Table 15.1 Differences in regulations in EU and US side turn-signal lamps*

Property	EU (UN Regulations)**	US (FMVSS/SAE Standards)§	Comparison
Applicability	Optional, option of AM/RM1/RM2 category lamps	Optional	Identical for applicability The EU permits the use of variable intensity rear end outline marker lamps, while the US prohibits their use
Number	4–8	2x Front 2x Rear	No. of side marker lamps can range from 4–8 in the EU, but must be 4 (2x rear and 2x front) in the US
Colour	Front: White Rear: Red	Front: Amber Rear: Red	Colour must be white at the front and red at the rear in the EU, while the colour must be amber at

			the front and red at the rear in the US
Position			
Height	Front: Upper edge not lower than upper edge of wind-screen Rear: At maximum height possible	As near the top as practicable	Minimum height at front is lower in the EU Identical for the rear
Width	Outer: ≤400 mm and as close as possible to the extreme outer edge of the vehicle	Indicate the overall width of the vehicle and symmetric about the vertical centre line	Widths are more prescriptive in the EU, while the US is more subjective
Length	–	Front: On the front Rear: On the rear Other: Any other location to ensure that overall width of vehicle is indicated	Lengths are not defined in the EU, while the US provides subjective length definitions
Other	Distances must be ≥200 mm vertically from position lamps	–	Minimum vertical distance from position lamps are prescribed in the EU, while the US does not define these minimum distances
Geometric visibility	H: O80° V: D20° to U5°	–	Geometric visibility ranges are prescribed in the EU, while the US does not define geometric visibility ranges
Photometric visibility	H: 0° to O20° V: D10° to U5°	H: I45° to O45°† V: D10°$ to U10°	Smaller horizontal and upward photometric visibility angles required in the EU
Photometric Minima∆	≥4 cd @ H: 0°, V: 0°	Front: ≥0.62 cd Rear: ≥0.25 cd	Photometric minima are greater in the reference

	≥0.4 cd @ H: O20°, V: D/U 5°		axis for all lamps in the EU Absolute photometric minima for all lamps in the EU are smaller than photometric minima for front end-outline marker lamps and greater than photometric minima for rear end-outline marker lamps
Photometric MaximaΔ	AM: ≥140 cd @ H: 0°, V: 0° ≥14 cd @ H: O20°, V: D/U 5° RM1: ≥17 cd @ H: 0°, V: 0° ≥1.7 cd @ H: O20°, V: D/U 5° RM2: ≥42 cd @ H: 0°, V: 0° ≥4.2 cd @ H: O20°, V: D/U 5°	Front: - Rear: ≥15 cd	Front photometric maxima are prescribed in the EU, while the US does not define front photometric maxima Rear photometric maxima are greater in the reference axis for all lamps in the EU Absolute rear photometric minima for all lamps in the EU are smaller than photometric minima for rear end-outline marker lamps

* Current EU regulations and US end-outline marker lamps [clearance lamps] (R48: UN Regulation No. 48; F108: FMVSS Standard No. 108; R7: UN Regulation No. 7; SAE Standard No. J2042)

** Applicable for vehicles that are between 1.8–2.1 m in length

§ Applicable for vehicles that are ≤2302 mm in width

† May be reduced to D0° if lamp is mounted at locations other than the front or rear

$ May be reduced to D5° when lamp is mounted below 750 mm

Δ UN: for single function lamps tested at voltage supplies of 6.75v, 13.5v and 28v; US: for non-reflecting single function lamps with photometric measurements made at ≥1.2m

Directional nomenclature: I, inboard; O, outboard; D, downward; U, upward; B, backward; F, forward; L, left; R, right. Applicable for right hand traffic lamps only, reverse left and right directions for left hand traffic lamps. H, horizontal (longitudinal) plane about a polar axis in a spherical coordinate system centred on the illuminating surface of the lamp; V, vertical (latitudinal) plane perpendicular to a polar axis in a spherical coordinate system centred on the illuminating surface of the lamp

Source: European Commission (2015, Table 33).

Ultimately, what matters is the outcome of the requirements: Are passengers safe in vehicles meeting European or US regulations? To answer this question, we compare auto fatality data across countries. Figure 15.1a shows fatalities per 100,000 vehicles across EU countries. Figure 15.1b shows the same across US states. The EU rates are very similar to US rates, with 15.8 fatalities per 100,000 vehicles in the European Union versus 13.6 fatalities in the United States. Figure 15.1c shows fatality rates and GDP per capita of the individual EU countries and US states, indicating that rates vary far more with stage of development than with auto regulations, which are largely the same within Europe and the United States. This suggests that country-specific variables, such as age of the fleet on the road, quality of roads, terrain, weather, and enforcement of laws are far more important in safety than regulation of the vehicles.

To test whether fatalities per motor vehicle are fewer in the United States or the European Union, we regress the fatality rate on an indicator variable for the European Union—this variable takes the value 1 for EU members and zero otherwise. If the United States and the European Union have different safety regulations, the EU dummy should be negative and significant if the European Union is safer, and positive and significant if the European Union is more dangerous. The results, reported in Table 15.2, show no significant difference across EU countries and US states. Next, we control for GDP per capita. The point estimate on "ln GDP" is negative and highly significant; suggesting that a 10% increase in GDP per capita saves 2 to 3 lives per 100,000 vehicles. The third column measures fatalities in logs and results remain similar, though in this case the interpretation is slightly different. The results show that a 1% increase in per capita income reduces fatalities by more than 1%. In both specifications, per capita income explains more than 50% of the variation in fatality rates across countries. The coefficient on the EU variable remains insignificant in all specifications, and is very small when income is included in the regression, suggesting that auto safety in EU countries is not statistically different from US states.

Figure 15.1 Auto fatalities per 100,000 vehicles, US and EU, 2013

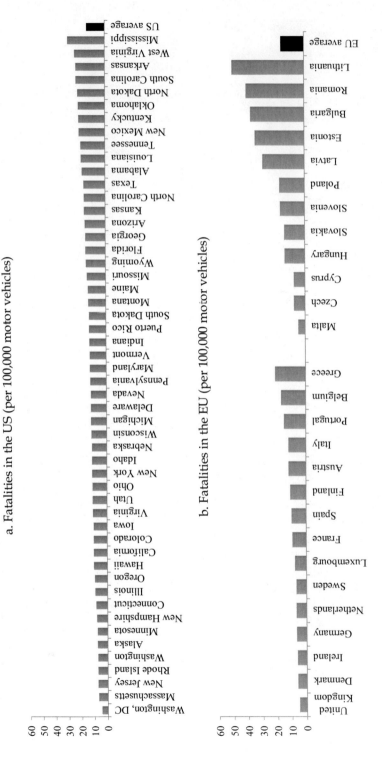

a. Fatalities in the US (per 100,000 motor vehicles)

b. Fatalities in the EU (per 100,000 motor vehicles)

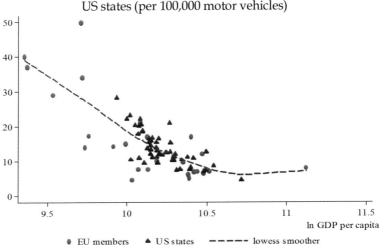

c. Fatality rates and GDP per capita in individual EU countries and US states (per 100,000 motor vehicles)

Data sources: World Health Organization Global Health Observatory Data Repository, 2010 (http://apps.who.int/gho/data/node.main.A997); authors' calculations using data from US National Highway and Traffic Safety Administration, 2012, FARS database (www.nhtsa.gov/FARS), and US Census Bureau, 2012 (www.census.gov/popest/data/historical/2010s/index.html).

Table 15.2 Fatalities US versus EU regression results

	(1)	(2)	(3)
	Fatality rate per 100,000 vehicles	**Fatality rate per 100,000 vehicles**	**ln fatality rate**
EU dummy	2.192	–0.190	–0.156
	[2.393]	[1.609]	[0.102]
ln GDP per capita		–22.673***	–1.373***
		[4.020]	[0.217]
Observations	78	78	78
R-squared	0.017	0.554	0.544

Notes: Robust standard errors in brackets. *** p<0.01, ** p<0.05, * p<0.1

Data sources: World Health Organization Global Health Observatory Data Repository, 2010 (http://apps.who.int/gho/data/node.main.A997); authors' calculations using data from US National Highway and Traffic Safety Administration, 2012 FARS database, (www.nhtsa.gov/FARS) and US Census Bureau, 2012, (www.census.gov/popest/data/historical/2010s/index.html).

3. Economic benefits: Evidence from the 1958 Agreement

The economic argument against different regulations is that instead of making one model for both markets, car producers make two separate models. Returns to scale are underutilised, some processes are duplicated, producers can price discriminate, and inventory cannot be reallocated across markets. As a result, consumers face higher average prices and less variety.

Regulatory barriers are especially burdensome for small producers or in small markets. Some models are not sold in markets where there is demand because sunk costs of adjusting the models to those markets are too high. For example, while the Canadian market adheres to US regulations, demand for subcompact and compact cars is higher in Canada than in the United States (representing 65% and 41% of market share, respectively). European manufacturers are unable to take advantage of this demand for smaller cars in Canada, because as Canadian car sales were less than 5% of US auto sales in 2014, the sunk cost of adjusting a subcompact European car to US regulations (in order to sell in the Canadian market) is higher than the relative gains in the Canadian market.[1]

Regulatory differences also affect consumers: When there is demand for the same car in both markets, consumers may not be able to take advantage of price differentials across markets due to the cost of recertification in the new market. This allows producers to price discriminate, selling a Mercedes for the profit-maximising price in each market, which leads to higher average prices.[2]

Regulatory differences also impede market integration, preventing companies from selling new products in both markets. For example, if a specific new technology is approved under European regulations, such as Mercedes-Benz LED Intelligent Light System, but not under US regulations, the new technology is not available for sale

---

[1] Canadian light vehicle sales in 2014 were 0.55 million units (0.23 million passenger cars and 0.32 million light trucks); US light vehicle sales in 2014 were 16.8 million units (7.7 million passenger cars and 9.1 million light trucks). *Sources:* Desrosiers Automotive Reports (www.desrosiers.ca/pdfs/sales.pdf) and WardsAuto Reports (http://wardsauto.com/public-data).

[2]. The welfare consequences of price discrimination can be positive if poor consumers receive a lower price, which may be socially optimal. See Bradford &Lawrence (2004) for a detailed analysis of the welfare effects from removing price differentials across markets.

in the United States. US consumers thus cannot enjoy the new technology because markets are not integrated.

Increased integration of markets promotes rapid innovation. Previous work on auto emissions regulations shows that convergence of regulation leads to increased technology transfer and motivates export-oriented car industries in smaller countries to adopt higher emissions regulations to converge with the US and EU markets, creating a race to the top. Using data on automobile emissions regulations between 1992 and 2007, Antoine Dechezleprêtre, Eric Neumayer and Richard Perkins (2015) find that technological developments, measured as cross-border patents, are more likely to flow between countries where regulatory standards are similar, rather than the level of regulations themselves. Perkins & Neumayer (2012) find that small and developing countries with export-oriented auto industries are more likely to have stricter auto emissions regulations and their auto sectors receive higher levels of inward foreign direct investment (FDI). The authors argue that export-oriented firms whose main target markets include countries with higher emissions standards have an incentive to raise standards in their home markets since these firms already have the infrastructure in place to produce higher-standard vehicles and therefore would be more competitive than strictly domestic producers. Better regulatory coherence will also promote research and development because instead of spending on adapting models to different regulatory regimes, companies will channel resources toward finding safer and more fuel efficient technologies.

While an increasing number of countries have adopted the UN Regulations associated with the 1958 Agreement, some such as Chile (and some small countries) follow US regulations. Regulatory convergence will not only help the US and EU markets but also may draw smaller countries into their standardised framework, thus spreading the high standards.

3.1 Quantifying the Gains from Integration of Regulations

To estimate the gains from having a single market, we use data on trade to evaluate the effect of becoming a contracting party to the 1958 Agreement. Along with its subsequent revisions in 1967 and 1995, the 1958 Agreement has gone a long way towards completely harmonising

regulatory standards.[3] Individual governments and governing bodies
(such as the European Union) that are parties to the agreement verify
that automobiles meet the regulations before they are certified for sale
to consumers. The agreement was made under the United Nations
Economic Commission for Europe (UNECE) and originally allowed
participation only by UNECE members, but since 1995 has accepted
non-European members, such as Japan (1998) and South Korea (2004).
Table 15.3 lists the countries that are currently contracting parties to the
1958 agreement, by order of accession date.

Table 15.3 Members of the 1958 Agreement (as of February 2014)

Country	Date of accession	Country	Date of accession
Belgium	1959	Estonia	1995
France	1959	Belarus	1995
Sweden	1959	Turkey	1996
Hungary	1960	Ireland	1998
Netherlands	1960	European Union	1998
Spain	1961	Japan	1998
United Kingdom	1963	Latvia	1999
Italy	1963	Bulgaria	2000
Germany	1966	Australia	2000
Austria	1971	Ukraine	2000
Luxembourg	1971	Serbia	2001
Switzerland	1973	South Africa	2001
Norway	1975	Azerbaijan	2002
Finland	1976	New Zealand	2002
Denmark	1976	Lithuania	2002
Romania	1977	Cyprus	2004
Poland	1979	Malta	2004
Portugal	1980	South Korea	2004
Russia	1987	Thailand	2006
Croatia	1991	Montenegro	2006
Macedonia	1991	Malaysia	2006

[3] There is also a 1998 Agreement, which is more limited in scope than the 1958
Agreement and calls for the establishment of global technical regulations (GTR)
but does not include legally binding global regulations or provide for mutual
recognition, as the 1958 Agreement does. The United States is a contracting
member of the 1998 Agreement, along with the European Union, Japan, Canada
and a host of other countries.

Slovenia	1991	Tunisia	2008
Greece	1992	Albania	2011
Bosnia and Herzegovina	1992	Kazakhstan	2011
Czech Republic	1993	Egypt	2013
Slovakia	1993		

Data source: UN Economic Commission for Europe (www.unece.org/fileadmin/DAM/trans/main/wp29/wp29regs/updates/E CE-TRANS-WP.29-343-Rev.22.pdf).

The variation in accession dates helps to isolate the effect on auto trade of signing the 1958 Agreement. Figure 15.2 shows the average and median of the log of real exports versus time relative to accession year. Year 0 is the year a country joined the agreement, year 1 is the year after, year -1 is the year before and so forth. The figure shows that after joining the agreement countries tend to increase exports with members, from a similar starting level. The graph is in logs indicating that member exports doubled around accession and exports of non-members remained unchanged. Figure 15.3 shows that joining the agreement leads to a shift in exports to other agreement members. Both show a clear effect of the agreement on trade flows between contracting parties.

Figure 15.2 Export expansion relative to accession to 1958 Agreement

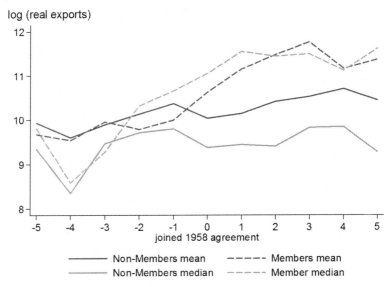

Source: Authors' own calculations.

Figure 15.3 Export share to 1958 Agreement members relative to accession year

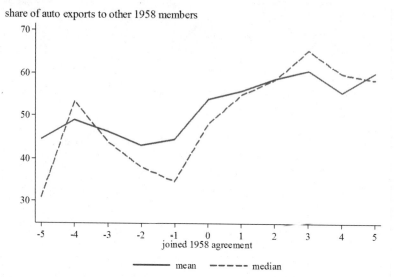

share of auto exports to other 1958 members

Source: Authors' calculations.

3.2 Estimating the Magnitude of the UN58 Effect

To estimate the size of the effect, controlling for supply and demand shocks to trade, we use a difference-in-differences approach. The difference-in-difference approach allows for a near experimental research design. While ideally we would like to randomly assign some countries the same regulatory standards and then observe what happens to auto trade, this type of experimental research design is obviously not feasible. This methodology is as close as you can get to experimental design using data. It compares trade growth between a new member and an existing member to trade growth between the new member and an otherwise similar country that is not a member.

In particular, we use the following regression equation on exports from country i to country j in year t (*exports$_{ijt}$*):

$$\ln(exports)_{ijt} = \gamma_{it} + \gamma_{jt} + +\gamma_{ij} + UN58_{ijt} + \varepsilon_{ijt}, \qquad (1)$$

where US58 is a dummy for two countries being members of the 1958 agreement, γit is an exporter-year fixed effect, γjt is an importer-year fixed effect, and γij is an country-pair fixed effect, and the final term is the error. When Greece joined the agreement in 1992 the *UN58* variable switched from 0 to 1, on bilateral trade flows with another agreement member. The variable remains 1 when trade is between Greece and other agreement members for all subsequent years that Greece is a member of the agreement.

We also include a dummy for the European Union to ensure that *UN58* does not pick up EU effects, as a number of countries that joined the 1958 Agreement also joined the European Union over the period. The EU dummy is one for the year of accession and all years after for trade between the new member and other EU members, and zero otherwise.[4]

Data are from UN Comtrade for trade in passenger cars (SITC 7321) and include total value of bilateral exports for all country pairs. Data are drawn as mirror import data, which is better reported, and range from 1970 to 2013, over which period 41 countries acceded to the agreement. Because of the large number of fixed effects, we cannot estimate the regression on the full sample. We include all exporters that exported an aggregate of $1 million in automobiles in at least one year of the sample, and all importers that imported at least $1 million in one year. These countries account for on average 97% of total auto trade over the period.[5] Errors are clustered at the country-pair level, consistent with our variable of interest.[6]

The advantage of this approach is that importer-year fixed effects control for demand shocks, for example, because of a rise in income or a change in most-favoured nation (MFN) tariffs. Exporter-year fixed effects pick up supply shocks, such as a productivity boost. The country-pair fixed effect controls for average trade between two countries and picks up non-time-varying factors, such as distance, common language, and other static linkages, such as the pair's membership in the European Union over the whole period. The variable of interest, *UN58*, picks up the long-run effect on annual bilateral trade flows between members from signing the agreement.

---

[4] During the sample period, the following countries became EU members: United Kingdom and Ireland in 1973, Greece in 1981, Portugal and Spain in 1986, Austria, Finland, and Sweden in 1995, a group of 10 mainly Eastern European countries in 2004, and Bulgaria and Romania in 2007.

[5]. This yields 35 exporters, listed in appendix Table 15.A1, and 69 importers. In the robustness section we also split the period and drop countries with less than $100,000 exports or imports in any year, which yields 77 exporters and 142 importers.

[6]. In the robustness section, we also cluster errors at the reporter (importer) level, and results remain robust.

The results are reported in Table 15.4. The first column reports results with only the *UN58* variable, the coefficient of 0.21 implies a trade effect of the agreement of 23% (exp(.21)-1). The next column repeats the exercise including the EU dummy in the regression and the result remains unchanged.

Table 15.4 Effect of the 1958 Agreement on auto trade

Variable	(1)	(2)	(3)	(4)	(5)
Dependent variable: *ln(exports$_{ij}$)*					
UN58	0.205*	0.197*	0.388***	0.456***	0.448***
	[0.118]	[0.118]	[0.138]	[0.148]	[0.148]
EU		0.662***	0.626***	0.613***	0.691***
		[0.134]	[0.134]	[0.134]	[0.154]
Left-Right*UN58			−0.393**	−0.368**	−0.368**
			[0.156]	[0.156]	[0.156]
Share*UN58				−1.737*	−1.663*
				[0.977]	[0.982]
Share*EU					−2.238*
					[1.296]
Observations	50,467	50,467	50,467	50,467	50,467
R-squared	0.85	0.85	0.85	0.85	0.85
Trade effect (percent)	23	22	47	58	57

Notes: Standard errors in brackets clustered at the exporter-importer level.
*** p<0.01, ** p<0.05, * p<0.1.

The effect on auto trade of joining the 1958 Agreement is large and significant but smaller than the effect of EU accession. The EU membership effect is more important in this sector because the auto sector relies on distribution and service, and over our sample period relatively high tariffs and other regulations were limiting cross-border auto trade. The EU coefficient found here is comparable to estimates of the gains to trade associated with EU membership in manufacturing sectors.[7]

---

[7] Freund & Portugal-Perez (2013) find a 52% increase in imports associated with EU membership, while Baldwin & Taglioni (2006) find a smaller effect (27%)

A potential concern about our methodology is that joining the 1958 Agreement might be endogenous. Countries that have increasing auto trade with agreement members might be more likely to join the agreement. This could overestimate the effect of the agreement on trade. To some extent the exporter-year and importer-year effects should pick this up, as they control for countries that become increasingly involved in auto trade over time. But if the effect is group-specific they may not.

In the absence of a good instrument for joining the agreement, we exploit an additional feature of the data to control for potential endogeneity. In 10 countries in the 1958 Agreement, people drive on the left side of the road.[8] For trade between these countries and the rest, the agreement should be less effective because inventory cannot be redeployed across markets and two separate models still need to be created. It is impossible for regulations to be the same when an important feature such as the steering side of the car is different, which results in differences in dashboards, mirrors, pedals, stick shift, etc. We thus create a dummy for trade between a left-hand driving country and a right-hand driving country. We interact this dummy with the *UN58* variable and include the interaction in the regression (country-pair fixed effects eliminate the need to include the dummy itself). If the effect of the agreement is about trends among members, we expect the interaction effect to be insignificant. If it is about regulatory convergence, we expect the variable to be negative and significant, indicating that these country pairs do not experience the full effect of the agreement. The result is shown in the third column of Table 15.4. The negative and significant effect of the interaction shows that the agreement has no effect on trade between left-hand and right-hand driving countries. In addition, controlling for the mixed pairs, the overall effect of the agreement is larger and closer to the EU effect. This strongly suggests that we are picking up the effect of the agreement and not general trends in the group.

---

over the period 1980–2004. Using auto data over the same period (1980–2004), we find no significant effect of EU membership on auto exports, but this is not surprising considering new EU members over this period were not major auto producers. The *UN58* effect remains robust and highly significant in this period with a coefficient of 0.34.

[8] These are the United Kingdom, Ireland, Japan, Australia, South Africa, New Zealand, Cyprus, Malta, Thailand and Malaysia.

The results suggest that the boost in trade from joining the 1958 Agreement has been at least 20%. But using the effects of the agreement to predict what would happen to the United States may be problematic because the United States is a relatively large exporter, accounting for 8% of auto exports on average to the sample group over the period. If small exporters are affected differently from large exporters then the results might not transfer. Indeed, a standard trade model would suggest larger effects on small exporters if the agreement is largely about fixed costs, as these producers can now access more markets. We next interact average market share over the period with the *UN58* effect. Average market share is defined as a country's total exports of autos in a given year relative to the world total, averaged over the whole period. We use average market share because market share in any year is endogenous to the agreement. If the effect is larger for small exporters we expect the coefficient to be negative. Interacting market share with the *UN58* dummy variable also enables us to estimate the effect on trade for a relatively large exporter like the United States.

The results are reported in column 4. Larger exporters experience a smaller boost to exports from regulatory convergence, but the overall effect is still positive for all exporters. Figure 15.4 shows how the effect varies with average market share over the period. Exports of a country with a market share of 8% like the United States would increase by about 35% with other countries that drive on the right side of the road. The largest exporters, Germany and Japan, still receive a 7% boost from membership.

Figure 15.4 Trade effect by average market share

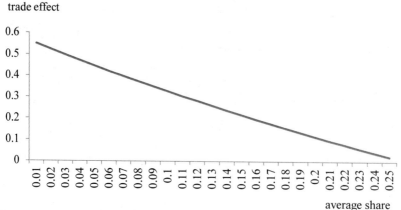

The results above offer strong evidence that regulatory harmonisation has strong positive effects on trade. We subject the results to further robustness tests, including more conservative treatment of errors, alternative time periods, controlling for trade policies, and a placebo test. All results remain robust.[9]

3.3   Comparison with other estimates

Using the 1958 Agreement as an example produces larger effects on trade than results based on tariff equivalents. Ecorys (2009) estimates trade gains associated with EU and US auto regulatory convergence of about 10%. After designing and collecting data from a business survey of 5,500 NAFTA and EU member firms, Ecorys constructed an index ranking restrictiveness of nontariff regulations for bilateral trade between countries, ranging from 0 (completely open) to 100 (completely closed), for 23 sectors. The individual responses are aggregated by sector country-pair, and added to a gravity model, which predicts trade after controlling for GDP of trading partners and the distance between them, using data from 2008. The gravity model was run individually for each of the sectors to generate a set of tariff equivalents. In the auto sector, Ecorys finds a 25.5% increase in costs of US exports to the European Union, and a 26.8% increase in costs of EU exports to the United States. That is, they estimate that regulations affect trade in the same way as an ad valorem tariff of about 25%.

Using this tariff equivalent, Ecorys then uses computable general equilibrium (CGE) analysis to predict the medium-run increase in exports between the United States and European Union following a reduction in non-tariff measures between the two countries through 2018. In an ambitious scenario, where all automotive regulations are eliminated, EU exports increase by 10.7% a year, while US exports increase 9.1%. A limited scenario, which sees only half of non-tariff regulations eliminated, still has a positive impact on EU exports (4.3% increase per year) and US exports (5.3% per year).[10] Following the model, this export increase corresponds to an increase in sector output of 0.7% per year for the United States and a 2.2% increase for the European Union, which translates into an increase in national income of $2.1 billion and $15.6 billion for the two markets, respectively. In

---

[9] For details, see this chapter's original complete text in Freund & Oliver (2015).

[10] For the entire economy, Ecorys predicts a 6.1% increase in US exports versus a 2.1% increase for the European Union following the elimination of non-tariff barriers.

comparison, our model cannot be used like a CGE model to predict changes in output or income, but given the much larger export boost we estimate from regulatory convergence, the Ecorys' predictions likely represent the minimum increases in output and income. Our estimates, which are based on an actual harmonisation event, may be larger than theirs for a number of reasons. The most important are that 1) the restrictiveness index from survey evidence is likely to be very noisy and not necessarily linked to the production costs associated with regulatory differences. Perceived regulations may not affect trade in a monotonic way as their model assumes. For example, a small regulatory difference in one sector may affect production costs more than a large regulatory difference in another sector because of the production process. 2) Using a gravity equation to turn the survey into a tariff equivalent forces regulatory barriers to affect trade in a very restrictive way, as an iceberg cost that affects trade in the same way across sectors, when regulatory differences affect production structure, returns to scale, and variable and fixed costs.

In contrast, our estimate is the long-run trade effect of harmonisation, as estimated from an actual agreement. As these are historical effects, the actual effect could still differ if modern supply chains have reduced the importance of trade restrictions. The short- to medium-run effects might be significantly smaller if foreign investment has already adjusted to segment the US and EU markets. To the extent these investments are irreversible in the short run, production will take some time to adjust to changes in the regulatory system. In light of this, the next section looks at production chains across markets and the trends in FDI in the auto sector between the United States and European Union.

4.   Foreign direct investment and industry trends

FDI in both directions is substantial. FDI stocks between the United States and European Union in the transportation sector have steadily increased over time in both directions, with an increase in both US direct investment in the European Union and EU investment in the United States. In particular, European investment has increased in recent years, while US FDI stock in the European Union has declined since 2007 (Figure 15.5). For European carmakers, particularly German firms Volkswagen and BMW, revenue from US sales has also steadily increased over the past 10 years (Figure 15.6).

Figure 15.5 Foreign direct investment position in transportation equipment, 1982-2013

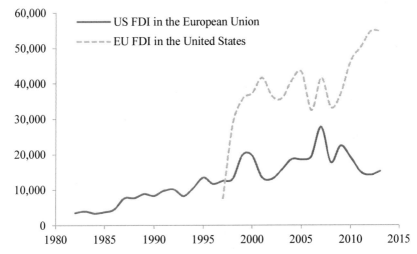

FDI stock (millions of US dollars)

Source: Authors' configuration based on data from US Bureau of Economic Analysis, International Data, Direct Investment and MNE (www.bea.gov).

Figure 15.6 EU manufacturers' revenue from US operations, 2004-13

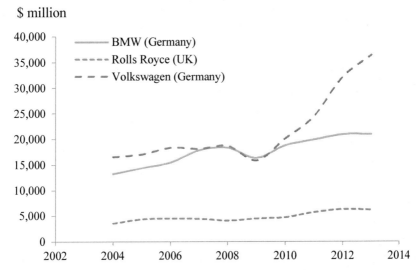

$ million

Source: Authors' configuration based on data from Bloomberg.

US and European manufacturers use different supply chains for cars produced for the US consumer. The 1992 American Automotive Labeling Act (AALA) requires all automobiles sold in the United States to be labelled with the percent of US and Canadian content that makes up each type of automobile sold in the United States, in order to encourage US consumers to buy cars with high levels of US content. Figure 15.7 shows the average share of US and Canadian content of the 'big three' US automakers (Chrysler, GM and Ford). In 2007, the big three produced car models that contained 70% US or Canadian content on average. By 2015 models, that share had declined in all three companies, as production shifted to Mexico. So, while US carmakers' production for US consumption has shifted away from the United States, there has been little movement outside NAFTA.

Figure 15.7 Average share of US and Canadian content, by company, 2007-2015 models

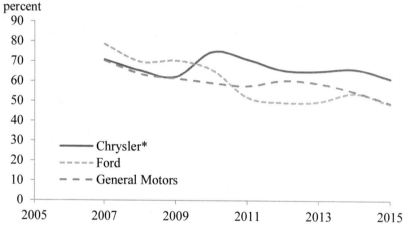

* Chrysler 2015 average includes Fiat models, following the merging of the two companies in 2014.

Source: Data from the 1992 American Automotive Labeling Act.

The AALA data show that compared with US or Japanese automobile manufacturers, European firms still tend to produce the majority of their parts in the European Union for cars sold in the United States. Table 15.5 compares the US content of the top-five models sold in the United States in 2014, separated into US, EU, and other non-US manufacturers. Of the top-five European cars sold, only Volkswagen has a significant share of its content from outside of Germany and produces cars for the US market in both Germany and Mexico.

Table 15.5 US content of top-selling US, EU and other non-US car models, 2014

Model	Models sold	US/ Canadian content (%)	Other content[a] (%)	Final assembly location(s)	Engine source(s)	Trans-mission source(s)
United States						
Ford F-Series	753,851	75		US	US	US
Chevrolet Silverado	529,755	40	51, Mexico	US, Mexico	US	US
Dodge Ram 1500-3500	439,789	66	23, Mexico	US, Mexico	Mexico, Italy	US
Ford Fusion	306,860	75	15, Mexico	Mexico	Romania, UK, Spain, Mexico	US, UK
Ford Escape	306,212	60		US	Mexico, Spain, UK	US
Europe						
Volkswagen Jetta	141,354	6–12	37-41, Mexico, up to 26, Germany	Mexico	Mexico	Japan, Argentina, Germany
BMW 3 Series	100,902	5	60-65, Germany	Germany	Germany	Germany
Passat Volkswagen	96,649	40–45	21, Mexico; 26-41, Germany	US	Germany, Mexico	Germany, Argentina, Japan
Mercedes-Benz "C" Class	75,066	0	73, Germany	Germany	Germany	Germany
Mercedes-Benz "E" Class	66,403	0	73, Germany	Germany	Germany	Germany

Other non-US						
Toyota Camry	428,606	75	20, Japan	US	US, Japan	US, Japan
Honda Accord	388,374	70	15, Japan	US	US, Japan	US, Japan
Toyota Corolla	339,498	60	30, Japan	China, US	US	Japan
Nissan Altima	335,644	60	15, Japan	US	US	Japan
Honda Cr-V	335,019	70	15, Japan	US, China, Mexico	US	US, Japan

ᵃ To be included in the other content category, an individual country must produce at least 15% of the parts included in the car model.

Data sources: 1992 American Automotive Labeling Act, National Highway Traffic Safety Administration (www.nhtsa.gov/Laws+&+Regulations/Part+583+American+Automobile+Labeling+Act+(AALA)+Reports) and Bloomberg (www.bloomberg.com/graphics/2015-auto-sales).

The high share of US content among Japanese firms relative to European carmakers is related to historical restrictions on Japanese car imports and a volatile yen. As trade tensions between Japan and the United States flared, the Japanese government agreed to VERs on the number of Japanese cars that could be exported to the United States, while European carmakers had no similar legislation in place. VERs were in effect from 1981 to 1994. Additionally, in 1985, the United States and Japan realigned exchange rates in the Plaza Accord. The significant appreciation of the yen removed the cost advantage of producing in Japan for export to the United States and led to a less stable yen/dollar exchange rate. The three biggest Japanese carmakers opened factories in the United States to get around VERs, (Honda in 1980, Nissan in 1983, and Toyota in 1986) and continued producing in the United States to some extent because of the exchange rate adjustment. In contrast, VW closed its only US plant in the United States in 1988 and did not open another US plant until 2011.[11]

Although the differences in regulations require separate car models for the US markets, European firms still choose to produce cars

---

[11] Schaede (2010); James Healy, "'Transplant' Auto Factories in USA Turn 30 This Year," *USA Today*, 3 April 2012; Andrew Pollack, "Japan to End Restraints on Auto Exports to US", *New York Times*, 29 March 1994.

bound for the US market through EU supply chains perhaps because of fewer historical restrictions on trade (and indeed Korean-made cars also tend to have lower levels of US content than Japanese-made ones). If regulations were mutually recognised, pre-existing supply chains, which currently produce two versions of the same model of cars sold in both markets, would become more efficient as they would be able to halve the number of different models they produce along these supply chains.

While European cars sold in the United States are largely European-made, what about US cars sold in Europe? The European Union does not have similar content-reporting regulations in place, making it difficult to determine precisely the European content of US branded cars sold in Europe. However, one way of determining if US auto firms are any more reliant on production in Europe than EU auto firms are on production in the United States is to compare sales of multinationals outside of their home countries, which is likely to move with foreign production, and exports. The higher the ratio of exports to sales, the more foreign affiliates rely on imports from the parent company for sales, rather than producing cars in the market they sell in.

Table 15.6 uses US Bureau of Economic Analysis data on multinationals operating in the United States and US companies abroad to calculate the ratio of exports to sales in 2012, the most recent year for which data are available. These BEA data are for both US affiliates operating abroad and foreign affiliates operating in the United States and report total sales in transport equipment for both groups (NAICS 366). For European parents and their US affiliates, exports are of all transport equipment and wholesale trade in motor vehicles and motor vehicle parts and supplies. This matches closely data from Comtrade on transportation exports from the European Union to the United States. However, these data are not available for US parents and their European affiliates. To calculate the ratio of exports to sales in this case, we instead use Comtrade data on total EU-27 exports of transport equipment to the United States (SITC 73).

Despite exports to total sales of just one-third of European sales, local content data reveal that European cars are still made of largely EU content. This may be because final assembly is often the most cost-effective stage of production to move. As a result these ratios may offer a good sense of relative differences across markets but may be less useful as an indication of home-country content.

Table 15.6 Ratio of exports to total sales, 2012

	Exports by parent to affiliate company ($ million)	Total sales by affiliate ($ million)	Exports/total sales
All transportation equipment			
European parent, US affiliate	56,860	165,066	0.34
US parent, European affiliate	28,837[a]	166,788	0.17

[a] Total EU imports of transportation equipment from the United States (SITC code 73).

Source: Authors' calculations using data from Bureau of Economic Analysis and UN Comtrade Database.

The ratio of exports to total sales is higher in Europe than in the United States. This suggests that US car sales in Europe have relatively higher levels of foreign content than European cars have non-European content in the United States. The estimates from the model of large long-run trade gains from regulatory harmonisation, significantly larger than from tariff reductions, therefore may be more delayed in the United States than Europe, because the United States produces vehicles in Europe with less US content compared with the EU content of European vehicles for the US market. European producers are therefore likely to adjust more rapidly to a new integrated terrain than US producers, where production is separated.

Beyond the firms with production abroad, firms that do not currently export to the United States, such as French motor company Renault, could increase variety in the US market without incurring the costs associated with building cars to US specification. As noted earlier, the market for compact and subcompact cars in the United States is very small, but if firms that produce such vehicles following EU regulations can sell in North America, they will be able to reach the US and Canadian consumers who prefer smaller cars without incurring the high costs of modifying the car models. Since regulations provide similar levels of safety, and harmonised regulations bring trade gains, the United States and European Union should work towards making US and European cars available in both markets without having to make separate versions of each model.

5.   Policy proposal

Considering the large gains from harmonisation, one proposal for the US and EU automotive sector is for the United States to join the 1958 Agreement. However, this approach has high logistic and legal costs. In addition to the technical differences in regulations, such as the turn signal light example in Table 15.1, EU and US regulations on vehicle safety certification also differ in implementation. The United States operates under a self-certification system for vehicle regulations. The National Highway and Traffic Safety Administration (NHTSA) issues safety regulations for US vehicles, but calls on automakers to certify that their new vehicles conform to these safety regulations. Firms are responsible for both testing of new vehicles and liable for any penalties associated with vehicles that are found not in compliance with NHTSA regulations. On the other hand, under the 1958 Agreement, the European Union operates under a type-approval system, where firms submit samples of new cars to government testing facilities, which formally approve these new models. Once approved by any government in the European Union, that car model is considered to have met the safety regulations of all EU members and can be sold in all EU countries (Canis & Lattanzio, 2014).

As demand for vehicles shifts away from the US market, there is less of an incentive to produce models specifically designed to meet US safety regulations and approval systems. However, logistically, it would likely be infeasible to switch from a self-certification to a type-approval system, as the United States would need to establish a new government entity to handle auto safety regulations, rewrite laws to regulate changes in liability for faulty vehicles and parts, and build new infrastructure for safety testing.

An alternative approach would be to leave established regulatory systems in place in both the United States and the European Union but have both countries accept the other's regulations as valid in their own market. Such a policy could be adopted either for all vehicle regulations or for a range of particular components. Currently, few cases of such mutual recognition are in place, but it is not without precedent, and this approach is gaining ground. New Zealand, which signed on to the 1958 Agreement in 2002, also imports vehicles certified under US regulations.[12] Mexico allows sales of vehicles with either

---

[12] New Zealand Transport Agency, "Guide to importing a vehicle" (www.nzta.govt.nz/vehicle/importing).

Mexican or European certification.[13] Additionally, free trade agreements have facilitated some of this mutual recognition. The Korea-US Free Trade Agreement allows Korea to import 25,000 vehicles per automaker that meet US regulations, without having to also meet Korean regulations (Schott, 2010). Canada is moving toward mutual recognition of EU and US regulations. While Canadian regulations generally mirror US regulations, the Canada-European Union Comprehensive Economic and Trade Agreement, signed in October 2014, lists 17 UNECE safety regulations that are considered an allowable alternative to current Canadian regulations (Foreign Affairs, Trade and Development Canada, 2013).

There is evidence that both the United States and the European Union would accept such of agreement. In September 2009, the European Communities brought a proposal to the World Trade Organization (WTO) to supplement the existing text of the December 2008 Negotiating Group on Market Access, in order to reconcile type-approval (1958 Agreement) and self-certification (US regulations) frameworks in the auto industry.[14] The proposal recognised both systems as valid auto regulatory frameworks and allows for three paths for potential signatories: 1) members with type-approval systems already in place must sign the 1958 Agreement; 2) members with self-certification systems may join the 1958 Agreement, then nominate a national regulatory body to deliver type-approval of automobiles produced in that member state; and 3) members with self-certification systems may maintain them while recognising UN Regulations as equally valid as their own regulations in their market (Negotiating Group on Market Access, 2009a).

The proposal also presents a method for documenting member country adoptions of mutually recognised equivalent regulations for EU and US technical requirements. Each member is required to certify that it will accept a particular EU regulation as equivalent to a US regulation. For each requirement, the United States must document each safety requirement that is considered equivalent to the EU requirement in order for a car that meets either regulation to be sold.

---

[13] Jeremy Cato, "Mexico accepts European vehicle standards, why doesn't Canada?" *Globe and Mail*, 5 November 2014.

[14] The 2008 negotiations provide a framework for proposing and adopting regulatory harmonisation in the automotive sector but does not itself propose steps for convergence.

At the same time, the European Union must recognise that the same US regulation is equivalent to the EU regulation to sell a car that meets either requirement in the market.

For example, the United States requires that the colours of the front and rear end-outline marker lamps be amber and red, respectively.[15] The corresponding EU requirement is white and red, respectively. If both the United States and the European Union recognised each other's regulations, firms from both countries would be able to sell cars with either type of lights in both markets and not have to change the colours.

The US response to the WTO framework was positive. The United States circulated a response outlining a procedure for transparently reporting changes in regulation and conformity assessment procedures, noting transparency was particularly necessary when countries were adopting another member's regulations. This communication also added that when members propose to adopt a technical regulation, they should also consider the costs of complying with this regulation and consider any already available alternatives that fulfil the same objective. A revised version of the proposal, circulated in December 2009, incorporated these US proposed changes (Negotiating Group on Market Access, 2009b).

While this proposal has not moved forward in the WTO, there is potential for a similar bilateral proposal of mutual recognition either within the TTIP framework or in an auto sector-specific agreement.

From an economic perspective, assuming the safety and environmental outcomes of the regulations are the same, harmonisation and mutual recognition have similar economic results. In both cases, inventory can be redeployed. In both cases, only one model needs to be created for both markets. In both cases, models with low demand in a foreign market can still be exported without costly adjustments. Mutual recognition will be much easier to achieve in this case, especially with respect to the approval system, because shifting from government to self-approval or vice versa would require the trade agreement to impinge on legal systems, which are part of national sovereignty. For members the main economic concern with mutual recognition is that if one system is significantly cheaper to use than the

---

[15] Outline marker lamps are placed on the front and rear of the vehicle to indicate the overall width of the vehicle.

other, it could draw investment away from the region with the more costly regulation.

Mutual recognition also has important implications for outside producers. If the agreement extends only to the European Union and the United States, outside producers will still be required to produce for two different systems. For example, if Korea-manufactured automobiles that meet EU regulations are not eligible for the mutual recognition agreement, then Korean producers will still be required to produce separate models for each market. This will put them at a cost disadvantage relative to US and EU producers. Not extending mutual recognition will also prevent the 'global standard-setting' that the US and EU governments have used to motivate the agreement. It is therefore important that a mutual recognition agreement is extended to outside producers as well. Of course, they would not be permitted to follow their own unique regulations and be granted recognition privileges, but provided they adhere to either US or EU regulations, automobiles produced outside the TTIP area should be subject to the same restrictions as US- or EU-produced vehicles.

Mutual recognition, particularly with enhanced technical harmonisation, would require time to achieve. Kenneth Feith, Daniel Malone, and John Creamer (2014) offer a starting point of trust and cooperation, where US and EU regulators considering new technologies keep each other informed and work together on the rulemaking process and commit to bridging the type-approval and self-certification systems, and build in steps towards mutual recognition.

6.   Conclusion

Regulatory convergence or mutual recognition of regulations between the European Union and the United States would bring larger welfare gains than tariff reduction. The gains are in efficiency, variety, and innovation. We estimate that harmonisation of auto regulations would increase US-EU auto trade by at least 20%. These gains can be achieved through the TTIP, which also aims at setting rules for global trade. To maximise auto market integration, greater harmonisation would be preferable, with the United States becoming a contracting member of the 1958 Agreement. However, recognising differences in legal systems and approval systems implies that the greatest benefit at the least cost is likely to come from the harmonisation of technical regulations, where overlap already exists, and the mutual recognition of regulations and approval methods across countries. This approach allows firms to streamline production and offers increased variety for consumers without implicitly favouring either the existing EU or US systems. We also recommend that outside producers are extended the same treatment, provided they adhere to the US or the EU system.

References

Baldwin, Richard and Daria Taglioni (2006), "Gravity for Dummies and Dummies for Gravity Equations", NBER Working Paper 12516, National Bureau of Economic Research, Cambridge, MA.

Bradford, Scott and Robert Lawrence (2004), *Has Globalization Gone Far Enough? The Costs of Fragmented Markets*, Institute for International Economics, Washington, D.C.

Canis, Bill and Richard Lattanzio (2014), "US and EU Motor Vehicle Standards: Issues for Transatlantic Trade Negotiations", CRS Report R43399, Congressional Research Service, Washington, D.C.

Dechezleprêtre, Antoine, Eric Neumayer and Richard Perkins (2015), "Environmental regulation and the cross-border diffusion of new technology: Evidence from automobile patents", *Research Policy* 44: 244–257 (www.sciencedirect.com/science/article/pii/S0048733314001383).

Ecorys (2009), "Non-Tariff Measures in EU-US Trade and Investment", report prepared for the European Commission (http://trade.ec.europa.eu/doclib/docs/2009/december/tradoc_145613.pdf).

European Commission (2015), "Second Test Case on Recognition of Equivalence in Relation to US and EU Lighting and Vision Standards", Technical Non-Paper, 30 January (http://trade.ec.europa.eu/doclib/docs/2015/february/tradoc_153168.4.9%20Vehicles%20paper%20second%20test%20case.pdf).

Feith, Kenneth, Daniel Malone and John Creame (2014), "America's Disconnect between Domestic and Global Automotive Rulemaking: Time to Pull in the Same Direction", Bloomberg Government.

Foreign Affairs, Trade and Development Canada (2013), Canada-European Union: Comprehensive Economic and Trade Agreement. Technical Summary of Final Negotiated Outcomes, October (http://international.gc.ca/trade-agreements-accords-commerciaux/agr-acc/ceta-aecg/understanding-comprendre/technical-technique.aspx?lang=eng),

Freund, Caroline and Alberto Portugal-Perez (2013), "Assessing MENA's Trade Agreements", in Michael Gasiorek (ed.), *The Arab Spring: Implications for Economic Integration*, Centre for Economic Policy Research, London.

Freund, Caroline and Sarah Oliver (2015), "Gains from Harmonizing US and EU Auto Regulations under the Transatlantic Trade and Investment Partnership", Policy Brief 15-10, Peterson Institute for International Economics, Washington, D.C., June (www.piie.com/publications/interstitial.cfm?ResearchID=2797).

Negotiating Group on Market Access (2009a), Communication from the European Communities. TN/MA/W/188, 9 September, World Trade Organization.

_____ (2009b), Communication from the United States. TN/MA/W/120, 15 September, World Trade Organization.

Perkins, Richard and Eric Neumayer (2012), "Does the 'California Effect' Operate Across Borders? Trading- and Investing-Up in Automobile Emission Standards", *Journal of European Public Policy*, Vol. 19, No. 2. 217–237 (http://ssrn.com/abstract=1546558).

Schaede, Ulrike (2010), "Globalization and the Reorganization of Japan's Auto Parts Industry" *International Journal of Automotive Technology and Management*, Vol. 10, Nos. 2/3.

Schott, Jeffrey (2010), "KORUS 2.0: Assessing the Changes", PIIE Policy Brief 10-28, Peterson Institute for International Economics, Washington, D.C.

Appendix

Table 15.A1 List of exporters

Argentina	United Kingdom
Belgium	India
Belgium-Luxembourg	Italy
Brazil	Japan
Canada	South Korea
China	Mexico
Germany	Netherlands
Spain	Portugal
France	Thailand
United States	Finland
Australia	Hungary
Romania	Morocco
Austria	Poland
Sweden	Russia
South Africa	Serbia/Montenegro
Indonesia	Slovak Republic
Turkey	Slovenia
Czech Republic	

ABOUT THE CEPS-CTR PROJECT: TTIP IN THE BALANCE

The Centre for European Policy Studies (CEPS) and the Center for Transatlantic Relations (CTR) at the School for Advanced International Studies (SAIS) of Johns Hopkins University in Washington, D.C. set up a joint project in 2014 to explore the Transatlantic Trade and Investment Partnership (TTIP), under negotiation between the European Union and the United States. Its aim was to promote a deepening of the TTIP debate, a comprehensive approach – also sectorally – to the negotiations, a far more detached perspective on the substance of TTIP (than found in numerous circles) and concrete analytical output as a support for negotiators on both sides. It also aspired to improve the quality of the policy discussions.

The project was directed by Jacques Pelkmans from CEPS and Daniel S. Hamilton from CTR. Some 13 papers were produced in the context of the project and published simultaneously on the websites of CEPS and of CTR. Most or all papers have both US- and EU-based authors. Both institutes supported the project, which was co-funded by AMCHAM-EU, Repsol and the Konrad Adenauer Foundation. The Center for Transatlantic Relations also gratefully acknowledge funding from the European Commission and the Transatlantic Program of the German government, with funds from the European Recovery Program of the German Ministry for Economics and Technology. The organisation, substance and editing of the project results, however, are entirely independent.

INDEX